Criminal Justice in Canada

SEVENTH EDITION

Criminal Justice in Canada

SEVENTH EDITION

Colin Goff

University of Winnipeg

Criminal Justice in Canada
Seventh Edition

by Colin Goff

VP, Product and Partnership Solutions:
Anne Williams

Publisher, Digital and Print Content:
Leanna MacLean

Executive Marketing Manager:
Amanda Henry

Content Development Manager:
Suzanne Simpson Millar

Photo and Permissions Researcher:
Natalie Barrington

Production Project Manager:
Jennifer Hare

Production Service:
SPi Global

Copy Editor:
Kelli Howey

Proofreader:
SPi Global

Indexer:
SPi Global

Design Director:
Ken Phipps

Managing Designer:
Franca Amore

Interior Design:
Deborah Brock

Cover Design:
Deborah Brock

Cover Image:
IgorKozeev/Thinkstock

Compositor:
SPi Global

Printed and bound in the United States

1 2 3 4 19 18 17 16

For more information contact Nelson Education Ltd., 1120 Birchmount Road, Toronto, Ontario, M1K 5G4. Or you can visit our Internet site at http://www.nelson.com

Library and Archives Canada Cataloguing in Publication Data

Goff, Colin H., 1949–, author
Criminal justice in Canada / Colin Goff, University of Winnipeg. — Seventh edition.

Includes bibliographical references and index.
ISBN 978-0-17-658294-4 (paperback)

1. Criminal justice, Administration of—Canada—Textbooks. I. Title.

HV9960.C2G63 2016
364.971 C2015-907534-3

ISBN-13: 978-0-17-658294-4
ISBN-10: 0-17-658294-0

To Sarah, whose kindness and support will always be remembered,
and to Buddy and Robley, for their continued encouragement.

CONTENTS

LIST OF EXHIBITS

PREFACE

Criminal Justice in Canada has now been an ongoing project for 20 years. The seventh edition continues to chronicle the operation of the Canadian criminal justice system and, as with all previous editions, the various components of our justice system are described and updated. Since the publication of the previous edition, the federal Conservative government continued to pass legislation altering the nature of crime control policy in this country. As well, the Supreme Court, through its decisions, continues to influence the operations of various criminal justice agencies. The seventh edition of *Criminal Justice in Canada* attempts to identify the significant issues, crime control policies, and Supreme Court decisions that have had and will continue to have a fundamental impact upon our criminal justice system.

Although this text covers many of the changes found within our justice system over the past few years, it addresses many of the same fundamental questions that appeared in the previous editions. Issues such as why and how a certain type of behaviour becomes a crime. Who is a criminal? How are decisions made about whom to charge and whom to release? Do our criminal justice policies promote justice? Do our criminal justice agencies follow the rule of law? Whom should we punish, and how? Do some of the new policies introduced by the federal government "work" in the way they were intended to? How is public safety best achieved? Should we incarcerate those individuals who commit crimes by placing them in custodial facilities? What is the role of community corrections, and should we place as many offenders in the community as possible? Is it better to incarcerate for lengthy periods of time those individuals who commit serious crimes or who continue to commit more crimes after they have been released from a custodial facility? Should there be more community alternatives, such as problem-solving courts? Should we rehabilitate all offenders? And, if so, should the same type of treatment be applicable to all offenders, or should we recognize differences among offenders, such as gender and race?

With each new edition, attempts are made to update as many of the changes and rulings that impact the Canadian criminal justice system as possible, and not to simply repeat many of the issues that have been resolved and are no longer contentious. This seventh edition of *Criminal Justice in Canada* continues with the same approach used in previous editions by describing in as much detail as possible how our criminal justice system attempts to bring "justice" in its policies, operations, and court decisions. This approach involves a discussion of the major agencies of our justice system and the manner in which they operate to identify, apprehend, process, and control offenders while at the same time protecting the rights of individuals. The text does not describe every aspect and nuance of each criminal justice agency, but rather highlights many of the major policies, legal cases, decisions, and issues that shape the Canadian criminal justice system. Various research studies are used, as are government statistics.

In this seventh edition, some of the recent initiatives to control crime and criminals are discussed and updated: anti-terrorism legislation, mandatory minimum sentences, and problem-solving courts such as mental health courts. In addition, various new initiatives attempting to better deal with crime and criminals are reviewed, such as community courts, human trafficking, and gender-responsive programming. Issues related to decisions made by the Supreme Court of Canada are discussed, such as the criminalization of HIV, physician-assisted suicide, and search warrants for electronic devices. Finally, responses made by the various criminal justice agencies to certain issues, such as the way in which the police conducted themselves during the G20 protests, are reviewed, along with how Parliament has responded with new legislation in order to combat such cybercrimes as Internet luring.

NEW TO THE SEVENTH EDITION

As the demands of and challenges to the Canadian criminal justice system emerge, the inevitable result is seen in various types of change: changes to legislation, changes to available services, changes in the policies used to direct criminal justice agencies, as well as changes in the types of behaviours that are being criminalized. To keep this textbook current with these demands and challenges, the seventh edition includes a number of the changes that have occurred over the past few years. A new chapter has been added that reflects new updates to the police. In addition, chapters have been altered to better reflect the actual chronological processing of individuals through the various parts of the criminal justice system.

Some important changes are found in each chapter of the seventh edition:

- Each chapter is divided into various thematic subsections, and at the end of the subsections are *Summing Up and Looking Forward* features in which the highlights of the previous section are reviewed and then related to the next section of the chapter or the theme of the next chapter.
- Chapters now contain *Criminal Justice Focus* and *Criminal Justice Insight* sections, both of which are designed to give more detail to topics identified in that chapter.
- Each chapter has a new *Summary*, in which each subsection is briefly reviewed and key words are listed.
- *Exhibits* present short, illustrative boxes such as excerpts from the Charter of Rights and Freedoms and bulleted lists, whereas *Investigating* boxes are longer features that provide more in-depth coverage of an issue or concept.

As well, at the end of each chapter, a section entitled *Critical Issues in Canadian Criminal Justice* highlights a specific issue relevant to our criminal justice system. This section hopefully allows students to discuss each of these issues in detail and apply some of the concepts they have learned in that particular chapter.

The following is a chapter-by-chapter list of some of the new and updated content added to the seventh edition.

Chapter 1 *(An Overview of the Criminal Justice System in Canada)* has a new introduction highlighting some of the issues related to the role of "justice" within our criminal justice system. Both the rule of law and access to justice are now included in this chapter. In addition, there are updated discussions of physician-assisted suicide and euthanasia as well as Canada's anti-terrorism legislation.

Chapter 2 *(Criminal Law and Criminal Justice in Canada)* discusses issues such as the response of the criminal justice system to sexual assault, whether or not the criminal law can cause harm, and criminal law reform (specifically, legislation passed by the former federal Conservative government and the Safe Streets Act). There are also updated sections on sexual assault, the Charter of Rights and Freedoms, and the issue of criminalization.

Chapter 3 *(Control Philosophy and Criminal Justice Policy)* updates the information about how policies concerning sex offending or sex offenders are approached by the various control philosophies. The issue of whether or not information about sex offenders should be released to the public is highlighted in *Critical Issues in Canadian Criminal Justice*.

Chapter 4 *(Crime Rates, Crime Trends, and Criminal Victimization in Canada)* contains the most recent police-recorded crime statistics and Crime Severity Index for crime rates and victimization in Canada available when the manuscript was completed. Ethnographic research has been added to the ways in which investigators collect crime about crime and criminals. Police-reported cybercrime in Canada and legislative responses to this crime are highlighted in *Critical Issues in Canadian Criminal Justice*.

Chapter 5 *(The Context of Policing)* starts with a brief discussion of the importance of the legitimacy of the police. It contains expanded and new sections concerning how the idea of policing emerged, the principle of policing by consent, plural policing, private policing, diversity in policing, women and policing, and gender conflicts. Sections on the police culture and the police personality are now included in this chapter. The chapter closes with an updated *Critical Issues in Canadian Criminal Justice* relating to the expansion of the role of DNA data banks in Canada.

Chapter 6 *(The Practice of Policing)* contains updated information concerning how police agencies put their activities into practice. This chapter starts by discussing the history and importance of reactive-style policing, and what led to changes in this dominant policing practice. This is followed by experiments conducted by the police with different practices (i.e., proactive and hot spots policing). The chapter concludes with a discussion of recent types of policing practices, including intelligence-led policing. The critical issue focuses upon policing public protests, examining the police role in the G20 protests in Toronto, and how the legal system has responded to the actions of the police.

Chapter 7 *(The Police and the Law)* starts by discussing the legal powers of the police, including the decision to arrest, investigative detention, and search warrants. Recent Supreme Court decisions in the area of search warrants and electronic devices are examined. This is followed by discussion of the law governing the right to legal counsel and police interrogations. The police interrogation technique known as "Mr. Big" and the Supreme Court ruling in this are reviewed. The chapter next considers issues such as the use of deadly force by the police, police misconduct, "problem" police officers, and police accountability. The impact of body-worn cameras upon the police is assessed.

Chapter 8 (*Pretrial Criminal Procedure*) provides an overview of the experiences of the accused as they are processed into the next stage of the criminal justice system: the courts. This involves considerations about pretrial release, the first appearance, and legal aid. Prosecutors begin to screen cases and make decisions about how to proceed with a case. Other considerations covered in this chapter include plea bargains, the right to a speedy trial, and juries. The critical issue discusses the issue of credit for pretrial custody.

Chapter 9 *(The Courts and Criminal Trial Procedure)* begins with the issue of the increasing number of self-represented accused in our criminal justice system. The various models of the criminal courts and how the court system operates in Canada are covered. This is followed by a discussion of the roles of the defence lawyer, the Crown prosecutor, and the judge. The various components of the criminal trial procedure are then reviewed, as are the major aspects of the right to a fair trial. The critical issue details judicial independence and the mandatory victim surcharge.

Chapter 10 *(Sentences and Dispositions)* includes the most updated statistics available pertaining to the operation of the adult criminal courts in Canada. This chapter starts with a brief discussion of the importance of the role of sentencing within the criminal justice system. Updated sections found throughout this chapter that include sentencing patterns, victim participation, the constitutionality of mandatory minimum sentences for gun-related crimes, and miscarriages of justice (wrongful convictions). New information includes the sentencing of multiple murderers.

Chapter 11 *(Offenders Supervised in the Community: Alternative Sanctions and Conditional Release Programs)* features two groups of offenders: those who serve their sentence or part thereof as part of their sentence (e.g., probation), and those who are released from custody on a conditional release program (e.g., parole). As such, it includes parts of two chapters previously found in the sixth edition. Most sections in this chapter have been updated, including the discussions of probation, the conditional sentence of imprisonment, conditional release programs such as full parole, and problem-solving courts.

***Chapter 12** (Corrections in Canada: History, Facilities, and Populations)* contains updates throughout. As well, there are revisions to the sections discussing inmate society and the legal rights of inmates. New sections discuss Black inmates, use-of-force reviews, and self-injury as found in federal correctional facilities. The critical issue focuses upon the issue of solitary confinement (administrative segregation).

***Chapter 13** (Community Reintegration)* contains updates to a number of sections, including conditional release programs, the risk of recidivism, the "faint hope" clause, and issues related to older inmates. New sections deal with community correctional centres, pardons, and desistance from criminal activity.

INSTRUCTOR RESOURCES

The **Nelson Education Teaching Advantage (NETA)** program delivers research-based instructor resources that promote student engagement and higher-order thinking to enable the success of Canadian students and educators. Visit Nelson Education's **Inspired Instruction** website at http://www.nelson.com/inspired/ to find out more about NETA.

The following instructor resources have been created for *Criminal Justice in Canada*, seventh edition. Access these ultimate tools for customizing lectures and presentations at www.nelson.com/instructor.

NETA Test Bank

This resource was written by Joanne Arbour, Durham College. It includes more than 1,000 multiple-choice questions written according to NETA guidelines for effective construction and development of higher-order questions. Also included are approximately 520 true/false questions and 130 essay questions.

The NETA Test Bank is available in a new, cloud-based platform. **Nelson Testing Powered by Cognero®** is a secure online testing system that allows instructors to author, edit, and manage test bank content from anywhere Internet access is available. No special installations or downloads are needed, and the desktop-inspired interface, with its drop-down menus and familiar, intuitive tools, allows instructors to create and manage tests with ease. Multiple test versions can be created in an instant, and content can be imported or exported into other systems. Tests can be delivered from a learning management system, the classroom, or wherever an instructor chooses. Nelson Testing Powered by Cognero for *Criminal Justice in Canada* can also be accessed through www.nelson.com/instructor.

NETA PowerPoint

Microsoft® PowerPoint ® lecture slides for every chapter have been created by Rochelle Stevenson, University of Windsor. There is an average of 23 slides per chapter, many featuring key figures, tables, exhibits, and photographs from *Criminal Justice in Canada*. The notes pages provide additional instructor support, with further lecture ideas, current topics, and suggestions for student engagement. NETA principles of clear design and engaging content have been incorporated throughout, making it simple for instructors to customize the deck for their curses.

Image Library

This resource consists of digital copies of figures, tables, exhibits, and photographs used in the book. Instructors may use these jpegs to customize the NETA PowerPoint or create their own PowerPoint presentations.

NETA Instructor Guide

This resource was written by textbook author Colin Goff, University of Winnipeg. It is organized according to the textbook chapters and addresses key educational concerns, such as typical stumbling blocks student face and how to address them. Other features include *What can I do in class?*, as well as a new section, *What can I do online?*

ACKNOWLEDGMENTS

Writing a text for an area as diverse and challenging as the Canadian criminal justice system often requires the assistance of people who are willing to share their knowledge, time, and support. Two individuals deserve recognition for their assistance in seeing this project through to its completion. In particular, the editorial assistance of Sarah Goff has been very much appreciated. Inspector Robert W. Bangs of the RCMP was more than generous in giving up his personal time to offer his expertise, and it, too, was always much appreciated.

The training given to me by Gilbert Geis of the University of California, Irvine, and continued support provided by Francis Cullen of the University of Cincinnati, both teachers and colleagues, have contributed to this text in many intangible ways.

Many individuals who work at Nelson Education deserve recognition. Their enthusiasm, patience, tact, and positive support was always appreciated. Maya Castle deserves special mention for supporting the seventh edition and making sure that the project was progressing. More than special thanks go to Suzanne Simpson Millar, whose excellent editorial advice and assistance was always insightful and welcomed. Her tireless efforts and advice throughout the development of the text were appreciated and added to the overall quality of the final product in so many ways. As well, the ability of Natalie Barrington to track down and secure permissions was an essential part of completing the seventh edition, while Leanna MacLean's vision of how digital resources could enhance the learning experience of students was both insightful and creative. At the production stage of the manuscript, the efforts of Kelli Howey, Jennifer Hare, and Mohan guided the successful transformation of the manuscript into the final text. I would also like to thank all the Nelson sales representatives across Canada for all their hard work in bringing this text to the attention of instructors.

Finally, the reviewers of this and past editions deserve special mention for their detailed comments. I appreciate all of their efforts, and many of their suggestions were incorporated into the final text. My thanks go to the following:

John Deukmedjian, University of Windsor

Thomas Groulx, University of Windsor

John Legault, Fanshawe College

John Martin, University of the Fraser Valley

Anne-Marie Singh, Ryerson University

Paul Wintemute, Niagara College

ABOUT THE AUTHOR

Colin Goff received his M.A. in sociology from the University of Calgary and his Ph.D. from the University of California (Irvine). Since graduating, he has taught at Simon Fraser University, the University of New Brunswick (Fredericton), and the University of Winnipeg. His areas of research include all aspects of the criminal justice system as well as corporate and white-collar crime, the history of criminology, and Aboriginal justice. In addition to *Criminal Justice in Canada*, he has published *Corporate Crime in Canada* (with C. Reasons) and *Corrections in Canada*. He has also published many articles on the work of Edwin H. Sutherland (many with Gilbert Geis), on the development of criminology as a discipline in the early twentieth century, and on corporate crime in Canada. He is currently studying life course criminology and the sentencing of white-collar criminals in Canada as well as the development of the discipline of criminology in the United States during the early twentieth century. With the assistance of Gilbert Geis, he has published manuscripts on Edwin H. Sutherland, Thorsten Sellin, and the Michael-Adler Report.

graphixmania/Shutterstock

CHAPTER

1

An Overview of the Criminal Justice System in Canada

Learning Objectives

After completing this chapter, you should be able to:

- Understand the importance of social control and its relationship to how crime is regulated.
- Differentiate among the different definitions of crime.
- Summarize how legal change can occur by discussing assisted suicide and euthanasia.
- Summarize the major components of the normative system of our criminal justice system.
- Differentiate among the models focusing on the goals of our criminal justice system.
- Summarize the major components of the formal criminal justice system.
- Summarize the major components of the informal criminal justice system.
- Critique anti-terrorism legislation according to the due process model.

This chapter provides an overview of some of the essential themes and practices found within our criminal justice system. It includes a preliminary examination of how our system of justice operates by discussing what the core components of "criminal justice" are. Our criminal justice system has developed as a response by the state to alleged and actual violations of the criminal law. It contains various agencies, processes, and practices focused upon those individuals who are charged for (or suspected of) breaking the law or who are victims of criminal activity. How our criminal justice system operates is important: we expect our system of justice to follow the rule of law and uphold the legal rights of all individuals.

Changes to our criminal law and new legislative initiatives impact criminal justice policies and processes. In recent years, the federal government has taken a "law and order" approach to criminal justice and as a result many practitioners debate the veracity of these changes. Regardless of the direction of these changes, we expect the criminal justice system to search for truth and uphold justice by, for example, ensuring that the innocent are not wrongfully punished or that the outcomes of decisions are not inaccurate. Our laws, legislation, and practices have to achieve justice, ensure legal rights are upheld, and implement both fairness and equality. A criminal justice system is one that operates according to the rule of law and achieves justice for all. The following chapters will elaborate on many of the major issues facing our criminal justice system by placing them within the context of each of the major institutions (the police, the courts, and corrections).

Since our criminal justice system deals with individuals who are suspected of committing a crime, arrested by the police, or convicted of an offence in a court of law, an important task at the outset is to examine what exactly is meant by "crime." Some people answer this question by stating that it is an act that is in violation of the criminal law. Yet, when asked to give examples, most people think about crimes committed by strangers in public spaces. Alternatively, a more critical analysis recognizes there are many other criminal offences (e.g., domestic violence and corporate crime) that may not be as visible but are just as or more harmful than street crimes. Another question we could ask is who decides "what is crime"? It is important to recognize that crime is not a fixed, objective entity but rather the result of laws created by changing views of what is acceptable behaviour in society or changes in the enforcement patterns of certain types of behaviour. A key point is that the way in which people decide to respond to crime has a profound impact upon the way in which our criminal justice system operates.

What, then, is criminal justice and what is its purpose? The most common answer to this question is to look at the formal response to crime by the state and/or the functions of its various agencies (i.e., the police, courts, and corrections). Criminal justice in this view is

> (t)he process through which the state responds that it deems unacceptable. Criminal justice is delivered through a series of stages: charge, prosecution; trial; sentence; appeal; punishment. These processes and the agencies which carry them out are referred to collectively as the criminal justice system. (Hudson 2006:93–94)

Others prefer to answer the above question by identifying what they feel are the most important forms of our criminal justice system, including:

> *Substantive law*: The content of the criminal law provides the starting point . . .
>
> *Form and process*: Who responds to crime and what procedures must be used?
>
> *Functions*: What are the intended consequences and aims of the system?
>
> *Modes of punishment*: What sentences are available to the courts? (Davies et al. 2005:8)

But what is "justice" in the context of "criminal justice"? We have all probably experienced someone asking us what we understand by criminal justice. Some of us may have responded by identifying the following as essential aspects of justice within our criminal justice system: *fairness*, *personal liberty*, *respect*, *tolerance*, *equality*, *public safety*, *rights*, *due process*, and *appropriate punishment*. You might have also added to your answer that criminal justice serves as a way to enforce a system of rules and laws to protect the well-being of both individuals and communities.

What is the best way for our criminal justice system to achieve justice? When deciding to determine how justice might be achieved, responses usually include the importance of having a criminal justice system that treats everyone equally. This concern about achieving justice is fundamental to the way our criminal justice system operates. While all of the major institutions in our criminal justice system (the police, the courts, and the correctional system) have differing organizational structures and goals, each tries to achieve justice. All of these institutions are concerned with who deserves justice, how people should receive justice, and how justice is to be delivered.

Who *deserves justice*? Almost everyone would agree that people who experience harm or suffer an injury at the hands of someone who has been charged with a criminal offence deserve justice. And most would support the idea that people who have allegedly broken the law also deserve justice while they are investigated and tried in a court of law, as they are presumed to be innocent. We could also add that justice also means that there is an impartial and deliberate process that provides each individual with the same access to justice as everyone else. That is, people deserve justice by being treated equally, having the same rights, privileges, and opportunities. But are there limits as to who deserves justice? Some people would argue that once a person is convicted of a crime, they don't deserve the same extent of justice as law-abiding citizens. This distinction has led to debates about whether or not, at some point, individuals convicted of certain types of crimes could be treated differently from others.

Another question is *how should people receive justice?* To facilitate an impartial and deliberate process in which people are treated impartially and equally, a number of institutions and procedures have emerged and evolved in Canada. We could point out that people in our society receive justice through the operation of the criminal justice system; that is, through the practices of such agencies as the police and the courts, as well as the various individuals who work within these agencies, such as lawyers. When someone is convicted of a crime they enter into the correctional system, and here, too, they should receive justice.

Who makes sure that the system of criminal justice *delivers justice* in a fair and impartial manner? In our society, it is usually the federal or provincial governments that take on the responsibility of making sure justice is achieved and maintained. But what are the best policies that will allow a society to attain social control as well as to manage risk? What approach is best when it comes to protecting law-abiding citizens and ensuring that those who are charged and found guilty of a crime are treated fairly?

In summary, in our society when most people speak of justice they are referring to an expectation that the law, relevant institutions, and the criminal justice system apply to all individuals equally and all are entitled to equal protection of the law. Before we can explore in detail various issues related to the Canadian criminal justice system, we need to ask broader questions, such as "What are the essential characteristics of our criminal justice system?" and "How are cases processed through our criminal justice system?" In order to do so, we need to look at a number of questions pertaining to our criminal justice system. It is these questions that are the focus of this chapter.

What Is Crime and How Is It Regulated in Canada?

In order to understand our criminal justice system, we need to ask the question, "What is crime and how is it regulated?" To answer this question, we need to look first at the meaning of social control, and second at some of the different ways to define crime. Ideas about what types of behaviour should be socially controlled and criminalized may change over time. Two related activities (euthanasia and assisted suicide) are discussed (see *Investigating: Physician-Assisted Suicide and Euthanasia in Canada* on page 5) to highlight how our criminal law changes over time, from criminalization of certain types of behaviour to decriminalization. This issue leads us to consider that the primary regulation of behaviour in our society can change from one group (i.e., the Criminal Code) to other groups (i.e., committees of medical experts).

It is important to recognize that behavioural patterns of a society are shaped by common ways of thinking, feeling, and acting. Since some individuals engage in activities that are inconsistent with the welfare of society, systems have been developed that indicate the disapproval of those who break with approved ways of thinking and acting. In Western societies, an important function of governments has been to develop systems of social control. Various formal and informal social control systems have emerged over time—in Canada the most common form of social control system has been formal and this system includes the police, the courts, and the correctional system.

The term **social control** is commonly used to refer to the various types of organized reaction to behaviour viewed as problematic. As societies develop, they adjust the ways in which criminal behaviour is defined as well as how the social control systems respond to such behaviour. Historically speaking, criminal behaviour has been attributed to immorality, wickedness, and poverty (among other things). At the same time, the mechanisms for maintaining social control have also changed. For example, societies have attempted to socially control criminals through death (i.e., capital punishment) as well as rehabilitation. Whatever approaches are developed, the objective has always been to control behaviour viewed as criminal in some way. In our contemporary society, the most typical way of trying to control both crime and criminals is to establish a formal system of criminal justice that will enable the various institutions of social control—the police, the courts, and the correctional system—to investigate, detect, prosecute, and punish offenders. Remember, though, that these institutions do not enjoy a totally free hand—limits are always placed on them by various laws, such as the Charter of Rights and Freedoms.

How does a society define crime? And how should we deal with issues such as equality, justice, privacy, and security? There are no easy answers to these questions, as people hold different opinions on how we should define crime and achieve justice.

What Is Crime?

Criminal law is reserved for wrongful acts that seriously threaten the social values of Canadians. These wrongful acts are reflected in the various categories of crime found in the Criminal Code: weapons crime, property crime, crimes against persons, and so on. According to Bowal and Lau (2005:10), it is important to understand crime as it "largely defines a society because it mediates the powerful forces of security, morality, and control." They also point out that criminal law is not static, because as social attitudes change, "our definitions of crime are constantly refashioned in response."

There are two commonly used definitions of crime. The first focuses on the violation of a criminal law, the second on the determination of guilt in a criminal court. According to the first definition, an act can be called a crime only when it violates the existing legal code of the jurisdiction in which it occurs. However, breaking the law is not always regarded as a crime in our society. This is because criminal responsibility requires more than a "guilty act"—it also requires a "guilty mind" (see Chapter 2). The second approach—sometimes referred to as the **"black letter" approach**—stipulates that no act can be considered criminal until a duly appointed representative of the criminal court (e.g., a judge or a jury) has established the guilt of an offender and attached a punishment to that determination.

These two definitions have two important consequences. First, without the criminal law there would be no crime. In other words, no behaviour can be considered criminal "unless a formal action exists to prohibit it." Second, no behaviour or individual "can be considered criminal until formally decided upon by the criminal justice system" (Muncie 2002:10). In essence, then, a criminal act can be established only once it is determined that it violates the criminal law and/or when an accused person is found guilty in a court of criminal law.

A number of criticisms have been directed toward the use of these two definitions in determining crime. According to Muncie (2002), these criticisms include the fact that not every individual who violates the criminal law is caught and prosecuted. Another is the fact that many criminal acts are not prosecuted even after the authorities have discovered them. Muncie also raises the issue that these two definitions neglect "the basic issue of why and how some acts are legislated as criminal, while others remain subject only to informal control" (ibid.:12). Further, he points out that these definitions separate the criminal process from its social context—in other words, they don't consider the ways in which the law is not applied by the criminal court, but rather "is actively made and interpreted by key court personnel (for example, in plea bargaining, the quality of legal representation, and judicial discretion)" (ibid.).

According to other legal theorists, crime is better viewed as a violation of **social norms** (see Exhibit 1.1). This definition was first used by the criminologist Edwin Sutherland, whose research into corporate crime led him to argue that crime shouldn't be defined on the basis of criminal law, but rather on the basis of two more abstract notions: "social injury" and "social harm." He felt that the essential characteristic of crime is that it is "behaviour which is prohibited by the State as an injury to the state" (1949:31). He also noted that there are two abstract criteria that are necessary elements in a definition of a crime—the "legal descriptions of an act as socially harmful and legal provision of a penalty of an act." According to him, some sort of social normative criteria must be applied before any definition of crime can be developed. In part, this means that we need to consider how crime, law, and social norms are linked. We can do this by asking, "What behaviours should be regulated?" Today, this type of approach is visible in attempts to classify behaviour as "criminal" on the basis of normative decision making. For example, some Canadian cities now equate crime with disorderly conduct (such as panhandling), arguing that such conduct undermines public safety and security.

Crime has also been defined as a **social construct**. In other words, crime is viewed as a result of social interaction, the consequence of a negotiated process involving the alleged offender, the police, court personnel, and even lawmakers. According to this definition, the actions of alleged offenders are important, but so is how those actions are perceived and evaluated by those involved with the criminal justice system, including legislators, the police, and Crown prosecutors, who decide whether a crime has been committed as well as how serious it is. In this approach, crime is viewed as being dependent on those who possess the power to define what a crime is and therefore are able to direct the various institutions of the criminal justice system to enforce the law.

All of these definitions can be used to describe and analyze the nature of crime in our society. Since the three major institutions of social control in our society—the police, the courts, and the correctional system—are all involved with the control of crime and criminals, many questions can be raised about how we respond to crime and about the role of the criminal justice system. For example, is the criminal law applied equally to all, or unequally toward some? How does the use of discretion in our criminal justice system influence the processes and outcomes of that system? Can that system simultaneously promote liberty and security? Many people would agree that it is easy to declare that the planned and deliberate killing of one individual by another is a homicide and that the perpetrator of this act should be given a lengthy punishment. However, there may be other issues involved in the case that some people feel should be considered before guilt or punishment is determined. The *Investigating* feature highlights how a type of activity considered to be criminal can be altered as perceptions change, with the result that how that behaviour is regulated is revised.

EXHIBIT 1.1 Differing Definitions of Crime

Legal:

Crime is that behaviour prohibited by the Criminal Code.

Social norms:

Crime is that behaviour that violates social norms.

Social constructionist:

Crime is that behaviour so defined by the agents and activities of the powerful.

Source: Walklate, S. 2005. *Criminology: The Basics.* London, Routledge.

Investigating: Physician-Assisted Suicide and Euthanasia in Canada

During the past 20 years a number of cases in Canada have led some persons to question existing Canadian laws about the "right to die" and to suggest that laws relating to assisted suicide and euthanasia be decriminalized. In essence, these arguments have centred upon assisted suicide and euthanasia. Assisted suicide involves the intentional act of providing a person with the medical knowledge to commit suicide. According to s. 241(b) of the Criminal Code, it is illegal to aid or abet a person to commit suicide (although the act of suicide is legal). The relevant section of the Criminal Code states that everyone who (a) counsels a person to commit suicide, or (b) aids or abets a person to commit suicide, whether suicide ensues or not, is guilty of an indictable offence and liable to imprisonment for a term not to exceed 14 years.

Euthanasia (sometimes referred to as "mercy killing") is the act or practice of causing or hastening the death of a person who suffers from an incurable or terminal disease or condition, especially a painful one, for reasons of mercy. The word "euthanasia" derives from the Greek *euthanos*, which refers to "good death." Euthanasia is not a crime specifically defined in the Criminal Code. It is, however, related to other Criminal Code offences such as murder; manslaughter; assault; criminal negligence; poisoning; and helping, encouraging, or advising someone to commit suicide.

Criminal cases involving charges of either assisted suicide or euthanasia are not common in Canada. Eckstein (2007) has studied the history of euthanasia in Canada and reports finding only 40 reported cases that relate to euthanasia and patient-assisted suicide. Of these 40 cases, 8 involved either doctors, nurses, or nurses' aides; 15 involved "mercy killings" (7 of which involved parents deciding that their children had had enough suffering and pain and were alleged to have assisted in their suicide; 5 involved an individual who alleged their spouse had experienced enough suffering; and 3 in which children felt their parent had experienced enough pain and suffering); 11 were classified as "assisted suicides"; 5 were considered to be a murder-suicide; and 1 case involved infanticide. Eckstein points out that many more cases of euthanasia are thought to have occurred in Canada. For instance, she notes a member of the Special Senate Committee on Euthanasia and Assisted Suicide stated that "there are thousands of cases in Canada in which doctors have illegally helped patients to die" (Eckstein 2007:1). In Canada, there have been three individuals who, after performing an assisted suicide, were convicted and sentenced to a period of incarceration. In addition, at least 18 other cases have come to the attention of the authorities in which the defendants were acquitted, the charges were stayed or dropped, or a charge was not laid (Royal Society of Canada 2011:35).

Assisted Suicide

The constitutionality of the prohibition found in the Criminal Code on assisted suicide was originally tested in 1993 by Sue Rodriguez. She suffered from amyotrophic lateral sclerosis (ALS) and when informed that she had 14 months to live, requested assistance to commit suicide and applied for an order that would find s. 241(b) of the Criminal Code invalid as it violated her rights under ss. 7, 12, and 15(1) of the Charter of Rights and Freedoms. The Supreme Court held, in a 5–4 decision, that "a Charter violation was present but that the violation was necessary in order to protect society's weak, vulnerable and disabled" (Canadian Bar Association 2003:28). She committed suicide in 1994 with the assistance of an anonymous physician.

In 2009, the Quebec College of Physicians surveyed more than 2,000 of its members and found that 75 percent favoured euthanasia as long as it occurred within clear legal guidelines. Eighty-one percent informed the pollsters that they had seen euthanasia practised in Quebec, with most of the cases involving the suspension of medical treatment accompanied by sedation (Peritz 2009). One month later, it was reported that Quebec doctors had "issued a cautiously worded policy . . . suggesting Criminal Code changes to protect doctors who follow an 'appropriate care logic' to end the life of suffering patients facing 'imminent and inevitable death'" (Perraux 2009:A5). In June 2014, Quebec became the first jurisdiction in Canada to legalize physician-assisted death by placing the new law into the provincial health legislation.

The next constitutional challenge to Canada's Criminal Code that makes physician-assisted suicide illegal occurred in 2011. Gloria Taylor, who was suffering from ALS, was told in January 2010 she would likely die within a year. In December 2011, the Supreme Court of British Columbia agreed to expedite her case for assisted suicide (Hume 2011). In June 2012, the B.C. Supreme Court declared the Criminal Code provisions prohibiting doctors from assisting their patients commit suicide to be unconstitutional. The B.C. Supreme Court held that the provisions discriminate against people who are too ill to take their lives. The Court granted Ms. Taylor the right to assisted suicide, and she became the first Canadian to win the legal right to receive a doctor's help to die. She died from her illness in 2012, without assistance. The federal government appealed the B.C. Supreme Court ruling, and in October 2013 the B.C. Court of Appeal overturned the lower court's ruling, citing it was bound by the Supreme Court of Canada's Rodriguez decision. The Supreme Court of Canada agreed to hear an appeal of this and other similar cases, and in early 2015 unanimously held in *Carter v. Canada (Attorney General)* that adults facing "enduring and intolerable suffering" have the right to end their life with a doctor's assistance. They

Continued on next page

Investigating: Physician-Assisted Suicide and Euthanasia in Canada (*Continued*)

also stated that individuals with a "grievous and irremediable" medical condition suffering from needless pain is a denial of their rights and dignity.

Euthanasia

Perhaps the most controversial case in Canada involving involuntary euthanasia occurred in 1993, when Robert Latimer killed his severely disabled daughter to end her suffering (Wilson 2011). During police questioning, Mr. Latimer admitted to the police that he had planned the death of his 12-year-old daughter, Tracy, as he believed she was suffering from the most extreme form of cerebral palsy and he wanted to deliver her from constant pain. Eleven days later he confessed to the police that he had poisoned his daughter with carbon monoxide after placing her in a pickup truck with a hose connected to the exhaust pipe. Mr. Latimer was charged with first degree murder and was found guilty of second degree murder and given the minimum sentence of life imprisonment with no eligibility for parole for 10 years. The case was appealed to the Saskatchewan Court of Appeal, and then to the Supreme Court of Canada. When it was discovered that the Crown prosecutor in the trial had improperly asked potential jurors about their beliefs on mercy killing, the Supreme Court put Mr. Latimer's conviction aside and returned the case to Saskatchewan for a new trial.

In October 1997, Mr. Latimer was again tried, but this time on a charge of second degree murder. He was found guilty of the charge, but the judge decided that in Mr. Latimer's situation his Charter right not to be subjected to "cruel and unusual punishment" would be violated by the 10-year minimum sentence without parole eligibility. The judge granted Mr. Latimer a constitutional exemption and sentenced him to one year's imprisonment and one year of house arrest. The case was appealed to both the Saskatchewan Court of Appeal and the Supreme Court of Canada, both of which restored the statutory minimum sentence of life imprisonment and no parole eligibility for 10 years. The Supreme Court held that mercy killing was legally murder, whatever the motive.

Jurisdictions in Which Assisted Suicide and Voluntary Euthanasia Have Been Legalized

Prior to the legalization of physician-assisted suicide in Quebec, only a limited number of other jurisdictions had legalized physician-assisted suicide and/or euthanasia, specifically Belgium, the Netherlands, and Oregon, Washington, and Vermont in the United States. In 1984, the Netherlands Supreme Court approved voluntary euthanasia and physician-supported suicide under strict guidelines, and in 2002, Belgium passed a similar law. In the United States, Oregon voters approved the Death with Dignity Act in 1994, allowing terminally ill patients, under certain safeguards, to obtain a physician's prescription to end their lives in a humane and dignified manner. The law was challenged and it was not until January 1, 1998, that Oregon's Death with Dignity Act came into force. By the end of 2012, 673 people died by making use of its provisions. In March 2009, Washington State passed a physician-assisted suicide law (the Death with Dignity Act) similar to that in Oregon, and 616 people have been recorded as dying since the law was enacted until the end of December 2012. Vermont was the third state in the United States to enact such a law, enacting legislation in May 2013.

SUMMING UP AND LOOKING FORWARD

The very concept of "justice" is challenging as it raises questions about how it should be received and delivered. The way in which we conceive of justice in our society is important, as the way in which we interpret it raises questions about the best way to approach social control. Despite the fact that we may agree on how we interpret justice, differing definitions of crime have emerged. As a result, we can consider a variety of ways to be the best approach to study and understand crime in our society. Many people prefer the "black letter" definition as it focuses upon those convicted in a court of criminal law; others prefer to identify more with the social constructionist approach, as they feel by studying the actions of lawmakers in terms of what behaviours they view as problematic (i.e., the creation of laws) and how different agencies (e.g., the police, Crown prosecutors) use their powers gives us a better understanding of crime in our society. The legal response to certain types of behaviours (e.g., physician-assisted suicide) can change over time, from one in which there is a blanket prohibition to one in which there are exceptions.

So, what are the essential characteristics we have developed in the hopes our criminal justice system operates as a just system? This question is the subject of the following section.

Review Questions:

1. What is justice and how should it be delivered and received?
2. What is social control and what is its relationship to our understanding of crime?
3. What are the differing definitions of crime and how do they influence our understanding of what "crime" is?

What Is the Normative Framework of Our Criminal Justice System?

Our criminal justice system is not a series of unrelated ideas and decisions that are placed together in a haphazard fashion. A number of key characteristics form the basis of our criminal justice system, and while some of these may be more recognizable than others each one impacts the decisions made throughout the entire system. These characteristics are important in the sense that they are not to be treated as facts, but rather as "criteria by which to judge the performance and practices of a criminal justice system" (Davies et al. 2005:17). This approach establishes our **normative approach to criminal justice**: this includes discovering the truth, the rule of law, protecting the legal rights of individuals, ensuring that everyone can access justice, and guaranteeing fairness and equality.

The Adversarial System

An **adversarial system** of justice has a number of components. Both parties involved hope to win the case and have the right to argue about what evidence the court will consider. A feature of this system is that a prosecutor (representing the state) is concerned initially that justice be done (e.g., that charges are laid only where enough evidence exists to support them) and later on with the successful prosecution of the case. Second, the trial is heard by an impartial fact finder—the judge—who is trained in the law and who is not involved in presenting evidence or questioning witnesses. This guarantees that the defendant receives a fair trial. The judge ensures that the appropriate questions are asked and that the rules of a criminal court case are followed.

In theory, all levels of our court system operate in an adversarial manner. The purpose of the adversarial system is to search for the truth—specifically, to determine the guilt or innocence of the accused. This system has been designed to ensure that the accused's fundamental legal rights are protected, that the trial is fair, and that the final decision is impartial. Significant issues have been raised about the benefits and limitations of the adversarial system of justice and some of these are outlined in Exhibit 1.2.

EXHIBIT 1.2 Benefits and Limitations of the Adversarial System of Justice

Benefits

- A clear division exists among the various actors and agencies.
- As much evidence as possible is looked at in each case, particularly as it benefits each side, since each is committed to winning.
- The legitimacy of the criminal justice system is promoted through the appearance of fairness operating throughout the criminal justice system.

Limitations

- The opposing sides often cooperate in order to reach a desired result, thereby undermining procedural justice in favour of efficiency.
- The length of a trial becomes a concern, since each side has to present as much information as possible in the hope that they will be able to win the case.
- Relevant evidence may be excluded if the judge considers that its use will violate the Charter of Rights and Freedoms.

Substantive and Procedural Justice

How does our criminal justice system operate to make sure that its decisions are fair and equal and do not discriminate? The answer to this question is found in part by looking at what our society considers the most important components of justice. The first component is **substantive justice**—specifically, the accuracy or correctness of the *outcome* of a case and the appropriateness of a judgment, order, or award. If a criminal suspect is in fact guilty, a verdict of "guilty" is a just decision. However, if the suspect is in fact innocent of the charge, then the verdict of "not guilty" is just. Substantive justice is primarily concerned with the truthfulness of the allegation, the accuracy of the verdict, and the appropriateness of the sentence. The high expectations we have of our criminal justice agencies to make correct decisions are the result of our concern with substantive justice.

The second component is **procedural justice**, which refers to the decisions made by courts and the government impacting "the rights and interests of individuals" and, as such, it "seeks to preserve, above all else, the fundamental fairness of the process" and is the "main method by which we enforce and observe the fundamentals of fair trials and other proceedings" (Davison 2006:17, 19). If fair procedures aren't used the trial cannot be just, whether or not substantive justice was attained. For example, a person who is found guilty could in fact have violated the law (substantive justice), but if unfair procedures were used at some point during the investigation and/or trial, the conviction will be considered unjust according to procedural justice. This situation is sometimes brought to our attention when a higher court in this country such as a provincial appeal court or the Supreme Court of Canada rules that there was a problem with the procedural fairness in a case (e.g., the interrogation of the suspect by the police did not follow appropriate procedures). In Canada today, issues involving procedural justice are more common than those involving substantive justice. The importance of procedural justice is clear in those situations when it has not been followed. For example, the Anti-terrorism Act, when it was introduced, gave the federal government powers allowing them to ignore certain aspects of procedural justice when national security was considered to be at stake (see the *Critical Issues in Canadian Criminal Justice* feature at the end of this chapter).

The Rule of Law

According to the rule of law, in our system of justice there is a "sense of orderliness, of subjection to known legal rules and of executive accountability to legal authority" (*Resolution to Amend the Constitution* [1981]). In other words, society must be governed by clear legal rules rather than by arbitrary personal wishes and desires. Central to this is that no one individual or group has a privileged exemption from the law unless an exception is identified. Everyone is subject to the laws that have been introduced by the government. To protect society from the self-interest of individuals or groups, the rule of law ensures that laws are created, administered, and enforced on the basis of acceptable procedures that promote fairness and equality. The **rule of law** plays a central role in our society as it "forms part of the supreme law of our country, binding on all levels of government and enforceable by the courts" (Billingsley 2002:29). Davison (2006:11) points out that the rule of law means that "all members of society must follow and obey the law no matter what their area of activity or endeavour . . ." and that it "provides certainty and stability in our dealings with one another."

The basic elements of the rule of law include the following:

- *Scope of the law.* This means that there should be no privileged exemptions to the law. All people come under the rule of law. There are political and social aspects to this statement. Government under law is the political component. Both the government and public officials are subject to the existing law. The social aspect is equality before the law.
- *Character of the law.* This means that the law should be public, clear enough that most people can understand it, and relatively clear and determinate in its requirements.
- *Institution of the law.* In the Anglo legal system, this means that there are certain rules that the institutions of the law must produce in order for the law to be fair and just. These include an independent judiciary, written laws, and the right to a fair hearing.

Access to Justice

One component of the rule of law is **access to justice**, which involves the idea of legal equality, found in Section 15 (the equality section) of the Charter of Rights and Freedoms. This section sets out that each individual is equal under the law and is entitled to be treated without discrimination based on, for example, age, sexual orientation, sex, race, religion, and mental or physical disability.

The Supreme Court of Canada has held that the right of access to our courts is an essential aspect of the rule of law. In *B.C.G.E.U. v. B.C. (A.G.)* (1988), the Supreme Court ruled on an issue involving the right of unionized civil servants to picket in front of their place of work, in this case the courts in British Columbia, with the rights of other people to access the courts. They upheld a lower court's injunction against picketing in front of courts, stating that although the injunction infringed on the right to peaceful assembly under s. 2(b) of the Charter, the infringement was a justifiable limit based on s. 1 of the Charter. The decision was based on the fact that the assertion of one right could not be at the expense of another important right, in this case access to justice (Seaman 2006). In their judgment, the Supreme Court held that "there cannot be a rule of law without access, otherwise the rule of law is replaced by a rule of men and women who decide who shall and who shall not have access to justice."

Parker (1999:31) points out that the "history of access to justice movement can be read as an ongoing struggle to overcome the discrepancy between the claims of substantive justice and the formal legal system." Since a key aspect of access to justice in our criminal justice system institution involves the provision of legal services, "much access to justice policy relies either directly or indirectly on reorganizing institutions of legal professionalism and legal service delivery" (ibid). The three components of the access to justice movement are (1) legal aid; (2) public interest law; and (3) informal justice.

Starting in the mid-1960s, demands for better access to justice began to increase with demands for improved systems of **legal aid**. While the state has had a responsibility to provide effective, efficient, and accessible courts since the time of the Magna Carta (1215), historically the ideal of equal justice has oftentimes favoured the socio-economic elite since it was they who possessed the resources to access and enjoy the benefits of individual rights and liberty. In the mid-1960s the obligation to ensure legal representation was introduced, leading to an increase in the ability of people to access the courts.

Public interest law focuses on achieving justice by emphasizing group participation in law and placing traditionally underrepresented and marginalized members

The World Justice Project: Rule of Law Index 2014

The World Justice Project (WJP) is an independent organization that attempts to advance the rule of law in 99 countries and jurisdictions. According to the WJP, when the rule of law is weak there are numerous problems, including high rates of criminal violence and the unequal access to laws. Where the rule of law is strong, there are few injustices and a lack of corruption.

The WJP bases its rankings on the following four universal principles*:

- The government and its officials and agents as well as individuals and private entities are accountable under the law.
- The laws are clear, publicized, stable, and just; are applied evenly; and protect fundamental rights, including the security of persons and property.
- The process by which the laws are enacted, administered, and enforced is accessible, fair, and efficient.
- Justice is delivered by competent, ethical, and independent representatives and neutrals who are of sufficient number, have adequate resources, and reflect the makeup of the communities they serve.

Overall, where does Canada rank in the world in terms of the rule of law? See Figure 1.1.

One of the areas measured by the WJP in the rule of law is criminal justice, which is based on seven separate factors. How does Canada rank among the 99 countries and jurisdictions when it comes to delivering justice? Overall, Canada is tied for 11th (see Figure 1.2).

Which groups are discriminated against in Canada? And what can we do to improve our ranking so that the discrimination that exists in our criminal justice system is reduced to the point of elimination?

* *The World Justice Project Rule of Law Index* 2014, p. 4, http://worldjusticeproject.org/sites/default/files/wjp_rule_of_law_index_2014_report.pdf. Used with permission of The World Justice Project.

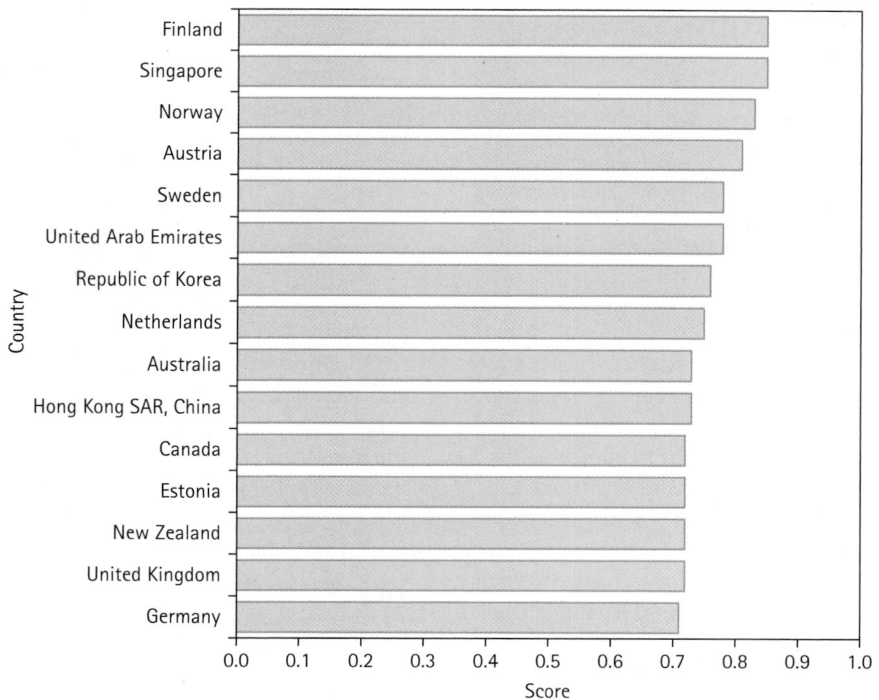

FIGURE 1.1 The Global Rule of Law, Overall Top 15 Rankings, 2014

Source: The World Justice Project Rule of Law Index 2014, p. 185, http://worldjusticeproject.org/sites/default/files/wjp_rule_of_law_index_2014_report.pdf.

Continued on next page

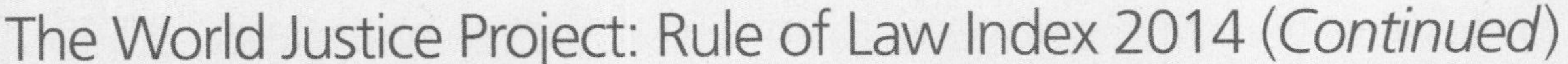

The World Justice Project: Rule of Law Index 2014 (*Continued*)

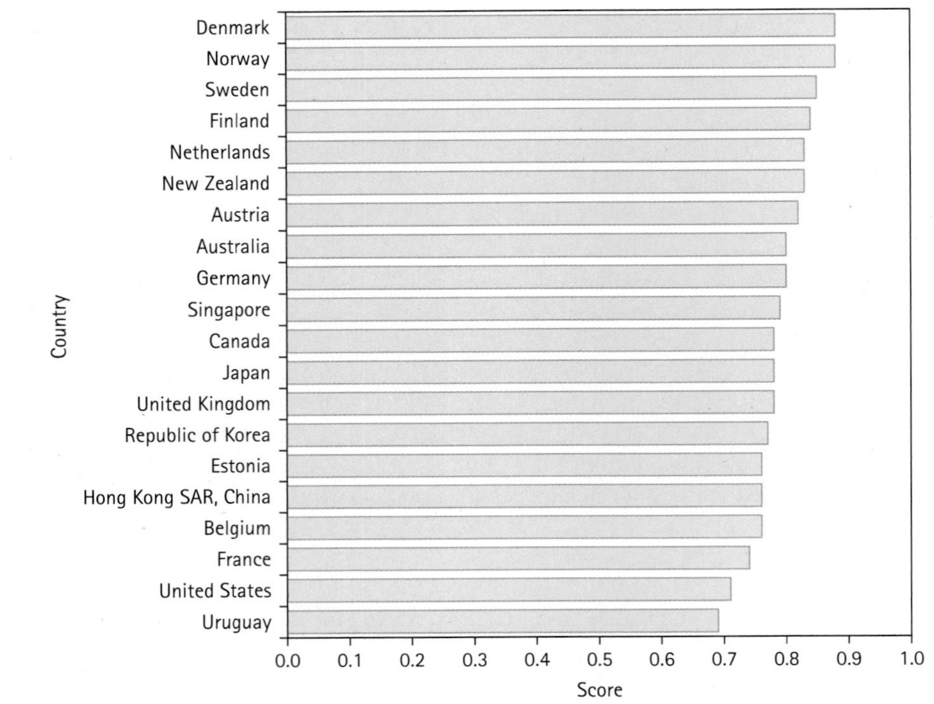

FIGURE 1.2 The Global Rule of Law, Criminal Justice Top 20 Rankings, 2014

Source: The World Justice Project Rule of Law Index 2014, p. 172, http://worldjusticeproject.org/sites/default/files/wjp_rule_of_law_index_2014_report.pdf.

into groups in order that they be better represented in the legal process. Since the Charter of Rights and Freedoms can lead to issues of "fundamental societal significance, access to Charter justice enables the resolution of public interest issues important to the whole community . . . public interest litigants are crucial to realizing the Charter's democratic potential because they illustrate the systemic impacts of the law on the most vulnerable people" (Phillips 2013:23). This approach attempts to change laws, court procedures, and the nature of legal practices in order that access to justice can be attained by the members of various groups whose voices have traditionally not been heard in court, such as consumer action groups and environmental and women's movements.

A third type of approach that attempts to increase access to justice is **informal justice**, which has attempted to increase access to justice through the creation of alternatives to the traditional criminal justice system. A significant and successful part of this approach was the introduction of restorative justice (see Chapter 3). Other examples include the introduction of mediation and arbitration services, alternative dispute resolution, and community justice centres.

Legitimacy of Criminal Justice Institutions

Another component of the rule of law is the degree to which people consider the criminal justice institutions to be legitimate. **Legitimacy** is important as it refers to the agreement with and support of the social regulatory efforts of the police, courts, and corrections. Without legitimacy people question the rule of law. What, then,

iStock/Thinkstock

The physical presence of our courts conveys their importance and high status in our society.

encourages people to have this legitimacy? People have been found to be very sensitive to the way these institutions (and the people who work within them) exercise their authority—that is, to issues of **procedural justice** (Tyler 1990). Support for the legitimacy of our criminal justice institutions is based on citizens' perceptions of fairness and equity, particularly on the basis of the fairness of procedures. Tyler (ibid.) believes four elements (participation, neutrality, trustworthiness of authorities, and treatment with dignity and respect) are key to understanding procedural fairness and why people perceive criminal justice institutions to have legitimacy. What are these four elements and what do they refer to?

- *Participation* refers to the extent to which individuals believe they have control over the process, especially in terms of having the opportunity to present their side of the story to the decision makers.
- *Neutrality* occurs when decision makers do not allow the personal characteristics of individuals to influence decisions and treatment during the process.
- *Trustworthiness of authorities* refers to the degree to which decision makers can be trusted to behave fairly.
- *Treatment with dignity and respect* is based on whether or not decision makers treat individuals with dignity and respect for their rights.

These four elements apply to all stages of the criminal justice system. If people feel an institution is not fair or is disrespectful in its actions, their level of legitimacy decreases. If, for example, members of a minority group feel they are discriminated against they will believe the authorities do not act in a procedurally just manner. This has significant implications for the way people view the legitimacy of criminal justice institutions as it has been found to impact the willingness of some groups to cooperate with the authorities. If the public questions the legitimacy of these institutions they question the use of their legal authority, in particular how they use their discretionary powers.

SUMMING UP AND LOOKING FORWARD

How does our criminal justice system operate to ensure that its decisions are fair and equal? The answer to this question is found in part by looking at what our society considers the most important characteristics of justice. The critical characteristics of our system of justice include the adversarial system, substantive justice, procedural justice, the rule of law, access to justice, and feelings of legitimacy toward criminal justice institutions. These are some of the essential aspects of the normative framework of our criminal justice system. While there is almost total agreement on the above characteristics, there is not necessarily as much agreement on what the goals of our criminal justice system should be. Various goals have been identified and these have allowed different conceptualizations to be put forward about what our criminal justice system should achieve. This has led to the identification of principles and characteristics that ultimately provide for different understandings of the role of criminal justice in our society. It is these approaches, referred to most commonly as "models," that is the focus of the next section.

Review Questions:

1. Identify each of the major characteristics of our criminal justice system.
2. Do you think that the adversarial system always leads to the discovery of truth?
3. To what extent do you think the normative framework is practised throughout our criminal justice system on a daily basis?

What Are the Goals of Our Criminal Justice System?

Before discussing our criminal justice system, we should identify what we expect it to achieve. If you were asked to identify the goals of our criminal justice system, you may decide that it is to attain fairness and equality, or perhaps the prevention and reduction of criminal behaviour or the identification and punishment of the guilty. A useful place to start to examine the goals of the criminal justice system is Herbert Packer's (1968) influential discussion of two models of the criminal justice system. Packer, who was both legally and academically trained, attempted to answer this question by developing two ideal models of criminal justice (see Exhibit 1.3). He called these two models the **due process model** (Figure 1.3) and the **crime control model** (Figure 1.4). These two models were developed to explain not two polar opposites but insights into the relative priorities that each possesses, as well as the shared commitment both possess in terms of reaching the goals of the system. They are best viewed as "ideal types," which means that they don't exist in reality but are viewed as explanatory tools. Packer himself stated that most of what occurs in the criminal justice system is found somewhere between the extremes outlined by the models. He also pointed out that different agencies can prioritize a different model than other agencies, although they are able to co-exist. For example, the police prefer the crime control model, while prosecutors follow the due process model.

The due process model closely resembles the way most people view our criminal justice system operating. This model emphasizes the rule of law and the protection of the legal rights of the accused. It is viewed as being just and fair by upholding the ideal of equality throughout all areas of the criminal justice system. This approach operates on the basis of "the need to administer justice according to legal rules and procedures which are publicly known, fair and seen to be just" (Hudson 2001:104). The most important goal of this model is not to reduce crime but to see that justice is done—specifically, by protecting the legal rights of the accused. This ensures that innocent people are not convicted. If they are, a serious wrong has occurred somewhere in the justice system and it needs to be corrected immediately. The best way to protect the rights of the accused is to limit the powers of criminal justice officials. The criminal

EXHIBIT 1.3 Goals of the Criminal Justice System

MODELS	GOALS
Crime Control Model (Packer)	Assembly line (efficient) justice Factual guilt Public safety Punish offenders High rate of conviction
Due Process Model (Packer)	Fairness, equality, and justice Obstacle course Legal guilt Protection from the powers of the state Search for truth
Medical (Rehabilitation) Model (King)	Needs of the offender Treatment of the offender Discretion of judges Expertise of treatment personnel Community reintegration
Bureaucratic Model (King)	Management of criminals Speed of case processing Efficiency of system Management of resources Administrative discretion
Punitive Model (Roach)	Roller coaster Factual guilt Victims' rights Victim focus throughout the system Greater punishment
Non-Punitive Model (Roach)	Circle (healing, cooperation, restoration) Victims' needs Reduction of harm Non-adversarial emphasis Reduced involvement of criminal justice actors

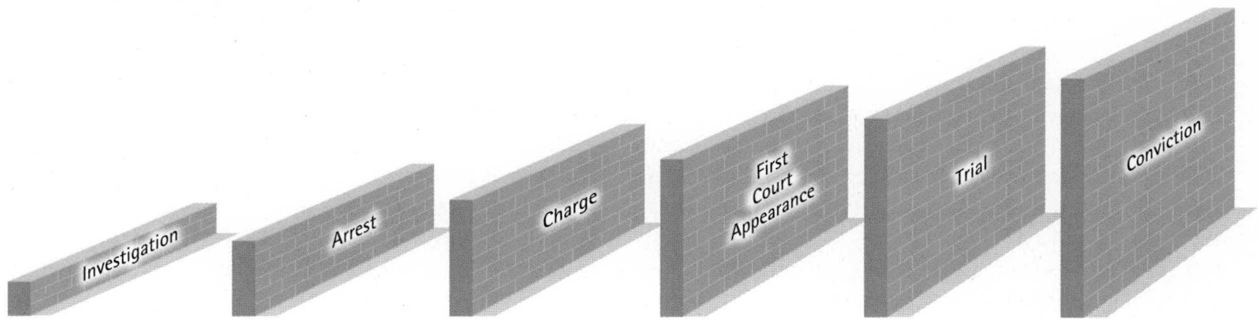

FIGURE 1.3 The Due Process Model
The due process model is an obstacle course.

justice system under this model operates very differently than it would under the crime control model—it's like an obstacle course.

According to Sykes and Cullen (1992), the crime cont-rol model is best characterized by such statements as "get tough on crime" and "the criminal justice system is weak on criminals." It holds that the most important goal of the criminal justice system is to reduce crime by incarcerating criminals for lengthy periods of time. This reduces lawlessness, controls crime, and protects the rights of law-abiding citizens. To achieve this goal, the criminal justice system operates like an assembly line—it moves offenders as efficiently as possible to conviction and punishment so that effective crime control is attained. Certainty of punishment is achieved through mandatory sentences, longer prison terms, and the elimination of parole.

The crime control model rests on the presumption of guilt. That is, most individuals who are arrested are in fact guilty. Thus the model places great trust in the decisions made by criminal justice officials, who wish to protect society. To ensure conviction very little if any attention is

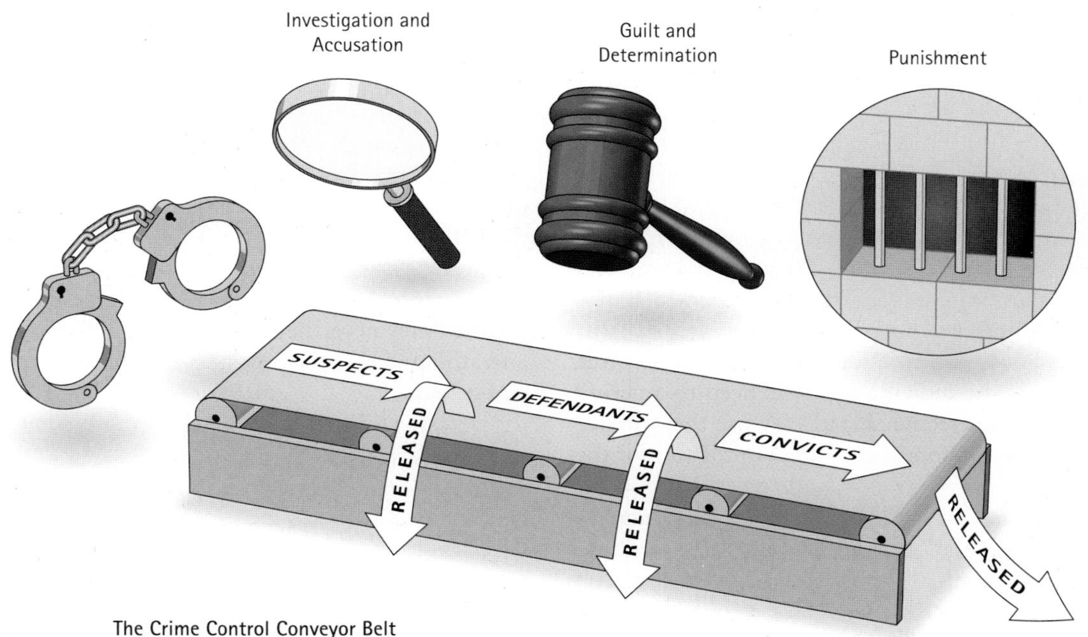

FIGURE 1.4 The Crime Control Model
The crime control model highlights law and order and that the focus of the criminal justice system should be to eliminate crime and to convict and incarcerate all offenders.

placed upon the legal rights of individuals being processed through the system. The model assumes that these individuals make few if any errors, since most defendants are guilty. Each stage of the criminal justice system involves a series of uniform and routine decisions made by officials. Finality is important to officials, because it indicates that there are few problems with the system and that, as a result, there will be few challenges to the system. Support for the use of discretion throughout the system is a key feature of this model, since legal technicalities would reduce its efficiency. When the criminal justice system is allowed to operate as efficiently as possible, it is thought that a reduction in the crime rate results. It follows that concerns for legal rights should not be allowed to erode the system's ability to reduce crime. Furthermore, when issues about the administration of justice come into conflict with the goal of protecting society, the crime control model errs in favour of protecting the rights of the lawabiding citizenry.

There have been recent attempts to develop more models over time, largely on the grounds that they fail to take into account the current realities of the criminal justice system. Some believe that the criminal justice system possesses a multitude of goals beyond due process and crime control, while others focus on the impact of scarce resources. For example, Ashworth and Redmayne (2010) point out that these models fail to consider how limited resources are managed as well as the interests of victims.

King (1981) identified a number of other models, one of which is what he referred to as the **medical (rehabilitation) model**, whose goal it is to rehabilitate those convicted of a criminal offence. The majority of the activity associated with this model is found at the latter stages of the system, after the individual has been convicted and is being assessed by those who work in the court system or in corrections. Probation officers assist judges by providing presentence reports, providing information to the judge about an offender's needs. They may recommend release into the community with conditions, which may include attending appropriate treatment programs or involvement in a therapeutic court such as drug court (see Chapter 10). If the individual is sentenced to a period of incarceration, correctional staff may use their discretion to select the appropriate treatment program for the offender.

Another model forwarded by King is the **bureaucratic model**, which emphasizes the pressures felt by those working in the criminal justice system to work within numerous restrictions such as scarce resources as well as the intense pressure placed on them by the public to solve crimes. Cost effectiveness has increasingly become a major issue for the various agencies in the criminal justice system over the past few decades. According to King, these restrictions lead various agencies to create meas-ures of bureaucratic efficiency, such as making sure that those charged with a criminal offence are tried within a reasonable period of time. Otherwise, charges may be dropped on the basis that the government has taken too long to try their case. In some cases, "the interests of just-ice may conflict with those of efficiency" (Davies et al. 2005:26). If defendants decide to plead not guilty both the prosecution and defence have to prepare a case, which may involve the expenditure of significant amounts of resources. However, if the defendant pleads guilty (even if the Crown predicts that, based on the evidence, it may be hard to gain a conviction), much of this cost can be avoided. As a result, guilty pleas are more cost effective than prosecuting the majority of cases.

Others have attempted to update the models to reflect more contemporary goals relevant to the criminal justice system. Roach (1999), for example, has proposed an alternative model: the **punitive model of victims' rights** and the **non-punitive model of victims' rights**. Roach views the punitive model as more of a roller coaster approach to punishment, in a continual state of crisis as the rights of victims and potential victims are in constant conflict with the rights of the accused. The non-punitive model is portrayed as a circle that "symbolizes successful crime prevention through family and community-building and successful acts of restorative justice" (Roach 1999:699). For Roach, the benefit of an emphasis upon a non-punitive approach is that it would lead to a reduced tendency to rely upon the constant use of the criminal sanction.

Ruth and Reitz (2003) prefer to ignore differentiating between separate models and instead offer a unified set of goals they believe should be shared among all major agencies operating within the criminal justice system. They identify five goals; the first four are the ones the criminal justice system should achieve, while the fifth goal focuses upon the proper size and scope of the system itself (see Exhibit 1.4). Each goal is interrelated with the others, and while they may never be attained they nevertheless serve as a guide to the formal and affiliated agencies working within the criminal justice system.

What Is Criminal Justice?

In Canadian society today, when most people speak of justice they are referring to the fairness of our criminal law system, and their view is informed by three different assumptions. First, guilt, innocence, and the sentence should be determined fairly and in accordance with the available evidence. Second, punishment should fit the offence as well as the offender. Third, like cases should be

EXHIBIT 1.4 Ruth and Reitz's Unified Goals of the Criminal Justice System

Goal #1: to reduce the amount of crime. The response must include not only immediate reactions (e.g., arresting, prosecuting, and punishing) but also activities that are not connected to traditional activities, such as alternative dispute resolutions.

Goal #2: to confront fear. Fear can lead to a society that is "divided, distrustful, and distracted."

Goal #3: justice needs to include the crime victim, potential future victims, and the offender. It also requires just laws, fair processes for their enforcement, and the even-handed administration of those processes.

Goal #4: the justice system must operate in a way that creates and sustains broad faith in its moral legitimacy. Perceptions of injustice as the outcomes of our criminal justice system are problematic, as they reduce the perception of legitimacy within our justice system.

Goal #5: the proper scope of the crime response. Criminal justice should be used only if the behaviour in question is severe enough to be condemned as criminal.

treated alike and different cases differently (Law Reform Commission of Canada 1977). The primary principle of the justice model is that punishment should be proportional; that is, "commensurate to the seriousness of the offence" (Hudson 2003:40).

This view of criminal justice currently guides most Canadians' thinking regarding the most appropriate form for justice to take in our society. It is most closely related to what is called the **justice model** (see Chapter 3). This approach emphasizes that justice is achieved when the various agencies of our criminal justice system follow legal rules and procedures that are publicly known, fair, and just. Key components of this approach are ideas such as the presumption of innocence, procedural fairness, and the need to follow legal rules. Discretion and unequal treatment must be reduced as much as possible. It is argued that when these rules and procedures are followed, our criminal justice system operates in an efficient, fair, and impartial manner (von Hirsch 1976). An important component of the justice model is "justice as fairness," or equality before the law. Here, the rule of law dictates that justice prevails in every stage of the criminal justice system, so no one person experiences discrimination.

SUMMING UP AND LOOKING FORWARD

What does our criminal justice system seek to achieve? Is it to reduce the amount of crime and to prevent crime in the future? Models have been developed in order to offer explanations about the proper role of the various agencies as well as what policies should be adopted. Various models allow us to recognize different conceptualizations of goals in our criminal justice system. Some focus on specific approaches (e.g., the crime control model, the bureaucratic model, or the punitive model of victims' rights), while others focus on having all criminal justice agencies working together to achieve agreed-upon goals.

Now that the essential characteristics and models have been discussed we need to outline some other information about our criminal justice system, including the major agencies as well as how cases are processed at both the pretrial and trial stages.

Review Questions:

1. Identify the major elements of the crime control, due process, rehabilitation, and bureaucratic models.
2. What is the importance of including victims into the goals of our criminal justice system?
3. Do you think that all of the central actors in our criminal justice system can agree on what the most important goals are?

The Structure of the Criminal Justice System

In order to understand the structure of the Canadian criminal justice system, we need to first look at its three major agencies: the police, the courts, and corrections.

The Police

Three main levels of police agencies exist in Canada: municipal, provincial, and federal. Although police agencies vary in their organizational structures and mandates,

Onfokus/iStock

The RCMP are responsible for all federal policing across Canada.

they usually cooperate with one another should the need arise. The most common type of police agency is found at the municipal level. Some municipalities establish their own police force and hire their own police personnel; others contract with the RCMP to provide police services. In 2013, just over 66 percent of sworn police personnel in Canada were employed by municipal police services (Hutchins 2014). Municipal police services are found in almost every major Canadian city, including Vancouver, Calgary, Edmonton, Winnipeg, Toronto, Montreal, and Halifax. The 10 regional police services in southern Ontario (including the Halton Regional Police and the Peel Regional Police) are classified as municipal police services. Some larger municipalities (including Burnaby and North Vancouver, B.C.) contract out with the RCMP, but most municipalities that do so have a population between 50,000 and 100,000. Most jurisdictions in Canada have some municipal police services; the exceptions are Newfoundland and Labrador, Yukon, the Northwest Territories, and Nunavut.

Each province is responsible for developing its own municipal and provincial policing services (ibid.). This means that a province may require all cities within its jurisdiction that reach a certain population size (e.g., any city with more than 10,000 people) to form and maintain their own municipal police service. Provincial police services enforce all relevant laws in those parts of the province that are not under the control of a municipal police service. Besides the RCMP, which operates at the provincial level in most provinces, there are currently three provincial police services: the Ontario Provincial Police, the Sûreté du Québec, and the Royal Newfoundland Constabulary.

The federal government, through the RCMP, is responsible for enforcing laws created by Parliament. The RCMP is organized under the authority of the RCMP Act and is part of the portfolio held by the Solicitor General of Canada. The RCMP, while involved in municipal and provincial policing across Canada, is also charged with other duties such as enforcing federal statutes, carrying out executive orders of the federal government, and providing protective services for visiting dignitaries. In addition, it operates forensic facilities and an educational facility in Ottawa (the Canadian Police College), as well as the Canadian Police Information Centre (CPIC), the automated national computer system used by all Canadian police services.

The Courts

The adult criminal courts across Canada process a significant number of cases each year. During 2011–12, the adult criminal courts in five provinces and all of the territories processed 386,451 cases involving almost 1,160,307 charges in all (Boyce 2013).

All provincial/territorial court systems in Canada with the exception of that of Nunavut have three levels, though their formal titles differ by province (Russell 1987). The **lower courts** are called the provincial courts in most jurisdictions, although in Ontario they are referred to as the Court of Justice and in Quebec as the Court of Quebec. One level higher are the **superior courts**, usually known as the Court of Queen's Bench or Supreme Court (Trial Division). In Ontario, these courts are called the Superior Court of Justice, and in Quebec, the Superior Court. The highest level of criminal court in any province or territory is the appeal court. The court with the greatest authority in any criminal matter is the Supreme Court of Canada. The Nunavut Court is unique in Canada in that it consists of a single-level trial court. Superior court judges hear all criminal, family, and civil matters. This system was introduced in order to simplify the structure of the courts, improve accessibility to the court, and reduce the travel of judges.

The provincial courts are the first courts most Canadians encounter when they are charged with a criminal offence. These courts are typically organized into specialized divisions that deal with different areas of the law. For example, a province may decide to divide its provincial court into a criminal court, a family court, a small claims court, a youth court, and a family violence court. These courts deal with the majority of criminal cases, including disorderly conduct, common assaults, property offences, traffic violations, municipal bylaws, and provincial offences (Figure 1.5).

Corrections

An accused, having been found guilty, may be sentenced to a term in the federal or provincial/territorial correctional system. In Canada, the correctional system involves a vast array of facilities, agencies, and programs. The responsibility for adult corrections is divided between the provincial/territorial governments and the federal government. Provincial and territorial governments are responsible for any individual serving a term of incarceration under two years and for all non-custodial sentences (e.g., probation). The federal government, through the Correctional Service of Canada, is responsible for any adult sentenced to a prison term of two years or more. A person sentenced to a term of two years or more who decides to appeal the conviction or sentence will first be incarcerated in a provincial facility. Those who waive the right to an appeal are sent directly to a federal institution to start serving the sentence.

The majority of individuals in the correctional population are serving all or part of their sentence under community supervision (Figure 1.6). Community supervision includes parole, probation, conditional sentence, statutory release, and temporary absences.

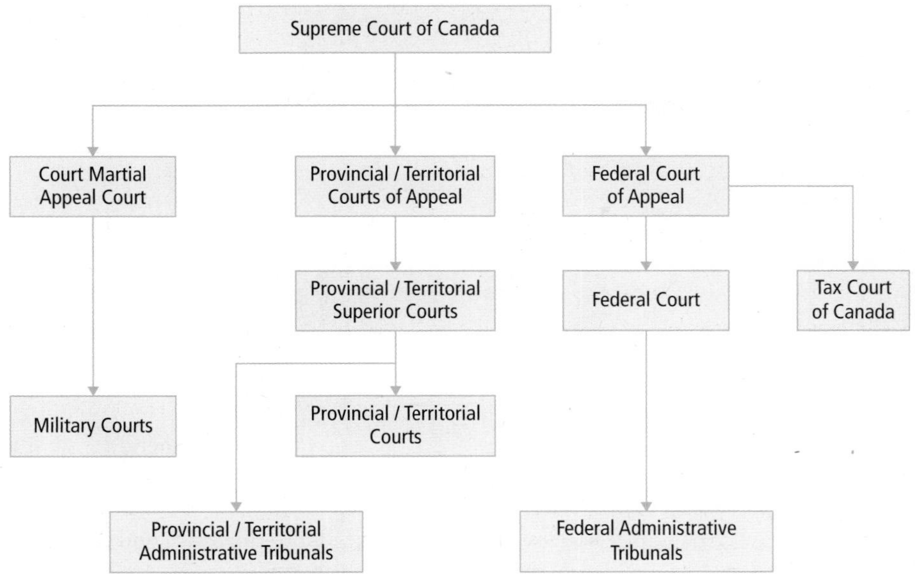

FIGURE 1.5 Canada's Court System: How the Courts Are Organized

The highest level of court in a province or territory—the appeal court—hears appeals from the superior courts and occasionally from provincial courts. These courts do not try criminal court cases; rather, they deal with issues concerning sentence lengths and the possibility of procedural errors. Defendants rarely appear in cases heard in appeal courts. Instead, lawyers representing the Crown and the defendant argue the case before a panel of appeal court judges.

Source: Canada's Court System, http://www.justice.gc.ca/eng/csj-sjc/ccs-ajc/pdf/courten.pdf, Outline of Canada's Court System. Department of Justice Canada, 2015. Reproduced with the permission of the Department of Justice Canada, 2015.

The Formal Organization of the Canadian Criminal Justice System

According to the Law Reform Commission of Canada (1988), a key function of our criminal justice system is to bring offenders to justice. At the same time, our legal system has developed a number of legal rights and protections for those accused of crimes. Various fundamental principles exist that attempt to ensure that no arbitrary actions violate these principles. Our criminal justice system is based on the presumption of innocence of all defendants and is supposed to conduct itself in a manner that is fair, efficient, accountable, participatory, and protective of the legal rights of those arrested and charged with the commission of a criminal action.

An integral part of these guarantees is found in what is known as **criminal procedure**. Criminal procedure is concerned with how criminal justice agencies operate during the interrogation of suspects, the gathering of evidence, and the processing of the accused through the courts. Criminal procedure also ensures that the agents of the state act in a fair and impartial manner in their

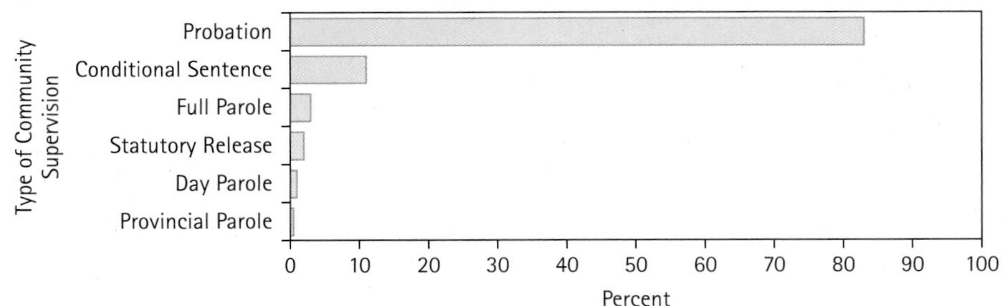

FIGURE 1.6 Average Counts of Adults in Correctional Services, by Community Supervision, Canada, 2010–11

Source: Mia Dauvergne, "Adult correctional statistics in Canada, 2010/11." *Juristat* (May 2012), Statistics Canada Catalogue no. 85-002-X, p. 20, http://www.statcan.gc.ca/pub/85-002-x/2012001/article/11715-eng.pdf. Reproduced and distributed on an "as is" basis with the permission of Statistics Canada.

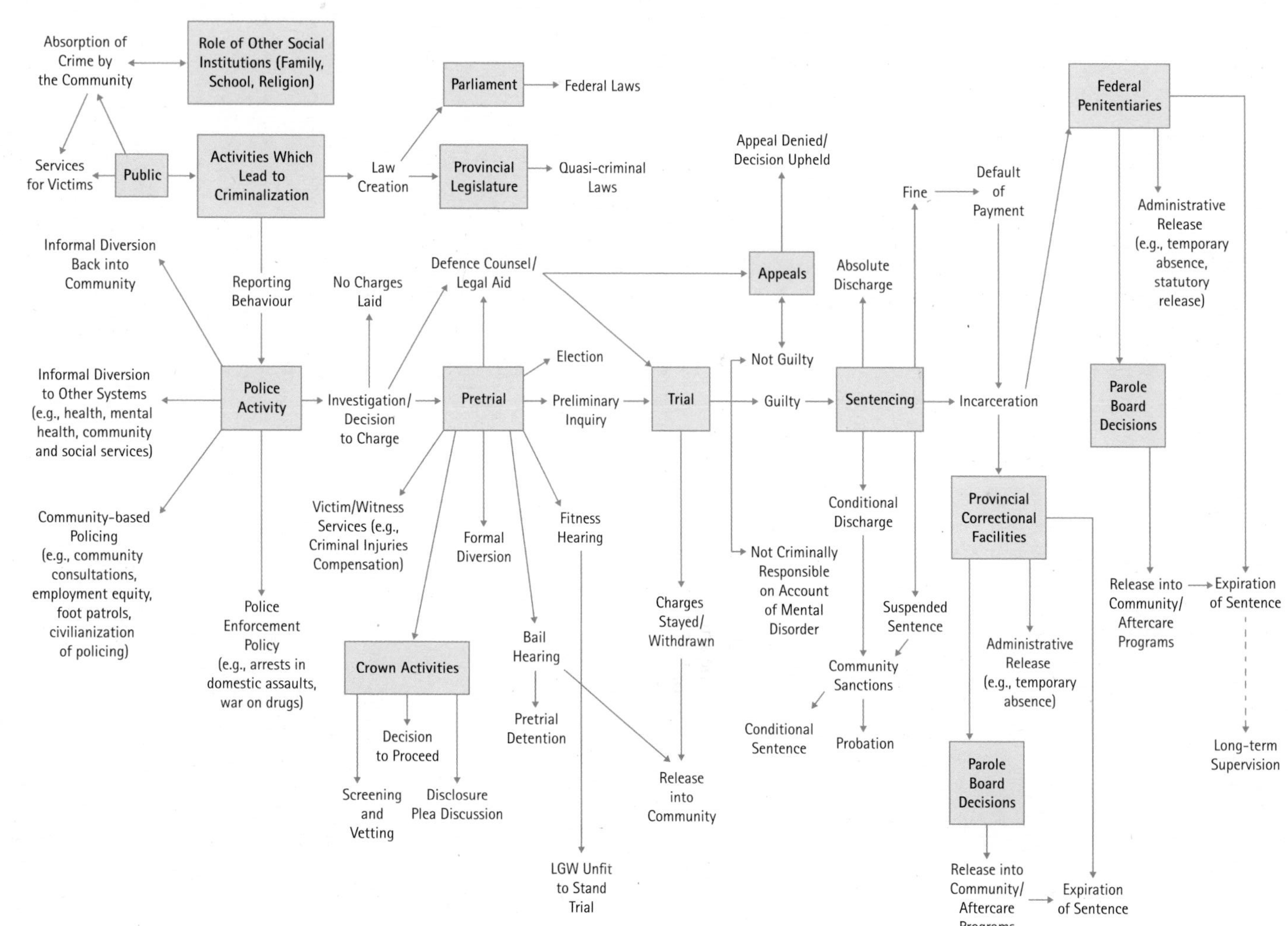

FIGURE 1.7 Overview of the Operation of the Canadian Criminal Justice System

search for truth. Our system of criminal procedure has two major parts: **pretrial procedure** and **trial procedure**. What follows is an overview of the pathway people experience as they are processed through our criminal justice system. One can think of this as a horizontal approach (see Figure 1.7), which includes numerous formal decision making points before they move on to the next stage.

Pretrial Criminal Procedure

Arrest, Appearance Notice, and Summons

The main purpose of arresting someone is to ensure that the accused appears in a criminal court, in which that person's guilt or innocence will be determined. Another purpose of **arrest** is to prevent the commission of any further crimes. With or without a warrant, police officers can arrest a suspect for violating the law.

A **warrant** is issued after a crime has been committed and the police, through their subsequent investigation, have collected enough evidence that they have reasonable and probable grounds to suspect that a certain person committed the offence. Once the evidence has been collected, the police must go to a justice of the peace and **lay an information** against the suspect, indicating why they feel it is in the public interest to arrest the suspect. After the arrest warrant has been signed, the police execute the order by arresting the individual named on the warrant. Most warrants are issued only for the province in which the police investigated the crime. A Canada-wide warrant is issued only after an individual fails to appear in court after being charged with a violent or serious property offence. Even without a warrant, police can arrest an individual. This generally occurs when police officers have no chance to lay an information—for example, when they discover a crime in progress.

Shutterstock

An arrest involves the words of arrest along with the touching of an individual with the purpose of detaining them or the individual submitting to the arrest.

Police officers need not arrest an individual when the offence in question is either a summary conviction offence or an indictable offence that does not allow the accused to choose a jury trial. Nor do police officers need to arrest a suspect (1) when they are certain the suspect will appear in court at the designated time and date, (2) when the prosecutor can proceed by way of a summary or indictable offence (that is, a hybrid offence), or (3) when the offence involves a charge of keeping a gaming or betting house, placing bets, or keeping a common bawdyhouse.

Police may issue an **appearance notice** to a suspect or request a justice of the peace to issue a summons. An appearance notice is given to the suspect by a police officer at the scene of the crime. In these cases, the police officer hands the accused a form with information pertaining to the offence as well as the time and place the accused has to appear in court to answer the charge (or charges). The police officer must lay an information with a justice of the peace as soon as possible thereafter. Another alternative to an arrest is a **summons**. Here the accused is ordered to appear in court by a justice of the peace. The summons must be handed to the accused by a police officer or person granted special powers by provincial authorities. It can also be left at the accused's last known address with an individual who appears to be at least 16 years old. When this document is served, the accused is compelled to appear in court at a designated time and place (Barnhorst and Barnhorst 2004).

Detention

After an individual is arrested, the police have a number of decisions to make about the suspect. For one, they have to determine whether the person arrested should be held in custody before the trial. The law in Canada states that the accused must be released unless there is good reason for keeping him or her in **detention**. The police cannot hold an individual for an undetermined reason; Section 9 of the Charter of Rights and Freedoms states that "everyone has the right not to be arbitrarily detained." In addition, Section 10(a) states that "everyone has the right on arrest or detention to be informed promptly of the reasons thereof." If the arresting officer decides that the accused is to be formally detained, the officer in charge at the police station to which the accused is taken has the discretion to release the suspect. The officer usually exercises that discretion unless the suspect is being charged with a criminal offence punishable by imprisonment of five years or more, the suspect is felt to pose a threat to the public, or the suspect is believed unlikely to appear in court. If the officer decides the accused is to remain in custody, the accused must be taken before a justice of the peace within 24 hours or—if this is not possible—at the earliest possible time. While the accused is in detention, the police may take fingerprints and photographs if the individual is charged with an indictable offence.

Bail or Custody

The purpose of bail is to make sure that the accused appears at the ensuing trial. In Canada today, the Criminal Code requires all individuals arrested to be brought before a justice of the peace, who decides whether the accused is to be released before trial. This hearing is form-ally known as the **judicial interim release hearing**, but is commonly referred to as the bail hearing. The justice of the peace is expected to release the accused unless the prosecutor supplies evidence to show either that the individual should not be released or that conditions should be attached to the release. Those charged with first or second degree murder can be released on bail only by a superior court judge.

Bail is such an important part of the Canadian legal process that s. 11(e) of the Charter of Rights and Freedoms guarantees the right of the accused "not to be denied reasonable bail without just cause." According to s. 457 of the Criminal Code, bail may not be granted when it can be shown to be in the public interest or necessary for the protection or safety of the public, and/or when denial is necessary to ensure the appearance of the accused on the designated date of the trial. In certain circumstances, it is up to the accused to inform the judge why he or she should be released pending trial.

Whether the accused is granted bail or is held until the trial, almost all criminal prosecutions in Canada start with an **information**. According to Mewett and Nakatsuru (2000), this serves two important purposes in the Canadian legal system. First, it compels the accused to appear in court on a specific date and at a designated time. Second, it forms the written basis for the charge that the accused faces in court.

Fitness Hearings

In Canada, an accused person is presumed to be **fit to stand trial**—that is, able to understand the trial proceedings and to instruct defence counsel throughout the trial. If this fitness comes into doubt, there is a system in place to establish whether the accused should have a trial. If issues about the ability of the accused to stand trial are raised at the bail hearing, an assessment can be ordered "on the court's own motion, on application by the accused, or on application of the prosecutor but the latter may apply only if the accused puts it into issue or there are reasonable grounds to doubt fitness" (ibid.:192).

As a result, if there is a **preliminary inquiry**, or a trial where there is no jury, there will be some evidence concerning the fitness of the accused to stand trial. In these instances, the judge alone will make the decision after hearing all the evidence. As we have seen, however, trials involving a judge alone are not as common as trials by judge and jury. If the trial involves a jury, and the issue arises before the trial starts (which is the usual case), a special jury is empanelled to determine whether the accused should be tried. If the jurors agree that the accused is unfit, there won't be a trial; if they agree the accused is fit, the trial will proceed. If the issue is raised during the trial itself, the same jury hearing the trial will determine whether the accused is fit to stand trial.

If it is determined that the accused is fit, there is a trial (or the trial continues). However, if the accused is determined to be unfit, special provisions exist: a judge may decide he or she has enough information to make a decision right away, or may order a review board to formally assess the accused and provide the court with the necessary information—a process that usually takes no more than 45 days. If the accused is found to be unfit to stand trial, there will be no verdict one way or other. Technically, the accused is ordered to be returned to court for trial when it is decided that he or she is fit—although based on a number of factors, such as the seriousness of the charge, the prosecution may decide not to try the accused.

Trial Procedure

The First Court Appearance

In most jurisdictions, the accused is *arraigned*—that is, hears the charges that are being brought and enters a plea in response—not at the first appearance in court but at the preliminary hearing or at trial. During the **arraignment**, the accused is brought before a provincially appointed judge. All formal charges are read by the court clerk at this time and the accused (or the accused's lawyer) makes the initial plea.

Sometimes the defence counsel or prosecutor indicates to the judge that they are not ready to proceed. This usually happens in cases that involve complex issues, where more time is needed to prepare the defence or prosecution. In such cases, the presiding judge agrees to set aside the case until a later date. During the postponement, the conditions that governed the accused individual before the initial appearance will apply. The Charter of Rights and Freedoms guarantees the right to a trial within a reasonable period of time; for this reason, the accused may be asked to waive for the record that Charter right before the court proceeds further (see Chapter 8). Only for that particular adjournment is the right waived; it can be raised again with respect to subsequent delays.

If a plea of not guilty is entered, a trial date is specified. However, if the accused decides to enter a plea of guilty, the judge sets a sentencing date and decides whether the accused is to be held in custody until sentencing. If a plea of not guilty is entered, an information is drafted; but before the actual trial takes place, the accused may have the right to a preliminary inquiry. (It is only when a case goes to the Supreme Court that an indictment is drafted.)

The Indictment and Preliminary Inquiry

When the charge involves an **election indictable offence**—that is, when the accused has the right to choose between trial by judge alone and trial by judge and jury—the next step is to hold a preliminary inquiry. Few cases in Canada involve a preliminary inquiry. However, a preliminary inquiry is a right of the accused and is supposed to be held prior to the formal trial. Preliminary inquiries are heard by a provincial court judge. Summary conviction offences proceed differently from indictable offences in our court system and don't involve a preliminary inquiry.

The purpose of a preliminary inquiry is not to determine the guilt or innocence of the individual charged with a crime but rather to determine whether there is enough evidence to send the accused to trial. During a preliminary inquiry, a prosecutor attempts to show the judge that enough evidence exists for a criminal trial. The prosecution has the power to call as few or as many witnesses as it thinks necessary to prove to the judge that a case merits a trial. Once a witness testifies for the prosecution, defence counsel has the right of cross-examination.

The defence has the right to call witnesses to support a claim of innocence. If the defence can prove to the judge that the prosecution doesn't have a good case, there won't be a trial. Thus, a good defence during the preliminary inquiry can lead to the discharge of the accused. Another reason why the defence may call witnesses is to get their testimony on record, especially if witnesses are sick or about to leave the country. The evidence provided by witnesses during the preliminary inquiry may be used during the trial. Most preliminary inquiries last less than a day, and only rarely does a preliminary inquiry end in a judicial decision to discharge the accused or withdraw the charges. An inquiry is important to defendants because it allows them to "hear the nature and judge the strength" of much of the evidence that the prosecution will use during the trial (Barnhorst and Barnhorst 2004:21). The defendant may then decide to plead guilty. In a study by the Law Reform Commission of Canada (1984), 71 percent of preliminary inquiries resulted in a plea of guilty once the case reached the actual court trial.

When the judge decides that enough evidence exists to proceed to a trial, the offence for which the accused is to stand trial is written in the form of an indictment. The indictment, which replaces the information, forms the basis of the prosecution. It is a formally written allegation that states that the accused has committed a particular offence.

However, even if the judge decides to discharge the accused, this does not mean that the accused is acquitted. It simply means that insufficient evidence exists at this time to proceed to trial. Mewett and Nakatsuru (2000:88) point out that a discharge means that "the accused cannot be tried on that information and that proceedings on that information are terminated." If, at a future date, new evidence is produced and strongly indicates the accused was involved in the crime, the prosecution usually proceeds by way of a direct indictment instead of requesting another preliminary inquiry. Whichever avenue is chosen, the attorney general or a senior official in the provincial justice department is required to give personal approval of the Crown's actions.

The Trial

For most indictable offences, the accused can elect trial by judge alone or by judge and jury. Some exceptions apply—for example, with first and second degree murder charges the accused must be tried by judge and jury unless both the defendant and the attorney general of the province agree to proceed with a judge alone. Some indictable offences (e.g., gaming offences) are considered so minor that they are almost always heard by a judge alone.

In Canada, the accused has the right to change his or her mind about the type of trial chosen, although some restrictions apply. In a re-election, as this process is called, an accused who initially selected trial by a provincial court judge has 14 days to change his or her mind and request a trial by a judge and jury. An accused who originally selected trial by judge and jury has 15 days after the completion of the preliminary inquiry to change his or her mind and select a trial heard by a provincial court judge alone.

Once the indictment is read to the accused in court, that person has to plead to the charge(s) by entering a plea of either guilty or not guilty. If the accused pleads not guilty, the prosecution has to prove that the defendant is guilty of the offence beyond a reasonable doubt. In this

rubberball/Getty Images

A witness is sworn in during trial. All individuals who give evidence in court must swear or, if they object to taking an oath, make a solemn affirmation to tell the truth.

situation, no reasonable amount of doubt concerning the guilt or innocence of the accused can be left unresolved. If reasonable doubt exists, the accused is acquitted of all charges.

Sentencing

If the accused is found guilty, the judge has numerous **sentencing** options available. Commonly applied sentences in Canada include an **absolute** or **conditional discharge**, **probation**, **incarceration**, a **suspended sentence**, and a **fine**. A judge may decide to combine two of these sentences, such as a period of incarceration with a fine. The sentence depends in large part on the charges the individual was found guilty of and the prior record of the offender. In a few instances, a judge has no choice in setting the penalty. For example, a judge who finds an offender guilty of first or second degree murder must sentence the accused to life imprisonment.

In many instances, a judge also relies on a presentence report compiled by a probation officer. This report may evaluate such things as the employment record of the offender and any family support. Other sources of information that a judge may use to determine a sentence include a victim impact statement, information given about the accused at the sentence hearing by the Crown prosecutor or the defence lawyer, and any mitigating or aggravating circumstances surrounding the commission of the crime. These can be significant factors in the sentencing.

Incarceration

If the sentence involves a period of incarceration, the offender is sent to either a provincial jail or a federal institution. If sentenced to a federal institution, the offender can apply for **day parole** six months before being eligible to make an application for full parole. **Full parole** is possible for most offenders after one-third of the sentence or seven years, whichever period is shortest. Most offenders in Canada do not serve the full term of their sentence; if they don't receive full parole, they receive **statutory release** after serving two-thirds of the sentence. While incarcerated, offenders can receive some form of rehabilitation or treatment. Programs have been designed to help offenders reintegrate into society. The amount of treatment given to offenders varies, however. After their release, offenders on parole must contact their parole officer on a regular basis. They may be required to spend some time in a halfway house or under some other form of community supervision.

SUMMING UP AND LOOKING FORWARD

A key function of our criminal justice system is to bring offenders to justice. It closely follows the justice model, which emphasizes legal rights and protections for those accused of crimes. Our criminal justice system is based on the presumption of innocence of all defendants and is supposed to conduct itself in a manner that is fair, efficient, accountable, participatory, and protective of the legal rights of those arrested and charged with the commission of a criminal action.

Much of what we learn about the criminal justice system is formal in nature; that is, the vast majority of those individuals charged are processed through each stage of the system. This system can be divided into two major categories: pretrial procedure and trial procedure.

Pretrial procedures typically involve an individual being investigated by the police, who determine whether or not charges should be laid. They may decide to detain a person, or they may decide to arrest an individual and take them to the police station for further questioning or receive an appearance notice or a summons for a later court date. In those situations where a crime has already been committed, the police may decide to obtain a warrant to arrest someone or to gather evidence. Individuals who are arrested may be placed into custody or apply for bail to ensure that they will appear at a later court hearing.

Once a case reaches court, there are a number of trial procedures. At the first court appearance the individual charged will enter a plea. If it is "not guilty" there usually is a preliminary inquiry. If a decision is made to proceed, there is a trial. If there is a finding of guilt at trial, the individual will be sentenced. In these situations, an individual may be incarcerated for a period of time; prior to completing all of their sentence, they may be released on either day parole, full parole, or statutory release.

This is not always what people experience as they are processed through the system, however. Alternative interpretations have been developed in order to explain a different approach, which is premised on the argument that not all criminal cases are handled in the exact same way by either the police or judiciary. This approach argues that the type of treatment received by an accused is commonly based on their group membership, the seriousness of the charge, the personal status of the individual, as well as their resources. Commonly referred to as the "informal criminal justice system," this model is discussed in the next section.

Review Questions:

1. How has the justice model become the dominant approach taken by our criminal justice system today?
2. What model(s) of criminal justice is (are) most closely associated with the way our criminal justice system operates today?
3. Identify and briefly describe the major components of criminal procedure in our criminal justice system. How does each of these contribute to our understanding of the operation of justice?
4. What are the possible ways of dealing with a suspect after a crime has been committed?
5. What are the most common features of our trial procedure when someone makes the plea of "not guilty"?

The Informal Organization of the Canadian Criminal Justice System

The previous section illustrated the steps through which an accused moves through our criminal justice system in a horizontal fashion. Those who focus upon the informal processing tend to look at our system vertically; that is, some cases are very common and are treated as such, while other high-profile cases and/or defendants are given greater attention. The system operates like a **wedding cake**: Layer 4, the lowest level (where most cases are located), involves lesser offences; Layer 3 includes the less serious crimes; Layer 2 includes the more serious crimes; and Layer 1, the top level, is where the most celebrated cases are and where most of the media attention is focused, since these crimes involve celebrity defendants or unique factors (see Figure 1.9).

The reality of this informal processing has been recognized not only by researchers but also by some members of the legal profession. For example, the Law Reform Commission (1977:12–13) has recognized that, despite the belief that only those who commit crimes are formally charged, processed, and tried, and only those convicted of a crime are punished, "reality falls short of aspiration" . . . and . . . "our picture of the criminal justice system bears little resemblance to reality." An important aspect of this approach is its attention to the ways in which the organizational and institutional cultures found within criminal justice agencies can affect the services provided to offenders. A variety of approaches have been forwarded that attempt to explain the operations of the informal system of criminal justice.

People researching our criminal justice system believe that almost everyone who enters it experiences quite a different process than that pictured by the formal system. For example, Ericson and Baranek (1982) argue that the formal system operates only in theory and that the legal protections given to the accused are frequently ignored

Criminal Justice Insight

The Crime Funnel

The criminal justice funnel reveals how decisions made at one stage in our criminal justice system impact the next stage by sorting out who should and should not continue (Figure 1.8). This is referred to as *case attrition*; that is, at each stage of the funnel, there are fewer people than before, as more people are released or placed into other parts of the system—for example, when a judge decides to sentence someone to a community sanction instead of sending them to a correctional facility. The decisions made throughout the criminal justice funnel by authorities oftentimes reflect the strength of the case. For example, prosecutors may decide that there is not enough evidence to proceed with the charges and judges may decide that the crime was not serious enough to send the person convicted to a correctional facility, especially after looking at their (non-existent) prior record. In other words, the criminal justice system is considered to be fair and just.

Decisions made by lax officials also may lead to reductions throughout the funnel. There are too many loopholes in the system and the result is offenders being dealt with "too easily." This leads to claims that the criminal justice system is unfair and unjust.

Does the criminal justice funnel represent a system operating in a fair and just way, according to formal rules, or does it represent an informal system where fairness and justice is compromised?

Continued on next page

Criminal Justice Insight (*Continued*)

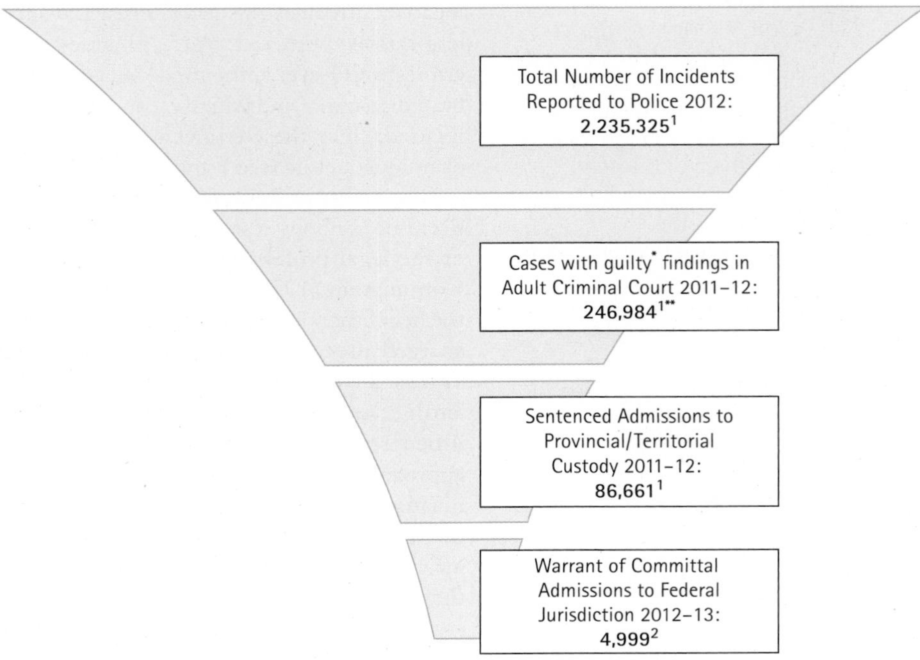

FIGURE 1.8 The Criminal Justice Funnel

The criminal justice funnel reveals that at each stage in the criminal justice system, fewer numbers of people are processed at the next stage.

[1] Uniform Crime Reporting Survey, Adult Criminal Court Survey, and Adult Correctional Services Survey, Canadian Centre for Justice Statistics, Statistics Canada.

[2] Correctional Service Canada.

* The type of decision group "guilty" includes guilty of the offence, of an included offence, of an attempt of the offence, or of an attempt of an included offence. This category also includes cases where an absolute or conditional discharge has been imposed.

** This figure only includes cases in provincial court and partial data from Superior Court. Superior Court data are not reported to the Adult Criminal Court Survey for Quebec, Ontario, Manitoba and Saskatchewan. Information from Quebec's municipal courts is not collected.

Source: Corrections and Conditional Release Statistical Overview Annual Report 2013, Fig. A-7, p. 13, http://www.publicsafety.gc.ca/cnt/rsrcs/pblctns/crrctns-cndtnl-rls-2013/crrctns-cndtnl-tls-2013-eng.pdf. Reproduced with the permission of the Minister of Public Safety and Emergency Preparedness, 2015.

or plea bargained away by the defence counsel and prosecutor. As such, "**legal justice**" does not exist. Instead, most defendants receive a form of "**bargain justice**," where the accused is encouraged to plead guilty in return for a reduced sentence or the dropping of a number of charges. These critics argue that the final result is a court system in which the vast majority of the accused plead guilty before any item of evidence is contested in open court. Guilty pleas usually involve a reduction in the number of charges or a recommendation to the judge that the sentence be reduced.

Provincial criminal court dockets are crowded with individuals who are charged with lesser offences and waiting to have their cases heard. The courtrooms themselves have an air of "assembly-line justice"; defendants line up to enter the courtroom, only to have their cases summarily dispatched. Defendants in these courts rarely contest their cases in front of a judge. Researchers and observers report that most defendants who enter the provincial courts plead guilty to the charges during their initial appearance or find the charges either stayed (postponed indefinitely) or withdrawn by a prosecutor (Desroches 1995; Ericson and Baranek 1982; Ursel 1994; Wheeler 1987). Desroches (1995:252) reported that 90 percent of the 70 robbers he interviewed pleaded guilty in provincial court, quickly averting any argument over

FIGURE 1.9 The Wedding Cake Model of Crime

The wedding cake model of criminal justice features a four-tiered hierarchy of criminal cases, with the tiers decreasing in size as the severity of the cases increases. A small number of celebrated cases make up the highest tier level.

the charges in an open courtroom. Most indicated they pleaded guilty simply because they wanted to "get the thing over with." Most criminal cases in Canada end up being heard in the provincial courts, which handle routine criminal cases. This is the extent of most Canadians' involvement in the court system.

One of the first approaches developed to explain the informal nature of our justice system is the **courtroom work group**. The existence of this group disputes the belief that the criminal courts operate as a formal, rational legal system (i.e., a bureaucracy) with all of its members following the rule of law and well-defined rules as they go about their daily work roles. Instead, courts consist of informal work groups whose members hold considerable discretion, largely as a result of professional bonds that have developed among the members (Eisenstein and Jacobs 1974). One important feature of this group is group cohesion—that is, everyone involved cooperates with everyone else, and the members establish shared methods and values that help the group as a whole achieve its goals. As a result, the needs of the group members take precedence over concerns about the system's fairness and equality. The relationships among the individuals in this group have a significant impact on the day-to-day operations of the various criminal justice agencies and on the outcomes of individual cases.

An essential component of the courtroom work group is that it develops a shared understanding of **normal crimes**, which refers to the social characteristics of the individuals who have been charged with a criminal offence, the settings in which the alleged crime has occurred, and the types of victims that are involved. In these cases, the members of the courtroom workgroup "make sense" of the individuals and cases being processed through the courts, an assessment that may only in part be influenced by legal (statutory) definitions of crime (Sudnow 1965).

Three other characteristics of the courtroom work group essentially allow its members to accomplish their tasks: (1) there is an emphasis on speed—that is, on disposing of cases rather than dispensing justice; (2) guilt is presumed—in other words, it is generally understood that individuals charged by the police are in fact guilty; (3) secrecy is prized, because it enables all members to decide cases among themselves and to keep these negotiations private. All of these have a significant impact on the daily operations of our justice system and on the type of justice administered to and experienced by both offenders and victims.

An alternative approach to explaining the processing of cases through the criminal justice system is referred to as the **criminal justice funnel** (see *Criminal Justice Insight* on pp. 23–24). When a crime is committed and the offender is charged by the police, the case enters the top of the funnel. From there, it passes through ever-narrowing stages until it exits. Sometimes this exiting occurs at the bottom of the funnel, with the offender being sent to a correctional facility, but it can also exit higher up the funnel, such as when all charges are dropped because a witness refuses to testify or because the prosecutor feels the evidence is not sufficient. Between the top and bottom of this funnel, then, are key decision-making points; at each, the case load has the potential to be reduced.

The actors and agencies in our criminal justice system are controlled by the formal rules of law; that said, they enjoy considerable leeway in how they prioritize and carry out their activities. According to those who study the informal criminal justice system, the system as a whole is best perceived as a process. This view emphasizes the key decision points through which cases pass. Each decision point is, in effect, a screening stage that involves a series of routinized operations; its efficacy is gauged primarily in terms of its ability to move a case to its next stage and a successful conclusion. The processing of individuals through our criminal justice system has in effect become a system of human resource management. The various actors go about their daily activities without stepping on toes, all the while bending informal social and agency rules. Part of this system is dedicated to the search for simple solutions. Simple routine justice treats similarly situated defendants in the same ways. Its central elements correspond more to the personal and political needs of justice personnel than to any abstract concept of justice or the rule of law.

For others, a characteristic of our criminal justice system is that people are treated unfavourably on the basis of a number of factors, such as their gender, social class, race, ethnicity, and sexual preference. This is due to **discretion**, i.e., the ability of an individual or organization within our criminal justice system to take alternative courses of action beyond the formal rules and procedures. This discretion leads to disparity and discrimination, both of which occur "where the law is permissive and individual discretion wide, and that where there are few guidelines as to how a decision should be taken, decision making is often based on subjective judgments. . . ." (Gelsthorpe and Padfield 2003:4).

Disparity

Disparity refers to a difference, but one that doesn't necessarily include discrimination. Concerns about disparity in our criminal justice system arise when inconsistencies appear as a result of the authorities using illegitimate factors when making their decisions. In the area of criminal justice, disparity has most commonly been raised with sentencing, most specifically whether people receive different sentences for similar offences. However, it has also been used to analyze a broader issue, notably whether individuals, such as offenders and victims, are treated equally or unequally when there are similar circumstances. As Gelsthorpe and Padfield (ibid.) note, when a disparity is found it "strikes at the heart of the ideal . . . that all are equal before the law."

Legitimate reasons for differences include appropriate legal factors such as the seriousness of the offence and the prior record of the offender. These are considered to be legitimate reasons for differences in our treatment of alleged offenders and those convicted of a crime within our criminal justice system since they are specifically concerned with the criminal behaviour of the offender. Illegitimate factors are extralegal factors, such as race, religion, and gender, which involve decisions about the group the alleged offender belongs to and are unrelated to the criminal activity of any particular individual. For example, our criminal justice system is not supposed to operate or decide about a person's criminality on the basis of his or her social class. If it did, it is entirely possible that middle and upper-class individuals who commit crimes would serve their sentence within the community, while members of the working class would receive a prison sentence.

Discrimination

Discrimination refers to the differential treatment of individuals based on negative judgments relating to their perceived or real membership in a group. In other words, something about an individual (e.g., race) overrides their other qualities (e.g., educational attainment). Most research efforts in the area of discrimination focus upon gender and race, while less has studied sexual orientation, age, religion, and disability. Discrimination can occur when individuals or groups are perceived as inferior or difficult (Gelsthorpe and Padfield 2003).

Various types of discrimination have been identified, and each has the potential to influence fairness in a variety of different ways in our criminal justice system. **Systemic discrimination** refers to discrimination (e.g., race and/or gender) existing in all aspects of the operations of our criminal justice system. This means that discrimination can consistently be found in the rates of arrest, the type of charges laid, and the decision to prosecute or stay charges, as well as in the conviction rates and types of sentences given to those convicted without any significant variation over a selected time period. Provincial inquiries into the treatment of racial minorities within the Canadian criminal justice system during the 1990s (e.g., the Manitoba Aboriginal Justice Inquiry) reported the existence of systemic discrimination.

With **institutionalized discrimination**, disparities appear in the outcomes of decisions. Such disparities are the result of established (i.e., institutionalized) policies in the criminal justice system. These policies do not directly involve extralegal factors such as an individual's employment status, race, gender, or religion. The main issue here is one of system outcomes or results rather than any intent to discriminate against a specific individual or member of a group. One example involves decisions made within the criminal justice system based on the employment status of those accused of a crime when they are applying for bail. A policy granting bail made on the basis of the employment status of the accused can be legitimized on the basis of research showing that employed persons are better risks for showing up for trial than those who are unemployed. But what if all men are employed and very few women are? Since women are disproportionately overrepresented among the unemployed, they are more likely to be denied bail. This result is referred to as a *gender effect*, which means that discrimination is the result of a policy that is not concerned with the gender of those who apply for bail. Institutional discrimination is the result of a policy; it does not exist because of individuals who are prejudiced.

Contextual discrimination arises from organizational policies within criminal justice agencies such as

In its study of the treatment of Aboriginal peoples in the criminal justice system in Manitoba, the *Aboriginal Justice Inquiry* found evidence of systemic discrimination across the province.

the police and the courts. One example is when a police service fails to enforce the criminal harassment (or anti-stalking) provisions of the Criminal Code simply because it foresees the complainant dropping charges before the case enters the courts. Another example is when a judge sent-ences the members of one racial minority group more harshly when they victimize the members of another racial group, but less severely when they victimize a member of their own racial group.

Individual discrimination occurs when an individual employed within the criminal justice system acts in a way that discriminates against the members of certain groups. For example, a police officer may discriminate against members of a certain social class and/or ethnic group by arresting them in all circumstances while only giving warnings to all others.

It is important, however, to recognize that discrimination and disparities can be permitted under exceptional conditions in our criminal justice system. For example, an individual who is found not criminally responsible for committing a crime may in fact face a longer sentence than a criminally responsible offender convicted of the same offence. This is because the potential exists for the individual found not criminally responsible to receive an indeterminate sentence, whereas the criminally responsible offender receives a designated term of punishment. It has been argued (*Winko v. Forensic Psychiatric Institute* [1999]; *R. v. LePage* [1999]) that this policy discriminates against the mentally disordered. The Supreme Court of Canada upheld the relevant Criminal Code provision (s. 672.65) even though a disparity resulted. The Court held that for an individual convicted in a criminal court, a specific period of incarceration is punishment for the criminal act. A more flexible approach is warranted for offenders who are not criminally responsible, given that they are not morally responsible for their actions. In such cases, the purpose of punishment is the protection of society and the treatment of the offender (Mewett and Nakatsuru 2000).

SUMMING UP AND LOOKING FORWARD

Not all criminal cases are viewed or processed in the same manner despite claims to the contrary. The type of treatment given to any particular case may be determined by such factors as an individual's membership in a particular group, their social status, the seriousness of the offence and the defendant's ability to use their personal resources. For many critics, then, the processing of cases through our criminal justice system does meet the expectations set out in the essential characteristics of justice. This has been referred to as the informal criminal justice system and a number of explanations have been forwarded to try to explain it, such as the courtroom work group and the criminal justice funnel. Discretion is a common feature in these approaches, and the concern is that disparity and various types of discrimination may occur.

This chapter has largely focused upon an approach to achieving and delivering justice through the normative framework of the criminal justice system. It was also noted that this approach can be ignored by those working within the criminal justice system and who decide to use informal mechanisms to control offenders. This section presents yet another perspective: a response (typically called "tough on crime") developed by the federal Conservative government largely based upon public attitudes about the importance of increasing punishments for offenders. This approach to criminal justice policy is largely based upon the belief that there are increasing levels of crime (see Chapter 4 for the most recent crime statistics), the reoffending rates of serious, violent offenders, as well as a decline in the "moral framework" of society. Some have questioned this approach by arguing that it contravenes many aspects of our normative framework of our criminal justice system and that it has no correspondence to crime rates. As later chapters are considered, it will be possible to assess many of these new directives to achieving and delivering justice.

Review Questions:

1. Is our criminal justice system always "just"?
2. Is it inevitable that discretion will exist in our criminal justice system? Is it possible for significant amounts of discretion to coexist with the essential characteristics of our criminal justice?
3. Define disparity and discrimination. What is the potential negative impact of each on our criminal justice system?

Critical Issues in Canadian Criminal Justice

ANTI-TERRORISM LAWS: CRIME CONTROL OR DUE PROCESS?

Laws usually evolve in a deliberate manner in our society. However, this approach has changed in Canada following two events. The first occurred immediately after 8:45 A.M. on the morning of September 11, 2001, when American Airlines Flight 11 was flown into the North Tower of the World Trade Center in New York City by hijackers. The second was after two members of the Canadian Armed Forces, Warrant Officer Patrice Vincent and Corporal Nathan Cirillo, were killed in attacks in Saint-Jean-Sur-Richelieu, Quebec, and Ottawa, respectively, in October 2014.

Both of these events led the federal government and many Canadians to ask whether we are sufficiently prepared to handle such actions. More specifically, if laws had been in place in Canada, could these attacks have somehow been prevented? How should we react to such actions in the future? Even in situations like this, with almost all Canadians demanding some form of legal response, the creation of new legal powers can involve difficult decisions about how anti-terrorism laws should be enacted. Should the government pass laws that place some restrictions on the principles of fundamental justice, as found in the Charter of Rights and Freedoms, for an accused? Or should the laws follow these principles, thereby guaranteeing the accused a trial with all of the safeguards found in our criminal justice system?

Maxime Deland/QMI Agency

Fred Lum/The Globe and Mail

The deaths of two soldiers in the fall of 2014 led the Canadian Government to introduce new anti-terrorist legislation (Bill C-51).

The Government's Response

After 9/11, the federal government introduced two pieces of legislation to deal with terrorism in Canada. The first, introduced on October 15, 2001, was the Anti-terrorism Act (Bill C-36), which created measures to (1) identify, prosecute, convict, and punish terrorists and terrorist organizations; and (2) give new investigative powers to law enforcement and security agencies. Some of the measures included the following:

- Defining and designating terrorist groups to make it easier to prosecute terrorists and their supporters.
- Making it an offence to knowingly participate in, contribute to, or facilitate the activities of a terrorist group or to instruct anyone to carry out a terrorist activity or an activity on behalf of a terrorist group.
- Creating tougher sentences and parole supervision for terrorist offenders.

- Cutting off financial support for terrorists by making it a crime to knowingly collect or give funds to them, either directly or indirectly.

The second proposal to extend law enforcement and security agencies involves powerful new investigative tools to collect information about and prosecute terrorists and terrorist groups. These tools included the following:

- Making it easier to use electronic surveillance against terrorist organizations.
- Creating new offences targeting unlawful disclosure of certain information of national interest.
- Amending the Canada Evidence Act to guard certain information of national interest from disclosure during courtroom or other judicial proceedings.
- Within certain defined limits, allowing the arrest of suspected terrorists and their detention for 72 hours without charge, in order to prevent terrorist acts and save lives.
- Establishing investigative hearings with the power to compel individuals possessing information about a terrorist organization to disclose that information to a judge even in the absence of a formal trial.

Some criticized these new measures, arguing that Bill C-36 violated human rights in Canada, as well as failing to balance individual liberties with the security interests of the country.

Preventive Detention and Investigation Hearings

In the Anti-terrorism Act, many considered the "investigation hearings" and "preventive detention" sections to be the most controversial. Investigative hearings (s. 83.28 of the Criminal Code) are designed to allow the Crown to approve an application for an order requiring an individual who has not yet been charged with an offence to appear before the court for questioning about a terrorist offence. After an order is granted under s. 83.28, the individual in question could be arrested, compelled to give answers to questions, and charged with contempt for refusing to testify or for providing false testimony (Diab 2008:65).

The preventive arrest clause (s. 83.3 of the Criminal Code) enables the police to arrest suspects without a warrant and detain them for up to 72 hours without charge before a judge has to decide to impose a peace bond if the authorities had reason to believe a terrorist act would be committed. Once a peace bond is issued, the detention ends. Bonds can be used to impose stringent conditions on individuals up to a maximum of 12 months. If the bond's conditions are violated or refused, the judge can extend it. See Exhibit 1.5 for a timeline of Canada's anti-terrorism measures.

EXHIBIT 1.5 Timeline for Selected Anti-terrorism Measures in Canada

October 2001	Bill C-36 Anti-terrorism Act introduced into Parliament
December 2001	Bill C-36 enacted
May 2004	Bill C-42 Public Safety Act enacted
February 2007	Parliament defeats a motion that proposed extending the preventive arrest and investigative hearing provisions
October 2007	Federal government introduces Bill C-3, reintroducing both the preventive arrest and investigative hearing provisions
September 2008	Bill C-3 dies on the Order Paper with the call for a federal election
March 2009	Bill C-3 reintroduced as Bill C-19; this bill dies on the Order Paper in December 2009
April 2010	Bill C-19 reintroduced as Bill C-17; this bill dies on the Order Paper in March 2011
November 2011	Bill S-215 An Act to amend the Criminal Code (suicide bombings) enacted
February 2012	Bill C-17 Combating Terrorism Act reintroduced as Bill C-7
February 2012	Bill C-13 Protecting Canadians from Online Crime Act introduced
March 2012	Bill C-10 Justice for Victims of Terrorism Act enacted
July 2013	Bill C-7 Combating Terrorism Act enacted
November 2013	Bill S-9 Nuclear Terrorism Act enacted
October 2014	Bill C-44 Protection of Canada from Terrorists Act introduced
December 2014	Bill C-13 passes; comes into force in March 2015
January 2015	Bill C-51 Anti-terrorism Act, 2015 is introduced
April 2015	Bill C-44 receives Royal Assent and becomes law
June 2015	Bill C-51 passes and becomes law

Continued on next page

Critical Issues in Canadian Criminal Justice *(Continued)*

When the investigative hearing and preventive arrest sections were included in the Anti-terrorism Act, concerns were expressed that they would override civil liberties. As a result, the federal government placed a "sunset" clause on the provisions of the law enabling "preventive arrests" and "investigative hearings." Both provisions were to expire at the end of February 2007, unless the House of Commons and Senate passed a resolution to extend them.

After five years, neither one had been used; nevertheless, the federal government decided to attempt to renew both the investigative arrest and preventive arrest clauses of the Anti-terrorism Act. In its House of Commons Committee Interim Report on Preventive Arrests and Investigative Hearings (2006), all members of the committee agreed that investigative hearings be extended to December 31, 2011, but recommended that such hearings should be held only when there is reason to believe that there was "imminent peril that a terrorist offence would be committed." A majority of the Committee also agreed that the preventive arrests should be continued, but some members pointed out that they could be used to label an individual as a terrorist on the basis of a reasonable suspicion.

In February 2007, when the two provisions were close to expiring, the minority Conservative federal government introduced a motion into Parliament extending preventive arrests and investigative hearings for the next three years (Bill C-3). A few weeks later this motion was defeated. In July 2007, the federal government stated that it intended to reintroduce both provisions. They added that they did not intend to include review and sunset provisions to the proposed legislation. This Bill was introduced but did not pass due to the fact that a federal election was called in September 2008.

After forming a majority government in 2011, the Conservative federal government in February 2012 introduced legislation designed to bring back preventive detentions. The preventive detention clause allows the police to arrest suspects without a warrant and hold them for up to 72 hours without charge if they believe that a terrorist act has been committed. The individual can then be released after a judge stipulates a number of conditions for them to follow. It is also required compelled testimony when requested by a judge, but this testimony could not be used against an individual in a future criminal case. The new provisions also created a number of new offences, such as making it an offence to leave, or attempt to leave, Canada to attend a terrorist training camp, leaving Canada to facilitate a terrorist activity, and leaving Canada to commit an offence for the benefit of a terrorist group. To date, only four verdicts have been reached in cases involving a terrorism charge and only six peace bonds have been imposed.

Security Certificates

Security certificates were introduced in the Immigration Act in 1988. This provision was strengthened in 2002 after the 9/11 attacks in order to give authorities a faster and more efficient way to remove non-citizen terrorist suspects from Canada without having to lay charges and then process the accused through the criminal justice system as they would a citizen of Canada. Two cabinet ministers view secret intelligence and sign a certificate declaring a non-resident a national security risk, leading to potential deportation. Suspects who argue that they would face torture in their homelands could spend an indefinite amount of time in jail, without criminal charges, as their cases work their way through the courts. This process was described by some as "draconian" as accused persons and their counsel are provided with only a vague summary of the allegations against them. Evidence to back up the allegations is received in secret by a judge, and neither the accused nor his or her lawyer can attend (Makin 2007).

Security certificates were challenged in the Supreme Court (*Charkaoui v. Canada [Minister of Citizenship and Immigration]* 2007). On February 23, 2007, the Supreme Court, in a 9–0 ruling, invalidated provisions of the Immigration and Refugee Protection Act that denied persons named in security certificates a right to a fair hearing—the right to know and to be able to rebut the information against them. In its decision, the Supreme Court wrote that "the state can detain people for significant periods of time; it must accord them a fair judicial process." They also decided that "without this information, the named person may not be in a position to contradict errors, identify omissions, challenge the credibility of the informants or refute false allegations." The court also stated that foreign nationals who do not live in Canada should be treated on par with permanent residents and given the chance to file applications for judicial review of a security certificate immediately after being detained, instead of having to wait 120 days to make any filing, as they do under the post-9/11 rules.

In its decision, the Supreme Court made several suggestions to "Charter-proof" the certificates, including allowing a security-cleared "special advocate" into a hearing to look out for the interests of the accused, a system that existed in the United Kingdom. At the same time, the court cautioned that a suspect's right to the government's case "is not absolute" and some evidence may have to remain secret to protect national security (Tibbetts 2007). The Supreme Court suspended its ruling for one year in order to allow the government to introduce new legislation in its place.

In October 2007, the Conservative government introduced Bill C-3, An Act to amend the Immigration and Refugee Protection Act (certificates and special advocates), in response to the Supreme Court ruling. It received Royal Assent on February 13, 2008. The new legislation introduced a special advocate into the certificate process. The role of the special advocate is to protect the interests of those individuals subject to a certificate hearing during the closed proceedings. They are also able to argue before federal judges that certain evidence should not be secret, and they could cross-examine government witnesses. They are able to cross-examine witnesses, make submissions to the Court, and communicate with the individual in question until such time that they are allowed to view the confidential information.

Less than a week following the deaths of the two soldiers and the attack on Parliament Hill, the federal government tabled a new bill, Bill C-51 (Anti-terrorism Act, 2015). The bill, prepared prior to the shootings in October, proposes to give new powers to the police and the Canadian Security Intelligence Service (CSIS). In the bill, the police and CSIS are given greater authority, while requiring less evidence in their counterterrorism investigations. Critics argued that these new powers give the authorities too much power, and have too little oversight by Parliament (Wingrove 2014). Bill C-51 became law in June 2015.

Questions

1. Do you think that the provisions found in the Anti-terrorism Act will help deter terrorist acts?
2. Do you believe that the creation of "special advocates" for the accused under the Anti-terrorism Act is sufficient to ensure that the due process of rights of the accused is upheld?
3. In the wake of terrorist acts, how can the federal government protect the legal rights of all residents of Canada while at the same time ensuring the safety of the rest of the public?
4. In a time of crisis, should the federal government be allowed to give itself extraordinary legal powers even if they violate individual rights?

SUMMARY

What Is Crime and How Is It Regulated in Canada?

What Is Crime? (p. 3)

In order to understand our criminal justice system, this section explored the importance of social control as well as differing definitions of "crime" and their impact upon the role of criminal legislation and what we perceive to be behaviour that has to be regulated.

KEY WORDS: social control, "black letter" approach, social norms, social construct.

What Is the Normative Framework of Our Criminal Justice System?

The Adversarial System (p. 7)
Substantive and Procedural Justice (p. 7)
The Rule of Law (p. 8)
Access to Justice (p. 8)
Legitimacy of Criminal Justice Institutions (p. 10)

A number of key characteristics form the basis of our criminal justice system, and while some of these may be more recognizable than others, each impacts the decisions made throughout the entire system. This section explored these characteristics of our system of criminal justice.

KEY WORDS: normative approach to criminal justice, adversarial system, substantive justice, procedural justice, rule of law, access to justice, legal aid, public interest law, informal justice, legitimacy, procedural justice.

What Are the Goals of Our Criminal Justice System?

This section explored what our criminal justice system seeks to achieve. Is it to reduce the amount of crime and to prevent crime in the future? A number of models of the criminal justice system have been developed in order to offer explanations about the proper role of the various agencies as well as what policies should be adopted.

KEY WORDS: due process model, crime control model, medical (rehabilitation) model, bureaucratic model, punitive model of victims' rights, non-punitive model of victims' rights.

What Is Criminal Justice?

The Structure of the Criminal Justice System (p. 15)
The Formal Organization of the Canadian Criminal Justice System (p. 17)
Pretrial Criminal Procedure (p. 18)
Trial Procedure (p. 20)
Sentencing (p. 22)
Incarceration (p. 22)

What are the key points that people experience as they are being processed in our criminal justice system? This section focused upon the dominant interpretation of criminal justice in Canada, how the criminal justice system is structured in terms of the major agencies (the police, courts, and corrections), as well as the formal procedures and decision points people experience as they are being processed through the criminal justice system.

KEY WORDS: justice model, lower courts, superior courts, criminal procedure, pretrial procedure, trial procedure, arrest, warrant, lay an information, appearance notice, summons, detention, judicial interim release hearing, bail, information, fit to stand trial, preliminary inquiry, arraignment, election indictable offence, sentencing, absolute discharge, conditional discharge, probation, incarceration, suspended sentence, fine, day parole, full parole, statutory release.

The Informal Organization of the Canadian Criminal Justice System

Disparity (p. 26)
Discrimination (p. 26)

The operation of our criminal justice system may be more informal than formal, which means that the majority of people being processed in our criminal justice system receive bargain justice rather than legal justice. This section provided an overview of how the informal system operates and what impact it might have upon individuals and groups.

KEY WORDS: wedding cake model, legal justice, bargain justice, courtroom work group, normal crimes, criminal justice funnel, discretion, disparity, discrimination, systemic discrimination, institutionalized discrimination, contextual discrimination, individual discrimination.

Critical Thinking Questions

1. In order to understand our criminal justice system we need to explore the differing definitions of "crime" and the impact these have upon the role of criminal legislation and what we perceive to be behaviour that has to be regulated. What definition of crime best describes how our criminal justice system operates?
2. A number of key characteristics form the basis of our criminal justice system, and while some of these may be more recognizable than others, each impacts the decisions made throughout the entire system. What are the essential characteristics of the normative approach to our criminal justice system?

3. What does our criminal justice system seek to achieve? Is it to reduce the amount of crime and to prevent crime in the future? Is it to treat all people equally and achieve equal justice for all?
4. According to the crime control model, the primary focus of our criminal justice is a safe and secure society, while the due process model guarantees that fair procedures will be used throughout the system. Based on these two models, what should be the primary focus of our criminal justice system? Should it include goals from other models discussed in the text?
5. What are the key points that people experience as they are being processed through the formal structure of our criminal justice system? In the formal criminal justice system, courts are legal institutions where lawyers fight to defend their clients, prosecutors fight to protect society, and neutral judges act as referees to make sure the system is fair and operates according to the principles of fundamental justice.
6. The operation of our criminal justice system may be more informal than formal. In the informal criminal justice system, trials are conducted for the purpose of sanctioning what was decided behind closed doors. Once defendants are charged, prosecutors, defence lawyers, and judges agree they are guilty of something so the main issue is to determine the appropriate punishment. Defendants are outsiders in this process. What are the implications of an informal approach for our system of criminal justice?

Weblinks

The issue of assisted dying has been of great interest to Canadians in recent years. To understand many of the legal issues surrounding this issue, watch the following video on YouTube: "Mini Law School: A Conversation about Assisted Dying: What Does the Law Have to Say?" (1:18:09).

Court Cases

B.C.G.E.U. v. B.C. (A.G.) (1988), 2 S.C.R. 214.

Carter v. Canada (Attorney General) (2015), S.C.C. 5.

Charkaoui v. Canada (Minister of Citizenship and Immigration) (2007), 1 S.C.R. 350.

R. v. Latimer (2001), 1 S.C.R. 3.

R. v. LePage (1999), 2 S.C.R. 744.

Rodriguez v. British Columbia (Attorney General) (1993), 3 S.C.R. 519.

Winko v. Forensic Psychiatric Institute (1999), 2 S.C.R. 625.

Suggested Readings

Bauslaugh, G. 2010. *Robert Latimer: A Story of Justice and Mercy*. Toronto: James Lorimer & Company.

Ericson, R.V. and P.M. Baranek. 1982. *The Ordering of Justice: A Study of Accused Persons as Dependants in the Criminal Justice Process*. Toronto: University of Toronto Press.

Godfrey, R. 2006. *Under The Bridge*. Toronto: HarperCollins.

Mallea, P. 2011. *Fearmonger: Stephen Harper's Tough-on-Crime Agenda*. Toronto: James Lorimer.

Roach, K. 2010. *The 9/11 Effect: Comparative Counter-Terrorism*. Cambridge: Cambridge University Press.

Royal Society of Canada. 2011. *The Royal Society of Canada Expert Panel: End of Life Decision-Making*. Ottawa: The Royal Society of Canada.

References

Ashworth, A. and M. Redmayne. 2010. *The Criminal Process: An Evaluation Study*. 4th ed. Oxford: Oxford University Press.

Barnhorst, R. and S. Barnhorst. 2004. *Criminal Law and the Canadian Criminal Code*. 4th ed. Toronto: McGraw-Hill Ryerson.

Billingsley, B. 2002. "The Rule of Law: What Is It? Why Should We Care?" *LawNow* 26:27–30.

Bowal, P. and B. Lau. 2005. "The Contours of What Is Criminal." *LawNow* 29:8–10.

Boyce, J. 2013. *Adult Criminal Court Statistics in Canada, 2011/2012*. Ottawa: Canadian Centre for Justice Statistics.

Canadian Bar Association. 2003. "Euthanasia: The Debate Is Far from Over," *National*, August/September, p. 28.

Dauvergne, M. 2012. *Adult Correctional Statistics in Canada, 2010/2011*. Ottawa: Canadian Centre for Justice Statistics.

Davies, M., H. Croall, and J. Tyrer. 2005. *Criminal Justice: An Introduction to the Criminal Justice System in England and Wales*. 3rd ed. Essex: England.

Davison, C.B. 2006. "Procedural Justice Preserves Fundamental Fairness." *LawNow* 30:17–19.

Desroches, F.J. 1995. *Force and Fear: Robbery in Canada*. Scarborough, ON: Nelson Canada.

Diab, R. 2008. *Guantanamo North: Terrorism and the Administration of Justice in Canada*. Halifax: Fernwood.

Eckstein, C. 2007. *History of Euthanasia, Part 1*. Retrieved May 9, 2009 (www.chninternational.com).

Eisenstein, J. and H. Jacobs. 1974. *Felony Justice: An Organizational Analysis of Criminal Courts*. Boston: Little Brown.

Ericson, R. and P.M. Baranek. 1982. *The Ordering of Justice: A Study of Accused Persons as Defendants in the Criminal Process*. Toronto: University of Toronto Press.

Gelsthorpe, L. and N. Padfield. 2003. *Exercising Discretion: Decision-Making in the Criminal Justice System and Beyond*. Devon: Willan.

Hudson, B. 2006. "Criminal Justice." Pp. 93–95 in *The Sage Dictionary of Criminology*, 2nd edition, edited by E. McLaughlin and J. Muncie. London: Sage.

Hudson, B. 2003. *Understanding Justice: An Introduction to the Idea, Perspective, and Controversies in Modern Penal Theory*. Milton Keynes: Open University Press.

Hudson, B. 2001. "Crime Control, Due Process, and Social Justice." Pp. 104–5 in *The Sage Dictionary of Criminology*, edited by E. McLaughlin and J. Muncie. London: Sage.

Hume, M. 2011. "Right-to-Die Case Gets Early Court Date," *The Globe and Mail*, August 4, p. A5.

Hutchins, H. 2014. *Police Resources in Canada*. Ottawa: Canadian Centre for Justice Statistics.

King, M. 1981. *The Framework of Criminal Justice*. London: Croom Helm.

Law Reform Commission of Canada 1988. *Compelling Appearance, Interim Release, and the Pre-Trial Detention*. Ottawa: Law Reform Commission of Canada.

Law Reform Commission of Canada. 1984. *Questioning Suspects—Working Paper 32*. Ottawa: Minister of Supply and Services.

Law Reform Commission of Canada. 1977. *Our Criminal Law*. Ottawa: Minister of Supply and Services Canada.

Makin, K. 2007. "Top Court to Rule on Security Certificates," *The Globe and Mail*, February 20, p. A10.

Mewett, A.W. and S. Nakatsuru. 2000. *An Introduction to the Criminal Process in Canada*. 4th ed. Scarborough, ON: Carswell.

Muncie, J. 2002. "The Construction and Deconstruction of Crime." *In the Problem of Crime*, 2nd ed., edited by J. Muncie and E. McLaughlin. London: Sage.

Packer, H.L. 1968. *The Limits of the Criminal Sanction*. Stanford, CA: Stanford University Press.

Parker, C. 1999. *Just Lawyers: Regulation and Access to Justice*. New York: Oxford University Press.

Peritz, I. 2009. "Majority of Quebec Specialists Favour Euthanasia," *The Globe and Mail*, October 14, p. A7.

Perraux, L. 2009. "Quebec Doctors Cautiously Back Euthanasia," *The Globe and Mail*, November 4, p. A5.

Phillips, D. 2013. "Public Interest Standing, Access to Justice, and Democracy Under the Charter: *(AG) v. Downtown Eastside Sex Workers United Against Violence*." *Constitutional Forum* 22:21–31.

Roach, K. 1999. "Four Models of the Criminal Process." *Journal of Crime and Criminology* 89:671–715.

Royal Society of Canada. 2011. *The Royal Society of Canada Expert Panel: End of Life Decision-Making*. Ottawa: The Royal Society of Canada.

Russell, P. 1987. *The Judiciary in Canada: The Third Branch of Government*. Toronto: McGraw-Hill Ryerson.

Ruth, H. and K. Reitz. 2003. *The Challenge of Crime: Rethinking our Response*. Cambridge, MA: Harvard University Press.

Seaman, B. 2006. "Legal Equity, Poverty, and Access to Justice." *LawNow*, June/July, pp. 20–21.

Sudnow, D. 1965. "Normal Crimes: Sociological Features of the Penal Code in a Public Defender's Office." *Social Problems* 12:255–277.

Sutherland, E. 1949. *White Collar Crime*. New York: Dryden.

Sykes, G.M. and F.T. Cullen. 1992. *Criminology*. 2nd ed. Fort Worth, TX: Harcourt Brace Jovanovich.

Tibbetts, J. 2007. "Supreme Court Strikes Down Security Law," *National Post*, February 24, p. A13.

Tyler, T. 1990. *Why People Obey the Law*. New Haven, Conn.: Yale University Press.

Ursel, J. 1994. *The Winnipeg Family Violence Court*. Ottawa: Canadian Centre for Justice Statistics.

von Hirsch, A. 1976. *Doing Justice: The Choice of Punishments*. New York: Hill and Wang.

Walklate, S. 2005. *Criminology: The Basics*. London, Routledge.

Wheeler, G. 1987. "The Police, the Crowns, and the Courts: Who's Running the Show?" *Canadian Lawyer*, February.

Wilson, G. 2011. "Crime and Punishment: The Latimer Case Underlines Hard Truths about Canada's Legal System." *Literary Review of Canada*, March, pp. 7–8.

Wingrove, J. 2014. "Anti-terrorism Bills Expected to Pass Quickly." *The Globe and Mail*, November 25, p. A17.

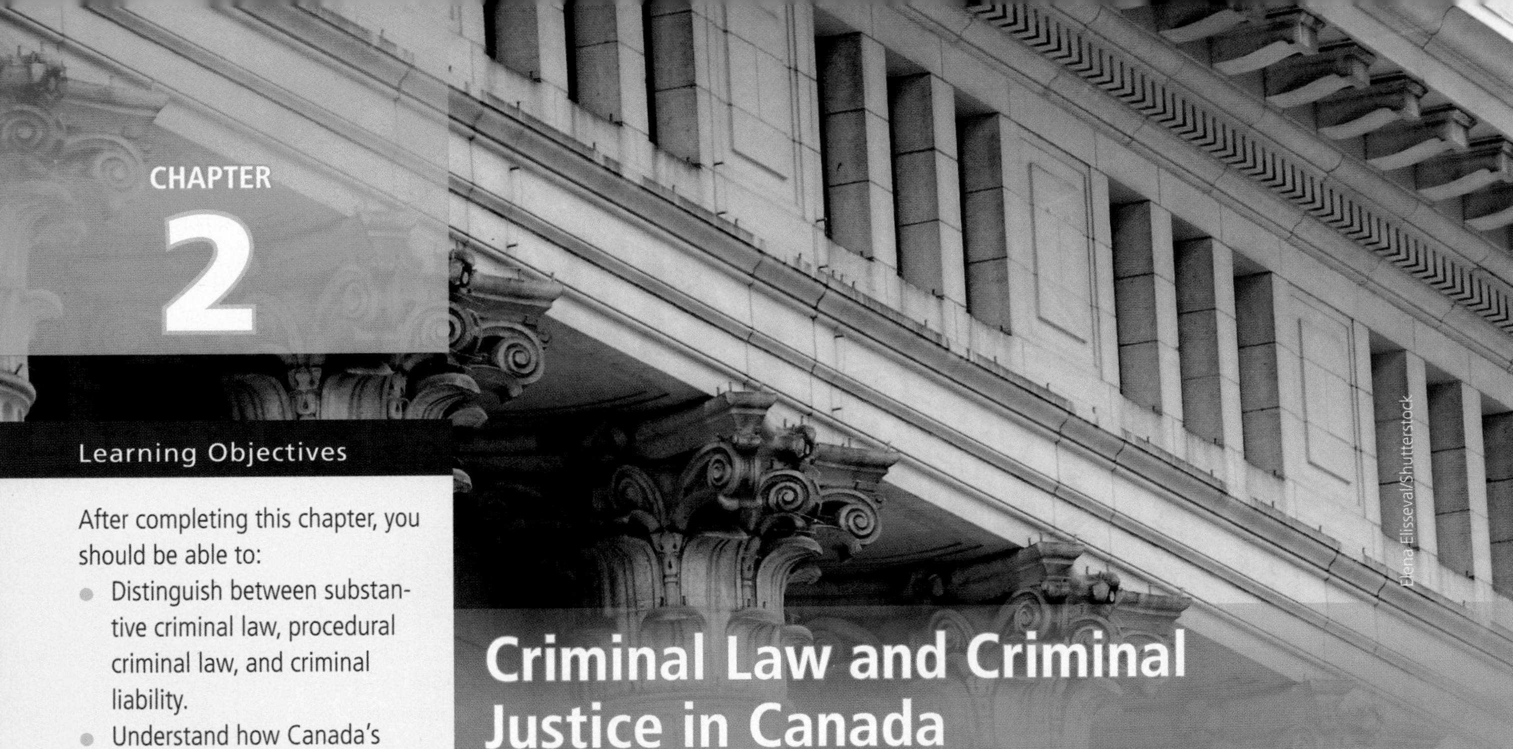

CHAPTER 2

Criminal Law and Criminal Justice in Canada

Learning Objectives

After completing this chapter, you should be able to:

- Distinguish between substantive criminal law, procedural criminal law, and criminal liability.
- Understand how Canada's sexual assault legislation developed and the relevant decisions made by the Supreme Court.
- Summarize the various elements of the legal definition of crime.
- Understand the developments in the principles of fundamental justice since the introduction of the Charter of Rights and Freedoms.
- Differentiate between the two main categories of legal defences and summarize the various types of legal defences.
- Understand of the sources of criminal law.
- Understand the classifications of the criminal law.
- Understand how the focus of recent federal criminal law legislation and Ontario's Safe Streets Act emphasize placing greater controls on individuals.
- Summarize the legal approach to the treatment of HIV nondisclosure and why some people want to decriminalize the law as it applies in this area.

In Chapter 1, we learned that societies are concerned with the social control of behaviour. When certain behaviours are identified as serious, dangerous, or harmful, people oftentimes demand that the government do something to control them. Sometimes the government decides to define such behaviour as a criminal offence by passing legislation. This is the beginning of a process known as **criminalization**, which involves

1. identifying problematic behaviour,
2. defining certain behaviour as crimes through legislation,
3. regulating this behaviour through law enforcement, and
4. punishing those who are found guilty in a criminal court.

The criminal law gives our criminal justice agencies the powers to regulate behaviour. These include the power to detain, stop and search, arrest, and prosecute. Enforcement agencies can use their powers to deal with, for example, normal crimes, organized crimes, and disorderly conduct. At the same time, the criminal law guarantees that those who are suspected of criminal activity, arrested, charged, and prosecuted have certain legal rights, known as procedural safeguards. The criminal law has been defined as "those formally established norms according to which individuals are adjudged guilty or innocent" (Lacey 2007:181). It is concerned about criminal liability, such as the *mens rea* (i.e., the guilty mind) and *actus reus* (i.e., the act) of a person suspected of committing a criminal offence. It also has an impact upon criminal procedure, those various arrangements about how crimes should be investigated and how any person charged with a criminal offence should be processed through the court system.

The criminal law is also "the jumping-off point for all other criminal justice practices—crime prevention, reporting, investigation, prosecution, punishment" (Lacey 2007:183). Ashworth and Zedner (2008:22) point out that a relationship exists between the roles of the criminal law and our criminal justice system. While the criminal law provides the basis for determining which behaviours are illegal, the criminal justice system ensures that individuals are not "liable to conviction and/or punishment unless the charge has been duly tried in a criminal court according to . . . procedural safeguards. . . ." Through the creation of legal and criminal justice systems, then, the government creates laws to protect society as well as to guarantee procedural safeguards for those charged and convicted of crimes.

What Are the Major Categories of the Criminal Law?

Despite the fact that the criminal law is exceedingly complex, it is possible to determine some of its basic processes when we wish to control harmful behaviour. This involves dividing the criminal law into three main categories: the first recognizes that *substantive criminal laws* need to be designed to govern and control individual conduct; the second focuses upon the *procedural criminal laws* created to determine what legal rights individuals should have if they become involved with the criminal justice system; and the third looks at how *criminal liability* should be attributed to individuals.

Substantive and Procedural Criminal Law

The first category, the **substantive criminal law**, refers to those laws which forbid particular types of conduct. In essence, the substantive criminal law informs us as to "what we can and cannot do in our everyday lives and the potential consequences for wrongdoing" (Horner 2007:79). It is what legally defines crime in our society. This is the written law that defines behaviours as criminal—in other words, it is the very substance of the criminal law. The source of the substantive criminal law is those basic values that are agreed upon by people in our society, such as which conduct is to be tolerated and what behaviour is to be condemned (Davison 2011). Therefore, these laws provide a basis of legitimacy for the various institutions (e.g., the police, the courts, and the correctional system) that are involved in the investigation, prosecution, and punishment of individuals. The majority of our substantive criminal laws are now enacted by Parliament, but at one time the courts were able to create new criminal offences, such as murder. Today, the courts are able to influence our criminal law through their interpretation of statutes.

An example of the substantive criminal law is found in s. 7 of the Charter of Rights and Freedoms, which states that individuals cannot be deprived of life, liberty, and security of the person except in accordance with the principles of fundamental justice. As Roach (2009:6) points out, "it is necessary that the criminal law be in accord with the principles of fundamental justice." These principles "address the substantive fairness of criminal laws to ensure that morally innocent people are not convicted and that people who could have reasonably been expected to obey the law are not punished for conduct committed in a mortally involuntary fashion" (Roach 2012:7). Substantive criminal law is not static, as Parliament is constantly passing new laws and the courts are interpreting them. The courts also play a role in substantive criminal law as the principles of fundamental justice are "to be found in the basic tenets of our legal system and that it is up to the courts to develop the limits of these tenets" (Barnhorst and Barnhorst 2004:10).

The second category, **procedural criminal law** (sometimes referred to as "procedural fairness" or "due process") in essence establishes the procedures necessary for processing cases throughout the entire criminal justice system. The individuals who drafted the Charter chose not to use terms such as "due process" or "procedural criminal law"; instead, they preferred (and this is the most common term used in Canada today) the words "principles of fundamental justice." The procedural criminal law gives legality to the actions of the various criminal justice agencies, such as the power to arrest, but they can also constrain their actions by establishing procedural safeguards for those suspected of a committing a crime and accused of a crime. The procedural criminal law is an important part of our criminal justice system as it highlights "the primacy of demonstrating **legal guilt** rather than **factual guilt**, and raises a number of obstacles to conviction in order to protect the rights of criminal suspects" (Hiebert 2002:135).

Sexual Assault Legislation

Since the Charter's introduction, the constitutionality of both substantive and procedural criminal laws have been challenged in many criminal court cases. This is illustrated in the history of Canada's **sexual assault** laws, during which both types of criminal law have been examined and, in some cases, redrafted by Parliament after rulings by the Supreme Court of Canada. Before 1983, the common law allowed legal counsel for the accused in rape cases to question the complainant about her reputation and prior sexual activity in the hope of convincing the jury that she had consented to the sexual activity in question. It was an ordeal for the victim of a sexual assault to testify in court since her reputation and prior sexual history could be held against her. As a result, many sexual assaults were not reported to the police since the trial itself "could be almost as agonizing to a victim of sexual assault as the offence itself" (Bowland 1994:245).

Offences of sexual aggression were dealt with in Sections 139 to 154 of Part VI of the Criminal Code. The offences in those sections dealt with "Sexual Offences, Public Morals and Disorderly Conduct." Four principal offences were recognized by the courts as relating to rape. Rape itself was one of them. The key provision of the

Criminal Code dealing with rape was found in s. 143. It stated that before a person could be found guilty of rape, the following general conditions needed to be established:

1. The complainant had to be female.
2. The accused had to be male.
3. The complainant and accused were not married to each other.
4. Sexual intercourse occurred.
5. The act of intercourse occurred without the consent of the woman.

The other three principal offences in Part VI were attempted rape (s. 145), indecent assault against a female (s. 149), and indecent assault against a male (s. 156). The penalties for these four offences were life, 10 years, 5 years, and 10 years, respectively.

Many criticisms were raised against these laws over the decades. For example, some argued that they reflected "the gender dichotomy and cultural perceptions of gender relations that were functional to the male status maintenance" (Los 1994). In response, the federal government enacted new legislation (Bill C-127) that was proclaimed on January 1, 1983. Bill C-127 introduced a number of significant changes—for example, sexual assault was reclassified and placed in Part VIII of the Criminal Code ("Offences against the Person and Reputation"), so as to emphasize that "sexual assault involves physical violence against another person." Other significant changes included the recognition that the victim could be male or female and that a spouse could be charged with sexual assault. The changes also established protections for women against cross-examination in criminal court trials regarding their past sexual history. These changes were designed to eliminate the practices and beliefs that perpetuated violence against women. According to Hodgson and Kelley (2001:114), the purpose of these changes was to "seek justice in sexual assault trials and to settle on fair rules and procedures to do so. . . ."

The new legislation also included three degrees or levels of harm, in order to reflect the seriousness of the incident. Level 1 sexual assault (s. 271) refers to incidents in which the victim suffers the least physical injury; it carries a maximum punishment of 10 years' imprisonment. Level 1 is the most common charge for sexual assault. Ninety-eight percent of all sexual assault charges in 2012 were Level 1.

Level 2 sexual assault (s. 272) involves the use of a weapon, threats to use a weapon, or bodily harm; it carries a maximum punishment of 14 years' imprisonment.

Level 3 sexual assault (s. 273) involves wounding, maiming, disfiguring, or endangering the life of the victim. An offender convicted of this offence can receive a maximum term of life imprisonment.

Level 1 sexual assault is a hybrid offence (see *Criminal Justice Insight*), which means that a Crown prosecutor has the power of discretion to proceed by way of indictment or summary conviction. That decision has a huge impact on the offender in terms of penalties. If the prosecutor proceeds by way of indictment, the maximum punishment is 10 years' incarceration, but if the case proceeds by way of summary conviction, the maximum punishment is 18 months.

There have been many legal changes and challenges to the sexual assault legislation over its brief history (see Exhibit 2.1). In 1991, for example, the Supreme Court of Canada struck down s. 276 of the Criminal Code, ruling that it favoured the victim at the expense of the accused. In its decision involving the cases of Seaboyer and Gayme, for example, two men who had been accused of rape argued successfully that their right to a fair trial had been violated, since they were prevented from cross-examining the complainant about her prior sexual conduct during the preliminary hearing. The following year, amendments were made through the introduction of Bill C-49, which outlined "the legal parameters for determining the admissibility of a victim's past sexual history as evidence in sexual assault trials" (Mohr and Roberts 1994:10). In addition, "implied consent" was eliminated as a defence; actual consent would now be required.

Following the 1992 legislation, defence lawyers attempted to obtain the confidential files of complainants in order to raise issues at trial. This approach was appealed to the Supreme Court of Canada, and in 1995, in *R. v. O'Connor*, the Supreme Court, in a 5–4 decision, ruled that a woman's records must be handed over to a judge if the defence can persuade the judge the records may contain information useful to the defendant. This ruling was based on the logic that barring such records from the proceedings would violate the defendant's right to a fair trial. After this decision, it became common practice for judges to order full disclosure of records. This ruling created difficulties for complainants as they did not want their personal information given to the defence and publicized. As a result, it acted as a deterrent to many women who decided that pursuing criminal complaints through the criminal justice system was problematic (Busby 1997). Critics argued that Parliament and the courts were not doing enough to make the criminal justice system more effective for protecting the interests of women who had been sexually assaulted, calling for a re-examination of how the justice system operates. "The more general indictment of the current criminal justice process is that

Criminal Justice Insight

Reporting Sexual Assault: The Response of the Criminal Justice System

While the trend in the police-recorded rate of sexual assaults has declined over the years (see Figure 2.1), it is not clear if this reflects a real decline "in the occurrence of sexual assault in the population, changes in the way the police respond to the assaults reported to them, or a rise and fall in women's confidence in the criminal justice system reflected in their reporting behaviour" (Johnson 2012:617). Evidence from the self-reports of victims of sexual assault reveals that the majority of all sexual assaults are not reported to the police. The General Social Survey (GSS) (see Chapter 4) reveals that the majority of women who are the victims of sexual assault do not report them to the police (see Figure 2.2). In the 2009 GSS, it was revealed that only 10 percent of women aged 15 and over who reported being sexually assaulted by non-spouses during the previous 12 months said they reported the incident to the police (Perreault and Brennan 2010).

According to Makin (2013:F1), while there were good intentions in the changes made to better protect victims of sexual assault when they report the offence, these have "backfired" and "(m)ore attacks are going unreported than ever, and sentencing is radically softer." He states than 90 percent of all sexual assaults are unreported, and that when a complaint is made to the police, fewer than half "result in criminal charges and, of those charges, only about one in four leads to a guilty verdict." What changes are necessary in our criminal justice system to protect women?

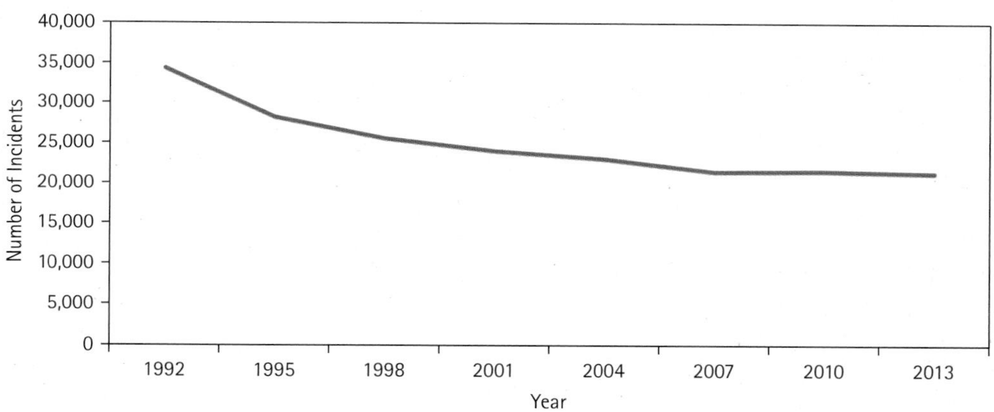

FIGURE 2.1 Police-Recorded Incidents of Sexual Assault, 1992–2013

Source: Uniform Crime Reports, Canadian Centre for Justice Statistics. Reproduced and distributed on an "as is" basis with the permission of Statistics Canada.

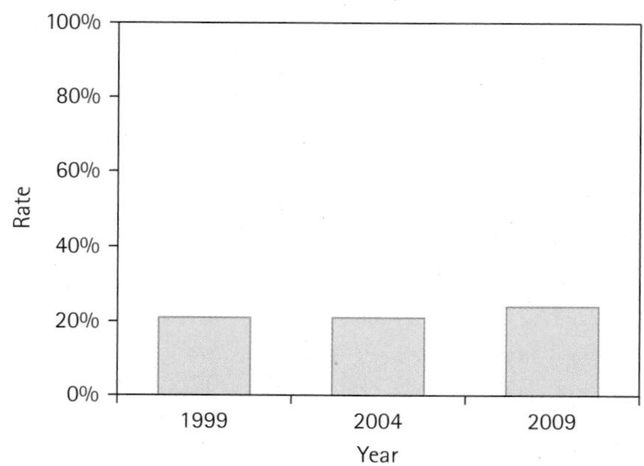

FIGURE 2.2 Self-Reported Sexual Assaults, 1999, 2004, 2009

Rates are calculated per 1,000 population age 15 years and older.

Source: S. Perreault and S. Brennan, "Criminal Victimization in Canada, 2009." *Juristat* (September 2010), Statistics Canada, Catalogue no. 85-002-X, p. 24, http://www.statcan.gc.ca/pub/85-002-x/2010002/article/11340-eng.pdf. Reproduced and distributed on an "as is" basis with the permission of Statistics Canada.

EXHIBIT 2.1 Sexual Assault Legislation In Canada

Since the enactment of sexual assault legislation in 1983, numerous changes have occurred:

1991	The Supreme Court of Canada rules that the law favours the victim at the expense of the accused (*Seaboyer v. R.* [1991] and *Gayme v. R.* [1991]). The Supreme Court strikes down s. 276 of the Criminal Code, which limits the questioning of victims in sexual assault trials by the defence.
1992	Bill C-49 is passed, allowing sexual history to be introduced in a case but only when strict guidelines are used. It also provides a legal definition of consent specific to the offence of sexual assault.
1995	The Supreme Court rules that counselling records of the victim must be produced when requested by the court (*R. v. O'Connor*).
1997	An Alberta judge in *R. v. Mills* rules that the new law covering the disclosure of third-party therapy or counselling records is unconstitutional on the basis that they violated ss. 7 and 11 of the Charter, as it places too much of the burden of proof on the accused. The Supreme Court of Canada decides that when a sexual assault victim cannot produce her counselling records at the request of the court, the case must be thrown out of court (*R. v. Carosella*). The Criminal Code is amended (Bill C-46) to introduce guidelines that instruct all parties on when the sexual assault victim's records are relevant during a trial.
1999	The Supreme Court of Canada upholds, in *R. v. Mills*, the constitutionality of the Bill C-46 provisions. The Supreme Court of Canada, in *R. v. Ewanchuk*, rejects the defence of implied consent.
2000	The Supreme Court of Canada, in *R. v. Darrach*, upholds the provision of the sexual assault law that restricts defence lawyers in their questioning of sexual assault victims about their past sexual history.
2014	The Supreme Court of Canada, in *R. v. Quesnelle*, rules that sexual assault victims cannot have police occurrence reports used against them when they are not related to the case in question.

Sources: Bowland 1994; Los 1994; Makin 1999; Majury 1994; Roberts and Mohr 1994.

the law and legal doctrines concerning sexual assault have acted as the principal systemic mechanisms for invalidating the experiences of women . . . it is necessary to re-examine the existing doctrines . . . that have preserved dominant male interests . . ." (Renner et al. 1997:100).

As a result of O'Connor, in 1997 the federal government passed new legislation (Bill C-46) that amended the Criminal Code to include ss. 278.1 to 278.91, which govern the production of records related to both complainants and witnesses in sexual offence cases. This resulted in the protection of the privacy interests of complainants by restricting the full disclosure of records. This bill established a two-stage process under s. 278.1 for judges to determine whether the victim's records would be disclosed to the defendant. In the first stage, the accused must convince the trial judge that the documents are likely relevant to their defence. In the second stage, the judge must consider whether it is "necessary in the interests of justice" to view them.

In November 1999, the Supreme Court upheld Bill C-46 in *R. v. Mills*, stating that when judges decide to order the production of records concerning a complainant, they must consider "the rights and interests of all those affected by disclosure" and that the three relevant principles in this are (1) full answer and defence, (2) privacy, and (3) equality.

In 1997, in *R. v. Carosella*, the Supreme Court threw out a case involving sexual assault in which the victim's counselling records had been destroyed. This decision placed any third-party records on the same standard as police and Crown prosecutor documents. The federal government then passed amendments to Bill C-46, in an attempt to clarify when records concerning the victim should be given restricted access to the defendant. The amendments introduced a two-stage application process. In the first stage, trial judges have to decide whether the sought-after record is likely to be of sufficient relevance to the defence. The second stage involves balancing information contained in the document with the position forwarded by the defence on the basis of its importance to the defence, as well as with the threat its exposure might pose to the complainant's right to privacy, dignity, and security of the person.

In the fall of 2000, the Supreme Court unanimously upheld the 1992 law that restricted the freedom of defence lawyers to question sexual assault victims about their past sexual history. The Court ruled that forcing the victim to give such evidence invaded her right to privacy and would discourage the reporting of crimes of sexual violence (Anderssen 2000:A7). In this case (*R. v. Darrach*), the defendant argued that he had been denied a fair trial because he had been unable to raise specific aspects of his prior sexual relationship with the complainant. Darrach argued that he had formed the "honest but mistaken belief" that the incident was consensual. His argument failed to influence the Court that the evidence was of significant probative value. In its ruling, the Supreme Court considered s. 276 to be "carefully crafted to comport with the principles of fundamental justice. It protects the integrity of the judicial process while at the same time respecting the rights of the people involved. The complainant's privacy and dignity are protected by a procedure that also vindicates the right of the accused to make full answer and defence" (*R. v. Darrach*, 2000 2 S.C.R.).

What about other records concerning the complainant, such as police occurrence reports? In *R. v. Quesnelle* (2014), the defence argued that relevant police occurrence records concerning the complainant should be made in accordance with the rules concerning full disclosure (see below) while the prosecution stated that any application for these types of records fell under s. 278.1. In her decision, the trial judge agreed with the prosecution but her decision was overturned by the Ontario Court of Appeal. In its decision, the Supreme Court held that, as a general rule, police occurrence reports should be kept from the accused and their lawyer as such reports could reveal private information about complainants, which would harm their "dignity rights" and discourage women from reporting sexual violence (Fine 2014).

How have the courts reacted to these decisions by the Supreme Court? One result of the Supreme Court's decision in Darrach is that judges can hold "different views on the issue of the relevance and probative value of evidence of prior sexual history with the accused on the issue of consent. . . ." (Stuart 2010:238). Gotell (2002:257) studied 37 trial and appellate sexual assault cases between 1999 and 2002 where there had been requests for records by the accused after the Supreme Court decision in *R. v. Mills* and concluded that complainants "remained vulnerable to disclosure post-*Mills*. . . ." In another research study of 16 sexual assault cases where there had also been requests from the defence for records about the complainants between 2002 and 2006, Gotell (2008:153) concluded that it "was clear from a detailed reading of these recent decisions that records continue to be produced to judges and disclosed to the accused on the basis of bare assertions and discriminatory rationales." Hodgson and Kelley (2001:114) observe that the "determination of the relevance of (third party records) and of the extent to which their disclosure is deemed 'in the interest of justice' rises and falls in judicial discretion."

SUMMING UP AND LOOKING FORWARD

A key concept for understanding our criminal justice system is criminalization. That is, the behaviour in question must be defined in legislation as a criminal offence and there must be a criminal sanction attached to it. Once a behaviour is defined as criminal, it becomes part of the substantive criminal law. These refer to the laws that define criminal behaviours—that is, it is the very substance of the criminal law. Certain legal rights are given to those suspected of breaking the law: these are known as the procedural criminal law. These are the rules that specify how substantive laws are to be enforced. Numerous challenges to both substantive and procedural criminal laws passed by Parliament in the area of sexual assault legislation have led to changes in those laws, for example in the production of records relating to the complainant.

The criminal law also establishes criminal liability. This refers to those ideas that form a core framework concerning the nature of crime, which sets out those general conditions or principles in which criminal liability is established. What are these ideas? These are discussed next.

Review Questions:

1. What does criminalization refer to and what is its impact on the operation of our criminal justice system?
2. Are there any crimes that are inherently evil?
3. What are the substantive and procedural criminal law and how are they an issue in the sexual assault legislation?

Criminal Liability and the Legal Elements of a Crime

The third basic process of the criminal law is **criminal liability**. Criminal laws are typically organized around a set of ideas that form a core framework concerning the nature of crime, which sets out those general conditions or principles in which criminal liability is established.

These are the rules that apply to all aspects of the criminal law as opposed to any one specific offence. They are important for the study of criminal law as they contain "an implicit set of assumptions about what makes the imposition of criminal liability legitimate" and, as such, most criminal law follows from them (Lacey 2007:187).

Different approaches—the *general* and the *legal*—are used to explain what a crime is in our society. The **general definition of a crime** has it that a crime can be defined as any action

1. that is harmful;
2. that is prohibited by the criminal law; and
3. that can be prosecuted by the state
4. in a formal court environment
5. for which a punishment can be imposed. (Senna and Siegel 1995)

The **legal definition of a crime** encompasses mental and physical elements as well as "attendant circumstances"—that is, a causal link between the act and the harm that resulted. It also specifies that certain aspects of the criminal act in question must be proven in a court of law. Criminal law is founded on seven principles traditionally determined and followed by legislators and the courts. Our system of criminal law is based on the existence of these essential features in every criminal act. These principles are summarized by the term ***corpus delecti***, which means literally "the body of the crime," and they are all central to the rule of law. In order to convict someone, the state must usually prove each of the following seven elements:

1. legality
2. *mens rea*
3. *actus reus*
4. concurrence of *mens rea* and *actus reus*
5. harm
6. causation
7. punishment

As Hall (1947:17) noted, "[the] harm forbidden in penal law must be imputed to any normal adult who voluntarily commits it with criminal intent, and such a person must be subjected to the legally prescribed punishment."

Legality

Legally, a crime is defined as "an intentional act or omission in violation of the criminal law, committed without defense or justification and sanctioned by the state" (Tappan 1946:10). This means that an act, to be

Sean Kilpatrick/THE CANADIAN PRESS

considered criminal, must be "forbidden in a penal law" (Brannigan 1984:25). The idea is that there can be no crime unless a law forbids the act in question. This is embodied in the phrase nullum crimen sine lege, or "no crime without a law."

Mens Rea

A fundamental principle of our criminal law is that no person should be punished unless they committed the act or omission and is blameworthy for it; that is, they are "at fault." What this means is that it must be established that an individual not only has committed an offence (the *actus reus*—see below), but also is responsible for it (the *mens rea*). An assumption found in the Criminal Code is that the act of becoming involved in a criminal act results from a guilty mind. This is referred to as ***mens rea***, or the fault or mental element of a crime. *Mens rea* is commonly translated as "guilty mind," although it is often referred to as intent. It rests on the idea that a person has the capacity to control their behaviour and has the ability to choose among different courses of action.

The criminal law recognizes two types of fault: **specific intent** and **general intent** (see Table 2.1), each of which requires a different amount of proof. Some offences require only general intent, which means that *mens rea* is inferred from the action or inaction of the accused. In these crimes (e.g., manslaughter), there is no need for the prosecution to prove, through an independent investigation, the state of the defendant's mind at the time of the offence.

In contrast, specific intent offences (e.g., murder) require, in addition to the general intent, a further intention or purpose. For example, the intent to commit a murder is inferred from the fact that the accused pointed

TABLE 2.1 Selected Specific and General Intent Offences

Specific Intent Offences	General Intent Offences
Arson	Aggravated assault
Attempted murder	Assault causing bodily harm
Murder	Manslaughter
Robbery	Sexual assault
Sexual exploitation	Unlawful confinement

a weapon at the victim and discharged it. Specific intent requires that the prosecution prove beyond a reasonable doubt the intent specified in the statute's definition of the elements of a crime. These offences are identified by phrases such as "with intent" or "for the purpose of" (Barnhorst and Barnhorst 2004). In these cases, the prosecution must prove "not only an intention to commit an *actus reus* of the crime in question but also the 'intention' to produce some further consequence beyond the *actus reus*" (Verdun-Jones 1989:121).

Intent is commonly confused with **motive**, although the two concepts are distinct. Intent refers to an individual's mental resolve to commit a criminal offence; motive refers to the reason for committing the actual illegal act. While motive is distinct from *mens rea*, Barnhorst and Barnhorst (2004:42–43) contend that it is relevant to the criminal justice system in two ways. First, motive provides evidence of intent by establishing a reason why a person committed a crime (e.g., out of greed or jealousy). Second, motive may assist a judge in sentencing the accused in the same way—by providing a reason why the person committed the crime. As a result, the accused may receive a lighter sentence if there was a good reason for committing the crime (e.g., mercy killing, compared to killing someone out of financial greed).

In addition to the concepts of general and specific intent, there are three distinct levels or degrees of *mens rea*, ranging from the most to the least culpable states of mind: *intent*, *knowledge*, and *recklessness*. The highest level of **culpability** is purposefully or intentionally causing harm, and such offences are identified with the word *intent*. These offences are indicated in the Criminal Code by words such as "intentional" and "willful" and refer to those actions that purposefully or intentionally cause harm (see Table 2.2).

Knowledge is used to indicate that the accused possessed an awareness of a particular circumstance. For example, if someone utters a threat to another individual, the question is whether the accused knowingly stated the threat. According to s. 264.1 of the Criminal Code:

> 264.1 (1) Every one commits an offence who, in any manner, knowingly utters, conveys or causes any person to receive a threat
>
> (a) to cause death or serious bodily harm to any person
>
> (b) to burn, destroy or damage real or personal property, or
>
> (c) to kill, poison or injure an animal or bird that is the property of any person[.]

Recklessness refers to a situation in which an individual violates a law simply by lacking the appropriate care about and attention to something they are doing. For example, a person who decides to practise shooting a weapon in a crowded schoolyard during a lunch break, and who kills a child, may argue that they did not have the intention to harm anyone. Yet they would probably be charged with the criminal offence of manslaughter because they were acting with reckless disregard for the safety of those nearby but death was not actually intended.

Some legal defences in court can be made on the basis that the *mens rea* element does not apply (see below). The

TABLE 2.2 The Levels of Culpability

Highest ↓ Lowest		
	Purposeful	An individual did (or caused) it on purpose
	Knowledge	An individual is committing an act or causing a harm but they're not acting for that purpose
	Recklessness	An individual is consciously creating a risk or causing a criminal harm
	Negligence	An individual unconsciously creates a risk, that is, should have known, ("a reasonable person would have known"

issue concerns the notion of criminal responsibility, and Canadian law recognizes certain individuals to be unable to form the mental state necessary to commit a crime. This means that a person might be excused for committing an action that would normally be classed as criminal. For example, children under 12 cannot be charged with a criminal offence in Canada. *Mens rea* is also lacking when people commit a crime in self-defence or while under duress.

Actus Reus

Another criterion that has to be met before a criminal charge can be laid against a suspect is known as ***actus reus***. This is the physical or action element of a crime, and it is generally referred to as the "guilty act" or "evil act." In the Criminal Code, *actus reus* usually refers to the physical act performed by the accused—a punch, shove, or similar type of action directed against another individual. The actor, and the actor alone, is responsible for their actions. In other words, a person cannot blame someone else for the criminal act they have carried out.

Actus reus usually involves the commission of an illegal act; however, it also refers also to the failure to do something—in other words, an omission of an act when the Criminal Code specifies that there is a duty to act. Section 219 of the Criminal Code, for example, refers to the offence of criminal negligence and criminal negligence causing death:

> 219. (1) Every one is criminally negligent who
>
> (a) in doing anything, or
> (b) in omitting to anything that it is his duty to do,
> shows wanton or reckless disregard for the lives or safety of other persons.
>
> (2) For the purposes of this section, "duty" means a duty imposed by law.

For some criminal offences a person doesn't have to become physically involved in an action. The Criminal Code specifies that in certain circumstances the mere act of talking (or speech) can be interpreted as a physical act. In fact, a crime can be committed by speech (as opposed to thought) in our legal system. Section 465 of the Criminal Code specifies that it is illegal for two or more persons to agree to commit a crime. If both individuals are in agreement about the plan, the act of criminal conspiracy has transpired. In addition, s. 131 of the Criminal Code specifies that an individual is guilty of a criminal offence when they commit perjury, while s. 225 states that any individual who causes the death of another individual through threats, fear of violence, or deception is guilty of a crime.

Concurrence between *Mens Rea* and *Actus Reus*

While not an "official" element of a crime, **concurrence** requires that "intent both precede and be related to the specific prohibited action or inaction that was or was not taken" (Brown et al. 1991:68). Concurrence is usually not considered a controversial issue, since in most instances the connection between act and intent is obvious.

Harm

An important element in our legal system is that conduct is criminal only if it is harmful. This idea is "reflected in the notion of due process, which holds that a criminal statute is unconstitutional if it bears no reasonable relationship to the matter of injury to the public" (Territo et al. 1995:33–34). This means there has to be a victim for the action to be harmful. Others argue that if the offence is a "victimless" crime—for example, gambling, abortion, prostitution—it is "not the law's business" (Geis 1974). The basis for this view is that **victimless crimes** violate morality, not the law, and that making them illegal doesn't contribute to the good of society.

Criminal harm may result in physical injury, but such harm is by no means restricted to such injuries. For example, physical injury is not inflicted when perjury is committed, yet perjury is still considered harmful. This is because the criminal law has to deal with intangibles, such as harm to public institutions and the harm resulting from the fear for one's own well-being. An example is Canada's anti-stalking law, the purpose of which is to protect citizens from criminal harassment (see Chapter 4). In addition, Canada has developed "hate laws." These are usually attached as a sentence enhancement to acts of violence or crimes against property if such crimes are committed because of the victim's race, gender, or sexual preference. Recent social scientific research documented the harm experienced by prostitutes as a result of the criminal law, resulting in the Supreme Court of Canada deciding that the laws at issue were unconstitutional (see *Criminal Justice Focus*).

Causation

Causation refers to the requirement that the conduct of the accused produce a specific result (i.e., a crime). In other words, when the act (or omission) of the accused started a series of events that led to harm, there is causation. Important concerns have been raised about causation when a long time has passed between the *mens rea* and the *actus reus*. Sometimes it is easy to see the harm that has resulted from an act, but it is not so easy to

Criminal Justice Focus

Can the Criminal Law Cause Harm?

As we have seen in this chapter, one of the areas of concern for the criminal law is when someone harms another person. However, other questions about harm can be raised. For example, is it possible for a criminal law to cause harm? More specifically, is "the harm caused by a criminal law grossly disproportionate to the harms that the law avoids?" (Editorial 2014:321). The Supreme Court of Canada has determined that this may sometimes be the case. For example, in *Canada (Attorney General) v. PHS Community Services Society (Insite)* (2011), the Supreme Court of Canada held that drug laws can cause grossly disproportionate harm by preventing medical personnel from giving injections in a manner that protects individuals from contracting potentially deadly diseases.

In another case, *Canada (Attorney General v. Bedford)* (2013), the Supreme Court of Canada held that the criminal offence outlawing the ability for prostitutes to have a steady place of business in a location such as a home (i.e., a common bawdy house) as well as the criminal offence of prostitutes being an employer of individuals such as a bodyguard (i.e., living off the avails of prostitution) and soliciting offences in the Criminal Code caused grossly disproportionate harms to prostitutes. In their ruling, the Supreme Court of Canada considered these offences were too restrictive, thereby endangering the life, liberty, and security of prostitutes.

Les Bazso/The Province

The North Vancouver RCMP Youth Intervention Unit, concerned about an apparent increase among youths participating in the sex trade, many of whom are advertising on Craigslist, announced that there appears to be a small group of individuals within the community who are pressuring women as young as 16 to prostitute themselves online.

What led to this decision? The answer lies in how the activities of prostitutes have been governed by the Criminal Code of Canada. From 1892 until 1972, the Criminal Code contained a provision (s. 175(1)(c)) that treated the actions of prostitutes as a form of vagrancy. In 1972, this provision was replaced by another provision (s. 195.1), known as the soliciting law. According to the new provision, "everyone who solicits any person in a public place for the purposes of prostitution is guilty of an offence punishable on summary conviction." The enforcement of this legislation was problematic, as there were difficulties determining exactly what was meant as a "public place" and whether or not the legislation applied to male prostitutes and their clients. In *Hutt v. R.* (1978) the issue of what was meant by solicitation was raised and the Supreme Court held that for solicitation to be illegal, it must be "pressing and persistent." Later, in 1983, an amendment was passed recognizing that a prostitute could be a person of either sex as well as clarifying what constituted a "public place." Questions remained about whether or not clients could be charged.

In the early 1980s, the federal government established the Fraser Committee whose task it was to assess the adequacy of the laws related to both prostitution and pornography. Soon after, the Badgley Committee was formed to report on the then existing laws in terms of protecting children and youths from sexual abuse and youth prostitution. As a result, the federal government, in December 1985, passed new legislation (Bill C-49) that replaced the soliciting law with the "communicating law." The purpose of this law was to make prostitution less visible, and as a result, less of a nuisance, to the majority of citizens. It became illegal to communicate with another individual in public to purchase or sell sexual services. This led some to argue that it would be difficult to enforce prostitution-related laws. Figure 2.3 shows police-recorded crime for prostitution-related offences.

Continued on next page

Can the Criminal Law Cause Harm? (*Continued*)

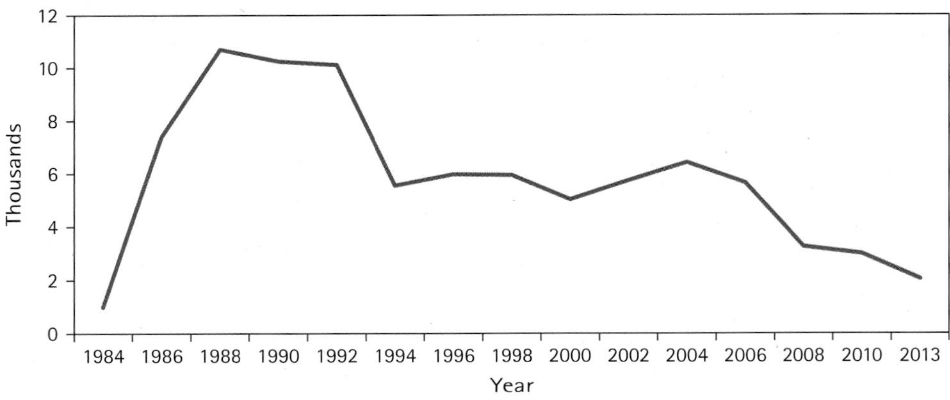

FIGURE 2.3 Police-Recorded Crime—Prostitution-Related Offences, 1984–2013

In 1990, in a reference case (*Reference Re Sections 193 and 195.1(1)(c) of the Criminal Code*) the Supreme Court of Canada ruled on various aspects of the communicating law that were being challenged under the Charter of Rights and Freedoms. The Supreme Court held that the bawdy house law was not unconstitutionally vague, and while it found the communication law violated s. 2(b) of the Charter (the right to freedom of expression), it was a reasonable limit under s. 1 of the Charter.

This decision forced prostitutes into situations that oftentimes resulted in their becoming victims of severe violence. Between 1991 and 2002 the Canadian Centre for Justice Statistics reported that 73 prostitutes in Canada were killed while working (Kong et al. 2003; Savoie 2003). In 2002, police in Vancouver arrested Robert Pickton in a case that would ultimately involve the murders of 26 women, most of them prostitutes. In 2007, Pickton was convicted of six murders and sentenced to life imprisonment. This case highlighted the dangerous conditions facing street prostitutes.

In 2009, a case was heard in the Ontario Superior Court that involved a suit by three former and current Ontario sex workers who wanted to overturn the prostitution laws. The following year, in her ruling in *Bedford v. Canada* (2010), the judge held that Canada's criminal laws governing prostitution violate s. 7 of the Charter of Rights and Freedoms. She struck down three provisions of the Criminal Code associated with prostitution, including communicating in a public place for the purpose of prostitution (the communicating law, s. 213 [1][c]), keeping a common bawdy house (s. 210), and living off the avails of prostitution (s. 212 [1][j]). The Crown argued that prostitution is "inherently harmful." In her decision, the judge paid particular attention to the harm prostitutes experience as a result of being prevented by the criminal law to increase their safety. She held that the impact of the three provisions under consideration were disproportionate in terms of their legislative intent, and as a result not in accordance with the principles of fundamental justice.

Adrian Wyld/THE CANADIAN PRESS

Terri-Lynn Bedford, one of the three principal complainants to challenge the prostitution laws in Canada, celebrates the Supreme Court of Canada decision.

Criminal Justice Focus

Can the Criminal Law Cause Harm? (*Continued*)

The federal government appealed this decision to the Ontario Court of Appeal, which upheld the lower court ruling in part (*Bedford v. Canada (Attorney General)* (2012). They unanimously held that the common bawdy house provision should be struck down. But they decided that the living off the avails provision of the Criminal Code could be maintained if it applies "in circumstances of exploitation." The majority held that communicating law should remain illegal. In December 2013, the Supreme Court of Canada unanimously threw out all three provisions as violating constitutional guarantees to life, liberty, and security of the person. The Supreme Court held that the existing laws placed prostitutes in potentially great harm and that the harm of the existing laws was disproportionate in terms of deterring a social nuisance. In June 2014 the federal government introduced new legislation (the Protection of Communities and Exploited Persons Act) in an attempt to amend the existing laws, and received Royal Assent in December 2014.

establish the *mens rea* element. This is particularly true for actions generally referred to as corporate crime.

Take, for example, an employee of a corporation who is told that because the spraying of a particular chemical mixture is "safe," they need not wear safety equipment. If they die immediately after applying the chemical, concurrence can easily be determined. But what if that worker suffers no ill health for 15 years and then suddenly dies from a blood disease associated with exposure to the chemical? The lack of concurrence will make it difficult to prove that a crime was committed. This situation can be further complicated if many other workers applied the spray at the same time without contracting a terminal disease, or if some suffered from seemingly unrelated illnesses.

R. Gino Santa Maria/Shutterstock

What are the challenges facing criminal justice officials if they decide to prosecute corporate actions harmful to humans?

Punishment

The law must state the sanctions for every crime so that everyone is aware of the possible consequences of certain actions. The Criminal Code therefore specifies the sanctions for every crime. In Canada, there are sanctions for two types of offences: indictable and summary conviction offences. These are discussed in detail later in this chapter.

SUMMING UP AND LOOKING FORWARD

The criminal law encompasses criminal liability; that is, the legal definition of crime, which is a key component of the rule of law. One element of the legal definition of a crime is legality: no act is inherently a crime. Another is responsibility, which includes *mens rea* (i.e., intent, recklessness, and knowledge) and *actus reus* (i.e., the guilty act). The other elements of the legal definition of crime are the concurrence between *mens rea* and *actus reus*, harm, causation, and punishment. Some people argue that criminal laws can create harms, such as in Canada's prostitution laws prior to the Supreme Court's ruling in Bedford.

Criminal liability is based on the idea that an individual is in some sense responsible (or "at fault") for committing an act specifically stated in the substantive criminal law. But what happens if the defence argues that while the defendant did commit the act in question, they had an excuse for doing so? In these cases, defence lawyers may use arguments, referred to as legal defences, in order to try to prove to the court that the defendant was not responsible for their actions. The two major categories of legal defences are the subject of the next section.

Review Questions:

1. How is criminal liability associated with the rule of law?
2. Do you agree that acts are defined as criminal because they constitute actions that almost everyone in society regards as problematic? Include the actions of corporations in your answer.
3. Can the criminal law itself cause harms?

Legal Defences and the Law

Legal defences fall into two categories, excuse *defences* and justification *defences*. The difference between these "is that where conduct is justified, it is not wrong in the context in which it occurs," whereas conduct that is excused is wrong "but because certain circumstances exist, the actor is excused from criminal liability" (Barnhorst and Barnhorst 2004:65) (see Table 2.3).

Excuse Defences

With **excuse defences**, the defendant admits to committing a criminal act but contends that they cannot be held criminally responsible for it because there was no criminal intent. In these cases, then, the disposition of the accused is an important consideration. The two most common examples of excuse defences are age and mental disorder.

TABLE 2.3 The Legal Defences to Crime

Even if the prosecution proves all of the elements of a crime, defences can avoid conviction if they can prove a defence of excuse or defence of justification.

Defences of Excuse
Defendants admit what they did was wrong but they argue, under the circumstances, they weren't responsible for their actions.

Excuse defences are:

Age
Mental Disorder
Automatism
Mistake of fact
Mistake of law

Defences of Justification
Defendants admit that while they did commit the criminal act in question, their act was justified in the circumstances.

Justification defences are:

Duress
Necessity
Self-Defence
Provocation
Entrapment

Age

In Canada, there are three distinct stages of criminal responsibility. The law considers people (i.e., children) under the **age** of 12 to lack criminal responsibility. This is sometimes referred to as being *doli incapax*. Thereafter, until their 18th birthday, they are classified as youths and have limited criminal accountability (or "diminished responsibility") under the Youth Criminal Justice Act. Adulthood starts when a person turns 18, at which point people face full legal accountability; however, they also possess full legal rights. These distinctions of legal accountability based on age are part of the very foundations of our criminal law. The fundamental criminal law concept "of moral accountability and the policy objective of social protection through deterrence of crime and rehabilitation apply differently to children and youth than to adults, because youths are different than adults" (Bala 1997:2).

Mental Disorder

A controversial legal defence involves **mental disorder**. Recent cases involving this defence (e.g., Vince Li in Manitoba and Luka Magnotta in Quebec) have been highly publicized in the media. An accused with a mental disorder lacks the *mens rea* to commit the offence. Section 16(1) of the Criminal Code sets out the defence:

> 16. (1) No person is criminally responsible for an act committed or an omission made while suffering from a mental disorder that rendered the person incapable of appreciating the nature and quality of the act or omission or of knowing that it was wrong.

This section of the Criminal Code also states that everyone is presumed not to be suffering from a mental disorder unless that issue is raised. If the issue is raised, the burden of proof rests with the party that raises the issue. Mental disorder is defined as a disease of the mind. Whether a specific condition is a disease of the mind is a question of law, and two important aspects of a judge's determination are expert medical evidence and public safety (Barnhorst and Barnhorst 2004). Examples of mental disorder include schizophrenia, paranoia, and melancholia. Self-induced states caused by alcohol or drugs are excluded, as are temporary conditions such as hysteria. "Appreciating the nature and quality of the act" refers to the defendant's capacity to perceive the consequences, impact, and results of the physical act. If it is determined that the accused was incapable of knowing the act was wrong, this defence may succeed. This defence is rarely successful, as indicated in Figure 2.4, which reveals

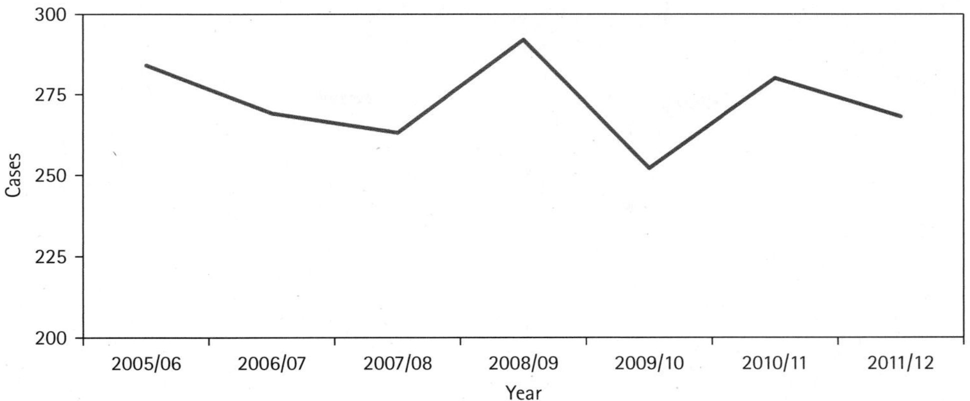

FIGURE 2.4 Total Number of Adult Cases in Which There Was a Final Decision of Not Criminally Responsible on Account of Mental Disorder, 2005–06 to 2011–12

Source: Z. Miladininovic and J. Lukassen, "Verdicts of not criminal responsible on account of mental disorder in adult criminal courts 2005/06 - 2011/12." *Juristat* (September 18, 2014), http://www.statcan.gc.ca/pub/85-002-x/2014001/article/14085-eng.htm. Reproduced and distributed on an "as is" basis with the permission of Statistics Canada.

that between 2005–06 and 2011–12 the success of this defence was less than 1 percent nationally.

When someone is found not criminally responsible on account of a mental disorder, they are neither acquitted nor found guilty. The court or a review board makes one of three dispositions: absolute discharge, conditional discharge, or detention in a hospital.

Automatism

Automatism (or dissociative amnesia) refers to unconscious or involuntary behaviour. People who are in a dissociative state are not in conscious control of their bodily movements, and thus they act abnormally. This defence is rarely used because there must be strong evidence from expert witnesses affirming the condition. The accused's behaviour is considered "automatic" because they did not have the *actus reus* of the crime (Barnhorst and Barnhorst 2004). The Supreme Court of Canada has defined automatism as "unconscious, involuntary behaviour, the state of a person who, though capable of action, is not conscious of what they are doing. It means an unconscious, involuntary act, where the mind does not go with what is being done" (*R. v. Rabey* [1977]). When this defence is used, it cannot be based on a mental disorder or voluntary intoxication by alcohol or drugs. If this defence succeeds, the accused is immediately released from custody. Examples of automatism include someone who commits a crime while sleepwalking (*R. v. Parks* [1992]), while in a dazed condition following a concussion (*R. v. Bleta* [1965]), or who has taken a drug without knowing its effects (*R. v. King* [1962]). In *R. v. Graveline* (2006), the Supreme Court upheld a 2001 jury verdict that acquitted a defendant charged with second degree murder for shooting her sleeping husband after suffering from years of mental and physical abuse. Automatism is sometimes confused with self-defence (see below). The fundamental premise of automatism is that the behaviour is involuntary; in contrast, self-defence implies deliberate conduct (Tibbetts 2006:A6).

Mistake of Fact

Someone who commits an illegal act while believing that certain circumstances exist may use the defence of **mistake of fact**. This defence focuses on the *mens rea* of the offence. It is a defence to a criminal charge if (1) the mistake was an honest one, and (2) no offence would have been committed if the circumstances had been as the accused believed them to be.

The Criminal Code limits the use of this defence. For example, an accused person cannot use this defence when charged with touching a young person under the age of 14 for a Sexual purpose unless the accused took all reasonable steps to determine the age of the youth. In addition, there are special rules for using this defence when the charge is sexual assault (see s. 150.1[4]).

Mistake of Law

The general rule that "ignorance of the law is no excuse" is found in s. 19 of the Criminal Code. That is, everyone is presumed to know the criminal law. If a **mistake of law** defence is used, it concerns an error regarding the legal status of a circumstance or fact. The Supreme Court of Canada has stated that the mistake of law defence is no excuse by noting that "it is a principle of our criminal law that an honest but mistaken belief in respect of the legal consequences of one's deliberate actions does not furnish a defence to a criminal charge, even when the mistake cannot be attributed to the negligence of the accused" (*R. v. Forster* [1992]). Individuals "rely on their own knowledge of the law, or even a lawyer's advice, at their peril," even when they have "made genuine and reasonable attempts to ascertain what the law is and to comply with it" (Roach 2004:82).

Justification Defences

Justification defences involve a defendant admitting that while they did commit the criminal act in question, that act was justified in the circumstances. There are five justification defences: duress, necessity, self-defence, provocation, and entrapment. Three of these defences (duress, necessity, and self-defence) are known as "complete defences" because if they are accepted by the court, they result in acquittal. The Supreme Court of Canada has ruled that a defendant who is acquitted after arguing justification will not be punished because "the values of society, indeed of criminal law itself, are better promoted by disobeying a given statute than by observing it" (*R. v. Perka* [1984]). The exceptions here are the defences of provocation and entrapment. Provocation is a partial defence, which means that, if the accused is successful in this defence, it will partly exonerate the defendant. This defence arises in cases involving murder, and if successful reduces that charge to manslaughter. Entrapment results in a permanent stay of proceedings rather than acquittal.

Justification defences "to some extent require a person to have acted reasonably in response to external pressures" (Roach 2004:278). The Supreme Court of Canada in *R. v. Hibbert* (1995) ruled that three of these defences—self-defence, necessity, and duress—"all arise under circumstances where a person is subjected to an external danger that otherwise would be criminal as a way of avoiding the harm the danger presents." In all justification defences, the burden of proof is on the Crown to prove guilt beyond a reasonable doubt.

Duress

Duress exists when the wrongful threat of one person makes another person commit a crime he or she would not otherwise have committed, when there was an imminent threat of death or bodily harm (*R. v. Ruzic* [2001]), and when there was no realistic alternative course of action (*R. v. Hibbert* [1995]). In these situations, duress is seen as negating the *mens rea* necessary to commit a crime. The rationale for duress is "a plea for absolution where the accused's actions are considered blameworthy but forgivable" as long as "the only reasonable avenue of escape is to commit the crime" (*R. v. Ryan* [2011]).

Necessity

Necessity is related to the defence of duress because duress is actually a type of necessity. In cases of duress, the danger is caused by intentional threats of bodily harm, while in cases involving necessity, the danger is caused by forces of nature or human conduct other than the intentional threats of bodily harm.

The defence of necessity is rarely used (Barnhorst and Barnhorst 2004:80). The Supreme Court decided in *R. v. Perka* (1984) that the defence of necessity applies in those cases where:

- there was imminent peril or danger;
- the accused had no reasonable legal alternative to the course of action he or she took; and
- there was proportionality between the harm inflicted and the harm avoided.

One of the most controversial Canadian cases involving the defence of necessity occurred in November 1993, when Robert Latimer was charged with first degree murder for the death of his 12-year-old daughter. She was suffering from a severe form of cerebral palsy that had left her physically and developmentally disabled and in extreme pain, a condition that could not be helped by medication. During the first trial, Latimer's lawyer offered the defence of necessity, arguing that his client was attempting to prevent a tragedy greater than that of his daughter's death. The Supreme Court, however, disagreed, deciding that there had been no imminent threat to Tracy's life because her pain was ongoing—that is, it was not an emergency. It also ruled that there were reasonable legal alternatives for Tracy. Finally, it considered that the harm avoided was "completely disproportionate to the harm caused" (Sneiderman 2000:513–14).

Self-Defence

Self-defence (which involves defending oneself as well as others and property) justifies the use of force against another person. The general rule, found in s. 26 of the Criminal Code, is that only as much force as necessary can be used in the circumstances. If excessive force is used, the individual can be charged with a criminal offence (e.g., an assault) or be subject to a lawsuit in a civil action. Section 27 of the Criminal Code states that anyone can use as much force as is reasonably necessary to prevent the commission of certain offences that are likely to cause severe harm to a person or to property (Barnhorst and Barnhorst 2004:82). Other sections of the Criminal Code also deal with self-defence. For an example, force can be used to protect oneself against assault, be it provoked or not, or to prevent an assault from occurring. Also, individuals can use force to defend movable property in their possession as well as a dwelling house or real property.

Self-defence has been successfully used to acquit women who used force to protect themselves from aggressors. The case of *R. v. Lavallee* (1990) involved a woman using force to protect herself. The accused was unable to leave her husband despite being constantly abused by him over the previous four years. On the day of the killing, he found her hiding in a closet. He then gave her a gun and dared her to shoot him, saying that if she didn't shoot him, he would kill her later. When he started to leave the room, she shot him in the head. During the trial, experts testified that the accused felt "trapped, vulnerable [and] worthless." The Supreme Court of Canada accepted the evidence of **battered woman syndrome** and upheld her acquittal. It ruled that battered woman syndrome can be resorted to when there is a well-founded anticipation of peril—in other words, the accused does not have to prove imminent peril.

A controversial aspect of the self-defence law concerns the issue of a citizen's arrest. In 2009, Mr. Bennett stole $72 worth of house plants from a store owned by Mr. Chen in Toronto. The theft was recorded by the store surveillance cameras. An hour later Mr. Bennett returned to the store and Mr. Chen told him to pay for the items he had taken, but he refused, denied stealing the plants, and then ran away. Mr. Chen and another employee gave chase, and then the delivery van driver from the same store came upon the scene and blocked the path of Mr. Bennett. Once surrounded, Mr. Bennett fought back, but the three men were able to subdue him. They then tied his feet and legs and placed him in the van. Bystanders called 911, thinking they were witnessing a kidnapping. The police arrived within minutes, and arrested the three men and charged them with assault, forcible confinement, kidnapping, and carrying concealed weapons (two of the men were carrying box cutters on them). The kidnapping and weapons charges were later dropped. At trial, the three men were acquitted of the remaining charges (*R. v. Chen et al.* [2010]). As a result of the ensuing public and political outcry, Parliament introduced Bill C-26, The Citizen's Arrest and Self-defence Act, which contained a number of revisions to the existing law, specifically ss. 34 and 35 of the Criminal Code. One of the revisions was that self-defence can now be claimed for any offence, not just for violent crimes such as assault or murder. Another change is that acts of self-defence have to be "reasonable in the circumstances." How the courts will interpret the new provisions will be determined in future cases.

Provocation

Provocation, as defined in s. 232 of the Criminal Code, involves a wrongful act or insult that deprives an ordinary person of the power of self-control. It is a partial defence only, as it can only be used for the offence of murder and, if it succeeds, the accused will be found guilty of the less serious offence of manslaughter.

Tony Bock/Getstock

David Chen stands outside his food store in Toronto. He was charged with assault and forcible confinement because of his citizen's arrest he made after a man stole items from his store. He was later acquitted of the charges.

According to s. 232 of the Criminal Code, provocation consists of the following elements:

- a wrongful act or insult . . .
- sufficient to deprive an ordinary person of the power of self-control . . .
- that actually provoked the offender, who acted in response to it . . .
- on the sudden, before there was time for his or her passion to cool.

These four elements are used to form two tests—(1) "a wrongful act or insult" and (2) "upon the sudden"—both of which must be satisfied if the defence of provocation is to be used successfully. In *R. v. Tran* (2010), the Supreme Court of Canada agreed with an Alberta Court of Appeal decision to overturn an Alberta lower court finding where the trial judge had agreed with the argument of provocation and convicted Mr. Tran of the lesser offence of manslaughter. Mr. Tran was estranged from his wife but knew she was seeing another man. One afternoon, he let himself into her locked apartment and discovered her in bed with her boyfriend. He then stabbed both of them, killing the man. At trial, Mr. Tran used the defence of provocation, pointing out that he had lost his self-control after seeing his wife in bed with another man. On appeal, the Alberta Court of Appeal overturned the lower court decision and substituted a conviction for second degree murder. The Supreme Court pointed out that Mr. Tran had kept his wife under surveillance and had eavesdropped on her private conversations and, as such, the surprise was on the part of both victims, not Mr. Tran.

Entrapment

Entrapment is a justification defence and it arises when a police officer or government agent deceives a defendant into committing a wrongful act. The police can use legitimate means to gain information to arrest a suspect, but only up to a point. Entrapment occurs when an agent of the state (such as a police officer) offers an individual an opportunity to commit a crime without reasonable grounds to suspect that the individual in question was involved in a criminal activity. Entrapment also occurs when the state actually induces the individual to commit a crime. In *R. v. Mack* (1988), for example, the Supreme Court of Canada held that this defence exists as part of the doctrine of abuse of process.

The entrapment defence may be available when someone has been "set up" to commit a crime by the police or police informants. The defendant must prove that he or she was entrapped on a balance of probabilities. The finding that entrapment occurred is always reached by a judge, and only after the guilt of the accused has been determined.

SUMMING UP AND LOOKING FORWARD

Our criminal justice system allows people charged with crimes to offer defences for their behaviour. Since defendants claim such defences, they typically have the burden of proving them. This means that even if the prosecution proves all of the elements of crime beyond a reasonable doubt, defendants can avoid conviction. There are two categories of defences that allow people to avoid being held liable for criminal offences as they are not seen as responsible for their actions. In excuse defences, defendants admit to committing a criminal act but argue they cannot be held criminally responsible since there was no criminal intent. The two most common examples of excuse defences are age and mental disorder. There are also situations where people can argue that their actions are justified under the circumstances. There are five justification defences: duress, necessity, self-defence, provocation, and entrapment.

So far in this chapter we have been discussing the major categories of the criminal law and legal defences, but what are the sources of our criminal laws? These are discussed in the next section.

Review Questions:

1. Do you think old age should be an excuse to criminal liability?
2. Do you agree with the recent revisions to the self-defence provisions? What should happen if a suspect is only offering mild resistance to a citizen's arrest and is seriously injured?
3. Should there be a legal defence for those individuals who commit a crime against someone who consents to it, such as assisted suicides (see Chapter 1)?

What Are the Sources of the Criminal Law in Canada?

Canadian criminal law is derived from British common law. Thus, the structure of our criminal law is modelled closely on the British experience. The **common law** is an important source of our criminal law and is an important component of the substantive law in Canada. It originated during the reign of Henry II (1154–1189) as a result of his desire to establish a strong central government. Part of his vision was a court system that would try cases on the basis of laws passed by the government and applicable to all citizens. To this end, he appointed judges to specific territories (or circuits) to hear cases in order to ensure that the "King's Law" was administered and enforced. Over time, judges exchanged information about their legal decisions, and this growing body of knowledge slowly began to replace laws based on local customs. In the traditional system, serious crimes such as murder, rape, and assault had been viewed as wrongs between private citizens. Judges now began to redefine these as wrongs against the state—that is, as criminal offences. A common law gradually developed, forming legal principles that were equally applicable to all citizens regardless of local customs or place of residence.

Another significant change emerged about this same time. A system gradually developed in which judges decided cases on the basis of previous judgments in similar cases. Crimes had general meanings attached to them, so that most people now knew what was meant by murder and other criminal offences. This shared knowledge resulted in a practice that continues today in our system of criminal law: deciding trials on the basis of precedents, even if such precedents are not necessarily binding. This practice evolved into a principle or rule known as ***stare decisis*** ("based on situations of similar facts"), which requires the judiciary to follow previous decisions in similar cases. Thus, by a process of making decisions in case after case, and guided by the rule of precedent, these early English judges created a body of law that applied to all the people of England. This law was common to all. Today, judges in Canada still follow precedent. This generally means that the lower courts must follow the decisions of higher courts and that courts of equal rank should try to follow one another's decisions.

The principle of *stare decisis* is still in use today. When a criminal court has to make a decision, the judge will research how other courts have reached their decisions in similar cases, and these earlier decisions will be used as guides. This principle lends itself to stability in the legal system, since it allows one to predict how a court will probably decide a case. This practice does not necessarily lead to a rigid system of criminal law, because a judge can still make rulings that deviate from existing precedent. This can happen when, for example, conditions in a society have changed so that a judge feels warranted in departing from existing precedents.

Written Sources of the Criminal Law

Originally, the common law was uncodified—in other words, it was not written down and preserved in a central location. This meant that judges had to discuss the rulings among themselves, a situation that often led to long waiting periods before a final judgment was given. This system proved to be extremely cumbersome and led to the creation of written sources of the criminal law.

Contemporary Canadian criminal law has four main sources: the Constitution, statute law, case law, and administrative law. Canadian criminal law is modelled closely on the British experience and makes use of British legal precedents and procedures. However, changes were gradually introduced when it became apparent that some legal issues facing Canadians were inapplicable to the British experience and British precedents and procedures. Clearly, some of the legal issues facing Canadians were unique and called for made-in-Canada alternatives.

The Constitution

The Constitution is the supreme law in Canada. The fundamental principles that guide the enactment of laws and the application of those laws by the courts are found in the Constitution Act. While only the federal government can enact criminal laws and procedure, a criminal law may be found to be unconstitutional by the courts "if it infringes upon a right or a freedom protected under the Canadian Charter of Rights and Freedoms [see below] and if it cannot be justified under s. 1 of the Charter as a reasonable and demonstrably justified limit on a right" (Roach 2004:6).

Statute Law

Another source of criminal law is **statutes**. Statutes are laws that prohibit or mandate certain acts. These laws are systematically codified and placed in a single volume, such as our Criminal Code. Most offences are updated over time so that they can include more detailed definitions of a criminal act. In order to change the existing law, governments must either modify existing laws or introduce new ones by enacting statutes. Statute law is today considered the most important source of law in Canada. It is through the use of statutes that criminal law is created, changed, or eliminated.

The power to enact statute law in Canada is divided among the federal government (that is, Parliament), the provinces, and municipalities. However, only Parliament has the power to enact criminal law. Statute law always overrules case law, except in conflicts over the Canadian Charter of Rights and Freedoms. Under the Charter, citizens possess certain rights and freedoms "that cannot be infringed upon by the government"; in this way, the Charter "limits the legislative authority of the government" (Barnhorst and Barnhorst 2004:8). In Canada, all statutes are consolidated about every 10 years when Parliament replaces the existing statutes with revised versions.

Case Law

Case law involves the judicial application and interpretation of laws as they apply in a particular case. Every time a judge in Canada makes a decision in a court case, they have the discretion to interpret the relevant statutes. Statutes may need to be interpreted, because they are stated only in general terms while the court case may call for a specific meaning. For example, a judge may decide that all previous decisions are problematic because they are outdated or vague, given the facts of a case at hand. As a result, the law may be redefined to make it reflect specifics. Once a judge makes a decision that changes the traditional legal definitions, an appeal is usually made to the provincial court of appeal in that jurisdiction. The appeal court decision too will likely be appealed to the Supreme Court of Canada. If the Supreme Court refuses to hear the case, the ruling made by the provincial court of appeal stands. However, if the Supreme Court decides to hear the case, its decision becomes law. This occurred in *Canada (Attorney General) v. Bedford* (2013), which challenged Canada's prostitution laws (see *Criminal Justice Focus* previously in this chapter). In this case, the Ontario Superior Court judge, in order to achieve justice, did not follow legal precedent and held that the laws violated s. 7 of the Charter of Rights and Freedoms. On appeal, the Supreme Court justified the lower court judge's decision on the basis that Charter rulings had developed since 1990, when it had last heard a case challenging the constitutionality of laws related to prostitution. In its decision, the Supreme Court of Canada stated that

> . . . a trial judge can consider and decide arguments based on Charter provisions that were not raised in the earlier case; this constitutes a new legal case. Similarly, the matter may be revisited if new legal issues are raised as a consequence of significant developments in the law, or if there is a change in the circumstances or evidence that fundamentally shifts the parameters of the debate.

Administrative Regulations (Regulatory Offences)

Another source of criminal law is **administrative regulations.** These regulations are considered to have the power of criminal law, since they can include criminal penalties. Laws are written by regulatory agencies that have been given the power by governments to develop and enforce rules in specific areas, such as the environment, competition policy, and protection from hazardous products. Violations of administrative laws are sometimes referred to as regulatory offences. The federal government, the provinces, and municipalities can enact them. The purpose of these offences is to deter behaviour felt to be risky in order to prevent harmful acts before they occur.

SUMMING UP AND LOOKING FORWARD

The common law, an important source of the criminal law, refers to those legal principles equally applicable to everyone. Starting in the late 12th century, judges in England began to exchange their decisions with other judges. Over time, a law common to all emerged and developed, and these laws were based on previous cases, or precedent. When precedents are applied in contemporary cases, it is referred to as ***stare decisis***. Precedents are supposed to be followed, but when the current case significantly differs from the precedent, judges are able to depart from it. In Canada today, there are four main sources of the written law. The Constitution is the supreme law, and its fundamental principles guide the enactment and application of the law. Statute law refers to laws that prohibit or mandate certain actions. Case law involves the judicial application of laws as they apply in particular cases. Administrative regulations are written by regulatory agencies that possess the power to develop and enforce rules in certain areas, such as the environment.

The above types of laws are mainly concerned with the substantive criminal law. But what about the procedural criminal law? Procedural safeguards for suspects and the accused are mainly found in the legal rights sections of the Charter of Rights and Freedoms. These are discussed in the next section.

Review Questions:

1. Why is the Constitution considered to be the supreme law in Canada?
2. Under what conditions can judges break with precedent in their decisions?
3. What is the primary purpose of regulatory offences? How does this differ from the criminal law?

The Canadian Charter of Rights and Freedoms

One of the most important additions to the Canadian legal system was the Charter of Rights and Freedoms, enacted on April 17, 1982. The Charter differs from common law and statute law in that it applies mainly to the protection of the **legal rights** of criminal suspects and convicted persons, the powers of the various criminal justice agencies, and criminal procedure during a trial. It is a complex piece of legislation, and only parts of it deal with issues relevant to the criminal justice system. However, the sections concerned with the operation of the criminal justice system have had a tremendous impact on criminal procedure issues in Canada, especially as they apply to the rights of the accused and the powers of criminal justice agencies involved in detecting and prosecuting criminals (see Figure 2.5).

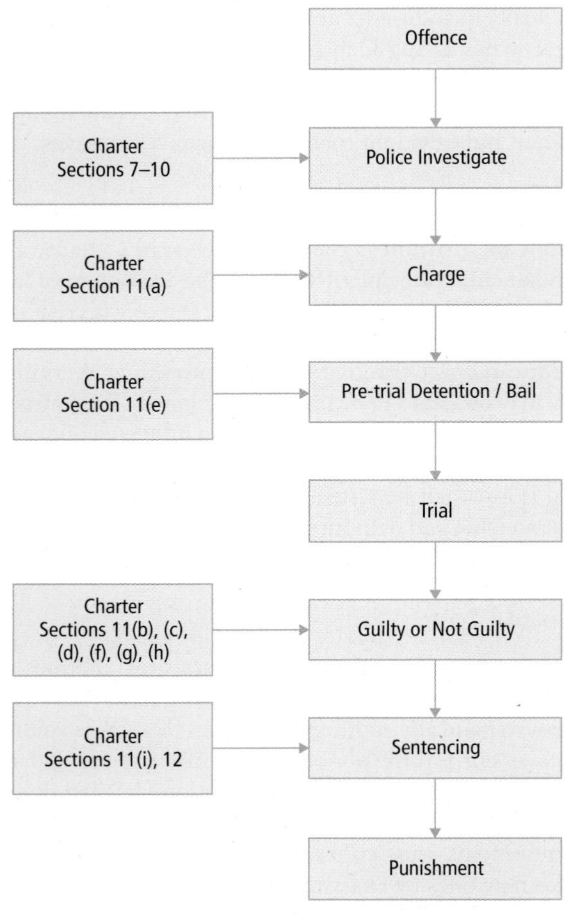

FIGURE 2.5 The Criminal Process and the Charter

Source: Roach 2012:4.

THE CANADIAN PRESS/stf

Prior to the Charter coming into force, the criminal law was determined by lawmakers (as long as it was within their proper scope of authority). The operation of our criminal justice system before the Charter is best described as following a **crime control model** (see Chapter 1), as the criminal courts were in most cases not concerned with the legal rights of those being investigated or charged with a criminal offence by the police.

Since its introduction, the Charter has done much to establish and enforce certain fundamental principles relating to the operation of the criminal justice system—principles such as a fair trial and freedom from cruel and unusual punishment (see Exhibit 2.2). The rights guaranteed by the Charter are of fundamental importance to the criminal law, as they apply to all parts of it (e.g., the substantive criminal law and the procedural criminal law). Section 1 discusses the kinds of acceptable limits that may be made to the Charter and are intended to give judges direction in such matters. There are three key features in this section. First, if someone (typically a government) wishes to limit a right they need to prove that the limitation is reasonable. Second, any limit must expressly be provided or implied by a law or regulation (i.e., "prescribed by law"). This means that "under the principle of rule of law, government may not take action, including action to limit rights, except through law" (Greene 2014:76). Third, "reasonable limit" refers to what is considered to be a justifiable limit in our society. Section 7 of the Charter is a general guarantee of the principles of fundamental justice. It states that everyone has the right to life, liberty, and security of the person unless deprived thereof pursuant to "fundamental justice."

EXHIBIT 2.2 The Charter of Rights and Freedoms: Legal Rights of the Accused and the Canadian Criminal Justice System

Procedural safeguards are found in the legal rights sections of the Charter of Rights and Freedoms. They are designed to protect individuals from government intrusion. While the government can restrict freedoms, they must follow the procedures to ensure that any freedoms are not unduly restricted.

Legal Rights

1. The Canadian Charter of Rights and Freedoms guarantees the rights and freedoms set out in it subject only to such reasonable limits prescribed by law as can be demonstrably justified in a free and democratic society.
7. Everyone has the right to life, liberty and security of the person and the right not to be deprived thereof except in accordance with the principles of fundamental justice.
8. Everyone has the right to be secure against unreasonable search or seizure.
9. Everyone has the right not to be arbitrarily detained or imprisoned.
10. Everyone has the right on arrest or detention
    - (a) to be informed promptly of the reasons therefore;
    - (b) to retain and instruct counsel without delay and to be informed of that right; and
    - (c) to have the validity of the detection determined by way of habeas corpus and to be released if the detention is not lawful.
11. Any person charged with an offence has the right
    - (a) to be informed without unreasonable delay of the specific offence;
    - (b) to be tried within a reasonable time;
    - (c) not to be compelled to be a witness in proceedings against that person in respect of the offence;
    - (d) to be presumed innocent until proven guilty according to law in a fair and public hearing by an independent and impartial tribunal;
    - (e) not to be denied reasonable bail without just cause;
    - (f) except in the case of an offence under military law tried before a military tribunal, to the benefit of trial by jury where the maximum punishment for the offence is imprisonment for five years or a more severe punishment;
    - (g) not to be found guilty on account of any act or omission unless, at the time of the act or omission, it is constituted an offence under Canadian or international law or was criminal according to the general principles of law recognized by the community of nations;
    - (h) if finally acquitted of the offence, not to be tried for it again and, if finally found guilty and punished for the offence, not to be tried or punished for it again; and
    - (i) if found guilty of the offence and if the punishment for the offence has been varied between the time of the commission and the time of sentencing, to the benefit of the lesser punishment.
12. Everyone has the right not to be subjected to any cruel and unusual treatment or punishment.
13. A witness who testifies in any proceedings has the right not to have any incriminating evidence so given used to incriminate that witness in any other proceedings, except in a prosecution for perjury or for the giving of contradictory evidence.
14. A party or witness in any proceedings who does not understand or speak the language in which the proceedings are conducted or who is deaf has the right to the assistance of an interpreter.

Equality Rights

15. (1) Every individual is equal before and under the law and has the right to the equal protection and equal benefit of the law without discrimination and, in particular, without discrimination based on race, national or ethnic origin, colour, religion, sex, age or mental or physical disability.

    (2) Subsection (1) does not preclude any law, program or activity that has as its object the amelioration of conditions of disadvantaged individuals or groups including those that are disadvantaged because of race, national or ethnic origin, colour, religion, sex, age or mental or physical disability.

Enforcement

24. (1) Anyone whose rights or freedoms, as guaranteed by this Charter, have been infringed or denied may apply to a court of competent jurisdiction to obtain such remedy as the court considers appropriate and just in the circumstances.

    (2) Where, in proceedings under subsection (1), a court concludes that evidence was obtained in a manner that infringed or denied any rights or freedoms guaranteed by this Charter, the evidence shall be excluded if it is established that, having regard to all the circumstances, the admission of it in the proceedings would bring the administration of justice into disrepute.

The criminal law as it is structured within the Charter can be divided into two general categories, (1) the investigation of crime and (2) the criminal trial process. The sections of the Charter applicable to the investigation of crime includes the right to be secure from unreasonable search and seizure (s. 8); the right not to be arbitrarily detained and imprisoned (s. 9); and the rights of individuals when they are arrested or detained, specifically the right to be informed for the reasons on arrest and detention (s. 10[a]), the right to counsel (s. 10[b]), and the right to **habeas corpus** (the right to be released if the detention is not lawful (s. 10[c]).

The Investigation of Crime and the Charter

Sections 8–10 of the Charter deal with the rights of individuals when they are detained and arrested by the police. Section 8 provides everyone with the right to be secure against unreasonable search or seizure. It involves the protection of citizens' property and privacy against unwarranted intrusions by state agents. This section has generated a significant amount of case law, since most criminal trial evidence is collected by the police and the propriety of how they obtained that evidence is often raised in court. According to s. 8, a "search" occurs when a government action invades a person's reasonable expectation of privacy, while a "seizure" involves the taking of something from an individual by a state authority, but no consent has been given. This section concerns an individual's right to privacy; however, this right has to be balanced with the need for the police to be able to conduct searches and seize evidence as a part of their law enforcement activities. Section 8 is therefore referred to as a "relative" right, since an individual is protected only against unreasonable searches and seizures. It applies to personal information (where an individual has a right to be protected from intrusive activities by the authorities) as opposed to commercial records (which are not subject to this protection).

Whether or not a search is "reasonable" under s. 8 is determined by balancing the public interest of having privacy with the reason for the government's intrusion by law enforcement officials. The Supreme Court set out the basic framework for police searches and seizures in one of its earliest decisions, *Hunter v. Southam Inc.* (1984). In this case, the Supreme Court outlined three basic criteria to be considered when balancing these interests:

- Where possible, the search must have been approved by prior authorization;
- The person authorizing the search need not be a judge but must act in a judicial manner; and
- There must be reasonable and probable grounds, established upon oath, to believe that an offence has been committed and that evidence of this is to be found at a particular place.

The Court, while agreeing that individuals have a right to be secure from an unreasonable search and seizure, established that certain procedural elements must exist in order for the police to do their work. As a result, the police are now required to justify their need to search by producing sworn evidence that meets an objective standard. The Court also recognized that in some exigent circumstances (such as a "hot pursuit") the police need not have a warrant before they act. Other limitations surround a citizen's right to privacy—for example, if there is the threat or danger that evidence connected to a crime will be destroyed or removed, if a person has contacted the police because of an emergency, or if the police are involved in a reasonable search.

Section 8 is designed to protect all reasonable expectations of privacy, and it is not to be ignored even when an individual is caught committing a crime. In *R. v. Duarte* (1990), the police placed a body-pack recorder on an informer to record a conversation with a suspect. No warrant had been obtained; the police assumed that their action was legal because one of the individuals involved had given consent to being taped. The Supreme Court, however, ruled that the individual in question had the right to a reasonable expectation of privacy.

Section 8 protections are not absolute; the Supreme Court has determined that in certain situations individuals have diminished or no expectations of privacy. For example, in *R. v. Lawrence and Belnavis* (1998), the Supreme Court held that passengers in a vehicle normally have no reasonable expectation of privacy—only the owner of the vehicle or those individuals able to exercise control over the vehicle are likely to have s. 8 rights. In *R. v. Tesling* (2004) (see Chapter 7), the police use of forward looking infrared (FLIR) technology to detect heat coming from a private home where a marijuana grow operation was suspected did not violate s. 8.

Section 9 guarantees that everyone has the right to be free from arbitrary detention or imprisonment. A "detention" occurs when a law enforcement official takes some type of control over an individual through some form of compulsion or coercion which may have legal consequences for that individual, such as a request for a breath sample. The Supreme Court has determined that a detention can be both physical and psychological. In *R. v. Therens* (1985), the Supreme Court identified three different types of detention.

- The first occurs when an individual is subjected to physical restraint (detention by physical restraint) by

the police; in other words, when someone is arrested, they are detained.
- The second type of detention (detention by legal compulsion) occurs when there are legal consequences for an individual if they decide to not comply with a request from a police officer.
- The third type of detention occurs when an individual is psychologically detained.

If an individual is detained, it is necessary to determine whether or not it was "arbitrary." An early Charter case involving s. 9 involved the provincial power of the police to conduct random "spot checks" in order to identify impaired drivers. In *R. v. Hufsky* (1988), the Supreme Court ruled that randomly stopping a driver was in fact an arbitrary detention under s. 9 of the Charter since it represented total discretion on the behalf of the police officer as to who would be stopped. However, the Court then stated that randomly stopping a driver thought to be impaired could be justified under s. 1 of the Charter due to the importance of highway safety and the need to protect other citizens from potential harm. However, the police should possess reasonable suspicion based on objective standards (*R. v. Duguay* [(1985]).

Prior to detaining and arresting someone, the police must have reasonable grounds or else their actions will be judged as arbitrary and in violation of s. 9. *R. v. Simpson* (1993) focused on the meaning of reasonable grounds for an arrest. In this case, a police officer observed a man leaving a house reputed to be inhabited by persons selling drugs. While he was driving away, the police officer pulled him over and asked to see his driver's licence and registration. The man informed the officer he was driving without a valid driver's licence. He was arrested and subsequently charged with driving while under suspension. The officer then continued her search under the assumption that he had bought drugs at the residence. She discovered several grams of crack cocaine, which led to additional charges. When the case reached court, all charges were dropped; it was ruled that the police officer had conducted an improper investigation that violated the suspect's s. 9 Charter rights. Educated "guesses" do not constitute reasonable grounds to arrest someone.

Psychological detention is seen as happening in two situations. The first is when an individual, during a formal investigation, voluntarily agrees to go to the police station to answer questions. If the individual is subsequently considered a suspect (e.g., because the police determine there are reasonable grounds they were somehow connected to the crime) and placed under arrest, there is probably no issue related to s. 9 of the Charter since this type of detention is no doubt lawful and, as a result, not arbitrary. What happens when, during a sidewalk stop, an individual makes an incriminating statement, or they are carrying an item (e.g., drugs) found by the police during a search? In such cases, questions are raised as to whether or not being stopped and questioned by the police on the sidewalk involved an arbitrary detention. Until recently, most lower courts in Canada ruled that such instances of detaining someone did not necessarily make the police actions arbitrary under s. 9. However, in *R. v. Grant* (2009), which involved a sidewalk stop, the majority of the Supreme Court explained that psychological detention is established either where an individual has a legal obligation to comply with the restrictive request or demand, or when a reasonable person would conclude by reason of the state conduct that they had no choice but to comply. As a result, the detention of the individual was held to be arbitrary and violated s. 9 of the Charter.

Section 10 rights are guaranteed only when someone is arrested or detained. Similar to s. 9, this section deals with a detention when an agent of the state gains control over an individual by a demand or a request that may have significant legal consequences, but here the focus is upon actions that prevent an individual's access to legal counsel. Similar to s. 9, either physical or psychological aspects can be considered.

Three subsections of s. 10 deal with certain specific rights given to individuals when they are arrested or detained by the police. Section 10(a) stipulates that everyone who is arrested has the right to be informed as soon as possible of the reasons for that arrest. Arrest and detention constitutes a significant intrusion into a private citizen's life, and it is a basic right for that person to know why he or she has been arrested and detained (*R. v. Borden* [1994]). When there is reasonable suspicion that an individual was somehow involved in "a recent or ongoing criminal offence" and the detention is brief (i.e., an "investigative detention"), the detention is not arbitrary (*R. v. Mann* [2004]).

Section 10(b) states that "everyone has the right on arrest or detention to retain and instruct counsel without delay and to be informed of that right." According to this section of the Charter, the police are not permitted to question an individual who has been detained or is under arrest until that person understands they have the right to counsel as well as having the opportunity to use that right. This section has been one of the most controversial in the Charter. Its purpose is to control police conduct after initial charges have been laid against the suspect. In *R. v. Therens* (1985), the Supreme Court ruled that evidence obtained by the police without first informing the suspect of his or her right to a lawyer cannot be used. This interpretation was expanded in *R. v. Manninen* (1987), in which the right to legal counsel was extended to all persons detained by the police. Law enforcement officers were later instructed that before conducting questioning, they had to inform all persons in their custody as to how they could exercise this right. In *R. v. Brydges* (1990), the Court extended the police duty to advise individuals of their right to legal counsel by giving the accused a reasonable length of time to retain and instruct counsel. The police now have to refrain from questioning any suspect until the accused has been given a reasonable opportunity to exercise this right. The police are also now required to provide *access* to counsel at the first practical moment (*R. v. Taylor* [2014]).

However, certain limits have been placed on the rights of the accused to obtain legal counsel. The Supreme Court has ruled that the rights set out in this section of the Charter are not absolute and that a suspect's right to retain and instruct counsel must be exercised diligently by the suspect. This means that a suspect cannot refuse the opportunity to contact legal counsel, be questioned by the police, and then complain about having said things he or she should not have said because no lawyer was present. Sections 10(a) and 10(b) have sometimes been referred to as "gateway" rights since the Supreme Court has indicated the purpose of these two sections is to ensure suspects be given their other Charter rights. Section 10(c) is concerned with habeas corpus, a common-law remedy against unlawful detention. Habeas corpus entitles an individual who is detained to request an assessment as to whether they are being unlawfully detained. The rights provided by this rule of common law are guaranteed by other Charter provisions, such as the right to be secure from arbitrary arrest and detention and the right not to be denied reasonable bail. In *Charkaoui v. Canada* (2007), the Supreme Court dealt with security certificates under the Immigration and Refugee Protection Act, which authorizes the indefinite detention of noncitizens suspected of terrorism (see Chapter 1). The Supreme Court held that the 120-day delay for review of detentions for noncitizens (in contrast to 48 hours for permanent residents) violated s. 10(c) as well as other sections.

SUMMING UP AND LOOKING FORWARD

Prior to the Charter of Rights and Freedoms, the criminal courts were in most cases not concerned with the legal rights of those being investigated or charged with a criminal offence by the police. With the introduction of the Charter, this system changed dramatically as legal rights were now guaranteed to all suspects and those who were charged with a criminal offence. The rights guaranteed by the Charter are of fundamental importance to the criminal law, as they apply to all parts of it (e.g., the substantive criminal law and the procedural criminal law). Procedural safeguards are found in the legal rights sections (ss. 7–14) of the Charter of Rights and Freedoms. They are designed to protect individuals from government intrusion. While the government can restrict freedoms, they must follow the procedures to ensure that any freedoms are not unduly restricted.

Sections 8 through 10 (inclusive) deal with the rights of suspects and the accused during the investigation of crime. These sections include the right to be secure from unreasonable search and seizure (s. 8); the right not to be arbitrarily detained or imprisoned (s. 9); and the rights of individuals when they are arrested or detained, specifically the right to be informed for the reasons on arrest and detention (s. 10[a]), the right to counsel (s. 10[b]), and the right to habeas corpus (the right to be released if the detention is not lawful (s. 10[c]).

In the next section, the procedural safeguards for those who have been charged and are going to have their case heard in a criminal court are discussed. A violation of any of these rights can result in the exclusion of evidence from the criminal trial if it is decided that it brings the administration of justice into disrepute (s. 24[2]).

Review Questions:

1. Do ss. 8–10 of the Charter benefit the interests of law enforcement (i.e., the crime control model) or better reflect the legal rights of the accused (i.e., the due process model)?
2. What is the boundary between being detained by the police and being placed under arrest?
3. Should the legal protections governing the right of an accused to contact a lawyer be expanded in favour of those charged with a criminal offence?

© Gaetano/Corbis

An accused person is led into court in order to give a judge his initial plea.

The Criminal Trial, Punishment, and the Charter

Sections 11, 12, 13, and 14 outline the rights of individuals charged with a criminal offence and as they proceed through the criminal courts. Section 11 deals with the rights that come into effect upon being charged with an offence, such as the presumption of innocence, court delays, and the right not to be denied reasonable bail. Section 11(a) states that the police must inform the accused the precise nature of the charges they are facing without unreasonable delay. This enables the accused to challenge the proceedings if they are unlawful or to prepare a defence if the case is proceeding to court. There are three parts to this right:

- the right to be informed of the charge;
- the right to specificity in the allegation of the offence; and
- the right to be informed without unreasonable delay.

Section 11(b) includes the right of the defendant to be tried within a reasonable time (*R. v. Askov* [1990]). This section attempts to protect:

- the right to security of the person by minimizing the anxiety and stigma associated with a criminal charge;
- the right of liberty by minimizing the length of restrictions on liberty due to pretrial incarceration and restrictive bail conditions; and
- the right to a fair trial by ensuring that evidence is available and fresh at the proceedings (*R. v. Morin* [1992]).

The Supreme Court has drawn a distinction between pre-charge and post-charge delays. For example, over the past few years a number of charges have been laid against individuals years after the alleged incident. The Court has ruled that a delay in charging an individual will rarely lead to a successful challenge about an unreasonable delay (*R. v. Mills* [1986]), although unexplained or unjustified delays may lead to a successful challenge (*R. v. Kalanj* [1989]). When a delay is completely attributable to the actions of the Crown and unexplained, a court may stay the charges against the accused (*R. v. Godin* [2009]).

Section 11(c) refers to the right of a person charged with an offence not to be compelled to testify (known as the right of non-compellability). While this right protects the accused from having to testify during trial, it doesn't extend to persons charged as an accessory to a crime as they may be compelled to testify at the trial of the individual who was the principal offender. Section 11(d) deals with the presumption of innocence. The Supreme Court has held that the following elements are contained within this section of the Charter:

- an individual must be proven guilty beyond a reasonable doubt;
- the state must bear the burden of proof; and
- criminal prosecutions must be carried out in accordance with lawful procedures and fairness (*R. v. Oakes* [1986]).

Thus, an individual is innocent until proven guilty by an independent and impartial tribunal in a fair and public hearing. Concerns about the presumption of innocence led the Supreme Court of Canada, in *R. v. Oakes* (1986), to strike down a section of the Narcotic Control Act (now the Controlled Drugs and Substances Act) that presumed the guilt of the accused, in that it demanded that the accused prove to the court that they did not possess a narcotic for the purposes of trafficking. The other parts of Section 11 give the accused the right to reasonable bail (s. 11[e]) and the right to a jury trial for any offence for which the maximum punishment is five years or more (s. 11[f]). An individual's act or omission can be construed as an offence only if it was illegal at the time of the offence (s. 11[g]). Individuals are protected from double jeopardy; that is, an individual charged with an offence has the right, if acquitted of an offence, not to be tried or punished for it again (s. 11[h]). Section 11(i) states that the accused, if convicted, can be punished only on the basis of the penalties that were available at the time of the offence.

Section 12 protects individuals from any form of cruel and unusual punishment by restricting the state's power to punish people after they have been found guilty of a criminal offence. The criterion here is whether the punishment handed out is excessive—that is, violates our standards of decency. In *Smith v. R.* (1987), the Supreme Court ruled that laws mandating a minimum of seven years' punishment for importing narcotics were in violation of this section of the Charter. Its reasoning was based on the fact that this section of the relevant act included too many prohibited activities and did not distinguish between small amounts of drugs to be used for personal consumption and large amounts for trafficking. The Court regarded the minimum sentence as disproportionate to the seriousness of the offence. Other minimum sentences have been upheld by the Court, such as the mandatory minimum punishment of seven days' imprisonment for driving while under suspension (*R. v. Goltz* [1991]). Indefinite sentences for those classified by the system as dangerous offenders have also been upheld by the Court (*R. v. Luxton* [1990]).

Section 13 protects witnesses from self-incrimination and from having charges laid against them as the result of their statements. The right given to witnesses in this section is restricted to not having the evidence they give in one trial used against them in a later trial in order to prove their guilt (*R. v. Mannion* [1986]) (Sharpe and Roach 2005). Section 14 guarantees the accused and any witnesses the right to an interpreter; also, that interpreter must translate the key testimony in full instead of simply summarizing the accused's statements (*R. v. Tran* [1994]).

Equality, the Administration of Justice, and the Charter

Sections 15(1) and 15(2) of the Charter concern equality rights. They guarantee the equal protection of all individuals within our system of justice as well as for equality before and under the law. This section prohibits all types of discrimination. In *R. v. Rodriguez* (1993) (see Chapter 1), the majority of the Supreme Court held that any violation of the equality rights of the terminally ill by the Criminal Code offence against assisting suicide was not discrimination under s. 15, the true focus of which is to remedy or prevent discrimination against groups subject to historical disadvantage, stereotyping, and political and social prejudice in Canada.

Section 24 deals with remedies in the criminal process in the event of any violation of the above rights. Section 24(1) allows for a stay of proceedings so that a prosecutor cannot proceed with the case. This remedy is not common, as it is considered to be an extreme measure. In addition, the Supreme Court has stated that it can only be applied in "the clearest of cases" (*R. v. O'Connor* [1995]).

The most common remedy for a Charter violation is found in s. 24(2). A judge may decide to exclude evidence if its admission "would bring the administration of justice into disrepute." This usually occurs when the legality of the evidence collected by state agents is questioned at trial. In order to determine the legality of the evidence, judges apply a three-part test that examines

- the seriousness of the Charter violation;
- the impact of the Charter violation on the accused's Charter protected interests; and
- society's interest in an adjudication on the merits of the case (*R. v. Grant* [2009]).

Section 7: The Principles of Fundamental Justice

In addition to the rights guaranteed by the Charter reviewed above, s. 7 of the Charter has been applied by the Supreme Court of Canada to introduce and subsequently require certain procedural rights. These rights are not specifically guaranteed by ss. 8 to 14 of the Charter. However, the Court has determined that the principles of fundamental justice are broader than the rights provided by the Charter. The rulings made in this context have had a significant impact on the processing of defendants through the criminal justice system. Four areas have been affected: **the right to silence, the right to disclosure, the right to make full answer and defence,** and **the detention of those persons found not guilty by reason of insanity.**

The Right to Silence

In *R. v. Hebert* (1990), an undercover police officer posing as a fellow prisoner engaged the accused in a discussion about his activities. The officer was placed in the same cell in order to initiate conversations about the alleged offence and obtain incriminating evidence after the suspect (on instructions from his legal counsel) had refused to make a statement to the police. The Supreme Court ruled that in this case the Charter protections of s. 10(b) (the right to legal counsel) and s. 11(c) (the right against self-incrimination) did not apply. The Court, however, said that the principles of fundamental justice implicitly include a broader right to silence and that the police cannot use their "superior powers" in attempt to overstep the accused's decision to invoke his legal rights. The use of an undercover agent was ruled as "trickery," designed to deprive the accused of his choice to remain silent. The accused has a right not to be deprived of life, liberty, and security of the person except in accordance with the principles of fundamental justice, and in this case these rights were violated by the police. In this case, however, the Supreme Court was divided over the exact parameters of the right to silence. The Supreme Court used the same logic when the police hired an inmate (who was then placed in the same cell) to talk to the alleged offender in order to elicit incriminating evidence (*R. v. Broyles* [1991]).

In *R. v. Turcotte* (2005), the defendant was convicted of murder. During questioning by the police, he had refused to answer some questions. At trial, the judge suggested to the jury that it could draw an inference of guilt from Turcotte's refusal to answer, and he was convicted. On appeal, the Supreme Court ruled that Turcotte should be given a new trial. In their judgment, the Court stated that "the right to silence would be illusory if the decision not to speak to the police could be used by the Crown as evidence of guilt. . . . The right to silence . . . exists at all times against the state."

The Supreme Court once again dealt with the issue of right to silence in *R. v. Singh* (2007), but this time it involved a police interrogation. At the time of his arrest, Mr. Singh was given a Charter warning by the police and was permitted to talk to a lawyer. In one of his two interviews with the police, Mr. Singh repeatedly requested to the police that he no longer wanted to be interviewed and be returned to his cell but the police officer continued to interrogate him, ignoring Mr. Singh. In total, Mr. Singh asserted his right to silence 18 times during the lengthy police interrogation. During an interrogation, Mr. Singh made statements admitting his involvement in the crime, which the Crown later introduced into the trial. He was charged and convicted of second degree murder. The British Columbia Court of Appeal upheld the trial court judge's decision, pointing out that this case had to be distinguished from Hebert as that case involved police trickery but Mr. Singh had been aware of the police officer's intentions. Mr. Singh appealed to the Supreme Court of Canada, challenging the admissibility of his statements made during the interrogation as they were made involuntarily and violated his Charter right to remain silent. The Supreme Court of Canada, in a 5–4 decision, ruled against Mr. Singh. According to the majority, if the police cannot use "legitimate means of persuasion" to get a suspect to talk, "then the police will lose a valuable method of fighting crime. . . . One can readily appreciate that the police could hardly investigate crime without putting questions to persons from whom it is thought that useful information may be obtained" (Makin 2007:A6).

The Right of Disclosure

In a number of cases, the Crown failed to give all the relevant evidence in its possession to the defence. The Supreme Court responded by ruling, in *R. v. Stinchcombe* (1991), that s. 7 imposed a duty on the prosecution to disclose all the evidence it would be using in the trial as well as any other evidence the defence might find useful. This ruling has had a tremendous impact on the activities of both prosecutors and police (see Chapter 8 for a further discussion of disclosure).

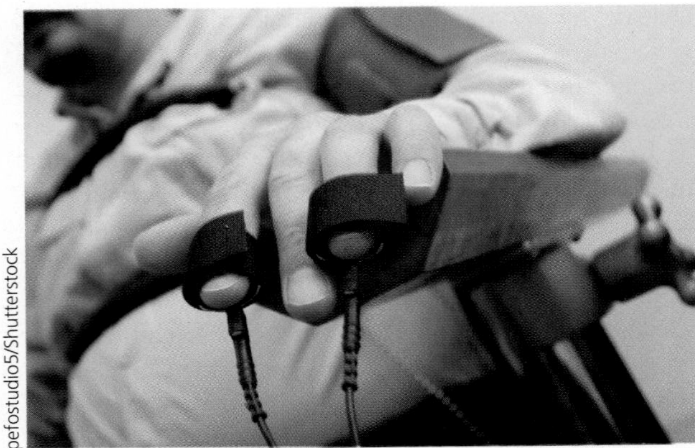
pefostudio5/Shutterstock

A polygraph (or lie detector) is a device that measures and records several physiological variables such as blood pressure during questioning. Are the results of polygraph tests admissible at trial in Canada?

The Right to Make Full Answer and Defence

One of the most significant common-law rights provided to a defendant is the right to question the complainant during a criminal trial. This became an issue in the sexual assault trials *R. v. Seaboyer* (1991) and *R. v. Gayme* (1991), mentioned earlier in this chapter. In these cases, the Criminal Code provision denying the accused's right to question the victim during the trial about her prior sexual conduct was found to be in violation of the principles of fundamental justice. The Supreme Court determined that a complete ban was excessive as it could prevent the accused from providing a legitimate defence. It ruled that this Criminal Code provision violated the principles of fundamental justice; however, it ultimately accepted strict guidelines detailing the specific circumstances in which such questions would be allowed.

The Detention of Those Found Not Guilty by Reason of Insanity

The principles of fundamental justice apply at the post-trial and pre-charge stages of the criminal justice system. Until recently, the law governing the detention of those found not guilty by reason of insanity stated that if an individual were found to be unfit to stand trial, he or she would be confined without a hearing and held indefinitely at "the pleasure of the Lieutenant-Governor." This meant that the accused could be held without the benefit of a trial to determine actual guilt or innocence (McKay-Panos 1998–99). This confinement amounted in most cases to an indefinite period of detention, since there was no provision for a hearing or for any procedural protections.

In *R. v. Swain* (1991), the Supreme Court ruled that this situation violated s. 7 of the Charter and instructed the provinces to change their legislation to alleviate it. The following year, the federal government mandated the creation of provincial review boards to take over the decision-making authority. One activity of these boards is to hold hearings no less often than every 12 months to review those individuals who are subject to their authority.

SUMMING UP AND LOOKING FORWARD

Sections 11, 12, 13, and 14 focus upon the rights of individuals as they proceed through the criminal courts. Section 11 is divided into 10 sections that focus upon the legal rights that come into effect after the suspect is charged, such as the presumption of innocence, court delays, and the right not to be denied reasonable bail. Section 12 protects individuals from any form of cruel and unusual punishment by restricting the state's power to punish people after they have been found guilty of a criminal offence, while s. 13 protects witnesses from self-incrimination and from having charges laid against them as the result of their statements. Section 14 guarantees the accused and any witnesses the right to an interpreter. Sections 15(1) and 15(2) guarantee the equal protection of all individuals within our system of justice as well as for equality before and under the law. Section 24(1) allows for a stay of proceedings so that a prosecutor cannot proceed with the case, while s. 24(2) permits a judge to exclude evidence if its admission would bring the administration of justice into disrepute. In addition to the legal rights guaranteed by the Charter noted above, s. 7 of the Charter has been applied by the Supreme Court of Canada to introduce and subsequently require certain procedural rights. While these rights are not specifically guaranteed by ss. 8 to 14 of the Charter, the Court has determined that the principles of fundamental justice are broader than the rights provided by the Charter. Four areas have been affected: the right to silence, disclosure, the right to make full answer and defence, and the detention of those persons found not guilty by reason of insanity.

Review Questions:

1. Should evidence be excluded from trial if a judge determines that it brings the administration of justice into disrepute?
2. Should the defence have to disclose all information it has collected in a criminal case to the prosecution and police?
3. Should the right to be silent mean that the police have to stop interrogating the suspect once that right is invoked?

How Are Criminal Offences Classified?

There are two major crime classification systems used in Canada. **Legal classifications** include summary conviction offences, indictable offences, and hybrid offences (see below); **general classifications** are employed by police and other criminal justice agencies to classify criminal offences, and include violent crimes and property crimes (see Chapter 4). Another way to classify criminal offences is much older than our criminal law and divides them on the basis of whether they are perceived as "evil." This approach overlaps summary, hybrid, and indictable offences. Some crimes are defined as inherently bad (***mala in se***) while other actions are crimes only because the law says it is (***mala prohibita***).

Summary Conviction, Hybrid, and Indictable Offences

There are two types of procedures by which an individual charged with a criminal offence may be prosecuted. There are three types of offences: (1) summary conviction only; (2) hybrid (or dual procedure) offences; and (3) indictable. **Summary conviction only offences** are prosecutable by summary conviction only. These offences are tried by a summary conviction court. These offences are generally punishable by a period of incarceration not exceeding six months and a maximum fine of $2,000, although for some offences (such as sexual assault level 1) the Supreme Court of Canada has increased the maximum punishment to 18 months. Summary conviction trials are always heard by a provincial court judge. In addition, charges for summary conviction offences must be laid within six months of the commission of the offence. If a period of imprisonment is part of the sentence, the offender serves the sentence in a provincial facility.

Hybrid offences allow prosecutors the discretion to decide whether they wish to proceed with a case as a summary conviction offence or an indictable offence. The prosecutor's decision is formally based on such factors as the previous record of the offender and any mitigating factors (e.g., the social status of the offender) or aggravating factors (e.g., crimes involving violence) associated with the crime. This decision has a significant impact on most of the procedures that apply to the accused. For example, the decision determines possible appeals, the maximum length of sentence, whether a fine is imposed in addition to imprisonment, and whether an offender can serve the sentence in the community.

There are three types of **indictable offences**. The less serious indictable offences (e.g., theft under $5,000) are also known as **absolute jurisdiction indictable offences.** The accused has to be tried by a provincial court judge. The most serious crimes (e.g., first and second degree murder) are referred to as **Supreme Court exclusive indictable offences.** These crimes must be tried by a federally appointed judge and a jury in a provincial superior court. The accused may sometimes request that the case be heard by judge alone, but this request has to be permitted by the provincial attorney general or the justice minister. For all other indictable offences, the accused can choose to have the trial by a provincially appointed judge without a jury, or by a federally appointed judge with or without a jury. These offences, which make up the majority of indictable offences in Canada, are known as **election indictable offences.** If convicted of an indictable offence, the accused may receive a variety of sentences. Some offences (e.g., homicide) bring life sentences; for others (e.g., sexual assault), the punishment depends on the degree of harm inflicted on the victim.

SUMMING UP AND LOOKING FORWARD

This section is concerned with the classification of criminal offences. One way to classify crimes is based on whether they are perceived as "evil." This approach defines some crimes as inherently evil (*mala in se* offences) and others only because the law says so (*mala prohibita* offences). The legal classification approach divides offences into three different types. Summary conviction only offences are tried by a summary conviction court. These offences are generally punishable by a period of incarceration not exceeding six months and a maximum fine of $2,000, although for some offences (such as sexual assault level 1) the Supreme Court of Canada has increased the maximum punishment to 18 months. Hybrid offences allow prosecutors the discretion to decide whether they wish to proceed with a case as a summary conviction offence or an indictable offence. There are three types of indictable offences. The less serious indictable offences (e.g., theft under $5,000) are also known as absolute jurisdiction indictable offences. The accused has to be tried by a provincial court judge. The most serious crimes (e.g., first and second degree murder) are referred to as Supreme Court exclusive indictable offences and are tried by a superior court judge. For all other indictable offences, the accused can choose to have the trial by a provincially appointed judge without a jury, or by a federally appointed judge with or without a jury. These offences, which make up the majority of indictable offences in Canada, are known as election indictable offences.

Review Questions:

1. Why would the Supreme Court increase the maximum punishment for some summary conviction offences to 18 months?
2. On what basis would a Crown prosecutor decide to elect to pursue charges against a defendant as indictable instead of a summary conviction offence?
3. In election indictable offences, when and why would a defendant select a trial by judge alone?

Criminal Law Reform

During the past few decades, the federal government has introduced and revised various substantive criminal laws and ruled on countless procedural issues in an attempt to deal with contemporary issues. As Davison (2005:18) has pointed out, the trend of these new laws has been toward increasing the crime control powers of the state. Rarely do these changes "involve decriminalizing prohibited conduct or enhancing and protecting the rights of those accused of crime." Instead, most of the recent changes reflect stricter laws and "a clear willingness on the part of government to listen to and accommodate the results or demands of law enforcement, victims' groups, and similar bodies and interests within society."

Criminal Law Reform in Canada: The Federal Conservative Approach

Since 2006, the federal Conservative party has actively pursued an agenda of revising various sections of the Criminal Code as well as introducing new criminal laws for the express purpose of "**tackling crime**" and "**making communities safer**." These changes are closely aligned to the crime control model as they include, for example, increasing the number of mandatory minimum penalty laws that remove judicial discretion from judges at the time of sentencing (see Chapter 10) and limiting the number of individuals who can be granted a conditional sentence (see Chapter 11). In addition, these pieces of legislation, in their attempt to control and solve the problem of crime, emphasize the placing of greater controls on individuals. The belief is that implementing legislation advocating greater use of punishment, especially incarceration, will lead to greater and more effective social control.

Initially, the Conservatives typically attempted to pass their proposed legislation as separate items. When their proposals were severely amended by Parliament or failed to pass, they resorted to combining a number of pieces of legislation into one bill, such as the Tackling Violent Crime Act in 2007 and the Safe Streets and Communities Act in 2012. The purpose of these pieces of legislation was to ensure that criminals "are held fully accountable for their actions and that the safety and security of law-abiding Canadians and victims comes first in Canada's justice system." According to federal justice minister Rob Nicholson, the federal government developed its "**tough on crime**" approach as "Canadians gave us a mandate to go after criminals in this country and that is exactly what we are going to do" (Howlett et al. 2011:A4). One of the ways in which the government has been so successful in terms of its crime agenda, according to one Conservative MP, is "by **standing up for victims**" (Brown 2011:F5).

It wasn't until early 2014 that the first challenges to the federal Conservatives' "tough on crime" approach were heard by the Supreme Court of Canada. In a period of 22 days, the Court delivered decisions on two cases that had a significant impact on the federal government's crime policy in Canada. The Court's response did not favour the government's legislation. The first case (*R. v. Whaling*) challenged the policy introduced by the Conservative government that eliminated access to early parole from non-violent, first time federal offenders, including those already sentenced. At the time of Mr. Whaling's conviction, individuals convicted of serious but non-violent crimes were eligible for accelerated parole review (see Chapter 11). Since 1997, non-violent, first time federal offenders have been allowed to apply for day parole at one-sixth of their sentence. All other offenders could not apply until six months prior to having served one-third of their sentence. In addition, non-violent, first time offenders do not have to apply for their release to the Canadian Parole Board.

Mr. Whaling was convicted of weapons trafficking and possession of firearms offences in September 2010, and received a sentence of four years and six months. After his conviction, Parliament repealed the accelerated parole revisions with the Abolition of Early Parole Act and with it the possibility of earlier release for everyone serving a sentence. This Act became effective on March 2011 and was retroactive, meaning that Mr. Whaling would not be able to apply for early release. It was argued that this new policy violated the right of Mr. Whaling, guaranteed by s. 11(h) of the Charter of Rights and Freedoms, not to be punished twice for the same offence. The trial court agreed, as did the B.C. Court of Appeal. This case was appealed to the Supreme Court of Canada, which unanimously upheld the previous decisions on March 20, 2014.

In the second case (*R. v. Summers*), the issue concerned whether or not the federal government could stop judges from routinely giving extra credit to offenders for the time they had served in custody before sentencing. For almost four decades, the Criminal Code has granted judges the power to give enhanced credit to individuals for time served in custody before sentencing. What emerged was a practice where judges typically gave double credit—two days' reduction in sentence for each day served. In February 2010, the Truth in Sentencing Act (see Chapter 10) was passed, effectively banning double credit. A policy of 1:1 was substituted—that is, each day in custody prior to sentencing should be worth no more than one day off in the sentence. However, the Truth in Sentencing Act also stipulates that judges could grant 1.5 days' credit for each day served under certain circumstances.

Mr. Summers was convicted of manslaughter and, prior to his sentencing, he requested to have 1.5 days' credit for each day he served while awaiting trial. The sentencing judge agreed, reducing his eight-year sentence by 15 months. The Crown subsequently appealed this ruling to the Ontario Court of Appeal. The Ontario Court of Appeal upheld the ruling of the trial court judge, holding that the time served by Mr. Summers was a circumstance that did in fact justify the decision to give him the enhanced credit of 1.5 days. The Supreme Court unanimously ruled on April 11, 2014 that judges have the discretion to grant 1.5 days for each day served.

The Safe Streets Act

Is it possible to regulate behaviour seen by some as disorderly, but by others as necessary to survive? In 1999, Ontario passed a law (the Safe Streets Act) that criminalized some behaviour viewed as disorderly. The source of concern about **disorderly conduct** and its relationship to crime emerged over 30 years ago with the publication of the **broken windows theory** in 1982 (see Chapter 6). This theory led both provinces as well as numerous cities to pass legislation attempting to control behaviour believed to contribute to disorder. The type of behaviour targeted by this legislation typically focuses upon "aggressive solicitation" and the "solicitation of a captive audience."

The Safe Streets Act attempts to control similar behaviour as well as any type of solicitation involving a "captive audience." This piece of legislation generated much controversy and led to court challenges based on questions about their constitutionality. The Safe Streets Act defines "aggressive" soliciting as soliciting in a manner likely to cause a "reasonable person" to be concerned about his or her personal safety. It also identifies numerous activities, all of which are automatically considered to involve aggressive soliciting, such as:

- threatening the person with physical harm.
- obstructing the path of the person who is being solicited.
- using abusive language during or after solicitation.

iStock/Thinkstock

Should the criminal law be used to socially control the homeless?

- continuing to solicit a person in a persistent manner after the person has said that they don't want to give any money.

The Act also identifies specific places where an individual cannot solicit a "captive audience." Examples include the following:

- near a pay telephone or in a public washroom facility
- near an automated teller machine
- on a public transit vehicle
- in a parking lot

The Safe Streets Act specifies that the first conviction is to be a fine not exceeding $500; subsequent convictions involve fines of up to $1,000 and a jail term of no more than six months.

Critics of the Safe Streets Act argue these laws discriminate against the poor and are essentially a continuation of laws that over the centuries have attempted to outlaw similar types of activities by applying various terms such as "vagrancy" and "homeless." In addition, they argue that these laws are vague, in that they do not define in any specific or detailed way exactly what types of activities are outlawed (Hermer and Mosher 2002). Others (e.g., Ruddick 2002) contend that this legislation lists so many prohibitions that it in effect controls the public places where homeless people can pursue their activities. Such laws, they point out, focus on those least able to defend themselves or pay fines (thereby raising the possibility of a jail sentence).

Supporters of this legislation argue that many citizens want these types of laws as they fear disorder and its effects. In addition, they believe that street crime increases as the result of disorder. In their view, to control activities in certain public places and times is not a blanket prohibition; it only controls certain undesirable actions in very specific locations.

Eighteen months after the Safe Streets Act was introduced in Ontario, more than 100 individuals who were panhandling or squeegeeing had been charged with an offence. In August 2001, 80 of the individuals charged decided to challenge the constitutionality of the Act. The facts surrounding the activities of 13 of these individuals were agreed upon by defence counsel and the Crown (the other 67 individuals had their charges withdrawn). In this challenge (*R. v. Banks et al.*), nine of the individuals were charged with "soliciting on the road-way," three were charged under the provincial Highway Traffic Act, and one was charged with soliciting "in a persistent manner." Defence lawyers challenged the act on the constitutional grounds that it denied freedom of expression, violated equality rights, and denied life, liberty, and security of the person. A provincial court judge ruled in August 2001 that the Safe Streets Act was constitutional. He agreed that while it limited people's freedom of expression, such infringement was justified in terms of public safety. In addition, he wrote that poverty "is itself not an analogous ground of discrimination under s. 15," that the defendants "failed to establish that the Act discriminates against the extremely poor," and that the Act "does not apply only to the poor." In 2007, the Ontario Court of Appeal unanimously agreed that concerns about public safety and the flow of traffic override violations of freedom of expression. Between 2000 and 2010, the number of tickets for violations of the Safe Streets Act issued by the police in Toronto increased over 2,000 percent; in 2010, 15,551 tickets were issued. In addition, between 2005 and 2010, 253 custody orders were issued by the courts in Ontario; in 2010, the average length of sentence for a custody order was almost 17 days (O'Grady et al. 2013).

SUMMING UP AND LOOKING FORWARD

Criminal law reform efforts in Canada have favoured increasing the crime control powers of the state. Rarely do these reforms involve decriminalizing prohibited conduct or granting better protections to those accused of crime. Instead, most of the recent changes reflect stricter laws that support the interests of certain groups, such as law enforcement agencies and victims' rights groups. The recent criminal law reforms passed by the federal Conservative government (typically called "tough on crime") are largely based upon the belief that there are increasing levels of crime (see Chapter 4 for the most recent crime statistics) and reoffending rates of serious, violent offenders, as well as a decline in the "moral framework" of society.

Provinces have also passed legislation in an attempt to control disorderly behaviour. In 1999, Ontario passed the Safe Streets Act in an attempt to control "aggressive solicitation" and the "solicitation of a captive audience." The Safe Streets Act defines "aggressive" soliciting as soliciting in a manner likely to cause a "reasonable person" to be concerned about his or her personal safety. This piece of legislation generated much controversy and led to court challenges based on questions about its constitutionality.

What is the best way to achieve justice in our criminal justice system? There is no agreed upon single approach; rather, a number of different approaches, both traditional and contemporary, provide different avenues in an attempt to achieve justice. These are the focus of the next chapter.

Review Questions:

1. Why do you think the trend in Canada during recent years is to introduce laws that promote the interests of certain groups, for example law enforcement and victims' rights groups, as opposed to other groups, for example, those convicted of criminal offences?
2. How did the decisions made by Supreme Court of Canada in *R. v. Whaling* and *R. v. Summers* challenge the legislation passed by the federal government in these areas? Considering the information provided earlier in this chapter, on what basis do you think the Supreme Court made their decisions in both of these cases?
3. Why did the provincial government of Ontario criminalize the behaviours included in the Safe Streets Act? Was there an alternative approach they could have taken to better deal with the same actions?

Critical Issues in Canadian Criminal Justice

SHOULD HIV NONDISCLOSURE BE DECRIMINALIZED?

Since the law reflects, in part, public opinion and morality regarding various forms of behaviour, what was considered to be criminal many—or even a few—years ago may not be considered so today. When a government decides to remove a crime from the Criminal Code, it is referred to as **decriminalization**. The traditional response by Parliament to HIV nondisclosure has been to treat such instances as a criminal offence. Others argue that, given our increasing ability to treat HIV-infected individuals, it is better to approach this issue from outside the criminal law. Decriminalization means a social policy response (as opposed to a crime policy response) is considered the best practice to deal with an issue (Lee 2006).

In April 2009, a Toronto jury of nine men and three women found 52-year-old Johnson Aziga guilty of two counts of first degree murder, ten counts of aggravated assault, and one count of attempted aggravated assault. Mr. Aziga's crime was spreading the HIV/AIDS virus and he became the first Canadian to be found guilty of murder for spreading the virus that causes HIV/AIDS (Prokaska 2009:A10). One of the women he infected died of AIDS-related cancer three weeks after the police videotaped an interview with her on November 19, 2002 about her relationship with Mr. Aziga. Prosecutors alleged that Mr. Aziga "failed to inform his partners about his HIV-positive status, although he had been aware of it since 1996 and was under public-health orders to do so" (Perkel 2009:A11). In August 2011, Mr. Aziga was declared a dangerous offender (see Chapter 3).

In recent years, a number of other Canadian men have received harsh sentences for similar repetitive duplicity resulting in HIV-infected women (Kay 2009). In April 2008, Carlos Leone pleaded guilty to 15 counts of aggravated sexual assault after failing to inform his sexual partners of his HIV status. He was sentenced to 15 consecutive terms ranging from two to five years each (which totalled 49 years), but then adjusted the prison term downward to 18 years ("Leone Jailed . . ." 2008).

In 1998, the Supreme Court decided to hear its first HIV-related case when an individual failed to disclose his condition to his sexual partners (*R. v. Cuerrier*). In this case, the accused had been charged with two counts of aggravated assault on the basis that the nondisclosure of his HIV-positive status constituted fraud under s. 265(3) of the Criminal Code. Mr. Cuerrier had been informed by public health officials in 1992 that he had tested positive for HIV and told to use a condom whenever he engaged in sexual intercourse and to inform any potential partners that he was HIV-positive. However, Mr. Cuerrier refused the advice and had unprotected sexual intercourse. Two complainants testified in court that they wouldn't have engaged in unprotected sex with Mr. Cuerrier if they had realized that he was HIV-positive. Mr. Cuerrier was acquitted by both the trial judge and the British Columbia Court of Appeal. The Supreme Court unanimously held that any individual who conceals or fails to disclose that they are HIV-positive has committed a type of fraud that vitiates any apparent consent on the part of the victim to engage in sexual activity. According to the Supreme Court, persons who know that they are HIV-positive and fail to inform their sexual partners may be found to fulfill the traditional requirements for fraud, namely dishonesty and deprivation. Section 265(3) states that an alleged consent obtained by fraud or by the use of authority is not real consent. The Supreme Court sent the case back to British Columbia on the charge of aggravated sexual assault, but the Crown decided not to retry the case.

Since *Cuerrier*, the Supreme Court of Canada has considered the willful transmission of HIV in two other cases (*R. v. Thornton* [1993]; *R. v. Williams* [2003]). In both of these cases, the Supreme Court upheld the convictions. In *R. v. Mercer* (1993), it denied leave to appeal in which the Newfoundland Court of Appeal had raised a sentence from 30 months to 11 years. According to Grant (2008:14), the decisions made by the Supreme

Continued on next page

Critical Issues in Canadian Criminal Justice *(Continued)*

Court indicate "we have a clear indication from the Court, without a single dissenting voice, that criminal law is an appropriate tool to use in the most serious cases involving an accused who knows he is HIV-positive but fails to inform that status to sexual partners. The majority of the Supreme Court has given short shrift to the various arguments against criminalization. . . ."

A number of arguments have been made in favour of removing HIV nondisclosure from the Criminal Code. Those who support the idea of decriminalization point out that recent research indicates "the possibility of transmitting HIV is dramatically reduced when treatments are used," the need to update the criminal justice system in order "to reflect the idea that HIV is no longer the immediate death sentence it was when the legal obligation to disclose HIV was set," as well as what the implications of criminalization "will be on public health strategies for HIV prevention" (Mykhalovskiy 2009:A12). Grant (2008) adds that issues such as the stigmatization of the offender need to be considered, as well as the difficulties in prosecuting these cases. The HIV/AIDS Legal Network argues that an absolutist approach to disclosure trivializes "the criminal process through a proliferation of prosecutions where the risk of harm is negligible . . . and cases where an HIV-positive person has taken steps to prevent transmission" (Makin 2012:A5). Advances in HIV medication and condoms have reduced the probability of transmission. In 2005, a judge in British Columbia instructed a jury that the accused had no duty to disclose his HIV-positive status if he used a condom at all times. Those who support the criminalization of HIV-nondisclosure argue that there is a need to isolate the accused, to deter others, as well as retribution (Grant 2008).

In 2012, the Supreme Court of Canada (in *R. v. Mabior* and *R. v. D.C.*) considered the medical advancements in the treatment of HIV when the accused did not reveal to their partners that they were HIV-positive. In their decisions, the Supreme Court refined the ruling (in *R. v. Cuerrier*) that had guided the courts for 14 years. In both of these cases, the Supreme Court held that failure to disclose an HIV-positive status constitutes fraud vitiating consent only when there is a "realistic possibility" of HIV transmission. The justices noted that with future medical scientific advancements in the area, failure to disclose HIV-positive status may no longer constitute "fraud vitiating consent." In other words, the decisions made in these two cases would not remain the precedent in the future.

Questions

1. Do you agree that individuals who know they are HIV-positive but fail to inform their sexual partners after they have been told to by the authorities should be dealt with in the criminal courts?
2. The Crown prosecutor wanted to apply the dangerous offender label to Mr. Leone. Do you believe that people with HIV and who fail to disclose that fact to their partners despite being warned to do so by the authorities should be given a dangerous offender status?
3. As medical treatment for those with HIV advances, do you think the criminalization of those who engage in sex without disclosure will end?
4. Do you believe that by implementing the nondisclosure law that individuals with HIV who practise safety in their relations with others will be stigmatized?

SUMMARY

What Are the Major Categories of the Criminal Law?

Substantive and Procedural Criminal Law (p. 37)
Sexual Assault Legislation (p. 37)

In order to better understand the legal basis of our criminal justice system we can divide the criminal law into three different categories, two of which are discussed in this section: the substantive criminal law and the procedural criminal law. Changes in the way in which defendants are treated in Canada's sexual assault legislation are used to highlight both types of criminal law categories.

KEY WORDS: substantive criminal law, procedural criminal law, legal guilt, factual guilt, sexual assault

Criminal Liability and the Legal Elements of a Crime

This section discusses criminal liability, the third category of criminal law to be examined. The general definition of a crime is briefly discussed, while the elements of the legal definition of a crime are discussed at length.

KEY WORDS: criminal liability, general definition of a crime, legal definition of a crime, *corpus delecti*, *mens rea*, specific intent, general intent, motive, culpability, knowledge, recklessness, *actus reus*, concurrence, victimless crimes, causation

Legal Defences and the Law

Although the prosecution can prove all of the elements of the legal definition of a crime beyond a reasonable doubt, defendants can avoid being convicted for a crime if they can prove one of the different kinds of legal defences.

KEY WORDS: excuse defences, age, mental disorder, automatism, mistake of fact, mistake of law, justification defences, duress, necessity, self-defence, battered woman syndrome, provocation, entrapment

What Are the Sources of the Criminal Law in Canada?

Attempts to create criminal law extend back many centuries. A key figure in the creation of our criminal law system was King Henry II, who felt a unified substantive law was necessary to establish a strong central government.

KEY WORDS: common law, *stare decisis*, the Constitution, statutes, case law, administrative regulations (regulatory offences)

The Canadian Charter of Rights and Freedoms

The Charter of Rights and Freedoms includes sections that safeguard individuals who experience governmental actions under the law. These sections of the Charter can be divided into two main categories: the investigation of crime and the criminal trial and punishment.

KEY WORDS: legal rights, crime control model, habeas corpus, the right to silence, the right of disclosure, the right to make full answer and defence, the detention of those found not guilty by reason of insanity

How Are Criminal Offences Classified?

Criminal offences can be organized into various categories. In this section two categories are used: whether they are "evil," and the type and duration of punishment (the latter being the approach taken in our criminal law).

KEY WORDS: legal classifications, general classifications, *mala in se*, *mala prohibita*, summary conviction only offences, hybrid offences, indictable offences, absolute jurisdiction indictable offences, Supreme Court exclusive indictable offences, election indictable offences

Criminal Law Reform

Criminal Law Reform in Canada: The Federal Conservative Approach (p. 64)
The Safe Streets Act (p. 65)

Over the past few decades the trend of criminal law reform has been to make our system "tougher." This section highlights the reforms introduced by the federal Conservative government, especially since it formed a majority government, and how the criminal law has been used to deal with disorderly conduct.

KEY WORDS: tackling crime, making communities safer, tough on crime, standing up for victims, disorderly conduct, broken windows theory

Critical Thinking Questions

1. Both our substantive and procedural criminal laws are designed to ensure that everyone is guaranteed certain legal protections. Do you think that complainants in sexual assault cases are afforded these legal protections?
2. A key element on the *corpus delecti* of the law is "harm." Do you think all harmful behaviour is considered to be criminal? Why might harmful behaviour not be considered criminal?
3. The Charter of Rights and Freedoms gives individuals certain legal rights to protect themselves from government intervention. Do you think these protections are adequate when considering the powers of state agents found in Sections 8 through 10 of the Charter?
4. One of the key section of s. 7 of the Charter of Rights and Freedoms is the right to silence. Why do you think that right was not included when the Charter was introduced?
5. Most of our criminal law reforms in recent years have made the laws governing specific parts of our criminal justice system "tougher." Do you think that this is the appropriate approach to take when reforming our criminal laws?

Weblinks

Many people think that our laws governing sexual assault are problematic and don't reflect the true nature of this serious crime. To gain a greater understanding of some of the issues related to our sexual assault laws, go to YouTube and watch the following video: "Mini Law School—Understanding Sexual Assault Law." (1:23).

Court Cases

Bedford v. Canada (2010), ONSC 4264.

Bedford v. Canada (Attorney General) (2012), ONCA 186.

Canada (Attorney General) v. Bedford (2013), 3 S.C.R. 1101.

Canada (A.G.) v. PHS Community Services Society (Insite) (2011), S.C.C. 44.

Canada (Attorney General) v. Whaling (2014), S.C.C. 20.

Charkaoui v. Canada (2007), SCC 9, 1 S.C.R. 350.

Gayme v. R. (1991), 6 C.C.C. (3d) 321 (S.C.C.).

Hunter v. Southam Inc. (1984), 2 S.C.R. 145, 11 D.L.R. (4th) 641.

Hutt v. R. (1978), 38 C.C.C. (2d) 418 (S.C.C.).

Reference Re Sections 193 and 195.1(1)(c) of the Criminal Code 1990, 1 S.C.R. 1123.

R. v. Askov (1990), 59 C.C.C. (3d) 449, 59 C.C.C. (3d) 449.
R. v. Banks et al. (2005), O.J. 98.
R. v. Bleta (1964), S.C.R. 561.
R. v. Borden (1994), 3 S.C.R. 145.
R. v. Broyles (1991), 3 S.C.R. 595, 68 C.C.C. (3e) 308.
R. v. Brydges (1990), 1 S.C.R. 190, 53 C.C.C. (3d) 330.
R. v. Carosella (1997), 112 C.C.C. (3d) 289 (S.C.C.).
R. v. Chen et al. (2010), ONCJ 641.
R. v. Cuerrier (1998), 2 S.C.R. 371.
R. v. Darrach (2000), 2 S.C.R. 443.
R. v. D.C. (2012), S.C.J. No. 48.
R. v. Duarte (1990), 1 S.C.R. 30.
R. v. Duguay (1985), 46 C.C.C. (3) 1 (S.C.C.).
R. v. Ewanchuk (1999), 131 C.C.C. (3d) 481.
R. v. Forster (1997), 70 C.C.C. (3d).
R. v. Gayme (1991), 2 S.C.R. 577, 7 C.R. (4th) 117.
R. v. Godin (2009), 2 S.C.R. 3.
R. v. Goltz (1991), 3 S.C.R. 485, 67 C.C.C. (3d) 481.
R. v. Grant (2009), 66 C.R. (6th) 1 (S.C.C.).
R. v. Graveline (2006), S.C.C. 16.
R. v. Hebert (1990), 2 S.C.R. 151, 57 C.C.C. (3d) 1.
R. v. Hibbert (1995), 2 S.C.R. 973.
R. v. Hufsky (1988), 40 C.C.C. (3d) 398 (S.C.C.).
R. v. Kalanj (1989), 1 S.C.R. 1594, 48 C.C.C. (3d) 459.
R. v. King (1962), 133 C.C.C. 1.
R. v. Lavallee (1990), 55 C.C.C. (3d).
R. v. Lawrence and Belnavis (1998), 10 C.R. (5th) 65 (S.C.C.).
R. v. Luxton (1990), 2 S.C.R. 711, 58 C.C.C. (3d) 449.
R. v. Mabior (2012), 2 S.C.R. 584.
R. v. Mack (1988), 44 C.C.C. (3d).
R. v. Mann (2004), 3 S.C.R. 59.
R. v. Manninen (1987), 34 C.C.C. (3d) 385.
R. v. Mannion (1986), 2 S.C.R. 272, 28 C.C.C. (3d) 353.
R. v. Mercer (1993), 84 C.C.C. (3d) 41.
R. v. Mills (1986), 1 S.C.R. 863, 29 D.L.R. (4th) 161.
R.v. Mills (1997), 1 S.C.R. 771.
R. v. Mills (1999), 3 S.C.R. 668.
R. v. Morin (1992) 12 C.C.R. (5th).
R. v. Oakes (1986), 24 C.C.C. (3d) 321.
R. v. O'Connor (1995), 123 C.C.C. (3d) 487 (B.C.C.A.).
R. v. Parks (1992), 75 C.C.C. (3d) 287.
R. v. Perka (1984), 2 S.C.R. 232.
R. v. Quesnelle (2014), S.C.C. 46.

R. v. Rabey (1977), 37 C.C.C. (2d) 463.
R. v. Rodriguez (1993), 24 C.R. (4th) 281 (S.C.C.).
R. v. Ruzic (2001), 1 S.C.R. 687.
R. v. Ryan (2011), NCSA 30.
R. v. Simpson (1993), 79 C.C.C. (3d) 482 (Ont. C.A.).
R. v. Seaboyer (1991), 66 C.C.C. (3d) 321 (S.C.C.).
R. v. Singh (2007), S.C.C. 48.
R. v. Stinchcombe (1991), 3 S.C.R. 326, 68 C.C.C. (3d) 1.
R. v. Summers (2014), S.C.C . No. 26.
R. v. Swain (1991), 1 S.C.R. 933.
R. v. Taylor (2014), SCC 50.
R. v. Tesling (2004), 23 C.R. (6th) 207 (S.C.C.).
R. v. Therens (1985), 18 C.C.C. (3d) 481.
R. v. Thornton (1993), 2 S.C.R. 445.
R. v. Tran (1994), 2 S.C.R. 951, 117 D.L.R. (4th) 7.
R. v. Tran (2010), 3 S.C.R. 350.
R. v. Turcotte (2005), 2 S.C.R. 519.
R. v. Whaling (2014), S.C.C. 20.
R. v. Williams (2003), 2 S.C.R. 134.
Seaboyer v. R. (1991), 6 C.C.C. (3d) 321 (S.C.C.).
Smith v. R. (1987), 34 C.C.C. (3d) 97 (S.C.C.).

Suggested Readings

Barnhorst, R. and S. Barnhorst. 2004. *Criminal Law and the Canadian Criminal Code*. 4th ed. Toronto: McGraw-Hill Ryerson.

Mewett, A. and S. Nakatsuru. 2000. *An Introduction to the Criminal Process in Canada*. 4th ed. Scarborough, ON: Carswell.

Roach, K. 2012. *Criminal Law*. 5th ed. Toronto: Irwin Law.

Sheehy, E., ed. 2014. *Defending Battered Women on Trial*. Vancouver: UBC Press.

Van der Meulen, E., E. Durisin, and V. Love, eds. 2013. *Selling Sex: Experience, Advocacy, and Research on Sex Work in Canada*. Vancouver: UBC Press.

References

Anderssen, E. 2000. “Supreme Court Upholds Rape-Shield Law,” *The Globe and Mail*, October 13, p. A7.

Ashworth, A. and L. Zedner. 2008. “Defending the Criminal Law: Reflections on the Changing Character of Crime, Procedure, and Sanctions.” *Crime, Law and Philosophy* 2:21–51 .

Bala, N. 1997. *Young Offenders and the Law*. Concord, ON: Irwin Law.

Barnhorst, R. and S. Barnhorst. 2004. *Criminal Law and the Canadian Criminal Code*. 4th ed. Toronto: McGraw-Hill Ryerson.

Bowland, A.L. 1994. “Sexual Assault Trials and Protection of ‘Bad Girls’: The Battle Between the Courts and Parliament.” Pp. 241–67 in *Confronting Sexual*

Assault: A Decade of Legal and Social Change, edited by J.V. Roberts and R.M. Mohr. Toronto: University of Toronto Press.

Brannigan, A. 1984. *Crimes, Courts, and Corrections: An Introduction to Crime and Social Control in Canada*. Toronto: Holt, Rinehart, and Winston.

Brown, I. 2011. "Unlocking the Crime Conundrum," *The Globe and Mail*, April 9, pp. F1, F5.

Brown, S., F.A. Esbensen, and G. Geis. 1991. *Criminology: Explaining Crime and Its Content*. Cincinnati, OH.: Anderson.

Busby, K. 1997. "Discriminating Uses of Personal Records in Sexual Violence Cases: Notes for Sexual Assault Counsellors on the Supreme Court Decision in *R. v. O'Connor* and *L.L.A. v. A.B.*" *Canadian Journal of Women and the Law* 9:148–177.

Davison, C. 2011. "Multiculturalism and Criminal Law." *LawNow* 36:16–18.

Davison, C. 2005. "Developments in Criminal Law." *LawNow* 29:18–20.

Editorial. 2014. "The Changed Nature of the Harm Debate." *Criminal Law Quarterly* 60:321–323.

Fine, S. 2014. "Judges Side with Sex-Assault Victims," *The Globe and Mail*, July 10, p. A4.

Geis, G. 1974. *Not the Law's Business*. New York: Schocken.

Gotell, L. 2008. "Tracking Decisions on Access to Sexual Assault Complainants' Confidential Records: The Continued Permeability of Subsections 278.1–278.9 of the Criminal Code." *Canadian Journal of Women and the Law* 20:111–54.

Gotell, L. 2002. "The Ideal Victim, the Hysterical Complainant, and the Disclosure of Confidential Records: The Implications of the Charter for Sexual Assault Law." *Osgoode Hall Law Journal* 3&4:251–95.

Grant, I. 2008. "The Boundaries of the Criminal Law: The Criminalization of the Non-disclosure of HIV. *Dalhousie Law Journal* 31, Spring. www.lexisnexis.com. Retrieved April 5, 2009.

Greene, I. 2014. *The Charter of Rights and Freedoms: 30+ Years of Decisions That Shape Canadian Life*. Toronto: Lorimer.

Hall, J. 1947. *Theft, Law and Society*. 2nd ed. Indianapolis: Bobbs-Merrill.

Hermer, J. and J. Mosher. 2002. *Disorderly People: Law and the Politics of Exclusion in Ontario*. Halifax: Fernwood.

Hiebert, J. 2002. *Charter Conflicts: What Is Parliament's Role?* Montreal: McGill-Queen's University Press.

Hodgson, J. and D. Kelley. 2001. *Sexual Violence: Policies, Practices, and Challenges in the United States and Canada*. Westport, CT: Praeger.

Horner, J. 2007. *Canadian Law and the Canadian Legal System*. Toronto: Pearson.

House of Common Debates. 1986. 26 May. Hansard VI: 62.

Howlett, K., R. Seguin, and D. LeBlanc. 2011. "East-West Rift Opens over Crime Bill." *The Globe and Mail*, November 3, p. A4.

Johnson, H. 2012. "Limits of a Criminal Justice Response: Trends in Police and Court Processing of Sexual Assault." Pp. 616–634 in *Sexual Assault in Canada: Law, Legal Practice and Women's Activism*, edited by E. Sheehy. Ottawa: University of Ottawa Press.

Kay, B. 2009. "A Fraudster, Not a Murderer," *National Post*, April 8. www.nationalpost.com. Retrieved May 1, 2009.

Kong, R., H. Johnson, S. Beattie, and A. Cardillo. 2003. *Sexual Offences in Canada*. Ottawa: Canadian Centre for Justice Statistics.

Lacey, N. 2007. "Legal Constructions of Crime." Pp. 179–200 in *The Oxford Handbook of Criminology* (4th ed.), edited by M. Maguire, R. Morgan, and R. Reiner. Oxford: Oxford University Press.

Law Reform Commission of Canada. 1974. *Discovery in Criminal Cases*. Ottawa: Justice Canada.

Lee, M. 2006. "Decriminalization." Pp. 114–115 in *The Sage Dictionary of Criminology* (2nd ed.), edited by E. McLaughlin and J. Muncie. London: Sage.

"Leone Jailed 18 Years for HIV Sex Crimes." 2008. *National Post*, April 4. www.nationalpost.com. Retrieved May 1, 2009.

Los, M. 1994. "The Struggle to Redefine Rape in the Early 1980s." Pp. 20–56 in *Confronting Sexual Assault: A Decade of Legal and Social Change*, edited by J.V. Roberts and R.M. Mohr. Toronto: University of Toronto Press.

Majury, D. 1994. "Seaboyer and Gayme: A Study Inequality." Pp. 268–92 in *Confronting Sexual Assault: A Decade of Legal and Social Change*, edited by J.V. Roberts and R.M. Mohr. Toronto: University of Toronto Press.

Makin, K. 2013. "Sexual Assault Rape," *The Globe and Mail*, October 5, 2013, pp. F1, F6–F7.

Makin, K. 2012. "HIV-Disclosure Obligations under Scrutiny in Separate Cases," *The Globe and Mail*, February 6, p. A5.

Makin, K. 2007. "Top Court Ruling Criticized as Attack on Right to Silence," *The Globe and Mail*, November 2, p. A6.

Makin, K. 1999. "Top Court Bows to Will of Parliament," *The Globe and Mail*, November 26, pp. A1, A7.

McKay-Panos, L. 1998–99. "Indefinite Sentence/No Criminal Conviction." *LawNow* 23:24–31.

Mohr, R. and J. Roberts. 1994. "Sexual Assault in Canada: Recent Developments." Pp. 3–19 in *Confronting Sexual Assault: A Decade of Legal and Social Change*, edited by J.V. Roberts and R.M. Mohr. Toronto: University of Toronto Press.

Mykhalovskiy, E. 2009. "HIV Legal Policy Needs Debate," *The Globe and Mail*, April 9, p. A12.

O'Grady, B., S. Gaetz, and K. Buccieri. 2013. "Tickets . . . and More Tickets: A Case Study of the Enforcement of the Ontario Safe Streets Act." *Canadian Public Policy* XXXIX:541–558.

Perkel, D. 2009. "AIDS-Trial Jury Asks to Review Deathbed Interview," *The Globe and Mail*, April 3, p. A11.

Perreault, S. and S. Brennan. 2010. *Criminal Victimization in Canada, 2009*. Ottawa: Canadian Centre for Justice Statistics.

Prokaska, L. 2009. "HIV Murder Conviction the Right Thing to Do," *Winnipeg Free Press*, April 9, p. A10.

Renner, K., C. Alksnis, and L. Park. 1997. "The Standard of Social Justice as a Research Process." *Canadian Journal of Psychology* 38:91–102.

Roach, K. 2012. *Criminal Law*. 5th ed. Toronto: Irwin Law.

Roach, K. 2009. *Criminal Law*. 4th ed. Toronto: Irwin Law.

Roach, K. 2004. *Criminal Law*. 3rd ed. Concord, ON: Irwin Law.

Roberts, J. and R. Mohr, eds. 1994. *Confronting Sexual Assault: A Decade of Legal and Social Change*. Toronto: University of Toronto Press.

Ruddick, S. 2002. "Metamorphosis Revisited: Restricting Discourses of Citizenship." Pp. 55–64 in J. Hermer and J. Mosher, eds., *Disorderly People: Law and the Politics of Exclusion in Ontario*. Halifax: Fernwood.

Savoie, J. 2003. *Homicide in Canada*. Ottawa: Canadian Centre for Justice Statistics.

Senna, J. and L. Siegel. 1995. *Essentials of Criminal Justice*. Minneapolis, MN: West.

Sharpe, R. and K. Roach. 2005. *The Charter of Rights and Freedoms*. 3rd ed. Toronto: Irwin Law.

Sneiderman, B. 2000. "Latimer in the Supreme Court: Necessity, Compassionate Harm and Mandatory Sentencing." *Saskatchewan Law Review* 64:511–44.

Stuart, D. 2010. *Charter Justice in Canadian Criminal Law*. 5th ed. Toronto: Carswell.

Tappan, P. 1946. "Who Is the Criminal?" *American Sociological Review* 12:96–102.

Territo, L., J. Halsted, and M. Bromley. 1995. *Crime and Justice in America*. 4th ed. Minneapolis, MN: West.

Tibbetts, J. 2006. "Top Court Clears Wife Who Killed in a Trance," *National Post*, April 28, p. A6.

Verdun-Jones, S. 1989. *Criminal Law in Canada: Cases, Questions, and the Code*. Toronto: Harcourt Brace Jovanovich.

CHAPTER

3

Control Philosophy and Criminal Justice Policy

Learning Objectives

After completing this chapter, you should be able to:

- Understand the differences and similarities among the four different punitive models of criminal justice in terms of criminal sanctions and the operations of the major components of the criminal justice system.
- Differentiate between the two different non-punitive models in terms of criminal sanctions and the operations of the major components of the criminal justice system.
- Identify the differences between the punitive and non-punitive approaches to crime control in society.
- Recognize the basic elements of an Aboriginal justice system and how they differ from those in all other approaches.
- Recognize how each of these models approaches the general category of "sex offenders."

As we have noted so far, society imposes laws governing acceptable behaviour, particularly through the criminal law. When certain behaviours are criminalized, a number of social institutions—the police, the courts, and corrections—become involved. Before we start to examine in some detail how each of these institutions operate, it is important to examine the role each of these institutions has in delivering and achieving justice. When examining these roles, it is important to understand the major philosophies that provide differing justifications about how a criminal justice system should actually operate. While each of these philosophies overlap in some regards (e.g., all recognize the principles of fundamental justice), they all vary in important ways. For example, one model emphasizes that all sentences for convicted offenders (except those convicted of first degree murder) should be short (the justice model), while others highlight the importance of using informal sanctions (restorative justice).

Since the 1960s, our criminal justice system has experienced a number of changes in terms of what philosophy is dominant at any given time. For much of the 20th century, the rehabilitation philosophy dominated our criminal justice system. Starting in the 1970s the justice model challenged this tradition, criticizing the lack of legal rights afforded to offenders as well as the lack of alternatives to incarceration. This was quickly followed by the re-emergence and widespread acceptance of the deterrence philosophy. At the beginning of the 1980s, criminal justice administrators began to focus on individuals they saw as chronic criminals, who not only commit the bulk of criminal offences but also the majority of serious, violent crimes. The result was the introduction and growth of the selective incapacitation philosophy to deal with chronic offenders.

In time, this emphasis by the deterrence and selective incapacitation philosophies (referred to as the **new punitiveness**) on punishment was criticized. Two alternative philosophies gained popularity, both of which support the belief that harsher punishments have little or no effect or actually increase criminal activity when offenders are released. For these the important consideration is not the *quantity* (i.e., length) of punishment but rather the *quality* of the punishment. Each of these offers a different perspective to a number of central questions about our criminal justice system, including the best way to control, reduce, and prevent crime as well as the most appropriate way to punish offenders. This chapter summarizes how each of these major crime control philosophies would operate in Canada today if it operated as a "stand-alone" system. The discussion of each of these crime control philosophies also features an example: how does each deal with sexual offenders?

What Is the Extent and Response to Sexual Offending in Canada?

Concerns about how our criminal justice system should respond to sexual offenders and sexual offending have become a major issue in Canada in the past decade or so. Sexual offences do not account for a large number of the crimes reported to the police annually—25,543 incidents involving sexual offences were reported to the police in Canada during 2013, accounting for just over 1 percent of total Criminal Code incidents. Due to the high-profile nature of some of the cases reported by the media, **moral panic** occurs as members of the public perceive our criminal justice system to be inefficient in controlling these offenders. As a result, a significant amount of pressure is placed upon politicians to pass laws that will criminalize the behaviours in question and introduce harsh sanctions to control them. Consequently, new laws, policies, and programs have been introduced (some of which are discussed later in this chapter) in the past few decades in order to allow the authorities more control over sexual offenders.

Sexual offences involve violent behaviour—in 2013 sexual offences accounted for slightly more than 6 percent of all incidents reported to the police in the category "Violent Crime." The majority of these offences were sexual assaults. Sexual assault (level 1) was the most frequently reported of these offences, accounting for 85 percent of all reported sexual offences; the category "sexual violations against children" accounted for 17 percent, while sexual assault (levels 2 and 3) accounted for the remaining 2 percent (Boyce et al. 2014). Most sexual offences reported to the police are against children and youths (see Figure 3.1).

A significant number of victims of sexual offences do not report their victimization to the police. In 2009, for example, it was reported that spousal violence was less likely to be reported to the police than in the past—in 2009, 22 percent of spousal violence victims said the police learned of the incident, down from 28 percent in 2004 (Brennan 2011). In addition, it may be difficult to gain a conviction. Daly and Bouhours (2010:602), in their analysis of convictions for sexual assaults in Canada since 1983, found that there has been "a significant decrease in rates of conviction from the early to later periods (from 26.5 percent to 14 percent)."

Sexual offenders are often charged with committing more criminal offences than are other types of offenders. For example, Kong et al. (2003) report that during 2001–02, adult sexual offenders—in particular those charged with offences in the category of "other sexual offences"—appeared in criminal court with a higher percentage of multiple charges per case, "indicating a higher tendency toward repeat offending prior to being reported to the police." They also found that in those same years 33 percent of all individuals appearing in adult criminal courts across Canada charged with a sexual offence as the most serious charge faced three or more charges—a figure higher than for those individuals convicted for either violent or property offences. Sexual offences are less likely to be cleared by the police than other types of offences. Brennan and Taylor-Butts (2008) studied 11 sexual offences included in the 2004 General Social Survey as well as in both the 2007 aggregate and incident-based Uniform Crime Reporting Surveys

FIGURE 3.1 Victims of Police-Reported Sexual Offences, by Age, Canada, 2012

Source: Adam Cotter and Pascale Beaupre, "Police-reported sexual offences against children and youth in Canada, 2012." *Juristat* (May 2014), Statistics Canada Catalogue no. 85-002-X, p. 10, http://www.statscan.gc.ca/pub/85-002-x/2014001/article/14008-eng.htm. Reproduced and distributed on an "as is" basis with the permission of Statistics Canada.

(see Chapter 4). They found that criminal charges were laid in just over 33 percent of all sexual offences reported to the police, compared to almost 50 percent of all other types of violent crime.

Once individuals charged with a sexual offence appear in court, a high percentage of cases result in a finding of guilt. In 2011–12, for example, 74 percent of all sexual offence cases against children and youths in Canada ended with a determination of guilt (Cotter and Beaupre 2014). The three highest guilty findings were for luring a child (83 percent), followed by the offence of sexual interference of a child under the age of 16 (78 percent) and child pornography under the age of 18 (77 percent). Those individuals found guilty of a sexual offence in the adult courts are more likely to receive a custodial sentence compared to those found guilty of another violent crime. In 2011–12, almost 81 percent of those found guilty of a sexual offence in the adult criminal courts were sentenced to custody (ibid.).

A major concern is the reoffending rate of sexual offenders. Kingston and Bradford (2013) report that 16.7 percent of the adult males convicted of a sexual offence against an adult (86 individuals) or a child (500 individuals) were later charged or convicted of another sexual offence against a victim of any age. In their overview of research studies which included information about the recidivism rates of sex offenders, Harris and Hanson (2004) found that the majority of individuals convicted of a sexual offence had not been recharged or re-convicted for a sexual offence. The average recidivism rate during a 15-year time span was 24 percent. The category of sex offenders with the highest rate of recidivism was the offenders who had committed offences against boys under the age of 18 (35 percent recidivism rate).

One of the biggest questions facing policymakers is how best to control criminal behaviour. In attempting to exert this control, policymakers must consider an array of choices. For example, should they try to rehabilitate offenders? Or should they try to develop prevention programs in an effort to stop criminal activities before they start? Sometimes it might be better to sentence offenders to very long periods of incarceration since this would protect society over the long term. Other times, however, depending on the type of offence and the background of the offender, it may be better to consider alternative approaches, such as restorative justice. Whichever approach is chosen, the legal rights of the offender must always be considered.

This chapter presents different ways of understanding how each of the crime control philosophies has the potential to influence the criminal justice system. First, the four major contemporary criminal justice policies—the justice model, deterrence, selective incapacitation, and rehabilitation—are presented in as pure a form as possible. This discussion is followed by a review of the two most recent models to emerge—restorative justice and Aboriginal justice. Each of these crime control philosophies is considered in the context of a single issue: What is the best way to deal with sexual offenders? Is it best to improve the conventional responses, such as the operation of the criminal justice system by improving existing prosecution services and trials to make it more accountable for victims? Or is it better to introduce innovative responses that integrate informal justice approaches in an attempt to better protect victims' justice needs?

Achieving Justice: Crime Control Philosophy and Criminal Justice Policy

Four main philosophies guide our criminal justice system: the justice model, deterrence, selective incapacitation, and rehabilitation. Because these philosophies are constantly being revised and updated, many people speak of "neo-deterrence" and "neo-rehabilitation" systems. While legislators and other policymakers use these models to guide their policies, none of the philosophies exclusively guides our criminal justice system. Usually, two or more are combined. This is referred to as a multi-approach (or **bifurcation**) to crime control—less severe policies are reserved for low-risk criminals while tougher and much longer measures are given to criminals identified as posing a significant threat to public safety. For example, when the Young Offenders Act was enacted in 1984, it was grounded almost exclusively in the strategies of the deterrence and justice philosophies—in fact, the rehabilitation of young offenders was rarely mentioned. In 2003, when the Youth Criminal Justice Act was introduced, replacing the Young Offenders Act, deterrence, rehabilitation, and the justice model were combined to form the Act's Declaration of Principles (s. 3[1]). In addition, s. 4 of the new Act added restorative justice principles to the Declaration of Principles. Combining models leads to confusion about which strategy is most important in a given situation; it also raises questions about what leads to the success or failure of any particular crime control. In practice, these control philosophies may be combined by criminal justice practitioners. When Daly (1994) studied the New Haven, Connecticut courts, she had to "read the sentencing transcripts many times before I could identify the category (or categories) in which a sentencing justification fell . . . What I found was that judges combine various punishment theories" (Daly 1994:182). These philosophies address different issues, although some share certain features. For example, only rehabilitation focuses on the criminal actor, so it emphasizes treating most convicted criminals. The other three philosophies focus on the criminal act, albeit in different ways. For example, the justice model focuses exclusively on the criminal act committed by the alleged perpetrator, with punishment based on the seriousness of the offence. The deterrence and selective incapacitation philosophies, like the justice model, focus on the act, but for the purpose of preventing future crimes. In contrast to the justice model, however, the issue of the current criminal offence is of secondary importance.

Though some overlap exists among these philosophies, they are better understood in terms of their differences. Price and Stitt (1986) developed a framework for comparing the philosophies and policies, showing how each strategy approaches crime control through criminal sanctions and showing the policy implications of each. The following description of the four philosophies follows the Price and Stitt outline.

The Justice Model

History

The justice model, though a recent creation, has had a strong impact on the criminal justice system. The first important document to offer support for the justice model appeared in *Struggle for Justice* (1971), written by the American Friends Service Committee. This committee concluded that the existing criminal justice system was discriminatory as it treated members of marginalized groups more harshly. They also noted the existing system was unable to deliver justice to offenders, particularly in the protection of due process rights of those charged and convicted of crimes. In its conclusion, the Committee recommended that the criminal justice system be guided by the ideals of justice, fairness, and the need to protect human rights and dignity. It also recommended the elimination of the discretionary powers held by prosecutors, the judiciary, and parole boards. One of its important findings was that a sentence needed to fit the offence, not the offender. All individuals convicted of a certain offence must receive the same sentence; however, repeat offenders ought to be given longer sentences than first-time offenders for the same crime.

Perhaps the most influential argument for a justice model–based criminal justice system came from the Committee for the Study of Incarceration. It published a book, *Doing Justice* (1975), which proposed the creation of sentencing guidelines based on the seriousness of the crime and the prior record of the offender. It also proposed shorter punishments for most crimes as well as the expansion of alternative sanctions. According to the Committee, the best way to achieve justice was to punish criminals for the crime committed. There was to be no attempt to either to reform or deter individuals. Punishments should fit the crime committed, not the criminals.

The first criminal justice systems based on the justice model emerged in the United States during the 1970s and early 1980s. While these systems varied in the particulars, they shared a number of features—namely, the elimination or control of prosecutorial discretion, the abolition of individualized sentencing practices, limited treatment programs for prisoners, and the termination of early-release programs such as parole (Griset 1991). The justice model was also explored by other nations. During the late 1980s in Canada, the Canadian Sentencing Commission (1987) proposed a similar approach, but it was never introduced into public policy.

The Criminal Sanction

According to the justice model, the essential factor "is to punish offenders—fairly and with justice—through lengths of confinement proportionate to the gravity of their crimes" (Logan 1993). The punishment must be proportionate to the crime—specifically, the most serious crimes deserve the most severe punishments, in accordance with the doctrine of **proportionality**. In addition, the rights of the accused must be guaranteed through due process protections, from arrest to incarceration (Hudson 1987).

The justice model assumes that a direct relationship exists between the seriousness of the offence and the severity of the punishment. Ideally, any personal circumstances of those involved in the crime are ignored. The only information the justice model needs to know about an offender is that person's prior record. This "ensures the individual is not made to suffer disproportionately for the sake of social gain" and that "disproportionate leniency" as well as "disproportionate severity" are not allowed (Hudson 1987). An example of a violation of the principle of proportionality would be a mandatory five-year prison term for parking violators; here, the punishment would far outweigh the seriousness of the offence, since we can assume that parking violators could be dissuaded by other, lighter sanctions, such as towing or fines.

In Canada, the federal government determines the proportionality of sentences that link a criminal offence to its punishment. While it is easy to conclude that a violent criminal should receive a more severe punishment than an individual convicted of a lesser offence, such as an act of vandalism, the development of a comprehensive scale of proportional punishments is a difficult task, given the wide variety of crimes found in our Criminal Code. Should a person who sexually assaults a child receive a longer sentence than a person who robs a bank at gunpoint? If we are to create a workable system of punishment based on proportionality, much discussion will be required, since the seriousness of crimes and the unpleasantness of crimes are not objective facts.

One major contribution of the justice model to the area of punishment is that it supports the creation and proliferation of **alternative sanctions**, such as when a convicted person is allowed to serve part or all of the punishment in the community. The justice model prefers alternative sanctions for minor offences. Thus, any individual who is convicted of an offence in those categories designated as minor usually receives an alternative sentence allowing them to serve the sentence in the community. Community service orders and probation orders are favoured for many first- and second-time property offenders. This means that many offenders don't serve time in a prison facility, unless of course the number of their prior convictions grows beyond a certain point. Dangerous violent offenders, however, will always be incarcerated for the longest periods of time, even if they have no prior convictions.

One significant aspect of the justice model is that it guarantees due process rights for all individuals accused of committing a crime (see *Investigating: Have the Legal Rights of Sex Offenders Gone Too Far?*). Pretrial, trial, and posttrial procedural rights are guaranteed, so that every suspect receives protections to ensure that criminal justice officials do not overextend their powers. In addition, anyone under investigation or charged with an offence is presumed to be factually innocent before proven legally guilty. Thus, although someone may admit to police investigators that he or she committed the crime (i.e., **factual guilt**), that person's guilt nonetheless has to be established (i.e., **legal guilt**) in a court of law. Due process ensures that only the facts of the case are at issue, that evidence is collected according to the rules established by the courts, that formal hearings with impartial arbitrators are held, and that procedural regularity is maintained. Extralegal issues are considered to be inconsistent with fundamental justice.

Investigating: Have the Legal Rights of Sex Offenders Gone Too Far?

There will always be a debate between those who advocate for the accused's legal rights and those who argue that crime control should take precedence in judicial decisions. But can one side be taken too far? Many Canadians feel that the courts have gone too far in protecting the accused, much to the detriment of the law-abiding. In particular, some decisions made by the Supreme Court of Canada have been criticized for expanding the rights of the accused too far. This has led supporters of crime control to argue that Canada's top court is focusing too much on the principles of justice in its decisions while ignoring the reality of horrific crimes committed by sex offenders. Some of the most controversial decisions made by the Supreme Court in this area follow.

R. v. Borden

This case had a strong impact on the legal system because it created a law according to which bodily substances can be legally taken by the police for DNA analysis (see Chapter 6). Police in Nova Scotia were investigating two sexual assaults that occurred within a few months of each other. The police arrested a suspect for the second sexual assault, and they were certain that the same individual had committed the first, which involved a 69-year-old woman who had just returned from a prayer meeting. They requested a blood sample from the accused, but informed Borden that they only wanted it for the second investigation. The police didn't inform him that they really wanted to use the DNA analysis in connection with the sexual assault on the senior citizen. DNA linked this individual to both sexual offences. Borden was convicted and sentenced to six years' imprisonment, based on the results of the DNA test. The Appeal Division of the Supreme Court of Nova Scotia overturned Borden's conviction on the grounds that his legal rights had been violated under s. 8 of the Charter of Rights and Freedoms, which controls unlawful searches and seizures. The Crown appealed this verdict, but the Supreme Court of Canada agreed in a 7–0 ruling that the DNA evidence could not be admitted as evidence because the police did not tell Borden that the blood sample and the subsequent DNA analysis could be used against him. Although the suspect had voluntarily signed a consent form for the police, the Supreme Court ruled that the proper test was not consent but rather whether or not the suspect had enough information to give up the right to be secure from unreasonable seizure. It was up to the police to inform the suspect that they were going to use his consent for a DNA test for both offences, not just the second one.

R. v. Spencer

The police discovered that someone was using a sharing program on the Internet to share child pornography. Having the IP address of the network connection being

Continued on next page

Investigating: Have the Legal Rights of Sex Offenders Gone Too Far? *(Continued)*

used, the police were able to obtain the name of the individual (Mr. Spencer) through a request (no court order or warrant was used) sent to an Internet service provider (ISP). Following what was then standard policy, based on previous court decisions and the Personal Information Protection and Electronic Documents Act (PIPEDA), the police requested the name of the suspect as well as their ISP records, address, and phone number. Using this information, they obtained a search warrant and during a search of Mr. Spencer's residence, seized his computer and found evidence of child pornography. Mr. Spencer was charged and convicted of possession of child pornography (he was acquitted of a charge of making available child pornography).

Mr. Spencer appealed this decision to the Saskatchewan Court of Appeal, arguing that the disclosure of his name to the police by the ISP was an unreasonable search under s. 8 of the Charter. He argued that he had a reasonable expectation of privacy and that PIPEDA protected his personal information from being disclosed to the police. The Court of Appeal upheld the conviction, but set aside the acquittal and ordered a new trial based on this charge.

On appeal, the Supreme Court of Canada agreed with Mr. Spencer, ruling that the request by the police to the ISP did breach his reasonable expectation of privacy under s. 8 of the Charter.

R. v. James

James was a junior hockey coach who was charged and convicted in 1997 of sexually assaulting two of his players. After pleading guilty to over 350 counts of sexual assault he received a 42-month prison sentence. He served 20 months before being released on parole and later received a pardon and then left Canada to coach hockey. In 2011, Mr. James was again charged with sexually assaulting two players he coached almost 20 years ago. Once again, he pleaded guilty to the charges. His lawyer requested that the judge sentence him to a conditional sentence for 18 months, while the prosecutor sought six years' imprisonment. Toward the end of March 2012, the judge sentenced Mr. James to two years' imprisonment. When she handed down her sentence, the judge informed the court of the factors she took into account when deciding the sentence for Mr. James.

THE CANADIAN PRESS/John Wood

Graham James on his way to court to be sentenced for pleading guilty to sexually assaulting two hockey players.

First, Mr. James had been convicted in 1997 for sexually assaulting two other players around the same time he had also been sexually assaulting the two players involved in the current case. If Mr. James had been tried in 1997 for the four assaults, the judge calculated that Mr. James would have been sentenced to six years' imprisonment. Second, Mr. James had not reoffended since 1994. He had also received treatment, surrendered to the police, pleaded guilty to the charges, understood that what he had done was wrong, and apologized in court for the latest offences (Waldie 2012). The judge pointed out that her sentence would no doubt anger many citizens, but that sentencing is not supposed "to be about vengeance, anger, or revenge, . . ." but that "it is about public safety, and about separating individuals who have shown a repeated pattern of behaviour that is extremely dangerous to vulnerable victims" (Boesveld 2012:A1).

On appeal, the Manitoba Court of Appeal increased the sentence for Mr. James to five years. The justices said that the judge misapplied the totality principle s. 718.2(c), which is used in cases where multiple convictions could lead to a sentence that is considered excessive. According to the Court of Appeal, the judge gave Mr. James too much credit for his previous convictions (Pritchard 2013). In June 2015, two years were added onto Mr. James' sentence after he admitted to sexually assaulting another hockey player.

The Operations of a Justice Model–Based Criminal Justice System

One of the main goals of the justice model is to eliminate or control **discretion** within the criminal justice system, particularly as exercised by prosecutors, the judiciary, and parole boards. Supporters of the justice model argue that the main barrier to the attainment of justice is the discretion held by the key agencies in the criminal justice system. This concern about discretion led to another goal, specifically the protection of **legal rights** for all accused. The solution is to operate the justice system in a fair and equitable manner. The main recommendations concerning how the justice model is to operate are (1) to eliminate or control discretion; and (2) to enhance due process protections for all who enter the criminal justice system.

The role of the police is pivotal here, because their decisions affect all other groups involved in the later stages of the crime control process. The police will allocate most of their resources to investigating crimes classified as the most serious. Justice model considerations also will direct the way the police react to a crime, with minor offenders being recommended for diversion or other similar types of alternative sanction programs. Arrest and prosecution is more likely if the individual commits a serious crime and has an extensive criminal record.

Prosecutors would then have to prosecute the accused on the basis of all charges laid. This means that plea bargaining would be eliminated or strictly controlled by guidelines enacted by the legislative authorities. In reality, however, plea bargaining has proved to be difficult to ban. The State of Alaska banned all forms of plea bargaining in 1975, but the policy lasted only a few years, because, among other problems, the ban had no influence on the disposition of cases involving serious crimes. In addition, other criminal justice agencies (notably the police) increased their discretion prior to laying any charges (Rubenstein et al. 1980). The most popular policy has been to permit some plea bargaining but to control it by developing strict guidelines to govern its use as it allows prosecutors to bargain with the accused about their knowledge of other, more serious crimes or to gain evidence about other criminals who would otherwise not be charged.

Supporters of the justice model argue that the problem with traditional sentencing approaches is the great amount of discretion held by judges. This discretion has led to concerns about discrimination in sentencing, as some defendants receive more severe punishments apparently on the basis of their group characteristics—such as race or gender—instead of their crimes. To eliminate this problem, the justice model favours a **determinate sentencing** approach, in which all judges are required to follow sentencing guidelines. When deciding how much punishment a convicted offender receives, judges are to be influenced by the crime committed and the offender's prior record. Once the seriousness of the crime and prior record is established, the judge refers to the sentencing guidelines to determine the actual sentence. The research evaluating whether or not judges follow sentencing guidelines has found that they do (Kramer and Ulmer 1996).

The seriousness of the crime and the blameworthiness of the offender are the most significant criteria for determining the type of correctional facility or diversion program to which an offender is sent. Canadian correctional facilities are classified by security risk: maximum, medium, and minimum, with the most serious of all offenders being sent to a Special Handling Unit located in Quebec (see Chapter 13). Since most sentences in Canada only specify the maximum amount of time an individual is to serve before being released, the decision about the exact length of an inmate's period of incarceration is actually made by the parole board rather than a judge. The discretionary powers held by parole boards are of concern to justice model advocates, since those boards can decide to release inmates before they have served the full length of their sentence. The justice model's solution is either to eliminate the parole board altogether (by eliminating parole) or to remove it from the decision to release an inmate. In the latter case, the parole board would be responsible only for parole supervision. It is conceivable, however, that the elimination of parole could lead to prison overcrowding, since no prisoners would be released early. To prevent overcrowding, convicted criminals would serve all their sentences, but sentence lengths would be shortened. Finally, while treatment programs would be offered to inmates, such programs would be limited in scope and voluntary in nature.

Deterrence

History

Deterrence is the oldest of the four major criminal justice philosophies. Its roots are in 18th-century Europe, where two reformers, one Italian (Cesare Beccaria) and the other English (Jeremy Bentham), proposed significant reforms to the criminal justice system. Both argued that the goal of the criminal justice system should be to prevent future crimes by individuals who had already been caught (i.e., **specific or individual deterrence**) and by members of the broader society who might contemplate committing a crime (i.e., **general deterrence**). Specific deterrence is largely based on the idea that individual wrongdoers realize the pain of punishment outweighs the benefits or pleasures of offending, leading to a reduction in criminal activity. General deterrence is based on the idea of social control of the general population, with the intent that punishing a person will deter them from committing a similar offence.

Faced with a biased and barbaric system, Beccaria wrote *On Crimes and Punishment* (1764) in the hope of achieving equitable reforms that would eliminate favouritism. Note that Beccaria's recommendations became the source of modern criminal justice systems, including those in Canada and the United States. His book was the first widely read text to demand that due process rights be placed throughout the criminal justice system, that sentences reflect the harm done to the state and the victim, and that punishments be quick, certain, and contain a degree of deterrence. His key points (Beirne and Messerschmidt 1991:290) were as follows:

- The right of governments to punish offenders derives from a contractual obligation among the citizenry not to pursue self-interest at the expense of others.
- Punishment must be constituted by uniform and enlightened legislation.
- Imprisonment must replace torture and capital punishment as the standard form of punishment.
- The punishment must fit the crime. It must be prompt and certain, and its duration must reflect only the gravity of the offence and the social harm caused.

Bentham argued that legislators must calculate the amount of punishment required to prevent crimes and punish criminals. This system, which he referred to as a calculus, could include both positive sanctions (rewards) and negative sanctions (punishment). In addition, he argued that the criminal justice system should operate in a manner that allows it to catch suspects with certainty, process criminal cases in a speedy yet efficient manner, and punish those convicted of a crime with an appropriate (not excessive) amount of punishment. While Bentham and Beccaria shared a commitment to deterrence, a key difference between them involved the type of punishment they supported. For Beccaria, punishment should not be used to imprison a convicted offender but only as a temporary mechanism to ensure that the accused would appear at trial. Bentham supported the idea of imprisoning convicted offenders; his idea, along with others, led to a transformation in the type of punishment in Western societies at the end of the 18th and the beginning of the 19th centuries: from a system based on the **corporal punishment** of individuals to a system favouring placing convicted offenders into separate facilities (**carceral punishment**) (Cohen 1985).

An important basis of this approach was the reformers' strong belief that all people are rational—that is, possess **free will**. Criminals differ from law-abiding individuals only because they choose to engage in criminal as opposed to non-criminal activities. Over time, however, legislators have recognized a number of limitations to these arguments. Today most Western legal codes recognize limits to **criminal liability**, including such factors as age, duress, and mental disorder (see below).

Today, the **deterrence model** assumes that people participate in an action only after carefully considering the risks (or costs) and the benefits (or rewards). Punishment is supposed to induce **compliance** with the law, since people fear punishment and do not want to jeopardize their stake in conformity. According to the deterrence model, then, the point of punishment is to affect future behaviour rather than to inflict any pain that offenders might deserve as a result of their prior actions.

In reality, however, not all criminal actions are governed by careful consideration of the costs and benefits—some of them are unplanned and habitual. Some individuals choose not to engage in illegal behaviour because they lack the skills or opportunities to commit an act. At the same time, **rational choice** is involved in some criminal activity. Some offenders try to minimize the risks by planning their crimes, and select their targets on the basis of what they are to gain. However, many of these individuals make poor selections because they lack good information or overestimate what they will gain. On the other hand, they may underestimate the risk of punishment. In addition, many offenders have been found to act on impulse.

The Criminal Sanction

It is possible that a criminal penalty can act as a negative inducement, by discouraging people from engaging in behaviour that violates the law. According to Grasmick and Green (1980), deterrence is actually the threat of legal punishment, or fear of physical and material *deprivation* through legally imposed sanctions. Deterrence is an objective phenomenon, as it implies a behavioural result—specifically, the potential offender acts (or chooses not to act) because of fear that the illegal act could lead to capture and punishment. Supporters of the deterrence doctrine hope that any individual contemplating a crime will be deterred because of the certainty, or risk, that they will be caught and punished. Deterrence is also a perceptual phenomenon in the sense that potential criminals decide not to commit crimes on the basis of their perception that they may be caught and punished. Gibbs (1975:2), a strong advocate of this model, defines deterrence as "the omission of an act as a response to the perceived risk and fear of punishment for contrary behavior."

The deterrence approach assumes a direct relationship between the **certainty of punishment** and the **severity** and **swiftness of punishment**. The severity is set at a level that maximizes its deterrent effect—that is, where "the pain of punishment would exceed the pleasure of the offense for a majority of potential offenders" (Price and Stitt 1986:26). The deterrence philosophy places great emphasis on the efficient operation of the criminal justice system—specifically, on a reduction in court delays and in the time between arrest and trial (Feeley and Simon 1992). Yet researchers report that individuals have imperfect knowledge of the maximum penalties for various crimes. Behaviour choices are based on perceptions about the severity of sanctions, the certainty that the punishments will be applied, and the swiftness of the punishment (Apospori and Alpert 1993; Sherman and Berk 1984). The greater the degree of perceived risk of being caught, the more likely potential offenders will be deterred from committing wrongful acts in the future (Andeneas 1974). Chambliss (1969) was one of the first to point out that the effects of deterrence can vary, recognizing that some crimes are more easily deterred than others. Instrumental or goal-oriented behaviour, such as robbing a bank, is more easily deterred than expressive behaviour that results from the inner needs of the offender, such as a violent outburst. This distinction between **instrumental** and **expressive acts** is not easy to make: a person might commit a robbery to gain a sense of superiority over others (an expressive act) rather than to gain any material item (an instrumental act). Chambliss also states that the success or failure of deterrence is linked to the offender's commitment to crime. Offenders who are highly committed to a criminal lifestyle are more difficult to deter than those offenders who do not see crime as a way of life. Others (e.g., Mathiesen 2006) point out that the effects of deterrence are not universal, as differences in deterrence have been found, for example, on the basis of the strength of prosocial and support ties. Thus, the impact of deterrence can vary, based on such issues as the types of norms being punished, the seriousness of the wrongdoing, and the perception of being caught.

The Operations of a Deterrence-Based Criminal Justice System

Any deterrence-based criminal justice system would introduce policies to achieve the greatest certainty of capture, swiftness of prosecution, and—in cases of conviction for a crime—severity of punishment. The goal of this system is to prevent future crime. More emphasis is placed on protecting society and the law-abiding public than on protecting the individual rights of defendants. To ensure that the justice system and its agencies work to their maximum efficiency, more money would have to be spent on all criminal justice agencies. More police officers, prosecutors, judges, and correctional personnel would be hired, and more facilities such as jails, courts, and prisons would be built. Furthermore, the government would have to revise existing statute laws and pass new ones that would grant more powers to the police in the areas of investigation and apprehension, for the sole purpose of increasing the likelihood that suspected criminals are caught (see *Investigating: The DNA Data Bank*). Essentially, the criminal justice system would operate like an assembly line, pushing offenders as efficiently as possible from arrest through conviction to punishment.

Investigating: The DNA Data Bank

Attempting to deter sex offences and sex offenders has been "a front and center issue in criminal justice discussions and debates" for over a decade (Tewksbury 2014:135). Efforts to control sex offenders have led to the creation of a number of programs being introduced by both federal and provincial governments in Canada, including DNA data banks and sex offender registries (see below). Within the past 20 years, the federal government of Canada has established a national DNA data bank that contains the profiles of individuals convicted of the most serious crimes in Canada. The purpose of the DNA bank is to help the police by:

- linking crimes when there are no suspects;
- identifying suspects;
- eliminating suspects (i.e., when there is no match between crime scene DNA and a DNA profile in the National DNA Data Bank); and
- determining whether a serial offender is involved.

Prior to the DNA Identification Act being introduced on December 10, 1998, DNA samples could only be taken from declared dangerous offenders and those convicted of murder, attempted murder, sexual assault, robbery, assault, and break and enter with intent to commit an offence. Since this Act and the one establishing the Sex Offender Registry are both federal, both the bank and the registry are maintained by the RCMP.

The DNA Identification Act provided the legal framework to regulate the storage and the collection of DNA samples and created the national DNA data bank (which became operational on June 30, 2000). The law requires convicted persons to provide blood or other bodily samples, which are then placed in the data bank. In other words, persons convicted of the most serious criminal offences in Canada (referred to as primary offences) are required to provide samples for the data bank. **Primary compulsory offences** are those offences to which the court is compelled to make an order to obtain a DNA sample, such as murder, manslaughter, sexual assault, and aggravated sexual assault (see s. 487.04 of the Criminal Code). For certain offences (known as **presumptive primary offences**), for example, breaking and entering into a dwelling house and hostage taking, the court shall make an order for a DNA sample unless the accused can convince the court that the impact of the order upon their privacy and security of the person is "grossly

Continued on next page

Investigating: The Dna Data Bank (*Continued*)

disproportionate" to the public interest in the protection of society and the proper administration of justice. In addition, a judge can order an individual convicted of a less serious offence (i.e., a **listed secondary offence**) to provide a DNA sample as long as the facts of the case warrant it. Secondary offences include possession of child pornography, indecent acts, criminal negligence causing death, assaulting a peace officer, and robbery (see s. 487.04 of the Criminal Code). The information in the data bank can then be used to ascertain whether someone previously convicted of an offence is involved in a current case. For **generic secondary offences** (e.g., pointing a firearm, theft over $5,000) the court may, after an application by a Crown prosecutor, make an order if they are satisfied that it is in the best interests of the administration of justice.

The DNA bank consists of two distinct indexes. The Convicted Offender Index has been developed from the DNA profiles collected from offenders convicted of designated primary and secondary offences. The Crime Scene Index consists of DNA profiles collected through investigations of criminal acts mentioned in the DNA Act. As of March 31, 2014, the DNA Data Bank had given the police 32,757 "offender hits" (i.e., convicted offender to crime scene hits) and 3,713 "forensic hits" (i.e., crime scene to crime scene hits) (Figure 3.2). Over the same period, 300,853 DNA profiles have been entered into the Convicted Offender Index and another 100,708 DNA profiles into the Crime Scene Index.

Bill C-13 (passed by Parliament in May 2005) expanded the criteria regarding who could be included in the DNA bank. DNA samples can now be gathered from all persons convicted before June 30, 2000, of murder, manslaughter, or a sexual offence who are still under sentence. This policy was upheld by the Supreme Court of Canada in April 2006 in *R. v. Rodgers* (2006). In *Rodgers*, a repeat sex offender challenged the constitutionality of the provisions requiring him to hand over a DNA sample although he had been convicted before Parliament passed the new law. In a written opinion, one Supreme Court justice stated that the DNA database does in fact create a "proper balance" among the principles of privacy, individual security, and procedural fairness guaranteed by the Charter of Rights and Freedoms, as a sample can be obtained only through a judge's order and for those convicted of certain crimes. In addition, individuals convicted of serious offences have a reduced expectation of privacy and can't expect their identity to remain secret from the police. On March 31, 2014, 6,224 retroactive samples of convicted offenders were in the National DNA Data Bank.

TEK IMAGE/Getty Images

DNA has greatly assisted the police in their criminal investigations. In addition, it has exonerated over 200 wrongfully convicted persons in North America.

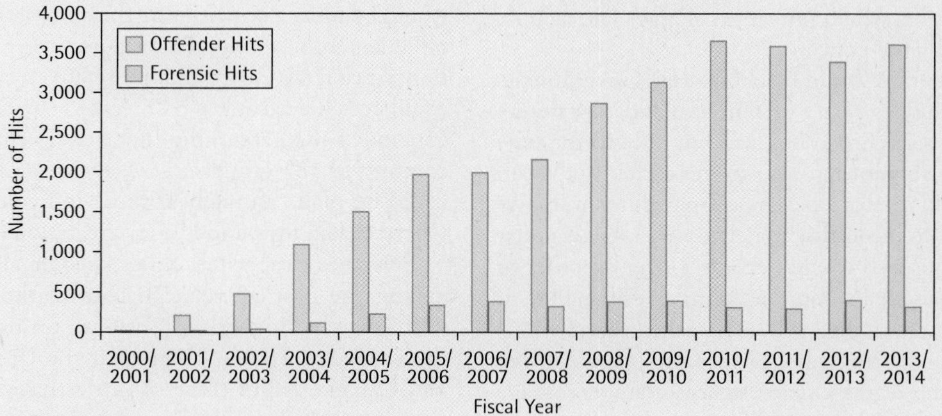

FIGURE 3.2 Offender and Forensic Hits

Source: National DNA Data Bank of Canada, *Annual Report 2013–2014: DNA: then and now*, http://www.rcmp-grc.ca/pubs/nddb-bndg/ann-13-14/index-eng.htm, graph titled "Offender and Forensic Hits." Reproduced with the permission of the RCMP.

The number of police officers and resources involved in crime detection within a deterrence-based criminal justice system would increase, since police are the frontline agency in the "war on crime." Police patrol tactics would change to ensure that the maximum deterrent effect would be achieved by highly visible patrol vehicles. Police officers would be better educated and better trained, and receive the latest technology in order to increase the certainty of capture of criminals. But not all the new resources given to the police would be involved in actual crime fighting. Procedural laws that inhibit the police during their search for and arrest of criminals would be reduced. Emphasis would be placed on **crime control** and **factual guilt**. If, for example, a police officer accidentally violated the rights of an alleged offender during an investigation, this violation would probably be overlooked, assuming that the individual in question is guilty of the offence.

Not all of this increase in police resources would go to hiring more police for street-level patrols. The deterrence doctrine also supports the prevention of crime. As a result, more money would be given to **proactive policing** activities such as Neighbourhood Watch, Operation Identification, and Crime Stoppers programs. These programs, because they involve members of the community in the fight against crime, enable police to spend more time pursuing criminals, thereby increasing the probability of capture and subsequent punishment.

Deterrence advocates the control of all forms of plea bargaining. Price and Stitt (1986:27) point out that controlling plea bargaining "could be the greatest single step to increase both certainty and severity of punishment." In addition, suspects awaiting trial would find it more difficult to receive bail, since they are presumed guilty. This means that most of the individuals arrested are guilty, particularly as they move past arrest and into the court system (Packer 1968). As was the case in the justice model, prosecutors would pursue all charges laid against the defendant by the police.

Judicial discretion would be eliminated. Governments would provide judges with a system of mandatory **determinate sentences**. This would lead not only to the uniformity of punishment but also to the certainty that an individual would receive a designated punishment. However, in contrast to the justice model, most sentences under a deterrence approach would become longer, in order to impress on individuals contemplating a crime that, if caught and convicted, they will be punished severely.

Parole would be abolished. More prisons would be built to house those guilty of an offence and to discourage potential criminals from committing a criminal offence by making them fearful of being caught and incarcerated. Risk assessments of offenders would become normal practice. Offenders would be placed into groups based on their predicted future behaviour. All sanctions would therefore be viewed in terms of their effectiveness at reducing the risk of further offences. At one extreme would be secure incarceration; at the other would be probation, with levels of intermediate punishments between (Morris and Tonry 1990).

Selective Incapacitation

History

Selective incapacitation policies attempt to separate high-risk offenders from low-risk ones and to incarcerate for a long time those who are most likely to be dangerous once released. This approach is very recent in criminal justice; it emerged as a major force only in the 1970s. James Q. Wilson, a prominent criminologist, gave this model strong support in *Thinking about Crime* (1975). He wrote that serious crimes could be reduced by about one-third if each individual convicted of a violent crime received a sentence of three years and was not paroled. Then a study conducted by the Rand Corporation and authored by Peter Greenwood, titled *Selective Incapacitation*, appeared in 1982. This study became famous because on the basis of their investigations the researchers devised a system that they felt would successfully separate those offenders who should be "incapacitated" because they posed a long-term threat to society from those who should serve shorter sentences because they could be successfully reintegrated back into society once released. Greenwood determined that a sentencing approach based on the Rand formula could reduce robberies by 15 percent and prison populations by 5 percent. An increase in the imprisonment of chronic offenders would be more than offset by the elimination of low-risk offenders from prisons. This report received strong attention, since it suggested that more effective crime control could be achieved at less cost. A study by E.D. Zedlewski concluded that, assuming the average chronic offender committed 187 crimes a year, a saving of $430 million could be made annually if these individuals were sentenced to lengthy periods of incarceration (Walker 1994).

Selective incapacitation has become a popular policy during the past 30 years to control those individuals deemed to be "high-risk," "serious," or "dangerous," first in the United States, followed by the United Kingdom, and Canada. All of these countries have adopted some type of approach combining a number of elements found in different crime control philosophies—less severe policies are reserved for "ordinary" and low-risk criminals, while tougher and much longer measures are given to criminals presumed to pose a significant threat to public safety. This approach favouring harsher punishments (referred to as a **law and order ideology**) creates policies such as mandatory prison sentences as well as extended prison sentences in order to keep the public safe from those individuals who commit designated serious crimes.

Despite these policies which intend to control and reduce crime in society, critics argue that many errors are made since predictions can never be precise. In other words, there will always be some "high-risk" individuals who would never commit another crime, and some "low-risk" individuals who would do so soon after being returned to the community (Ashworth 2005). Zimring and Hawkins (1988) have argued that the reduction in crime promised by supporters of selective incapacitation has not materialized. They contend that the figures used by this theory's proponents are based on estimates of the number of crimes a chronic offender remembered committing each year. Many of the critics' harshest criticisms are based on their contention that attempts at reducing crime may be limited by a number of factors. These include problems in the identification of high-risk offenders and the possibility that one offender, if arrested, will simply be replaced by another. Also, if the offender who is incarcerated is a gang member, the gang may continue to commit the same amount of crime. Selective incapacitation no doubt has some limited influence on the crime rate, but its success depends on the ability of the criminal justice system to identify chronic offenders in the early stages of their career (Visher 1995).

The Criminal Sanction

The selective incapacitation approach focuses on those few individuals who commit the greatest number of crimes, be they property crimes or violent crimes. Most of the attention to date has been on individuals classified as **chronic**, **career**, or **repeat offenders**.

According to the criminal sanction approach, the crime rate is a function of the total number of offenders less those imprisoned (i.e., incapacitated), multiplied by an average number of crimes per offender. It follows that if chronic criminals are incarcerated for long periods of time, the crime rate will go down. Research has shown that a relative handful of offenders are responsible for the vast majority of violent offences. An example of that research is a book by Wolfgang et al. titled *Delinquency in a Birth Cohort* (1972), which has been lauded as "the single most important piece of criminal justice research in the last 25 years" (Walker 1993:55). Focusing on 10,000 juvenile males born in Philadelphia in 1945 and living in that city between the ages of 10 and 18, the researchers measured crime as the number of times the police took a juvenile into custody. They discovered that nearly 35 percent of all males had a record of an offence. At least 627 of them had committed at least five offences. Even more important was their finding that only 6 percent of the males in the study accounted for more than half of all offences committed by the entire group, and that 6 percent accounted for well over half of all violent crimes. Other studies (Hamparian et al. 1978; Tracy et al. 1990) turned up similar findings for both juveniles and adults. These studies identified small groups of high-rate offenders who were responsible for most criminal offences as well as most violent crimes.

The selective incapacitation philosophy does not apply to all offenders; it focuses only on those who are deemed the most dangerous and/or who pose the greatest risk to society. A key feature of this approach is that individuals are considered dangerous not only because of their deeds in the past but also because of the crimes they are likely to commit in the future. Future crimes are determined either by the number of prior convictions or by the number of crimes that similar offenders committed once they were released from prison.

In 1990, the Solicitor General of Canada recommended the elimination of parole for those convicted of dealing drugs. This policy was to be instituted if members of the National Parole Board suspected convicted drug dealers would be at risk to sell drugs after they were released. Such individuals were to be denied parole—they were to be punished, in essence, for crimes they had not yet committed. An example of this type of philosophy is found in the State of Washington's "sexual predator" law, which allows the state to "indefinitely lock up anyone who has committed at least one violent sex crime—after he has served his time" (Richards 1992:A1). Legislation in Canada permits the authorities to identify potential high-risk individuals being released from a correctional facility to be closely controlled when they are in the community (see *Investigating: Dangerous Offender Designations and Long-Term Supervision Orders*).

© Don Hammond/Design Pics/Corbis

Selective incapacitation advocates support much longer prison terms for criminals who have committed serious crimes. Inmates will serve their sentences in prison cells like the one pictured above.

Investigating: Dangerous Offender Designations and Long-Term Supervision Orders

In Canada, the sentencing of an individual most commonly involves a judge evaluating the past behaviour of an individual convicted of a crime and then determining the appropriate punishment (this assumes that a convicted person can be held responsible for his or her actions). However, there are currently two sentencing options in Canada that treat the risk of reoffending as the principal factor. One relates to dangerous offenders, the other to long-term-supervision offenders. This focus on the risk of future criminal behaviour is sometimes referred to as "actuarial justice," an approach that places people in categories and then estimates the risk these groups present.

In the case of dangerous offenders (Figure 3.3), over the past 60 years Canada has used various laws to allow the indeterminate confinement of those considered to be a danger to the public. In 1947, the term "habitual offender" was introduced to the Criminal Code; a year later, "criminal sexual psychopath" provisions were introduced into the Criminal Code. In 1962, a new definition, "dangerous sexual offender," replaced "criminal sexual psychopath." Then, in 1977, new amendments to the Criminal Code replaced the designations of "habitual offender" and "dangerous sexual offender." This new designation, "dangerous offender," focused on those individuals considered dangerous because they had committed a "serious personal injury offence"—a category that included a number of violent offences as well as several sexual offences stipulating a maximum punishment of at least 10 years. This legislation, which was in force between 1977 and 1997, meant that when an offender was declared a dangerous offender, a judge could sentence him or her to either a determinate or indeterminate sentence. The dangerous offender classification was upheld by the Supreme Court of Canada in *R. v. Lyons* (1987), in which the plaintiff argued that these provisions violated ss. 7, 9, and 12 of the Charter of Rights and Freedoms.

The current legislation on dangerous offenders, introduced in 1997, retains many of the provisions passed in 1977. One of the most important changes is that once an individual is classified as a dangerous offender, an indeterminate sentence is automatic. Another important change is that when a finding of dangerous offender is not warranted, a court may declare an individual a long-term offender, which means that the offender receives a determinate sentence of at least two years as well as a lengthy supervision order (up to 10 years) after release. This new provision allows court officials to evaluate patterns of offending over time.

If the Crown wants someone classified as a dangerous offender, it must apply for a dangerous offender hearing

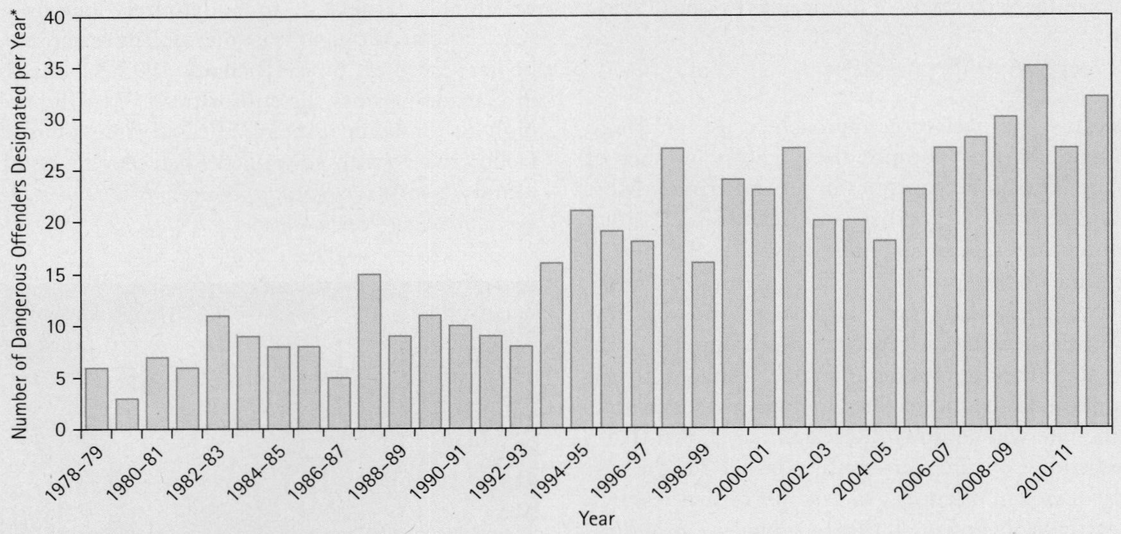

FIGURE 3.3 The Number of Dangerous Offender Designations Has Increased since 2011–12

*The number of Dangerous Offenders designated per year does not include overturned decisions.

Source: Corrections and Conditional Release Statistical Overview Annual Report 2012, Figure E3, p. 103, http://www.publicsafety.gc.ca/cnt/rsrcs/pblctns/2012-ccrs/2012-ccrs-eng.pdf. Reproduced with the permission of the Minister of Public Safety and Emergency Preparedness Canada 2015.

Continued on next page

Investigating: Dangerous Offender Designations and Long-Term Supervision Orders (*Continued*)

after the offender has been convicted of a "serious personal injury offence." Before the dangerous offender hearing, the individual in question is remanded for up to 60 days so that court-appointed experts can conduct a behavioural assessment. It is possible for an offender to become classified as a dangerous offender after committing one offence; however, most such individuals have long criminal histories. There are four possible criteria for a finding of dangerous offender. They are found in s. 753(1)(a) of the Criminal Code:

1. (a) that the offence for which the offender has been convicted is a serious personal injury offence described in paragraph (a) of the definition of that expression in s. 752 and the offender constitutes a threat to the life, safety or physical or mental well-being of other persons on the basis of establishing

   (i) a pattern of repetitive behaviour by the offender, of which the offence for which he or she has been convicted forms a part, showing a failure to restrain his or her behaviour and a likelihood of causing death or injury to other persons, or inflicting severe psychological damage on other persons, through failure in the future to restrain his or her behaviour,

   (ii) a pattern of persistent aggressive behaviour by the offender, of which the offence for which he or she has been convicted forms a part, showing a substantial degree of indifference on the part of the offender respecting the reasonably foreseeable consequences to other persons of his or her behaviour, or,

   (iii) any behaviour by the offender, associated with the offence for which he or she has been convicted, that is of such a brutal nature as to compel the conclusion that the offender's behaviour in the future is unlikely to be inhibited by normal standards of behavioural restraint; or

   (b) that at the offence for which the offender is convicted is a serious personal injury offence described in paragraph (b) of the definition of that expression in s. 752 and the offender, by his or her conduct in any sexual matter including that involved in the commission of the offence for which he or she has been convicted, has shown a failure to control his or her sexual impulses and a likelihood of causing injury, pain or other evil to other persons through failure in the future to control his or her sexual impulses.

A long-term supervision order application may be made if an offender has been convicted of an offence listed in s. 753.1(2)(a) of the Criminal Code: sexual interference (s. 151), invitation to sexual touching (s. 152), sexual exploitation (s. 153), exposure (s. 173[2]), sexual assault (s. 271), sexual assault with a weapon (s. 272), and aggravated sexual assault (s. 273). The offender may also have "engaged in serious conduct of a sexual nature in the commission of another offence of which the offender has been convicted" (s. 753.12[a]).

Long-term offender legislation is also found in s. 753.1:

1. The court may, on application made under this Part following the filing of an assessment report . . . find an offender to be a long-term offender if it is satisfied:

   (a) it would be appropriate to impose a sentence of imprisonment of two years or more for the offence for which the offender has been convicted;

   (b) there is substantial risk that the offender will re-offend; and

   (c) there is a reasonable possibility of eventual control of the risk in the community . . . If the court finds an offender to be a long-term offender, it shall: impose a sentence for the offence for which the offender has been convicted, which sentence must be a minimum punishment of imprisonment for a term of two years; and order the offender to be supervised in the community, for a period not exceeding ten years . . .

As of April 14, 2013, 538 individuals were classified as "active" dangerous offenders, with 507 serving an indeterminate sentence. Of the 538 individuals classified as dangerous offenders, 512 were incarcerated, one had been deported, one had escaped, and 24 were being supervised in the community.

In comparison, on April 14, 2013, there were 722 offenders with a long-term supervision order. Of these offenders, 482 (67 percent) had at least one current conviction for a sexual offence, as reported by Trevethan et al. (2002) who noted that most long-term supervision orders have involved sex offenders. There are currently 370 offenders being supervised on their long-term supervision order. These include 337 offenders released into the community, 24 offenders temporarily detained, five who have been deported, and four offenders unlawfully at large.

While there is undoubtedly support for such policies, there are potential pitfalls to such laws as well as problems associated with implementing them. The most serious criticism of the selective incapacitation of violent offenders is that the criminal justice system lacks the capacity to accurately predict future violent behaviour. This criticism directly challenges the legitimacy of selective incapacitation as a legal sanction. The judicial maxim that "it is better to let ten guilty people go free than to let one innocent person suffer" embodies the value that our society places on individual liberty. The criminal sanction approach would extend judges the power "to prevent violent offenders . . . and drug offenders from obtaining parole until they have served half of their sentences." Those identified as dangerous would be incarcerated longer than those who are not. For Price and Stitt (1986:28), this would mean that "two offenders could commit the same act but receive different sentences because one is thought to be more likely to commit that or a related act in the future."

The Operations of a Selective Incapacitation–Based Criminal Justice System

According to Price and Stitt (1986), the selective incapacitation approach is based on the idea that the best predictor of future behaviour is past behaviour. For the vast majority of offenders, the criminal justice system would operate on the basis of the deterrence doctrine. However, once an individual entered the system and was considered dangerous, the system would assign special resources and individuals to process the case as quickly as possible. Thus, only some of the resources of the criminal justice system would be dedicated to the selective incapacitation approach.

Furthermore, because it contained such a narrow interest, this approach could easily be attached to any of the other three models. Such is the case in Washington, which employs the justice model for most offenders but also has a sexual predator law to ensure that certain sex offenders are not released for a long time. This is the most specific of all the models in the sense that it looks only at a narrow group of criminals.

The role of the police would be to arrest suspected offenders, conduct careful background checks, and then place offenders in a pretrial detention centre if they are considered to be chronic offenders. Plea bargaining would be eliminated, enabling prosecutors to process all such cases as quickly as possible in order to ensure that offenders aren't released back into the general population. Judges would have little discretion in these cases. Once an offender was perceived as a chronic offender, he or she would be sentenced to a lengthy determinate prison term. Parole would be abolished and the correctional system would become little more than a holding facility for such offenders. Policies such as "three strikes and you're out" are consistent with the selective incapacitation approach.

The Rehabilitation Approach

History

According to the rehabilitation approach, punishment is able to reduce the amount of crime by improving offenders in a way that makes them less likely to commit crimes in the future. Supporters of this model assume that crime is a result of factors outside the control of the individual and deny that individuals are responsible for their actions (referred to as the **doctrine of determinism**). They argue that since criminals don't freely choose their behaviour, punishment is the wrong policy. Instead, they recommend the **individualized treatment** of offenders in the hope that the causes of their criminal behaviour can be discovered and eliminated. As Allen (1981:2) points out, a central purpose of the rehabilitative approach "is to effect in the characters, attitudes, and behavior of convicted offenders, so as to strengthen the social defense against unwanted behavior [as well as] to contribute to the welfare and satisfaction of the offenders."

Under the **rehabilitation model**, more attention is placed on the offender than on the criminal act itself. Criminal sanctions are intended to meet the needs of the offender instead of being "based on considerations of social harm and deterrence" (Cullen and Gilbert 1982:34). To facilitate this approach, indeterminate sentences are essential—specifically, offenders must remain in prison for as long as it takes to find the appropriate "cure." Treatment specialists therefore take on an important role within the criminal justice system as they are able to influence the early release of offenders serving their sentence in a correctional facility.

In the late 19th and early 20th centuries, to facilitate an individual-based justice system, probation and parole were introduced as well as indeterminate sentences. The idea behind these policies was that the type of punishment (probation or incarceration) would be based on an offender's need for treatment. If the individual needed treatment, the duration of that person's punishment "would be determined by his or her behavior after sentencing as much as by the crime itself" (Clear 1995:460). Inmates who showed improvement would be released earlier than those who resisted treatment or who failed to respond to it. Treatment at the turn of the century involved "programs of work, moral instruction, discipline, and order," all designed "to develop those personal habits that were prerequisites to a useful law-abiding life" (Carrigan 1991:356).

Probably the test most often used to evaluate the success of rehabilitation programs is whether the offender recidivates—that is, is convicted of another offence after the sentence is completed. Indicative of the results is the success rate of federal parolees who completed their first year while on full parole (see Chapter 13). In 2011–12, the success rate for 1,021 individuals released from a federal correctional facility was 78.7 percent. Of those who had their parole revoked, 16 percent (204 individuals) was for breach of conditions, 5 percent (65 individuals) was for committing a non-violent offence, while 0.5 percent (7 individuals) was for a violent offence (Public Safety Canada 2012). The debate over the effectiveness of rehabilitation continues to this day between advocates of rehabilitation and those of the other three models.

The Criminal Sanction

Supporters of rehabilitation see this approach as necessary if we are to understand why people commit crimes. Once we understand what causes criminal behaviour, society will be able to apply appropriate sanctions. To this end, punishment needs to be flexible as well as based on the needs of the individual. This means that two individuals could commit the identical crime but end up with completely different punishments—perhaps because one individual requires a lengthy treatment program while the other needs some other treatment. A rehabilitation system is best described as discretionary, with all court and correctional agencies having the power to determine the type and length of sentence to individualize the punishment.

Once the dominant approach to punishment, rehabilitation was challenged and then discredited in the 1970s. It was then replaced by policies that first favoured the justice model then later deterrence and selective incapacitation. In the past 20 years, however, rehabilitation has experienced a resurgence in popularity and has gained support. A number of national surveys have found that about an equal number of Canadians support rehabilitation as they do punishment-oriented approaches. In 1997, 37 percent of Canadians identified public safety as the primary goal of incarceration, compared to 34 percent who felt it was rehabilitation (Stein 2001). Roberts (2005) notes that when Canadians were asked their opinions about the purpose of corrections in 2002, almost the same number identified rehabilitation (34 percent) compared to punishment (36 percent).

The Operations of a Rehabilitation-Based Criminal Justice System

Rehabilitation sets out to enhance the discretionary powers of the principal agencies of the criminal justice system. Since the focus of this model is on the needs of the offender, each agency must make decisions to enhance the chances that the individual will return to society as a better person.

As Price and Stitt (1986) point out, a system based on rehabilitation would require the criminal justice system to focus on the criminal more than on the act committed. Agencies would intervene in the offender's life in order to change the offender, the hope being that the pressures that forced the individual to commit crime would be reduced and finally eliminated. Much of this model's emphasis would thus be on the sentencing and correctional stages of the criminal justice system.

The role of the police would not change dramatically. Police would continue to arrest criminals and lay charges. Prosecutors would be allowed to plea bargain as much as they wish and would encounter few if any restrictions in this regard. A case could easily be terminated or the total number of charges reduced if the prosecutor felt that it would be in the best interests of the offender. Prosecutors would rely on the presentence report and make recommendations on the type of treatment needed. Both the prosecutor and judge would make use of this report during the sentencing of the offender.

Judicial discretion is an essential component of the rehabilitation approach. Prior to handing out a sentence, the judge would receive a presentence report from a probation officer. Any recommendations made in this report would be carefully considered by the judge in the sentencing decision, as would any statements made by the defence lawyer and the Crown prosecutor. The sentence would reflect the "best interests" of the offender and would involve an **indeterminate sentence** that best fits the needs of the offender. As such, offenders would have to serve only the minimum length of their sentence. Under a rehabilitation approach, the correctional system and its related services would probably become the most important agencies of the criminal justice system. Parole services would be expanded, since they would be required in order to individualize the treatment program for each offender. This individualization would add discretion to the system, since offenders could be released at any time by the parole board after serving the minimum sentence.

Correctional services within the prison would become more treatment-oriented. The correctional system would discover the needs of offenders before proceeding with a course of treatment (see the *Investigating* feature on the next page). Since treatment would be personalized, it could take a long time before that treatment succeeded for any individual. Thus, the treatment services might vary for each offender and the length of treatment as well.

Investigating: Are Rehabilitation Programs More Effective in Reducing Sex Offender Recidivism Than Selective Incapacitation Punishments?

A common topic of debate over the past few decades has been the best way to control criminals convicted of sexual offences. Is it better to selectively incapacitate offenders or to rehabilitate them? Some researchers argue that psychological assessments reduce the recidivism risk of sexual offenders (e.g., Hanson et al. 2002), while others believe that the current research evidence does not support such a position (Rice and Harris 2003). As a result, many believe that sex offenders should be incarcerated for lengthy periods of time since in their view punishment is the only approach that "works" in the sense of keeping sex offenders from recidivating. However, they sometimes ignore the fact that sex offenders will be released once they have completed their sentence. The feeling is that if they are not treated, many will reoffend.

Other correctional experts are now questioning the success of deterrence-based punishment systems, arguing that they have only a marginal positive effect and do not save any money in either the short or long term (e.g., Cullen and Applegate 1997). Problems have been discovered in deterrence-based punishments, most notably the failure to properly implement programs. Some (e.g., Andrews and Bonta 1998) argue that deterrence-based punishments fail to significantly reduce recidivism rates because they do not focus on any of the known predictors of recidivism, such as antisocial values and the influence of negative peer groups. Others believe that "the deterrence approach ignores the criminological evidence showing that the roots of crime among serious offenders typically extend to childhood or early-adolescent activities, where youths develop propensities and associations that stabilize their involvement in crime" (Cullen and Applegate 1997:xxi). This debate over the appropriate approach to reducing recidivism rates has been going on for decades in the field of corrections, ever since the publication of Robert Martinson's research (1974), which questioned the success of rehabilitation programs (see Chapter 13).

Extensive empirical data now exist indicating that rehabilitation programs focusing upon offenders can and do work—if they are well designed and effectively implemented. Paul Gendreau found that "appropriate" treatment programs can reduce recidivism rates by 53 percent within six months to two years. Gendreau and Andrews (in Freiberg 1990) found that the most successful programs employ behavioural modification techniques that reward prosocial behaviour and that "target those anti-social attitudes and values that fuel criminal behaviour." Gendreau noted that these techniques vary—in some correctional settings, prisoners are given more privileges or money for prosocial behaviour. Often, role-playing exercises are conducted to influence an offender's thinking and values.

Gendreau and Goggin (1996) found that rehabilitation-based programs attain better results when programs operate with optimal theoretical integrity. In other words, programs need to be properly constructed, operated by qualified and well-trained staff who provide intensive treatments, and evaluated by experts in behavioural intervention. In their analyses of rehabilitation-based programs, Gendreau and Goggin reported that those programs with therapeutic integrity are much more successful than programs that ignore or contain only partial program integrity. Programs with proper therapeutic integrity reduce recidivism by 20 to 35 percent compared to between 5 and 15 percent for those without program integrity.

But if successful sex offender treatment programs can be implemented, will the recidivism rates of sex offenders be reduced? In Canada, sex offenders incarcerated in federal correctional facilities who want to apply for conditional release (e.g., parole) are expected to attend relevant institutional programs. Their progress in these programs helps correctional and parole officials determine whether a sex offender should be released on a conditional program

Seto (2003) reported on sex offenders released from the Warkworth Sexual Behaviour Clinic, a treatment program offered by a Canadian federal correctional facility. The main treatment approaches involved in that program included acceptance of responsibility for offences, victim empathy, understanding one's own offence cycle, and the development of an individual relapse prevention program. The performances of those who attended were evaluated at 32 and 62 months. It was found that treatment performance was not related to either general or serious recidivism—specifically, sex offenders who scored high in psychopathy were roughly twice as likely to seriously reoffend as those who scored lower in psychopathy.

Some studies report lower recidivism rates for sex offenders released into the community on a conditional release program. A study of a treatment program for high-risk sex offenders (recidivist rapists and pedophiles serving a federal sentence) conducted at CSC's maximum-security Regional Psychiatric Centre (Prairies) compared one treatment group to another group of federal offenders released from federal correctional facilities. Over three years, the treatment group had a 59 percent lower rate of sexual recidivism than the comparison group, even though they were followed up for more than two years longer. At the same time, however, no differences were reported in a comparison of a similar program comparing sexual and non-sexual offenders sentenced to provincial facilities (Nicholaichuk 1995).

SUMMING UP AND LOOKING FORWARD

Much has been written in an attempt to answer the question, "How can our criminal justice system achieve justice?" A common way of answering this question is by looking at a single control philosophy. Four major control philosophies rely upon the state and the operations of the major criminal justice agencies in order to achieve justice. These four control crime philosophies are the justice model, deterrence, selective incapacitation, and rehabilitation.

The justice model looks backward to punish offenders for their criminal behaviour because they deserve it. This model highlights the necessity for the following: (1) legal rights for both those charged and convicted of a criminal offence; (2) limits to the amount of discretion held by officials; and (3) proportionality between the criminal sanction and the seriousness of the offence. It is important to establish the legal guilt of individuals as opposed to factual guilt.

The deterrence model looks forward to change criminals, punishing them in the belief that this will prevent future crimes. The aim of this control philosophy is to prevent future crimes by inflicting the appropriate amount of pain (or the threat of pain) in order to make people consider the potential implications of their criminal actions. The selective incapacitation model focuses upon a selective group of offenders—repeat, dangerous, and/or high risk offenders who commit serious violent crimes in our society. It tries to prevent crime by incarcerating individuals for long periods or by placing legal controls such as a long-term supervision order to restrict their actions upon release.

The rehabilitation model differs from the three models discussed above because it is the only one that focuses upon the actor; all of the others focus upon the criminal act. Another difference is that this model favours discretion as each person is unique and may need a sentence based on their own risk level and personal needs. As a result, sentences are indeterminate.

In recent decades two alternatives, Aboriginal justice and restorative justice, have emerged. Both of these alternatives believe that restoration and healing will improve the quality and outcome of the criminal justice process. These approaches both start with a similar idea—that crime harms people and their relationships. As such, harms have to be healed, repaired, and restored. These alternative control philosophies will be explored in the next section.

Review Questions:

1. Do you think the justice model achieves justice?
2. What are the strengths and limitations of relying on a deterrence-based approach?
3. Do you think the selective incapacitation approach makes society safer?
4. Do you think it is best to focus on the actor (as rehabilitation does) in our criminal justice system?

Aboriginal and Restorative Justice Systems: An Introduction

Aboriginal and restorative justice systems represent a significant shift from the above-mentioned crime control philosophies. They share several principles, including the belief that governments need to give up their monopoly over our society's response to crime and must stop being the sole regulator of those who are most directly affected by the crime—the victim and the offender. Another principle involves gathering people in a circle to eliminate the hierarchical relationships that exist in today's legal system (Roach 1999). Yet another principle is that the relationship between victims and offenders must be restored in a process that allows both to participate (Van Ness and Heetderks Strong 1997; Zehr 1990). The importance of these principles was formally recognized in 1996, when they were incorporated into the sentencing principles of the Criminal Code, in particular into s. 718(e) (the provision of reparations for harm done to victims or to the community) and s. 718(f) (the promotion of responsibility in offenders, and acknowledgment of the harm done to victims and the community).

Programs based on restorative justice are guided by a number of factors, including the following:

- Victims and offenders must give and also be able to withdraw their free, voluntary, and informed consent to participate in the restorative justice process; they must be fully informed about the process and its consequences.
- Offenders must admit responsibility for the offence, and both the victim and offender must agree on the essential facts of the case.
- Offenders and victims can have legal advice at any time and can withdraw if they so wish.
- Admissions of guilt cannot be used as evidence in any later legal proceedings.
- Failure to reach an agreement should not be used in any subsequent legal proceedings to justify a harsher sentence than would otherwise be given.
- The consequences of failing to honour an agreement should be clearly stated.

Aboriginal justice systems differ from restorative justice systems in a number of ways, including their histories—the colonization of Aboriginal peoples in Canada and the **residential school system** resulted in the devaluation of their cultures and the destruction of traditional methods of social control. Justice systems developed by Aboriginal peoples involve the idea that crime devastates a community's quality of life and that **informal sanctions** play a pivotal role in restoring harmony. Instead of focusing on the formal punishment of offenders (as in the Western-based criminal justice system), they support a healing process involving victims, offenders, and the community. Many (e.g., Monture-Angus 1995; Proulx and Perrault 2000) recognize the importance of spirituality within Aboriginal justice. Another fundamental belief of Aboriginal justice systems is that local communities should be able to determine what happens to offenders who commit crimes within their boundaries. Roach (2000), for example, states that Aboriginal justice differs from the Western legal system through its attention on renewing **collective identity** and **community**. Monture-Angus and Turpel (1994) point out that Aboriginal peoples should have the power to develop and administer the criminal justice system within their communities in accordance with their particular history, language, and social and cultural practices of that community.

Aboriginal Justice Systems

Many Aboriginal communities have traditionally emphasized elements of restorative justice. The Supreme Court of Canada, in *R. v. Gladue* (1999) (see Chapter 10), commented that in general terms restorative justice can be described as an approach to remedying crime in which it is understood that all things are interrelated and that crime disrupts the harmony that existed prior to its occurrence, or at least that should have existed. The appropriateness of a particular sanction is determined largely by the needs of the victims and the community as well as those of the offender. The focus is on the human beings closely affected by the crime. In this case, the Supreme Court cited a statement made by the Royal Commission of Aboriginal Peoples in their report *Aboriginal Peoples and the Justice System*, in which they wrote that the Canadian criminal justice system is in conflict with Aboriginal perspectives on justice and that this conflict is rooted in **differing world views**: "The Canadian criminal justice system has failed the Indigenous peoples of Canada. . . . The principal reason for this crushing failure is the fundamentally different world views of Indigenous and non-Indigenous people with respect to such elemental issues as the substantive content of justice and the process of achieving justice" (Royal Commission on Aboriginal Peoples 1993:4). These differing world views in the context of justice refer to differences that include a **spiritual-based** versus a secular-based system, healing versus punishment, and community interdependence versus individualism (Taraschi 1998). Recently there has been discussion about the development of formal Aboriginal justice systems throughout Canada. These systems—specifically those administered by Aboriginal courts—have become a major area of interest, as they would honour traditional methods for resolving conflicts. At the same time, there is recognition that the Western criminal justice system, while attempting "to provide justice on the principle that all Canadians share common values and experiences cannot help but **discriminate** against Aboriginal people, who come to the system with cultural values and experiences that differ substantially from those of the dominant society" (Hamilton and Sinclair 1991:86–87).

A number of provincial and federal public inquiries and reviews have reported on the relationship between Aboriginal people and the Western justice system. In 1991, the *Aboriginal Justice Inquiry of Manitoba* (AJI) reported that the Manitoba criminal justice system was "decidedly unequal" and that Aboriginal peoples suffered from systemic discrimination (see Chapter 2). In its final report, the AJI made almost 300 recommendations, including the creation of a separate Aboriginal justice system. That same year, the *Task Force on the Criminal Justice System and Its Impact on the Indian and Metis People of Alberta* (Alberta Task Force) published its findings on the impact of the Alberta criminal justice system on Aboriginal peoples, concluding that "the imposition of the majority's justice system on the Aboriginal minority results in unfairness and inequity" (Alberta Task Force vol. 1:1–2). It made almost 350 recommendations concerning improving the entire operation of the criminal justice system. The next year, Saskatchewan released two reports, the *Saskatchewan Indian Justice Review Committee* and the *Saskatchewan Metis Justice Review Committee*, recommending in part that there had to be Aboriginal involvement "in deciding what changes are to be made, how they are to happen, and shares responsibility for the changes" in order to bring about meaningful changes in the administration and operation of the justice system.

At the federal level, the Law Reform Commission of Canada published a report (*Aboriginal Peoples and Criminal Justice*) in December 1991 that supported the concept of Aboriginal justice as the "present system fails the Aboriginal peoples" and that the "current regime fails to respect the Charter's guarantees of equality and fundamental justice in a number of important respects" (Law Reform Commission 1991:16, 75). It did not, however, indicate which type of system it supported. The commission did, however, discuss the reasons why such a justice system was needed in Canada: "From the Aboriginal perspective . . . the system is deeply insensitive to their traditions and values: many view it as unremittingly **racist**" (Law Reform Commission of Canada 1991:5). The Royal Commission on Aboriginal Peoples, appointed by the federal Conservative government in 1991, published a report (*Bridging the Cultural Divide: A Report on Aboriginal People and Criminal Justice in Canada*) stating that the criminal justice system was failing the Aboriginal peoples of Canada.

CP PHOTO/Winnipeg Free Press - Ken Gigliotti

Inmates at the Aboriginal Healing Range Home at the Stony Mountain Institution participate in a drum circle on May 19, 2006, in Stony Mountain, Manitoba. The inmates have committed to a lifestyle behind bars that follows traditional teachings, while also participating in mainstream correctional programs. Visits with Elders, cultural and spiritual ceremonies, sharing circles, stints in a sweat lodge, drumming, and arts and crafts are all part of the path to healing.

To date, most of the efforts in the area of Aboriginal justice systems in Canada have focused on the existing criminal justice system accommodating Aboriginal approaches to justice (referred to as **indigenization programs**). In Manitoba, for example, the AJI recommended sweeping changes in the criminal justice system; these changes failed to materialize, however. The provincial government turned down a proposal for an Aboriginal court in January 1993, proposing instead a three-year pilot project that would combine Aboriginal approaches to resolving conflict with principles found in the Western legal system. This led one of the original authors of the Aboriginal Justice Inquiry to speculate that such a system would never be introduced (Hamilton 2001).

An Aboriginal justice system inevitably involves more than having justice programs in Aboriginal communities delivered by Aboriginal organizations. As Rudin (2005:109) points out, in order for justice programs "to be successful, Aboriginal people must control the alternative justice processes." This involves governments and justice system providers allowing Aboriginal communities themselves "the time, opportunity and funding to determine how they wish to approach justice issues." Also, Aboriginal justice programs need to "be developed and controlled by Aboriginal organizations and communities" (ibid.:111).

Models of Aboriginal Justice Systems

How would an Aboriginal justice system operate? What shape would it take? There are many views regarding what would constitute an effective Aboriginal justice system, but "fundamental is the belief that the system must be faithful to aboriginal traditions and cultural values, while adapting them to modern society" (Law Reform Commission of Canada 1991:7). Other essential components of an Aboriginal justice system include care for the interests of the collectivity, the reintegration of the offender into the community, mediation and conciliation within the community, and the importance of the role of community Elders and leaders (ibid.) (see Table 3.1).

According to Meyer (1998:44), while there would be diversity among the justice systems developed by Aboriginal communities, they would all focus on certain elements. For example, all would "focus on **reparations** and making the parties 'whole' after the injury." And all would avoid, as a basic principle, blaming the offender for the harm they had done, as efforts would be made to **repair the injury** and make the community whole again. Such approaches would address the need to emphasize persuasion over coercion, with the goal of restoring the parties involved. They would also recognize the need for respected community members to serve as decision makers.

Manitoba's Aboriginal Justice Inquiry found that the meaning of justice in an Aboriginal society differs greatly from that of the broader society. European adversarial systems attempt to "prevent or punish harmful or deviant behaviour"; in contrast, Aboriginal systems attempt "to **restore the peace and equilibrium** within the community, and to reconcile the accused with his or her own conscience and with the individual or family who has been wronged." Thus, the underlying notion of Aboriginal justice systems when dealing with crime is "the resolution of disputes, the healing of wounds and the **restoration of social harmony**" (Hamilton and Sinclair 1991).

The Alberta Task Force recognized that important differences exist between European and Aboriginal approaches to justice. It noted (Bryant 1999:20–21) that the Aboriginal model incorporates different goals:

1. It focuses on problem solving and the restoration of harmony.
2. It uses restitution and reconciliation as means of restoration.
3. The community acts as a facilitator in the restorative process.
4. The impact of the actions in question is impressed on the offender.
5. The holistic context of an offence—its moral, social, economic, political, and religious and cosmic considerations—is carefully considered.
6. The stigma of the offence is removed through conformity.
7. It is important for the offender to express remorse, repentance, and forgiveness and for the community to recognize it.
8. The offender must play an active role in the restorative process.

TABLE 3.1 Differences in Justice Paradigms

Aboriginal Justice Approach	Western Justice Paradigm
Communication is fluid.	The paradigm is vertical.
Native language is used.	Communication is rehearsed.
Oral customary law learned as a way of life, by example.	English or French language is used.
Law and justice are part of the whole.	Written statutory law is derived from rules and procedure.
The spiritual realm is invoked in ceremonies and prayer.	The paradigm features separation of power.
Trusting relationships are built to promote resolution and healing.	The process is adversarial, conflict-oriented, argumentative.
Talk and discussion is necessary.	Isolated behaviour is considered—freeze-frame acts.
Problems are reviewed in their entirety; contributing factors are examined.	A fragmented approach is taken to process and solutions.
Comprehensive problem-solving is undertaken.	The process is time-oriented.
No time limits are put on the process; it includes all individuals affected and solutions.	Limits are imposed on the number of participants in the process.
All extended-family members are represented.	Representation is by strangers.
The focus is on victim and communal rights.	The focus is on individual rights.
The process is corrective; offenders are accountable and responsible for change.	The paradigm is punitive and removes the offender.
Customary sanctions are used to restore the victim–offender relationship.	Penalties are prescribed by and for the state.
Offender is given reparative obligations to victims and community.	Rights of the accused are defended, especially against self-incrimination.
	Society is vindicated.

Source: Melton, A.P. 1998. *Indigenous Justice Systems and Tribal Society*. Washington, DC: National Institute of Justice.

Ross (1994:262) has identified two essential features of Aboriginal justice systems:

1. A **dispersal of decision making** among many people, as suggested by a repeated emphasis on **consensus of decision making** and a regular denunciation of such hierarchical decision-making structures as those created by the Indian Act.
2. A belief that people can neither be understood nor assisted so long as they are seen as isolated individuals. People must be seen as participants in a broad **web of relationships**.

According to Ross it is important to see justice **relationally**, and he notes that Aboriginal justice programs recognize three relational goals:

- having offenders . . . understand, on an emotional level, the relational damage that their crimes have created in others;
- looking at the relational disharmonies in the offender's life that spawned the crime; and
- searching for ways to move both parties out of the relational disfigurement that has bound them together . . . (Ross 2014:20–21).

A number of key components of Aboriginal justice systems have been recognized. One is **healing**, which allows the spiritual needs of the individual to be addressed. Healing refers to "a means of reconciling wrongs within a person or a community" (Proulx 2003:35). According to Waldrum (2008:6), healing involves an individual's desire to be accepted back into the "web of relationships" and "is ultimately about the reparation of damaged and disordered social relations." Healing and the use of specific Indigenous-based cultural practices lead to wellness, which involves "restoring connection to the original pattern of relationships to others, including spiritual family and community" (Dumont and Hopkins, in Ross 2014:204). The other component is referred to as **cultural imperatives**. According to Clare Brant, a Mohawk psychiatrist, these consist of four major rules in the area of conflict suppression that maintain harmony in the group. Together, they form the very basis of Aboriginal community life. The four rules (Hamilton and Sinclair 1991) are these:

1. The **ethic of non-interference**—that is, the promotion of "positive interpersonal relationships by discouraging coercion of any kind, be it physical, verbal, or psychological."
2. The **rule of non-competitiveness**, which acts to eliminate internal group conflict by "averting intragroup rivalry."
3. **Emotional restraint**, which controls those emotional responses that may disrupt the group.
4. **Sharing**, which means that those who are rich give away much of their wealth to ensure the survival of the group.

Much diversity underlies these general characteristics. Green (1998), who studied Aboriginal communities throughout Saskatchewan and Manitoba, found four approaches in use, all of which involved community participation. These included **sentencing circles**, an **Elders' or community sentencing panel**, a **sentence advisory committee**, and a **community mediation committee**. Both the circle and mediation are important elements in these practices, as they represent a more egalitarian approach, one that reflects the communal nature of the group. A variety of offences were heard by these groups. Some heard cases for which the period of incarceration is less than two years; others dealt with more serious offences, such as sexual assault. All of these different approaches incorporated certain features of Aboriginal practices, including spirituality, grassroots consultations, community consensus, and sharing (ibid.:134).

Ross (1994), discussing the operation of different Aboriginal justice systems, found they utilized various approaches when dealing with offenders. The Hollow Water First Nation (see *Investigating: Hollow Water Community Holistic Circle Healing and Sexual Abuse*), located in eastern Manitoba, developed its justice system by requesting that some of the practices of the Western legal system be "modified to accommodate . . . what they wanted to continue doing on their own" (ibid.:248). In comparison, the Sandy Lake and Attawapiskat communities (both located in northern Ontario) requested that they be "granted roles within the Western legal system" in order to cooperate with selected functionaries of the Western legal system.

The Sandy Lake and Attawapiskat justice systems focus on integrating traditional Aboriginal values into the Western legal system by placing Aboriginal people in selected advisory roles. At Sandy Lake, the emphasis is on involvement not in the trial process but rather at the time of sentencing. A panel of Elders acts together with a provincial court judge or justice of the peace to deliver the sentence. Recommended sentences usually involve some interaction with the community, such as restitution and community service. Offenders who do not fulfill their obligation are "banished" to the Western legal system, where they are subject to incarceration.

At Attawapiskat, Ross found the Elders playing a different role during the sentencing of offenders. They hear most of the cases by themselves within a community court, complete with its own summonses and subpoenas. Charges are laid in provincial court, but are stayed; they can be reactivated within a year if the offender fails to follow the sentence of the Elders' court. The cases the Elders' court tries would not normally involve a period of incarceration. As in Sandy Lake, most of the sentences involve some form of community work.

The first Aboriginal court system in Canada opened in October 2000 on the Tsuu T'ina Nation, near Calgary. Referred to as "the first comprehensive justice system in Canada, it encompasses the desire of the Tsuu T'ina people to address the glaring problems affecting First Nations people within Canadian criminal justice" (Bryant 2002:16). Known as the **Peacemaker Court**, it consists of a First Nations judge and a Peacemaker program and controls its own administration. The court blends Tsuu T'ina cultural traditions with various components of the provincial court system (Mildon 2001). Since then, other Aboriginal courts have been created in Canada, for example, the Cree-Speaking Court and Dene-Speaking Court in northern Saskatchewan; the Gladue (Aboriginal Persons) Court in Toronto; the First Nations Court in New Westminster, B.C.; and Vancouver Aboriginal Transformative Justice Services in Vancouver.

The Tsuu T'ina court works in much the same way as the Alberta provincial court system. It has jurisdiction over summary conviction offences and over hybrid offences elected to be tried as summary conviction offences. Before any trial, however, all sessions begin with a Peacemaker (who has reviewed each case and whose role is in ways similar to that of the Crown prosecutor). The Peacemaker reviews cases and requests that suitable ones be transferred to the Peacemaker program. If the Crown prosecutor feels that the case should be held in a regular court, the outcome is decided by the First Nations judge. The court is set up in a circular arrangement, and its protocols reflect Tsuu T'ina traditions. Peacemaking is an integral component of the court process (Mandamin et al. 2003). The mandate of the Peacemaker program, which is modelled on

Investigating: Hollow Water Community Holistic Circle Healing and Sexual Abuse

The Hollow Water First Nation operates a program dealing with sexual abuse in the four communities surrounding Hollow Water, Manitoba. It is formally known as the Community Holistic Circle Healing Program (CHCH), and combines fundamental principles of Anishnawbe spirituality with a program designed to heal those individuals involved in the cycle of abuse and conflict. This system developed from the need to find a concrete solution to the community problem of sexual abuse. Studies in these four communities revealed that a significant number of people living in them had been sexually abused as children and were now themselves sexually abusing children (Royal Commission on Aboriginal Peoples 1996). In the past, when sexual abuse was detected, the police were called to arrest the individual, with the case heard in a court located outside of the community. Offenders who were found guilty were incarcerated in the provincial or federal correctional system. However, when they had completed their sentence, many of the offenders returned to Hollow Water and the surrounding communities and continued to engage in sexual abuse. As a result, a number of community members met during the mid-1980s and decided to set up a program to heal sexual abusers in a way that would keep both the offenders and their victims within the local communities.

According to the protocol of this justice system, disclosure about sexual abuse is first made to a community team rather than to the police. This community team consists of volunteers, mostly women, including a child protection worker, a community health representative, the nurse-in-charge, and representatives from the local school division and community churches, as well as the local detachment of the RCMP. Criminal charges are laid as quickly as possible after the act is disclosed. The alleged offender is then given a choice: proceed through the outside criminal justice system or proceed with the healing support of the team. Either way, the offender is ultimately sentenced in a court of law. Sentencing is delayed, however, if the individual decides to take part in the healing process.

There are four components to the CHCH. First, it brings together all of the resources in the community. It is available to any community member who is prepared to take full responsibility for his or her actions in the sexual victimization of another person. All members of the community participate in the healing process. Second, the CHCH is holistic—that is, it attempts to deal with all parties involved, including the victim, the victimizer, the families, and the community, as well as all aspects of the imbalance (physical, emotional, and spiritual). Third, the CHCH is a circle. This is the strength of tradition. In the circle everyone is equal and all similarities and differences are accepted. Within the circle, the power of one becomes the power of all. Finally, the CHCH is spontaneity from within, and all members follow their hearts. The CHCH uses principles that the Elders say would have been used in the past to deal with such issues. The traditional way was for the community to bring the issue out into the open; to protect the victim in such a way as to minimally disrupt the family and community functioning; to hold the person accountable for his or her behaviour; and to provide an opportunity for balance to be restored to all parties (Community Holistic Circle Healing 1997).

To be accepted into the healing program, an alleged abuser must accept full responsibility for their actions and enter a guilty plea as soon as possible. The abuser then enters a program that involves 13 different steps "from the initial disclosure to the creation of a healing contract." An individual who passes them then proceeds to the cleansing ceremony (Ross 1994:244). This process entails a painful stripping away of all the defences of the abuser over a long period of time; the rebuilding of the individual can then begin. Each case is seen as unique and is handled accordingly. Incarceration (as long as it includes input from the community) can be used as a part of this process, but only in those cases where the prognosis for healing is not good.

When the accused appears in court for sentencing, the team presents a report to the judge about the abuser's sincerity of effort and how much work, if any, still needs to be done. A Western court would sentence the offender; in sharp contrast, the healing circle fiercely rejects any recommendation of incarceration. Between 1986 and 1995, only five offenders selected to be tried by the Western courts; 48 others chose to enter the CHCH program (Moon 1995). An evaluation released in 2001 reported that since the beginning of the program, only 2 of the 107 participating offenders had recidivated (Couture et al. 2001).

the Navajo Peacemakers approach, is "to resolve problems, investigate and discover the root causes of the behaviour which has translated into criminal activity or disharmony in the community or among families" (Bryant 2002:17). The Peacemaking process focuses on community harmony and restorative justice. If this approach is successful, the Crown prosecutor withdraws the charges laid against the accused.

Restorative Justice

Restorative justice is another significant new development in the philosophy of crime control. This approach posits that an offender's conscience (i.e., internalized norms) and significant others (friends, family, and so on) can be incorporated into deterrence and serve as potential sources of punishment. Ideally, it attempts to **restore or repair relations** between offenders, victims, and the community. Supporters of this approach believe that criminal behaviour can be reduced by decreasing the expected utility of criminal activity. They argue that deterrence doesn't need to be restricted to legal sanctions; it can also come about when people refrain from acting on the basis of fear or of negative consequences such as **shame** (Grasmick and Bursik 1990).

Restorative justice provides a different way to achieve justice. The way in which our criminal justice system operates is "all about accountability to the state, but not to other members of the community . . . the state is not able to meet the needs of the community and the victim" (Morrison, in Benedict 2014). The Supreme Court of Canada has defined restorative justice as an attempt to remedy "the adverse effects of crime in a manner that addresses the needs of all parties involved. This is accomplished, in part, through rehabilitation of the offender, reparations to the victim and to the community, and the promotion of a sense of responsibility in the offender and acknowledgement of the harm done to victims and the community" (*R. v. Proulx* 2000).

History

In his theory of restorative justice, Braithwaite (1989) develops what he calls **reintegrative shaming**, a system of justice that is based on the idea that it is better to try to shame some offenders than to try to punish them within the formal criminal justice system. There are two types of shaming—reintegrative and disintegrative. **Disintegrative shaming** stigmatizes and excludes individuals, creating a "class of outcasts" (Braithwaite 1989:55). Reintegrative shaming, while first evoking community disapproval, attempts to "reintegrate the offender back into the community of law-abiding or respectable citizens through words or gestures of forgiveness or ceremonies to decertify the offender as deviant" (Braithwaite 1989:100–101). The criminal justice system stigmatizes people and turns offenders into outcasts; in this way it severs their ties to society and actually increases criminal behaviour. The offender is labelled as evil, and in this way *criminal* becomes the individual's **master status** trait. In contrast, shaming is "disapproval dispensed within an ongoing relationship with the offender based on respect" (Braithwaite 1993:1). This process involves victims and significant others confronting the offender in an attempt to moralize the individual and explain the harm the behaviour in question has caused. Disapproval of the offender's actions is counteracted by the community's efforts to build a moral conscience and strengthen social bonds (Makkai and Braithwaite 1994).

The key to reintegrative shaming, then, is to change perceptions of the offender. Instead of seeing the offender as someone to be punished (e.g., through incarceration), an attempt is made to reintegrate offenders by holding a "shaming" ceremony in which offenders realize the pain they have brought to the victim, the community, and society. Shaming is more likely to be reintegrative and successful when a high degree of **interdependence** exists between victim and offender, such as within a family, a group of relatives, or the community of which the offender is a member.

Restorative justice is a new approach to justice in North America. Its history is found in other nations, particularly Japan. Since the early 1950s, Western social scientists have been fascinated by the high level of social order—defined as the extent of citizens' compliance to important social norms—found in Japan. This compliance translates into a higher degree of social order and lower crime rates. Some (e.g., Befu 1990; Smith 1983) argue that the phenomenon is due to the religious ideals associated with Confucianism, an idea traditionally accepted by most Western social scientists. However, other Confucian nations have high levels of social disorder. Why, then, is Japan different?

Braithwaite (1989) points out that when someone is shamed in Japan, that shame is shared by the collectivity (e.g., family, friends, school, and the workplace) to which the individual belongs. In addition, the criminal justice authorities in Japan, notably the police, work with the offender and the victim to develop alternatives to formal punishment. According to Braithwaite, one of the powerful aspects of shaming is that social control is diverted back to the family, the community, and the social environment of the offender.

Hechter and Kanazawa (1993) believe that the answer lies in Japan's high rate of social conformity—higher than that found in either Canada or the United States. They explain this high rate of conformity on the basis of three principles of social control. The first principle is that of dependence, defined as the extent to which a group is the most important source of reward. Individuals conform more to group norms the more they are dependent on the group. The second factor involves visibility—the idea that behaviour that is easily observed and monitored by

CP Photo/AP Photo/John Bazemore

In 2003, NHL player Dany Heatley was charged with first degree vehicular homicide (which could have carried a prison sentence of 2 to 15 years if convicted) for a speeding accident that led to the death of his friend and teammate Dan Snyder. Mr. Heatley did not go to jail, as Dan Snyder's family chose to forgive him. Mr. Snyder's family and other people involved in restorative justice were able to persuade the judge not to send Mr. Heatley to jail as they favoured more constructive options.

the group is more likely to conform to group norms. The final factor involves how strongly norms are upheld by the group. According to Hechter and Kanazawa, the greater that strength, the greater the social order and the lower the crime rate.

Restorative Justice Sanctions

Restorative justice sanctions are developed to represent the interests of the victim, the public, and the community. The sanctions employed by restorative justice are **informal** as they are essentially alternatives to incarceration and generally involve sanctions served in the community or conveying to the community the decision of the court. The purpose of these sanctions is to make the offender aware of the moral wrong they have committed and to indicate that no more such actions are expected. There are two main types of objectives within restorative justice: reparations and reintegrative shaming. **Reparation** refers to those actions offenders have to undertake in order to "**repair the harm.**" This involves offenders recognizing and acknowledging the harm they have caused. It may lead the offender to directly compensate the victim, or to become involved in some form of community service. The purpose of reparations is to "address the full impact of crime on the victim . . . and to identify a way in which the offender can do something positive for them. Realization of the harm caused and the meaning of positive amends may also facilitate the social re-integration of the offender" (Sumner 2006:352).

Reintegrative shaming sanctions attempt to avoid **stigmatizing** the offender. The preferred approach is to shame the offender in order to have them accept what they have done wrong and subsequently be successfully reintegrated back into society. According to Karp (1998), three types of **shaming sanctions** are currently practised in North America. The first type (and the most common) is referred to as **public exposure sanctions**. The purpose of such sanctions is to bring the attention of the community and other parties to the offence, the offender, and the victim. The objective is to belittle the crime and therefore shame the offender.

Another shaming sanction involves **debasement penalties**. These typically involve shaming through embarrassment or humiliation. Usually the offender agrees to accept a penalty that compels reflection on the feelings that the victim may have experienced as a result of the offence. The third type of sanctions, **apology penalties**, typically has the offender writing an apology or making a public statement about the offence and how wrong it was to commit it. To date, evaluation studies have found that most of these agreements have been successfully completed. Bonta et al. (2006), on the basis of their analysis of 39 studies investigating the impact on recidivism of restorative justice interventions, concluded that (1) the effects of such interventions are small but significant, (2) the most significant reductions in reoffending occur when they are conducted in a non-coercive environment, and (3) restorative justice sanctions are more effective with low-risk offenders. Sherman and Strang (2007:8) take issue with the last point raised by Bonta et al. (2006), stating that their review of studies leads them to conclude that restorative justice "seems to reduce crime more effectively with more rather than less serious crimes."

The Operations of a Restorative Justice–Based Criminal Justice System

The focus of restorative justice is not on determining guilt and punishment but rather on addressing a harm. This approach provides an alternative to the traditional adversarial system.

Both the police and the courts operate in order to "restore" individuals to become law-abiding citizens. Only certain criminal acts are to be considered for processing in a shaming context, most commonly non-serious property crimes and minor forms of violent crime. One of the most common programs using restorative justice processes is **conferencing**. In this approach, certain criminal justice personnel, such as a police officer or a court worker, recommend that a conference take place and start the process of diverting the case to a trained facilitator. The facilitator then arranges a conference that involves the offender and the victim. A key component of the conference is the voluntary involvement of both the victim and the offender. In addition, a number of other individuals can be recognized as **stakeholders**, such as family members or close friends as well as community members. All stakeholders are able to have input to the decision about the appropriate way to repair the harm.

Most restorative justice approaches take the form of a diversion program that occurs prior to any criminal charge being laid against the alleged offender. If an agreement cannot be reached within a specified time, a criminal charge may be laid and the case heard in a criminal court. Certain restorative justice programs operate a bit differently, in that they start after a criminal charge is laid but before the case is heard in criminal court. Some restorative justice programs may not start until a finding of guilt is made; others don't start until a judge sends an offender to a program as part of his or her sentence. Latimer et al. (2001) have summarized the four entry points to restorative justice programs within our criminal justice system:

- Police (pre-charge)
- Crown (post-charge and pre-conviction)
- Courts (post-conviction and pre-sentence)
- Corrections (post-sentence and pre-reintegration)

Offenders can be referred to a restorative justice program at any one of these entry points, but the most common approach in Canada is for the police to make the decision. There are some exceptions to this approach: for example, in Manitoba, the Restorative Justice Act allows Crown prosecutors to make referrals to local restorative justice programs in order to divert certain offenders out of the court system.

Unlike Aboriginal justice systems, restorative justice programs are not an alternative to the current criminal justice system; rather, these programs are integrated into the current system. According to Latimer and Kleinknecht (2000:7), the "more serious the case, the more likely the case will be referred to a restorative justice program later in the process."

To participate in a restorative justice program, offenders have to accept responsibility for their actions. An important part of the shaming process involves the recognition of the community, so supporters of both the victim and the offender are invited to take part in the shaming process as well as serve as a social support mechanism. Professionals and law enforcement officials who have been involved or have assisted either party may also be invited. While 10 to 12 participants is the norm, 40 or more individuals may attend a conference. This group is expected to arrive at a consensus on the outcome of the case. In theory, there can be several benefits to using restorative justice programs in our criminal justice system. Victims receive the chance to participate in the system; normally they would not be allowed to take an active role. Offenders can find these programs "therapeutic" as they take responsibility for their actions and repair the harm their actions have caused. For members of the community, restorative justice programs can humanize the criminal justice system by giving them a voice in it. Latimer and Kleinknecht (ibid.:6) point out that restorative justice can be "an empowering experience" for all participants (see *Investigating: Restorative Justice and Sexual Violence*).

Goals of restorative justice conferences include **accountability**, **prevention**, and **healing**. The benefits of this approach are that it recognizes a larger group of people as victims, involves a wider group of participants than is normally the case, and acknowledges the importance of the family in the offender's life (Umbreit and Stacey 1996). At the end of the meeting a consensus is reached on the best way to deal with the harm, and a resolution document is signed by all participants.

Investigating: Restorative Justice and Sexual Violence

Some researchers have explored the possibility of using restorative justice to reduce the incidence of family violence. To date, there is more support for using restorative justice in the area of minor property crimes, not violent crime. However, a number of researchers have stated that restorative justice can benefit the adult victims of violent crimes. These benefits include social acknowledgment and support, a sense of power and control over their lives, the opportunity to present their story about what happened, and not having to directly confront the perpetrator (Herman 2005). Others (e.g., Koss 2006) believe restorative justice better serves victims' justice needs, such as having input into the resolution of the violation, receiving answers to questions, observing offender remorse, and experiencing a justice process that counteracts victim isolation.

Daly and Stubbs (2007:160) point out that although considerable debate exists on whether restorative justice should be used for partner, sexual, or family violence, "the empirical evidence is sparse." This is because many restorative justice programs rule ineligible or severely limit the number of cases involving sexual violence. Daly (2006), in her study of about 400 sexual violence cases finalized in court, by conference or caution, concluded that restorative justice conferences are a better option for victims as there is an admission to the offence and

Continued on next page

Investigating: Restorative Justice and Sexual Violence (*Continued*)

a penalty of some sort. Studies of a restorative justice approach to family violence in Newfoundland reported a significant reduction in child abuse and neglect as well as in the abuse of mothers and wives (Burford and Pennell 1998; Pennell and Burford 1995, 2000). The goal of this study was to test within different cultural contexts the ability of restorative justice programs to eliminate or reduce violence against child and adult family members as well as to promote their well-being. Thirty-two families participated in this program, and a total of 472 individuals (384 family members and 88 service providers). The program involved the following five stages:

1. The project coordinators received referrals from mandated individuals.
2. Conferences were organized by the project coordinators after consulting with family group members and involved service providers.
3. Conferences were then convened with the members of the family group as well as the service providers.
4. The referring agency personnel approved plans in terms of whether or not they met all of the areas of concern.
5. The program was then implemented. The programs typically involved services such as counselling, addiction treatment, in-home support, and child care.

The researchers, after evaluating the program and comparing the 32 families who participated with families who did not, reported that the restorative justice program protected children and adult family members while at the same time unifying family group members. There was a 50 percent reduction in all types of abuse and neglect for the 32 families involved in the study compared to the year before. In addition, the incidents among families involved in a comparison group that did not receive restorative justice programs increased markedly. The lowest success rates were found in those cases where young people were abusing their mothers.

The researchers, in an earlier study, reported that victims of family violence who participated in a restorative justice–based program had high levels of satisfaction. Ninety-four percent of family members were satisfied with the techniques used in the program; 92 percent said they were "able to say what was important"; and 92 percent said they agreed with the intervention plan that was offered to them. On the basis of all their studies, the researchers were able to conclude that their program led to a sense of shame throughout the extended families since they had not acted to protect their relations. This research suggests the power of restorative justice programs in the area of violent crime.

SUMMING UP AND LOOKING FORWARD

When people violate the law, our traditional response has been to apprehend the suspects and then process them though the criminal justice system. The basis of this belief is the idea that state intervention reduces crime. In the past few decades a number of alternatives have emerged to challenge these responses. Those who advocate alternative approaches argue that placing people into the criminal justice system makes them worse, not better.

Aboriginal justice differs in its worldview of justice compared to the Western legal system. Fundamental to Aboriginal justice is the recognition of Aboriginal traditions and cultural values. The healing of offenders is a key component of this approach, as is the recognition of cultural imperatives and relationships. Many believe that the best way for Aboriginal justice systems to operate is for Aboriginal peoples themselves to develop and have control over these systems.

Supporters of restorative justice believe that the best way to reduce crime is to decrease harm by bringing victims and offenders together in order to restore victims to their prior unharmed status. Informal processes are favoured, such as conferences in which the state acts more as a mediator. In these conferences, the actions of the offenders are shamed, and offenders are encouraged to take responsibility for their actions, express remorse, and apologize to the victim. Harm is repaired by creating a plan for how offenders will make reparations to the victims.

The next chapter deals with crime statistics and what this means for our understanding of crime in Canada. The way we respond to crime depends in part on their knowledge and interpretation of the types and extent of crime. It also provides us with a framework to inquire about the practices and policies of the various agencies of our criminal justice system and whether or not their actions deliver and achieve justice.

Review Questions:

1. How does the concept of justice differ in Aboriginal justice systems compared to mainstream Western approaches?
2. What is the importance of offender accountability in both the alternative approaches discussed in the last section? How does this approach differ from the mainstream approaches?
3. Why do you think many believe that Aboriginal-operated and -controlled systems increase justice?
4. Why do you think many believe that restorative justice systems increase justice?

Critical Issues in Canadian Criminal Justice

SHOULD INFORMATION ABOUT SEX OFFENDERS BE MADE PUBLIC?

Sex offender registries are a response by politicians to concerns voiced by community members about the risk of sex offenders residing in or visiting their area and committing sex offences. For the police, sex offender registries provide useful information about sex offenders' locations in the case of a sex crime being committed (Murphy et al. 2009). Others have pointed out that such registries may have a deterrent effect by reducing the potential of a sex offender committing a crime by having a list of their photos, names, and addresses (Cole and Petrunik 2006). The first sex offender registry in Canada was established in Ontario in 2001 and is maintained by the Ontario Provincial Police. The Ontario Sex Offender Registry (also known as "Christopher's Law") was introduced after the brutal slaying of 11-year-old Christopher Stephenson in 1988. During the 1993 inquest into the slaying, the coroner's jury recommended the creation of a national registry for convicted sex offenders. The Ontario registry compiled the names of those individuals convicted of sexual assault, child molestation, and other sex offences. These registries were established owing largely to public concern about the exploitation, assault, and murder of children by sex offenders. The Ontario registry requires all those convicted of a sex offence to register with the local police within 15 days of moving into a community; this enables the police to access the names and addresses of convicted sex offenders released into the community. Failure to register can result in fines of up to $25,000 and/or a jail term of up to one year, or both, for a first offence. In its first 12 months, the Ontario registry placed more than 5,000 names on its list; by March 31, 2011, there were 13,900 registered offenders. In 2008, the Ontario Court of Appeal upheld the constitutionality of the Ontario sex offender registration legislation (*R. v. Dyck* [2008]).

The federal government has passed three laws to help the police monitor convicted sex offenders who had been released into the community. In 1994, the National Screening System was introduced; this allows volunteer and other community organizations to access the criminal records of applicants for positions of trust with children and vulnerable adults. The second piece of legislation, Bill C-7, established a special flagging system within the Canadian Police Information Centre for those offenders who had been pardoned of offences against children and vulnerable adults. Both of these laws were quickly criticized. According to an OPP spokesperson, both lacked a search capability: "Without a name of the offender you can't do anything" (Elliott 2001). Another criticism was that the system did not force offenders to report a change of address. Not until February 2002 did the federal Solicitor General announce—after two years of intense pressure from federal opposition parties, provincial governments, and public organizations—that the federal government would introduce a national registry system. The new national system would require all convicted sex offenders to register their new addresses with local law enforcement officials when they move, along with other information such as a name change. This system would also allow police investigators to search by geographical area, such as postal code, so that when a sex crime was committed they would be able to determine quickly whether anyone who had been convicted of a similar offence was living in that area (Clark 2002).

The national Sex Offender Information Registration Act (Bill C-16) came into force on December 15, 2004. The legislation states that any individual convicted of a designated sexual offence may be ordered by the court to register with the registry within 15 days of conviction and/or after release from prison. Pertinent information such as address and telephone number, past offences, alias(es), and identifying marks are to be included in the national database. In addition, persons convicted of any designated sex offence are required to reregister or notify the provincial or territorial registration centre any time they change their address or their name. Persons convicted of a sexual offence are required to remain registered for periods of 10 years, 20 years, or life depending on the maximum length of the sentence for their crime.

The third piece of legislation, Bill S-2 (Protecting Victims from Sex Offenders Act) received Royal Assent in December 2010 and came into force in April 2011. It included the following:

- Convicted sex offenders are automatically included in the Sex Offender Registry.
- Convicted sex offenders are automatically included in the DNA Data Bank.
- Authorities can include in the registry those returning to Canada after being convicted of a sex offence outside the country.
- The registry contains information regarding the offender's vehicle(s), including company vehicles—licence plate, make, model, body type, year of manufacture, and colour.
- The registry contains information on how offenders committed their crimes (method of operation) to help police investigate subsequent cases.

The National Sex Offender Registry is retrospective—that is, it includes the names of offenders convicted

Continued on next page

of sex offences who were incarcerated, on parole, on probation, or under another form of sentence when the law came into force. As of March 31, 2011, there were 26,548 offenders registered federally. In Canada, the National Sex Offender Registry is not yet public, while certain information contained in the Ontario Sex Offender Registry is now public. The issue of allowing public access to these registries has occasionally been raised. During the 2011 Ontario provincial election, the leader of the provincial Progressive Conservative party pledged to allow the public to see online the locations of sex offenders living in their communities and place GPS tracking devices on the ankles of registered sex offenders. In 2014, the Supreme Court ruled that the provisions within the Ontario Sex Offender Registry allowing the provincial government to keep the names of all registered sex offenders private will not be strictly protected (*Ontario [Community Safety and Correctional Services] v. Ontario [Information and Privacy Commissioner*] [2014]). While the Supreme Court decision held that the names and addresses of sex offenders in Ontario are not to be identified, other limited information can be accessed using the Freedom of Information and Protection of Privacy Act. After a six-year court battle initiated by Global News, Ontario's corrections ministry released the numbers of registered sex offenders in the province (based on 2008 data) and their locations per the first three digits of postal codes.

A national public sex offender registry may soon be a reality in Canada. In February 2014, the federal government introduced new legislation (Tougher Penalties for Sexual Predators Act) that included proposals to share information on certain sex offenders with the United States and to establish a publicly accessible database of high-risk child sex offenders who have been the subject of a public notification in a province or territory.

Individuals who want public access to information pertaining about sex offenders usually point to the United States, where a number of state jurisdictions provide such information online. Researchers have studied the effects of such a policy, with most concluding no significant changes in the rates of sex offences in terms of the compliance and recidivism rates of offenders. In Ontario, there was a 97 percent compliance rate among sex offenders prior to the Supreme Court decision, whereas in those jurisdictions in the United States in which sex offenders are identified by their address, there is a 60 percent compliance rate. In their study of adult males registered on the Ontario Sex Offender Registry, the National Sex Offender registry, or both, Murphy and Fedoroff (2013) report that while 7 of the 21 respondents said they would be more likely to be deterred from reoffending if the registries were made public, the other 14 said they would be more likely to recidivate. In the United States, Barnoski (2007) reported that sex offenders who had gone "underground" were more than twice as likely to recidivate as those who complied with the Sex Offender Registry requirements. Other researchers point out that while it may be able to detect the deterrent effects of sex offender registries, they do give victims and concerned citizens a clear message that sexual victimization is important to lawmakers and politicians. As such, the importance of sex offender registries is found not in their instrumental effects, such as lower recidivism rates, but rather in their symbolic effects (Sample and Kadleck 2008).

Various provinces in Canada (e.g., Manitoba and Alberta) have allowed some degree of public disclosure to be released concerning offenders considered to be high risk to reoffend with a sexual offence. Manitoba introduced a community notification policy in 1995, when it created the Community Notification Advisory Committee (CNAC) to review cases of convicted sex offenders considered to be at high risk to reoffend (Figure 3.4). There are a number of options available to the CNAC to inform the public, including full public notification (a provincewide warning) and may include a photograph and physical description of the offender). In 2002, the Alberta government allowed the public to access information on the Internet about high-risk offenders. The information on the website includes the offender's name, a photograph, their offence, and the area where they were released or live. The Alberta legislation also includes prohibition orders (under s.161 of the Criminal Code) that restrict designated individuals from residing in certain geographical areas.

Questions

1. Do you think that publishing limited geographical information identifying the general areas where sex offenders live achieves justice?
2. Do you think that publishing limited geographical information identifying the general areas where sex offenders live reduces the risk of recidivism?
3. What are some of the benefits of publishing limited geographical information identifying the general areas where sex offenders live?
4. What are some of the limits of publishing limited geographical information identifying the general areas where sex offenders live?

Critical Issues in Canadian Criminal Justice (*Continued*)

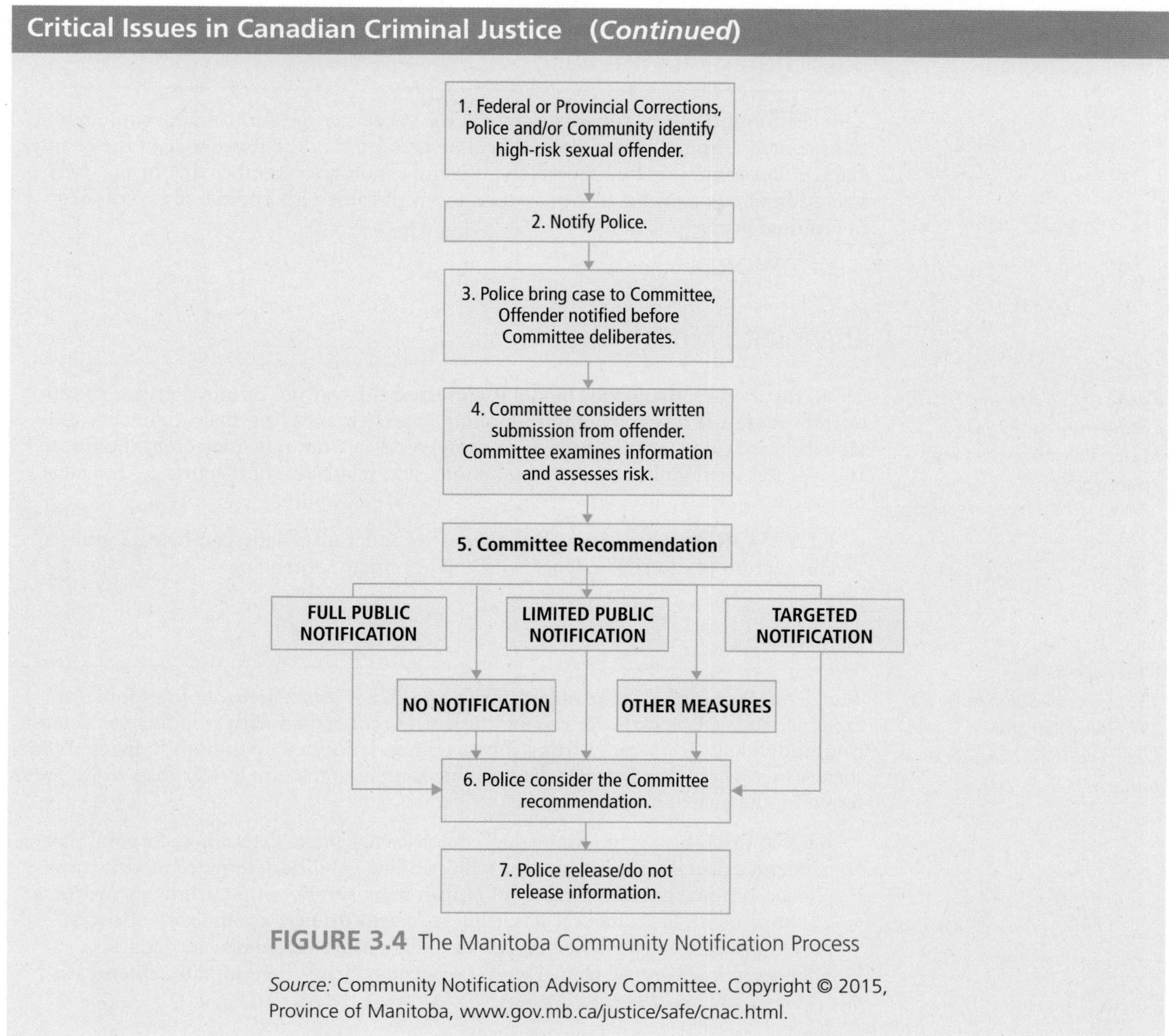

FIGURE 3.4 The Manitoba Community Notification Process

Source: Community Notification Advisory Committee. Copyright © 2015, Province of Manitoba, www.gov.mb.ca/justice/safe/cnac.html.

SUMMARY

What Is the Extent and Response to Sexual Offending in Canada?

This section overviews the extent of sexual offending in Canada and, in part, the response of our criminal justice system. It is important to consider all victims of sexual offending: children, youths, and adults. In addition, the rates of recidivism are outlined.

KEY WORD: moral panic

Achieving Justice: Crime Control Philosophy and Criminal Justice Policy

This section introduces the way in which the various crime control philosophies and their related criminal justice policies will be presented in the remainder of the chapter. Each philosophy is treated separately; it is important to remember that in the daily operation of our criminal justice system, many of these philosophies are combined in criminal justice policies.

KEY WORD: bifurcation

The Justice Model

History (p. 79)
The Criminal Sanction (p. 79)
The Operations of a Justice Model–Based Criminal Justice System (p. 81)

Of all the models, the justice model is closest to the way our criminal justice system operates today. It takes a backward looking approach, meaning that it punishes individuals based on what they have done as opposed to what they may do in the future. It advocates legal guilt, alternative sanctions, and relatively short sentences for most offenders.

KEY WORDS: proportionality, alternative sanctions, factual guilt, legal guilt, elimination of discretion, legal rights, determinate sentencing

Deterrence

History (p. 82)
The Criminal Sanction (p. 83)
The Operations of a Deterrence-Based Criminal Justice System (p. 84)

The deterrence model is the oldest of the four major crime control philosophies in existence today. It is forward looking in that it is concerned with stopping (or deterring) individuals from committing future crimes. It focuses upon both individuals and society as a whole. It advocates determinate sentences that are longer than those preferred by the justice model.

KEY WORDS: specific (individual) deterrence, general deterrence, corporal punishment, carceral punishment, free will, criminal liability, deterrence model, compliance, rational choice, certainty of punishment, severity of punishment, swiftness of punishment, instrumental acts, expressive acts, primary compulsory offences, presumptive primary offences, listed secondary offences, generic secondary offences, crime control, factual guilt, proactive policing, determinate sentences

Selective Incapacitation

History (p. 86)
The Criminal Sanction (p. 87)
The Operations of a Selective Incapacitation–Based Criminal Justice System (p. 90)

The selective incapacitation model is an outgrowth of the deterrence model. Instead of focusing upon all offenders, it is concerned with chronic or repeat offenders; that is, those individuals who repeat their illegal behaviour at a high rate and who are responsible for most serious offences. This particular philosophy supports determinate sentences and the longest and most severe punishments.

KEY WORDS: selective incapacitation, law and order ideology, chronic offenders, career offenders, repeat offenders

The Rehabilitation Approach

History (p. 90)
The Criminal Sanction (p. 91)
The Operations of a Rehabilitation-Based Criminal Justice System (p. 91)

The rehabilitation model is the only model that focuses upon the actor. It is forward looking as it attempts to change the behaviour of people so they won't commit a crime in the future. It believes in discretion as well as indeterminate sentences in order that responses to each person convicted of a crime can be individualized.

KEY WORDS: doctrine of determinism, individualized treatment, rehabilitation model, indeterminate sentence

Aboriginal and Restorative Justice Systems: An Introduction

Aboriginal Justice Systems (p. 94)
Models of Aboriginal Justice Systems (p. 95)

Aboriginal justice systems have a differing worldview of justice compared to Western approaches. It is recognized that Aboriginal approaches to justice will reduce crime and recidivism. For example, rather than focusing upon punishment, they promote healing and informal processes to better approach behaviour that is negatively impacting other individuals as well as the community. Key components of Aboriginal justice systems include spirituality, cultural imperatives, and relationships.

KEY WORDS: residential school system, informal sanctions, collective identity, community, differing world views, spiritual-based, discrimination, racism, indigenization programs, reparations, repair the injury, restore the peace and equilibrium, restoration of social harmony, dispersal of decision making, consensus of decision making, web of relationships, relational-based justice, healing, cultural imperatives, ethic of non-interference, rule of non-competiveness, emotional restraint, sharing, sentencing circles, Elders' or community sentencing panel, sentence advisory committee, community mediation committee, Peacemaker Court

Restorative Justice

History (p. 99)
Restorative Justice Sanctions (p. 100)
The Operations of a Restorative Justice–Based Criminal Justice System (p.100)

Supporters of restorative justice feel that the guiding principles of sanctions should be to decrease harm by restoring the victim to their prior unharmed status as well as the offender to the community. Victim–offender conferences are preferred over a criminal trial. It is believed that this approach will reintegrate offenders into society and will increase justice.

KEY WORDS: restore or repair relations, shaming, reintegrative shaming, disintegrative shaming, master status, interdependence, informal, reparation, repair the harm, stigma, shaming sanctions, public exposure sanctions, debasement penalties, apology penalties, conferencing, stakeholders, accountability, prevention, healing

Critical Thinking Questions

1. The differing approaches to crime control discussed in this chapter have fluctuated in their popularity over time. Why do you think this happens?
2. Numerous observers believe a trend in our criminal justice system is bifurcation. Using the first four crime control philosophies discussed in this chapter, construct a bifurcated system that you think would be the most effective in terms of preventing crime.
3. Restorative justice can take place within a variety of contexts. Do you think that if this approach to justice were more consistently used and applied in our criminal justice system we would have a better system of delivering and achieving justice?
4. A number of Aboriginal communities are now operating their own justice systems. What Aboriginal principles of justice do you think are superior to those held by Western-based legal systems?

Weblinks

In Canada, there are a number of Aboriginal justice systems in operation. Watch Jonathan Rudin discuss how the Aboriginal Transformative Justice of Toronto and other Ontario locations work within the criminal justice system (https://www.youtube.com/watch?v=Dy92vtcdBBY) (15:27).

Issues within Aboriginal communities are oftentimes resolved differently than in the Western adversarial system. One particular dispute resolution program is practised by the Hopi; a video of their program can be watched at www.nakwatsvewat.org. Click on the link to "A Way Out of Conflict" (10:14).

Court Cases

Ontario (Community Safety and Correctional Services) v. Ontario (Information and Privacy Commissioner) (2014), SCC 31.

R. v. Borden (1994), 3 S.C.R. 145.

R. v. Dyck (2008), ONCA 309.

R. v. Gladue (1999), 1 S.C.R. 688.

R. v. James (2012), MBPC 31.

R. v. Lyons (1987), 2 S.C.R. 309.

R. v. Proulx (2000), 1 S.C.R. 61.

R. v. Rodgers (2006), S.C.C. 15.

R. v. Spencer (2014), S.C.C. 43.

Suggested Readings

Cullen, F. and K. Gilbert. 1982. *Reaffirming Rehabilitation*. Cincinnati: CJ Anderson.

Elliott, E. and R. Gordon, eds. 2005. *New Directions in Restorative Justice: Issues, Practice, Evaluation*. Devon, U.K.: Willan.

Green, R. 1998. *Justice in Aboriginal Communities: Sentencing Alternatives*. Saskatoon: Purich.

Hudson, B. 1987. *Justice through Punishment: A Critique of the "Justice" Model of Corrections*. London: Macmillan.

Ross, R. 2014. *Indigenous Healing: Exploring Traditional Paths*. Toronto: Penguin.

Wilson, J.Q. 1975. *Thinking About Crime*. New York: Basic Books.

References

Aboriginal Justice Inquiry of Manitoba. 1991. *The Justice System and Aboriginal People, Volume* 1. Winnipeg: Queens's Printer.

Allen, F. 1981. *The Decline of the Rehabilitative Ideal: Penal Purpose and Social Purpose*. New Haven: Yale University Press.

American Friends Service Committee. 1971. *Struggle for Justice*. New York: Hill and Wang.

Andeneas, J. 1974. *Punishment and Deterrence*. Michigan: The University of Michigan Press.

Andrews, D. and J. Bonta. 1998. *The Psychology of Criminal Conduct*. 2nd ed. Cincinnati: Anderson.

Apospori, E. and G. Alpert. 1993. "Research Note: The Role of Differential Experience with the Criminal Justice System in Changes in Perceptions of Severity of Sanctions Over Time." *Crime and Delinquency* 39:184–94.

Ashworth, A. 2005. *Sentencing and Criminal Justice*. 4th ed. Cambridge, U.K.: Cambridge University Press.

Barnoski, R. 2007. *Sex Offender Sentencing in Washington State: Failure to Register as a Sex Offender—Revised*. Olympia, WA: Washington State Institute for Public Policy.

Beccaria, C. 1764. *On Crimes and Punishment*. Indianapolis: Bobbs-Merrill, 1978.

Befu, H. 1990. "Four Models of Japanese Society and Their Relevance to Conflict." In *Japanese Models of Conflict Resolution*, edited by S.N. Eisenstadt and E. Ben-Ari. London: Kegan Paul.

Beirne, P. and J. Messerschmidt. 1991. *Criminology*. San Diego, CA: Harcourt Brace Jovanovich.

Benedict, M. 2014. "Opening the Gate Wider Is the Aim of Restorative Justice Advocates: New Legislation Focused on Easing Burdened System, Reducing Costs." *The Lawyers Weekly*, July 4.

Boesveld, S. 2012. "Of Graham James, Sentencing and Common Sense," *National Post*, March 21, p. A1.

Bonta, J., R. Jesseman, T. Rugge, and R. Cormier. 2006. "Restorative Justice and Recidivism: Promises Made, Promises Kept?" Pp. 108–120 in *Handbook of Restorative Justice*, edited by D. Sullivan and L. Tiff. New York: Routledge.

Boyce, J., A. Cotter, and S. Perreault. 2014. *Police-Reported Crime Statistics in Canada, 2013*. Ottawa: Canadian Centre for Justice Statistics.

Braithwaite, J. 1993. "Shame and Modernity." *British Journal of Criminology* 33:1–18.

Braithwaite, J. 1989. *Crime, Shame, and Reintegration*. New York: Cambridge University Press.

Brennan, S. 2011. "Self-Reported Spousal Violence, 2009." In Statistics Canada, *Family Violence in Canada: A Statistical Profile*. Ottawa.

Brennan, S. and A. Taylor-Butts. 2008. *Sexual Assault in Canada 2004 and 2007*. Ottawa: Canadian Centre for Justice Statistics.

Bryant, M.E. 2002. "Tsuu T'ina First Nations Peacemaker Justice System." *LawNow* 26(4):16–17.

Bryant, M.E. 1999. "Sentencing Aboriginal Offenders." *LawNow* 24:20–22.

Burford, G. and J. Pennell. 1998. *Family Group Decision Making Project: Outcome Report*, vol. 1. St. John's: Memorial University.

Canadian Sentencing Commission. 1987. *Sentencing Reform: A Canadian Approach*. Ottawa: Ministry of Supply and Services Canada.

Carrigan, D.O. 1991. *Crime and Punishment in Canada: A History*. Toronto: McClelland & Stewart.

Chambliss, W.J., ed. 1969. *Crime and the Legal Process*. New York: McGraw-Hill.

Clark, C. 2002. "Ottawa to Create National Sex-Offender Registry," *The Globe and Mail*, February 14, pp. A1, A8.

Clear, T. 1995. "Correction beyond Prison Walls." *In Criminology*, 2nd ed., edited by J.F. Sheley. Belmont, CA: Wadsworth.

Cohen, S. 1985. *Visions of Social Control*. Cambridge: Polity Press.

Cole, M. and M. Petrunik. 2006. "Sex Offender Registration and Privacy Rights." *Criminal Justice Reports* 21:30–33.

Committee for the Study of Incarceration. 1975. *Doing Justice*. New York: Hill and Wang.

Community Holistic Circle Healing. 1997. *History*. Wampigoux, MA.

Cotter, A. and P. Beaupre. 2014. *Police-Reported Sexual Offences against Children and Youth in Canada, 2012*. Ottawa: Canadian Centre for Justice Statistics.

Couture, J., T. Parker, R. Couture, P., Laboucane and Native Counselling Services of Alberta. 2001. *A Cost-Benefit Analysis of Hollow Water's Community Holistic Circle Healing Process*. Ottawa: Ministry of the Solicitor General.

Cullen, F. T. and B.K. Applegate. 1997. *Offender Rehabilitation*. Aldershot: Ashgate.

Cullen, F. T. and K. Gilbert. 1982. *Reaffirming Rehabilitation*. Cincinnati, OH: Anderson.

Daly, K. 2006. "Restorative Justice and Sexual Assault: An Archival Study of Court and Conference Cases." *British Journal of Criminology* 46:334–56.

Daly, K. 1994. *Gender, Crime and Punishment*. New Haven CT: Yale University Press.

Daly, K. and B. Bouhours. 2010. "Rape and Attrition in the Legal Process: A Comparative Analysis of Five Countries." Pp. 565–650 in *Crime and Justice: A Review of Research*, Volume 39, edited by M. Tonry. Chicago: University of Chicago Press.

Daly, K. and J. Stubbs. 2007. "Feminist Theory, Feminist and Anti-Racist Politics, and Restorative Justice." In *Handbook of Restorative Justice*, edited by G. Johnstone and D.W. Van Ness. Cullompton, Devon: Willan.

Dauvergne, M. 2008. *Crime Statistics in Canada, 2007*. Ottawa: Canadian Centre for Justice Statistics.

Elliott, L. 2001. "Ontario Willing to Foot Bill for National Offender Registry," *Winnipeg Free Press*, September 7, p. B4.

Feeley, M. and J. Simon. 1992. "The New Penology: Notes on the Emerging Strategy of Corrections and Its Implications." *Criminology* 30:449–75.

Freiberg, P. 1990. "Rehabilitation Is Effective If Done Well, Studies Say." *American Psychological Association Monitor*. September.

Gendreau, P. and C. Goggin. 1996. "Principles of Effective Correctional Programming." *Forum on Corrections Research* 8:38–41.

Gibbs, J. 1975. *Crime, Punishment, and Deterrence*. New York: Elsevier.

Grasmick, H. and R. Bursik. 1990. "Conscience, Significant Others, and Rational Choice: Extending the Reference Model." *Law and Society Review* 24:837–61.

Grasmick, H. and D.E. Green. 1980. "Legal Punishment, Social Disapproval and Internalization as Inhibitors of Illegal Behavior." *Journal of Criminal Law and Criminology* 71:325–35.

Green, R.G. 1998. *Justice in Aboriginal Communities: Sentencing Alternatives*. Saskatoon: Purich.

Greenwood, P. 1982. *Selective Incapacitation*. Santa Monica, CA: Rand.

Griset, P.L. 1991. *Determinate Sentencing: The Promise and the Reality of Retributive Justice*. Albany: State University of New York Press.

Hamilton, A.C. 2001. *A Feather Not a Gavel: Working Towards Aboriginal Justice*. Winnipeg: Great Plains Publishing.

Hamilton, A.C. and C.M. Sinclair. 1991. *The Justice System and Aboriginal People: Report of the Aboriginal Justice Inquiry*, vol. 1. Winnipeg: Queen's Printer.

Hamparian, D.M., R.S. Schuster, S. Dinitz, and J.P. Conrad. 1978. *The Violent Few: A Study of Dangerous Juvenile Offenders*. Lexington, MA: Lexington Books.

Hanson, R.K., A. Gordon, A.J.R. Harris, W. Murphy, V.L. Quinsey, and M.C. Seto. 2002. "First Report of the Collaborative Outcome Data Project on the Effectiveness of Psychological Treatment of Sex Offenders." *Sexual Abuse: A Journal of Research and Treatment* 14: 169–94.

Harris, A., and R.K. Hanson. 2004. *Sex Offender Recidivism: A Simple Question.* Ottawa: Public Safety and Emergency Preparedness.

Hechter, M. and S. Kanazawa. 1993. "Group Politics and Social Order in Japan." *Journal of Theoretical Politics* 5:455–93.

Herman, M. 2005. "Justice from the Victim's Perspective." *Violence Against Women* 11:571–602.

Hudson, B. 1987. *Justice through Punishment: A Critique of the "Justice" Model of Corrections.* London: Macmillan.

Karp, D.R. 1998. "The Judicial and Judicious Use of Shame Penalties." *Crime and Delinquency* 37:449–64.

Kingston, D.A., and J.M. Bradford. 2013. "Hypersexuality and Recidivism among Sexual Offenders." *Sexual Addiction and Compulsivity* 20:91–105.

Kong, R., H. Johnson, S. Beattie, and A. Cardillo. 2003. *Sexual Offenders in Canada.* Ottawa: Canadian Centre for Justice Statistics.

Koss, M. 2006. "Restoring Rape Survivors: Justice, Advocacy, and a Call to Action." *Annals of the New York Academy of Sciences* 1087:206–34.

Kramer, J.H. and J.T. Ulmer. 1996. "Sentencing Disparity and Departures from Guidelines." *Justice Quarterly* 13:81–106.

Latimer, J., C. Dowden, and D. Muisse. 2001. *The Effectiveness of Restorative Justice Practices: A Meta-Analysis.* Ottawa: Department of Justice.

Latimer, J. and S. Kleinknecht. 2000. *The Effects of Restorative Justice Programming: A Review of the Empirical.* Ottawa: Department of Justice.

Law Reform Commission of Canada. 1991. *Aboriginal Peoples and Criminal Justice.* Ottawa: Law Reform Commission of Canada.

Logan, C. 1993. *Criminal Justice Performance: Measures for Prison.* Washington, DC: Bureau of Justice Statistics.

Makkai, T. and J. Braithwaite. 1994. "Reintegrative Shaming and Compliance with Regulatory Standards." *Criminology* 20:361–413.

Mandamin, Judge T.L.S., E. Starlight, and M. One-spot. 2003. "Peacemaking and the Tsuu T'ina Court." *Justice as Healing* 8.

Martinson, R. 1974. "What Works? Questions and Answers about Prison Reform." *Public Interest* 35:22–54.

Mathiesen, T. 2006. *Prison on Trial.* 3rd ed. Winchester, UK: Waterside Press.

Melton, A.P. 1998. *Indigenous Justice Systems and Tribal Society.* Washington, DC: National Institute of Justice.

Meyer, J.A.F. 1998. "History Repeats Itself: Restorative Justice in Native American Communities." *Journal of Contemporary Criminal Justice* 14:42–57.

Mildon, M. 2001. "First Native Court Set Up in Alberta." *LawNow* 25(5):6.

Monture-Angus, P. 1995. *Thunder in My Soul: A Mohawk Woman Speaks.* Halifax: Fernwood.

Monture-Angus, P. and M.E. Turpel. 1994. "Thinking about Aboriginal Justice: Myths and Revolution." Pp. 222–31 in *Continuing Poundmaker and Riel's Quest*, edited by R. Gosse, J.Y. Henderson, and R. Carter. Saskatoon: Purich.

Moon, P. 1995. "Natives Find Renewal in Manitoba Prison," *The Globe and Mail*, July 20, pp. A1, A4.

Morris, N. and M. Tonry. 1990. *Between Prison and Probation: Intermediate Punishments in a Rational Sentencing System.* New York: Oxford University Press.

Murphy, L. and J.P. Fedoroff. 2013. "Sexual Offenders' Views of Canadian Sex Offender Registration: A Survey of a Clinical Sample." *Canadian Journal of Behavioural Sciences* 45:238–49.

Murphy, L., J. P. Fedoroff, and M. Martineau. 2009. "Canada's Sex Offender Registries: Background, Implementation, and Social Policy Considerations." *The Canadian Journal of Human Sexuality* 18:61–72.

Nicholaichuk, T.P. 1995. "Sex Offender Treatment Priority: An Illustration of the Risk/Need Principle." *Forum on Corrections Research* 8: 30–32.

Packer, H.L. 1968. *The Limits of the Criminal Sanction*. Stanford, CA: Stanford University Press.

Pennell, J. and G. Burford. 2000. "Family Group Decision Making: Protecting Children and Women." *Child Welfare* 79:131–58.

Pennell, J. and G. Burford. 1995. *Family Group Decision Making: New Roles for "Old" Partners in Resolving Family Violence*. St. John's: Memorial University, School of Social Work.

Price, A.C. and B.G. Stitt. 1986. "Consistent Crime Control Philosophy and Policy: A Theoretical Analysis." *Criminal Justice Review* 11(2):23–30.

Pritchard, D. 2013. "Sentence for Graham Jones Upped to 5 Years on Appeal," *Winnipeg Sun*, February 15, p. 1.

Proulx, C. 2003. *Reclaiming Aboriginal Justice, Identity, and Community*. Saskatoon: Purich.

Proulx, J. and S. Perrault. 2000. *No Place for Violence: Canadian Aboriginal Alternatives*. Halifax: Fernwood.

Public Safety Canada. 2012. *Corrections and Conditional Release Statistical Overview*. Ottawa.

Rice, M.E. and G.T. Harris. 2003. "The Size and Sign of Treatment Effects in Sex Offender Therapy." *Annals of the New York Academy of Sciences* 989:428–40.

Richards, B. 1992. "Burden of Proof." *The Wall Street Journal*, December 8, pp. A1, A8.

Roach, K. 2000. "Changing Punishment at the Turn of the Century: Restorative Justice on the Rise." *Canadian Journal of Criminology* 42:249–80.

Roach, K. 1999. "Four Models of the Criminal Process." *Journal of Criminal Law and Criminology* 89: 671–716.

Roberts, J. 2005. Public Opinion and Corrections: Recent Findings in Canada. Ottawa: Correctional Service of Canada.

Ross, R. 2014. *Indigenous Healing: Exploring Traditional Paths*. Toronto: Penguin.

Ross, R. 1994. "Duelling Paradigms? Western Criminal Justice versus Aboriginal Community Healing." Pp. 241–68 in *Continuing Poundmaker and Riel's Request*, edited by R. Gosse, J. Youngblood Henderson, and R. Carter. Saskatoon: Purich.

Royal Commission on Aboriginal Peoples. 1996. *Bridging the Cultural Divide*. Ottawa: Minister of Supply and Services.

Royal Commission on Aboriginal Peoples. 1993. *Aboriginal Peoples and the Justice System*. Ottawa: Canada Communications Group.

Rubenstein, M.L., S.H. Clarke, and T.J. White. 1980. *Alaska Bans Plea Bargaining*. Washington, DC: Government Printing Office.

Rudin, J. 2005. "Aboriginal Justice and Restorative Justice." In *New Directions in Restorative Justice: Issues, Practice, Evaluation*, edited by E. Elliott and R.M. Gordon. Devon, U.K.: Willan.

Sample, L.L. and C. Kadleck. 2008. "Sex Offender Laws: Legislators' Accounts of the Need for Policy." *Criminal Justice Policy Review* 19:40–62.

Saskatchewan Indian Justice Review Committee. 1992. *Report*. Regina: Province of Saskatchewan.

Saskatchewan Metis Justice Review Committee. 1992. *Report*. Regina: Province of Saskatchewan.

Seto, M.C. 2003. "Interpreting the Treatment Performance of Sex Offenders." In *Sex Offenders in the Community*, edited by A. Matravers. Devon, U.K.: Willan.

Sherman, L.W. and R. Berk. 1984. "The Specific Deterrent Effects of Arrest for Domestic Assault." *American Sociological Review* 49:261–72.

Sherman, L. and H. Strang. 2007. *Restorative Justice: The Evidence*. London: The Smith Institute.

Smith, R.J. 1983. *Japanese Society: Individual, Self and the Social Order*. Cambridge: Cambridge University Press.

Stein, K. 2001. *Public Perceptions of Crime and Justice in Canada: A Review of Opinion Polls*. Ottawa: Department of Justice.

Sumner, M. 2006. "Reparation." In *The Sage Dictionary of Criminology*, 2nd ed., edited by E. McLaughlin and J. Muncie. London, U.K. Sage.

Taraschi, S. 1998. "Peacemaking Criminology and Aboriginal Justice Initiatives as a Revitalization of Justice." *Contemporary Justice Review* 1:103–121.

Task Force on the Criminal Justice System and Its Impact on the Indian and Metis People of Alberta. 1991. *Justice on Trial*. Edmonton: Province of Alberta.

Tewksbury, R. 2014. "Evidence of Ineffectiveness: Advancing the Argument Against Sex Offenders Residence Restrictions." *Criminology & Public Policy* 13:135–38.

Tracy, P., M.E. Wolfgang, and R.M. Figlio. 1990. *Delinquency in Two Birth Cohorts*. New York: Plenum.

Trevethan, S., N. Crutchon, and J.-P. Moore. 2002. *A Profile of Federal Offenders Designated as Dangerous Offenders or Serving Long-Term Supervision Orders*. Ottawa: Correctional Service of Canada.

Umbreit, M. and S. Stacey. 1996. "Family Group Conferencing Comes to the U.S." *Juvenile and Family Court Journal* 47:29–38.

Van Ness, D. and K. Heetderks Strong. 1997. *Restoring Justice*. Cincinnati, OH: CJ Anderson.

Visher, C. 1995. "Career Offenders and Crime Control." In *Criminology*, 2nd ed., edited by J.F. Sheley. Belmont, CA: Wadsworth.

Waldie, P. 2012. "The Shame of Graham James," *The Globe and Mail*, March 21, pp. A1, A4.

Waldrum, J., ed. 2008. *Aboriginal Healing in Canada: Studies in Therapeutic Meaning and Practice*. Ottawa: Aboriginal Healing Foundation.

Walker, S. 1994. *Sense and Nonsense about Crime*, 3rd ed. Belmont, CA: Wadsworth.

Walker, S. 1993. *Taming the System.* New York: Oxford University Press.

Wilson, J.Q. 1975. *Thinking about Crime*. New York: Basic Books.

Wolfgang, M.E., R.M. Figlio, and T. Sellin. 1972. *Delinquency in a Birth Cohort*. Chicago: University of Chicago Press.

Zedlewski, E.D. 1987. *Making Confinement Decisions*. Washington, D.C.: National Institute of Justice.

Zehr, H. 1990. *Changing Lenses: A New Focus for Criminal Justice*. Scottsdale, PA: Herald Press.

Zimring, F.E. and G. Hawkins. 1988. "The New Mathematics of Imprisonment." *Crime and Delinquency* 34:425–36.

CHAPTER

4

Crime Rates, Crime Trends, and Criminal Victimization in Canada

Learning Objectives

After completing this chapter, you should be able to:

- Understand the various ways criminal incidents are reported in Canada.
- Differentiate among violent, property, and "other" Criminal Code incidents.
- Differentiate between police-reported crime statistics and victimization statistics.
- Understand the changing patterns and extent of the major types of crime in Canada.
- Identify the strengths and shortcomings of official crime statistics.
- Understand the importance of studying the nature and impact of crimes not usually included in official crime statistics such as white-collar crime and money laundering.
- Identify the efforts made by the federal government to control cybercrime.

If the criminal justice system is to control and prevent crime, we need current and accurate information on the patterns and extent of crimes in particular locations across Canada. In order to understand the dimensions of any type of crime, accurate information about crime has to be obtained. There are, however, different measures that have been developed to collect and interpret crime statistics. One type of measure of crime statistics is referred to as **official crime statistics** (also referred to as the **institutionalist approach**), which are collected by the police and other justice officials from crimes reported to them or through interviews with individual citizens about instances in which they were victimized. Advocates of this approach believe official crime statistics constitute accurate measures about crime upon which crime policy can be based. Other types of measures have been developed because many feel that official crime statistics do not give an accurate portrayal of crimes. One of their arguments is based on the **crime funnel**—that is, the procedures found within the criminal justice system that reduce the number of people being processed at each stage—and so presents only a partial picture of criminal activity. These other approaches are referred to as **unofficial crime statistics**, since they measure crime by other means such as self-report studies (see below). Supporters of these alternative measures believe that crime statistics are *socially constructed* (see Chapter 1), which means that official crime statistics reflect responses to criminal behaviour that change over time as opposed to any objective criteria (see Exhibit 4.1).

The crime rate has decreased in Canada in recent years, and 2014 was no exception. Compared to 2013, the rate of all criminal incidents reported to the police in 2014 decreased by 5 percent, while between 2004 and 2014 the rate of crime decreased by 34 percent. All major categories of crime (violent crime, property crime, and other Criminal Code offences) declined between in the decade between 2004 and 2014. Violent crime declined by 26 percent, property crime experienced a 40 percent decrease, and other Criminal Code offences dropped by 15 percent.

Violent crime is usually the crime category that is given the most attention in our society. What is the perception of the rates of violent crime by the public—is it increasing or decreasing? In a poll conducted for the *National Post*, it was found that 54 percent of the 1,639 Canadians participating felt that violent crime was increasing, 33 percent felt

EXHIBIT 4.1 The Social Construction of Crime Statistics: Selected Elements

When people say that crime statistics are socially constructed, they are generally referring to the belief that official crime statistics are not an accurate portrayal of crime in society. Instead, they are the "outcomes of social and institutional processes" (Coleman and Moynihan 1996:16). According to social constructionists, crime statistics are not a true representation of all crimes that occurs in society (e.g., the overemphasis of street crimes and the de-emphasis of white-collar crimes). Rather, official crime statistics reflect attitudes toward certain types of behaviour that change over time. A number of factors influence the production of official crime statistics, including:

- The reasons why the behaviour in question was criminalized in the first place
- Changes over time in society's attitudes about what is acceptable and unacceptable behaviour
- Which social groups created the laws, the infraction of which is defined as criminal
- The criminalization of behaviour through a process of social perception and reaction as interpreted and applied by the various criminal justice agencies
- Police responses that vary over time with the priorities of the police operations
- Changes in the public's reporting practices

it was decreasing, and the remaining 13 percent were not sure (Edmiston, 2012). The poll also asked respondents their political affiliation, and discovered that 60 percent of federal Conservative supporters felt crime was increasing, while the corresponding figure for both Liberal and NDP supporters was 50 percent. The following sections will discuss how crime is officially measured in Canada, followed by alternative sources of collecting crime statistics.

Investigating: The Fear of Crime in Canada

As the crime rate has been declining across Canada, how have people been responding to this change? Are people becoming more confident in their safety, or are the levels of fear about crime remaining the same? A direct correspondence does not always occur between the crime rate and the fear of crime.

Fear of crime is usually measured in two ways: (1) by feelings of satisfaction with personal safety from crime, and (2) by an individual's anticipated fear or worry about becoming a victim. The 2009 General Social Survey on Victimization (GSS) asked respondents about their overall satisfaction with their own personal safety from crime as well as their level of fear of crime in three situations that focused on general feelings of security (as opposed to fear of certain types of crime): (1) being home alone at night, (2) taking public transportation at night, and (3) walking alone after dark.

In the 2009 GSS, Canadians aged 15 and over living in the 10 provinces were asked about their perceptions concerning their levels of personal safety from crime. Overall, 93 percent of Canadians indicated they held high levels of satisfaction about their personal safety, a small decrease from 94 percent in 2004. In addition, the fear of crime is not experienced by every citizen in the same way, and may differ on the basis of sex, age, and household income (Scarborough et al. 2010). In the 2009 GSS, younger Canadians were more likely than older Canadians to express satisfaction with their personal safety from crime. More specifically, 94 percent of those aged 15 to 24 indicated that they felt very or somewhat satisfied with their personal safety from crime, compared to 90 percent of those individuals aged 65 and over. Higher levels of satisfaction with safety were found among males, as well as among individuals who had household incomes of $20,000 or more, non-Aboriginals, and those who did not have an activity limitation, such as a physical or mental disability. Certain sociodemographic characteristics were found not to be associated with lower levels of satisfaction—sexual orientation, visible minority status, and immigrant status (Brennan 2011). Experiences of victimization during the previous 12 months led to less satisfaction about one's own level of personal safety. Ninety-four percent of Canadians who weren't victimized reported feeling satisfied compared to those who had been victimized once (92 percent) and those who had been victimized at least twice (87 percent). Individuals who had been the victim of a violent crime had the same level of satisfaction as those who had been the victim of a non-violent crime.

The 2009 GSS also asked respondents about their level of fear of crime in three situations that focused on general feelings of personal security (as opposed to fear of certain types of crime): (1) being home alone at night, (2) taking public transportation at night, and (3) walking alone after dark. Eighty-three percent of those who stayed at home alone in the evening indicated

Continued on next page

Investigating: The Fear of Crime in Canada (*Continued*)

that they were not worried about crime, slightly higher than the 80 percent who said the same thing in 2004. Waiting for and using public transportation alone after dark was the most fear-inducing activity of the three situations presented to the respondents. Only 58 percent of the respondents indicated that they weren't worried about becoming a victim of a crime when using public transportation alone at night, a slight increase from 2004, when 57 percent of individuals indicated that they weren't worried when in the same situation. Ninety percent of the respondents stated that they felt safe walking alone in their neighbourhood at night, the same level as in 2004.

Feelings of safety were lower among women (76 percent) than among men (90 percent). Ninety-five percent of men and 85 percent of women said they felt safe or reasonably safe when walking alone in their neighbourhood after dark. The greatest difference was found when people were waiting for public transportation: 73 percent of men compared to 42 percent of women said they weren't worried about using public transportation at night.

Official Crime Statistics

The most anticipated crime statistics are the annual national crime statistics, which are usually released to the public during the early summer. Criminologists are interested in the yearly annual crime rates as they allow them to investigate and analyze a number of issues about crime, such as how much crime occurs; whether overall crime rates are increasing or decreasing; the rate of violent crime; which crimes are committed most often; how many crimes are "cleared" (i.e., solved) by the police; and which cities have the highest and lowest crime rates. But what do these national crime statistics mean? What problems and limitations are associated with them? Can the figures be manipulated? Much of this chapter discusses the official crime reporting system in Canada. Official crime figures include police-generated crime data and data collected from victimization surveys. Self-reported criminal behaviour, another method of collecting crime data, is also discussed.

Police-Reported Crime Statistics

In 2014, just under 1.8 million Criminal Code incidents were reported to the police (excluding traffic incidents and those involving other federal statutes such as drug offences), reaching the lowest level since 1969 (see Figure 4.1). Overall, the volume of crime reported to and by the police decreased by 3 percent (or approximately 33,000 Criminal Code incidents) compared to 2013. Almost 21 percent of all offences were classified as violent crimes, property crimes accounted for 61 percent of offences, and the remaining 18 percent were classified as "other" Criminal Code offences. Together, eight offences accounted for approximately 81 percent of all reported crime in Canada during 2013: theft under $5,000

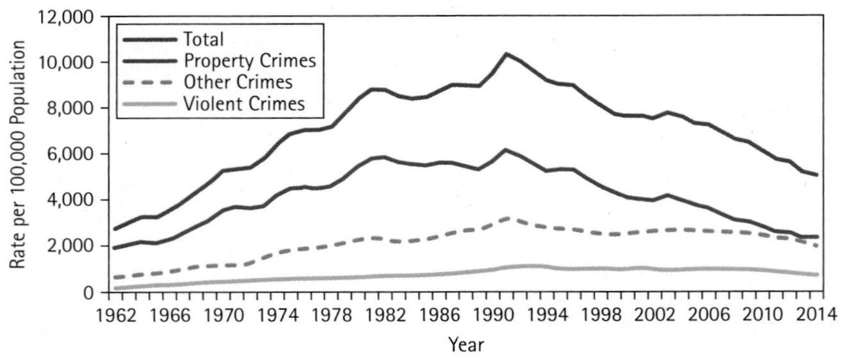

FIGURE 4.1 Police-Reported Crime Rates, Canada, 1962–2014

Source: Jillian Boyce, "Police-reported crime statistics in Canada, 2014." *Juristat* (July 22, 2015), Statistics Canada Catalogue no. 85-002-X, p. 6, http://www.statcan.gc.ca/pub/85-002-x/2015001/article/14211-eng.pdf. Reproduced and distributed on an "as is" basis with the permission of Statistics Canada.

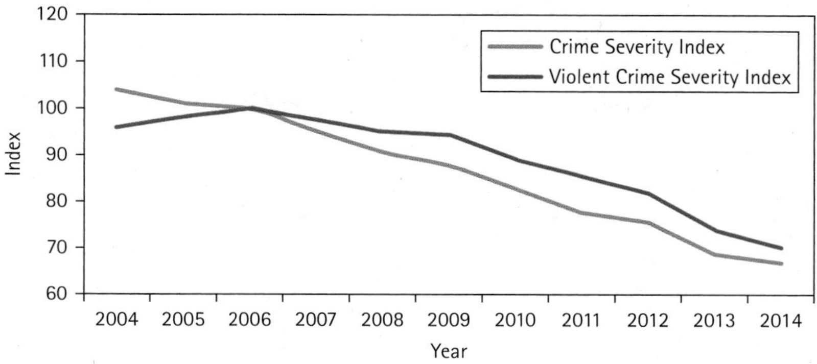

FIGURE 4.2 Police-Reported Crime Severity Indexes, Canada, 2004–14

Source: Jillian Boyce, "Police-reported crime statistics in Canada, 2014." *Juristat* (July 22, 2015), Statistics Canada Catalogue no. 85-002-X, p. 4, http://www.statcan.gc.ca/pub/85-002-x/2015001/article/14211-eng.pdf. Reproduced and distributed on an "as is" basis with the permission of Statistics Canada.

(26 percent), mischief (15 percent), administration of justice offences (9 percent), common assault or Assault – Level 1 and breaking and entering (both at 8 percent), disturbing the peace (6 percent), fraud (excluding identity fraud), and motor vehicle theft (4 percent) (Boyce 2015).

In 2008, a **Crime Severity Index** (CSI), which measures the seriousness of crime, was included for the first time to the annual crime statistics. In the CSI, each offence is assigned a weight, with the most serious offences being assigned a higher weight (see *Investigating: The Police-Reported Crime Rate and the Police-Reported Crime Severity Index*). Changes in the more serious crimes have a greater impact on the police-reported CSI compared to the police-reported crime statistics. In 2014, the CSI decreased by 3 percent compared to the previous year (see Figure 4.2).

Investigating: The Police-Reported Crime Rate and the Police-Reported Crime Severity Index

The new police-reported Crime Severity Index (PRCSI) adds to existing measures of crime—namely, the traditional police-reported crime rate (PRCR) and victimization data from the General Social Survey. The index was developed in response to a request by the police community to create a measure of crime that reflects the relative seriousness of different offences and addresses limitations of the current PRCR.

The PRCR is based upon all criminal incidents, excluding Criminal Code traffic offences, drug offences, other federal statute offences, as well as provincial statute offences. It measures changes in the volume of crime and counts each criminal incident equally. For example, one incident of homicide equals one incident of mischief. As a result, the rate is dominated by high-volume, less-serious offences. The PRCR is expressed as a rate per 100,000 population. In addition to the overall crime rate, there are three subtotals: violent, property, and other Criminal Code.

The PRCSI measures changes in the severity of crime from year to year. It takes into account not only the volume of crime but also the seriousness of crime. In the calculation of the PRCSI, each is assigned a weight derived from average sentences handed down by the criminal courts in all provinces and territories. Weights are calculated using the five most recent years of available sentencing data. More serious crimes are assigned higher weights; less-serious offences lower weights. As a result, when all crimes are included, more serious offences have a greater impact on changes in the Index.

Separate severity indexes have also been created: one for overall police-reported crime, one for violent crime including only crimes against the person, and one for non-violent crime such as property and drug offences. Drug offences are excluded from the traditional crime rate, along with federal statutes and Criminal Code traffic offences. In the PRCSI, all offences, including traffic and drug offences, are included.

Continued on next page

Investigating: The Police-Reported Crime Rate and the Police-Reported Crime Severity Index (*Continued*)

In contrast to the PRCR, which uses a rate of 100,000 population, the PRCSI is calculated by summing the weighted offences and dividing them by the population. The CSI is then standardized to a base year of "100," which is 2006. In addition to the overall CSI, both a violent CSI and a non-violent CSI have been created. In 2009, a Youth Crime Severity Index was introduced, using the same approach as described above for the CSI of adult offences.

Sources: Marnie Wallace, "Police-Reported Crime Statistics in Canada, 2008." *Juristat,* Vol. 29, no. 3, p. 7. Statistics Canada Catalogue No. 85-002-X; Mia Dauvergne and John Turner, "Police-Reported Crime Statistics in Canada, 2009." *Juristat,* Vol. 30, no. 2, p. 9; Shannon Brennan and Mia Dauvergne, "Police-Reported Crime Statistics in Canada, 2010." *Juristat,* July 2011, p. 4. Reproduced and distributed on an "as is" basis with the permission of Statistics Canada.

Violent Crime

There were approximately 369,000 violent Criminal Code violations reported to the police in 2014, a decrease of roughly 15,000 violent crimes compared to the previous year. Overall, the violent crime rate declined 5 percent in Canada in 2014 compared to 2013 (see Table 4.1). Both the volume and severity of police-reported violent crime decreased during 2014. Among the violent crimes that decreased were sexual assault (Level 3) (−22 percent), threatening or harassing phone calls and sexual assault (Level 2) (both −14 percent), robbery (−11 percent), and criminal harassment (−10 percent). Increases were recorded in three offences: extortion (+16 percent), sexual violations against children (+6 percent) and abduction (+4 percent). The rate of forcible confinement or kidnapping remained stable.

The **Violent Crime Severity Index** decreased by 5 percent in 2014, largely due to the decreases in the offence of robbery (see Table 4.2). The Violent Crime Severity Index in 2014 was 27 percent lower than it was a decade before. The severity of violent crime remained

TABLE 4.1 Police-Reported Crime Severity Indexes, Canada, 2004–14

Year	Total Crime Severity Index		Violent Crime Severity Index		Non-Violent Crime Severity Index	
	index	percent change from previous year	index	percent change from previous year	index	percent change from previous year
2004	104.1	−3	96	−2	107.2	−3
2005	101.3	−3	98.5	3	102.4	−4
2006	100	−1	100	2	100	−2
2007	95.3	−5	97.8	−2	94.3	−6
2008	90.6	−5	95.1	−3	88.9	−6
2009	87.8	−3	94.3	−1	85.3	−4
2010	82.9	−6	89.2	−5	80.5	−6
2011	77.6	−6	85.7	−4	74.5	−8
2012	75.4	−3	81.9	−5	72.9	−2
2013*	68.8	−9	73.9	−10	66.8	−8
2014	66.7	−3	70.2	−5	65.2	−2
Percent change 2004 to 2014	−36	not applicable	−27	not applicable	−39	not applicable

*revised

Note: Data on the Crime Severity Indexes are available beginning in 1998. The base index was set at 100 for 2006 for Canada.

Source: Jillian Boyce, "Police-reported crime statistics in Canada, 2014", *Juristat* (July 22, 2015), Statistics Canada Catalogue no. 85-002-X, p. 29, http://www.statcan.gc.ca/pub/85-002-x/2015001/article/14211-eng.pdf. Data from Uniform Crime Reporting Survey, Statistics Canada. Reproduced and distributed on an "as is" basis with the permission of Statistics Canada.

TABLE 4.2 Police-Reported Crime Rate, Canada, 2004–14

Year	Total Crime (Crime rate)			Violent Crime			Property Crime			Other Criminal Code Offences		
	Number	Rate	Percent change in rate from previous year	Number	Rate	Percent change in rate from previous year	Number	Rate	Percent change in rate from previous year	Number	Rate	Percent change in rate from previous year
2004	2,427,370	7,600	−2	448,514	1,404	−2	1,636,363	5,123	−3	342,493	1,072	3
2005	2,361,974	7,325	−4	447,857	1,389	−1	1,574,808	4,884	−5	339,309	1,052	−2
2006	2,359,804	7,245	−1	451,652	1,387	0	1,566,315	4,809	−2	341,837	1,050	0
2007	2,271,754	6,908	−5	445,252	1,354	−2	1,488,103	4,525	−6	338,399	1,029	−2
2008	2,204,479	6,631	−4	443,608	1,334	−1	1,415,572	4,258	−6	345,299	1,039	1
2009	2,172,809	6,461	−3	444,533	1,322	−1	1,386,184	4,122	−3	342,092	1,017	−2
2010	2,094,338	6,159	−5	439,220	1,292	−2	1,305,150	3,838	−7	349,968	1,029	1
2011	1,984,790	5,779	−6	424,338	1,236	−4	1,214,312	3,536	−8	346,140	1,008	−2
2012	1,957,227	5,632	−3	416,147	1,197	−3	1,193,600	3,434	−3	347,480	1,000	−1
2013*	1,826,431	5,195	−8	384,385	1,093	−9	1,106,509	3,148	−8	335,537	954	−5
2014	1,793,534	5,046	−3	369,359	1,039	−5	1,100,403	3096	−2	323,772	911	−5
Percent change 2004 to 2014	not applicable	−34	not applicable	not applicable	−26	not applicable	not applicable	−40	not applicable	not applicable	−15	not applicable

*revised

Note: Crime rates are based upon Criminal Code incidents, excluding traffic offences. Counts are based upon the most serious violation in the incident. One incident may involve multiple violations. Data for the rates of total, violent, property, and other crime categories are available beginning in 1962. Rates are calculated on the basis of 100,000 population. Percent changes are based on unrounded rates. Populations are based upon July 1st estimates from Statistics Canada, Demography Division.

Source: Jillian Boyce, "Police-reported crime statistics in Canada, 2014", *Juristat* (July 22, 2015), Statistics Canada Catalogue no. 85-002-X, p. 29, http://www.statcan.gc.ca/pub/85-002-x/2015001/article/14211-eng.pdf. Data from Uniform Crime Reporting Survey, Statistics Canada. Reproduced and distributed on an "as is" basis with the permission of Statistics Canada.

stable or decreased in all provinces and territories in 2014 compared to the previous year with the exception of Yukon (+50 percent), Prince Edward Island (+3 percent), and Alberta (+1 percent).

The homicide rate (which includes first and second degree murder, manslaughter, and infanticide) was the same in 2014 as it was in 2013. There were 516 homicides reported, an increase of 4 over the previous year, resulting in a homicide rate of 1.45 per 100,000 population. In both 2013 and 2014 Canada experienced its lowest homicide rate since 1966. The number of attempted murders declined in 2014, from 636 to 617. The attempted murder rate was 1.74 per 100,000 population, a 4 percent decrease compared to 2013; this is the lowest attempted murder rate in Canada since 1971 (Boyce 2015). In 2014, the police reported just under 213,000 assaults, the majority of which were classified as common assaults (assault Level 1), a decrease of just over 4 percent. The number of assaults reported to the police declined by 4 percent in 2014 compared to 2013. Police-reported robberies also declined in 2014, down 11 percent from 2013, continuing a downward trend that started in 1998. Sexual assaults experienced a decrease of just over 3 percent in 2014. Decreases were recorded in sexual assault level 1 (−4 percent) and sexual assault level 2 (−4 percent).

Property Crime

Most crimes (61 percent) reported by the police in 2014 were property crimes. Property crimes are committed with the intent to acquire property without violence or the threat of violence. The most common property crimes were theft under $5,000 (non-motor vehicle), followed by mischief, break and enter, and fraud (excluding identity fraud). These four offences accounted for just over 88 percent of all property crimes in 2014. All offences in the property crime category declined in 2014 compared to 2013 (see Table 4.1), with the exception of the offences of fraud, identity fraud, and theft of a motor vehicle. The largest rate decreases were found in arson (−6 percent), mischief and break and enter (both at −4 percent), and theft over $5,000 (non-motor vehicle), which declined by 2 percent.

Other Criminal Code

Eighteen percent of all police-reported crime in Canada during 2014 was classified as other Criminal Code offences. The total number of other Criminal Code offences in 2014 declined by 5 percent compared to 2013. The rate of all other Criminal Code offences declined in 2014, with the exception of two offences. The largest declines were recorded in prostitution (−48 percent) and counterfeiting (−10 percent). Terrorism offences and child pornography were the only offences to record an increase (+39 percent and +41 percent, respectively). The rate of weapons violations remained stable.

Factors Affecting Police-Reported Crime Rates

The crime statistics discussed above were those recorded by the police. However, the police are often **reactive** when it comes to recording crime—that is, in many instances they realize that a crime has been committed only after they have been told about it by a member of the public (see Chapter 5). A number of other factors affect police crime statistics (see *Criminal Justice Focus*). **Behavioural patterns**, such as variations in the number of individuals committing offences, as well as society's

Criminal Justice Focus

Factors Affecting Police-Reported Crime Statistics

Many factors can influence the prevalence of police-reported crime statistics:

Demographics—changes in the age structure of the population, particularly for high-risk (15–24) and low-risk (over 50) offender groups can influence crime rates.

Public reporting rates to police—changes in societal responses and perceptions of certain crimes (such as sexual assault or spousal violence) can lead to differences in reporting rates to police.

Local police policies and procedures—some police services maintain call centres to receive and record criminal incidents, while others require victims to report crimes in person. The ease of public reporting can impact whether a criminal incident becomes known to police and subsequently reported to Statistics Canada through the UCR Survey. Also, internal police records management system (RMS) and processes can impact on whether or not a criminal incident is entered into the local RMS.

Legislative changes—changes to the criminal justice system, such as the introduction of a new offence, can impact the number of police-reported criminal incidents.

Social and economic factors—various social and economic factors can influence crime statistics. For example, a study examining patterns in crime data found that shifts in inflation were associated with changes in financially motivated crime (namely robbery, break and enter, and motor vehicle theft) and that alcohol consumption and unemployment rates were correlated with homicide rates (Pottie-Bunge et al. 2005). Other studies have found an association between neighbourhood crime rates and access to socioeconomic resources (Charron 2009; Savoie 2008).

Technological change—with continuing advances in technology, opportunities for new, more complex crimes have developed.

Source: Mia Dauvergne and John Turner, "Police-reported crime statistics in Canada, 2009." *Juristat,* Vol. 30, no. 2, p. 9, Statistics Canada catalogue no. 85-002-X. Reproduced and distributed on an "as is" basis with the permission of Statistics Canada.

responses to criminal behaviour, can influence the crime rate. Moreover, crime rates can be influenced by the **age structure** of the population, particularly among the higher-risk ages (15 to 24 years) and the lower-risk ages (over 50 years) (Blonigen 2010). Other possible influences include neighbourhood crime rates and income levels as well as access to socioeconomic resources (Charron 2009; Savoie 2008). This is why researchers look for correlates of criminal behaviour; they want to understand why crime rates fluctuate over time.

Crime rates in Canada typically follow shifts in the population, although there is a bit of a **lag effect**. For example, Pottie Bunge et al. (2005) concluded that the overall crime rate was influenced by the age cohort referred to as the baby boomers. After all ages in this cohort reached 15 years of age (between 1960 and 1980), the violent and property crime rates also increased almost every year. Then the overall crime rate for property and violent crimes began to change, each following its own separate path over the next decade. Property crime rates stabilized during the 1980s as the proportion of 15- to 24-year-olds began to decline, then increased for a few years during the early 1990s, then declined again. Violent crime rates, however, increased steadily until 1993, several years following the decrease in the proportion of individuals aged 15 to 24 and 25 to 34 in Canadian society.

Pottie Bunge and colleagues (ibid.) also discovered links between certain social factors and types of crime. They reported that trends in financially motivated criminal offences, such as robbery and break and enter, were positively correlated with changes in Canada's inflation rate. This could be explained by the reduction in purchasing power for goods and services, uncertainty about the economy's future, and the resulting attractiveness of illegal criminal activity to obtain desired material goods. And while many might think that the age structure of society would have a strong impact on financially motivated crimes, this was not the case in Canada between 1962 and 2003. In fact, the researchers found that only one financially motivated crime—break and enter—was heavily influenced by the number of individuals between 15 and 24, the most criminally active age group.

The number of 15- to 24-year-olds in the population was also found to have an impact on violent crime, notably the homicide rate. The same researchers also noted two other studies that found a similar relationship between age and homicide in Canada. Leenaars and Lester (2004) noted that the proportion of the Canadian population between 15 and 24 years of age was the most significant predictor of homicide rates in Canada. Sprott and Cesaroni (2002) estimated that 14 percent of the reduction in Canadian homicide rates between 1974 and 1999 could be explained by changes in the age composition in the population.

Decreases in the public's tolerance for certain offences—such as domestic violence, child abuse, and other offences committed within the family—can lead to an increase in the number of cases reported to the police. In addition, victims' expectations of how the police will handle a complaint can increase or decrease the likelihood that they will report a crime to the police. Other factors that can influence crime rates include new laws—for example, the sexual assault laws introduced in 1983 (see Chapter 2)—or modifications to existing laws that make it easier to file a complaint and/or for the police and Crown to enforce the law; the latter can increase the number of criminal incidents reported. Changes in enforcement tactics as well as targeted operations can also have a significant impact on crime rates. Examples of offences that reflect the level of police enforcement activities as opposed to any increase or decrease in criminal activity include drug offences and prostitution (e.g., Duchesne 1997).

The Official Crime Reporting System

One of the most basic questions asked about crime in Canada, but one of the hardest to answer, is whether we know what the actual crime rate is. The question is difficult to answer as it depends on the type of crime data we are using. If those data come from the police, they represent those crimes the police are told about or discover themselves. If we use an alternative source of data, such as self-reports, ethnographic research, or victimization reports, they usually discover numerous criminal incidents that don't come to the attention of the police. By themselves, none of these sources of crime data provides an accurate view of the amount of crime; in combination, we get better accuracy, but it is no doubt still incomplete.

The **Uniform Crime Reporting (UCR) system** was launched in Canada in 1961 and continues, with some modifications, to this day. The UCR is designed to generate reliable crime statistics for use in all aspects of law enforcement. In order to ensure reliability in the reporting of crime data, it applies standard definitions to all offences. This approach eliminates regional and local variations in the definitions of offences. All police agencies are required to submit their crime statistics in accordance with the UCR definitions. Since some offences are "hybrid" (see Chapter 2), the UCR does not distinguish between indictable and summary conviction offences.

In order to classify crimes, the police use a guidebook, the Uniform Crime Reporting Manual, which contains definitions of crime as determined by Statistics Canada and the Canadian Association of Chiefs of Police (Silverman et al., 1991). Between 1961 and 1988, all police departments in Canada summarized their crime data on standardized forms on a monthly basis and forwarded those forms to Statistics Canada. Since 1982, the responsibility for collecting and reporting these data has fallen to an affiliated agency, the Canadian Centre for Justice Statistics. This organization produces the annual crime statistics as well as a bulletin known as *Juristat*. This publication, which is published numerous times a year, provides reports that offer insight into specialized areas of Canadian crime statistics as well as the operations of various aspects of the criminal justice system, such as corrections.

For its first 27 years, the UCR reported crime on the basis of aggregated statistics. This survey, known as the Aggregate UCR Survey, is still used today alongside a revised system referred to as the UCR2 (see below). The **Aggregate UCR Survey** records the number of incidents reported to the police and includes the number of reported offences, the number of actual offences (i.e., excluding those that are unfounded), the number of offences cleared by charge, the number of adults charged, the number of youths charged, and the gender of those charged. It doesn't include victim characteristics. This approach to collecting statistics has been criticized for being "less useful for analytic purposes than information based on characteristics of individual crimes" (ibid.:62).

A new system for collecting and reporting crime statistics was introduced in 1988 but wasn't fully operational until 1992. The new system—referred to as the **Incident-Based UCR Survey**, or UCR2—incorporated a key change: it collected incident-based data rather than summary data and thus allowed for better analyses of crime trends. This revised UCR system also added the following:

1. Information on victims: age, sex, victim-accused relationship, level of injury, type of weapon causing injury, and drug and/or alcohol use.
2. Information on the accused: age, sex, type of charges laid or recommended, and drug and/or alcohol use.
3. Information on the circumstances of the incident: type of violation (or crime), target of violation, types of property stolen, dollar value of property affected, dollar value of drugs confiscated, type of weapon present, date, time, and type of location of the incident (ibid.:62–63).

Another difference between the aggregate survey and UCR2 relates to the number of police departments included. For example, while the aggregate survey reflects virtually 100 percent of the total caseload of every police service, the latter has historically consisted of only a number of police services. For example, in 2005, a sample of 127 police services in nine provinces was used in the UCR2. By 2007, 153 police services in all provinces and territories were forwarding data to the UCR2, representing 94 percent of the population of Canada (Wallace et al. 2009).

At least three major steps are involved in the process of recording a crime:

1. awareness that a crime occurred;
2. reporting the crime to the police; and
3. recording of a crime by the police.

In order for a crime to be recorded in the official crime statistics, it is first necessary for someone to know that a crime has been committed. This is not always apparent, as people may not be aware that a crime has occurred. A crime typically becomes known to the police when someone reports it. At best, the police discover only a minimal number of crimes by themselves, since many victims do not report the crimes committed against them. When the police do receive a report of a criminal incident, they have to decide whether to record it as such. Sometimes they may not believe the report; even if they do believe it, they may not feel that the incident really involved any criminal activity. Even if the police do believe that a crime occurred, they may be too busy to investigate it thoroughly or to complete all the necessary paperwork, especially if the incident is not that serious. If the police do not record it as a crime, it will not be included on the official UCR system. One study (Silverman 1980) found that about 6 percent of all information informally processed by the Edmonton police was lost somewhere on its journey to the records section; the corresponding figure for the Calgary police was closer to 20 percent. Differences in the crime rates between cities can be attributed to the structure, organization, and operations of the information system that each police service maintains.

And even when the police do record the crime, a case successfully cleared by a charge is the exception rather than the rule. Generally, the **clearance rate** (which represents the proportion of all crimes that are successfully cleared) refers to criminal incidents being cleared by the laying of a charge or by some other way, such as through extrajudicial measures. Various aspects of criminal incidents can influence a police service's clearance rate. For example, criminal incidents such as minor thefts and mischief are common and can be more difficult to solve compared to serious, violent crimes. As a result, police services with a higher number of minor offences may report a lower clearance rate in their jurisdiction. As a result, a weighted clearance rate was developed to provide a more meaningful picture of crime solved by police services.

Similar to the CSI (see above), the **weighted clearance rate** assigns values to crimes according to their seriousness, with the more serious crimes being given a higher statistical weight. Since 2004, the weighted clearance rate for police services in Canada has increased each year; in 2010, it increased by 2 percent, reaching 39 percent. Among the police services in areas with populations exceeding 100,000, the highest weighted clearance rates were all found in Ontario (Durham 48 percent; Guelph, London, and York 47 percent) with the exception of the Codiac Regional Police in New Brunswick (47 percent) (Burczycka 2011).

The UCR's accuracy is often questioned. How well does it measure Canada's crime rate? For the UCR to be accurate, citizens must report criminal activity to the police, and then the police must pass this information on to the Canadian Centre for Justice Statistics. Criminologists have long been aware that this is a highly discretionary area. Citizens may not report a crime—perhaps they are afraid to do so—and because of their discretionary powers, the police themselves may not report every crime that comes to their attention. One consequence is that many criticisms have been levelled against police-generated crime statistics. The most common of these criticisms are as follows:

1. An unknown (and no doubt large) amount of crime is not reported to the police and, as a result, is not recorded in the UCR. This problem can be alleviated through the use of victimization surveys.
2. For each single series of criminal actions reported to the police, only the most serious crime is included in the UCR. The most serious offence is usually the one that carries the longest maximum sentence under the Criminal Code. For example, if someone breaks and enters a house, sexually assaults a woman (level 1), and then kills her (homicide), only the murder is recorded. Although break and enter and homicide both have a maximum penalty of life imprisonment, violent offences take precedence in the record over non-violent offences. One exception to this approach is criminal harassment (stalking): all instances of this offence are recorded, whether or not it was the most serious violation in a series (Hendrick 1995).
3. The overall crime totals misrepresent the crime rate in any given year. When we talk of an increase or a decrease in any given year, we are comparing the totals of all crimes included in the crime statistics to totals from previous years. But what if an increase in break and enter corresponds with a decrease in level 1 sexual assault? It has been argued that since one offence is classified as a violent crime and the other as a property crime, these two offences shouldn't have the same weight.
4. There are problems with the way the UCR records criminal incidents for some crimes. For non-violent crimes, one incident is counted for every distinct or separate incident. But the UCR records violent incidents differently from other incidents. For violent crime, a separate incident is recorded for each victim, so if one person attacks and assaults five individuals, five incidents are recorded. But if five people attack and assault one person, only one incident is recorded. In the original Aggregate UCR Survey, robbery was an exception to this approach. One robbery was considered to equal one incident, regardless of the number of victims. This was because a single robbery can involve many victims, so to record the robbery by the number of persons it victimizes was thought to overstate the occurrence of robbery (Martin and Ogrodnik 1996). With the introduction of the UCR2, it became possible to distinguish between robbery cases in which multiple victims were robbed, and cases in which a number of persons were present when an establishment was being robbed. As a result, each victim of a robbery is now counted as a robbery. If a specific location is robbed, only one incident is counted. This change in the way robberies are counted has had a notable impact on the volume of robberies over the past 10 years. When the new definition was added to the number of robberies committed between 1998 and 2007, the amount of robberies increased by almost 12 percent for each year than was originally published in the Aggregate UCR Survey. Also, the total amount of overall violent crime for each of these years increased by approximately 1 percent as robbery accounts for about 1 of every 10 violent crimes (Wallace et al. 2009).
5. Crime rates are a more reliable way to measure crime than total numbers of crimes. This is because rates are not influenced by changes in the population, which can have a significant impact on the degree of risk faced by an individual. If, for example, you live in a town of 1,000 residents in which there were 200 break and enters, your chances of being a victim are 1 in 5. But if you live in a community of 10,000 with 200 break and enters, the risk is reduced

to 1 in 50, even though the number of break and enters is the same. Since the term "crime rate" is used so often, it is important to know exactly what it means. Crime rates are usually based on 100,000 population. This allows researchers to standardize and compare crime rates across Canada in any given year as well as across a number of years. For example, in 2014 there were 554 homicides in Canada, and the homicide rate was 1.45 per 100,000 population. The 2014 rate continues a decline in the rate of homicide starting in 1975, when the rate was 3.03 per 100,000.

What Victims Say: Victimization Data

One of the problems with using the UCR as the only basis for crime statistics in Canada is that not all victims report crimes to the police. For example, in 2009, there were 2,485,207 crimes recorded by the police in all of the provinces and territories across Canada; in comparison, there were just over 9.4 million criminal victimization incidents involving only eight criminal offences in the 10 provinces alone (Perreault and Brennan 2010). The exact number of unreported crimes is unknown, but these unreported crimes probably fluctuate in number and type from year to year. For example, the number of crimes that went unreported to the police in 2009 was estimated to be 88 percent for all types of sexual assaults, 77 percent for all household property thefts, and 66 percent for physical assaults (ibid.). The official crime rate generated by the UCR is only as accurate as the number of incidents reported to the police and the data the police decide to process. Asking members of the public about the crimes they do not report to the police contributes significantly to our understanding of the amount of crime. **Victimization surveys** (1) help estimate unrecorded crime; (2) help explain why victims do not report crimes to the police; (3) provide information about the impact of crime on victims; and (4) identify populations at risk (Hood and Sparks 1970:5).

Victimization studies also have a number of limitations, including the following:

1. *Underreporting to interviewers*. Victimization surveys always reveal more crime than the UCR does, yet they too underreport the crime rate. This is because many crimes are forgotten by victims or seem so insignificant to them that they do not report them (Sparks 1981).
2. *Response bias*. Critics of victimization surveys argue that the rate of underreporting is distributed unevenly in society. For example, White people are more likely than Black people to report having been victimized. Also, university graduates are more likely to report their victimization than those with less education (Beirne and Messerschmidt 1991).

Victimization surveys were originally used in Canada during the late 1970s and early 1980s in an attempt to gain more information about the volume, types, and rates of crime. The first national study was the **Canadian Urban Victimization Survey** (CUVS), conducted by the federal government in the late 1970s in various urban centres across Canada. It found that significant numbers of Canadians living in these areas were not reporting crimes—including large numbers of violent crimes—to the police. For example, it was revealed that victims had not reported 11,000 sexual assaults, 27,000 robberies, and 185,000 assaults to the police. Since 1988, the **General Social Survey** (GSS) has included questions asking respondents about their experiences as victims of crime.

The most recent GSS (2009) was based on a representative sample of about 19,500 Canadians aged 15 or older, from the non-institutionalized population in the 10 provinces. Interviewers asked the respondents about their experience with eight offence types, their risk factors associated with victimization, their reporting rates to the police, the nature and extent of spousal violence, the fear of crime, and public perceptions of crime and the criminal justice system during the previous 12 months.

There are a number of differences in how the UCR and the GSS collect data about crimes (see Table 4.3). One difference relates to the ability of the GSS (as compared to the UCR) to discover information about crimes not reported by victims to the police. The GSS collects data about personal and household risks. It also examines the prevalence and social and demographic distribution for eight types of criminal victimization: sexual assault, robbery, physical assault (all of which are categorized as "violent victimizations"), theft of personal property, and the following crimes classified as "household victimizations": break and enter and attempted break and enter, motor vehicle/parts theft, theft of household property, and vandalism. Information is also collected for other facets of criminal victimization as well, including fear and perceptions of crime and perceptions about the criminal justice system.

The GSS was not intended to replace the UCR but to complement it. Comparisons between the UCR and the GSS are of dubious value, because the ideas behind each

TABLE 4.3 Comparison of the GSS and UCR

UCR	GSS
Data Collection Methods	
Administrative police records Census 100% coverage of all police agencies Data submitted on paper or in machine-readable format National in scope Continuous historical file: 1962 onward All recorded criminal incidents regardless of victim's age Counts only those incidents reported to and recorded by police	Personal reports from individual citizens Sample survey Sample of approximately 10,000 persons using random digit dialling Computer-assisted telephone interviewing (CATT); excludes households without telephones Excludes Yukon, Nunavut, and the Northwest Territories Periodic survey: 1988, 1993, 1999 Target population: persons aged 15 and over, excluding full-time residents of institutions Collects crimes reported and not reported to police
Scope and Definitions	
Primary unit of count is the criminal incident Nearly 100 crime categories "Most Serious Offence" rule results in an undercount of less serious crimes. Includes attempts.	Primary unit of count is criminal victimization (at personal and household levels) Eight crime categories Statistics are usually reported on a "most serious offence" basis, but counts for every crime type are possible, depending on statistical reliability. Includes attempts.
Sources of Error	
Reporting by public Processing error, edit non-responding police department, police discretion, changes in policy and procedures Legislative change	Sampling error Non-sampling error related to the following: coverage, respondent error (e.g., recall), non-response, coding, edit and imputation, estimation.

Source: Statistics Canada, *An Overview of the Differences between Police-Reported and Victim-Reported Crime.* (1997). Catalogue No. 85–542. Reproduced and distributed on an "as is" basis with the permission of Statistics Canada.

system are different. Crime rates in the UCR emerge from reports of crime incidents by the public to the police; those in the GSS emerge from reports of victimizations to survey interviewers. In other words, GSS data originate from individuals who are actually victimized, whereas UCR data are based on criminal acts reported to the police. Because their sources of data differ, the GSS and UCR give us different information about crime in Canada.

Victimization surveys are able to focus on specific types of crimes. In 1993, for example, the federal government conducted a national victimization survey, the **Violence Against Women Survey** (VAWS), which focused on the amount of violence committed against women in Canada. After compiling and analyzing the information obtained from victims in the GSS, researchers working with the Canadian Centre for Justice Statistics oftentimes produce reports focusing upon certain aspects of victimization. For example, Perreault et al. (2009) studied multiple victimizations and found that certain groups are more vulnerable to violent victimization and that certain households possess characteristics which make them more susceptible to victimization.

SUMMING UP AND LOOKING FORWARD

Official crime statistics provide information about the amount of crime that exists in society on an annual basis. These statistics are based upon criminal incidents that the police are made aware of. The total amount of police-reported crime statistics have been declining in recent years and the official crime rate is now at its lowest level since 1961. Official crime statistics are divided into three main categories: violent crime, property crime, and other Criminal Code. In 2008, the Crime Severity Index, which measures the seriousness of crime, was introduced.

A major source of information about the amount of crime is provided through the amount and type of crimes that come to the attention of the police. Police-reported statistics are published on an annual basis and are known as the Uniform Crime Statistics. These statistics have been produced since 1961. Starting in the late 1980s, incident-based crime statistics have also been collected; these statistics provide more comprehensive information about the criminal incident.

The accuracy of police-reported statistics has been questioned. Among the concerns are that people may not report crimes to the police; it is rare for the police to record all of the incidents that occur in one crime—the most serious criminal offence is the one that is recorded; and violent crimes are counted differently compared to non-violent crimes. As a result of these issues regarding the accuracy of official crime statistics, a number of other approaches have been introduced in an attempt to better understand the level of crime in society. One of these alternative official crime statistics approaches is the victimization survey, which will be discussed in the next section. Also, two unofficial crime statistics, self-report and ethnographic research, will also be overviewed.

Review Questions:

1. What does the Aggregate UCR Survey measure?
2. What does the Incident-Based UCR Survey measure? Why was it introduced?
3. What is the Crime Severity Index? Why was it introduced?
4. What are the factors that may affect police-reported crime statistics?
5. What are some of the reasons why crime has declined in Canada during the past few years?

Criminal Victimization in Canada

Trends and Patterns of Victimization: The General Social Survey 1988–2009

According to Perreault and Brennan (2010), just over 25 percent of all Canadians aged 15 years and over in 2009 living in the 10 provinces were victimized by at least one crime during the previous 12 months. This was a decline of approximately 3 percent compared to 2004. The majority of all criminal incidents reported to the General Social Survey (GSS) were non-violent. Specifically, theft of personal property (34 percent), theft of household property (13 percent), vandalism (11 percent), break and enters, (7 percent), and theft of motor vehicles/parts (5 percent) accounted for 70 percent of all incidents recorded by the GSS in 2009. The highest rate of increase in victimization in 2009 compared to 2004 was for the theft of personal property, which increased by 16 percent. There were slight differences for sexual assaults, robberies, physical assaults, and break and enters in 2009, while the rates of motor vehicle/parts theft, theft of household property, and vandalism all declined.

The rate for those offences categorized as violent victimizations in 2009 was 118 per 1,000 Canadians 15 years or older, an increase from a rate of 106 in 2004. Physical assault incidents had the highest victimization rate (80 incidents per 1,000), followed by sexual assault and robbery (24 and 13 incidents per 1,000, respectively). Most individuals (74 percent) who experienced a violent victimization reported one violent incident, another 16 percent reported that they had been violently victimized twice, and the remaining 10 percent stated they had been victimized three or more times. The overall rate for household victimization was twice that of the rate of violent victimization. Overall, there were 237 incidents of personal victimization per 1,000 households. Theft of household property and vandalism had the highest rates (83 and 74 incidents per 1,000 households, respectively), while break and enter and motor vehicle/parts theft had the lowest (47 and 34 incidents per 1,000 households, respectively).

Young people were particularly vulnerable to violent crime in 2009. In this year, the rate for Canadians aged 15 to 24 who were victims of a violent crime was greater than the rates recorded for all other age groups. The rate of violent victimization declined with age—while Canadians between the ages of 15 and 24 had a violent victimization rate of 284 per 1,000 incidents, individuals between the ages of 25 and 34 had a rate of violent victimization of 165 per 1,000. Individuals 65 and older reported the lowest violent victimization rate: 19 per 1,000.

The number of evening activities people were involved with and marital status also influenced the rate of violent victimization. Individuals who participated in 30 or more evening activities in any given month reported the highest rates of violent victimization (202 per 1,000). This rate was over four times higher than for those who stated that they had been involved in fewer than 10 evening activities during a month (48 incidents per 1,000). People who were single faced a greater likelihood of being the victim of a violent crime (231 incidents per 1,000) compared to those who were separated or divorced (158 incidents), living common law (137 incidents), or married (62 incidents).

Some of the principal findings of the 2009 GSS are noted below (Perreault and Brennan 2010):

(1) Violent Victimization Rates:

- Violent victimizations are most often committed by males and young adults.
- Violent victimization rates of Aboriginal people were double that of non-Aboriginal people.
- Higher household income is associated with higher rates of violent victimization.

- Family members, friends, acquaintances, and neighbours were the perpetrators in 48 percent of violent victimizations.
- The most common location of a violent victimization was a commercial establishment.

(2) Household Victimization Rates:

- Home owners and renters had the same risk of household victimization.
- Individuals who had lived in their dwelling for 10 years or more reported the lowest rates of household victimizations while the highest rates were reported by those who had lived in their dwelling for less than six months.
- In terms of household income, the highest rates of household victimization were found in the highest category of household income ($100,000 or more), while the lowest rates were found among people whose household incomes were between $20,000 and $39,999.

(3) Theft of Personal Property:

- Females have a higher rate of theft of personal property than males.
- Individuals between the ages of 15 and 24 have the highest rates of personal property theft while those aged 65 and over have the lowest.
- Students have the highest rates of theft of personal property.
- Individuals with the highest household incomes ($100,000 or more) were more at risk of personal property theft compared to individuals with lower annual incomes.

The GSS also collects information from victims of crime about the impact of their victimization. In fact, victims of both household victimizations were just as likely as victims of violent crimes to be affected emotionally. Some of the findings concerning the consequences of self-reported victimization incidents from the 2009 GSS include the following:

- Overall, 28 percent of the victims of a violent crime reported that they found it difficult or even impossible to carry out their daily activities.
- When a victim of a violent crime found it difficult or impossible to carry out their everyday activities, the average time required for the victim to return to their regular routine was 11 days.
- For nearly one-third of all victims of household crime, the value of damaged or stolen property was over $500. For motor vehicle thefts (excluding the theft of parts and attempted thefts) the value of the damaged or stolen property exceeds $500 in 91 percent of all incidents.

Victimizations Not Reported to the Police

In 2009, almost 31 percent of all victimizations were reported to the police, a slight decrease from the 33 percent reported in 2004. Twenty-nine percent of all violent victimizations were reported to the police in 2009. Among the violent incidents, robberies (including attempted robberies) and physical assaults were most likely to be reported to the police (43 and 34 percent, respectively). In contrast, only 12 percent of sexual assaults were reported to the police. Just over one-half (51 percent) of violent crimes that occurred in the victim's home or in the immediate area were reported to the police. In comparison, only 20 percent of the incidents that occurred in a business or public institution were reported to the police.

Thirty-six percent of all household victimizations were reported to the police during 2009. According to Gannon and Mihorean (2005), this low rate of reporting can be explained in part by the fact that oftentimes no items are stolen in theft-related household crimes. When there is a significant loss of property, victims are more likely to report the crime. Almost 70 percent of all household incidents in 2009 were reported to the police when the value of stolen or damaged property exceeded $1,000. In comparison, when the stolen or damaged property was valued at less than $100, only 15 percent of the incidents were reported. Age is also a factor when reporting a victimization to the police. Perreault and Brennan (2010) found that older victims are more likely than younger victims to report a violent incident. Forty-six percent of violent incidents involving victims aged 55 years or older were brought to the attention of the police, compared to 20 percent of those involving victims between the ages of 15 and 24. In addition, the number of offenders involved in an incident influenced the reporting of an incident by the victim. In 2009, 49 percent of all violent incidents involving multiple offenders were reported to police, compared to 20 percent of those incidents committed by one offender.

The most common reason given by the victim of a crime for reporting it to the police was that it was their duty (86 percent said so). Sixty-nine percent said they reported the crime from a desire to see the offender arrested or punished. Victims of a violent crime were more likely than victims of household crime to report the incident due to a desire to receive protection, while the victims of household crime were more likely to report in order to obtain compensation or to file an insurance claim.

Why don't the victims of crime report crimes to the police? In 2009, the most common reason why victims did not report their victimization to the police is because they thought it wasn't important enough (68 percent).

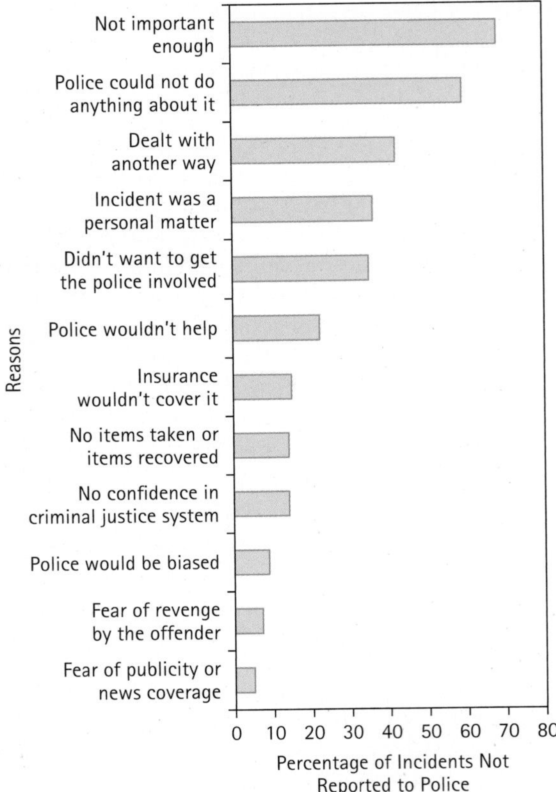

FIGURE 4.3 Reasons for Not Reporting Victimization Incidents to the Police, 2009

Source: "Criminal Victimization in Canada, 2009." *Juristat* Vol. 30, no.2 (Summer 2010), Statistics Canada Catalogue no. 85-002-X, p.16, http://www.statcan.gc.ca/pub/85-002-x/2010002/article/11340-eng.pdf. Reproduced and distributed on an "as is" basis with the permission of Statistics Canada.

The next most common reasons given were because they felt there was nothing the police could do about it (59 percent), they dealt with the situation in another way (42 percent), that the incident was a personal matter (36 percent), and they didn't want the police to get involved (35 percent) (see Figure 4.3). Of those who did report the incident to the police, 63 percent were satisfied with the response of the police.

Self-Report Surveys

Self-report surveys are another approach used by criminologists to collect information about victimizations not necessarily reported to the police. Such surveys are based on similar principles as victimization surveys, in that people are asked directly about any criminal activities they may have been involved with over a certain period, usually the previous year. Self-report surveys also include questions about subjects' attitudes, values, personal characteristics, and behaviours. The information obtained in this way is used for various purposes such as to measure attitudes toward criminal offences and to examine the relationship between crime and certain social variables such as family relations, income, and educational achievement.

This approach can be used to investigate the prevalence of offending among those who indicate that they have committed a criminal offence during the period under study. Most self-report surveys focus on youths and drug offenders. Youths are usually questioned about issues besides their offending, such as how their friends, schools, and families influence their law-breaking and/or law-abiding behaviours. Drug offenders are also oftentimes asked to self-report their activities since many of them have committed numerous crimes in order to pay for the drugs they use.

Self-report surveys help some researchers focus on specific criminological subjects. Some have used them to study the age (referred to as **age of onset**) at which youths first start offending. Frechette and LeBlanc (1987) studied male youths in Montreal and discovered that the annual rate of self-reported offending was approximately twice as high for those who started their involvement with youth crime earlier compared to those who started later. In the late 1980s, using the same approach, Hagan and McCarthy (1992) studied the criminal activities of 309 homeless youths in Toronto; they found that youths who had been homeless for one year or more were more likely to be involved in criminal activities.

Ethnographic Research

Ethnographic research also asks people if they were involved in any criminal activities during a certain period of time. This approach usually involves the study of small groups and the social context of their activity or activities (i.e., the **micro situations**) under study. This style of research conducted is a type of **field research**. Field research occurs when researchers obtain information about an issue through face-to-face contact between themselves and the individual(s) who are the object of the research. The aim of this approach is to discover information about

1. the social worlds of the subject(s) in order to find out why they act the way they do,
2. the meanings they attach to their activities, and
3. their perceptions and emotions about the particular situations in which they find themselves.

Information is usually obtained through a number of different techniques (Exhibit 4.2). One is via prolonged interviews (referred to as **unstructured interviews**) between the researcher(s) and the subject(s). Another is by the researcher becoming a **participant observer** of the group and gaining the members' consent by informing members of what the researcher is interested in studying (i.e., **overt research**). Alternatively, researchers may become participant observers by joining the group they are studying without getting permission from the members of the group and becoming accepted as member, an approach known as **covert research**.

Many famous studies in the area of criminal justice have used the ethnographic technique. For example, Clifford Shaw (1930) detailed a delinquent boy's own life experiences in *The Jack Roller*. Anderson (1999:9) studied for a number of years the issue of "why it is that so many inner-city young people are inclined to commit aggression and violence toward one another" in Philadelphia. Many ethnographic studies explore areas related to criminal justice in Canada that would otherwise be unknown to the outside world, such as research in the area of gangs, sex work, and prisons (e.g., Densley 2013; van der Meulen et al. 2013, and Garrison 2015).

EXHIBIT 4.2 Features of Ethnographic Research

Ethnographic research involves a number of methodological techniques:

- Studying the social world from the perspective of those being studied.
- The role of the researcher(s) is to understand the realities of those being studied.
- Researchers are interested in observing the ways the research subjects navigate their social world and the way in which they interact in various social contexts.
- It is important for the researcher(s) to study the ways in which the research subjects interact normally in their everyday situations.

SUMMING UP AND LOOKING FORWARD

Another type of official crime statistic is the victimization survey. They attempt to gain a better understanding of the level of crime in society by asking citizens if they were victimized during a certain period of time. The federal government collects victimization data every five years in the General Social Survey. Oftentimes, victimization surveys are used on a one-time basis to study the occurrence of a specific type of crime by interviewing a randomly selected group of people. These types of surveys have been conducted either by the government or by independent researchers. An example of a government victimization survey was VAWS, which studies the amount of violence experienced by women across Canada.

Victimization surveys generally report a higher amount of criminal activity than that recorded by police-reported crime statistics. A reason for this is because people may not feel comfortable reporting their victimization to the police or feel that the criminal justice system will not deal with the incident appropriately. In the 2009 General Social Survey, it was found that only 31 percent of all victimizations were reported to the police. The most common reason for victims to report a crime to the police was because they felt it was their duty to do so, while the most common reason for not reporting a victimization was because the victim didn't think it was important enough.

Two types of unofficial crime statistics are used to collect information about crime. Both of these approaches are able to collect data that usually aren't collected by official crime statistics. Self-report studies ask individuals to record their own involvement in criminal activities. These usually consist of a number of questions addressing members of selected groups about their personal involvement in crime. Ethnographies are another unofficial approach to the collection of crime statistics and usually involves the observation of someone or the members of a group by a researcher. Whatever method is used to collect data about crime, people oftentimes categorize this information on the basis of two categories, crimes against the person and crimes against property. Selected offences found within each of these categories are the subject of the next section.

Review Questions:

1. What are the benefits of victimization data for understanding crime? How does the federal government collect information about victimization?
2. What are the limitations of victimization studies?
3. Why don't victims report their victimization(s) to the police?
4. What are the advantages of self-report studies?
5. What is the purpose of ethnographic research?

Trends and Patterns of Selected Crimes in Canada: Crimes against the Person

Almost 21 percent of all crimes reported to the police in 2014 were classified as violent. The number of violent crime incidents reported to the police in 2014 was 369,359, a decrease of approximately 15,000 from the previous year and about 68,000 from 2010. The rate of violent crime decreased 5 percent between 2013 and 2014, and 26 percent from 2004 to 2014. This was largely due to decreases in the four most frequently committed violent crimes: assault Level 1 (−25 percent between 2004 and 2014), robbery (−39 percent from 2004 to 2014), uttering threats (−34 percent from 2004 to 2014), and assault Level 2 (−14 percent) (Boyce 2015).

Reuters/Andy Clarke

According to police officials, Robert Pickton was the focus of the largest serial killer investigation in Canadian history. He was charged with the deaths of 26 women and was tried and convicted on six counts of murder in 2007. The remaining 20 charges were stayed. Pickton once said that he had killed 49 women.

Homicide

Homicide occurs when a person directly or indirectly, by any means, causes the death of a human being. Homicide is either culpable (murder, manslaughter, or infanticide) or non-culpable (not an offence and therefore not included in the homicide statistics). Examples of non-culpable homicide include suicide, deaths caused by criminal negligence, and accidental or justifiable homicide (e.g., self-defence). A murder has been committed when a person intentionally, by a willful act or omission, causes the death of another human being, or means to cause bodily harm that the person knows is likely to cause death. Four Criminal Code offences are associated with homicide: *first degree murder*, *second degree murder*, *manslaughter*, and *infanticide*.

First degree murder occurs when the act is planned and deliberate; or the victim is a person employed at and acting in the course of his or her work for the preservation of and maintenance of the public peace (e.g., a police officer or correctional worker); or the death is caused by a person committing or attempting to commit certain serious offences (e.g., treason, kidnapping, hijacking, sexual assault, robbery, and arson).

Second degree murder is all murder that is not first degree murder.

Manslaughter is culpable homicide that is not murder or infanticide. It is generally considered to be a homicide committed in the heat of passion caused by sudden provocation.

Infanticide occurs when a female willfully causes the death of her newborn child (under 12 months of age), if her mind is considered disturbed from the effects of giving birth or from lactation.

Homicide is a unique crime for several reasons. First, it is widely perceived as the most serious of all criminal acts. Second, it is more likely than any other crime to be discovered by the police and to be the subject of a police investigation. Third, unlike other crimes, the definition of homicide tends to be fairly consistent across nations. As a result, homicide is important to examine, "not only because of its severity, but because it is a fairly reliable barometer of violence in society" (Dauvergne 2005:2). The incidence of homicide decreased gradually in Canada between 1975 and 2001, with some yearly fluctuations; in 2003, the homicide rate was 1.73 per 100,000 but then increased slightly in 2007 to 1.80 and to 2.0 per 100,000 in 2008 before dropping to 1.62 in 2010 and 1.45 in both 2013 and 2014, the lowest rate since 1966 (see Figure 4.4).

Methods Used to Commit Homicide

In 2013, 40 percent of all homicides involved a stabbing; 27 percent involved a shooting; and 21 percent involved beatings (see Figure 4.5). Since 1969, the Canadian government has introduced numerous pieces of legislation to restrict and regulate firearms (see Exhibit 4.3 and Figure 4.6). The use of firearms in homicides has declined since 1974. Homicides caused by firearms account for a relatively small percentage of all fatalities involving firearms. In 2013, there were 131 firearm-related homicides, and 195 homicides committed by stabbings (Cotter 2014).

When a firearm was used in a homicide, most common firearm used was a handgun—in 2013, these accounted for 68 percent of all firearm-related homicides; shotguns or rifles accounted for another 23 percent. In terms of victim–offender relationships, most victims (87 percent)

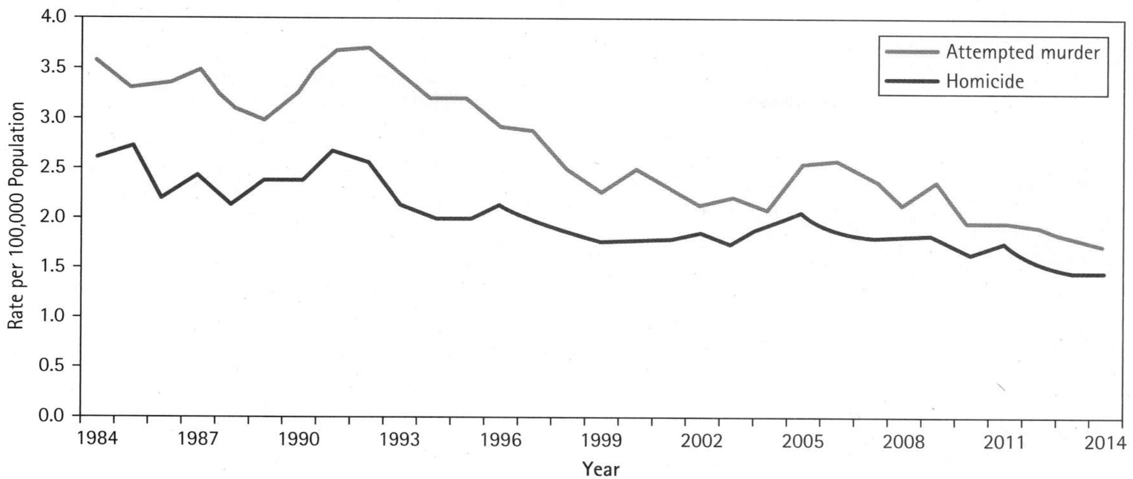

FIGURE 4.4 Homicides and Attempted Murders, Canada, 1984–2014

Source: Jillian Boyce, Canadian Centre for Justice Statistics, "Police-reported crime statistics in Canada, 2014." *Juristat* (July 22, 2015), Statistics Canada Catalogue no. 85-002-X, p. 14, www.statcan.gc.ca/pub/85-002-x/2015001/article/14211-eng.pdf. Reproduced and distributed on an "as is" basis with the permission of Statistics Canada.

knew their killer (Cotter 2014). There were 149 homicides committed by an acquaintance and 126 involving a family relationship, while another 82 homicides involved non-spousal relationships. Homicides involving a criminal relationship almost doubled in 2013 compared to 2012 (from 23 to 36 homicides) (see Table 4.4).

Sexual Assault

Sexual assault is committed when an individual is sexually assaulted or molested or when an attempt is made to sexually assault or molest an individual. In 2014, 20,735 sexual assault incidents were recorded by the police, or slightly over 5.5 percent of all violent crimes. This was a decrease of 3 percent in the number of sexual assaults reported by the police compared to 2013. Of the sexual assaults reported to the police in 2014, 98 percent were classified as level 1. The rates of all three levels of sexual assault decreased in 2014 compared to 2013: the rate of sexual assault level 1 decreased by 3 percent, level 2 by 14 percent, and level 3 by 22 percent. It is important to note that police-reported data significantly underestimate the true extent of sexual assault in Canada. According to the self-reported victimization data collected in the 2009 GSS, only 1 in 10 sexual assaults were brought to the attention of the police (Perreault and Brennan 2010).

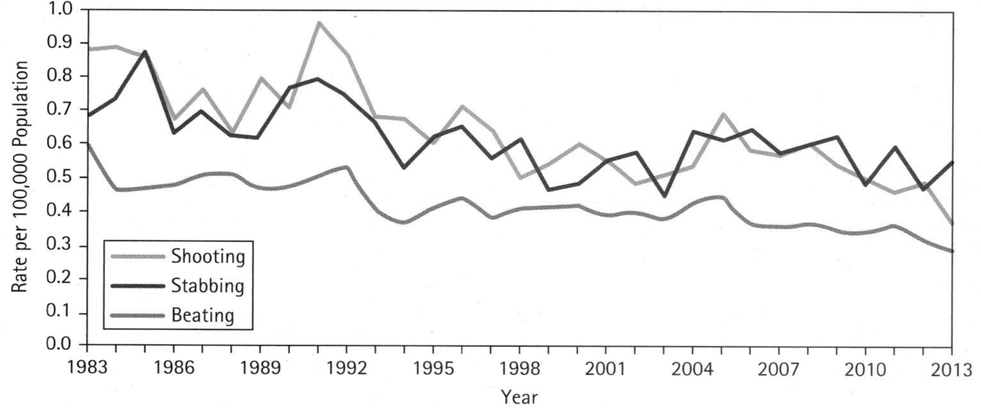

FIGURE 4.5 Homicides, by Most Common Method, Canada, 1983–2013

Source: Adam Cotter, "Homicide in Canada, 2013." *Juristat* (December 1, 2014), Statistics Canada Catalogue no. 85-002, p. 9, http://www.statcan.gc.ca/pub/85-002-x/2012001/article/11647-eng.pdf. Reproduced and distributed on an "as is" basis with the permission of Statistics Canada.

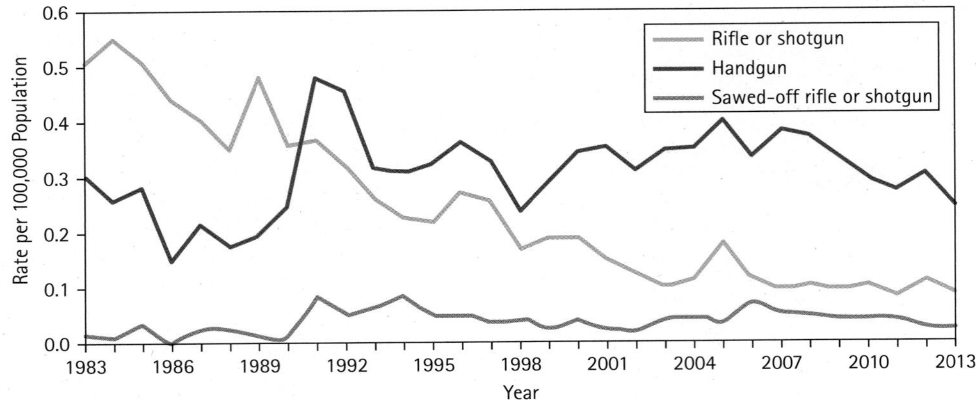

FIGURE 4.6 Firearm-Related Deaths, by Selected Type of Firearm, Canada, 1983–2013
Excludes homicides committed with the use of other types of firearm, such as fully automatic firearms or firearm-like weapons (i.e., nail gun, pellet gun).

Source: Adam Cotter, "Homicide in Canada, 2013." *Juristat* (December 1, 2014), Statistics Canada Catalogue no. 85-002, p. 10, http://www.statcan.gc.ca/pub/85-002-x/2014001/article/14108-eng.pdf. Reproduced and distributed on an "as is" basis with the permission of Statistics Canada.

EXHIBIT 4.3 Changes to Canadian Firearm Legislation 1969–2012

Important changes have been made to Canadian firearms laws in an effort to reduce the number of firearms-related injuries and deaths. To this end, the Criminal Code was amended in 1969, 1977, 1991, 1995, 1998, 2003, and 2012. These pieces of legislation are summarized below:

1969: Parliament enacted Bill C-150, which for the first time made it illegal to provide firearms to persons of "unsound mind" or to convicted criminals under a prohibition order. Also, the definition of a "firearm" was revised so that it now included non-restricted, restricted, and prohibited weapons.

1977: Amendments to Bill C-150 were introduced (Bill C-51) so that a firearms acquisition certificate (FAC) would now be required prior to obtaining a firearm. This legislation also introduced a variety of other provisions, including regulations on safe storage and display of firearms for businesses and bona fide gun collectors, and mandatory minimum sentences to deter the criminal use of firearms.

1991: With Bill C-17, Parliament strengthened the FAC screening provisions (Bill C-17) so that applicants now had to provide references, a personal and criminal history, and a photograph. Also, a mandatory 28-day waiting period was established.

1995: The Firearms Act (Bill C-68) was passed, establishing a licensing system for people wishing to possess firearms. Those who met the criteria could be licensed to possess firearms that were neither prohibited nor restricted. The Firearms Act also established a system for registering all firearms. The registration component of the Firearms Act was implemented and the deadline for all gun owners to register their non-restricted firearms was set for January 1, 2003. Three-quarters of all gun owners successfully registered their non-registered firearms by the designated date; in total, 5.8 million firearms were registered.

1996: The Canadian Firearms Centre was established to oversee the administration of Bill C-68.

1998: Part III of the Criminal Code was amended to create a variety of offences relating to the unauthorized possession, transfer, importing, or exporting of firearms and the use of firearms in the commission of offences.

2001: Starting January 1, 2001, Canadians needed a licence to possess and acquire firearms.

2003: In January, all firearms owners and users were required to obtain a firearms licence and registration certificate in their possession. All firearms now had to be registered (including non-registered rifles and shotguns).

2006: In June 2006, Bill C-21 was tabled in Parliament, with the intent of repealing the requirement to register non-restricted long guns. It died on the Order Paper.

EXHIBIT 4.3 Changes to Canadian Firearm Legislation 1969–2012 ***(Continued)***

2007: Bill C-21 was reintroduced as Bill C-24.

2008: Bill C-24 dies on the Order Paper in September.

2009: A Private Member's Bill (C-391) is introduced, proposing to repeal the portion of the requirement that requires the registration of non-restricted firearms, but would have continued the registration requirement for guns classified as restricted. The Bill reaches third reading, when it is narrowly defeated in the House of Commons.

2011: The Conservative government introduced Bill C-19, which would repeal the requirement to register non-restricted firearms (long guns), provide for the destruction of all records pertaining to the registration of long guns currently contained in the Canadian Firearms Registry, and maintain controls over restricted and prohibited firearms.

2012: In February, Bill C-19 was passed in the House of Commons. In April, Bill C-19 was given Royal Assent.

Sources: Pottie Bunge, V., H. Johnson, and T.A. Balde. 2005. *Exploring Crime Patterns in Canada*. Ottawa: Canadian Centre for Justice Statistics; Royal Canadian Mounted Police. 2009. *History of Firearms Control in Canada: Up to and Including the Firearms Act*. Ottawa.

TABLE 4.4 Homicides, By Accused-Victim Relationship, Canada, 2012 and 2013

Relationship Type[1] (victim killed by)	2013 number of victims	2013 percent[2]	2012* number of victims	2012* percent[2]	Average 2003 to 2012 number of victims	Average 2003 to 2012 percent[2]
Family relationship	126	32.8	145	35.3	150	33.4
Spousal relationship	44	11.5	62	15.1	69	15.4
Legal husband/wife	18	4.7	27	6.6	26	5.7
Common-law husband/wife	17	4.4	20	4.9	27	6.0
Separated or divorced husband/wife	3	0.8	11	2.7	11	2.4
Separated common-law husband/wife[3]	5	1.3	2	0.5	6	1.3
Same-sex spouse[4]	1	0.3	2	0.5	1	0.2
Other family relationship[5]	82	21.4	83	20.2	81	18.0
Father or mother	19	4.9	26	6.3	28	6.2
Son or daughter	32	8.3	30	7.3	21	4.9
Sibling	11	2.9	7	1.7	10	2.2
Extended family[6]	20	5.2	20	4.9	22	4.9
Intimate relationship[7]	24	6.3	20	4.9	21	4.6
Acquaintance	149	38.6	158	38.1	158	35.0
Close friend	34	8.9	44	10.7	33	7.4
Neighbour	15	3.9	12	2.9	13	2.9
Authority figure	3	0.8	0	0.0	2	0.4
Business relationship (legal)	3	0.8	10	2.4	8	1.7

(Continued on next page)

TABLE 4.4 Homicides, By Accused-Victim Relationship, Canada, 2012 and 2013 *(Continued)*

Relationship Type[1] (victim killed by)	2013 number of victims	2013 percent[2]	2012* number of victims	2012* percent[2]	Average 2003 to 2012 number of victims	Average 2003 to 2012 percent[2]
Casual acquaintance	94	24.5	92	22.4	102	22.7
Criminal relationship[8]	36	9.4	23	5.6	46	10.3
Stranger	49	12.8	65	15.8	74	16.4
Unknown relationship	2	...	4	...	4	...
Total solved homicides[9]	**386**	**100.0**	**415**	**100.0**	**452**	**100.0**
Unsolved homicides	119	...	128	...	143	...
Total homicides	**505**	**...**	**543**	**...**	**595**	**...**

... not applicable

* revised

[1] Includes homicides with a known accused. If there were more than one accused, only the closest relationship to the victim was recorded.

[2] Solved homicides where the type of relationship was unknown are excluded from the calculation of percentages.

[3] Response categories for "separated common-law husband" and "separated common-law wife" were introduced to the Homicide Survey in 2005. As such, the average number and percent are calculated from 2005 to 2012.

[4] Includes current and former same-sex spouses.

[5] Includes biological, adopted, step and foster relationships.

[6] Includes nieces, nephews, grandchildren, uncles, aunts, cousins, in-laws, etc. related by blood, marriage (including common-law) or adoption.

[7] Includes dating relationships (current and former) and other intimate relationships.

[8] Includes, for example, sex workers, drug dealers and their clients, loan sharks, or gang members. Where more than one relationship applies (e.g. criminal relationship and close friend), police are asked to report the primary relationship.

[9] Includes homicides with a known accused.

Note: The sum of averages may not add up to the total average due to rounding. Percentages may not add up due to rounding. Figures prior to 2013 may differ from previously published figures due to ongoing updates to the data files as new information becomes available.

Source: Adam Cotter, "Homicide in Canada, 2013", *Juristat* (December 1, 2014), Statistics Canada Catalogue no. 85-002, p. 32. http://www.statcan.gc.ca/pub/85-002-x/2014001/article/14108-eng.pdf. Reproduced and distributed on an "as is" basis with the permission of Statistics Canada.

Assault

Assault is the most frequently occurring crime in the violent crime category. In 2014, 201,382 incidents of assault were reported to the police, which accounted for just over 54 percent of all violent crimes reported in the year. The most frequently occurring type of assault reported to the police in 2014 was assault level 1 (or common assault), which accounted for all assault offences. The next most frequent category was assault with a weapon or causing bodily harm, or assault level 2, which accounted for 22 percent of all assault offences. Aggravated assault, or assault level 3 (2 percent of all assault offences) involves the wounding, maiming, or disfigurement of the victim (see Figure 4.7). Since 2000, level 1 assaults have gradually declined—there was a 4 percent decrease in 2014 compared to 2013, marking the seventh consecutive year that these rates have decreased.

Data from the 2009 GSS indicate that males are more likely than females to be the victim of a physical assault. Most of the perpetrators were strangers and the most common location of the incident was at a commercial establishment. About half of all victims who had been injured as a result of a physical assault reported the incident to the police. In general, incidents involving physical assault that result in an injury to the victim are most likely to be reported to the police compared to those who are not physically injured (Perreault and Brennan 2010).

Assaults occur at every age. The number of victims of police-reported assaults against children and youths (ages 0–17) by age and gender of victim in 2011 is shown in Figure 4.8. As both children and youths age increases,

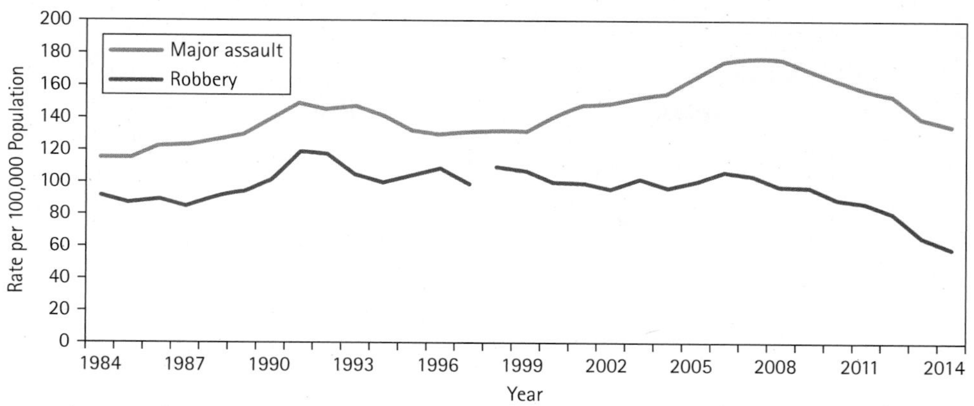

FIGURE 4.7 Major Assault (Levels 2 and 3) and Robbery, Police-Reported Rates, Canada, 1984–2014

Source: Jillian Boyce, Adam Cotter, and Samuel Perreault, "Police reported crime statistics in Canada, 2013." *Juristat* (July 23, 2014), Statistics Canada Catalogue no. 85-002-X, p. 16, www.statcan.gc.ca/pub/85-002-x/2014001/article/14040-eng.pdf. Reproduced and distributed on an "as is" basis with the permission of Statistics Canada.

the number of victims reported to the police increases. At every age and for both males and females, common assault accounted for the greatest percentage of all assault types (about 78 percent in 2011).

Robbery

Robbery is defined as an incident of theft that also involves violence or the threat of violence. In 2013, there were 20,929 robbery incidents reported to the police, an 11 percent decrease from the previous year. The robbery rate has been declining—the rate of robbery decreased by 39 percent from 2004 to 2014 (see Figure 4.7). The overall decline in police-reported robberies over the past 10 years has been due primarily to fewer robberies committed in commercial or institutional facilities. In 2008, "robbery to steal a firearm" was introduced as a new Criminal Code offence. In that year, 55 robberies (less than 1 percent of all robberies) involving the theft of a firearm were reported to the police.

Criminal Harassment (Stalking)

In 2014, there were 19,653 incidents of **criminal harassment** reported to the police, a 10 percent decrease compared to 2013. Just over 5 percent of all violent crimes during 2014 involved criminal harassment incidents reported to the police. Youths, in particular adolescent women, are also the victims of criminal harassment. Figure 4.9 shows that while

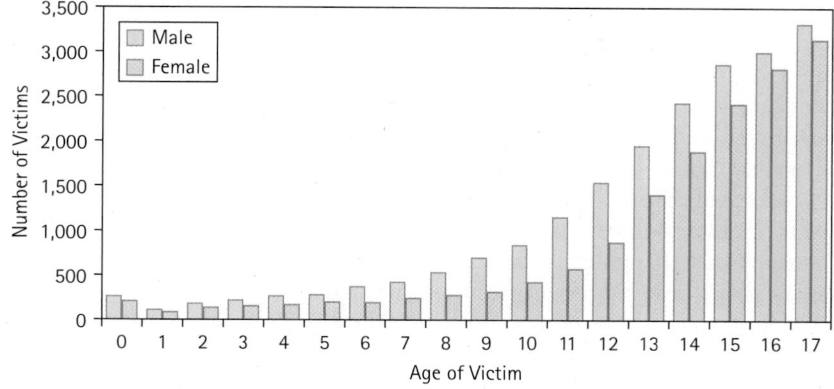

FIGURE 4.8 Number of Victims of Police-Reported Assaults against Children and Youth (0–17) by Age and Gender of Victim, 2011

Source: From Department of Justice Canada, "Child and Youth Victims of Criminal Harassment." *Building Knowledge*, Issue 4 (June 2013), http://www.justice.gc.ca/eng/rp-pr/cj-jp/victim/knowledge-savoir/issue4-vol4/BuildingKnowledge4.pdf. Data from *Incident-based Uniform Crime Reporting Survey 2011*, Statistics Canada. Reproduced and distributed on an "as is" basis with the permission of Statistics Canada.

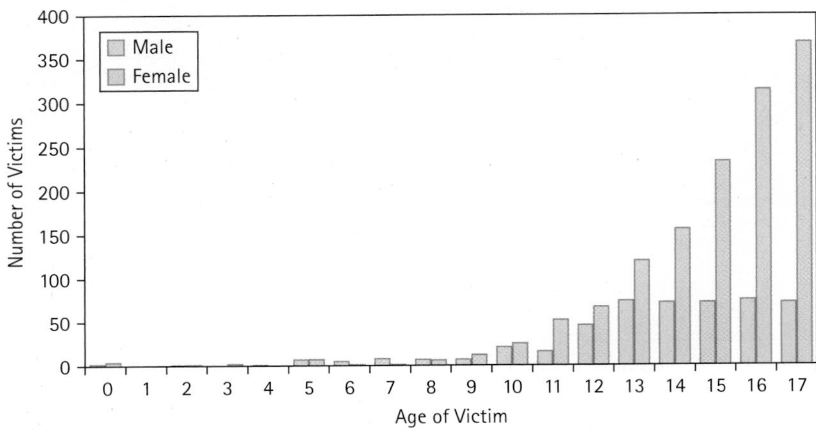

FIGURE 4.9 Number of Victims of Police-Reported Criminal Harassment, by Gender and Age, 2011

Source: From Department of Justice Canada, "Child and Youth Victims of Criminal Harassment, 2011." *Building Knowledge*, Issue 2 (February 2013), http://www.justice.gc.ca/eng/rp-pr/cj-jp/victim/knowledge-savoir/issue4-vol4/BuildingKnowledge4.pdf. Data from *Incident-based Uniform Crime Reporting Survey 2011*, Statistics Canada. Reproduced and distributed on an "as is" basis with the permission of Statistics Canada.

incidents of criminal harassment involving adolescent men remained stable between the ages of 12 and 17, this was not the case for adolescent women. The number of incidents of criminal harassment for adolescent women continually increased throughout their teenage years.

Criminal harassment most commonly is committed against women. Female victims accounted for 76 percent of criminal harassment incidents reported to the police in 2009, compared to just over half (51 percent) of the victims of overall violent crime. The relationship between victims and those accused of criminal harassment varies based on the sex of the victims. In 2009, 45 percent of female victims were harassed by a former intimate partner, while an additional 6 percent were harassed by a current intimate partner. Male victims were more often harassed by a casual acquaintance (37 percent) than by a former (21 percent) or current (2 percent) intimate partner.

Threats (38 percent) or physical force (12 percent) were more commonly used against victims of criminal harassment than a weapon (3 percent of the cases) in 2009. Neither weapons nor threats of physical force were involved in almost half (48 percent) of the incidents. Twenty-seven percent of these incidents involved other offences in 2009, the most common of which was uttering threats. Most victims of criminal harassment (69 percent) were harassed in their own home or at another residence, such as a friend's home. Sixteen percent occurred in a commercial or corporate location as well as a transit area, while another 11 percent of the incidents occurred in an outdoor public location such as a street or parking lot. Four percent occurred at a school or university (Milligan 2011).

Forcible Confinement

Forcible confinement is one of the few violent crimes that increased in Canada over the past three decades until recently—in 2014, the rate of forcible confinement was the same compared to the previous year. In Canada, it is a criminal offence to unjustly hold an individual against his or her will by the use of threats, duress, force, or the exhibition of force. This offence, "forcible confinement," is defined by the Criminal Code (s. 279) as depriving an individual of the liberty to move from one point to another by unlawfully confining, imprisoning, or forcibly seizing that person. According to Dauvergne (2009), the offence of forcible confinement is similar to kidnapping in that a person who is kidnapped is held against his or her will, but kidnapping also involves the act of transporting the victim from one location to another. Police reports do not distinguish these two offences; however, information about these two offences from the Adult Criminal Courts Survey data shows that the majority of these two offences are forcible confinement (94 percent).

One of the unique aspects of forcible confinement is that it usually involves other offences. For example, in 2007, 78 percent of all forcible confinement charges also involved offences such as assault, uttering threats, sexual assault, and robbery. In comparison, only about 25 percent of all other violent crimes occurred in conjunction with other offences. There are three primary situations in which forcible confinement occurs. The most common involves individuals being held against their will by a spouse or intimate partner (48 percent).

Most of these incidents happened in conjunction with another violent offence, such as an assault (70 percent) or uttering threats (28 percent). Seventy-one percent of all victims were in a current relationship with the perpetrator. The second forcible confinement situation occurs during disputes between friends and acquaintances (20 percent of all forcible confinement charges), while the third type of situation is associated with robberies and

Investigating: Home Invasions

In recent years, Canada has been experiencing a new criminal phenomenon: the home invasion. Home invasions are generally thought to be different from break and enters in that there is premeditated confrontation with the intent to rob and/or inflict violence on the occupants of the household. In this context, a home invasion is actually more like a robbery than a break and enter. In any case, few robberies or break and enters are characterized as home invasions.

While no official definition of this crime exists, based upon the UCR Survey, home invasion is typically defined in two ways. The first (or "narrow") definition includes all robberies that occur in a private residential building. The second (or "broad") definition includes robberies that occur in a private residential building or break and enters with an associated violent offence. This definition is normally characterized by the forced entry into a private residence while the occupants are home and involves violence against the occupants. The broad definition accounts for the majority of police-reported home invasions in Canada (see Figure 4.10).

Regardless of the definition used, this type of crime is particularly frightening to the victim, as it involves an attack within the sanctity of one's home. Some police services do record the number of home invasions in their jurisdiction, although the definitions they use may vary across police agencies. Researchers have tried to use GSS data to study this type of crime, but the number of such incidents reported by victims has been too small to allow for any analysis.

A number of provinces have recognized the seriousness of home invasions, and individuals convicted of such offences are being given longer sentences. In Alberta, for example, the Court of Appeal has established a minimum of eight years for this offence. On June 10, 2002, the Criminal Code was amended so that it now specifically identifies home invasion as an aggravating circumstance for judges to consider at the time of sentencing.

Using the narrow definition of home invasion, the rate of police-reported home invasions increased by 38 percent between 1999 and 2005 and has remained stable since. In 2008, almost 2,700 such incidents came to the attention of the police. Information about home invasions solved by the police indicates that most are committed by strangers. Home invasions are not as likely to involve strangers—in 2008, 63 percent of all home invasions were committed by strangers compared to approximately 90 percent of all other robberies. A substantial amount of home invasions were committed by acquaintances of the victim (28 percent).

Sources: Dauvergne 2010; Fedorowycz 2004:7; Kong 1998:6; Kowalski 2000:4–5.

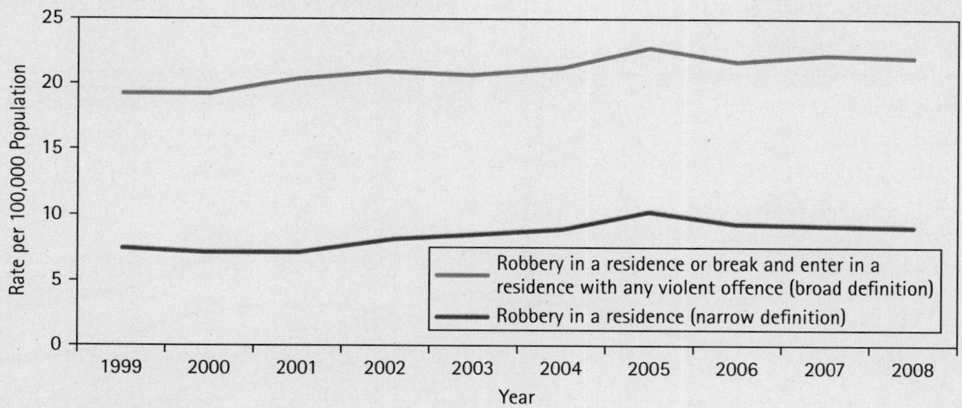

FIGURE 4.10 Police-Reported Home Invasions, Canada, 1999–2008

Source: Mia Dauvergne, "Police-reported robbery in Canada." *Juristat*, Volume 30, no. 1, (Spring 2010), Statistics Canada Catalogue no. 85-002-X, p. 12, http://www.statcan.gc.ca/pub/85-002-x/2010001/article/11115-eng.pdf. Reproduced and distributed on an "as is" basis with the permission of Statistics Canada.

break and enters. When these types of incidents occur in a private residence they are sometimes classified as **home invasions** (see *Investigating: Home Invasions*). In 2007, 46 percent of all robberies involving forcible confinement and 96 percent of all break and enters involving forcible confinement occurred in a private residence. There were just over 4,300 incidents of forcible confinement reported in 2010. The rate of forcible confinement in 2010 was eight times higher than what it was a decade ago.

Trends and Patterns of Selected Crimes: Crimes against Property

Property crimes account for the majority of all serious crimes. Property incidents involve unlawful actions with the intent to gain property, but do not involve the use or threat of violence. Nine crimes comprised the category of property crime in 2014: theft $5,000 or under, theft over $5,000, fraud, breaking and entering, motor vehicle theft, possession of stolen goods, identity fraud, arson, and mischief. Theft under $5,000 is the most common property crime. In 2014, 1.1 million property crime incidents were reported to the police, accounting for just over 61 percent of all Criminal Code incidents. The rates for all types of property crime decreased in 2014 with the exception of identity fraud, which increased by 8 percent, fraud (+12 percent), and theft of a motor vehicle (+1 percent). The rate for the offence of possession of stolen property remained stable. The greatest declines were for arson (−6 percent), breaking and entering, and mischief (both −4 percent). Property crimes heard in adult court tend to receive more custodial sentences than offences in the category of crimes against persons; in 2008–09, 40 percent of individuals found guilty of a property crime were sentenced to prison, compared to 32 percent of those found guilty of a violent crime (Thomas 2010). Fedorowycz (2004:8) states that this difference can be explained in large part by the fact that adults charged with a property offence tend to have longer criminal records. In 2008–09, 57 percent of those found guilty of break and enter cases and 49 percent of those found guilty of possession of stolen property were sentenced to a term of custody.

Breaking and Entering

Breaking and entering occurs when a dwelling or other premise is illegally entered by a person who intends to commit an indictable offence. Break and enter is considered the most serious of all property crimes. This is reflected in the severity of the sentencing provisions in the Criminal Code. The maximum penalty for an offender convicted of breaking and entering into a dwelling is life imprisonment. In comparison, the maximum punishment for breaking and entering into a business or any other premise is 14 years. In the UCR, breaking and entering is divided into three classifications: business, residential, and "other."

Breaking and entering is the fourth largest offence category in the UCR (after theft under $5,000 [non-motor vehicle], mischief, and assault level 1). In 2014, it accounted for approximately 8 percent of all Criminal Code incidents and approximately 14 percent of all property crimes. There were 151,921 break and enter incidents in 2014, the lowest number in four decades. Between 2004 and 2014, the rate of break and enters decreased by 51 percent, including a 4 percent decrease in 2014 from 2013 (see Figure 4.11).

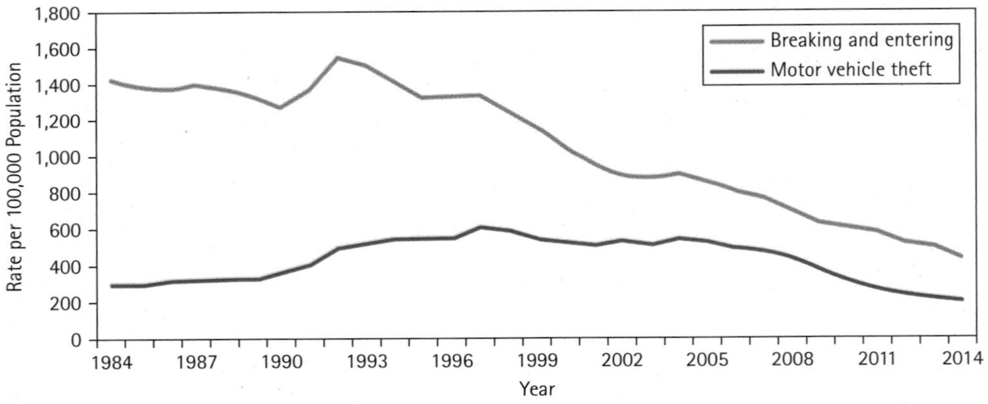

FIGURE 4.11 Breaking and Entering and Motor Vehicle Theft, Police-Reported Rates, Canada, 1984–2014

Source: Jillian Boyce, Adam Cotter, and Samuel Perreault, "Police reported crime statistics in Canada, 2013." *Juristat* (July 23, 2014), Statistics Canada Catalogue no. 85-002-X, p. 18, http://www.statcan.gc.ca/pub/85-002-x/2014001/article/14040-eng.pdf. Reproduced and distributed on an "as is" basis with the permission of Statistics Canada.

According to Sinha (2015), one possible reason why the rate of breaking and entering is declining is because fewer people may be reporting this offence. In 2009, only 54 percent of all break-ins were reported to the police, despite the fact that it had the highest rate of reporting for all household victimizations according to the 2009 GSS (Perreault and Brennan 2010).

In 2010, nearly 61 percent of all break-ins occurred in residences; 28 percent occurred in businesses; and the remaining 11 percent occurred in other locations such as schools, sheds, and detached garages. In 2010, the rate for break-ins decreased in all types of locations, declining by 4 percent for residences and 13 percent for businesses (Brennan and Dauvergne 2011). This decrease could be explained in part by an increase in the use of home security systems and devices (Gannon and Taylor-Butts 2006). Others (e.g., Fedorowycz 2004) have suggested that rising insurance deductibles could lead to fewer incidents being reported to the police.

CP PHOTO/New Brunswick Telegraph-Journal/Noel Chenier

An RCMP officer speaks at a crime scene. Do you think the police should release all the information they collect about a crime, or withhold information until they arrest a suspect?

Theft

Theft comprises two separate offences—"theft over $5,000" (non-motor vehicle) and "theft under $5,000" (non-motor vehicle). The cutoff point of $5,000 was established in 1995. Incidents of theft under $5,000 accounted for almost 43 percent of all property crimes in 2014, a 7 percent decrease compared to 2013. Since 2004, the rate of theft has decreased for both offences—the rate of theft over $5,000 has fallen by 24 percent, while the rate of theft under $5,000 has fallen by 37 percent. The decrease in reported incidents of theft under $5,000 has strongly influenced the decrease in both the property crime rate and the overall crime rate, as the number of "thefts under $5,000" is so large (Tremblay 1999).

Motor Vehicle Theft

Motor vehicle theft involves taking, or attempting to take, a vehicle without the permission of the owner. In 2014, there were 73,064 incidents of motor vehicle theft reported to the police, an increase of 1 percent compared to the previous year and a 61 percent decline in the rate since 2004 (see Figure 4.11). Theft from a motor vehicle involves the theft of automobile accessories as well as personal property found inside the vehicle. Motor vehicle theft is an expensive crime. In 2007, the Insurance Bureau of Canada estimated the direct and indirect financial costs of motor vehicle theft to consumers, police, insurance companies, and governments to exceed $1 billion annually (Dauvergne 2008).

Other Criminal Code Offences

"Other" Criminal Code offences include **counterfeiting**, **weapons offences**, **child pornography**, **disturbing the peace**, **administration of justice violations**, and **prostitution**. Eighteen percent of all Criminal Code incidents recorded in 2013 included one of these. Offences in this category declined by 5 percent compared to the previous year. Large increases were recorded in child pornography incidents (+41 percent) and terrorism-related offences (+39 percent), while the greatest decrease was found in prostitution offences (−48 percent). There was also a decrease of 3 percent in the administration of justice violations, the most common offence in this category, which accounted for 53 percent of all of these offences during 2014. It should be noted that while the police reported 100 terrorism incidents during 2014 (an increase from the 71 reported in 2013), the rate of these offences remained below one incident per 100,000 population. This increase is attributed to the new anti-terrorism laws (see Chapter 1) (Boyce 2015).

Other Types of Crime

So far we have been looking only at the most serious violent and property crimes. For obvious reasons, these receive the greatest amount of attention from the public, the police, and politicians. However, other types of crimes are emerging and are posing significant threats. They can be assigned to two categories: white-collar (or economic) crime and money laundering.

White-Collar (or Economic) Crime

White-collar crime is a generic term that encompasses a variety of activities. It was originally defined as "a crime committed by a person of respectability and high social status in the course of his occupation" (Sutherland 1949:9). Today, there are a number of meanings people attach to white-collar crime, including the following:

1. ***Occupational crime***: this most commonly refers to employees within a workplace who attempt to gain personal advantage at the expense of their employer. These individuals do not have to be of high social status; they could be, for example, individuals who are in charge of a warehouse.
2. ***Corporate crime***: these are activities carried out by employees of a corporation whose criminal activities benefit the company rather than personal gain. These actions may involve price-fixing between corporations so that one receives a large contract; another example is compromising safety standards that lead to serious injuries or the death of workers in order to maximize corporate profits.

The term "white-collar crime" is commonly used within the criminal justice system to describe crimes of fraud that are carried out during the course of a (seemingly) legitimate occupation. White-collar criminals exercise deceit (as opposed to force or stealth) in an effort to trick their unsuspecting victims. White-collar crimes receiving significant attention today include investment and securities fraud, market manipulation, consumer and business fraud, theft of telecommunication services, and the manufacture and use of counterfeit currency and payment cards.

Perhaps the most notorious case of white-collar crime in recent years was the securities fraud conducted by Bernie Madoff, who ran the operation from his New York City office. Madoff operated a **Ponzi scheme** that defrauded investors of an estimated $65 billion. For decades he had been paying substantial returns to investors from their own investments or from those of other investors rather than from any profits earned. His scam came to the attention of the authorities only as a result of too many investors requesting their money be returned due to the U.S. financial crisis of 2008. In December 2008, the U.S. Securities and Exchange Commission charged Madoff with securities fraud, and on March 3, 2009, he pleaded guilty to 11 criminal charges. Four months later, Madoff was sentenced to the maximum possible sentence of 150 years.

Canadians have also been victimized by individuals operating Ponzi schemes. In 2009, Earl Jones, who operated an asset-management and estate planning company

AP Images/Jason Decrow

Bernie Madoff was sentenced to a 150-year prison term for his $65 million (U.S.) Ponzi scheme that the sentencing judge termed "extraordinarily evil."

Dale Brazao/GetStock.com

RCMP recently seized these illegal cigarettes, packed in resealable bags, as well as the vehicle in which they were being smuggled.

Online Luring and Internet Use

The federal government introduced Bill C-15A, which was intended to protect children from sexual predators in cyberspace, in 2002. The bill addressed three issues: sexual exploitation, Internet luring, and child pornography. When Bill C-15A was proclaimed, the Canadian Criminal Code was amended to include the following:

- A new offence that targets individuals who use the Internet to lure and exploit children for sexual purposes.
- A new offence that makes it a crime to transmit, make available, export, or intentionally access child pornography on the Internet.
- Allows judges to order the forfeiture of any materials or equipment used in the commission of a child pornography offence.
- Enhances the ability of judges to keep known sex offenders away from children by making prohibition orders, long-term offender designations, and one-year peace bonds available for offences relating to child pornography and the Internet.
- Amends the child sex tourism law enacted in 1997 to simplify the process for prosecuting Canadians who sexually assault children in other countries (Kowalski 2002).

The new amendments were created in order to assist justice officials in their efforts to crack down on the problem of children and youth under the age of 18 being exploited via the Internet. They also made it illegal to communicate over the Internet with children for the purpose of committing a sexual offence. Under s. 172.1 of the Criminal Code (Luring of Children on the Internet), the age (real or believed) of the intended victim varies from 14 to 17, depending on the offence. When the crime of luring came into force in 2002, the maximum punishment was five years; in 2007, the punishment was doubled to 10 years. Bill C-10 (The Omnibus Crime Act) established new mandatory minimum penalties when a child is lured through the use of a computer, to 90 days on summary conviction and one year for indictable offences. See Figure 4.12 for statistics on child luring.

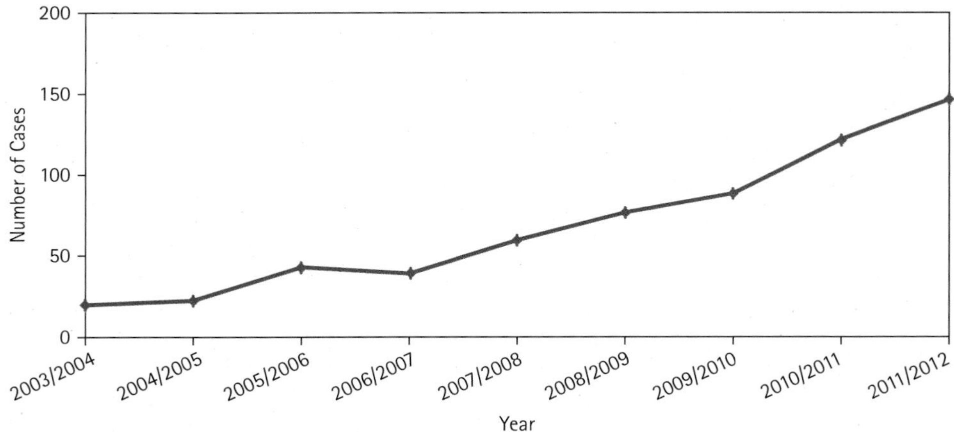

FIGURE 4.12 Number of Child Luring Cases Completed in Adult Criminal Court, 2003–04 to 2011–12

Note: Represents all completed cases containing at least one *Criminal Code* child luring charge. Data represent the 10 jurisdictions that have consistently reported to the Integrated Criminal Court Survey since 2001/2002. The jurisdictions not covered are Manitoba, Northwest Territories, and Nunavut.

Sources: Department of Justice Canada, "Online Luring and Internet Use." *Building Knowledge,* Issue 6 (Winter 2013/2014), p. 2, http://www.justice.gc.ca/eng/rp-pr/cj-jp/victim/knowledge-savoir/issue6-vol6/index.html. Data from *Integrated Criminal Court Survey, 2003/2004 to 2011/2012,* Statistics Canada. Reproduced and distributed on an "as is" basis with the permission of Statistics Canada.

in Quebec, was charged with operating an alleged Ponzi scheme. It was alleged that Jones had run this scheme for over 25 years, promising investors returns as high as 12 percent, which resulted in more than 150 of his clients losing just over $50 million. Jones pleaded guilty to two fraud charges in early 2010 and was sentenced to 11 years in prison. He received full parole in early 2014. After his conviction, the victims of Jones's Ponzi scheme started a class action lawsuit against Jones's bank, arguing that the Royal Bank of Canada was aware of irregularities in his account but did nothing. The victims demanded $40 million in their lawsuit, but in early March 2012 the bank agreed to pay them $17 million in an out-of-court settlement.

Money Laundering

According to the Criminal Code, **money laundering** occurs when an individual or group uses, transfers, sends, delivers, transports, transmits, alters, disposes, or otherwise deals with any property or proceeds of any property that was obtained as a result of criminal activity. The intent is to conceal or convert illegal assets into legitimate funds. According to the Financial Transactions and Reports Centre of Canada (FINTRAC), money laundering is often associated with the illegal drug trade or the defrauding and manipulation of Canada's financial institutions. The RCMP believe that money laundering is often related to organized crime and/or terrorist activity. They estimate that between $5 billion and $15 billion is laundered in Canada every year. While the focus in traditional policing is upon the person committing the crime and the commodity involved (e.g., stolen property), this area concentrates on a third component—the illicit wealth that flows from these criminal activities (Royal Canadian Mounted Police 2011).

According to Brennan and Vaillancourt (2011), incidents involving money laundering are extremely difficult to solve. In 2009, the police were able to identify an accused person in 18 percent of all money laundering incidents, compared to 39 percent for crime in general. Money laundering cases are complicated and difficult to prosecute, and typically involve multiple charges. For example, of the 85 completed money laundering cases in 2009–2010, 81 included charges other than money laundering. Only 29 (or 34 percent) of money laundering cases completed in the adult criminal courts resulted in a finding of guilt, compared to 65 percent of all other cases. The majority of money laundering cases (64 percent) resulted in charges being stayed or withdrawn, more than twice the proportion of cases in general (30 percent).

Money laundering involves a number of different criminal activities, generally around the provision of illegal goods or services as well as the infiltration of legitimate businesses. In Canada, various laws have been introduced to govern such activities. The Proceeds of Crime (Money Laundering) Act (PCMLA) created a mandatory system for reporting suspicious financial transactions, large cross-border currency and monetary instruments transfers, and suspicious financial transactions. The legislation also created FINTRAC to collect and analyze these financial transactions and disclose relevant information to various law enforcement agencies. In December 2001, the PCMLA was amended to include measures that would focus on terrorist financing activities and was subsequently renamed the Proceeds of Crime (Money Laundering) and Terrorist Financing Act. In the United States, law enforcement agencies operate under more sweeping laws, such as the Racketeer Influenced and Corrupt Organization (or RICO) provisions of the Organized Crime Control Act, which make it illegal for people to engage in racketeering activities. These laws are meant to make it difficult for people to organize to violate the law.

SUMMING UP AND LOOKING FORWARD

Criminal activities are often placed into different categories, most commonly based upon the degree of seriousness. A typical way that crime is referred to in Canada is on the basis of "crimes against the person" (i.e., violent crimes) and "crimes against property." This approach most typically combines summary data reported by the UCR and information about the actual incidents from the UCR2. As there are numerous offences found in each category, it allows a more detailed analysis of certain types of these crimes. For example, while the overall crime rate has declined, not every criminal offence has declined, or perhaps declined only slightly, relative to other types of criminal offence. In addition, certain information about the incident is included, such as the relationship between the victim and offender or how the crime was committed (e.g., the type of method used to commit a crime), as well as the age and gender of the victim(s).

The crime statistics normally found in these two categories don't include all types of crimes. A few of these other types of crimes—white-collar crimes, online (Internet) luring, and money laundering—are briefly reviewed. These types of crime occur quite frequently and cause great harm among their victims. It is the police who investigate crime, but some of these types of crimes (e.g., various types of white-collar crime) are difficult to investigate and even more difficult to find evidence of who is responsible for committing them. One reason for this is due to the fact that the context of policing has historically focused upon street crimes and street criminals. The context of policing is the topic of the next chapter.

Review Questions:

1. What differentiates first degree murder from manslaughter?
2. What method is most commonly used to commit a homicide? Has this changed over time?
3. What is a home invasion and how is it defined?
4. What is the most common property crime? The second most common property crime?
5. Define money laundering. Why is it difficult to solve this type of crime?

POLICE-REPORTED CYBERCRIME IN CANADA

The rapid growth of the Internet has led to the emergence of new criminal opportunities. Eighty-three percent of all Canadians aged 16 and older accessed the Internet for personal use during 2012, and the total dollar value of online orders placed by Canadians in that same year was $18.9 billion. While there are different types of crimes committed over the Internet, such as fraud, identity theft, extortion, and offences related to child pornography, they are collectively referred to as cybercrimes.

The UCR definition of cybercrime used by the police is "a criminal offence involving a computer as the object of the crime, or the tool used to commit a material component of the offence" (Kowalski 2002). Cybercrimes are then divided into two general categories:

(1) incidents in which computers or the Internet are the target of a crime (referred to as **technology-as-target** by law enforcement agencies), for example computer hacking, and
(2) incidents in which computers or the Internet are used as an instrument to commit a crime (referred to as **technology-as-instrument** by law enforcement agencies), for example luring a child (Mazowita and Vezina 2014).

Of the above two types, 88 percent of all reported cybercrimes in 2012 were of the type described in category (2) while 10 percent of all cybercrimes were of the type described in category (1). The cybercrime type of the remaining 2 percent could not be determined.

In 2012, there were 9,084 incidents reported by the police. Property crimes accounted for the majority of cybercrime (61 percent). Fraud was the most common type of property cybercrime, accounting for just over half (54 percent) of all cybercrimes. Other property-related cybercrimes included identity fraud (5 percent), mischief (2 percent), and identity theft (1 percent) (see Figure 4.13). Thirty-six percent of all reported cybercrimes in 2012 were categorized as crimes against the person. Cybercrimes involving crimes against the person are oftentimes divided into two categories: intimidation violations, which consist of violations involving the threat of

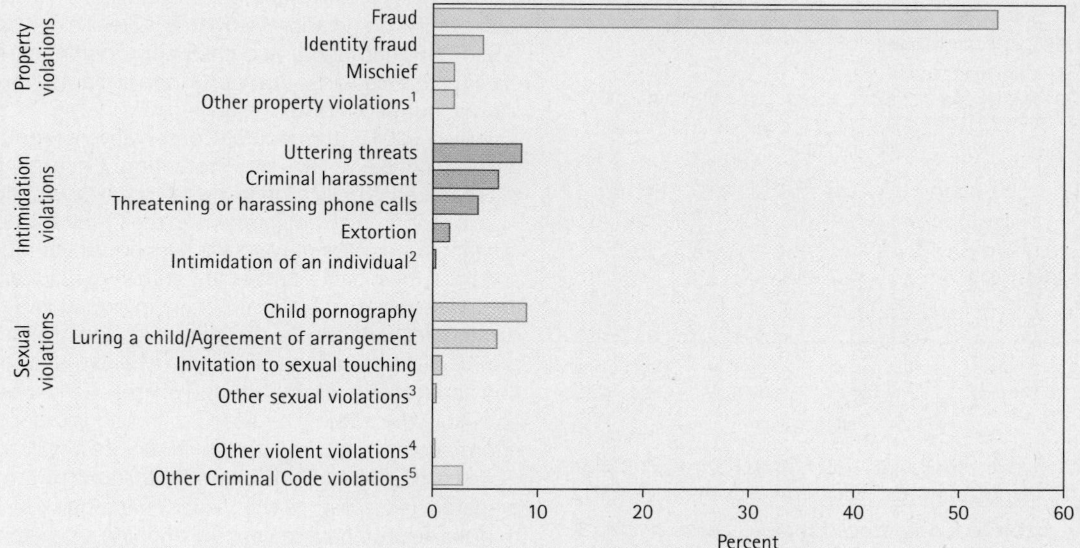

FIGURE 4.13 Police Reported Cybercrime, by Violation Type, Selected Police Services, 2012

[1] Other property violations include identity theft and trafficking stolen goods.
[2] Intimidation of an individual includes intimidation of a justice system participant or journalist and intimidation of a non-justice system participant.
[3] Other sexual violations include voyeurism, sexual exploitation, corrupting children, making sexually explicit material available to children, and bestiality—commit or compel person.
[4] Other violent violations include trafficking in persons and other violent violations.
[5] Other *Criminal Code* violations include offences such as corrupting morals, indecent acts, offences against the person and reputation, fail to comply with order, and breach of probation.

Note: This chart reflects data reported by police services covering 80% of the population of Canada.

Source: Bengamin Mazowita and Mirielle Vezina, "Police-reported cybercrime in Canada, 2012." *Juristat* (September 25, 2014), Statistics Canada Catalogue no. 85-002-X, p. 6, http://www.statcan.gc.ca/pub/85-002-x/2014001/article/14093-eng.pdf. Reproduced and distributed on an "as is" basis with the permission of Statistics Canada.

Continued on next page

violence, for example uttering threats and criminal harassment, and sexual violations, which include violations such as luring a child through a computer. Intimidation violations accounted for 20 percent of all police-reported cybercrimes in 2012 (or 1,839 incidents). Uttering threats and criminal harassment accounted for 8 and 6 percent of all cybercrimes, respectively. There were 1,441 incidents of cybercrime where the cyber-related violation was a sexual violation, and this type of cybercrime represented 16 percent of all police-reported cybercrimes. Other types of police-reported cybercrimes in 2012 included luring a child through the use of a computer (6 percent of all police-reported cybercrime incidents) (see Figure 4.13).

How likely is it that an individual is identified in incidents of cybercrime? Overall, an accused was identified in 21 percent of all police-reported cybercrime incidents during 2012 (see Figure 4.14). Six percent of all property-related cybercrimes were cleared by charge or otherwise. In comparison, 31 percent of all sexual cybercrime-related violations and 55 percent of all cybercrimes related to intimidation were cleared by charge or otherwise during 2012. The highest clearance rate was found in incidents of sexual violations (23 percent).

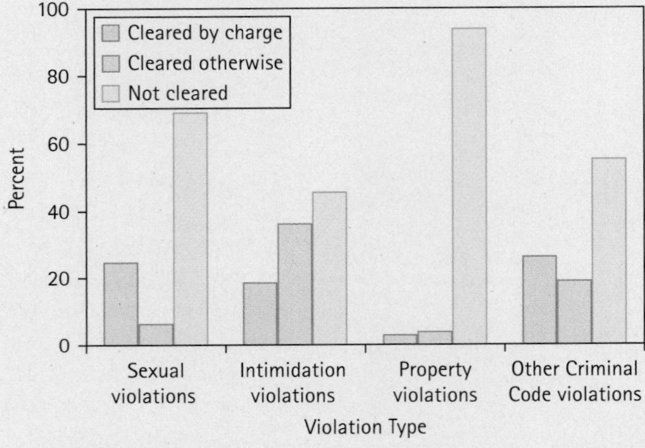

FIGURE 4.14 Police Reported Cybercrime, by Violation Type and Clearance Status, Selected Police Services, 2012

Note: This chart reflects data reported by police services covering 80% of the population of Canada. For an incident to be cleared, an accused must be identified and there must be enough evidence to lay a charge in connection with the incident. Incidents may be cleared by charge or processed by other means (i.e. cleared otherwise). Sexual violations include sexual violations against the person and child pornography related offences. Intimidation violations include violations against the person involving the threat of violence. The category Property violations includes fraud, identity theft, identity fraud, mischief and trafficking stolen goods. The category Other *Criminal Code* violations includes offences such as corrupting morals, indecent acts, and offences against the 1 for a list of offences in each violation type category.

Source: Bengamin Mazowita and Mirielle Vezina, "Police-reported cybercrime in Canada, 2012." *Juristat* (September 25, 2014), Statistics Canada Catalogue no. 85-002-X, p. 8, http://www.statcan.gc.ca/pub/85-002-x/2014001/article/14093-eng.pdf. Reproduced and distributed on an "as is" basis with the permission of Statistics Canada.

The accused is most likely to be a male—76 percent of the 2,051 individuals accused of a cybercrime incident in 2012 were men. Men were the accused in 94 percent of cyber violations of a sexual nature. In the same year, the police identified 2,070 victims of violent incidents involving a cybercrime-related incident. Almost 70 percent of the victims of all incidents of cybercrime were women. They accounted for 84 percent of all victims of sexual violations associated with a cybercrime and 65 percent of those involving a non-sexual violent violation. Forty-two percent of the victims of cybercrime were aged 17 years and under, and another 17 percent of victims were between the ages of 17 and 24.

In addition, 73 percent of the victims of violent violations of a police-reported cybercrime knew the accused. For sexual violations, 57 percent of the victims knew the accused, most commonly as an acquaintance (45 percent of the time) or as a current or former intimate partner (24 percent).

In response to the increasing number of violations using the Internet, the federal government has introduced a number of bills in an attempt to control such activities. Bill C-15A, which was intended to protect children from sexual predators in cyberspace, was introduced in 2002 and addressed three issues: sexual exploitation, Internet luring, and child pornography (see the *Criminal Justice Focus* previously in this chapter for specifics about Bill C-15A).

In early 2012, the federal Conservative government introduced Bill C-30, the Protecting Children from Internet Predators Act (originally titled the Lawful Access Act). It proposed an amendment to the Criminal Code by allowing authorities new warrantless powers to monitor and track the digital activities of Canadians, require mandatory disclosure of basic subscriber information by telecommunications service providers (i.e., Internet service providers and telephone providers) to hand over information about their customers to the police when requested and allow the authorities access to individuals electronic information, none of which would require a warrant.

Since the Bill did not mention children or Internet predators (except in its title), critics were quick to state that the federal government was hoping to overextend the powers of the government and various agencies involved in law enforcement. Due to the extent of criticism brought against the Bill by the other federal political parties as well as large sections of the public, particularly that the Bill violated the privacy rights of Canadians, the federal government withdrew it in February 2013.

Ten months later, in November 2013, the federal Conservative government introduced Bill C-13 (the Protecting Canadians from Online Crime Act) as a response to a number of high-profile cases involving adolescents who committed suicide due to cyberbullying. There were two parts to this Bill: one part was directed to cyberbullying and, in this context, created an offence to the Criminal Code of non-consensual distribution of intimate images of someone without their permission. It also made amendments to authorize the removal of such images from the Internet, the recovery of costs involved with removing those images, and the forfeiture of property used in the commission of the offence.

The other part of Bill C-13 contained a number of new investigative powers for authorities, such as new warrants for police access to online data, phone records, and for digital tracking. The Bill also makes organizations such as Internet service providers and telecommunications service providers to comply with orders made by the courts and demands made by law enforcement agencies and "public officers." Bill C-13 came into force in March 2015.

Questions

1. Do you believe that Canada's child luring laws are strong enough? If not, how do you think they can be improved?
2. Do you think that individuals convicted of Internet luring should be able to receive a long-term offender designation after they have finished serving their sentence?
3. Do you think the Canadian government is doing enough in terms of funding enforcement efforts to detect and control Internet luring?

SUMMARY

Information about the amount of crime at any one time or how it has changed over time is provided through crime statistics. There are, however, different approaches that are used to gather information about crime in our society. While some people consider crime statistics to be a realistic portrayal of crime in our society, others believe that crime statistics are a product of processes that don't accurately reflect the volume and type of crime, but rather attitudes toward social behaviour that change over time.

KEY WORDS: official crime statistics, institutionalist approach, crime funnel, unofficial crime statistics

Official Crime Statistics

Official crime statistics are based upon information obtained from the police, and these have usually been reported to them by the public. Official crime statistics provide us with information about the amount of crime occurring in one year; these can be combined with other years to reveal trends in crime patterns over time.

KEY WORDS: Crime Severity Index; Violent Crime Severity Index, reactive, behavioural patterns, age structure, lag effect, Uniform Crime Reporting system, Aggregate UCR Survey, Incident-Based UCR Survey, clearance rate, weighted clearance rate, victimization surveys, Canadian Urban Victimization Survey, General Social Survey, Violence Against Women Survey

Police-Reported Crime Statistics (p. 116)
Violent Crime (p. 118)
Property Crime (p. 119)
Other Criminal Code (p. 120)
Factors Affecting Police-Reported Crime Rates (p. 120)
The Official Crime Reporting System (p. 121)
What Victims Say: Victimization Data (p. 124)

Criminal Victimization in Canada

Difficulties in obtaining a complete picture of crime statistics by relying solely on police-reported crime statistics have led to the use of other approaches to discover a more accurate level of crime in society. The most common alternative is the victim survey; two other approaches are the self-report study and the ethnographic approach.

KEY WORDS: self-report surveys, age of onset, ethnographic research, micro situations, field research, unstructured interviews, participant observation, overt research, covert research

Trends and Patterns of Victimization: The General Social Survey 1988–2009 (p. 126).
Victimizations Not Reported to the Police (p. 127)
Self-Report Surveys (p. 128).
Ethnographic Research (p. 128)

Trends and Patterns of Selected Crimes in Canada: Crimes against the Person

Homicide (p. 130)
Sexual Assault (p. 131)
Assault (p. 134)
Robbery (p. 135)
Criminal Harassment (Stalking) (p. 135)
Forcible Confinement (p. 136)

One of the categories used to study crime is "crimes against the person." This category focuses upon those crimes classified as violent.

KEY WORDS: homicide, first degree murder, second degree murder, manslaughter, infanticide, sexual assault, assault, robbery, criminal harassment, forcible confinement, home invasion

Trends and Patterns of Selected Crimes: Crimes against Property

Breaking and Entering (p. 138)
Theft (p. 139)
Motor Vehicle Theft (p. 139)

One of the categories used to study crime is "crimes against property." This category focuses upon those crimes classified as property offences.

KEY WORDS: property crimes, breaking and entering, theft, motor vehicle theft

Other Criminal Code Offences

This category is used for those offences that do not fit into either the crimes against the person or crimes against property offences.

KEY WORDS: counterfeiting, weapons offences, child pornography, disturbing the peace, administration of justice offences, prostitution

Other Types of Crime

White-Collar (or Economic) Crime (p. 139)
Money Laundering (p. 142)

Many high-profile crimes today and in the recent past have involved financial transactions; these include white-collar crime and money laundering.

KEY WORDS: white-collar crime, Ponzi scheme, money laundering, technology-as-target, technology-as-instrument

Critical Thinking Questions

1. Why did government officials revise the UCRs?
2. What are the three categories into which all crimes in Canada are placed? Do you think the government should develop new categories, such as a sexual offence category or a white-collar crime category? Why or why not?
3. Why is the clearance rate for aggravated assault lower than the clearance rate for first degree murder?
4. Why is sexual assault level 1 one of the most underreported violent crimes?
5. What are the four categories of murder?
6. Why would a police force try to manipulate the number of crimes reported to the various categories?
7. Discuss the differences between the UCRs and victimization surveys.
8. What are the most common criticisms of UCRs?
9. Why is it important to study the fear of crime? Should statistics on the fear of crime be incorporated into official year-end measures of crime, as are the statistics in the UCRs?

Weblinks

To watch an example of ethnographic research and the insights it gives into crime, watch the following video on YouTube: "Street Codes—Code of the Street, Elijah Anderson" (6:26). To watch a video about Bernie Madoff and Ponzi schemes, watch the following on YouTube: "Bernie Madoff: Scamming of America—The $50 Billion Ponzi Scheme" (44:56).

Suggested Readings

Archer, N., S. Sproule, Y. Yuan, and K. Guo. 2012. *Identity Theft and Fraud: Evaluating and Managing Risk*. Ottawa: University of Ottawa Press.

Desroches, F. 2005. *The Crime That Pays: Drug Trafficking and Organized Crime in Canada*. Toronto: Canadian Scholars' Press.

Furnell, S. 2002. *Cybercrime: Vandalizing the Information Society*. Edinburgh: Pearson Education.

Goffman, A. 2014. *On the Run: Fugitive Life in American Cities*. Chicago: The University of Chicago Press.

Kenney, J. 2009. *Canadian Victims of Crime: Critical Insights*. Toronto: Canadian Scholars' Press.

Pawluch, D., W. Shaffir, and C. Miall. 2005. *Doing Ethnography: Studying Everyday Life*. Toronto: Canadian Scholars' Press.

References

Anderson, E. 1999. *Code of the Street: Decency, Violence, and the Moral Life of the Inner City*. New York: W.W. Norton.

Beirne, P. and J. Messerschmidt. 1991. *Criminology*. San Diego, CA: Harcourt Brace Jovanovich.

Blonigen, D.M. 2010. "Explaining the Relationship between Age and Crime: Contributions from the Developmental Literature on Personality." *Clinical Psychology Review* 30:89–100.

Boyce, J. 2015. *Police-Reported Crime Statistics in Canada, 2014*. Ottawa: Canadian Centre for Justice Statistics.

Boyce, J., A. Cotter, and S. Perreault. 2014. *Police-Reported Crime Statistics in Canada, 2013*. Ottawa: Canadian Centre for Justice Statistics.

Brennan, S. 2011. *Canadians' Perceptions of Personal Safety and Crime, 2009*. Ottawa: Canadian Centre for Justice Statistics.

Brennan, S. and M. Dauvergne. 2011. *Police-Reported Crime Statistics in Canada, 2010*. Ottawa: Canadian Centre for Justice Statistics.

Brennan, S. and R. Vaillancourt. 2011. *Money Laundering in Canada, 2009*. Ottawa: Canadian Centre for Justice Statistics.

Burczycka, M. 2011. *Police Resources in Canada, 2011*. Ottawa: Canadian Centre for Justice Statistics.

Charron, M. 2009. *Neighbourhood Characteristics and the Distribution of Police-Reported Crime in the City of Toronto*. Ottawa: Statistics Canada.

Coleman, C. and J. Moynihan. (1996). *Understanding Crime Data: Haunted by the Dark Figure*. Buckingham: Open University Press.

Cotter, A. 2014. *Homicide in Canada, 2013*. Ottawa: Canadian Centre for Justice Statistics.

Dauvergne, M. 2010. *Police-Reported Robbery in Canada, 2008*. Ottawa: Canadian Centre for Justice Statistics.

Dauvergne, M. 2009. *Forcible Confinement in Canada, 2007*. Ottawa: Canadian Centre for Justice Statistics.

Dauvergne, M. 2008. *Motor Vehicle Theft in Canada, 2007*. Ottawa: Minister of Industry.

Dauvergne, M. 2005. *Homicide in Canada, 2004*. Ottawa: Canadian Centre for Justice Statistics.

Dauvergne, M. and L. De Socio. 2008. *Firearms and Violent Crime*. Ottawa: Canadian Centre for Justice Statistics.

Dauvergne, M. and J. Turner. 2010. *Police-Reported Crime Statistics in Canada, 2009*. Ottawa: Canadian Centre for Justice Statistics.

Densley, J. 2013. *How Gangs Work: An Ethnography of Youth Violence*. London: Palgrave Macmillan.

Department of Justice Canada. 2013/2014. *Building Knowledge: Online Luring and Internet Use*. Ottawa: Department of Justice Canada.

Department of Justice Canada. 2013a. *Building Knowledge: Child and Youth Victims of Criminal Harassment, 2011*. Ottawa: Department of Justice Canada.

Department of Justice Canada. 2013b. *Building Knowledge: Child and Youth Victims of Assault*. Ottawa: Department of Justice Canada.

Duchesne, D. 1997. *Street Prostitution in Canada*. Ottawa: Canadian Centre for Justice Statistics.

Edmiston, J. 2012. "Canada's Inexplicable Anxiety over Violent Crime," *National Post*, August 4. Retrieved August 17, 2014 (http://news.nationalpost.com/news .canada/canadas-inexplicable-anxiety-over-violent-crime).

Fedorowycz, O. 2004. *Breaking and Entering in Canada, 2002*. Ottawa: Canadian Centre for Justice Statistics.

Frechette, S. and M. LeBlanc. 1987. *Delinquances et Delinquants*. Chicoutimi: Gaetan Morin.

Gannon, M. and K. Mihorean. 2005. *Criminal Victimization in Canada, 2004*. Ottawa: Canadian Centre for Justice Statistics.

Gannon, M. and A. Taylor-Butts. 2006. *Canadians' Use of Crime Prevention Measures, 2004*. Ottawa: Canadian Centre for Justice Statistics.

Garrison, G. 2015. *Human on the Inside: Unlocking the Truth About Prisons*. Regina: University of Regina Press.

Hagan, J. and B. McCarthy. 1992. "Streetlife and Delinquency." *British Journal of Sociology* 43(4):533–61.

Hendrick, D. 1995. *Canadian Crime Statistics, 1994*. Ottawa: Canadian Centre for Justice Statistics.

Hood, R. and R. Sparks. 1970. *Key Issues in Criminology*. London: Weidenfeld and Nicholson.

Kong, R. 1998. *Breaking and Entering in Canada, 1996*. Ottawa: Canadian Centre for Justice Statistics.

Kowalski, M. 2002. *Cyber-Crime: Issues, Data Sources, and Feasibility of Collecting Police-Reported Statistics*. Ottawa: Canadian Centre for Justice Statistics.

Leenaars, A. and D. Lester. 2004. "Understanding the Declining Canadian Homicide Rate: A Test of Hollinger's Relative Cohort Size Hypothesis." *Death Studies* 28:263–65.

Martin, M. and L. Ogrodnik. 1996. "Canadian Crime Trends." Pp. 43–58 in *Crime Counts: A Criminal Event Analysis*, edited by L.W. Kennedy and V.F. Sacco. Scarborough, ON: Nelson Canada.

Mazowita, B. and M. Vezina. 2014. *Police-Reported Cybercrime in Canada*. Ottawa: Canadian Centre for Justice Statistics.

Milligan, S. 2011. *Criminal Harassment in Canada, 2009*. Ottawa: Canadian Centre for Justice Statistics.

Perreault, S. 2011. *Self-Reported Internet Victimization in Canada, 2009*. Ottawa: Canadian Centre for Justice Statistics.

Perreault, S. and S. Brennan. 2010. *Criminal Victimization in Canada, 2009*. Ottawa: Canadian Centre for Justice Statistics.

Perreault, S., J. Sauve, and M. Burns. 2009. *Multiple Victimization in Canada, 2004*. Ottawa: Canadian Centre for Justice Statistics.

Pottie Bunge, V., H. Johnson, and T.A. Balde. 2005. *Exploring Crime Patterns in Canada*. Ottawa: Ministry of Industry.

Royal Canadian Mounted Police. 2011. *Money Laundering*. (Online: accessed May 2, 2011.)

Royal Canadian Mounted Police. 2009. *History of Firearms Control in Canada: Up to and Including the Firearms Act*. (Online: accessed Feb. 22, 2012.)

Savoie, J. 2008. *Neighbourhood Characteristics and the Distribution of Crime: Edmonton, Halifax, and Thunder Bay*. Ottawa: Statistics Canada.

Scarborough, B.K., T.Z. Like-Halslip, K.J. Novak, W.L. Lucas, and L.F. Alarid. 2010. "Assessing the Relationship between Individual Characteristics, Neighbourhood Context, and Fear of Crime." *Journal of Criminal Justice* 38:819–826.

Shaw, C. 1930. *The Jack Roller: A Delinquent Boy's Own Story*. Chicago: The University of Chicago Press.

Silverman, R. 1980. "Measuring Crime: A Tale of Two Cities." Pp. 78–90 in *Crime in Canadian Society*, 2nd ed., edited by R.A. Silverman and J.J. Teevan. Toronto: Butterworths.

Silverman, R., J.J. Teevan, and V.F. Sacco, eds. 1991. *Crime in Canadian Society*, 4th ed. Toronto: Butterworths.

Sinha, M. 2015. *Trends in Reporting Criminal Victimization to police, 1999 to 2009*. Ottawa: Canadian Centre for Justice Statistics.

Sparks, R. 1981. "Surveys of Victimization—An Optimistic Assessment." Pp. 1–60 in *Crime and Justice—An Annual Review of Research*, edited by M. Tonry. Chicago: University of Chicago Press.

Sprott, J. and C. Cesaroni. 2002. "Similarities in Homicide Trends in the United States and Canada: Guns, Crack or Simple Demographics." *Homicide Studies* 6:348–59.

Sutherland, E. 1949. *White Collar Crime*. New York: Dryden Press.

Thomas, J. 2010. *Adult Criminal Court Statistics, 2008/2009*. Ottawa: Canadian Centre for Justice Statistics.

Tremblay, S. 1999. *Crime Statistics in Canada, 1998*. Ottawa: Canadian Centre for Justice Statistics.

Van der Meulen, E., E. Durisin, and V. Love, eds. 2013. *Selling Sex: Experience, Advocacy, and Research on Sex Work in Canada*. Vancouver: UBC Press.

Wallace, M. 2009. *Police-Reported Crime Statistics in Canada, 2008*. Ottawa: Canadian Centre for Justice Statistics.

Wallace, M., J. Turner, A. Matarazzo, and C. Babyak. 2009. *Measuring Crime in Canada: Introducing the Crime Severity Index and Improvements to the Uniform Crime Reporting Survey*. Ottawa: Canadian Centre for Justice Statistics.

CHAPTER

5

The Context of Policing

Learning Objectives

After completing this chapter, you should be able to:

- Describe the functions and roles of the police in early England.
- Understand the principle of policing by consent and its importance to the development of modern police organizations.
- Identify and describe the problems associated with the earliest forms of public policing and understand the core elements of the professional model of policing.
- Describe the emergence and development of plural policing.
- Describe how the public police are distributed across Canada.
- Understand the barriers and issues in police organizations for women and members of visible minority groups.
- Understand the police culture and appreciate its importance for both police officers and citizens.
- Understand the working personality of the police, how it develops, and its impact upon police officers.

As with all of the social institutions in our criminal justice system, the police perform a number of necessary functions and tasks that contribute toward the achievement of justice in our society. How the public views the role of the police in society is important to consider, as citizens' views about the legitimacy of the police influence their level of confidence in the police as well as their willingness to obey the law. Much of the work of the police is based on the idea that both their organization and their practices have public support. Legitimacy is important for the police since it affects their ability to operate in our society. The police would find it difficult to perform many if not all of their practices if the general public did not accept their legitimacy to do so.

What is **police legitimacy**? It is those "judgments that ordinary citizens make about the rightness of police conduct and the organizations that employ and supervise them" (Skogan and Frydl 2004:291). Our society follows the Anglo-American tradition in which the source of police legitimacy derives from the general public. This is known as the **common law model**, as legitimacy is given to the police from below (i.e., the general public). Some other Western nations, particularly European countries, use a different approach (the Continental model), in which the legitimacy of the police is obtained from above—that is, the government.

In the common law approach, the police are typically subject to a certain amount of local control and accountability. Their most important purpose is to serve the public by dealing with problems identified by the community, whether they be crime prevention, crime detection, order maintenance, or the provision of services. The police perform their duties in these areas by engaging in what is known as *policing by consent* (see below).

Do Canadians support the legitimacy of the police? One approach is to ask people how much confidence they have in the police. The 2009 GSS (see Chapter 4) asked respondents about their confidence in their local police service and found that "being approachable" was considered to be most important (see Figure 5.1).

But what encourages people to see the police as a legitimate institution? The public has been found to view the police as legitimate when they act fairly toward them or by finding out how the police treat other people who live in their city and/or community. These views are important, since people who believe that the police are legitimate are

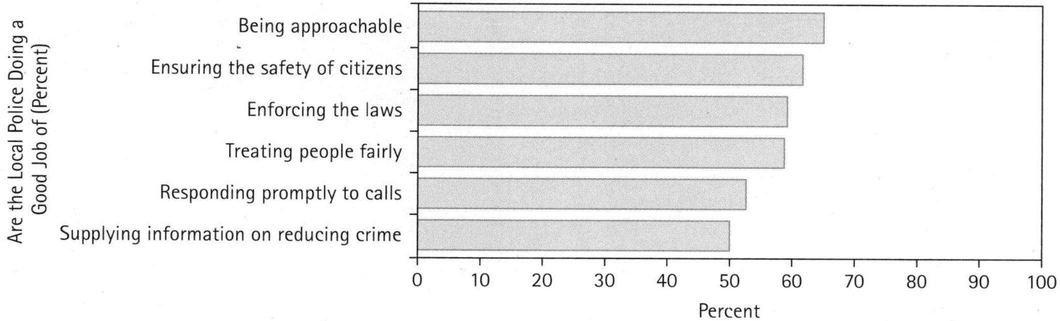

FIGURE 5.1 Perceptions of the Criminal Justice System, 2009

Source: Tina Hotton Mahony and John Turner, "Police-reported clearance rates in Canada, 2010." *Juristat* (June 7, 2012), Statistics Canada Catalogue no. 85-002-x, p. 23, http://www.statcan.gc.ca/pub/85-002-x/2012001/article/11647-eng.pdf. Reproduced and distributed on an "as is" basis with the permission of Statistics Canada.

more likely to defer to the legal authority of the police when they are requested to follow the instructions of police officers. In Canada, as in other common law countries, the legitimacy of the police is important as it is supported by the principle of **policing by consent**; that is, the police want the cooperation and support of the public when they are conducting their legal duties.

How Did the Idea of Policing Emerge?

The origins of Canadian police agencies, like our criminal law, can be traced back to early English society. Prior to the Norman Conquest of England in the 11th century, there was no regular police force. Justice was largely left in the hands of concerned citizens. Victims of a crime had to deal with the perpetrators without any assistance from the state, as there was no court system. The closest thing to a police agency was the **pledge system**, in which every person was responsible for assisting neighbours and protecting the village from thieves and other criminals. Gradually, however, a system of group protection emerged. Groups of 10 families (known as "**tithings**," or the *frank-pledge system*) were set up in villages in order to police their own minor problems. Ten tithings were then grouped in a larger area to a form a "**hundred**," whose affairs were looked after by a **constable** appointed by the local nobles. The constable, considered by many to be the first "real" police officer, dealt with the most serious law violations. The hundreds were then amalgamated into **shires** (the equivalent of modern-day counties), and the top law enforcement officials became known as **shire-reeves**, a position that (as the phonetics suggest) developed into the position of sheriff. This individual was appointed by the Crown or local landowner to supervise a specific area to maintain law and order and apprehend law violators.

At the end of the 12th century, the position of the **coroner** was created. Their job was to make sure that the interests of the Crown were upheld, including criminal matters. In serious (i.e., indictable) cases coroners were able to conduct preliminary hearings, and on such occasions sheriffs usually attended. This became known as the "coroner's inquest," and the participants attempted to determine the cause of death of the victim and who was responsible for it.

In the 13th century, the **constable-watch system** of protection was formalized by the **Statute of Westminster** (1285). This system was created in order to protect the property of people in larger English towns and cities. In the largest English cities, watchmen were organized within church parishes; usually they were residents of the parishes they were hired to protect. The statute allowed one man from each parish to be selected as a constable. It enabled constables to appoint citizens as **watchmen**, whose duties largely consisted of watching or guarding the local town or city. Watchmen patrolled predominantly at night and were responsible for protecting citizens from robbers, ensuring that citizens were safe, and detecting fires. They reported to the area constable, who ultimately became the primary law enforcement officer. These individuals were not paid, and as a result many did not perform their duties as instructed. The statute also required all males between 15 and 60 to possess weapons and to be ready to participate in the "hue and cry"; that is, to come to the assistance of a watchman when their assistance was needed. If they did not, criminal punishments could be handed out to the neglectful citizens on the reasoning that their inaction aided the offender. This system lasted until the 18th century.

In 1326, shire-reeves were replaced by **justices of the peace**, a position created to control an entire county. Over time, justices of the peace were assigned judicial functions. From this came the position of **parish constable**, who was expected to oversee criminal justice for his parishioners.

Parish constables were agents of the justice of the peace; they supervised night watchmen, investigated offences, served summonses, executed warrants, and ensured the security of those charged with crimes before their trial. This system has been credited with starting the separation of the police from the judiciary, a system that has continued in our legal system for almost 700 years.

What Is the Importance of the Principle of Policing by Public Consent?

As of the mid-1700s, cities in England still did not have an organized law enforcement system. Policing efforts were haphazard and organized in various ways in different locations. This continued into the early 19th century in both rural and urban areas. In London, criminal activity was commonplace, and when crime grew so common as to become unbearable, the only recourse open to city officials was to call in the military. This approach became unpopular among the local populace, however, as the soldiers used their powers in most cases to maintain a system of harsh control over those living in crime-prone areas, and they occasionally used their weapons to exert control in disorderly situations. So the military were placed under the direct control of city officials. It is a matter of historical record that these officials often abused the power of the military to their own purposes. As a result, many citizens in London were suspicious of any formal efforts to control their activities.

An alternative to calling in the military was introduced by Henry Fielding, Chief Magistrate of Bow Street, in 1748. Fielding decided to turn a group of men into professional law enforcement agents; their duties would be to catch criminals and recover stolen property. These individuals became known as the **Bow Street Runners** (also referred to as the "**Thief Takers**"), and they proved to be so successful that they were hired out to control crime in various other parts of England. Their efforts were largely unsuccessful; even so, the idea of a group of individuals tasked with apprehending criminals and with returning stolen property to its rightful owners helped develop the concept of a professional police force.

The Industrial Revolution dramatically increased the size of urban populations while at the same time traditional forms of social control broke down. At the same time, social problems such as poverty, crime, and disorder began to increase. Concerns over the rise of the "**dangerous class**" and crime and disorder drew the British Parliament into a debate about the best way to deal with criminal activity. But it wasn't until Sir Robert Peel was appointed to the position of Home Secretary

Georgios Kollidas/iStock/Thinkstock

Sir Robert Peel founded the London Metropolitan Police.

that a formal plan was approved. In 1829, Peel succeeded in having the London Metropolitan Police Act passed by Parliament (Exhibit 5.1).

This led to the creation of a 3,200-member professional police force which replaced the various law enforcement systems existing in London at the time. Members were easily recognized by their uniforms (which included blue coats and top hats). The new police force had a military structure, including ranks. Two magistrates (later known as "commissioners") were appointed to oversee the force.

EXHIBIT 5.1 The Mandate of the London Metropolitan Police Force (1829)

The **goals** of the police were to:

- prevent crime; and
- detect and apprehend offenders when crimes were committed.

The **success** of the police was based on:

- protecting life and property;
- preserving the public order; and
- eliminating crime. (Villiers 2009)

The creation of the London Metropolitan Police became the template for almost all police forces in common law countries. When the first professional police force was established in London during 1829, it was subject to a certain amount of local control and accountability. Only civilians were hired for the positions, and non-militaristic methods were used only when necessary. Their major responsibility was to serve the public by dealing with those issues which concerned them by engaging in the prevention and detection of crime. This approach to policing was based on the *principle of policing by public consent*. This principle emphasized the need for the police to have the support of the public; that is, the police act for citizens, not over them. In order to live up to this mandate, the police instituted a number of key features into the way they were organized and guided their operations (see Exhibit 5.2).

This approach to policing became so popular that in 1835 it expanded to locations outside London, where "new" police organizations replaced constables and watchmen. In 1856, police forces became compulsory in all counties. This approach to policing quickly spread into Canada, the United States, and Australia. One reason why the idea of the modern police became accepted so quickly was because the public accepted their role as legitimate; that is, the public accepted the "right" of the police to maintain law and order. As the professional police developed, large numbers of citizens, particularly in the middle class, viewed the police as a legitimate organization that upheld the law. Over time, consent to the police led citizens to consent to the rule of law.

What Was the Early Canadian Police Experience?

In colonial Canada, various law enforcement agencies were established. Before Canada joined the British Empire, settlers in New France created a system of policing that replicated the one in France. The first individuals involved in policing appeared in the settlement of Quebec in 1651. Twenty years later, that settlement developed police regulations (Kelly and Kelly 1976). The first permanent constables under the control of their respective town councils appeared in Quebec and Montreal in 1833.

Settlers in Ontario municipalities followed the law enforcement system being practised in England. In 1835, the City of Toronto hired six men to be its first constables; their task was to police the municipality at night. Other Canadian cities gradually formed their own municipal police forces, including Halifax (1841), Hamilton (1847), Saint John (1849), Victoria (1862), Winnipeg (1874), Calgary (1885), and Vancouver (1886). In the North-West Territories, there was no organized municipal policing. Most rural communities developed policing systems based largely on what the populace had experienced in their homelands. The Hudson's Bay Company formed its own policing system, approved by the federal government, in the areas surrounding its trading posts. In order to gain control over its western lands, Canada established the North-West Mounted Police (NWMP) in 1873. The NWMP was organized in a different way from the municipal police forces, as its founders applied a paramilitary structure

EXHIBIT 5.2 The Principles of Policing by Consent

In order to have the public trust and support, the first professional police departments were formulated around a number of ideas which became known as policing by public consent. Some of these principles were:

Methods of policing: In order to prevent crime the police patrolled small geographic areas on foot. The idea was that the physical presence of the police would deter crime.

Police powers: The police were bound by the rule of law. Early on, the first professional police did not have special powers granted to them; instead, they used common law powers to enforce the law.

Weaponry: The police operated on the principle of minimum force. The idea was that when the police maintained law and order, they would do so with the least possible force.

Service to the public: While law enforcement was central to police operations, they also provided a service function in order to gain and maintain the trust of the community.

Structure, control, and accountability: When the professional police were introduced to areas outside the large British cities, policing was oftentimes controlled by and accountable to the local authorities. This approach was developed in order to show that the police wouldn't challenge the rights and liberties of the people. (Reiner 2000)

SUMMING UP AND LOOKING FORWARD

The roots of some of the positions found in our criminal justice system originated in early England. This system gradually evolved over the centuries, but as societies industrialized, cities grew and presented new issues concerning crime control. The traditional social control systems did not work well in cities, and as a result the first professional police force was created in London in the 19th century. The "new" police introduced a number of features into policing, including (1) a formal organization (similar to the hierarchy found in the military), (2) control by federal or city governments, and (3) a preventive policing style. To overcome any potential resistance to the new police forces, the principle of policing by consent was established. In Canada, the first police forces were established in New France, and subsequently followed the professional policing model practised in Great Britain.

Why were these early police forces viewed as essential aspects of governance? And how did they develop and change over time? Municipal governments recognized the benefits of having police forces working to prevent crime, and soon the police started to serve the community in numerous ways. This type of policing became problematic, especially in the United States, and in many municipalities the public withdrew their consent to be policed. As a result, reformers introduced new ways or models of policing. These issues with early municipal policing are briefly discussed in the next section, as is the "new" style of policing introduced by reformers. But what, if any, problems existed in this new style of policing?

Review Questions:

1. How did the first public police force emerge and why was it considered to be a necessity?
2. What were the major police-related positions and their functions prior to the emergence of the first professional police force in 1829 in England?
3. What is meant by policing by consent and what is its importance to the emergence of the public police?
4. How was the early Canadian experience in policing different from its counterparts in Europe?

based on that of the Royal Irish Constabulary. This system was gradually adopted by all municipal forces across Canada (Guth 1994). The purpose of the NWMP (renamed the RCMP in 1920) was to police and control the lands purchased from the Hudson's Bay Company by the federal government in 1869 (Browne and Browne 1973; Kelly and Kelly 1976).

How Did Modern Policing Develop? The Rise of Municipal Policing

As the 19th century ended, the type of policing practised was **preventive** in nature. In this approach, police officers on patrol were assigned "beats" in a small geographical area and it was thought that their presence would deter crime. One important aspect of this style of policing was that it often helped to create good relationships between the police and the public. Police officers worked in the same areas where they lived, and provided a variety of services such as soup kitchens, homeless shelters, and ambulance services. "In a time before widespread and well-supported social work and social programs, and before municipalities has assumed many of their routine obligations, the police often filled important vacuums" (Sparrow et al. 1995:34). Perhaps the most significant development in this type of policing over the decades was the police adaptation of technological advances, especially in the area of communications. In their early stages of development, municipal police officers had to personally meet or write notes delivered by police runners in order to communicate with one another. The introduction of call boxes in the 1870s revolutionized policing. At first, patrol officers were only able to signal their location to police headquarters. Later, the call boxes were equipped with a bell system, which allowed patrol officers to send different signals to headquarters—for example, to call for backup or an ambulance. Finally, in the 1880s, telephones were placed in the call boxes, establishing a direct link between officers on the street and those at headquarters. Over the coming decades, the police introduced more technology into their operations as it became available. Patrol vehicles, two-way communication systems, fingerprinting, a criminal record system, and toxicological analyses were all introduced during and after the 1920s. Over time, these changes led to police officers reducing their close relationship, a situation that was to last until the introduction of community policing in the late 1980s.

This separation of the police from the community was the result of a number of problems that plagued the police in the early 20th century. Political influence over and corruption within many large urban police forces

Matthew McCarthy/Waterloo Record

The police have always been quick to embrace new technologies. Here, a police officer uses an e-ticket system for a speeding infraction.

in the United States became a concern during the last decades of the 19th century and the first decades of the 20th century. Essentially, in many major American urban areas, the police became part of dominant political machines. As a result, some of the police departments protected corrupt political practices, and some police officers used their position to profit individually by protecting criminals.

Many of these problems were ultimately traced to the lack of training for and qualifications among police officers. Around this time, then, a number of individuals set out to reform policing. These reformers believed they could improve the police by raising the educational requirements for police officers and improving the training they received. This led to the introduction of a "new" way of policing that many today see as being the "normal" policing role and function in our society. This approach, which was slowly and carefully developed over three decades (1920 to 1950), revolutionized how policing was practised. The police moved from a focus on a preventive style of policing to one that was predominantly **reactive** in nature. The components of this approach to policing (most commonly known as the "professional" or "reform" model of policing) changed the primary focus of the police, from **social service** and **order maintenance** to **crime fighting** exclusively (see Exhibit 5.3).

The professional model continues to play a dominant role in policing, although it has been criticized over the decades not only by the public but also by police officials. Why has it been criticized? Some of these reasons include:

- Police tactics at the core of the professional model (e.g., random patrol, rapid response) don't control crime or reduce fear of crime very well;
- Even if the police arrest suspects, it is unlikely that most individuals convicted of a crime will serve time in a correctional facility;
- The role of technology has changed both how the police operate and the types of criminal activity the police have to monitor;
- Private security is surpassing the police as a means to control crime, fear, and disorder; and
- The amount of transnational criminal activity requiring different police organizations to cooperate and share information is increasing.

Numerous changes have been made in the professional model since it was first introduced. Starting in the late 1970s new types of proactive policing (e.g., problem-oriented policing) have been implemented (see Chapter 6). In addition, the nature of policing has dramatically changed in recent decades, with more agencies (e.g., private security forces) becoming involved in social regulation than ever before as well as the changing scope of criminal activity (e.g., transnational crime). These changes have led to the rise of what is referred to as plural policing.

EXHIBIT 5.3 Selected Characteristics of the Professional Model of Policing

During the 1920s, three police chiefs in the United States, A. Vollmer, O.W. Wilson, and W. Parker, decided to bring about changes to the way police departments were organized. They ultimately created the **professional model of policing**. The expectations of this model were clearly stated: the police were to engage in crime control, specifically arresting people for committing crimes, especially the most serious crimes. This model changed how police organizations were structured and operated. At first the larger police organizations adopted it, but soon every police force, regardless of size, was using this approach.

- Centralization of police authority.
- Creation of specialized crime-fighting units such as homicide and robbery.
- Moving from foot patrols to motorized patrols.
- Creating patrol systems based on criteria such as crime rates, calls for service, and response times.
- Recruiting new officers through psychological testing and civil service tests.
- Reactive, incident-driven responses to crime.

Investigating: The Police Mandate

What is it that the police are supposed to do? The answer to this question refers to the role of the police in society. As we saw in Chapter 1, some form of social control is necessary and the police are the primary institution that formally regulates behaviour. Yet, police researchers have had a difficult time defining precisely the mandate of the police as their role in our society is a complex one. Most agree, however, that the following are three core aspects of the **police mandate**:

Criminal Law Enforcement

Criminal law enforcement is the most commonly identified police mandate. The police are responsible for enforcing the law and detecting those individuals who violate it. The police play a crucial role in our criminal justice system. They try to prevent crimes from occurring, investigate crimes and identify suspects, arrest the suspects, and assist prosecutors in developing a case against the defendants. Since it is their actions that ultimately decide whether or not the individual(s) in question are going to be processed, the police, then, can be viewed as the gatekeepers of the criminal justice system.

Order Maintenance

The police also maintain public order (also referred to as "order maintenance") so that the public can involve themselves with their everyday activities without being fearful of crime. When the police are called to deal with an issue, they don't necessarily arrest anyone. Instead, they may use their discretionary powers to decide what they consider to be the appropriate course of action.

Service

The police oftentimes help individuals who require assistance; this is referred to as the service role of policing. Since they are on duty throughout the day, the police can be called to deal with all sorts of situations requested of them by the public. These requests may include assisting the homeless find accommodation, resolving arguments between neighbours, responding to a noisy party, directing traffic when stop lights are not functioning, or informing people how to get to the nearest hospital. Many police organizations today want their officers to be involved in community service activities as it creates close ties between the police and the community.

What is the most important police mandate? Opinions are divided. Some (e.g., Kelling 1988) believe that the police should perform all aspects of their mandate, while others (e.g., Morris and Hawkins 1967) feel that the police should focus entirely on criminal law enforcement.

What Is Plural Policing?

While the criminal justice system is, in theory, the responsibility of governments, dealing with crime has never been entirely a state responsibility. In recent decades there has been an increasing amount of awareness about the expansion of different forms of policing in Western societies. It is now recognized that "policing" extends beyond the activities of the public police. While other types of policing (e.g., private security forces) have existed for long periods, some aspects of policing today extend across the globe, and as a result the police have had to reconfigure some of their practices to form close partnerships with other police agencies around the world. This has led to a transnational focus on policing.

The recognition that certain policing-style services are provided by a number of different (or "fragmented") agencies in Western societies is referred to as **plural policing**. Some believe that a new historical era of policing has emerged. Bayley and Shearing (1996:585) note that, in the final decades of the 20th century, advanced Western nations such as Canada, the United States, and Britain "have reached a watershed in the evolution of their systems of crime control and law enforcement. Future generations will look back on our era as a time when one system of policing ended and another took its place."

Plural policing consists of a variety of types; Loader has identified five different ones:*

- *Policing by government:* the traditional approach to policing;
- *Policing through government:* activities funded by the government but delivered by other agencies outside of the police;
- *Policing about government:* transnational policing actions involving international agencies;
- *Policing beyond government:* actions funded and delivered primarily by private security organizations; and
- *Policing below government:* community activities and self-policing.

Today, there are over 140,000 private security guards licensed in Canada, just over double the number of sworn police officers. Why has the growth of personnel

* Loader, I. 2000. "Plural Policing and Democratic Governance." Social and Legal Studies 9:323–345.

in the non-public police sector outstripped the growth in the number of sworn police officers in Canada? One answer is that, due in part to the breadth of their duties, the costs of the publicly funded police agencies are continually increasing. The total expenditures on policing in Canada during 2012 exceeded $13 billion, compared to $12.3 billion in 2009. While the costs of funding the police are rising, the amount and severity of crime has been decreasing in Canada. Some of this increase is due to the cost of dealing with new types of criminal activities, such as those related to the Internet and terrorism. In particular, the terrorist attacks on New York in 2001 led to significant changes in the role of policing in Western societies to include the collection of greater amounts of intelligence in order to better predict security threats (Murphy 2007).

One reason for the growth in plural policing is the idea of **mass private property** (Shearing and Stenning 1983). Consumers now go about many of their activities in private spaces (e.g., shopping malls). These private spaces are patrolled by private security agencies which monitor and provide surveillance services to the owners. Crawford and Lister (2006:165) believe that these **private security** organizations are members of an "extended policing family" since these types of policing "offer a tangible response to the public's quest for symbols of order and authority." This has led to the introduction of the term **security governance**, which refers to the "collective responsibility of networks of commercial and non-commercial 'partners'" (Johnston and Shearing 2003:141).

Criminal Justice Insight

The Private Police in Canada

In Canada, the number of private security personnel substantially outnumbers sworn police officers (see Figure 5.2). Why has this happened? There are a number of answers but the most common focuses upon the growth of *mass private property* (i.e., properties such as shopping malls that are privately owned but frequented by large numbers of the public).

What are the differences between the functions of private and public police? Over 30 years ago, Shearing and Stenning (1983) noted one difference: the private police have no duty to act in the public interest. Another difference is that the private police engage in what is known as **commercial policing**; that is, they make profits from those they protect. Another difference is that the private police are more concerned with loss prevention than crime prevention, anti-social behaviours, and housekeeping (i.e., maintaining the physical appearance of buildings and the safety of private operations) and customer care (Wakefield 2003).

Police Officers
Total Private Security
200,000
180,000
160,000
140,000
120,000
100,000
80,000
60,000
40,000
20,000
0
1991 1996 2001 2006 2013

FIGURE 5.2 Private Security Compared to Public Police

Source: Geoffrey Li, "Private security and public policing." *Juristat* (December 2008), Statistics Canada Catalogue no. 85-002-x, p. 33, http://www.statcan.gc.ca/pub/85-002-x/2008010/article/10730-eng.htm. Reproduced and distributed on an "as is" basis with the permission of Statistics Canada.

Balefire9/iStock

The private police are hired to ensure that buildings are secure even after employees have left.

Another reason has been the rise of global threats concerning the security of residents in Western nations, which have had a tremendous impact on the nature of policing. Concerns about higher levels of risk based on perceived threats from (largely) overseas organizations have led to demands for greater levels of policing and security. This has led to the creation and growth of transnational types of policing that enhances police cooperation across national boundaries. This is referred to as **high policing**, which recognizes that "enforcing the law in the global context is dependent on the gathering and sharing of intelligence . . ." (Brodeur 2000:43). "High" policing is characterized by

- a concern with both political intelligence and the disruption of suspicious activities as opposed to criminal prosecution;
- a potential to act outside the parameters of the law, such as questionable surveillance techniques;
- investigative methods that are more likely to be invasive or highly manipulative; and
- sharing intelligence between nations.

Investigating: Policing Human Trafficking: A Multi-Agency Approach

Ever since the professional or reform model of policing was introduced into police organizations, the police have created specialized policing units focusing upon a specific type of criminal activity or criminal offence. For decades, these units operated outside any permanent public or outside agency relationship; however, the complexity and expanse of criminal activities recently have led the police to create multi-agency partnerships reflecting plural policing initiatives both nationally and transnationally.

Human trafficking for sexual exploitation and forced labour are recognized as criminal activities requiring an integrated approach among various law enforcement and nongovernmental organizations (NGOs) both nationally and internationally. According to the United States Department of State, 2010 saw an estimated 12.3 million trafficked persons globally. According to the United Nations International Labour Organization, human trafficking is estimated to generate as much as $32 billion a year and is tied to the illegal arms trade as well as being the second largest criminal activity in the world, just behind the illegal drug trade.

What is human trafficking? It involves any person who recruits, transports, receives, holds, conceals, or harbours a person, or exercises control, direction, or influence over the movements of a person for the purpose of exploiting them or facilitating their exploitation. Trafficked persons typically are not able to, or perceive that they cannot, leave their situation. Trafficking has both international and domestic elements:

1. **International human trafficking** involves someone who, in the process of being trafficked, crosses an international border, regardless of the victim's immigration status. It is irrelevant if the victim had crossed the border legally or illegally.
2. **Domestic human trafficking** involves all stages of trafficking occurring within Canada, regardless of the victim's legal status. Vulnerable, economically exploited, and socially marginalized individuals of the Canadian population represent a potential source of domestic trafficking victims.

Human trafficking is often confused with human smuggling, which is a form of illegal migration involving the organized transport of a person across a border, usually in exchange for money and oftentimes using dangerous conditions and methods. For many persons, the key difference between human trafficking and human smuggling is whether or not the individual concerned is able to exercise freedom of choice (see Table 5.1).

It is not sufficient for governments to enact anti-human trafficking legislation and believe that this is a sufficient response. Trafficking victims can be difficult to locate and identify and they may feel wary about receiving assistance because of the threats against them or their families by the traffickers. Federal, provincial, and municipal government agencies have to work with private and community agencies to better facilitate victim cooperation with law enforcement agencies as well as providing the necessary services (e.g., emotional needs) for trafficking victims.

A large number of agencies are involved in human trafficking. International agencies, such as the United Nations, as well as national governments are usually informed by law enforcement agencies such as the police. NGOs tend to focus more on the rights and victims of the individuals trafficked. Efforts to combat such activities have led to global enforcement initiatives, with over 120 nations having adopted anti-trafficking legislation to date. In Canada, the federal government has

Investigating: Policing Human Trafficking: A Multi-Agency Approach (*Continued*)

TABLE 5.1 Differences between Human Trafficking and Human Smuggling

Trafficking	Smuggling
Must contain an element of force, fraud, or coercion (actual, perceived, or implied) unless under 18 years of age. Involved in commercial sex acts.	The person being smuggled is generally cooperating.
Forced labour and/or exploitation.	There is no actual or implied coercion.
Persons trafficked are victims.	Persons smuggled are violating the law, they are not victims.
Enslaved, subjected to limited freedom or isolation, or had documents confiscated.	Persons are free to leave, change jobs etc.
Need not involve the actual movement of person(s).	Facilitates the illegal entry of the victim from one country into another.
No requirement to cross an international border.	Always crosses an international border.
Person must be involved in labour/services; i.e., must be "working."	Person must only be in country or attempting entry illegally.

Source: U.S. Department of State. (2005). *Distinctions Between Human Smuggling and Human Trafficking*. Washington, D.C.: U.S. Department of State and Trafficking Center.

set up the Interdepartmental Working Group on Trafficking in Persons to coordinate 16 federal departments and agencies. This group develops government policy and responses to human trafficking as well as facilitating the cooperation and collaboration of the various federal agencies with other groups across Canada, including both provincial agencies and NGOs.

A key role in the enforcement and coordination of anti-human trafficking efforts in Canada is played by the RCMP. The strategic objective of the RCMP Immigration and Passport (I&P) Program is to investigate and disrupt human trafficking and human smuggling. Their mandate is the criminal enforcement of the Immigration and Refugee Protection Act, the Citizenship Act, and the Criminal Code. The RCMP established six regional offices across Canada, with a policy centre located at RCMP headquarters in Ottawa. In 2005, the Human Trafficking National Coordination Centre (HTNCC) was created with the I&P branch located at RCMP headquarters. The objectives of the HTNCC are

- The development of tools, protocols, and guidelines;
- The coordination of national awareness and training;
- The development and maintenance of international and national partnerships;
- The coordination of intelligence and the dissemination of information relating to human trafficking; and
- The identification and maintenance of lines of communication and as well as integrating coordination and providing support where needed.

At the international level, Canada is involved with the development and implementation of laws with the United Nations, the Organization of American States, the Regional Conference on Migration, and the Organization for Security and Co-operation in Europe. The most notable and widely accepted international framework was passed in 2000 by the United Nations—the Convention against Transnational Organized Crime and its Protocol to Prevent, Suppress and Punish Trafficking in Persons, Especially Women and Children.

As is the case with plural policing, a number of other federal agencies also are involved with the RCMP in anti-trafficking activities. These include

- The Department of Foreign Affairs and International Trade, which provides program support to combat trafficking in persons internationally through its Anti-Crime Capacity Building Program. This program provides financial assistance to regional cooperation to counter challenges associated with criminal activity in the Americas, including human trafficking.
- The Canadian International Development Agency, which provides project and program funding to a number of international organizations and nongovernmental organizations that work in the area of human trafficking with a

Continued on next page

Investigating: Policing Human Trafficking: A Multi-Agency Approach *(Continued)*

focus on prevention, protection, and the rehabilitation of trafficking victims.

- The Labour Program of Human Resources and Skills Development Canada developed and delivered training for provincial labour inspectors and other labour officials, with a particular focus on forced labour, industries at risk, and mechanisms for greater collaboration to address labour trafficking in Canada.
- Citizenship and Immigration Canada, in collaboration with Human Resources and Skills Development Canada, makes information available to temporary foreign workers informing them where they can get assistance on issues related to employment and health and safety standards.

In addition, the federal government provides assistance to victims of crime, including trafficking victims, via various programs and services through its Federal Victim Strategy. On November 1, 2010, the federal government started its national awareness campaign "Victims Matter," aimed at victims of crime, their families, and their supporters. Part of the new website created for the campaign included contact information about federal and provincial/territorial government websites set up for victim services, as well as the websites of nongovernmental organizations and other service providers.

Sources: Burgess 2006; Department of Justice 2011; RCMP 2010.

Another reason for the rise of plural policing is the difficulties the police face in terms of having a constant presence in each community on every shift. This has led to an enhanced role for citizens' groups in such activities as crime prevention and providing watch services within their neighbourhoods. Those involved are actually engaging in providing a semi-official presence for the police. Oftentimes, these groups are created due to the amount of disorderly and anti-social behaviours in their community, and it is the hope that actions of these groups will reduce these types of activities and lead to a reduction in the amount of fear about crime.

Neighbourhood empowerment teams in Edmonton have successfully supported crime prevention.

SUMMING UP AND LOOKING FORWARD

As societies became more urbanized in the later 19th century, city governments began to change the structure and operations of the police. As police organizations became formally organized they became part of municipal governments. The police established close ties to the communities they served, and their prime responsibility was to serve the public through the prevention and detection of crime. Police were active not only in enforcing the criminal law but also in order maintenance and service activities.

This approach ultimately declined as a result of corruption issues in the United States, where an alternative approach (the professional or reform model) emerged. According to this model, since the police are the gatekeepers of the criminal justice system, the police mandate includes criminal law enforcement. This approach led to reactive policing, which saw the police responding (i.e., reacting) to criminal incidents after they were committed. Speed of response became critical and the police began to adopt as many technological innovations as possible.

Recent events such as the increasing number of private security forces and the increasing amount of transnational crime has led to a reconceptualization of policing. This is referred to as plural policing. It includes patrolling private property such as shopping malls (mass private property) and sharing intelligence with other state police forces (high policing). Policing responsibilities are now carried out by a variety of local, private, regional, national, and transnational agencies.

How are the public police distributed in Canada, and what is their composition? For almost a century and a half after the modern police were first created, women and members of visible minority groups were rarely if ever employed as sworn officers. When and how did this change? What are their roles in the police today? And what challenges face women and members of visible minority groups in policing?

Review Questions:

1. What were the problems associated with early municipal policing?
2. What are the main characteristics and criticisms of the professional model of policing?
3. What are the different mandates of the police?
4. What are the different types of plural policing?
5. Why were private security agencies developed, and what are their purposes and roles in the area of policing?

How Are the Public Police Organized in Canada?

In 2013, 97,172 individuals were employed by police forces across Canada. Of this total, 69,272 were sworn police personnel and 27,900 were civilian employees. The number of sworn police officers was slightly lower compared to the previous year (a decrease of 1.5 percent), while the number of civilian employees employed by police organizations in Canada decreased by 2.5 percent. Figure 5.3 compares police strength in Canada with the police-recorded crime rate.

Three different jurisdictional levels of policing exist in Canada: **municipal, provincial**, and **federal**. In 2013, 45,795 (or 66 percent) of all police officers were involved with municipal police agencies. This total included more than 350 "independent" municipal police forces (i.e., non-RCMP), employing 40,567 officers—89 percent of all municipal police officers in Canada. There were also just over 200 RCMP municipal contract forces employing 5,228 officers. In addition, there were 6,815 RCMP officers (or 10 percent of all sworn police officers in Canada) working in various aspects of provincial policing beyond municipal policing.

Provincial police agencies employed 10,331 police officers, or almost 15 percent of all police personnel in Canada. Provincial police forces enforce the Criminal Code and provincial statutes within areas of a province not served by a municipal police force. The three provincial police forces are in Ontario (the Ontario Provincial Police [OPP]), Quebec (the Sûreté du Québec [SQ]), and Newfoundland (where the Royal Newfoundland Constabulary provides policing services to the three largest municipalities). For the other seven provinces and three territories, provincial policing is provided by the RCMP under contract.

The RCMP has complete responsibility in all provinces and territories for enforcing federal statutes, carrying out executive orders, and providing security for dignitaries. In 2013, 4,569 RCMP officers (6.7 percent of all police officers in Canada) were involved in federal

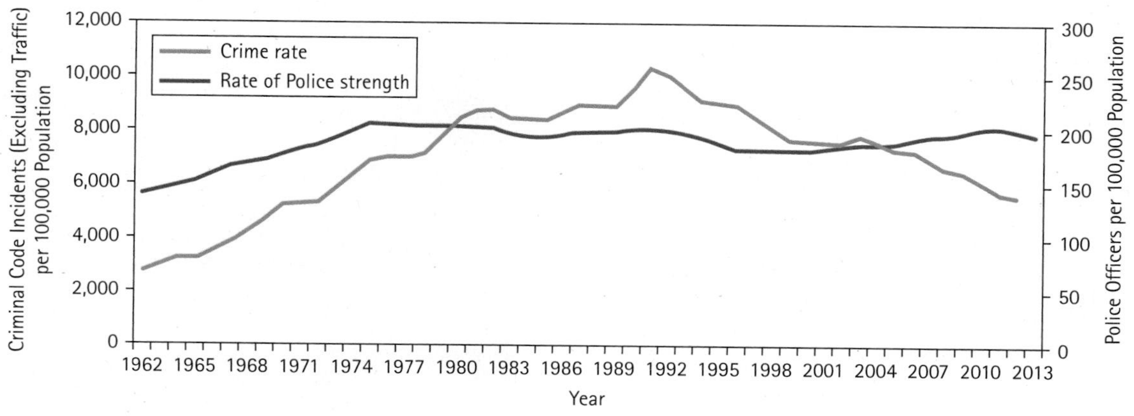

FIGURE 5.3 Crime Rate and Rate of Police Strength, Canada, 1962–2013

Source: Hope Hutchins, "Police resources in Canada, 2013." *Juristat* (March 2014), Statistics Canada Catalogue no. 85-002-x, p. 6, http://www.statcan.gc.ca/pub/85-002-x/2014001/article/11914-eng.pdf.

policing. Other responsibilities of the RCMP include forensic laboratory services, the operation of CPIC (an automated national computer system available to all police forces), and telecommunications services for data and radio transmissions to ensure that all detachments receive current information. The RCMP also maintains the National DNA Data Bank and the Sex Offender Registry. There were 1,762 RCMP officers stationed at RCMP headquarters and at the force's own training facility as well as in departmental and divisional administration in 2013 (Hutchins 2014).

The police agency with the greatest number of sworn police officers in Canada is the Toronto Police Service, with 9,967 officers. Montreal has the next largest police service, with 7,194 officers. The other police organizations with more than 2,000 sworn personnel in 2013 were Vancouver (3,645) and Calgary (2,130).

There is no single model for determining the appropriate size of a police force or its workload. One problem is determining the size of the population base. Census figures are commonly used, but every large city in Canada experiences a heavy influx of workers on most days as people who live outside the city limits drive in for work or pleasure. Police agencies vary significantly in size across Canada, both in terms of personnel and in terms of the number of officers per person served. For example, in 2014, both Thunder Bay and Winnipeg had the highest number of police officers for every 100,000 population (189); Regina was next with 185. Kingston, Ontario, Abbotsford-Mission in B.C., and Ottawa employed the lowest numbers of police officers for every 100,000 population (Kingston had 141, Abbotsford-Mission had 144, and Ottawa had 146).

Two measures are generally used to establish the appropriate size of a police force. Both measures are mainly used to analyze and identify trends in the population. The most common measure used is the population-to-police-officer ratio, which compares changes in the number of police officers with changes in the Canadian population. In 2013, the number of police officers per capita in Canada was 193 per 100,000 population, a decrease from 201.4 in 2011. The highest rate ever was 206 officers per 100,000, in 1975. By province/territory, the lowest numbers of police officers per 100,000 population in 2014 were found in Prince Edward Island (160 per 100,000) and Alberta (171 per 100,000). The highest rate among the provinces was for the Northwest Territories (441 per 100,000), followed by Nunavut and Yukon (both with 360 per 100,000).

The second method compares the number of Criminal Code incidents (excluding traffic incidents) reported to the police with the number of police officers in the force who handle those incidents. This ratio is used to indicate police workloads (Young 1995). The number of Criminal Code incidents per police officer increased from 20 in 1962 to a high of 51.1 in 1991. It has declined almost every year since, to 28.0 in 2012.

What Is the Extent of Diversity within Canadian Police Organizations?

The principle of policing by public consent creates a number of controversies for police organizations. One of these focuses upon how much **diversity** there should be in the internal composition of the police. The value of having police officers who reflect the composition of those they serve and protect in the wider community and society has long been recognized. Officers selected from diverse cross sections of various social groups will better understand, communicate with, and gain the trust of diverse members of communities. When there is greater diversity among police officers, the result is "a psychologically positive attitude on the part of visible minorities who have felt left out and alienated from the mainstream of society" (Jayewardene and Talbot 1990; Normandeau 1990). A police force that reflects the demographics of its community can do much "[to gain] the public's confidence by helping to dispel the view that police departments are generally bigoted or biased organizations" (Senna and Siegel 1995:239). Numerous benefits are associated with increasing the sexual and racial diversity

The Ontario Provincial Police (OPP) ensures that its police service reflects the diverse communities it serves and possesses the skills, knowledge, and ability to meet the needs of its diverse communities.

of police officers working in Canadian police organizations. These benefits extend to the police organization itself—the presence of such officers increases police effectiveness, prevents crime, and changes the image of the police among community members, especially youths (Jaccoud and Felice 1999).

Despite the recognition of the importance of diversity in police organizations, the numbers of women and visible minority group members joining the police for their careers in Canada (as in most other nations) have been low. In 1980, for example, only 2.2 percent of all police officers in Canada were women, and by 1986 only 1.1 percent of police officers were Aboriginal and members of visible minority groups. Why did this happen?

Historically, both women and members of visible minority groups faced significant barriers to employment within police organizations. It wasn't until the 1970s that pressure was placed on police organizations to hire more women and minority police officers. For women, it was the result of numerous organizations trying to eliminate legal and economic barriers to women's equality (Corsianos 2009). For example, the Royal Commission on the Status of Women (1970) recommended that all police organizations train and hire women as police officers. For visible minorities, this pressure was the result of increasing numbers of visible minority immigrants to Canada (Forcese 1992). For both, the equality section of the Charter of Rights and Freedoms guaranteed individuals fundamental rights and freedoms as well as full legal equality. The Charter also allowed for the creation of employment equity programs in order that equality would be achieved (Greschner 1985). The introduction of **employment equity** was a key factor in changing police organizations from exclusively hiring men. Employment equity involves the purposeful identification of any significant differences between the participation levels and the population figures of four targeted minority groups—people from visible minority groups, women, people with disabilities, and Aboriginal people. Employment equity aims to identify any employment policies and/or practices that disadvantage these groups. The legal foundation of employment equity is the Canadian Human Rights Act (1977). Section 16(1) of this act states that it is not discriminatory to start a program designed to prevent, eliminate, or reduce disadvantages experienced by individuals because of their race, national or ethnic origin, religion, age, sex, family status, marital status, or disability.

The number of women police officers is now over 20 percent of all officers; in addition, and as discussed in the next section, the number of women in the senior ranks has been increasing. In contrast, the proportion of police officers who are Aboriginal and members of visible minority groups is lower. In 2013, of the 48,710 police officers across Canada who provided information, 4,384 (or 9 percent) identified as a member of a visible minority group and 2,435 (or 5 percent) identified themselves as Aboriginal. The small number of visible minorities in Canadian police departments has been attributed to their restricted access to the law enforcement profession. Studies have found that unrelated job requirements have discouraged large numbers of visible minorities from applying to police forces across Canada (Jayewardene and Talbot 1990). For example, the debate over whether Sikh RCMP officers should be permitted to wear the turban as part of their uniform focused on the RCMP's traditions rather than on whether wearing a turban would interfere with the performance of duty. Hiring policies that create such obstacles for police officers are often viewed as a form of systemic discrimination, since these policies place an arbitrary barrier between people's abilities and their employment opportunities (Abella 1984). Cao (2011:1) found that visible minorities in Canada had lower levels of confidence in the police than non-members of visible

Courtesy Kai Liu.

Inspector Kai Liu was Ontario's first visible minority police chief.

members, and reported that "equal racial confidence in the police is yet to be achieved and continued reform measures are needed if the police force is to win the hearts and minds of visible minorities in Canada."

Women and Policing

The number of women police officers in Canada has slowly increased over the decades. Throughout the 1960s, the percentage of female police officers was below 1 percent, rising to 2.2 percent only in 1980. This figure has increased each year, to 20.2 percent in 2013 compared to 13.7 percent in 2000 (Hutchins 2014). In 2013, there were 14,004 women police officers, compared to 7,650 in 2000.

Women police officers are now entering the upper echelons of police administration in larger numbers (see Table 5.2). In 1997, 2.1 percent of all senior officers in Canada were women; by 2002, this figure had almost doubled to 4 percent, and in 2013 it had increased to 10.4 percent. Women police officers in non-commissioned ranks had increased their presence from 3.4 percent in 1997 to 17.1 percent in 2013. At the rank of constable, women made up 14.3 percent of all constables in 1997; in 2013, it was 21.9 percent.

In a comparison of the number of women police officers with 11 other countries in 2011, Canada ranked fifth (see Figure 5.4).

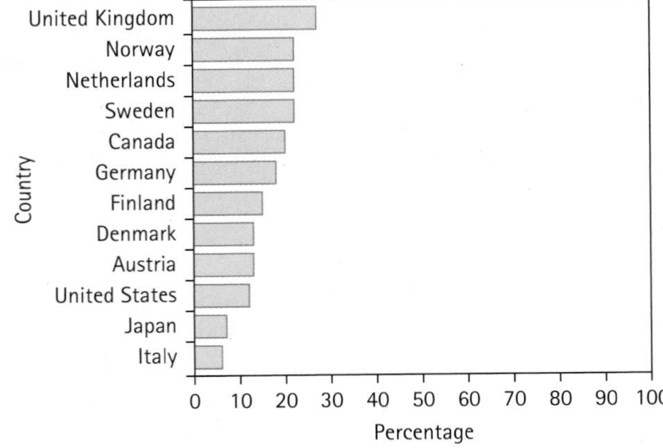

FIGURE 5.4 Female Police Officers as a Percentage of Total Police Officers, by Peer Country, 2011

Source: Hope Hutchins, "Police resources in Canada, 2013." *Juristat* (March 2014), Statistics Canada Catalogue no. 85-002-x, p. 31, http://www.statcan.gc.ca/pub/85-002-x/2014001/article/11914-eng.pdf. Reproduced and distributed on an "as is" basis with the permission of Statistics Canada.

TABLE 5.2 Male and Female Police Officers by Rank, Canada, 2013

Year	Senior officers[1]		Non-commissioned officers[2]		Constables	
	Male	Female	Male	Female	Male	Female
	percent					
	99.8	0.2	99.5	0.5	94.6	5.4
1987	99.8	0.2	99.4	0.6	93.9	6.1
1992	99.3	0.7	98.4	1.6	89.8	10.2
1997	97.9	2.1	96.6	3.4	85.7	14.3
2002	96	4	92.9	7.1	81.4	18.6
2007	92.8	7.2	88	12	78.5	21.5
2012*	90.1	9.9	83.6	16.4	78.2	21.8
2013	89.6	10.4	82.9	17.1	78.1	21.9

* revised

[1] Includes personnel who have obtained senior officer status, normally at the rank of lieutenant or higher, such as chiefs, deputy chiefs, staff superintendents, superintendents, staff inspectors, inspectors, lieutenants, and other equivalent ranks.

[2] Includes personnel between the rank of constable and lieutenant, such as staff-sergeants, sergeants, detective-sergeants, corporals and all equivalent ranks.

Notes: Prior to 1986, data on the rank of police officers was not available. Represents the actual number of permanent, fully-sworn police officers (or their full-time equivalents). This number also includes officers who are deployed to contract positions and who are not available for general policing duties in their community. Police officers on long-term leave who are not being paid by the police service's annual budget are excluded.

Source: Hope Hutchins, "Police resources in Canada, 2013." *Juristat* (March 2014), Statistics Canada Catalogue no. 85-002-x, p. 32. Figure abbreviated by author. http://www.statcan.gc.ca/pub/85-002-x/2014001/article/11914-eng.pdf. Reproduced and distributed on an "as is" basis with the permission of Statistics Canada.

Women Police Officers: Gender Conflicts at Work

Now that the legal barriers to entering policing have diminished, what has been the experience of policewomen as they have advanced in their policing careers? According to Balkin (1988:33), policewomen are perceived as lacking both the physical and emotional strength to perform well in violent confrontations. Overall, policemen hold "almost uniformly negative . . . attitudes toward policewomen." Petersen (1982) and Martin (1991) point out that since policemen associate masculinity with the use of physical force, and view the use of physical force as the defining feature of police work, they are concerned about and threatened by women's successful integration into police work. However, Hunt (1990) reports that policemen and policewomen develop similar attitudes toward their occupational duties and job satisfaction.

This is not to say that women officers no longer experience gender conflicts at work. For decades it has been reported that policewomen have had to face numerous obstacles such as sexism within police organizations. In her national assessment of women police officers in the United States in the 1980s, Martin (1991) reported a high percentage of women officers encountering some form of bias and that 75 percent of both new and experienced police officers reported being victims of sexual harassment. A higher proportion (35 percent) of rookie women officers than rookie men officers (8 percent) said that their biggest problem as new patrol officers was harassment by other police officers. This harassment included displays of pornography, jokes or comments based on sexual stereotypes of women, and remarks on women's sexuality. Throughout the 1990s other studies investigating sexual harassment reported that between 53 percent and 77 percent of women police officers had been subjected to some form of sexual harassment by their male co-workers (Bartol et al. 1992; Nichols 1995). Very few of these incidents were reported, with the most common reason being "nothing will be done" or that reporting the incident(s) "will make the situation worse" (Nichols 1995). Crawford and Stark-Adamec (1994) came to a similar conclusion in their study of 50 women and 68 men police officers and ex–police officers in four major Canadian police departments. Eighteen percent of the women in this study referred to experiencing sexually related problems on the job, including sexual harassment and sex discrimination.

CP PHOTO/Larry MacDougal

Women police officers have been found to experience **institutional sexism** in the workplace. Despite improvements in policies, institutional sexism continues to exist in practice through a variety of processes, attitudes, and behaviours which lead to discrimination against women. In March 2012, a notice of a class action lawsuit was filed in British Columbia, accusing the RCMP of systemic and persistent gender-based discrimination in its treatment of women members. More than 335 current or former women RCMP members, who have provided details of sexual harassment and assault, posttraumatic stress disorder, depression, anxiety, and attempted suicide, are currently seeking legal action against the RCMP in a class action suit.

What is the source of the problems faced by women, Aboriginals, and members of visible minority groups? Some aspects of the police occupational culture (see below), such as stereotypes and the prominence of masculinity, have been identified as the main source (Chan 1997).

Reprinted with the permission of the RCMP.

Brenda Butterworth-Carr became the first Aboriginal woman to lead an RCMP Division when she was appointed the Chief Superintendent of Saskatchewan in 2013.

The first woman chief of police in Canada was appointed in Guelph, Ontario, in 1994. Calgary became the first Canadian city with a population more than 100,000 to appoint a woman as police chief, in 1995. Since then, women have been appointed commissioner of the OPP (in 1998) and, in the RCMP, the first woman detachment commander was appointed in 1990, the first woman commissioned officer in 1992, and the first woman commanding officer of a division in 1998. In 2006, Bev Busson, a member of the first woman recruit class in the RCMP (1974), was appointed interim RCMP Commissioner.

Aboriginal (First Nations) Police Services

Few researchers have studied racial-minority communities in Canada to ascertain what residents expect from the local police forces in terms of racial composition. One such study was Manitoba's Aboriginal Justice Inquiry; the authors of its report wrote that Aboriginal people "consider the police to be a foreign presence and do not feel understood by it. They certainly do not feel that the police operate on their behalf, or that the police are in any significant manner subject to a corresponding Aboriginal influence in their communities" (Hamilton and Sinclair 1991:597). Due to these concerns, they recommended that police services in Aboriginal communities be delivered by professional regional Aboriginal police services that report to and service Aboriginal communities.

During the late 1980s and throughout the early to mid-1990s, a series of provincial and federal government commissions and reports considered the issue of First Nations policing. They concluded that First Nations communities were **underpoliced** (i.e., policing was inadequate), culturally insensitive, and **overpoliced**; that is, the police focused "their attention inordinately in one particular geographic area (or neighbourhood) or on the members of one particular racial or ethnic group" (Rudin 2007:28). In addition, these reports also stated that the justice system often discriminated against First Nations peoples, and that these communities were sorely lacking in crime prevention programs. These reports did not, however, agree on solutions. Some (e.g., Head 1989) felt that the best way was to make changes to the existing system, while others (e.g., Hamilton and Sinclair 1991) recommended a separate and First Nations-controlled policing service.

Aboriginal policing services, however, predate these inquiries. One of the earliest such services was founded in Quebec in 1978, when 25 First Nations communities began to receive policing services from a force known as the Amerindian Police. This force was established because it had been surmised that the dependency of Native communities on outside police forces "increases the likelihood of police interventions and 'criminalizes' behaviours that would not necessarily be considered criminal if other agencies were involved" (Hyde 1992:370). Aboriginal police forces were founded to change this approach and become more sensitive to the needs of Aboriginal communities.

Officers of the Amerindian Police were most often asked to perform service functions in the community. About one-third of the 17,000 requests for police assistance recorded between 1978 and 1983 were for non-criminal incidents. Almost 45 percent of these calls resulted in referrals to other agencies, such as social and health services, probation officers, and psychiatric specialists. According to Hyde (ibid.), "peace keeping, crime prevention, and crisis-intervention functions of

the police are, in part, the raison d'être for the establishment of the force."

The crimes committed involved the least serious Criminal Code and provincial offences—public order offences, interpersonal altercations, liquor and drug offences, and break and enters. The most typical police response to an incident was "no charge," meaning the police took no action; the next most common response was "suspect detained," meaning the individual was detained by the police overnight (Depew 1992). Clearly, the Amerindian Police played an important role in crisis intervention and in providing social services. LaPrairie and Diamond (1992) found that many criminal cases were dealt with outside the measures available through the formal criminal justice system. They also found that only about 33 percent of reported criminal or potential criminal offences were officially recorded and that only 12 percent of those officially recorded made it to court.

Recognizing the importance of Aboriginal police officers on First Nations communities, the federal government created the First Nations Policing Policy (FNPP) in June 1991 to allow Aboriginal communities more control over policing on reserves. The purpose of this policy was to improve the administration of justice and the maintenance of social order, public security, and personal safety on Aboriginal reserves. Specifically, the policy would

- help improve social order, public security, and personal safety in First Nations communities, especially for women, children, and other vulnerable groups;
- provide a practical way to improve the administration of justice for First Nations by establishing First Nations police services that were professional, effective, and responsive to the particular community's needs;
- ensure that First Nations peoples enjoyed their right to personal security and public safety. This would be achieved through access to policing services that were responsive to their needs and that met acceptable standards with respect to the quality and level of service;
- support First Nations in acquiring the tools to become self-sufficient and self-governing by establishing structures for the management, administration, and accountability of First Nations police services; and
- implement and administer the First Nations Policy in a manner promoting partnerships with First Nations based on trust, mutual respect, and participation in decision making (Solicitor General of Canada 1999).

By 1995, 41 agreements had been signed with 180 First Nations communities. In 2005, 319 Aboriginal communities with a total population of approximately 244,000 had signed agreements. Just under 10 years later, in 2012–2013, 396 First Nations communities with a total population of 341,942 residents were receiving policing services under the FNPP. There are 1,261 police officers, most of them of Aboriginal descent, employed under this program. Agreements exist both with single communities and with groups of communities; in one case, 44 communities joined together to establish one police service (see Figure 5.5).

Under the FNPP, two options are available to First Nations communities. One is the self-administered police service (also referred to as stand-alone police service), which allows a community or number of communities to have their own separate police force that is not affiliated with any other police force, be it federal, provincial, or municipal. In these arrangements, the First Nations community manages its own police service under provincial legislation. Independent police commissions oversee these self-administered police services. Another option is an agreement signed with an existing federal, provincial, or municipal police force. Agreements are signed between the federal government, the province or territory in which the First Nations community is located, and the governing body of the First Nations community, represented by the Band Council. These are known as **Community Tripartite Agreements**, and they usually involve the RCMP providing the policing services.

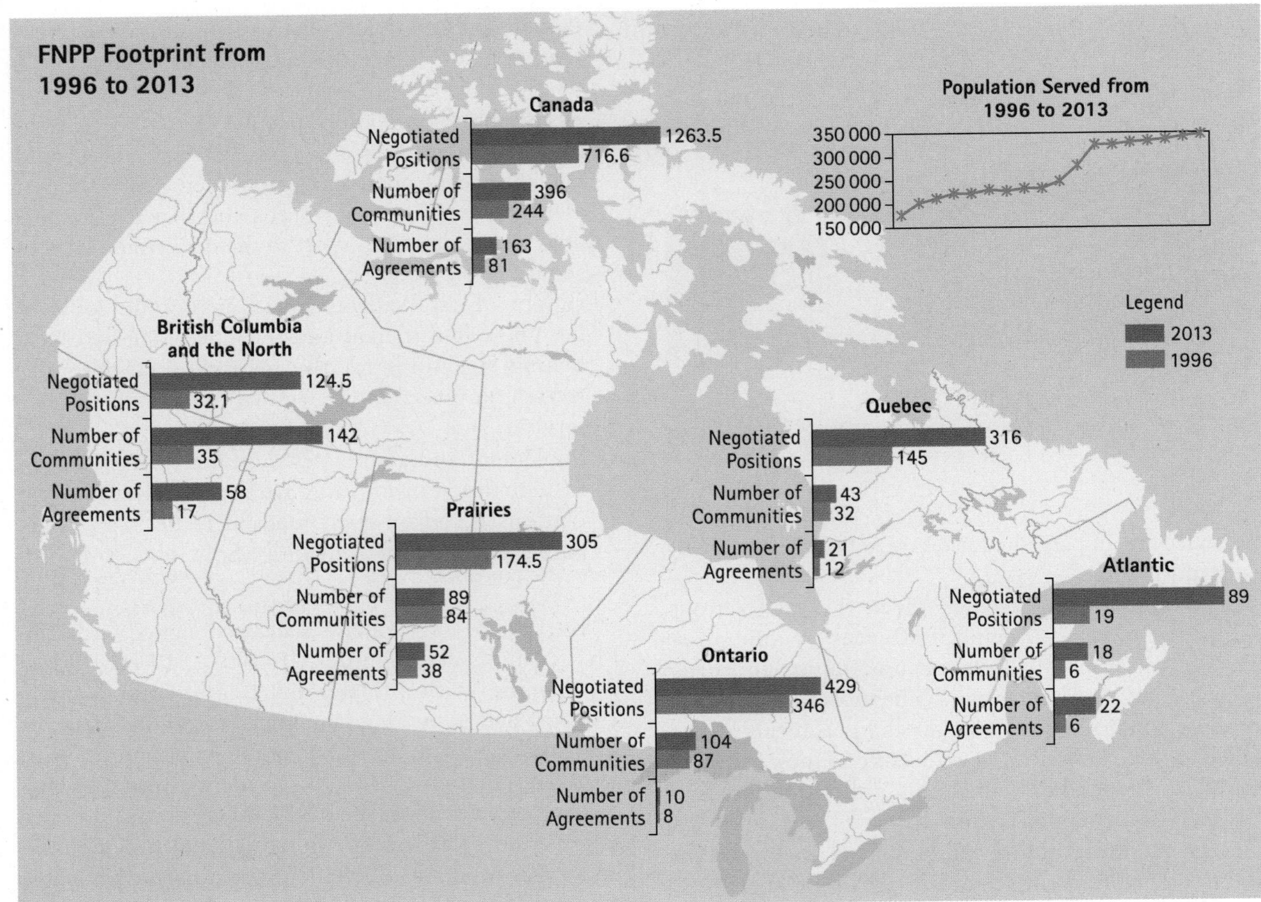

FIGURE 5.5 First Nations Policing Program Footprint, 1996–2013

Source: Aboriginal Policing: First Nations Policing Program, Public Safety Canada, http:www.publicsafety.gc.ca/cnt/cntrng-crm/plcng/brgnl-plcng/index-eng.aspx. Reproduced with the permission of the Minister of Public Safety and Emergency Preparedness Canada, 2015.

SUMMING UP AND LOOKING FORWARD

Most police officers in Canada provide municipal policing services. There are three provincial police departments; in the other seven provinces and three territories, the RCMP provides provincial policing services. The RCMP is responsible for some municipal and provincial policing in Canada as well; it also has complete responsibility in all provinces and territories for enforcing federal statutes, carrying out executive orders, and providing security for dignitaries.

The numbers of women and members of visible minority groups in the police have gradually increased. The equality provisions of the Charter of Rights and Freedoms led to changes in the hiring practices of the police, as has employment equity legislation. More than 20 percent of all police officers are women, and women currently make up slightly over 10 percent of all senior officers. Five percent of all police officers in Canada are Aboriginal, while 9 percent are members of visible minority groups. A number of barriers confront women, Aboriginals, and members of other visible minority groups in policing. These include isolation, marginalization, discrimination, and sexual harassment. While police organizations have attempted to address these issues, a large number of women officers experience institutional sexism in their workplace.

In an attempt to have more appropriate police services, numerous Aboriginal communities now have their own police organizations. The first Aboriginal police organizations were created during the 1970s; in 1991, the federal government created the First Nations Policing Policy to allow Aboriginal communities more control over policing.

This chapter has so far focused on the structural level of policing; that is, the context in which policing occurs in Canadian society. A micro-level analysis of policing is also important as it looks at the day-to-day nature of police work, how police officers experience their work, and how they cope with it. The next section looks at two micro-level areas of policing: the police culture and the police personality.

Review Questions:

1. What are the different jurisdictional levels of policing in Canada today?
2. What policing functions does the RCMP perform?
3. What is the history of diversity in police organizations in Canada?
4. What are the gender conflicts experienced by women police officers?
5. What are the reasons why the Aboriginal police were introduced in Canada?

What Is the Police Culture and Why Is It Important?

So far in this chapter the emphasis has been upon the ways in which police departments are organized and have changed. But what about the **micro-level processes**, such as the impact that police culture has upon everyday policing? Some feel that for the police organization to become more attuned to policing by consent, the police culture needs to change (e.g., Skogan and Frydl 2004). What is culture and why is it important to understand? Culture refers to such things as the understandings and interpretations shared by the members of a group, as well as the agreed-upon meanings about group activities and feelings about the broader society. Culture also guides how members of the group deal with each other and helps the group in a number of different ways, such as managing strains related to their work.

The two main ways researchers have used culture in the context of policing focus upon

- the **occupational culture** of policing, and
- the **subcultures** found within the police culture.

Occupational cultures consist of "accepted practices, rules and principles of conduct that are situationally applied, and generalized rationales and beliefs" (Manning 1995). The police culture is considered to be an important concept in terms of understanding a large number of issues surrounding policing, including how new members of the police organization "learn the ropes" of policing, the success or failure of attempts to reform the police, and how the police function on a day-to-day basis.

Members of the police culture share certain common values. These values, it is argued, arise from the hazards of police work and the ways in which officers attempt to minimize those hazards and protect the members of the subculture (Brown 1988). A number of these basic values have been identified:

- *Police are the only real crime fighters.* The public wants the police officer to fight crime; other agencies, both public and private, only play at crime fighting.
- *No one else understands the real nature of police work.* Lawyers, academics, politicians, and the public in general have little concept of what it means to be a police officer.
- *Loyalty to colleagues counts above everything else.* Police officers have to stick together because everyone is out to get the police and make the job more difficult.
- *It is impossible to win the war against crime without bending the rules.* Courts have awarded criminal defendants too many civil rights.
- *Members of the public are basically unsupportive and unreasonably demanding.* People are quick to criticize the police unless they themselves need police help.
- *Masculinity-based traits are idealized.* A strong masculinity focus is used to define much police work, with the result that sexist and racist attitudes are perpetuated.
- *Patrol work is the pits.* Detective work is glamorous and exciting (Skolnick 1966; Sparrow et al. 1995:51).

Studying the police culture is important for the insights it gives into the everyday activities of police officers. Researchers who have investigated the police culture have found both positive and negative aspects. Most, however, have discussed the negatives. For example, some have argued that this culture is a major reason why the police resist new or innovative ideas such as **community policing** (e.g., Skogan and Hartnett 1997), while others have pointed out that it is used to support violations of the legal rights of citizens as well as the misuse of police authority (e.g., Skolnick and Fyfe 1993). Others have commented that this culture is a major factor in police officers' resistance to police accountability. This has led to the "**blue curtain**" (also known as the "blue wall of silence"), a term referring to the value placed on secrecy and the general mistrust of the outside world shared by many police officers. The "blue curtain" is regarded as a major reason why the police are so deeply separated from the very citizens they are supposed to protect (Walker 2001).

Some researchers have examined the positive aspects of the police culture. It creates a sense of "collectiveness" that helps officers deal with their unique stresses (e.g., Waddington 1999), and it can be a mechanism for regulating and preventing inappropriate police actions (e.g., Crank 1997). Another positive aspect of the police culture is based on research that has found it enables new members of the police to learn the "craft" of policing (e.g., Manning 1995; Van Maanen 1974).

Most of the research on the police culture has focused on its use as a coping mechanism enabling the police to insulate themselves from the stresses and hazards of policing activities. In particular, two areas have typically been studied:

- the relationship of police officers to the citizens they meet in the course of their duties; and
- the organizational context in which police officers work.

The most commonly studied aspects of the police culture in terms of police–citizen relationships are the presence of or potential for danger (e.g., Skolnick 1994) and the coercive powers and authority that police officers possess over citizens (Bittner 1974). Skolnick (1994:42) points out that the police perceive their working environment as dangerous or as having a high level of risk, or as having the potential to escalate to high levels of dangerousness almost instantaneously. He states that the element of danger is so integral to the work of officers that explicit recognition of such situations can create an emotional barrier for some to the occupation of policing. In addition, the police are a unique institution in our society in that they have been given the power to use force legitimately—that is, they possess "a license to threaten drastic harm to others" (Muir 1977:37). This, in turn, reinforces the perception of police work as dangerous (Skolnick 1994).

The second component of the police environment is the organizational context in which officers work. Two major issues have been identified: (1) the unpredictable and punitive nature of the relationship between police officers and their supervisors, and (2) the ambiguity of the police role. Researchers have described the police–supervisor relationship as characterized by feelings of uncertainty. Police officers fully expect to deal with issues on the street in an efficient and timely manner, only to have their decisions and actions criticized later by a supervisor (Ericson 1982; Skolnick 1994). This can lead to organizational uncertainty, in that it appears to police officers that only their mistakes are noted by their superiors, and that their accomplishments go unrecognized. Another aspect of the organizational environment is the ambiguous role identification experienced by officers. This refers to the fact that officers use a number of policing styles (see Chapter 6) to accomplish their goals, but only the law enforcement–style functions are reinforced and recognized. The ambiguity exists because supervisors want the officers under their control to handle all their activities and roles on the street equally (Bittner 1974).

How do police officers—and their culture—cope with the stresses and hazards of their work? The police use two coping mechanisms in particular when dealing with citizens. Researchers refer to these as "suspiciousness" and "maintaining the edge." According to Skolnick (1994:46), in their attempts to reduce or control the uncertainty related to their work, the police have developed a conception of order that emphasizes "regularity and predictability. It is therefore, a conception shaped by persistent suspicion." Maintaining the edge refers to the tendency of police to use their authority when interacting with citizens. The police are able to handle situations by being in control—that is, by using enough of their authority that they can assert themselves to deal with the situation at hand. They achieve this by reading the people and the situations they come into contact with and always being "one up" on citizens (Muir 1977; Van Maanen 1974). Another coping mechanism, this one directed at avoiding the police supervisor's attention, is referred to as the "lay-low" attitude. Basically, this means that police officers learn when not to do something since it might draw undue attention to themselves (Brown 1988).

Many components of the police culture are transmitted through a socialization process that starts when an officer graduates from the training academy and that continues throughout their career. According to Van Maanen (1974:86), the socialization process gives new police officers "a set of rules, perspectives, techniques, and/or tools" that allow them to participate in the police organization. The socialization process starts in the training academies, where it is presented in a formal manner. Once the new recruits start their careers as probationary patrol officers, their field training officers offer them informal socialization—that is, "what to do and expect" versus "this is the way we really do it." Coping mechanisms within the police culture generally start during the first few months, while a new recruit is learning how to patrol, but they never really end (Brown 1988).

What Is the Police Personality?

Many researchers and citizens feel that police officers form a unique set of personality traits to help them in their work. The police are often criticized for the following traits, which are almost universally viewed as negative: cynicism, hostility, dogmatism, and conservatism. These attitudes are thought to influence police decisions to arrest, to contribute to poor relationships with the community, and to lead to police deviance as well as to greater use of deadly force. In particular, **police cynicism** is characterized by a rejection of the ideals of justice and truth—the very values that a police officer is sworn to uphold and protect. Officers who become cynical lose respect for the law and replace it with other "legal" rules formed in and promoted by the police culture. These values become more acceptable to some police officers because they think they offer a better representation of today's social realities. Police cynicism has been found at every level of policing, including among police chiefs, and throughout all stages of a police career (Regoli et al. 1990). Where police cynicism becomes entrenched, the result can be increased police misconduct, corruption, and brutality (Regoli 1977).

The existence of the police culture has led researchers to ask how it starts in the first place, prompting a study of the "police personality." This, in turn, has led to questions such as these: Do police officers and the general public have different attitudes? How do police officers develop these attitudes? Do the personality characteristics of officers influence their discretion and performance on the job? And do they acquire those characteristics from other officers while on the job?

"Police personality" refers to a value orientation that is unique to police—or at least to some police. It is the way in which the police look at the world, their standards of right and wrong, and the type of behaviours they have as they go about their duties (Skolnick and Fyfe 1993). Some believe that the police are cynical—that is, motivated entirely by self-interest—and are pessimistic about human behaviour. But how do police officers become cynical? Is it because they already hold a different attitude by the time they become members of a police force, or is it because they become that way once they have held the job and are exposed to negative public feelings and the police culture?

The earliest studies explored the possibility that police officers are exposed to negative social events and public responses and then learn from other police officers how to best deal with them, notably by becoming part of the police culture. The first major study of police cynicism was conducted by Niederhoffer (1967), who at the time was an NYPD officer. He believed there were two types of police cynicism: (1) general cynicism, i.e., cynicism directed against people in general; and (2) system cynicism, i.e., cynicism aimed at the police organization itself. Niederhoffer believed police officers embark on a policing career with a professional and committed attitude but experience frustrations on the job. This leads to disenchantment, which leads most officers to develop a cynical attitude. For a minority, however, it leads to a renewed commitment to the high standards with which they started.

What determines the degree of cynicism in a police officer? In Niederhoffer's view, is determined by age and experience. He discovered that new officers were less cynical compared to other police officers, even those who had limited amounts of experience. Almost 80 percent of new recruits questioned on their first day on the job responded that the police department was "an efficient, smoothly running organization"; less than two months later, however, fewer than one-third held this view. Niederhoffer also found that cynicism increased steadily during the first seven to ten years of a police officer's career; then, as years of experience increased beyond this time, cynicism decreased but never returned to the low levels found among the newly graduated recruits. In addition, he reported that college-educated patrol officers were more cynical than non-college-educated patrol officers and that police administrators had the lowest levels of cynicism. Based on his results, Niederhoffer concluded that police officers either left policing or were able to come to terms with the problems found within policing. While other researchers (e.g., Langworthy 1987; Rafky et al. 1976) have failed to replicate Niederhoffer's results regarding the length of service of police officers and cynicism, they have found differences between recruits at the beginning of their training compared to other officers with experience, including some who had just completed their training.

Cynicism may have a damaging impact on the job performance of a police officer. Feelings of cynicism appear to intensify the need to maintain respect and exert authority over others (Regoli and Poole 1979). And as this cynicism escalates, there can be a corresponding increase in citizens' distrust and fear of the police. This can ultimately result in the feeling that every contact with the public involves potential danger, a state of mind termed "police paranoia." All of these factors contribute to make the police conservative and resistant to change (ibid.).

The Working Personality of Police Officers

Probably the most important result of Niederhoffer's study is that it led to investigations on whether individuals who choose to become police officers possess personality characteristics that make them susceptible to cynicism. The classic work on the police personality was conducted by Jerome Skolnick (1966). Like Niederhoffer, Skolnick believed that the police personality emerges from certain aspects of police work, such as danger and isolation, rather than from pre-existing personality traits. Skolnick contended that the constant danger of the job leads police officers to be extremely suspicious of people, which has the effect of isolating them from the public. The fact that citizens constantly challenge their authority further isolates them. As a consequence, officers react to "vague indications of danger suggested by appearance," a feeling that is constantly reinforced by the police culture. Police officers also feel strongly that the public doesn't support them; this also leads to feelings of isolation, which in turn make police officers turn to one another for support (Skolnick 1966).

The works of Niederhoffer and Skolnick support the view that the police personality emerges as a product of the strains and pressures they encounter in their work. This view has become known as the **socialization model**. An alternative approach, referred to as the **predispositional model**, argues that the police personality is the product of the pre-existing personality traits of police officers.

One of the first tests of this model was conducted by Bennett and Greenstein (1975), who asked three groups of students at an American university—police officers (working toward a B.A. degree), police science majors, and non-police science majors—to assign priorities to the values that serve as guiding principles in their lives. These values included equality, happiness, freedom, a sense of accomplishment, a comfortable life, and so on. The researchers hypothesized that the police officers and police science majors would possess like-value orientations. However, the opposite was true, which led to a rejection of this model. The researchers found that the police science majors were most like the non-police science majors and that the values of both these groups were "markedly divergent from the value systems of experienced police officers." Other studies (e.g., Cochrane and Butler 1980) yielded similar results.

The significance of these studies is that any attempt to reduce value differences between the police and the community should be in the context of new training procedures rather than recruitment on the basis of personality characteristics alone. Furthermore, the training of new recruits should emphasize the social and legal aspects of policing (such as awareness of different cultures as well as the use of discretion) instead of focusing on changing personal values. Despite the evidence that police attitudes are learned on the job, most police forces today continue to rely on personality screening tests and similar interview questions when screening potential candidates for police academies (Ash et al. 1990; Sanders et al. 1995).

SUMMING UP AND LOOKING FORWARD

In order to understand the context of policing it is necessary to understand the police culture and how it sustains certain core values among police officers. Common values within the police culture lead to the maintenance of the police culture, which ultimately leads to the police being somewhat isolated (the blue curtain) from the communities they serve. The most studied aspects of the police culture in terms of police–citizen relationships are the presence of or potential for danger and the coercive powers and authority that police officers possess over citizens.

The police culture helps create the police personality, which is the way the police look at the world, their standards of right and wrong, and their behaviour as they carry out their various duties. How does the police personality translate into their working personality? It emerges as a product of the strains and pressures they encounter in their work. This view has become known as the socialization model. An alternative approach, referred to as the predispositional model, argues that the police personality is the product of the pre-existing personality traits of police officers.

But what about the manner in which policing is actually practised? As we saw earlier in this chapter, police departments historically favoured a preventive method of policing and later a reactive style. This latter style, however, neglected to practise the principles of policing by public consent, and as a result new practices of policing were introduced in the late 1970s to rebuild this principle. Many of these new practices were proactive, seeking not only to prevent crime but also to introduce practices that would re-establish positive relations with communities. The next chapter focuses upon the proactive police practices that emerged during the last three decades of the 20th century as well as innovations since the beginning of the 21st century.

Review Questions:

1. What is meant by the police culture and how does it function?
2. How are police recruits socialized into the police culture?
3. What is meant by the working personality of the police?
4. What are the functions of the working personality of the police?

EXPANDING THE ROLE OF DNA DATA BANKS

In January 2015, police officers in Windsor, Ontario, went door-to-door without a warrant in a neighbourhood in what is called a "DNA sweep," requesting residents to provide a blood sample in order to rule themselves out as a suspect in the murder of a pregnant woman (Humphreys 2015). What would happen if someone refused to give their sample? Would they become a suspect? And what would happen to all the DNA samples? Would they be destroyed after the person was cleared of the murder?

Some of the key issues regarding DNA data banks are determining who should be included and how long DNA samples should be retained. When DNA data banks were first developed, only those individuals who were convicted of selected criminal offences were included. In Canada, this remains the case today. DNA profiles and samples are included in the National DNA Data Bank's Convicted Offenders Index when individuals are convicted of a designated offence or when they become included under retroactive legislation. Under current Canadian legislation, DNA profiles and samples are no longer retained when the conviction or DNA order is quashed on appeal, the criminal record retention period has expired in the case of a youth, one year after an individual receives an absolute discharge, or three years after a conditional discharge unless there is on the criminal record a DNA sample collection order for another designated offence (Royal Canadian Mounted Police 2008). Since 2000, almost 7,000 DNA profiles have been removed from the Convicted Offenders Index of the National DNA Data Bank and destroyed. Questions have been raised about whether or not all the DNA samples are expunged in an efficient manner. For example, information supplied to an Ontario youth court indicated that the DNA of Canadian youths "convicted of crimes as minor as petty theft have been improperly retained by the federal DNA data bank . . . (violating) youths' constitutional rights to privacy. . . . In her ruling, Judge Cohen said . . . a senior data bank official stated that only 535 of 21,169 DNA samples seized from youths have been destroyed because their retention period has ended—a suspiciously small number." The judge also noted that when the data bank destroys DNA profiles taken from youths, it continues to hold a portion of the original biological material that was seized (Makin 2009).

The RCMP is responsible for operating the National DNA Data Bank.

Some countries, however, have expanded those who are included in their DNA data banks. Due to the fact that when DNA data banks were first established, the police found the information included in the data banks to be of limited assistance in their investigations. This was because there was a lack of having "an optimum size of sample and a means of storage" as well as the fact that the police also lacked the power "to compel suspects to give a suitable sample that could then be matched with samples found at the scene of a crime or on a victim" (Dovaston and Burton 1996).

In England and Wales, the Criminal Justice and Public Order Act was introduced in 1994 and gave the police the right to take samples from suspects for DNA analysis during investigations. If no criminal proceeding occurred, any samples taken were to be destroyed. In 1995, an amendment gave the police the power to take a DNA sample from offenders who had been convicted of a "recordable offence" (i.e., an offence punishable with imprisonment or as otherwise specified in law). Two years later, more legislation was passed allowing the taking of DNA samples from sex offenders currently in custody. The indefinite retention of samples was permitted by the Criminal Justice and Police Act (2001) and, as a result, the number of DNA samples increased dramatically. In early 1997, the National DNA Database had retained

Continued on next page

more than 112,000 samples; in 1999, this number had risen to over 600,000. By June 2003, the number of samples retained had reached 2 million; that number had more than doubled to 4.5 million DNA samples in 2009 and had reached 6.4 million by April 1, 2012. While most of the DNA samples were the result of convictions for criminal offences, the taking and retaining of DNA samples in other circumstances was voluntary, as when individuals allowed the police to take a sample of their DNA in order to assist the police in their investigation of a local sexual offence. As of March 2008, 857,000 people were on the database who had committed no crime (Moore 2009:19). In December 2008, in *S and Marper v. United Kingdom*, the European Court of Human Rights ruled that Britain's "blanket and indiscriminate" practice of collecting and retaining DNA profiles from innocent people, including children as young as 10, violated Article 8 of the ECHR which protects the right to privacy.

Concerns were raised about the retention of DNA samples collected during police investigations from volunteers and those samples held although the individuals in question had been acquitted of all charges. An investigation reported that "many thousands of samples, perhaps as many as 50,000, were being held on the database when they should have been taken off" (Thomas 2005:78). The government responded by passing the Criminal Justice and Police Act (2001), which legalized such activities as long as the retention of the samples was specifically for the purposes of the prevention or detection of crime. In addition, samples gathered to eliminate suspects of sex offences in a local area were also allowed to be retained if the person had given their written consent. In 2003, the Police and Criminal Evidence Act was amended in order to allow the police to take DNA (as well as fingerprints) without consent from anyone arrested for a recordable offence and detained in a police station. This led to a match at a crime scene in over 3,000 offences, including 37 murders, 16 attempted murders, and 90 rapes (British Home Office 2006).

The ruling by the European Court of Human Rights led England to re-evaluate its policies regarding the retention of DNA. In May 2012, England passed the Protection of Freedoms Bill, which made significant changes to the rules about the retention of DNA and DNA profiles in criminal matters. The intention of these provisions is to significantly reduce the number of DNA profiles kept in the National DNA Database. One part of the new legislation requires the government to delete DNA samples from the estimated one million innocent persons who are currently in the DNA data bank. A second provision states that in the future individuals arrested but not charged, or acquitted of minor offences, will have their records on the DNA database deleted when the charges are dropped or after an investigation is complete. Those individuals charged but not convicted of more serious offences will have their records on the DNA database deleted after three years unless the police apply for a further retention period of two years. This two-year extension has to be approved by a court and both the police and the individual can appeal.

In the United States, the FBI announced in April 2009 that it was going to expand its collection of DNA samples from an exclusive focus upon those convicted of certain crimes "to include millions more people who have been arrested or detained but not yet convicted" (Moore 2009:1). This move aligns the FBI collecting activities with a number of states that collect DNA samples from those awaiting trial. California is one such state, and in 2009 it started to collect DNA from individuals upon arrest. State officials predicted that the DNA database will increase to 390,000 by the end of the year, from 200,000 the year before.

Another issue concerning the use of DNA is whether forensic scientists should use a genetic analysis procedure known as "familial searching" or "kinship searching" to assist the police in identifying possible suspects. This procedure was first used in the United States when California officials solved a number of cold cases by using a DNA sample collected for another purpose to identify individuals who had so far eluded detection from serious crimes. In this case, the suspect's son had recently been convicted on a felony weapons charge, and his DNA gave authorities a partial match to the as-yet-unsolved murders, the last of which had been committed in 1985. California has developed precise guidelines that limit the use of familial searching. A committee of forensic and legal experts must meet at each stage of the proceedings to discuss the latest findings and decide whether or not the search should continue. This "widening of the genetic net" in the use of DNA has led some to argue that it can lead to guilt by genetic association and perhaps invade the privacy of individuals (Chamberlain 2012; Murphy 2012).

Questions

1. Do you think Canada should expand the use of its DNA database so that it would function in exactly the same way that the United States and England operate their DNA databases?
2. Do you believe that the familial search of DNA violates people's reasonable expectation to privacy as guaranteed by s. 8 of the Charter of Rights and Freedoms?
3. How strong is a person's privacy interest in their DNA? Does it matter that people leave traces of their DNA behind as they go about their day? Or that there are private DNA companies that use DNA for health screening for genealogical purposes?
4. With technology constantly evolving, what do you predict for the future of DNA databases?

SUMMARY

The institutional development of the police in Canada, the major practices of policing, and the micro processes occurring within police organizations are the focus of this chapter. A brief history of the police in Canada reveals that its practices have mirrored other common law countries (e.g., the professional model of policing) as well as specific police practices (e.g., Aboriginal [First Nations] policing). It is recognized that while the public police once dominated most types of policing activities, policing now involves numerous other providers (e.g., private security firms). The historical and contemporary record of women and visible minority group members in the police is discussed, as are the major micro processes associated with policing.

KEY WORDS: police legitimacy, common law model, policing by consent

How Did the Idea of Policing Emerge?

This section discusses the institutional history and development of policing in common law countries. A key idea is the development was the introduction of the principle of policing by consent. The initial police practices were preventive-based, which were designed to secure social control.

KEY WORDS: pledge system, tithings, hundred, constable, shires, shire-reeves, coroner, constable-watch system, Statute of Westminster, watchmen, justices of the peace, parish constable, Bow Street Runners (Thief Takers), dangerous class

What Is the Importance of the Principle of Policing by Public Consent? (p. 152)
What Was the Early Canadian Police Experience? (p. 153)

How Did Modern Policing Develop? The Rise of Municipal Policing

The various roles performed by the police include social service, order maintenance, and crime fighting (law enforcement). These are delivered most commonly through preventive, reactive, and proactive methods. The development of policing in the late 20th and early 21st centuries reveals that many other agencies are involved with the provision of security and policing services.

KEY WORDS: preventive, reactive, social service, order maintenance, crime fighting, professional model of policing, police mandate, plural policing, mass private property, private security, security governance, commercial policing, high policing

What Is Plural Policing? (p. 156)

How Are the Public Police Organized in Canada?

Three levels of jurisdiction exist among the police: municipal, provincial, and federal. Historically, the policies of police organizations have excluded women and members of minority groups from sworn officer positions. These policies began to change in the 1970s. The number of women and minority group police officers have slowly increased over the past few decades. However, women experience significant gender conflicts within police organizations. In order to overcome underpolicing and overpolicing, many First Nations communities have created their own police organizations.

KEY WORDS: municipal policing, provincial policing, federal policing, diversity, employment equity, institutional sexism, underpoliced, overpoliced, Community Tripartite Agreements

What Is the Extent of Diversity within Canadian Police Organizations? (p. 162)
Women and Policing (p. 164)
Aboriginal (First Nations) Police Services (p. 166)

What Is the Police Culture and Why Is It Important?

What Is the Police Personality? (p. 171)
The Working Personality of Police Officers (p. 171)

In this section, the emphasis is on micro processes found within police organizations. It is believed that jobs affect the way we interpret the world around us. Due to the nature of policing, officers form a culture in which they develop values and norms specific to their occupation. This leads to the police working personality, that is, their behaviour and standards of right and wrong as they go about their daily tasks.

KEY WORDS: micro-level processes, occupational culture, subcultures, community policing, blue curtain, police cynicism, socialization model, predispositional model

Critical Thinking Questions

1. How has the primary function of the police changed over time in our society?
2. Is the principle of policing by consent as valid in contemporary society as it was when it was first introduced?
3. What led to the success of the professional model of policing?
4. What has led to the expansion of plural policing in Canada? How has the rise of plural policing impacted public police services?
5. Why has the development of more diverse police services proved to be such a difficult challenge?
6. What are the differences among the various types of police cultures? How do these impact citizens?

Weblinks

DNA has changed policing in dramatic ways. Listen to Dr. John Butler's lecture on Forensic DNA and DNA databases. While his lecture is focused on the United States, he raises many issues that are applicable to Canada. Go to YouTube and watch Dr. John Butler "Forensic DNA & DNA Databases: An Introduction to the Use and Issues of DNA-Typing" (41:02).

Court Case

S and Marper v. United Kingdom (2009), 48 EHRR 50.

Suggested Readings

Chrismas, R. 2013. *Canadian Policing in the 21st Century: A Frontline Officer on Challenges and Changes*. Montreal: McGill-Queen's University Press.

Colvin, R. 2012. *Gay and Lesbian Cops: Diversity and Effective Policing*. Boulder, CO: Lynne Reinner.

Corsianos, M. 2009. *Policing and Gendered Justice: Examining the Possibilities*. Toronto: University of Toronto Press.

Sewell, J. 2010. *Policing in Canada: The Real Story*. Toronto: James Lorimer.

Trojanowicz, R.C., V. Kappeler, and L. Gaines. 2001. *Community Policing: A Contemporary Perspective*, 3rd ed. Cincinnati, OH: Anderson.

Whitelaw, B. and R.B. Parent. 2010. *Community-Based Strategic Policing in Canada.* Toronto: Nelson.

References

Abella, R. 1984. *Report of the Commission on Equality in Employment.* Ottawa: Supply and Services Canada.

Ash, P., K. Slora, and C. Britton. 1990. "Police Agency Selection Practices." *Journal of Police Science and Administration* 17:258–69.

Balkin, J. 1988. "Why Policemen Don't Like Policewomen." *Journal of Police Science and Administration* 16:29–38.

Bartol, C., G. Berger, J. Volkens, and K. Knoras. 1992. "Women in Small-Town Policing: Job Performance and Stress." *Criminal Justice and Behavior* 19:240–59.

Bayley, D. and C. Shearing. 1996. "The Future of Policing." *Law and Society* 30:585–606.

Bennett, R. and T. Greenstein. 1975. "The Police Personality: A Test of the Predispositional Model." *Journal of Police Science and Administration* 3:439–45.

Bittner, E. 1974. "Florence Nightingale in Pursuit of Willie Sutton: A Theory of the Police." In *The Potential for Reform of Criminal Justice*, edited by H. Jacob. Beverley Hills, CA: Sage.

British Home Office. 2006. *National Policing Improvement Agency: The National DNA Database Annual Report for 2006–07*. www.npia.police.uk. Retrieved April 23, 2009.

Brodeur, J-P. 2000. "Transnational Policing and Human Rights: A Case Study." In *Issues in Transnational Policing*, edited by J. Sheptycki. London: Routledge.

Brown, M. 1998. *Working the Street: Policing Discretion and the Dilemmas of Reform.* New York: Russell Sage.

Browne, L. and C. Browne. 1973. *An Unauthorized History of the RCMP.* Toronto: James Lewis and Samuel.

Burgess, J. 2006. "Putting the Brakes on Human Trafficking," *RCMP Pony Express*, 14–15.

Cao, L. 2011. "Visible Minorities and Confidence in the Police." *Canadian Journal of Criminology and Criminal Justice* 53:1–26.

Chamberlain, M. 2012. " Familial DNA Searching: A Proponent's Perspective." *Criminal Justice* 27:18, 25–30.

Chan, J. 1997. *Changing Police Culture: Policing in a Multiracial Society.* Cambridge: Cambridge University Press.

Cochrane, R. and A. Butler. 1980. "The Values of Police Officers, Recruits, and Civilians in England." *Journal of Police Science and Administration* 8:205–11.

Corsianos, M. 2009. *Policing and Gendered Justice: Examining the Possibilities.* Toronto: University of Toronto Press.

Crank, J. 1997. *Understanding Police Culture.* Cincinnati, OH: Anderson.

Crawford, A. and S. Lister. 2006. "Additional Security Patrols in Residential Areas: Notes from the Marketplace." *Policing and Society* 26:164–88.

Crawford, B. and C. Stark-Adamec. 1994. "Women in Canadian Urban Policing: Why Are They Leaving?" *In The Canadian Criminal Justice System: An Issues Approach to the Administration of Justice*, N. Larsen (ed). Toronto: Canadian Scholars' Press.

Department of Justice. 2011. *An Overview of Trafficking in Persons and the Government of Canada's Efforts to Respond to This Crime: 2010–2011*. Ottawa: Department of Justice. www.justice.gc.ca. Retrieved February 10, 2012.

Depew, R. 1992. "Policing Native Communities: Some Principles and Issues in Organizational Theory." *Canadian Journal of Criminology* 34(3–4):461–78.

Dovaston, D. and C. Burton. 1996. "Vital New Ingredient." *Policing Today*, 44–48.

Ericson, R. 1982. *Reproducing Order: A Study of Police Patrol Work*. Toronto: University of Toronto Press.

Forcese, D. 1992. *Policing Canadian Society*. Scarborough, ON: Prentice-Hall.

Greschner, D. 1985. "Affirmative Action and the Charter of Rights and Freedoms." *Canadian Women Studies* 6:34–36.

Guth, D. 1994. "The Traditional Common-Law Constable 1235–1829: From Bracton to the Fieldings of Canada." In *Police Powers in Canada: The Evolution and Practice of Authority*, edited by R.C. Macleod and D. Schneiderman. Toronto: University of Toronto Press.

Hamilton, A. and C. Sinclair. 1991. *The Justice System and Aboriginal People: Report of the Aboriginal Justice Inquiry of Manitoba*, vol. 1. Winnipeg: Queen's Printer.

Head, R. 1989. *Policy for Aboriginal Canadians: The RCMP Role*. Ottawa: RCMP.

Humphreys, A. 2015. "500 Samples of Blood DNA, and a Debate, in Murder Probe." *National Post*, January 30, pp. A1–A2.

Hunt, J. 1990. "The Logic of Sexism among the Police." *Women & Criminal Justice* 1:3–30.

Hutchins, H. 2014. *Police Resources in Canada, 2013*. Ottawa: Canadian Centre for Justice Statistics.

Hyde, M. 1992. "Servicing Indian Reserves: The Amerindian Police." *Canadian Journal of Criminology* 34(3–4):369–86.

Jaccoud, M. and M. Felice. 1999. "Ethnicization of the Police in Canada." *Canadian Journal of Law and Society* 14(1) (Spring):83–100.

Jayewardene, C. and C. Talbot. 1990. *Police Recruitment of Ethnic Minorities*. Canadian Police College.

Johnston, L. and C. Shearing. 2003. *Governing Security: Explorations in Policing and Justice*. London: Routledge.

Kelling, G. 1988. "Police and the Community: The Quiet Revolution." *In Perspectives on Policing, No. 1*. Washington DC: National Institute of Justice.

Kelly, W. and N. Kelly. 1976. *Policing in Canada*. Toronto: Macmillan.

Langworthy, R. 1987. "Police Cynicism: What We Know from the Niederhoffer Scale." *Journal of Police Science and Administration* 11:457–62.

LaPrairie, C. and E. Diamond. 1992. "Who Owns the Problem? Crime and Disorder in James Bay Cree Communities." *Canadian Journal of Criminology* 34(3–4):417–34.

Loader, I. 2000. "Plural Policing and Democratic Governance." *Social and Legal Studies* 9:323–45.

Makin, K. 2009. "Court Raises the Bar in Seizing DNA from Juveniles." *The Globe and Mail*, April 8, p. A7.

Manning, P. 1995. "The Police Organizational Culture in Anglo-American Societies." In *Encyclopedia of Police Science*, edited by W. Bailey. New York: Garland.

Martin, S. 1991. "The Effectiveness of Affirmative Action: The Case of Women in Policing." *Justice Quarterly* 8:489–504.

Moore, S. 2009. "F.B.I. and States Vastly Expanding Databases of DNA." *New York Times*, April 19, pp. 1, 19.

Morris, N. and G. Hawkins. 1967. *The Honest Politician's Guide to Crime Control.* Chicago: University of Chicago Press.

Muir, W. 1977. *Police: Streetcorner Politicians*. Chicago: University of Chicago Press.

Murphy, C. 2007. "'Securitizing' Canadian Policing: A New Policy Paradigm for the Post 9/11 Security State?" *Canadian Journal of Sociology* 32:449–75.

Murphy, E. 2012. "Familial DNA Searches: The Opposing Viewpoint." *Criminal Justice* 27:19–25.

Nichols, D. 1995. "The Brotherhood: Sexual Harassment in Police Agencies." *Women Police*, Summer:10–12.

Niederhoffer, A. 1967. *Behind the Shield: The Police in Urban Society*. Garden City, NY: Anchor Books.

Normandeau, A. 1990. "The Police and Ethnic Minorities." *Canadian Police College Journal* 14:215–29.

Petersen, C. 1982. "Doing Time with the Boys: An Analysis of Women Correctional Officers in All-Male Facilities." In *The Criminal Justice System and Women*, edited by B. Price and N. Sokoloff. New York: Clark Boardman.

Rafky, D., T. Lawley, and R. Ingram. 1976. "Are Police Recruits Cynical?" *Journal of Police Science and Administration* 4:352–60.

Regoli, R. 1977. *Police in America*. Washington, DC: R.F. Publishing.

Regoli, R., R. Culbertson, J. Crank, and J. Powell. 1990. "Career Stage and Cynicism among Police Chiefs." *Justice Quarterly* 7:592–614.

Regoli, R. and E. Poole. 1979. "Measurement of Police Cynicism: A Factor Scaling Approach." *Journal of Criminal Justice* 7:37–52.

Reiner, R. 2000. *The Politics of the Police*, 3rd ed. Oxford: Oxford University Press.

Royal Canadian Mounted Police. 2010. *Human Trafficking in Canada*. Ottawa: RCMP.

Royal Canadian Mounted Police. 2008. *The National DNA Data Bank of Canada Annual Report 2007–2008*. Ottawa: RCMP.

Rudin, J. 2007. *Aboriginal Peoples and the Criminal Justice System*. Ottawa, Ontario.

Sanders, B., T. Hughes, and R. Langworthy. 1995. "Police Officer Recruitment and Selection: A Survey of Major Police Departments in the U.S." *Police Forum* 5:1–4.

Senna, J. and L. Siegel. 1995. *Essentials of Criminal Justice*. Minneapolis: West.

Shearing, C. and P. Stenning. 1983. "Private Security Implications for Social Control." *Social Problems* 30:493–506.

Skogan, W. and Frydl, K. 2004. *Fairness and Effectiveness in Policing: The Evidence*. Washington, DC: National Academies Press.

Skogan, W. and S. Hartnett. 1997. *Community Policing: Chicago Style*. New York: Oxford University Press.

Skolnick, J. 1994. *Justice without Trial: Law Enforcement in Democratic Society*, 3rd ed. New York: Macmillan.

Skolnick, J. 1966. *Justice without Trial: Law Enforcement in Democratic Society*. New York: Wiley.

Skolnick, J. and J. Fyfe. 1993. *Above the Law: Police and Excessive Use of Force*. New York: Free Press.

Solicitor General of Canada. 1999. *The First Nations Policing Policy*. Ottawa: Solicitor General of Canada.

Sparrow, M., M. Moore, and D. Kennedy. 1995. *Beyond 911: A New Era for Policing*. New York: Basic Books.

Thomas, T. 2005. *Sex Crime: Sex Offending and Society*, 2nd ed. Cullompton, UK: Willan.

Van Maanen, J. 1974. "Working the Streets: A Developmental View of Police Behavior." Pp. 83–130 in *Potential for Reforming Criminal Justice*, edited by H. Jacobs. Beverly Hills, CA: Sage.

Villiers, P. 2009. *Police and Policing: An Introduction*. Hook, Hampshire: Waterside.

Waddington, P. 1999. "Police (Canteen) Sub-Culture: An Appreciation." *British Journal of Criminology* 39:287–309.

Wakefield, A. 2003. *Selling Security: The Private Policing of Public Space*. Cullompton, UK: Willan.

Walker, S. 2001. *Police Accountability: The Role of Citizen Oversight*. Belmont, CA: Wadsworth.

Young, G., 1995. *Police Personnel and Expenditures in Canada, 1993*. Ottawa: Canadian Centre for Justice Statistics.

CHAPTER 6

The Practice of Policing

Learning Objectives

After completing this chapter, you should be able to:

- Differentiate among the preventive, reactive, and proactive styles of policing.
- Understand the core components of reactive-style policing.
- Identify and describe the problems related to the reactive style of policing.
- Understand why the broken windows model became popular among police organizations.
- Differentiate between problem-oriented and community policing.
- Understand why zero tolerance policing became so controversial.
- Differentiate between intelligence-led policing and predictive policing.

Now that we have learned about the history of policing in common law countries, the way in which the police are organized, and the police culture, we will examine the practices used by the police to control crime in our society with an emphasis upon changes introduced since the 1970s. Interestingly, while the police have continued to integrate recent technology (e.g., forensics and computer analyses of crimes) into their practices, the "real" practice of policing mostly revolves around police patrols. Patrol has long been and remains today the dominant practice of policing. It is what the majority of police officers do when they are not actively involved with a specialized duty.

Throughout their existence, the police have practised preventive patrols; that is, uniformed police officers patrolling either by foot or in motorized vehicles to deter criminals. In the 1920s the police introduced reactive patrols, and integrated this approach with preventive patrols. Reactive patrols involved the police responding to criminal incidents after they had occurred rather than trying to prevent them. Rapid response to criminal incidents became the basis for evaluating the success of the police in controlling crime. Both of these used a **one-size-fits-all approach**—that is, they treated all crimes in all places in exactly the same way. For many decades, the effectiveness of the reactive approach in preventing crime went unquestioned. This changed during the last decades of the 20th century, when criticisms were raised about the continuing relevance of reactive-style policing.

Concerns about reactive-style policing practices were not evenly distributed among all communities. For middle and upper class communities few crimes were reported, and when they were, the police usually responded quickly much to the satisfaction of local residents. Residents of working class communities oftentimes had different experiences with the police. The police were viewed as unresponsive and when the police did arrive, their interactions with local residents were seen as disrespectful. This led residents to view the police (as well as the entire criminal justice system) as not working on their behalf, and as a result **legal cynicism** appeared. Legal cynicism is defined as a "cultural orientation in which the law and its agents are viewed as illegitimate, unresponsive, and ill equipped to ensure public safety" (Kirk and Matsuda 2011:443). If people feel that the police are unresponsive, they may not report crimes committed against them and may be more unlikely to intervene on the behalf of others (Kirk and Papachristos 2015). In essence, reporting a crime is seen as a waste of their time and people may take justice into their own hands.

This increasing frustration of the reactive style of policing led both public officials and citizens to demand that the police develop new approaches to better control crime. While it was agreed that the police could and should be responders to crime for justice reasons, people started to ask if there were better strategies for the police to practise. Changes were introduced, with patrols becoming **proactive**, an approach based on the idea that the police need to collect and analyze information in order to understand the nature of crime. Proactive policing led to changes in policing practices, including the creation of partnerships with other criminal justice agencies (an approach known as **multi-agency policing**) and the restoration of relationships with communities. Police departments quickly introduced proactive policing practices, and they were performed alongside (as opposed to replacing) reactive policing styles.

Other strategies introduced by the police focused upon specific types of criminals in specific areas at specific times in order to prevent or interrupt crimes and arrest criminals. These strategies (also referred to as *crime-attack strategies*) were welcomed as "smarter law enforcement" practices. Some, however, question how smart these strategies are, feeling they could potentially violate the civil and privacy rights of citizens in a variety of situations, such as policing public protests (see below), the collection and retention of DNA for future criminal investigations, the collection of personal data, and the interception of private communications.

The Professional Model of Policing: The Reactive Approach

While the professional model of policing continued to employ preventive patrols, it introduced a **reactive approach** (also referred to as **incident-based policing**) to criminal incidents. In the reactive approach, it was believed that since police patrols are able to quickly respond to criminal incidents in motor vehicles, the responding officers could catch suspects, collect evidence that would lead to the suspects being apprehended, or deal with situations before they escalated further (Spelman and Brown 1981). This introduction of the reactive style into preventive patrols was based in large part on the belief that the speed of response times to crime incidents was the superior way to apprehend suspects. By placing patrol officers in motor vehicles, any contact police officers enjoyed with citizens disappeared and they became removed from the communities they served. It was the position of police administrators that this loss of contact would be more than replaced by greater satisfaction with the police by the public.

When patrol officers are not responding to a criminal incident (which is estimated to make up only about 10 to 20 percent of their time), they continue to practise preventive patrols. By having the capacity to move around a designated geographic area in marked patrol vehicles in a random manner, it was thought that both the visibility of the police and their faster response time to crimes would deter would-be criminals. Successful crime control is seen as the result of marked patrol vehicles randomly patrolling within a designated area and reassuring law-abiding citizens that once they report a criminal incident, the police are able to respond quickly. The police response is facilitated by technology, through the use of land-line telephones and cell phones to contact the police (communications); patrol officers responding to the calls for service in automobiles (mobility); and police communications systems used to direct and monitor police officers. The professional model of policing is known as the standard model of policing, as it relies on interventions that are reactive and a one-size-fits-all approach in comparison to approaches focusing upon specific targets, such as a geographical area or a certain type of offender. Police patrols became the backbone of policing, and their role in policing was designed to achieve a number of goals, notably

- the maintenance of a police presence in the community,
- a quick response to emergencies, and
- the detection of crime (Langworthy and Travis 1994).

Patrol officers play an important role due to their ability to respond quickly to criminal incidents and emergencies. In addition, their preventive patrol function allows officers on patrol to observe what is going on in the community and hopefully prevent criminal activity. (See Exhibit 6.1 for a description of some of the activities of patrol officers.)

Patrol officers are the most visible component of the entire criminal justice system. When a criminal incident occurs, they are usually the first to arrive and deal with the incident as well as any victims or witnesses. They are typically seen in marked patrol vehicles, but they may also patrol on foot, on bicycle, or on horseback. They carry out their duties within a designated area, or beat, and rarely leave it unless in pursuit of a suspect or to back up other patrol officers. Police patrol 24 hours a day, by different shifts of officers. The activities of patrol officers are hard to enumerate, because their role is, in many ways, generalist—that is, a patrol officer plays a multitude of roles while on the job. (See Exhibit 6.2 for a typology of the

EXHIBIT 6.1 What Are the Activities of Patrol Officers?

The activities of patrol officers today are many and varied, but they can be divided into a few key areas:

- Deterring crime by maintaining a visible police presence.
- Maintaining public order within the patrol area.
- Enabling the police department to respond quickly to law violations or other emergencies.
- Identifying and apprehending law violators.
- Aiding individuals and caring for those who cannot help themselves.
- Facilitating the movement of traffic and people.
- Creating feelings of security in the community.
- Obtaining statements from crime victims and witnesses.
- Arresting suspects and transporting them to a police facility for investigation (American Bar Association 1974; Cordner and Hale 1992).

different types of roles that patrol officers might engage in during a shift.)

While patrol officers often receive a detailed assignment, such as traffic patrol or security checks at business establishments, these activities are usually short lived. Their most typical role is "routine observation"; that is, they drive around a particular beat and, when necessary, respond to citizens' calls for service. Most of the activities of patrol officers are unrelated to crime. This means that officers on patrol commonly deal with issues such as neighbourhood disputes, animal control, noise complaints, and locating lost children.

Police administrators firmly believed that the reactive approach lent itself to greater efficiency, most typically

EXHIBIT 6.2 What Are the Policing Styles of Patrol Officers?

In the 1960s researchers started to study the way in which patrol officers went about their duties. While they discovered preventive and reactive patrols taking up large amounts of patrol officers' time, they also found some patrol officers still engaged citizens. Wilson (1968) studied eight police departments and identified four policing styles: the social agent, the watchman, the law enforcer, and the crime fighter.

- **The social agent.** This style sees the need for police officers to be involved in a range of activities that are not necessarily attached to law enforcement. Instead, officers see themselves as problem solvers who work with community members. Generally, citizens expect officers working in this style to provide protection from outsiders and to respond to their concerns, whether they involve criminal violations or not. Police are also expected to direct their law enforcement actions toward strangers while giving local residents great latitude.
- **The watchman.** This style of policing emphasizes public order. It is tolerant of private matters between citizens as well as minor criminal offences. Much is left up to the citizenry. If the police respond for a second time to an altercation at an address, they may separate the parties involved but are unlikely to make an arrest unless a major incident occurs. This style of policing involves the restoration of "disruptive situations to normalcy without arresting the citizens involved" and "the management of situational tensions." Thus, for example, the police "move along" drunks to hostels instead of arresting them, and they escort mentally ill patients to their facilities when they wander away from them.
- **The law enforcer** (or **legalistic**) style. With this style, the police enforce all laws to the limit of their authority. All crime-related incidents and suspects are treated in accordance with the formal dictates of the law. This means that all suspects are arrested and charged if enough evidence is found, all traffic violators are issued tickets, and discretion is minimal. This approach involves investigating all criminal incidents, apprehending, interrogating, and charging suspects, and protecting the constitutional rights of suspects as well, because the law states that this is what police officers are supposed to do.
- **The crime fighter.** Here, the most important part of policing is the detection and apprehension of criminals. The focus is entirely on serious criminals, in the belief that without the "thin blue line," society would descend into chaos. Police who adopt this approach are opposed to any sort of social service function for the police, as this would diminish their effectiveness.

The police have a multitude of roles in our society, including responding to emergencies.

by increasing the mobility of police officers as well as response times, arrest rates, and public satisfaction with the police. If calls for service increased in one part of a city, patrol units could be moved to that location in order to better deter crime. Police organizations began to measure their efficiency using two measures: (1) response times, and (2) arrest rates. The first measure, **response time**, is the time elapsed between a citizen's call to police and the arrival of the police at the scene of the incident. The speed with which the police respond to calls for service is considered an effective response to crime control and prevention as the belief is that if the police can respond quickly, they will catch perpetrators at the scene of the offence.

Another measure used to assess police efficiency is **arrest rates**. Following the logic of the deterrence approach (see Chapter 3), it is assumed that when the police made more arrests there would be fewer numbers of criminals on the street. This approach, accepted for decades by police administrators, was later viewed as problematic as self-report and victim surveys (see Chapter 4) revealed that significant amounts of crime were not reported to the police. In addition, many people are arrested but not prosecuted; often offences cleared by charge do not result in a conviction when events and circumstances are beyond their control—for example, if witnesses or victims are reluctant to testify so prosecutors decide to stay the charges.

Reactive Criminal Investigations

Criminal investigation (or **detective work**) is the second main function of the police. In comparison to police patrols, which were considered an essential component of the earliest professional police forces in the early 1800s, detective work was largely conducted within the private sector. While some police departments did have a few detectives, the position was considered to be low status. It wasn't until J. Edgar Hoover reformed the Federal Bureau of Investigation in the 1920s that the type of work done by detectives gained high status. Today, criminal investigators are essential parts of police departments as they possess special expertise in a number of areas, including:

- interviewing skills,
- developing and managing informants,
- conducting covert surveillance,
- recreating the circumstances to identify perpetrators.
- identifying and locating potential witnesses and sources of intelligence, and
- preserving and developing evidence for court trials (Berg and Horgan 1998).

Criminal investigations typically have two components: (1) a preliminary investigation, which often is conducted by patrol officers; and (2) a follow-up investigation, which is conducted by detectives if the patrol officers are not able to apprehend the alleged perpetrator (Figure 6.1).

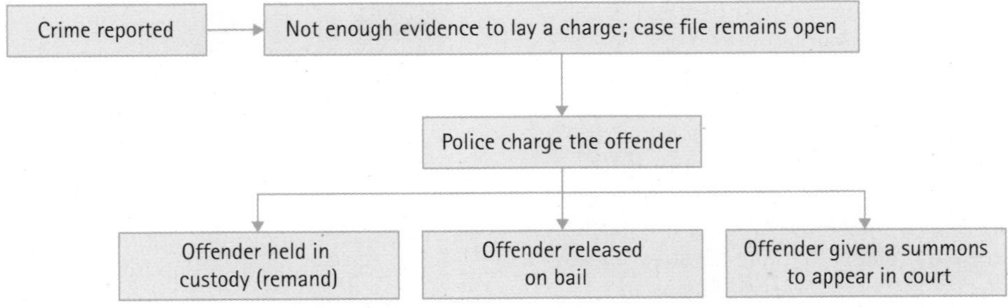

FIGURE 6.1 Criminal Investigations Usually Start Prior to an Offender Being Charged with a Criminal Offence

Preliminary Investigations

In **preliminary investigations**, patrol officers typically collect information where the criminal incident occurred and write up incident reports about what happened. Preliminary investigations usually involve five steps:

- identifying and arresting any suspects;
- providing assistance to any victims in need of medical attention;
- securing the crime scene to prevent the loss of any evidence;
- collecting any physical evidence; and
- preparing a preliminary report (Eck 1983).

Following the collection of this information, patrol officers often conduct preliminary investigations themselves, which may result in the arrest of the suspect(s). It is estimated that about 80 percent of all arrests of suspects are made by patrol officers rather than detectives. This is because when the patrol officers arrive, the suspect is often still near or at the crime scene or is readily identified by witnesses. If the patrol officers can't make the arrest, it can mean that very little is immediately known about the suspects and, as a result, it may be difficult to make an arrest.

Follow-Up Investigations

A case can be handed over to detectives for **follow-up investigation** after an arrest has been made or if further investigation is needed in order to identify the suspect(s). Follow-up investigations can be *routine, secondary*, or *tertiary*. **Routine activities** include interviewing victims and witnesses and examining the crime scene. **Secondary activities** include looking for people who may have witnessed the crime but who left the scene before the police arrived. **Tertiary activities** include discussing the case with patrol officers, interviewing suspects, checking police records and those of other agencies, interviewing informants, and staking out addresses or individuals.

In order to solve a crime, detectives may decide to **reconstruct a crime**. When they do this, detectives attempt to develop a theory about why a crime was committed, and this is typically based upon collected information and evidence. Detectives may then decide to focus the investigation with the hope of proving that one suspect is guilty of committing the crime (Weston and Wells 1986).

In most mid- to large-size police services today, 15 to 20 percent of the personnel are detectives. They have not been studied as closely as patrol officers, because the bulk of their work involves law enforcement and very little of their time goes into service and order maintenance activities. Detectives are usually organized in a different division of a police agency than patrol officers. They are often assigned to sections specializing in a particular type of criminal activity, such as vice, homicide, robbery, or prostitution; or they support services such as polygraph operations. While most of their investigative work is reactive, detectives are also involved in proactive activities. For example, a vice squad detective may pose as a prostitute in order to arrest customers; or in a sting operation, detectives may set up an operation that buys stolen goods and videotapes everyone who brings in those goods.

Advances in technology, such as DNA analysis, have allowed the police to maintain high clearance rates for certain crimes such as murder. Seventy-six percent of all murders in Canada were solved by the police between 2003 and 2013. Of these, the majority were solved within one week of their occurrence (see Figure 6.2).

Starting in the late 1960s, however, questions were raised about the reactive approach. This was largely the result of social and racial unrest, complaints about the lack of contact between police officers and citizens, and the inability of the police to control crime, despite growing budgets and increasing numbers of police officers. See Exhibit 6.3 for selected criticisms of reactive policing.

Due to these criticisms, police agencies began to reassess how they operated their patrols and criminal investigations. For patrols, response times to all calls for service were found to be a weak statistical measure of effectiveness. Alternatives were explored, with the result that a new system was introduced that distinguished between emergency and non-emergency calls. These systems utilize **management of demand** (also referred to

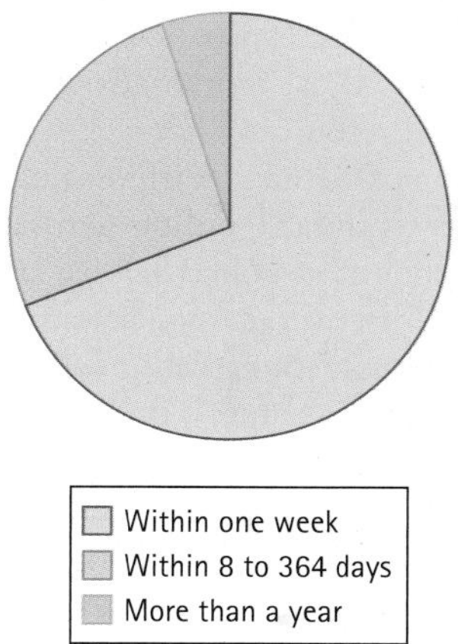

FIGURE 6.2 Length of Time to Solve Homicides, 2003–13

Source: A. Cotter, "Homicide in Canada, 2013." *Juristat* (December 2014), Statistics Canada Catalogue no. 85-002-x, p. 3, http://www.statcan.gc.ca/pub/85-002-x/2014001/article/14108-eng.pdf. Reproduced and distributed on an "as is" basis with the permission of Statistics Canada.

EXHIBIT 6.3 Selected Criticisms of Reactive Policing

When reactive policing was introduced, it was viewed by police administrators as an improvement in policing that would be embraced by the public. However, within a decade or so, criticisms of this model of policing began to appear:

- *Lack of knowledge about local communities:* Patrolling in vehicles made it difficult for the police to get to know and develop relationships with community residents. When the police did make contact with residents, it usually involved a criminal incident. This often-times led to complaints that the police were insensitive to the needs of residents. Ultimately, the police were viewed as "outsiders" by those they were meant to protect.
- *Fear of crime:* Officers patrolling in vehicles did not give community residents feelings of security, which had been the case with preventive policing. The result led to an increase in the fear of crime as crime rates started to increase.
- *Efficiency:* Evaluations of the response times of police to criminal incidents questioned the belief that reactive-style policing increased the chances of apprehending criminals. A number of studies found discovered that the key criteria for catching criminals at the scene of the crime was not the police response time, but instead the time it took for a member of the public to contact the police.
- *Community stereotyping:* The reduction and subsequent loss of community contacts led the police to classify certain neighbourhoods as "crime-prone" and "dangerous." This led to distrust between communities and the police. For example, incidents involving random stops and searches of people walking on the street led to people questioning the fairness of the police, leading to the erosion of trust in the police.

as **differential response**). Management of demand for services requires the police to categorize citizen demands for services and then match these with differential police responses. This means the police, after receiving a call for service involving an emergency, respond to it faster than for a non-emergency call. For non-emergency calls, for example, they may take the report over the telephone, request that the citizen go and file a report at a local police station, or ask the citizen to make an appointment for a police officer to come and talk to them when the level of calls for service is usually lower. This means the police are able to adjust workloads and thereby make better use of their resources.

Management of demand/differential response programs are now standard policy across Canada. For example, the Edmonton Police Service analyzed its calls for service and discovered "consistently, month after month . . . only about five percent of all incoming phone calls are high priority in nature" (Braiden 1993:219). If the police could identify the most serious criminal incidents, a rapid response might be the most efficient approach to apprehending offenders. In addition, by analyzing calls for service police, administrators can restructure their patrol activities without diminishing public satisfaction with the police. This approach gained support since it allows some patrol officers to become active in other areas of police operations, such as criminal investigation and crime prevention, when demand for immediate response is low.

Another change was the use of clearance rates as an indicator of police efficiency in crime control. The clearance rate, or the percentage of crimes solved over a specific period, allows the police to separate out and analyze various categories of crime, such as violent and property crimes (see Chapter 4).

SUMMING UP AND LOOKING FORWARD

The most common practice of policing has always been patrol work. In the early decades of the 20th century a reactive approach appeared, and it involved changing the focus of patrols to respond to incidents after they had occurred. This approach was based on a number of assumptions, including the belief that random patrols and rapid response rates would quickly apprehend criminals and better control crime. The reactive approach ultimately led to the demise of policing by public consent. Different styles of patrol work were practised by patrol officers.

Reactive-style policing also led to changes within police organizations, such as the growth of criminal investigators. While patrol officers usually conduct preliminary investigations, detectives are involved with follow-up investigations. Various types of follow-up investigations evolved over time.

A number of criticisms about reactive-style policing emerged, including lack of knowledge about the communities they served, increasing rates of fear, and questions concerning its overall efficiency. As a result of these criticisms, police organizations began to evaluate certain components of reactive-style policing, with unanticipated results. These evaluations are discussed in the next section.

Review Questions:

1. What is legal cynicism and what is its importance to the study of the practice of policing?
2. Why did police patrols become the "backbone" of policing in the reactive style, and what were the goals of this style of patrols?
3. What are the major styles of patrol officers?
4. Why do patrol officers usually become involved with preliminary investigations into crimes?
5. Why did the reactive style of policing begin to be criticized?

What Led to Changes in the Professional Model of Policing?

In the 1970s, a number of research studies were commissioned to empirically assess three core functions of the professional model of policing. These core functions are referred to as the **Three-R's strategy** and they relied heavily on interventions thought to achieve high levels of deterrence. The three components of this strategy were (1) **random preventive patrol**, (2) **patrol officer rapid response rates**, and (3) **criminal investigations**. The police used them in a similar fashion (a **"one-size-fits-all" approach**) regardless of what crimes were being investigated. The impact of these research studies led the police to introduce changes in their approach during the ensuing decades. This was in large part due to the fact that the police had, for at least 50 years, held on to the assumption that reactive policing practices were the best way to respond to criminal incidents and deter criminals.

Does Random Preventive Patrol Deter Crime?

A central purpose of police patrol is to prevent crime. It is assumed that the presence of officers on general patrol in marked vehicles prevents criminal activity and reduces the crime rate. This is a core assumption of the professional model of policing, and police organizations have for decades been using marked patrol vehicles as their principal tool for deterring crime. However, during the late 1960s and early 1970s, critics began to argue that this mainstay of policing operations was not in fact reducing crime rates. The assumption was not empirically evaluated until 1972 and 1973, when the Kansas City Police Department conducted perhaps the most famous of all police patrol studies, the Kansas City Preventive Patrol Experiment (Kelling et al. 1974). The results of this study forever changed how patrol officers in marked vehicles were used in both Canada and the United States.

During the one-year evaluation, the police studied the effects of preventive patrols by applying different patrol strategies in different areas. Three types of patrol were instituted: **reactive**, **proactive**, and **preventive patrol**. The reactive beats involved no preventive patrol activity whatsoever. Patrol officers who worked reactive patrol beats entered their beat only to respond to calls for assistance. When not responding to calls, the patrol officers patrolled neighbouring proactive police beats. Proactive beats were assigned two to three times the number of police patrol units through the addition of patrol vehicles from the reactive beats. Proactive patrols were highly visible, and the officers patrolled in an aggressive style, meaning they stopped vehicles and citizens if they felt there was reason to do so. The control beats maintained the normal level of patrols that were operational at that time—one car per beat.

Before this study started, most observers felt that preventive patrols would be the most successful in reducing crime and improving citizens' feelings of safety, due to the greater number of patrol vehicles and the more aggressive patrol approach. But the results of this experiment did not support the supposed superiority of this approach. In fact, the results revealed that, no matter what strategy

- crime rates stayed the same;
- crime reporting rates to the police remained constant;
- the level of fear of crime remained the same;
- opinions about the effectiveness of the police didn't change; and
- respect for the police increased in the control beats (i.e., the beats with traditional preventive patrol) (ibid.)

These findings were both revealing and controversial. They were revealing because the police had always considered routine preventive patrol to be the most effective approach to patrolling. Yet this study concluded that preventive patrol is no more effective than reactive patrol and that adding more patrol units does not automatically lead to a reduction in crime rates or in citizens' fear of crime. This study led Klockars and Mastrofski (1991:131) to conclude that it "makes about as much sense to have police patrol routinely in cars to fight crime as it does to have firemen patrol routinely in fire trucks to fight fire." The findings were controversial because they questioned traditional assumptions about preventive patrol. While it is necessary to have police patrols, the presence of more patrol officers doesn't lower crime rates. This finding led to the **"mayonnaise" theory of police patrol**, which states that the quantity of police patrols is similar to the amount of mayonnaise required to make a sandwich. If an area has no patrol, starting one there will reduce the crime rate, but adding more patrols to an area that already has some appears to have little if any impact on crime. This study gave police managers a reason to maintain a constant level of vehicles on patrol, but at the same time it allowed administrators to experiment with alternative tactics and strategies.

According to Walker (1994), there are several reasons why increasing police patrols have a limited impact on crime:

- Patrol officers are spread so thinly across a beat that a patrol vehicle may be seen only on chance encounters rather than as a daily occurrence;
- Many crimes cannot be deterred by police patrols. Crimes that occur in residences, such as murders, sexual assaults, and child abuse, are not going to stop because more police are patrolling the streets; and
- Some people are not deterred by increasing numbers of police. Robbers, for example, will change their approach to committing an offence rather than stop their criminal behaviour altogether (Desroches 1995).

Does Rapid Response Deter Criminals?

Another firmly held police belief in the professional model was that faster **response rates** to criminal incidents by patrol officers would lead to greater arrests and deter more criminals. In turn, this approach would allow officers to intervene before problems became more serious, arrest more suspects, and gather more information about potential suspects if they had left the scene prior to the police arriving. This approach was studied by the National Institute of Justice in 1977 in Kansas City. To determine the effects of rapid response rates, the researchers divided street crimes into two different categories: (1) victim–offender **"involvement" crimes** such as robbery, and (2) after-the-crime **"discovery" crimes** such as break and enter. Attention was then placed on the involvement criminal offences. The researchers divided these offences into three different categories:

- *Crime reporting:* the time it took from the crime occurrence to the time a call was made to the police;
- *Dispatch time:* the time it took from receiving the call to the patrol officers being dispatched to the crime scene; and
- *Travel time:* the time it took the police to arrive at the crime scene after they had been dispatched.

The researchers also interviewed crime victims in their study. Based on the information they collected, the researchers determined that the average reporting time for involvement crimes was 41 minutes. They concluded that there was no relationship between the likelihood of response-related arrests by patrol officers and reporting time after the reporting time exceeded nine minutes (Wilson and McLaren 1977).

Do Reactive Investigations Solve Crimes?

The "ideal" criminal case is one where the offender is arrested at the scene by a patrol officer, there are many witnesses, and the suspect quickly confesses. Such cases are, of course, rare; much more often, detectives must solve crimes by interviewing the victim and witnesses, doing background checks on potential suspects, and waiting for an analysis of any forensic evidence that was available at the crime scene. In the professional model of policing, it was thought that detectives solve a substantial amount of the crimes handed to them for investigation.

In 1975, a report was published that reported the results of an investigation into the role of detectives in terms of solving crimes in 150 police departments (Greenwood and Petersilia 1975). The research project studied whether detectives were able to find new information about crimes that could not be solved by patrol officers. It was discovered that it was rare for detectives to find new evidence that led to case being solved. In addition, they concluded that only about 20 percent of crimes handed to detectives were ultimately solved by them.

Upon further investigation, Eck (1983) found detectives categorized cases into the following types:

- *Unsolvable.* These cases are considered "weak" in the sense that they cannot be solved regardless of the amount of effort put into the investigation.
- *Solvable.* These cases can be solved with a moderate to considerable amount of investigation effort.
- *Already solved.* These cases have strong evidence and so can be solved with a minimum of investigation.

If a case was determined to be unsolvable, detectives worked fewer than 30 minutes on it.

What were the findings made from these and other similar studies? Bayley (1998), in his analysis of the major research studies, came to the following conclusions:

- Police discover very little crime on their own.
- Almost every crime is solved by the identification of a suspect by the public.
- The primary job of detectives is collecting information to successfully prosecute suspects.

- More crimes are solved through information provided by arrested or convicted offenders.

As a result of the findings of these research studies, police administrators started to look for alternatives, especially in the area of police patrols. Unlike patrol officers, the type of work done by detectives and described above has largely remained the same since the 1970s (Horvath et al. 2001). Police administrators began to recognize that traditional approaches to patrols were both ineffective and inefficient in controlling crime. Other policing strategies were subsequently introduced in the hope that they would be more effective and gain the support of the community.

Experimenting with Alternative Forms of Police Patrols

For over five decades, police officers on patrol engaged in reactive-style policing in the hope that this approach would deter criminals. When research studies questioned the viability of this approach, police administrators experimented with new styles of patrols. It was hoped that these alternative forms would bring about better crime control as well as reconnecting the police to communities. While a number of these experiments were short lived, they ultimately led to more permanent changes in how the police operated. One of the first changes was to attempt a return to a style of patrol first introduced in London during 1829, foot patrol, in order to re-engage the police with communities.

Foot Patrol

Foot patrol was the mainstay of police forces in the late 19th and early 20th centuries, but all disappeared when motor vehicle patrols were introduced in the 1920s. However, foot patrols began to reappear in the late 1970s in response to citizens' complaints about the lack of contact with patrol officers. A common feature of foot patrols today is the emphasis upon greater interaction with the community and the solving of underlying community problems that may lead to crime and disorder. Most municipal police forces in Canada today have foot patrols, although many forces maintain such patrols only in the downtown core or other densely populated areas.

An experiment involving foot patrol officers in Flint, Michigan, became the basis for the reintroduction of foot patrols across North America (Trojanowicz et al. 2001). An evaluation of the Flint Neighborhood Foot Patrol Program revealed that while foot patrol may reduce crime only slightly, it leads to a significant reduction in citizens' fear of crime and has a positive effect on police–citizen relationships. For example, it was found that foot patrol lowered crime rates by about 9 percent in all categories of crime except burglary and robbery, both of which increased by about 10 percent. Calls for service decreased by over 40 percent, and public support for the police increased. After four years, 64 percent of the citizens surveyed indicated they were satisfied with the police, and 68 percent felt safer in their neighbourhood.

Another early study on the effects of foot patrol was conducted in Newark, New Jersey (Kelling et al., 1981). In contrast to the Flint, Michigan study, this study found that foot patrol had little or no impact on crime levels. However, a number of positive effects were identified:

- Residents noticed when the foot patrol officers were in the immediate vicinity.
- Residents were more satisfied with the service they received from the police when foot patrol officers were involved.
- Residents who were in the area frequented by foot patrol officers were less fearful than citizens who received their police service from motorized patrol officers.

The evidence to date indicates that if foot patrol is to succeed, it must operate in locations where the possibility exists for frequent interaction with large numbers of community members, such as at shopping centres, in high-density neighbourhoods, and in the downtown core. The size of the foot patrol beat should be small, in some instances covering no more than a few blocks; this enables the police to walk their beat area at least once a day (Trojanowicz et al. 2001). In the Chicago Alternative Policing Strategy, 75 percent of police officers continued to be involved with the traditional model of patrolling, while the other 25 percent were assigned to beat teams and were assigned to less patrol duties in order that they use the extra time to engage in community policing (Skogan 2006).

Directed Patrol

With **directed patrols**, officers are given orders about how to use their time on patrol. For example, they are told to spend a certain amount of their patrol time in certain locations and to watch for specific crimes. This type of patrol is usually based on crime analyses. Results of directed patrols indicate that the police can reduce the target crime, although it is not known whether directed patrols actually reduce crime or merely force it into other areas. Studies have shown that this type of patrol activity can reduce certain types of crimes, such as thefts from automobiles as well as robberies (Cordner 1992).

Recent technological innovations have encouraged the increased use of directed patrols. One such innovation has been **crime-mapping systems** such as **geographic information systems** (GISs). This technology identifies crime patterns in specific geographic areas, such as neighbourhoods or larger districts of a city. The police can then develop and maintain an ongoing computer analysis of both crime and criminals and use this analysis to generate crime maps. The most common type of computer mapping is referred to as **resource allocation** mapping, which involves analyzing crime patterns and then sending police officers to designated geographical locations to keep watch on the preferred targets of criminal(s). It is thought that this system gives the police a better chance of arresting the individual(s) committing the crimes.

CP PHOTO/Toronto Star/Sean White

Helicopters are one resource used by the police in order to respond to calls for service and criminal incidents.

SUMMING UP AND LOOKING FORWARD

When questions about using reactive-style policing began to increase, evaluation studies were conducted to assess the effectiveness of certain police practices. The areas in question concerned the effectiveness of random police patrols, rapid responses to calls for service, as well as the activities of criminal investigators in terms of reducing crime. The results of these studies led to a number of changes in the area of policing, particularly police patrols, and new approaches started to be introduced, most notably foot and directed patrols.

Soon, pressures were placed on the police to dramatically change their practices. What emerged emphasized a style of policing known as "proactive policing." While reactive policing never completely disappeared, numerous proactive police practices were introduced in the hope that they would better control crime. These new police practices are the subject of the next section.

Review Questions:

1. How did preventive patrols and rapid response create difficulties with the police's relationship with the public?
2. Why did the police think that reactive approaches would improve the level of satisfaction by the public toward them?
3. Why was foot patrol so successful when it was introduced in Flint, Michigan?
4. How have technological innovations led to increased use of directed patrols?

Policing in Modern Society: The Emergence of Proactive Policing

Starting in the 1970s a "new" style of policing—**proactive policing**—was introduced, with the intention of rebuilding the principle of policing by consent. While the police continue to practise preventive policing, proactive policing requires the police to engage in positive measures in order to better control crime. This approach believes the police spent too much time focusing on how they were organized to do their work instead of focusing on the crime problems they needed to solve (Goldstein 1979). It argues that the police could be more effective by using detailed analyses of crime problems and developing appropriate solutions rather than focusing upon improving management techniques. An important component of proactive policing styles is the collection of information that in turn would be analyzed by the police in order for them to better control crime. At first, data collection and analyses of the data was rudimentary, but it wasn't long before the police started to use more sophisticated analytic systems in order that the information could be used as intelligence against crime and criminals.

One type of proactive policing is *hot spots patrols*, an idea based on the realization that crime is not a random

Do the Police Racially Profile?

In recent years, the issue of racial profiling, or discriminatory actions by the police toward members of minority groups, has made headlines in Western nations. Racial profiling occurs when a police action is initiated by a statistical profile of race, ethnicity, or national origin of a suspect, rather than by any evidence or information that the suspect had broken the law. According to Callahan and Anderson (2001), racial profiling involves the police moving from their standard practice of "case probability" to "class probability." Case probability is defined as those situations where some factors relevant to a particular event are comprehended, while class probability describes those situations where enough is known about a class of events to describe it using statistics, but nothing about a particular event other than the fact that it belongs to the class in question. That is, before the police have evidence of a crime, they start to "investigate a high proportion of people of some particular race, ethnic group, age group and so on. Their only justification is that by doing so, they increase their chances of discovering some crime" (ibid.:40). Once class probability or racial profiling occurs, "there is a strong claim that certain groups of people are being denied equal protection under the law."

CP Photo/Graham Hughes

Individuals protest against the alleged racial profiling by members of the police. Much of the controversy arises from what people say is racial profiling by police officers who are attempting to crack down on criminal activity.

A number of court cases have raised the issue of racial profiling. For example, in 1999, an African American member of the Toronto Raptors basketball team was stopped for going slightly over the speed limit. During the trial, his lawyer argued that his client was the victim of racial stereotyping and was stopped arbitrarily by the police because "black men in big cars must be criminals" (Mitchell 2002:8). The trial judge convicted the accused, dismissing the argument of racial profiling and said that such allegations were "distasteful" and "really quite nasty, malicious accusations based on, it seems to me, nothing" (ibid.). On appeal, race was held to be a factor in the actions of the police and the conviction was overturned (Makin 2003).

What actions of the police might lead to the overrepresentation of minority group members being arrested? Some argue (Engel et al. 2012) that both problem-oriented and hot spots policing require the police to have a greater presence in those areas where there are, for example, higher calls for service. This explanation, the **deployment theory**, argues that the police are placed in greater numbers in those neighbourhoods and communities where the residents are disproportionately members of minority groups. Another explanation, the **racial threat theory**, proposes that social control of minority groups rises as the number of minorities increases in an area (Feldmeyer and Ulmer 2011).

phenomenon but rather occurs at specific locations at certain times, which accounts for a majority of calls for service. Both problem-oriented and community policing, which attempt to close the gap between the police and the community, are also types of proactive policing. There are many types of proactive policing and almost all police forces in Canada are involved in some aspects of it. In fact, it is seen by some as the future style of policing; most, however, believe that it will enhance the standard approach already in use.

Hot Spots Patrol

Research has shown that many crimes tend to cluster in a few places, at particular times, and be committed by a few offenders. One type of proactive policing, referred to as **hot spots patrol**, was developed and is based on crime analyses. In this approach, police officers are directed to spend a certain amount of their patrol time in certain locations and to watch for specific crimes. Why? It is because crime isn't evenly distributed in either place or time. For example, Spelman and Eck (1989) studied a number of U.S. research efforts and estimated that 10 percent of all offenders are involved in more than 50 percent of serious crimes, and 10 percent of places are the source of approximately 60 percent of all calls for service.

Sherman and his colleagues (1989) discovered that in Minneapolis more than 50 percent of all 911 calls came from only 3 percent of its 115,000 addresses. He designed an experiment in which the police intermittently and unpredictably patrolled areas considered to be the worst hot spots in the city. Police officers patrolled in marked vehicles, but they never got out of their vehicles to, for example, talk to people or residents. Robberies declined by 20 percent while the crime rate decreased by 13 percent in these locations. Results of hot spots patrols indicate that the police can reduce the target crime, although it is not known whether they actually reduce crime or merely force it into other areas (known as the **displacement effect**). Studies have shown that this type of patrol activity can reduce certain types of crimes, such as thefts from automobiles as well as robberies (Cordner 1992).

Many communities have created programs to clean up signs of disorder in the hope that criminal activity will be reduced. Are these programs successful in reaching this goal?

The Broken Windows Model

Proactive policing goes beyond focusing upon certain types of crimes and criminals in specific locations. Perhaps the most important aspects of proactive policing are those types that begin to change much of the focus of the police by looking at broader issues. The concern with broader issues by the police can be traced to a 1982 article titled "Broken Windows: The Police and Neighborhood Safety," which argued that the police cannot combat crime successfully all by themselves (Kelling and Wilson 1982). The police need the assistance and support of the community; even more important, they need to change their basic approach by allowing for community involvement in policing. The authors argued that much of reactive policing focuses on the end result of policing activity—such as clearance rates. They contended it would be an improvement for the police to get involved at the beginning of the process of neighbourhood deterioration—that is, at the first signs of neglect and disorder. This article introduced the concept of **disorder** to policing by making the point that disorder, if left unchallenged, signals that no one cares about a neighbourhood. When that is the perception, disorder increases and so does crime (including violent crime). The police had traditionally ignored this element of community life, since it was not part of the reactive approach to policing.

The **broken windows model** posits that **social incivilities** (such as loitering and public drinking) and **physical incivilities** (such as vacant lots and abandoned buildings) cause residents and workers in a neighbourhood to be fearful of crime. This fear causes some residents to move out and others to live in fear and isolate themselves. The model has four components:

1. *Neighbourhood disorder creates fear.* Those areas in a city that are filled with criminals such as drug dealers are the areas that are most likely to have high crime rates.
2. *Neighbourhoods give out crime-promoting signals.* In other words, the appearance of a community can attract criminals. Deteriorated housing, disorderly behaviour, and unrepaired broken windows send the message that no one in the area cares about the quality of life. That message first attracts petty criminals, who feel they can go about their business without interference from the local residents.
3. *Serious criminals move in.* Once petty criminals begin to operate, local residents begin to withdraw from public spaces, and this offers an "invitation" to more serious criminals to move into the neighbourhood.
4. *Police need citizens' cooperation.* If the police are to reduce fear of crime and the crime rate, their policies must include the involvement and cooperation of local citizens.

This approach proposes that there is a significant correlation between disorder and perceived crime problems in a neighbourhood. This type of reasoning constitutes the basis of Ontario's Safe Streets Act (see Chapter 2), which targets panhandlers, homeless people, and squeegee kids as significant sources of disorder. Supporters of these laws point to the research on community policing; these studies have found that both serious crimes and fear of crime can be alleviated by reducing disorder (Pate et al. 1986; Skogan 1990). The broken windows model recommends that police administrators change some of their policies to include local residents in decisions about policing priorities in their neighbourhoods. This model also suggests that other areas of policing that had been largely ignored over the past four decades need to be reviewed in order to reduce fear of crime, increase levels of safety, and develop **order maintenance** policies. These should become the main focus of the police—and of patrol officers in particular.

Problem-Oriented Policing

In 1979, Herman Goldstein published an article in which he laid out a new style of policing that he called **problem-oriented policing**. This style, according to Goldstein, represented a fundamental change in the way the police operate. Instead of spending most of their time responding to citizens' calls about criminal incidents, the police would become more proactive by directing their energies to the causes of crimes and complaints in an attempt to modify them. It attempts to better understand the nature of the crime problem(s) by introducing a fundamental shift in the way the police operated. The underlying causes of crime has to be studied, for unless those causes were modified or eliminated the problems would persist, leading to more criminal incidents and to greater fear of crime. This type of policing was based on the idea that issues considered important to a community were often ignored by the police (Tilley 2003).

How were the police to operate in a problem-oriented approach? They were to talk to community residents in order to find out the problems that concerned them. The police would then decide which problems were to be targeted. But which problems would be selected? Although it is easy to point to criminal acts as problems, problem-oriented policing focuses strongly on those situations that are perceived as leading to criminal activity. See Exhibit 6.4 for a summary of the principles of problem-oriented policing.

As problem-oriented policing became more popular, four stages developed in the problem-solving process, known as **SARA** (see Figure 6.3). The first is referred to as *scanning*; here, a police officer identifies an issue and assesses whether it really is a problem. In the second stage, *analysis*, the officer collects as much information as possible about the problem. In the third stage, *response*,

EXHIBIT 6.4 The Principles of Problem-Oriented Policing

Five principles of problem-oriented policing have been identified, all of which are meant to turn the police away from an incident-based focus toward one that emphasizes the potential sources of criminal activity:

- A problem is something that concerns the community and its citizens, not just police officers.
- A problem is a group or pattern of incidents and therefore demands a different set of responses than does a single incident.
- A problem must be understood in terms of the competing interests at stake.
- Responding to a problem involves more than a "quick fix," such as an arrest. Problem solving is a long-term strategy.
- Problem solving requires a heightened level of creativity and initiative on the part of the patrol officer (Bureau of Justice Assistance 1993).

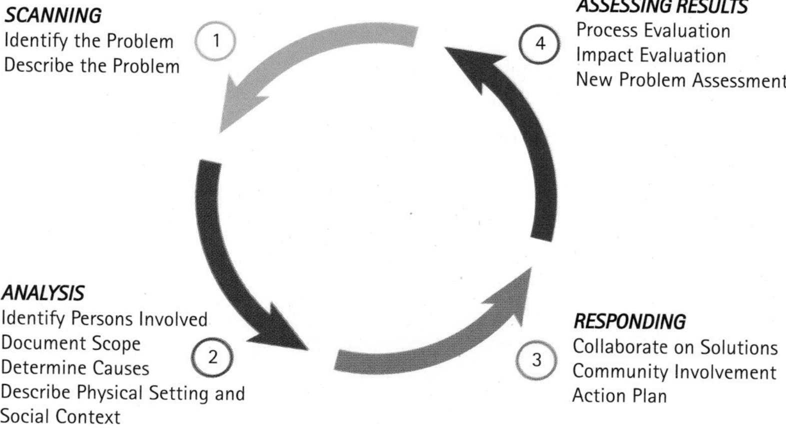

FIGURE 6.3 Scanning, Analysis, Response, and Evaluation Model (SARA)

Source: SARA Problem Solving Model, Office of Community Oriented Policing Services, U.S. Dept of Justice, http://ncjp.org/strategic-planning/justice-applications/sara-problem-solving-model.

all relevant information is collected and solutions are developed and implemented. In the final stage, *assessment*, officers collect information about the effectiveness of their approach, changing any particular tactics if doing so is considered necessary, or even developing an entirely new approach. This same approach is also found in the RCMP's CAPRA model. Many policing initiatives have used the problem-oriented approach, often with some success. Exhibit 6.5 lists some advantages of problem-oriented policing.

EXHIBIT 6.5 The Advantages of Problem-Oriented Policing

The introduction of problem-oriented policing created a number of advantages in the delivery of policing. It recognized that the police do things differently and, most importantly, started to create close relationships with community residents.

- *Better use of resources:* This approach allowed the police to focus on high-crime spaces or individuals who committed a large number of crimes without having to hire more police officers.
- *Decentralization of decision making:* Police decision making was removed from police administrators to front-line police officers, who in many cases possessed better knowledge of the problem. Police officers "must know the underlying issues locally, be in contact with the community, have information to help understand the nature of the underlying problems that generate clusters of incidents, be supported either by senior officers in attempting to solve problems imaginatively and tailor problem-solving to emerging local issues"(Jordan 1998:73).
- *Multi-agency approach:* While law enforcement may be used in any given situation, one of the strengths of this approach was that other non-police agencies may be asked to assist in the solving of crimes. Police officers in essence operate as "crime managers" as they become responsible for selecting problems, deciding what approach should be taken and what agencies could contribute to solving the issue.

Table 6.1 offers selected comparisons between problem-oriented and community policing.

TABLE 6.1 Selected Comparisons between Problem-Oriented Policing and Community Policing Principles

Principle	Problem-Oriented Policing	Community Policing
Primary emphasis	Substantive social problems within police mandate	Engaging the community in the policing process
When police and community collaborate	Determined on a problem by problem basis	Always or nearly always
Emphasis on problem analysis	Highest priority given to thorough analysis	Encouraged, but less important than community collaboration
Preference for responses	Strong preference that alternatives to criminal law enforcement be explored	Preference for collaborative responses with community
Role for police in organizing and mobilizing community	Advocated only if warranted within the context of the specific problem being addressed	Emphasizes strong role for police
Importance of geographic decentralization of police and continuity of officer assignment to community	Preferred, but not essential	Essential
Degree to which police share decisionmaking authority with community	Strongly encourages input from community while preserving ultimate decision-making authority to police	Emphasizes sharing decision-making authority with community
Emphasis on officers' skills	Emphasizes intellectual and analytical skills	Emphasizes interpersonal skills
View of the role or mandate of police	Encourages broad, but not unlimited role for police, stresses limited capacities of police and guards against creating unrealistic expectations of police	Encourages expansive role for police to achieve ambitious social objectives

Source: Michael S. Scott, *Problem-Oriented Policing: Reflections on The First 20 Years*, Washington, D.C.: U.S. Department of Justice, Office of Community Oriented Policing Services, 2000, p. 99, http://www.popcenter.org/library/reading/pdfs/reflectionsfull.pdf.

Community Policing

One flaw of the problem-oriented approach is that the police don't always include the community when studying a crime problem. A key aspect of community policing was that it attempted to restore public confidence and trust in the police. As Moore and Trojanowicz (1988) point out, **community policing** involves community groups, such as businesspeople, residents, and school teachers, as "key partners . . . in the creation of safe, secure communities. The success of the police depends not only on the development of their own skills and capabilities, but also on the creation of competent communities."

The goal of this style of policing is to encourage public safety and confidence, reduce citizens' fear of crime, and encourage citizen involvement. Community policing is a broad-based approach that can encompass many different policies and programs. One possible approach involves establishing decentralized, neighbourhood-based ministations or storefronts. Since community policing was introduced, a consensus has been reached regarding its basic elements and how it differs from past policing strategies. Key here is the change that community policing has brought to the role of policing in society. This new role embraces such issues as disorder, neighbourhood decay, the fear of crime, and order maintenance. This shift has been justified in two ways. The first is rooted in the belief that disorder leads to serious crime, as discussed earlier (the "broken windows" thesis). The second is that order maintenance contributes to the growth of civil society by promoting an environment in which citizens can, without fear, go about their lives (Greene and Mastrofski 1988).

Community policing has three basic aims:

1. the formation of community partnerships,
2. organizational change, and
3. problem solving.

Supporters of community policing view it as the most effective way to reduce disorder in communities; they contend that it does so by developing partnerships between the police and the community. The desired result is for the police and the community to become "**co-producers of crime control**."According to Bayley (1994), two elements are necessary in order to introduce community partnerships: consultation and mobilization. Consultation involves community meetings between the police and the community, while mobilization involves the introduction of community crime prevention programs that can increase neighbourhood cohesion.

Community policing also requires organizational change. Eck and Maguire (2000) contend that there are two reasons why such change is necessary:

1. to encourage officers to become active in community policing programs; and
2. to ensure that the organization is more flexible and open to developing community partnerships and creative problem-solving strategies.

In their opinion, before police agencies can successfully implement community policing, they will have to change

1. their structure,
2. their culture, and
3. their management approach.

Regarding the first, police agencies must abandon their traditional, strongly centralized structures. Regarding the second, those agencies must abandon their focus on crime fighting and begin to emphasize problem solving and community interaction. Regarding the third, management must reduce its emphasis on departmental rules and regulations and begin working more closely with community-based police officers as they develop programs and problem-solving initiatives.

The third aim, problem solving, refers to the police and the community participating in cooperative efforts to solve neighbourhood problems. Specifically, the problem-solving process involves police and community residents addressing chronic problems in the neighbourhood. Many of these programs focus on particular small-scale issues. Such programs identify the causes of problems instead of simply reacting to those problems.

Community policing also involves an important new role for the police, a role that focuses on reducing fear of crime in the community. There are three types of fear of crime. The first is the intense fear suffered by the victims of crime and by their family, friends, and neighbours. This fear comes from physical injury, property loss, economic costs (such as hospital bills and loss of wages at work), and psychological trauma (such as depression and anxiety). Some victims also suffer from **double victimization**—that is, when they report the crime they are treated as second-class citizens by agencies in the criminal justice system.

The second type is often referred to as the **concrete fear of crime**. Here, the fear is of specific crimes, especially violent ones. Various studies have found that women, the young, racial minorities, and metropolitan dwellers are most susceptible to this type of fear. Members of these groups fear being sexually assaulted, physically assaulted, robbed, and murdered. The third type—**formless fear**—is the general feeling that one is unsafe. Research has found that the elderly, the marginally employed, and those with low incomes experience the highest levels of formless fear. Studies that focus on the fear of crime note that while people are afraid of serious crimes, they are just as concerned—if not more so—about petty crimes and social disorder. In the past, the police failed to understand that when people say they are afraid of crime, they are talking about all types of crime and disorder, not just serious, violent crimes (Trojanowicz et al. 2001).

For community police officers, reducing the fear of crime is a core task. It's also a way to increase citizen–police cooperation. A variety of techniques can be employed to reduce the fear of crime in a community, including a police–community newsletter, a police–community contact centre staffed by patrol officers and civilians, and a variety of programs in which police officers contact victims of crime to inform them of police action on the case. Whatever programs are developed, the most successful seem to be those that allow officers the time to identify key issues with local residents and to use both personal initiative and community input to solve problems. While not all programs succeed, the evidence shows that foot patrol officers are actually able to reduce the level of fear in the community.

Critique of Problem-Oriented and Community Policing

Problem-oriented and community policing have been practised for a number of decades. What factors led to their introduction? One reason was the accusation that police practices were too coercive, especially in minority and marginalized neighbourhoods, and these were contributing to the ever-increasing estrangement of local residents from the police. Another reason was that despite increasing the number of police officers, crime rates continued to rise. As a result, police departments introduced both problem-oriented and community policing initiatives. Have both of these approaches worked? If by "work" we mean that community life is improved by a reduction in the amount of fear as well as crime and disorder, no systematic evidence consistently finds that these police practices "work."

Why is this so? Police researchers have come up with a number of reasons why they think both problem-oriented and community policing have not changed the police organization. One is that the police are paramilitary organizations, and their training and reward system is based on hierarchical decision making and strict obedience to departmental rules and regulations (Roberg 1994). Another reason is the fact that these approaches aren't considered by many police officers to be real police work. According to Klockars (1988), both of these approaches violate the very basis of what is considered to be "real" police work—coercive force.

In addition, police departments employing problem-oriented and community policing rarely if ever shifted their priorities or their resources from crime control to solving issues such as fear of crime, disorder, or neighbourhood quality of life concerns. Zhao et al. (2001), in their survey of 245 municipal police forces in the United States serving over 25,000 residents, concluded that (1) police departments rated crime control well above order maintenance or service despite the fact that crime rates were dropping and (2) when they introduced either problem-oriented and/or community policing initiatives, there was only a slight shift in priorities away from crime control. In essence, the core function of the police remained crime control and the structure of police organizations rarely changed.

Intelligence-Led Policing

A new proactive approach, **intelligence-led policing**, was developed in England in the early 1990s and gained prominence after the terrorist attacks on the World Trade Center in September 2001. After the U.S. government studied why the intelligence that could have prevented the attacks wasn't analyzed and/or brought to the attention of the authorities, it was concluded that the attacks might have been prevented if law enforcement agencies were not so "fragmented and uncoordinated" (Ratcliffe 2008:39). This approach to proactive policing emphasizes the **interagency sharing of information**, and **crime analysis** is used as the core of decision making. As a result, the police created formal relationships with other agencies not only to exchange information in a timely manner but also to arrive at strategic crime solutions. Intelligence-led policing advocates increasing the use of both intelligence and surveillance to create a pre-emptive approach to policing. According to Wood and Shearing (2007:53), intelligence-led policing "does not re-imagine the role of policing role so much as it re-imagines how the police can be smarter in the application of their unique authority and capacities."

Intelligence-led policing is based on the idea that reactive policing practices lack predictive value since they respond to criminal incidents after they have been committed. What is needed instead is the proactive targeting of the small number of offenders who commit the bulk of criminal offences as well as on the places and contexts in which they operate (Ratcliffe 2008).

Intelligence-led policing attempts to increase the effectiveness of the police by emphasizing

- the collection and analysis of vast amounts of intelligence (using techniques such as obtaining information from informants, various surveillance techniques, and technological applications such as offender profiling); and then
- using the information gained from this intelligence to target activities, individuals, or locations.

In the **Information Age**, police departments have now emerged as key agencies for managing information to achieve greater public safety. As part of the intelligence-led policing strategy, the police now consider the management of risk as part of their overall strategy (Neyroud 1999). Due to their involvement in risk management, the police are part of the **risk society** as they are in the best position to gather and store knowledge about crime and security, to assess that information, and to recommend how risks should be managed and controlled (Ericson and Haggerty 1997).

Over time, intelligence-led policing focused on the following:

- targeting repeat offenders, using both overt and covert techniques,
- managing crime and disorder hot spots,
- investigating the links among crimes and incidents, and
- developing and implementing preventive measures, especially through multi-agency partnerships.

Zero Tolerance Policing

While the police started to develop proactive policing practices such as problem-oriented policing and community policing, reactive policing did not disappear. In the 1990s a new form of reactive policing emerged: **zero tolerance policing** (also referred to as **quality-of-life policing**). While also based largely on the broken windows approach, zero tolerance policing takes a rigid and inflexible "law and order" approach to minor violations of the law, particularly those that are thought to cause fear of crime in neighbourhoods. It is actually a variant of problem-oriented policing, but instead of combating a problem by analyzing various features about it within the community, the police bypass most of the analysis stage and in its place apply traditional law enforcement methods. The focus of this style is order maintenance on the streets, and it narrows police attention to suppressing those individuals who are seen as the main sources of disorder in public places. This is based on the idea that safety on the streets is necessary to protect law-abiding citizens and to reduce fears about crime.

As shown in Table 6.2, zero tolerance policing differs from other forms of policing in a number of important ways. While problem-oriented and community policing emphasize crime prevention, zero tolerance policing embraces what has been termed the **crime-attack model**. In other words, it is based on suppression, which is closer to the traditional approach to policing in many Western countries. A second difference is that zero tolerance policing operates on the premise that not all communities may be able to provide support for crime prevention activities; thus, the police must take primary responsibility for crime control. A third difference is that zero tolerance policing focuses on specific types of behaviour instead of analyzing crimes to unearth their causes. Zero tolerance policing also concentrates more on place-specific interventions—that is, it maps crime and determines its hot spots. Another difference is that zero tolerance policing favours a more traditional organizational response to crime, one with an organizational structure that is both centralized and internally focused (Cordner 1998; Greene 2000).

To eliminate disorder, then, the police pursue an aggressive policy throughout certain designated neighbourhoods that are facing disorder problems. This leads to a confrontational style of policing, as the police target those individuals they feel are responsible for disorder and incivility in the community.

Zero tolerance policing gained the attention of police services across Canada and the United States after the results of this approach were published by the New York Police Department (NYPD). This style of policing started shortly after Rudolph Giuliani became mayor in 1993. He had promised the voters that he would make New York City a safe place to live. So he hired a new police commissioner, William Bratton, who had been the police chief in Boston. Bratton radically altered the way the NYPD approached crime by employing **COMPSTAT** (the acronym for "computer comparison statistics"), which places current crime data in the hands of precinct commanders. Commanders were held accountable if crime rates in their precincts did not decline within a certain time, and they were replaced if their actions were not deemed adequate. Bratton also increased the powers of police officers to stop, search, and question individuals who had violated the law, even if the infraction was minor. The belief was that by stopping and questioning suspects, the police might discover a weapon or information that could assist in solving a crime or in preventing a crime from occurring. To accomplish these goals, a large number of police officers were hired—the NYPD grew in size by 39.5 percent.

There was considerable interest in the NYPD's tactics because the crime rate had in fact decreased. Other cities rushed to introduce zero tolerance programs based on the fact that the zero tolerance approach apparently reduced crime in New York. Yet, it was also noted that remarkable reductions in crime rates were being recorded in cities that had not introduced zero tolerance policing. Critics of the NYPD approach pointed to the experience of the San Diego Police Department (SDPD). The SDPD had taken a more community-oriented approach to policing crime and disorder by trying to work closely with the community and to develop solutions acceptable to both groups. The results of its program were interesting: between

TABLE 6.2 A Comparison of Traditional Policing, Problem-Oriented Policing, Community Policing, and Zero Tolerance Policing

Social Interaction or Structural Dimension	Traditional Policing	Community Policing	Problem-Oriented Policing	Zero Tolerance Policing
Focus of Policing	Law enforcement	Community-building through crime prevention	Law, order, and fear problems	Order problems
Forms of Intervention	Reactive, based on criminal law	Proactive, on criminal, civil, and administrative law	Mixed, on criminal, civil, and administrative law	Proactive, uses criminal, civil, and administrative law
Range of Police Activity	Narrow, crime focused	Broad crime, order, fear, and quality-of-life focused	Narrow to broad—problem focused	Narrow—location and behaviour focused
Level of Discretion at Line Level	High and unaccountable	High and accountable to the community and local commanders	High and primarily accountable to the police administration	Low, but primarily accountable to the police administration
Focus of Police Culture	Inward, rejecting community	Outward, building partnerships	Mixed, depending on problem, but analysis focused	Inward, focused on attacking the target problem
Locus of Decision-Making	Police directed; minimizes the involvement of others	Community-police coproduction; joint responsibility and assessment	Varied, police identify problems but with community involvement/action	Police directed, some linkage to other agencies where necessary
Communication Flow	Downward from police to community	Horizontal between police and community	Horizontal between police and community	Downward from police to community
Range of Community Involvement	Low and passive	High and active	Mixed, depending on problem set	Low and passive
Linkage with Other Agencies	Poor and intermittent	Participative and integrative in the overarching process	Participative and integrative depending on the problem set	Moderate and intermittent
Type of Organization and Command Focus	Centralized command and control	Decentralized with community linkage	Decentralized with local command accountability to central admission	Centralized or decentralized but internal focus
Implications for Organizational Change/ Development	Few; static organization fending off the environment	Many; dynamic organization focused on the environment and environmental interactions	Varied; focused on problem resolution but with import for organization, intelligence, and structure	Few; limited interventions focused on target problems, using many traditional methods
Measurement of Success	Arrest and crime rates, particularly serious Part 1 crimes	Varied; crime calls for service, fear reduction, use of public places, community linkages and contacts, safer neighbourhoods	Varied; problems solved, minimized, displaced	Arrests, field stops, activity, location-specific reductions in targeted activity

Source: Greene, J. 2000. "Community Policing in America: Changing the Nature, Structure and Foundation of the Police" in J. Horney, ed., *Policies, Processes and Decisions of the Criminal Justice System*. Washington, DC: National Institute of Justice.

Criminal Justice Insight

The Impact of Zero Tolerance Policing

The results of the zero tolerance policing approach to controlling crime and disorder gained international headlines within a few years. Official police statistics indicated a dramatic reduction in the overall crime rate. Large reductions were recorded in homicides, robberies, and burglaries (see Table 6.3). This decrease was largely the result of the "stop, question, and frisk" approach used by police officers. Starting in the early 1990s, the number of these stops increased from just over 40,000 to nearly 600,000 annually (Zimring 2012).

Zero tolerance policing succeeded—but at a price. Minority neighbourhoods were most often the target of this style of policing, and as a result, the number of civil rights complaints against the NYPD had increased by 75 percent by the end of 1997. In the same time period, citizens' complaints filed with New York's Civilian Complaint Review Board rose by 60 percent. Complaints against the police in cases where no arrests were made had doubled by the end of the first year of the program. Amnesty International contended that this new policing approach had increased police brutality and the use of unjustifiable force. In addition, there was also an increased sense of injustice and legal cynicism among many minority group members whose communities were targeted by the police.

TABLE 6.3 COMPSTAT: Historical Perspective

(Historical perspective is a complete calendar year of data.)

	1990	1993	1998	2001	2014	% Chg '14 vs '01	% Chg '14 vs '98	% Chg '14 vs '93	% Chg '14 vs '90
Murder	2,262	1,927	629	649	333	−48.7	−47.1	−82.7	−85.3
Rape	3,126	3,225	2,476	1,930	1,352	−29.9	−45.4	−58.1	−56.7
Robbery	100,280	85,892	39,003	27,873	16,539	−40.7	−57.6	−80.7	−83.5
Fel. Assault	44,122	41,121	28,848	23,020	20,207	−12.2	−30.0	−50.9	−54.2
Burglary	122,055	100,936	47,181	32,694	16,765	−48.7	−64.5	−83.4	−86.3
Gr. Larceny	108,487	85,737	51,461	46,291	43,862	−5.2	−14.8	−48.8	−59.6
G.L.A.	146,925	111,622	43,315	29,607	7,664	−74.1	−82.3	−93.1	−94.8
TOTAL	527,257	430,460	212,913	162,064	106,722	−34.1	−49.9	−75.2	−79.8

All figures are subject to further analysis and revision. All degrees of rape are included in the rape category. As of January 2013, complaints occurring within the jurisdiction of the Department of Correction have been disaggregated from the borough and precinct crime totals and are displayed separately on the Department of Correction CompStat page. Crime statistics reflect New York State Penal Law definitions and differ from the crime categories used by the FBI Uniform Crime Reporting Program. All Crime statistics are translated to Uniform Crime Reporting categories for submission to the UCR Program.

Source:

1990 and 1995, both the crime rate and the number of complaints filed by citizens in San Diego had dropped 36.8 percent, and over the same years, the size of the SDPD had increased by only 6.8 percent. Central to the SDPD's success was that it had relied strongly on community participation when planning crime prevention efforts. In contrast, the approach taken by New York City alienated the residents of many communities (Greene 1999).

Predictive Policing

As the police have adopted a variety of technological systems, such as computerized records management systems and geographic information systems, their ability to assemble and analyze large amounts of crime and disorder data has increased. New technology and software allows the police to predict (or "forecast") crime by analyzing crime patterns that would otherwise go undetected by the police. This has led to the creation of a new police model referred to as **predictive policing**, which refers to a policing strategy or tactic that improves "the situational awareness of law enforcement concerning individuals or locations before criminal activity occurs" (National Institute of Justice 2009:3). Exhibit 6.6 explains the focus of predictive policing.

Sophisticated analytic technology and statistics are used to analyze this information and crime patterns; based on this information, predictions are made about locations where certain types of crime may occur. Predictive policing is largely based on the observation that the "most effective police strategies are focused and highly proactive, relying on crime analysis . . . police tend to be particularly successful when tailor-made efforts are concentrated on specific high violence street blocks, corners, and address clusters" (Telep in McCue 2011:5).

Predictive policing is not seen as a replacement to the other models of policing. Instead, it borrows from the principles of problem-oriented policing, community policing, and intelligence-led policing in order to "organize policing as an information-intensive business in an information age" (Pearsall 2010:17). This approach to policing connects technology, management practices, data analysis, problem solving, and information in an attempt to reduce crime.

The "strength" of predictive policing is that it gives the police the potential to use their knowledge and information not in a reactive way, but instead in a way that can "empower prevention strategies" (Casady 2011:2). These efforts will include city governments, as they must be committed to designating certain neighbourhoods as priorities for public monies. The police have to establish and develop relationships with other stakeholders in their efforts to enhance the collective efficacy of neighbourhoods. To date, while only a limited number of police agencies have reported the results of their predictive policing efforts, they have indicated that it has led to significant reductions of crime.

The key elements of predictive policing are:

- *Integrated information and operations:* Large police agencies maintain large numbers of databases. Yet, in the past the police have not used their computer systems in a way that links them together or to other agencies. As a result, poor information sharing prevents good analysis and investigation of crime. The most beneficial way to respond is to have a complete picture of the issue under investigation.
- *Seeing the big picture:* Very few crimes are isolated incidents. Rather, most crimes are part of a larger pattern of criminal activity and social issues. This means that the police have to be able to see these patterns in neighbourhoods and communities. Police can use predictive policing to avoid responding to issues on a reactive, isolated basis.
- *Cutting-edge analysis and technology:* Police agencies already possess large amounts of information but rarely analyze it to its fullest potential. Predictive policing requires the police to analyze all sources of their information. To be useful, this information has to be analyzed by the police and made into usable information for front-line police officers.
- *Linkage to performance:* Predictive policing places an emphasis upon the forecasting of crime trends. This leads to the police tracking performance based on expected outcomes as opposed to past outcomes. This

EXHIBIT 6.6 What Is the Focus of Predictive Policing?

Predictive policing is a type of data-based policing that attempts to forecast where their intervention efforts can be the most effective in preventing future crimes. What is the focus of predictive policing? There are two main parts to this approach to policing—one part makes predictions, while the other is intervention-based. The prediction component includes the following:

- Predicting crimes: the focus is upon forecasting the places and times with an increased risk of crime.
- Predicting offenders: identifying those individuals at risk of committing crimes in the future.
- Predicting perpetrators' identities: creating profiles that match likely offenders with specific crimes committed in the past.
- Predicting victims of crime: identifying those individuals likely to become victims of crime.

The intervention component is based on the prediction component. Interventions follow a process consisting of:

- Collecting and analyzing crime, incident, and offender data.
- Combining the above into a comprehensive analysis.
- Providing information leading to the development of an intervention plan.
- Implementing the intervention.
- Rapid assessment of the intervention.

allows the police to develop systems that allow them to adapt various tactics and strategies against criminal activity before they become major problems in a neighbourhood or community.

- *Adaptability to changing conditions:* The police must be able to recognize those conditions that are best responded to be a specific tactic or strategy. All officers must be trained and commit themselves to predictive policing.

SUMMING UP AND LOOKING FORWARD

The police began to develop and practise alternatives to reactive style policing in the 1970s. While these efforts were proactive in nature, they also re-introduced some of the principles of policing by public consent. These new approaches introduced positive measures in an attempt to control and reduce crime. Initially, various strategies were introduced that involved working with the community, including forming partnerships with various community groups as well as experts in the field of law and criminal justice, and creating formal relationships with other organizations that shared similar interests (multi-agency relationships). These approaches did not replace reactive policing style, but rather co-existed with it. Over time, new policing practices were introduced that focused upon certain types of offenders and offences (intelligence-led policing) as well to prevent crimes (predictive policing).

During their day-to-day activities, the police have the legal power to detain and arrest people. If cases proceed to trial, the police must be ready to inform the court they have followed proper legal procedures. When the police decide to use their legal powers, they create a relationship with the courts. The legal procedures that the police have to follow are the subject of the next chapter. In addition, during their activities, the police can engage in misconduct. The different types of misconduct as well as those systems that are in place to ensure the police are held accountable for their actions are also discussed in the following chapter.

Review Questions:

1. Why did the broken windows model have such an impact upon the practice of policing?
2. How did problem-oriented policing have such an impact upon the way the police operated in society?
3. Was community policing successful in restoring the contact between the police and local communities?
4. What are the differences between zero tolerance policing and both community and problem-oriented policing?
5. Do you think that police organizations will be able to successfully implement predictive policing?

Critical Issues in Canadian Criminal Justice

POLICING PUBLIC PROTESTS

As part of their role in our society, the police are placed into a variety of contexts, many of which may present complex and unique issues to them. One such context involves policing large public protests, situations in which the police have limited experience and expertise, but which may require significant amounts of planning by the police services, particularly if they require a multi-agency response. Two significant international events (the G8 and G20) were held in Ontario in June 2010, both of which had experienced mass public protests during their previous meetings. The G8 summit was held in Huntsville on June 25 and 26, while the G20 meetings were held in Toronto in late June.

Various local, regional, and national police and associated agencies were tasked to provide security for both

THE CANADIAN PRESS/Toronto Star-Bernard Weil

How have the courts responded to police actions during the G20?

Continued on next page

Critical Issues in Canadian Criminal Justice (*Continued*)

meetings. This included 6,200 personnel from the Toronto Police Service, 5,000 personnel under the deployment of the RCMP, 3,000 personnel from each of the Ontario Provincial Police and Canadian Armed Forces, and 740 personnel from the Peel Regional Police Force. Additional personnel were also brought in from police agencies from across Canada. Many of these personnel were present at both meetings. While there were public protests at the G8, they were small compared to the G20 summit. It was at the G20 where public protests took centre stage and presented the police with challenges to the security they had created for the participants. According to the Office of the Independent Police Review Director (OIPRD), two specific security challenges faced the police at the G20: (1) the short period of time the police had to plan their security and the fact that the G8 and G20 were scheduled virtually together; and (2) the difficulty of developing security for the G20 due to its downtown location (OIPRD 2012:10–11).

It was anticipated that there would be major protests at the G20 (a group of finance ministers and central bankers from 20 major economies who gather annually to discuss issues relating to the international financial system), as there had been protests at previous such gatherings. During these meetings, the actions of the police had been called into question; in particular, police actions during the previous G20 meeting in London, England during 2009 had been investigated as a passerby had died as a result of injuries sustained in an altercation with the London Metropolitan Police Service. The subsequent inquiry, led by Her Majesty's Chief Inspector of Constabulary (HMCIC), recommended that the primary objective of the police should be to facilitate rather than suppress the right to protest (HMCIC 2009).

This recommendation was largely based on the emergence of the use of a "negotiated management" style of dealing with protests in the United States (Farrow 2003). This particular negotiation style had been implemented in response to concerns that the model previously being used, the "escalated model," was undermining police legitimacy with the public. An approach emphasizing cooperation was viewed as best, even though it was recognized that this might lead to a certain amount of public disruption and ignoring peaceful activities that were, in fact, technically illegal.

A "negotiated management" model does not mean that the police would cooperate with all of the protesting groups, as they might decide not to negotiate with those they feel to be threats. It is recognized by the authorities that this new approach could be compromised by the fact that the G20 has to meet in a secure location. In such cases, the accepted police response to dealing with protestors who threaten the security of the G20 participants could be one of "strategic incapacitation," which includes a variety of crowd control measures such as preventive arrests and the creation of "no-go" zones. It could also include "kettling," which occurs when the police control large groups of people by containing them within a specific, small area where the people have, at best, one way to exit (or perhaps none at all) as determined by the police (Gillham and Noakes 2003). When the police use these techniques, it is because they consider them to be the best possible response to control protestors in a public space while minimizing disruption, as well as gaining control of a situation that may get out of control. By using these techniques, protestors are kept at a safe distance from the event.

In the situations where control measures such as preventive arrest and kettling are used, the protestors are viewed by the police in the context of a worst-case scenario in the sense that they are being confronted by an unruly, homogeneous group of protestors who have the potential to compromise the security zones. At the G20 meeting in Toronto, some protestors smashed windows and set police cruisers on fire. Due to these actions, police began to heighten their security measures, and as a result more than 1,000 individuals were arrested, with most being released without being charged; there were mass arrests of protestors and innocent passersby, arbitrary stops, searches of individuals in the street, and a raid at a university residence without proper warrants. As a result of the police actions during the G20, the OIPRD received hundreds of complaints. The function of the OIPRD (a civilian agency) is to process and oversee public complaints and, on occasion, investigate a public complaint itself. It was decided that it was in the public interest to conduct a review of the municipal, regional, and Ontario Provincial Police involvement. An investigation into the actions of the various Ontario police agencies by the OIPRD resulted in the conclusion that some police officers violated the civil rights of protestors, detained people illegally, and used excessive force. As a result of this report, it was expected that a number of police commanders and front-line police officers were to be charged and/or have disciplinary hearings for their actions during the G20.

The 42 recommendations made by the OIPRD were placed into six categories: planning; command and control; arrest and containment; tactics, equipment, and prisoner handling; communication and the public; and the media. The report pointed out that the police had only four months to plan the event, which was too short a period of time for the police to develop a proper strategy. As such, they recommended that the federal government make the decision about where it is holding such events much earlier in order to give the police more time to plan and prepare. The report is also critical of the actions of some members of the Toronto police, who had the main role of keeping order outside of the G20 security zone. The report found fault in a number of areas controlled by the Toronto police, including poor

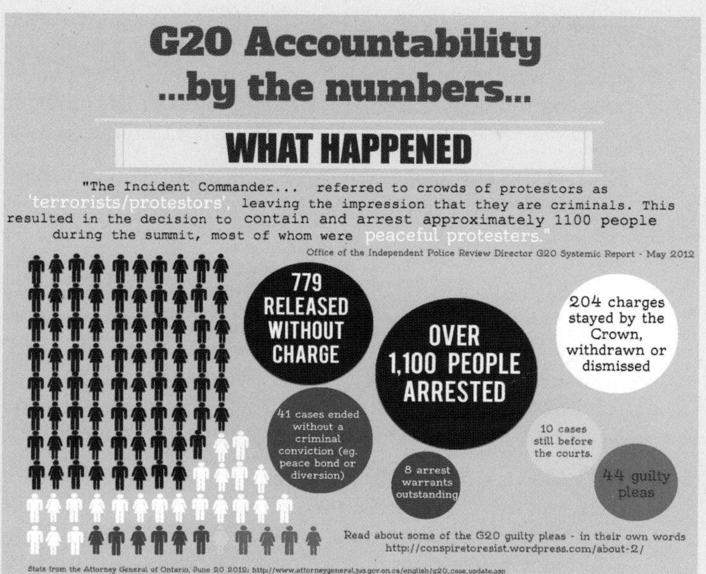

FIGURE 6.4 G20 Accountability By the Numbers . . . What Happened?

Source: Canadian Civil Liberties Association, https://ccla.org/cclanewsite/wp-content/uploads/lg_img/G20-infographic-large-final.png.

planning, gaps in communication, and problems with the incident command centre.

The actions of the RCMP, being a federal agency, were reviewed by a separate federal agency, the Commission for Public Complaints Against the RCMP. Their investigation concluded that personnel deployed by the RCMP acted in a reasonable and acceptable manner and that there were no incidents of unreasonable force. Most of the RCMP involvement focused upon the security planning for the event and the coordination and protection of the various participants and visiting dignitaries.

How the various police agencies responded to the protests during the G20 was largely the result of external factors, such as the large number of protestors, the possibility of certain groups trying to outmanoeuvre the police to gain access to the G20 location, and incidents of property damage. At the same time, however, internal characteristics of the police agencies themselves—such as their professional culture, policing style, and organizational resources—could have also played a role. And since this was a multi-agency action, exactly how each police agency interacted with the others could have led to some difficulties existing between them due to their differing policies. For example, members of the RCMP were found to have been involved in three incidents of kettling, a tactic contrary to RCMP policy. According to the Commission for Public Complaints Against the RCMP, the personnel in these situations acted reasonably based on the fact that the Toronto police were in charge of such activities.

An important issue in policing protests is how the police use their discretionary powers. In Toronto, the terms of the circumstances under which protestors and bystanders are allowed to leave a containment area were studied, and the report recommended that the police be able to use their discretion "to allow access and egress, trusting their own judgement and experience when necessary" (OIPRD 2012:xv). In addition, revised policies need to be introduced that contain more precise language in order to better guide and constrain the police use of discretion. For example, in terms of processing prisoners, the report recommended that the police should develop specific procedures for the processing of those detained that reflect "the circumstances, depth, and scope" of such events; they "should not use existing procedures that are meant for everyday scenarios" (OIPRD 2012:xvii). See Figure 6.4 concerning the aftermath of the G20 policing activities up to December 2012.

Questions:

1. Do you think the actions of the police during the G20 meetings in Toronto were warranted?
2. What other types of responses do you think the police should have used during the G20 protests?
3. How did the police use their discretionary powers during the G20 protests? How could the police have better used their discretion during this time?
4. How did the police response impact the legitimacy of the police?

SUMMARY

This chapter focuses upon the practices of the police in terms of controlling crime. During the early decades of policing in the 20th century the professional model (or reactive style) of policing was developed, which can be characterized as a one-size-fits-all approach. Various communities perceived the practice of police as problematic, and as a result during the latter decades of the 20th century the police introduced proactive style strategies.

KEY WORDS: one-size-fits-all approach, legal cynicism, proactive, multi-agency policing

The Professional Model of Policing: The Reactive Approach

Reactive Criminal Investigations (p. 184)
Preliminary Investigations (p. 185)
Follow-Up Investigations (p. 185)

The reactive style of policing dominated the practice of policing throughout most of the 20th century. The impact of this style of policing had a significant impact upon patrol officers and criminal investigators. This approach also led to the police successfully integrating advances in technology into their operations in this style of policing.

KEY WORDS: reactive approach, incident-based policing, the social agent style, the watchman style, the law enforcement (legalistic) style, the crime fighter style, response time, arrest rates, criminal investigation (detective work), preliminary investigations, follow-up investigation, routine activities, secondary activities, tertiary activities, reconstruct a crime, management of demand, differential response

What Led to Changes in the Professional Model of Policing?

Does Random Preventive Patrol Deter Crime? (p. 187)
Does Rapid Response Deter Criminals? (p. 188)
Do Reactive Investigations Solve Crimes? (p. 188)
Experimenting with Alternative Forms of Police Patrols (p. 189)

During the 1960s various questions were asked about the effectiveness of reactive-style policing. As a result, the police evaluated three different areas of this style of policing. What they found led to significant changes in the practice of policing. As a result, a number of new patrol strategies were introduced in the hope that would better control crime.

KEY WORDS: Three-R's strategy, random preventive patrol, patrol officer rapid response rates, criminal investigations, one-size-fits-all approach, reactive patrol, proactive patrol, preventive patrol, "mayonnaise" theory of police patrol, response rates, "involvement" crimes, "discovery" crimes, foot patrol, directed patrols, crime-mapping systems, geographic information systems, resource allocation

Policing in Modern Society: The Emergence of Proactive Policing

Hot Spots Patrol (p. 192)
The Broken Windows Model (p. 192)
Problem-Oriented Policing (p. 193)
Community Policing (p. 195)
Critique of Problem-Oriented and Community Policing (p. 196)
Intelligence-Led Policing (p. 196)
Zero Tolerance Policing (p. 197)
Predictive Policing (p. 199)

Proactive approaches to policing started to emerge in the late 1970s. Some of the new approaches were community policing and problem-oriented policing. One aspect of these new approaches that gained greater sophistication over the years involved the collection of information which was then analyzed by the police in the hope that they could better control and subsequently reduce crime.

KEY WORDS: proactive policing, deployment theory, racial threat theory, hot spots patrol, displacement effect, disorder, broken windows model, social incivilities, physical incivilities, order maintenance, problem-oriented policing, SARA, community policing, co-producers of crime control, double victimization, concrete fear of crime, formless fear, intelligence-led policing, interagency sharing of information, crime analysis, Information Age, risk society, zero tolerance policing (quality-of-life policing), crime-attack model, COMPSTAT, predictive policing

Critical Thinking Questions

1. Do you agree with the idea held by the legal cynicism approach the differences are found in some communities about the ability of the legal system, particularly the police, to be successful in controlling crime?
2. Why do the methods through which policing is practised exert a considerable impact upon the public's perception of the police?
3. Do you think the focus of the broken windows model can lead to a reduction of criminal behaviour in communities? Do you think it ignores the reasons why criminal behaviour exists beyond its focus on social disorder?
4. Do you think community policing reached its potential as a way in which to reduce crime?
5. Assuming that no one policing approach becomes dominant, how would you integrate the various types of proactive policing practices in order to successfully reduce the amount of crime?

Weblinks

According to Dr. Jerry Ratcliffe, while the primary focus of law enforcement has traditionally focused on reducing crime, almost 80 percent of all incidents the police respond to do not result in an arrest or other police investigations. Much of the remaining 20 percent involves protecting vulnerable individuals from many forms of harm. Dr. Ratcliffe notes that while people tend to focus their attention on the effects of serious crimes such as homicides, he believes that some long-term crime trends can cause serious harm to community residents as well. He argues that the future of policing should be harm-focused, intelligence-led, problem-oriented, and evidence-based. See his 47-minute video, available at the Police Foundation YouTube site—"Dr. Jerry Ratcliffe: Ideas in American Policing."

Suggested Readings

Beare, M., N. Des Rosiers, and A. Deshman. 2015. *Putting the State on Trial: The Policing of Protest during the G20 Summit*. 2015. Vancouver: UBC Press.

Goldstein, H. 1990. *Problem-Oriented Policing*. New York: McGraw-Hill.

Reber, S. and R. Renaud. 2005. *Starlight Tour: The Last, Lonely Night of Neil Stonechild.* Random House Canada.

Scott, I. 2014. *Issues in Civilian Oversight of Policing in Canada*. Aurora, ON: Canada Law Book.

Trojanowicz, R.C., V. Kappeler, and L. Gaines. 2001. *Community Policing: A Contemporary Perspective*, 3rd ed. Cincinnati, OH: Anderson.

Whitelaw, B. and R.B. Parent. 2010. *Community-Based Strategic Policing in Canada.* Toronto: Nelson.

References

American Bar Association. 1974. *Standards Relating to Urban Police Function*. New York: Institute of Judicial Administration.

Bayley, D. (ed.) 1998. *What Works in Policing?* New York: Oxford University Press.

Bayley, D. 1994. *Police for the Future*. Oxford: Oxford University Press.

Berg, B. and J. Horgan. 1998. *Criminal Investigation*, 3rd ed. Westerville: Glencoe/McGraw-Hill.

Braiden, C. 1993. "Community-Based Policing: A Process for Change." Pp. 211–32 in *Community Policing in Canada*, edited by J. Chacko and S.E. Nancoo. Toronto: Canadian Scholars' Press.

Bureau of Justice Assistance. 1993. *Problem-Oriented Drug Enforcement: A Community-Based Approach for Effective Policing*. Washington, DC: Office of Justice Programs.

Callahan, C. and W. Anderson. 2001. "The Roots of Racial Profiling." *Reason* 33(4):36–43.

Casady, T. 2011. "Police Legitimacy and Predictive Policing." *Geography & Public Safety* 2:1–2.

Cordner, G. 1998. "Problem Oriented Policing vs. Zero Tolerance." In *Problem Oriented Policing*, edited by T. O'Connor Shelly and A. Grant. Washington, DC: Police Executive Research Forum.

Cordner, G. 1992. "Patrol." In G. Cordner and D. Hale, eds., *What Works in Policing? Operations and Administration Examined.* Cincinnati, OH: Anderson.

Cordner, G. and D. Hale. 1992. *What Works in Policing? Operations and Administration Examined*. Cincinnati, OH: Anderson.

Cotter, A. 2014. *Homicide in Canada, 2013*. Ottawa: Canadian Centre for Justice Statistics.

Desroches, F. 1995. *Force and Fear: Robbery in Canada*. Scarborough, ON: Nelson Canada.

Eck, J. 1983. *Solving Crimes: The Investigation of Burglary and Robbery*. Washington, DC: Police Executive Research Forum.

Eck, J. and E. Maguire. 2000. "Have Changes in Policing Reduced Violent Crime?" In *The Crime Drop in America*, edited by A. Blumstein and J. Wallman. Cambridge, MA: Cambridge University Press.

Engel, R., M. Smith, and F. Cullen. 2012. "Race, Place, and Drug Enforcement: Reconsidering the Impact of Citizen Complaints and Crime Rates on Drug Arrests." *Criminology & Public Policy* 11:601–35.

Ericson, R. and K. Haggerty. 1997. *Policing the Risk Society*. Toronto: University of Toronto Press.

Farrow, T. 2003. "Negotiation, Mediation, Globalization Protests and Police: Right Processes; Wrong System, Issues, Parties and Time." *Queen's Law Journal* 50:665–703.

Feldmeyer, B. and J. Ulmer. 2011. "Racial/Ethnic Threat and Federal Sentencing." *Journal of Research on Crime and Delinquency* 48:238–70.

Gillham, P. and J. Noakes. 2007. "'More Than a March in a Circle': Transgressive Protests and the Limits of Negotiated Management." *Mobilization* 12:341–57.

Goldstein, H. 1979. "Improving Policing: A Problem-Oriented Approach." *Crime and Delinquency* 25:236–58.

Greene, J. 2000. "Community Policing in America: Changing the Nature, Structure and Foundation of the Police." In *Policies, Processes and Decisions of the Criminal Justice System*, edited by J. Horney. Washington, DC: National Institute of Justice.

Greene, J. 1999. "Zero Tolerance: A Case Study of Police Policies and Practices in New York City." *Crime and Delinquency* 45:171–88.

Greene, J. and S. Mastrofski. 1988. *Community Policing: Rhetoric or Reality?* New York: Praeger.

Greenwood, P. and J. Petersilia. 1975. *The Criminal Investigation Process*. Santa Monica, CA: Rand.

Her Majesty's Chief Inspector of Constabulary. 2009. *Adopting to Protest: Nurturing the British Model of Policing*. London: HMCIC.

Horvath, F., R. Meesig, and Y. Lee. 2001. *A National Survey of Police Policies and Practices Regarding the Criminal Investigation Process: Twenty-Five Years after Rand*. Washington, DC: National Institute of Justice.

Jordan, P. 1998. "Effective Policing Strategies for Reducing Crime." In P. Goldblatt and C. Lewis, eds., *Reducing Offending: An Assessment of Evidence on Ways of Dealing with Offending Behaviour*. London, UK: Home Office, Research Study 187.

Kelling, G., A. Pate, D. Dieckman, and C. Brown. 1974. *The Kansas City Preventive Patrol Experiment: A Summary Report*. Washington, DC: Police Foundation Report.

Kelling, G., A. Pate, A. Ferrara, M. Utne, and C.E. Brown. 1981. *The Newark Foot Patrol Experiment*. Washington, DC: The Police Foundation.

Kelling, G. and J.Q. Wilson. 1982. "Broken Windows: The Police and Neighborhood Safety." *The Atlantic Monthly* 249.

Kirk, D. and M. Matsuda. 2011. "Legal Cynicism, Collective Efficacy, and the Ecology of Arrest." *Criminology* 49:443–72.

Kirk, D. and A. Papachristos. 2015. "Concentrated Disadvantage, the Persistence of Legal Cynicism and Crime: Revisiting the Concepts of 'Culture' in Criminology." In F. Cullen, P. Wilcox, R. Sampson, and B. Dooley, eds., *Challenging Criminological Theory: The Legacy of Ruth Rosner Kornhauser (Advances in Criminological Theory, Vol. 19)*. New Brunswick, NJ: Transaction.

Klockars, C. 1988. "The Rhetoric of Community Policing." In J. Greene and S. Mastrofski, eds., *Community Policing: Rhetoric or Reality*. New York: Praeger.

Klockars, C. and S. Mastrofski. 1991. "The Police and Serious Crime." In *Thinking About Crime*, edited by C. Klockars and S. Mastrofski. New York: McGraw-Hill.

Langworthy, R. and L. Travis. 1994. *Policing in America: A Balance of Forces*. Don Mills, ON: Macmillan.

Makin, K. 2003. "Police Use Racial Profiling, Appeal Court Concludes," *The Globe and Mail*, April 17, pp. A1, A6.

Mitchell, T. 2002. "One Judge: Two Cases about Bias." *LawNow* 26(5):8.

Moore, M. and R. Trojanowicz. 1988. *Corporate Strategies for Policing*. Washington, DC: National Institute of Justice.

National Institute of Justice. 2009. *Solicitation: Predictive Policing Analytic and Evaluation Research Support*. Washington, DC: National Institute of Justice.

Neyroud, P. 1999. "Danger Signals." *Policing Today* 5:10–15.

Office of the Independent Police Review Director. 2012. *Policing the Right to Protest: G20 Systemic Review Report*. Toronto, Ontario.

Pate, A., M. Wycoff, W. Skogan, and L. Sherman. 1986. *Reducing Fear of Crime in Houston and Newark*. Washington, DC: Police Foundation.

Pearsall, B. 2010. "Predictive Policing: The Future of Law Enforcement." *NIJ Journal*. Washington, DC: National Institute of Justice, 266:16–19.

Ratcliffe, I. 2008. *Intelligence-Led Policing*. Cullompton, UK: Willan.

Roberg, R. 1994. "Can Today's Police Organizations Effectively Implement Community Policing." In *The Challenge of Community Policing: Testing the Premises*, edited by D. Rosenbaum. Thousand Oaks, CA: Sage.

Sherman, L., P. Gartin, and M. Buerger. 1989. "Hot Spots of Predatory Crime: Routine Activities and the Criminology of Place." *Criminology* 27:27–56.

Skogan, W. 2006. *Police and Community in Chicago: A Tale of Three Cities*. New York: Oxford University Press.

Skogan, W. 1990. *Disorder and Decline: Crime and the Spiral Decay in America's Neighborhoods*. New York: Free Press.

Spelman, W. and D. Brown. 1984. *Calling the Police: Citizen Reporting of Serious Crime*. Washington, DC: U.S. Government Printing Office.

Spelman, W. and J. Eck. 1989. "Sitting Ducks, Ravenous Wolves, and Helping Hands: New Approaches to Urban Policing." *Public Affairs Comment* 35:1–9.

Telep, C. 2009. "Police Interventions to Reduce Violent Crime: A Review of Rigorous Research." In C. McCue (ed.) 2011. "Proactive Policing: Using Geographic Analysis to Fight Crime." *Geography & Public Safety* 2:3–5.

Tilley, N. 2003. "Community Policing, Problem-Oriented Policing and Intelligence-Led Policing." In *Handbook of Policing*, edited by T. Newburn. Cullompton, UK: Willan.

Trojanowicz, R., V. Kappeler, and L. Gaines. 2001. *Community Policing: A Contemporary Perspective*, 3rd ed. Cincinnati, OH: Anderson.

Walker, S. 1994. *Sense and Nonsense about Crime*, 3rd ed. Belmont, CA: Wadsworth.

Weston, P. and K. Wells. 1986. *Criminal Investigation: Basic Perspectives*, 4th ed. Englewood Cliffs, NJ: Prentice-Hall.

Wilson, J.Q. 1968. *Varieties of Criminal Behavior*. Cambridge, MA: Harvard University Press.

Wilson, O. and R. McLaren. 1977. *Police Administration*, 4th ed. New York: McGraw-Hill.

Wood, J. and C. Shearing. 2007. *Imagining Security*. Cullompton, UK: Willan.

Zhao, J., N. Lovrich, and Q. Thurman. 2001. "Community Policing: Is It Changing the Basic Functions of Policing? Findings from a Longitudinal Study of 200+ Municipal Police Agencies." *Journal of Criminal Justice* 29:365–77.

Zimring, F. 2012. *The City That Became Safe: New York's Lessons for Urban Crime and Its Control*. New York: Oxford University Press.

CHAPTER 7

The Police and the Law

Learning Objectives

After completing this chapter, you should be able to:

- Understand the importance of police legitimacy.
- Understand the importance of police discretion and differentiate among the different factors that lead to discretion.
- Understand the importance of investigative detention for the police.
- Differentiate among ways in which the police arrest a suspect.
- Identify the differences among the requirements for search warrants.
- Understand the parameters of the right to legal counsel.
- Identify the various types of police interview techniques used during custodial interrogations.
- Identify the different types of police misconduct and how early warning systems operate.
- Understand the reasons for having civilian oversight of the police.

One of the most important questions for our criminal justice system concerns the **reasonable expectation of personal privacy**. That is, what protections do Canadians have against unreasonable police intrusion into their lives? This question has been raised in a number of significant cases since the Charter of Rights and Freedoms was introduced in 1982. While s. 8 of the Charter protects individuals against unreasonable search and seizure based on the reasonable expectation of privacy, "privacy" is not mentioned in the Charter and as a result the courts have had to interpret—and balance—this area of law between the rights of society to have effective police protection and the rights of suspects to their privacy. In *Hunter v. Southam Inc.* (1984), for example, the Supreme Court held that a reasonable expectation of privacy existed in s. 8 of the Charter and, for that reason, searches and seizures must be authorized by either statute or the common law in order to be constitutional. Since s. 8 of the Charter governs searches conducted by the police, questions can be raised as to whether or not the evidence collected by the police can be excluded from the trial if it was gathered in such a way that it violates a legal right of an individual protected by the Charter.

Privacy was a key issue in *R. v. Feeney* (1997), and the Supreme Court's ruling in that case led one legal observer to comment that the Court's decision was unprecedented (Coughlan 1998). In *Feeney*, a murder suspect was arrested without a warrant and evidence was seized from the location where the suspect was arrested. The decision of the Supreme Court, which favoured the defendant, was based on violations committed by the police, and its decision led to a restriction of police search powers. As a consequence, Parliament had to pass new legislation on warrants. In fact, the decision in this case reversed a rule previously established by the Supreme Court—that police could enter a residence to make an arrest without a warrant.

On June 8, 1991, the body of 86-year-old Frank Boyle was found in his mobile home in the B.C. Interior. He had been murdered. The police officer who arrived at the scene concluded from the amount of blood that Boyle's death had been extremely violent. A neighbour told the investigating officer that she had observed Michael Feeney, who lived nearby, walking away from Boyle's truck after it had been driven into a ditch earlier that morning. Another neighbour told the officer he had earlier seen Feeney enter a storage trailer. The officer knocked on the door of the trailer and yelled out "Police!" The officer heard nothing in response, entered without a warrant, and woke up Feeney by touching him on the leg. Feeney's shirt and shoes were covered with blood, and money stolen from the deceased was found under the suspect's mattress. Feeney was later charged and convicted of second degree murder.

However, on May 22, 1997, the Supreme Court of Canada, in a 5–4 ruling, ruled that the search had been unlawful because the police had violated ss. 8 and 10(b) of the Charter and ordered a new trial. The majority of the Court decided the police officer had acted on a hunch since he admitted that he did not have reasonable grounds for arresting Feeney and should have obtained a **search warrant** while waiting outside the storage facility. The Court's ruling was based on the arresting officer's statement that at the time he entered the suspect's trailer, he had reason to believe that the suspect was involved in the murder but did not have sufficient reason to make an arrest (he had reason only after he saw the bloodied clothing) (Hiebert 2002). The majority ruled that although the officer was correct in his "hunch" about the accused, this did not legitimize his actions. Since Feeney was asleep when the officer arrived, he did not pose a threat of flight and exigent circumstances (such as the need to prevent the destruction of evidence prior to the arrival of a warrant) were low. In addition, the police officer had not properly followed the Supreme Court's decision in *R. v. Brydges* (1990) that required them to inform the suspect of his right to free legal counsel. During the time they spent with Feeney before legal counsel arrived, the police officer had asked him a number of questions, and some of his answers were incriminating. Only after they took Feeney to the police detachment did the police ask for and receive a search warrant for the trailer.

The majority of the Supreme Court justices ruled that Feeney's fingerprints and incriminating statements would have to be excluded since they involved procedural violations on the part of the police. Mr. Justice Sopinka wrote in his decision that "in general, the privacy interest outweighs the interest of the police and warrantless arrests in dwelling houses are prohibited" (*R. v. Feeney* [1997], at 154). In addition, Mr. Justice Sopinka noted that Feeney had not spoken to a lawyer for two days following his arrest and detention; the fact that the police "did not cease in their efforts to gather information, indicates a lack of respect for the appellant's rights displayed by the police" (ibid.:15–17). Another issue of concern to the majority of Supreme Court justices was the police's delay in reading Feeney his rights. They ruled that it had taken too long for the officer to do so. They also ruled that as soon as the officer touched Feeney's leg to awaken him, Feeney had been "detained," and the law requires that the rights of a detained person be read immediately. Finally, the Supreme Court held that the police must receive prior authorization before entering the dwelling of an individual to gather evidence.

The minority of Supreme Court justices interpreted the actions of the officer quite differently. They based their opinion on a concern for the victim, and they believed the police officer had acted properly by ensuring that a suspect accused of murder was not at large in the community. Madame Justice L'Heureux-Dubé stated that the majority had seen the actions of the police officers involved "as [those of] lawless vigilantes, flagrantly and deliberately violating the Charter at every turn" (ibid.:204). Her concern extended beyond the police to the "helpless victim," whom she viewed as having suffered a "random" and "savage beating" (ibid.:205). The Supreme Court ordered a new trial but ruled the bloody shirt and shoes and the money inadmissible as evidence, because its continued use by the prosecution would bring the criminal justice system into disrepute.

Up until this case, the common law had permitted a police officer, in certain circumstances, to enter a private dwelling to arrest a suspect without a warrant. But now the majority of justices were ruling that the arresting officer had been incorrect to believe there were reasonable grounds to enter the dwelling and arrest the suspect. The police officer had been within the laws concerning the arrest and detention of a suspect as they had existed up until this case; with *Feeney*, the majority of the justices were overturning those rules. Based on the Supreme Court's decision in *Feeney*, the police would now be required to gain prior authorization to enter the private dwelling of an individual in order to search for and collect evidence. By the time of Feeney's second trial, DNA was well established and accepted by the courts. New DNA evidence, using saliva found on a cigarette collected from Mr. Boyle's yard, matched Mr. Feeney's DNA. His fingerprints were also found on a can of beer located in the victim's vehicle as well as on the refrigerator in Mr. Boyle's residence. These fingerprints were compared to Mr. Feeney's fingerprints held by the Calgary Police Service, as he had been fingerprinted in that city a year before in connection with another serious crime. In the second trial, the jury found Mr. Feeney guilty of second degree murder (Bowal and Bowal 2011).

The impact of the *Feeney* decision on police forces was potentially so devastating that the Supreme Court allowed the previous rules governing warrants to continue for six months. Parliament responded to this by passing Bill C-16, which allows a police officer to enter a residence or other dwelling to make an arrest without a warrant if exigent circumstances exist, such as the need to prevent the loss or destruction of evidence, and/or a belief that their warnings will lead to personal harm when they enter a dwelling, and/or an urgent call for assistance having been made, especially in the context of domestic violence. This latter exception was affirmed in *R. v. Godoy* (1997), a case that involved the police entering an apartment without a warrant after receiving a 911 call. A "nervous-looking man answered the door and suggested nothing was going on of interest to them," but "the police pushed past him" (Makin 1998). They discovered the woman who had made the call. She was sobbing and had a badly bruised eye. She told the police that the man who had tried to stop them at the door was responsible for her injury. The accused was acquitted by the lower court but on appeal was convicted by the appeal court. The accused argued that when the police entered his apartment they were infringing his constitutional right to be free of unreasonable search and seizure. The Supreme Court disagreed with the accused, and threw out his appeal.

Another exception to the decision made in *Feeney* involves the actions of police officers searching a motor vehicle without a warrant in certain circumstances. A **warrantless search** can often result in evidence being ruled inadmissible. One such case arose in October 1997 when a RCMP police officer on patrol arrested a man after he stepped out of a field of tall grass just outside Gimli, Manitoba. When questioned about his activities, the individual told the officer that he had gone into the field to relieve himself. After a quick search of the area, the officer discovered a bag containing 4 kilograms of marijuana and arrested him for marijuana trafficking. The officer then took the suspect to the police lockup in Gimli. The vehicle of the arrested individual was then towed to an impound lot; there, six hours after the arrest, the RCMP discovered cocaine and a large amount of cash during a routine inventory check of the arrested individual's vehicle. The cocaine and money were seized by the RCMP. Defence counsel later argued that since the RCMP did not have a search warrant, the cocaine and money should be returned.

Was the RCMP search of the suspect's vehicle lawful? Should the cocaine and money found in the vehicle have been returned? And could it be used as evidence for another criminal charge? Once again, these questions involve the conflict between an individual's right to privacy and the need for the police to have some leeway in the gathering of evidence. The answers to these questions are found in the interpretations of the Canadian Charter of Rights of Freedoms. This chapter reviews the principles of the Charter as they apply to the police collection of evidence that affect the freedom and privacy of Canadians.

In the case just outlined, *Caslake v. R.* (1998), the Supreme Court of Canada ruled that the seizure of the cocaine and money was unjust because the search was not connected to the arrest itself. However, the court also ruled that the evidence should not be excluded. Not only did the police act in good faith, but the evidence caused no harm to the administration of justice. The court felt that "excluding the evidence would have a more serious impact on the repute of the administration of justice than admitting it, for the prosecution had no case without the evidence." A main objective of police activities is to investigate criminal offences, search and seize evidence, identify and arrest suspects, and subsequently interrogate them. The information the police collect is essential for the operation of our criminal justice system. But while the police want to collect as much evidence as possible, suspects want to restrict as much as possible what the police can do.

Most of this chapter considers the legal constraints placed on the police when they decide to engage individuals. The ability of the police to follow the law as well as administrative regulations are typical standards used to evaluate whether or not policing is conducted properly. What happens when there are questions concerning police conduct? A discussion of police misconduct and problem police officers is the focus of the next section, which includes a review of the type of mechanisms (e.g., civilian oversight) put into place to potentially sanction such behaviour. Finally, there is a brief overview concerning the importance of moving beyond focusing exclusively on the legality of police actions to one which focuses upon what citizens themselves feel after coming into contact with the police. This involves a discussion of the procedural justice of police–citizen encounters, which can ultimately lead to greater support for the legitimacy of the police.

What Are the Legal Powers of the Police?

What powers do the police have to stop and search individuals? This is the topic of much of this chapter, and it includes the powers of investigative detention, arrest, search and seizure, and interrogation. When they decide to conduct an investigation, the police are required to follow the legal requirements in each of these areas. In addition, they are legally required to inform individuals about their right to legal counsel. While the police invoke these powers, they represent only one way they can respond to an incident, because much of police work involves officers using discretion to deal with specific situations.

Do the Police Have Discretion?

While the police operate according to formal rules and procedures, they also possess a certain amount of freedom in deciding what course of action to take. This is known as **discretion**, and it refers to police officers using their judgment when deciding whether or not to intervene in a situation. Discretion is a crucial part of policing since it is difficult to develop a system of laws and rules that divide appropriate from inappropriate behaviour in every context.

Attempts have been made to limit the use of police discretion as per the justice model (see Chapter 3). The most significant case involving this issue in Canada to date involved a decision by the Saskatchewan Court of Appeal, which ruled that the police possess too much discretionary power. The court ruled that while the power for this discretion is granted by the Criminal Code, in their opinion the police were using too much discretionary power in their daily decisions. This was particularly the case with decisions about reasonable grounds for believing the accused had committed an indictable offence (*Beare v. R.* [1988]).

On appeal, the Supreme Court of Canada disagreed with the Saskatchewan court. It ruled that "discretion is an essential part of the criminal justice system. . . . The Criminal Code provides no guidelines for the exercise of discretion in any of these areas. The day-to-day operation of law enforcement and the criminal justice system nonetheless depends upon the exercise of that discretion" (ibid.). In other words, police officers are in a unique position to use discretion in their decisions about enforcing the law.

Is it possible to challenge discretionary decisions made by the police? While it is possible to question the discretion of police during a case, this is not common in Canada. This is because the Supreme Court requires that a judicial stay be allowed only in cases where "compelling the accused to stand trial would violate those fundamental principles of justice which underlie the community's sense of fair play and decency" (*R. v. Mack* [1988]). Police discretion can be contested in court by an individual who feels that the police used their discretionary powers in a wrongful manner. Legal questions surrounding the discretionary powers of a police officer can be stayed on the basis of an abuse of process. Section 24 of the Charter is a remedy for cases involving the use of discretion in an "improper or arbitrary" manner.

While it was not developed to deal specifically with police discretion, the equality provision of the Charter stipulates that extralegal factors are not to be considered within the law or the application of the law. Police discretion may lead to the unequal enforcement of the law, specifically as it relates to possible discrimination against certain groups in our society. This would create unfairness within the criminal justice system, violating the various principles of fundamental fairness designed to protect individuals (see Chapter 2). If an appeal is made under s. 15(1), there must be clear evidence of discrimination (*R. v. Andrews* [1989]; *R. v. Turpin* [1989]).

What Factors Affect a Police Officer's Decision to Arrest?

Most studies on police use of discretion focus on the specific factors that led to an officer's decision to make an arrest. As Stansfield (1996:142) states, the focus should not be on whether or not the police decide to use discretion but "which criteria police use when enforcing the law." The factors most often influencing a police officer's discretion are **situational variables**, such as the presence of a complainant; **extralegal factors**, such as a suspect's social class and race; and **community factors**, such as the perception of danger perceived by police officers to exist within a community (see Exhibit 7.1).

What Is Investigative Detention?

Many people think that an arrest is the first step in criminal pretrial procedure, but often it is not. This is because Canadian courts have recognized that the police can detain, interrogate, and search an individual even "where there is less than reasonable grounds to believe that an offence has been committed" (Bilodeau 2001–02:42). Today in Canada, the police can hold a person for questioning even when they do not have grounds for an arrest. However, the legality of detaining a person in this way depends on the importance of the matter being investigated and on the amount of intrusion that is necessary.

THE CANADIAN PRESS/Jonathan Hayward

Police officers making an arrest of a suspect.

EXHIBIT 7.1 Factors Affecting Police Officers' Decisions to Arrest

What influences a police officer when they decide to arrest someone? We like to think that their decisions are always based on legal factors, but other factors may be considered by police officers. These are usually categorized into situational, extralegal, and community factors.

Legal Factors

- *Seriousness of the crime*. The more serious the crime, the more likely a police officer is to make an arrest.
- *Strength of the evidence*. The police are more likely to arrest a suspect when the evidence in a case is strong.

Situational Factors

- *Preference of the victim*. An arrest is more likely when a victim or the complainant requests that the officer make an arrest.

Extralegal Factors

- *Relationship between the victim and the suspect*. A police officer is more likely to arrest someone when the victim and offender are strangers, and least likely to do so if they are family members.
- *Demeanour of the suspect*. A number of researchers have found that the demeanour of the suspect can precipitate an arrest. In most cases, the argument goes that if a suspect is disrespectful toward the officer, it is more likely that they will be arrested.

Community Factors

- *The racial and social class composition of a neighbourhood*. Police officers are more likely to arrest someone in low-income as compared to higher-income neighbourhoods. The result is a greater likelihood of racial minority groups and poor people being arrested and processed through the courts.
- *The crime rate within a community.* Communities vary in their rates of reported crime and these higher rates can influence an officer's perception of danger and how best to respond to calls for service (McGahan 1984).

An **investigative detention** is defined as "a reactive power dependent upon a reasonable belief that the detained person is implicated in a prior criminal act" (*Brown v. Durham Regional Police Force* [1998]). The Charter is concerned about police officers misusing their powers, so s. 9 states that "everyone has the right not to be arbitrarily detained or imprisoned." According to Bilodeau (2001–02:42–43), the police are allowed to detain an individual due to safety concerns. If, for example, a suspect runs away from the police after leaving a crack house and being told to stop, the police are allowed to protect themselves by conducting a non-intrusive search for weapons. And if during this search illegal drugs are discovered, the police officer can legally arrest the person without fear of having the case thrown out of court on a Charter challenge to have the evidence excluded. Police officers risk having the evidence thrown out if they decide they are at risk when in fact they aren't (e.g., when the individual in question doesn't run away from the police after being told to stop). Another limit on police powers in this area is when the police decide to conduct an intrusive search, such as a strip search, which is more difficult to justify to the court. While an officer is allowed to detain an individual to determine whether they have been involved in a crime, this does not mean they have the right to make an intrusive search that does not involve issues of safety.

But what happens if the police "ask" an individual to accompany them to the police station? Has this person been arrested or detained? In either case, the s. 10 Charter rights of the individual in question must be observed (see below). When dealing with this question, the Ontario Court of Appeal in *R. v. Moran* (1987) listed several questions that should be considered, including these: What, precisely, was the language used by the police? Was the accused given a choice by the police? Did the individual go to the police station on their own free will? Was that individual free to leave at any time? And at what stage of the police investigation did this occur—that is, was it still a general investigation or did the police have reasonable grounds to believe that this individual was the actual offender? (Mewett and Nakatsuru 2000).

Why do the police resort to investigative detentions? As Nicol (2002:234) points out, "the opportunity to stop and confront suspects is an invaluable tool." Such detentions offer several benefits to the police. For example, they allow investigators the time and opportunity to use other search powers where the circumstances permit. If during their search of the individual they legally obtain evidence about a crime, they may then use a number of legal warrantless search and seizure powers they possess, such as the plain view doctrine (see below), certain exigent circumstances (see below), and powers relating to weapons and drugs. And if the police, during an investigative detention, find enough evidence to formally arrest an individual, then s. 495 of the Criminal Code permits them to conduct a search incident to an arrest (ibid.). Legal protections exist for those individuals detained or arrested and these are found in s. 10 (a) of the Charter:

> Everyone has the right on arrest or detention:
>
> (a) to be informed promptly of the reasons therefor;

How Do the Police Arrest Someone?

Once it is determined that an individual should be charged with an offence, an appropriate way must be chosen to ensure that person will appear at the trial. The police have several options at this point. They can seize the person and force them to appear, by way of an arrest and detention. Or they can arrest the individual but then release them with an order to appear if they are fairly certain that they will appear in court at the date and time given. Or they may decide not to arrest the individual, but require that they appear at a certain date and time in order to be tried. The Criminal Code tries "to ensure that the least unfair method is tried first before resorting to the most unfair, but at the same time [the] most certain method of arrest and pretrial detention" (Mewett and Nakatsuru 2000:56).

An **arrest** involves the police power to restrain an individual—in effect, to deprive an individual of liberty. Exactly how the police arrest someone depends on the case. When a crime has been committed, and the suspect is not known to any witness and/or the victim(s) or not apprehended at the scene of the crime, the police have to investigate and question people to discover the appropriate evidence. At this time, however, they can't go and arrest an individual right away. Once a suspect is identified, they have to go to a justice of the peace and **lay an information** against the person. The justice of the peace will determine whether the case has been properly made out and then either issue an arrest warrant authorizing the police to make an arrest or issue a **summons**—that is, an order directed to the accused requiring them to appear in court on a certain date. In both situations, the laying of the information occurs *before* the police have any procedural contact with the accused—this is referred to as **laying an information first**.

What happens when the police are able to arrest someone either at the scene of the crime or after they observe an individual committing a crime? In these cases it is not possible for the police to go to a justice of the peace, lay an information, and then obtain an arrest warrant. Instead, they arrest the individual and *then* go to a justice of the peace to lay an information. In these situations, an information is laid only after the police have had procedural contact with the accused. This is referred to as **laying an information second**.

The police must believe that they have **reasonable grounds** to make an arrest, and these grounds have to be justifiable from an objective point of view. This means a reasonable police officer must believe that the individual they are arresting has committed, is committing, or is about to commit a crime. This doesn't mean that an officer has to have proof beyond a reasonable doubt prior to arresting someone. For the police, the threshold to justify an arrest is relatively low; for example, they are not required to consider whether the person they are arresting will be convicted of a criminal offence. In *R. v. Golub* (1997), the Ontario Court of Appeal stated:

> [O]ften, the officer's decision to arrest must be made quickly in volatile and rapidly changing circumstances. Judicial reflection is not a luxury the officer can afford. The officer must make his or her decision based on available information which is often less than exact or complete. The law does not expect the same kind of inquiry of a police officer deciding whether to make an arrest that it demands of a justice faced with an application for a search warrant.

Arrest with a Warrant

For the police to arrest someone with a warrant, they must suspect on the basis of reasonable grounds that the individual in question committed a crime and that the suspect's appearance cannot be compelled by a summons (see above, and Chapter 1). To obtain a warrant, the police must ordinarily go before a justice of the peace and lay an information alleging that a criminal offence

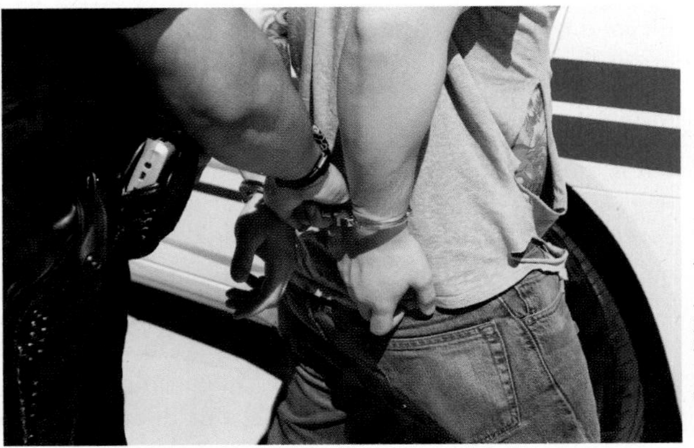

moodboard/Thinkstock

has been committed. After obtaining an arrest warrant, the officer who executes that warrant should have it in their possession in case the suspect asks to see it. If the police decide they are going to detain the individual for a period of time, the suspect must be brought before a justice of the peace as soon as possible.

Section 503.1 of the Criminal Code states that when a justice is available within 24 hours of an arrest, the accused must be taken before them within this period of time—or, if a justice is not available, within a reasonable period. If the accused does not appear before a justice within a certain amount of time, the case may be terminated on the grounds of "unreasonable delay." The Supreme Court of Canada dealt with the meaning of "unreasonable delay" in *R. v. Storey* (1990), where it ruled that the police could delay this process for 18 hours so that a line-up could be put together. However, when an accused was detained for 36 hours (*R. v. Charles* [1987]), the Supreme Court ruled that it was a violation of s. 9 of the Charter.

In order to arrest someone legally, the police officer has to verbally inform the suspect that they are under arrest. An arrest also involves the taking of physical control or custody of an individual with the intent to detain that individual. This action will require the use of force if the individual being arrested resists being taken into custody. If a person being arrested willingly accompanies the police officer, that officer will have no need to make physical contact, but at the same time the arrested person must acknowledge being in custody. If there is no such acknowledgment, a police officer has to make contact with the suspect.

Since s. 10(a) of the Charter of Rights and Freedoms stipulates that "everyone has the right on arrest or detention to be informed promptly of the reasons thereof," a police officer must inform an individual of their rights the moment that individual becomes a suspect in the crime under investigation. If the suspect is not informed of those rights, any evidence obtained from the suspect will be inadmissible as it would not stand the test of the Charter and would place the administration of justice in disrepute. On detaining or arresting a suspect, the police must read the following:

1. *Notice on arrest:* "I am arresting you for . . . [briefly describe reasons for arrest]."
2. *Right to counsel:* "It is my duty to inform you that you have the right to retain and instruct counsel without delay. Do you understand?"
3. *Caution to charged person:* "You [are charged, will be charged] with. . . . Do you wish to say anything in answer to the charge? You are not obligated to say anything unless you wish to do so, but whatever you say may be given in evidence."
4. *Secondary caution to charged person:* "If you have spoken to any police officer or anyone with authority, or if any such person has spoken to you in connection with this case, I want it clearly understood that I do not want it to influence you in making any statement."

Arrest without a Warrant

According to s. 495(1) of the Criminal Code, it is possible for a police officer to arrest someone without a warrant. A person may be arrested in this way when

- they are found committing any criminal offence (indictable, summary conviction, or federal statute);
- they are about to commit an indictable offence, on the basis of reasonable and probable grounds;
- the police officer, on reasonable and probable grounds, believes has an outstanding warrant within the territorial jurisdiction in which the person is located; and/or
- the police officer knows the individual has committed an indictable offence.

A police officer's power to arrest without a warrant is restricted by s. 495(2) of the Criminal Code, which states that no arrest shall occur, although they have the power to do so. Section 495(2) states:

> 495. (2) A peace officer shall not arrest a person without warrant for
>
> (a) an indictable offence mentioned in Section 553,
> (b) an offence for which the person may be prosecuted by indictment or for which he is punishable on summary conviction, or
> (c) an offence punishable on summary conviction, in any case where
> (d) he believes on reasonable grounds that the public interest, having regard to all the circumstances including the need to
>
> (i) establish the identity of the person,
> (ii) secure or preserve the identity of the person,
> (iii) prevent the continuation or repetition of the offence or the commission of another offence, may be satisfied without so arresting the person, and
>
> (e) he has no reasonable grounds to believe that, if he does not so arrest the person, the person will fail to attend court in order to be dealt with according to law.

Police officers then proceed to use one of three alternatives available to them. They can issue the suspect with an **appearance notice**; or they can release the suspect with the intention of applying for a summons from a justice of the peace; or they can release the suspect unconditionally. If the latter approach is selected, it means the police officer, after determining the identity of the suspect, can release the suspect and at a later date either issue an appearance notice or arrange for a justice of the peace to issue a summons.

Part of the tradition of our legal system is that the criminal process cannot begin until someone with the power of a judicial officer—a justice of the peace—is satisfied that a case exists against the accused. But in the above-mentioned situations, it is the police who actually are commencing the proceedings requiring the accused to appear in court. The Criminal Code (s. 505) requires any police officer who issues an appearance notice to lay an information as soon as it is practicable, but in all cases prior to the time indicated in the appearance notice for the accused's first court appearance.

SUMMING UP AND LOOKING FORWARD

The manner in which the police interact with people has an important influence upon the way citizens think about procedural fairness. Citizens feel it is important to tell their side of the story to the authorities, and this may influence how they feel about the legitimacy of the police. While the police possess discretion on how to proceed, they have legal powers to assist them when investigating and apprehending suspects. These legal powers require us to consider the balance between the power of the state to control crime and the right of citizens not to be subject to intrusive acts by the state. Since the introduction of the Charter of Rights and Freedoms, the Supreme Court of Canada has placed many constitutional limits on the police. For example, the police must now obtain properly authorized warrants to conduct searches except in clearly defined circumstances. These procedures are in place to ensure the police have to justify their right to interfere with citizens and their basic legal rights. Two of the legal rights citizens enjoy in our legal system are the right to be secure from unreasonable searches and seizures, and the right to legal counsel. These rights are discussed in the next section.

Review Questions:

1. What are the factors that influence police discretion?
2. How does discretion influence the criminal justice system?
3. How is an investigative detention different from an arrest?
4. When are the police required to apply for an information second?
5. What are the options for the police when they arrest someone?

Search and Seizure

One of the most fundamental rights of Canadians is the right to protection against unreasonable search and seizure. In other words, people have the right to be left alone by the government and its agents unless there are grounds for allowing such intrusion. A **search** is the intrusion of a government representative into an individual's privacy. A **seizure** is the exercise of control by a government representative over an individual and/or item. Three different legal areas govern searches and seizures in Canada: the Charter of Rights and Freedoms, the Criminal Code, and the common law.

Section 8 of the Charter of Rights and Freedoms is intended to protect an individual's reasonable expectation of privacy by guaranteeing that "everyone has the right to be secure against unreasonable search and seizure." When an investigative technique is classified as a "search" or "seizure," the constitutional requirement of "reasonableness" applies. The Supreme Court has found that a reasonable expectation of privacy exists in, for example, a person's home (*R. v. Feeney* [1997]), and also with regard to an individual's body and bodily fluids "harvested from the individual" (*R. v. Stillman* [1997]). A reduced expectation of privacy has been at border crossings (*R. v. Simmons* [1988]), as well as in prison cells housing inmates (*R. v. Wise* [1992]). There is no expectation of privacy for things in plain view in places where the public is ordinarily invited (*R. v. Fitt* [1996]), and in the use of infrared overhead technology (*R. v. Bryntwick* [2002]). All unreasonable searches will breach s. 8 of the Charter, but not every unreasonable search will lead to the exclusion of evidence. According to s. 24(2), when evidence "was obtained in a manner that infringed or denied any rights or freedoms guaranteed by the Charter, the evidence shall be excluded if it is established that . . . the admission of it in the proceedings would bring the administration of justice into disrepute."

Most of what the police do in this area of law is regulated by s. 487 of the Criminal Code.

The Criminal Code contains a number of specific provisions regarding the searches of places; there are fewer provisions concerning the searches of persons. The purpose of a search is not to allow the police to "fish" or look around for something that may be important to their investigation; rather, it is to collect evidence. Most often, the police obtain a search warrant from a justice of the peace allowing them to search any building, receptacle, or place named in the warrant. A search warrant is not automatic and a justice of the peace will issue one only if satisfied that there are reasonable grounds to believe that in the mentioned building, receptacle, or place one of the following four items will be found:

- Anything on or in respect of which an offence has been committed or is suspected to have been committed.
- Anything that there is reasonable grounds to believe will be evidence of an offence having been committed or that will reveal the whereabouts of a person believed to have committed an offence.
- Anything that there are reasonable grounds to believe is intended to be used in the commission of an indictable offence.
- Any property used or intended for use in any way with the commission of a criminal organization offence.

A search warrant must specify for what the police are looking. However, the police may seize not only what is mentioned in the warrant but also anything that they find and believe on reasonable grounds has been obtained or used in the commission of an offence.

The common law is concerned with the search of persons as well as places. Generally, the police must have a search warrant granted by the judiciary in order to search an individual. However, the common law gives police the right to conduct general body searches and searches of the immediate surrounding area when arresting a suspect. Searches of individuals oftentimes occur at the time of arrest or when an individual voluntarily consents to a police officer's request to conduct a search, which means that many searches take place without a warrant. When an individual is arrested without a warrant, the police are able to protect themselves by looking for weapons that a suspect may try to use against them and to preserve evidence that otherwise might be destroyed. If the police wish to conduct an invasive body search, special statutory authorization is required, and this is usually found in the Criminal Code. For example, in the case of the police requesting to gather a DNA sample, a search warrant has to be obtained from a provincial court judge to obtain such samples from a suspect for a number of specific offences, including murder and sexual assault (s. 487.5 of the Criminal Code). Judges considering a DNA warrant request have to consider whether or not it is in "the best interests of the administration of justice" by looking at, for example, the seriousness of the offence and the circumstances of the offence as well as whether a specially trained officer is available who will obtain the sample. In these cases the police have a duty to explain in detail to the individual the purposes why the sample(s) are being taken.

Laws governing privacy are always evolving as the police are constantly facing challenges about their

Investigating: The Seizing of DNA Samples: *R. v. Stillman* (1997)

Early decisions by the courts across Canada took conflicting positions on the taking of DNA samples by the police. In Ontario, the Court of Appeal ruled in *Alderton v. R.* (1985) that the police could take hair samples for DNA testing as part of their powers of search incident to an arrest. But the New Brunswick Court of Appeal, in the case of Alan Legere, a serial killer, held that the police violated s. 8 of the Charter of Rights and Freedoms when they took hair and bodily samples without a warrant or the consent of the accused. However, they admitted the evidence into court under s. 24(2) of the Charter. And in *Borden v. R.* (1994), the Supreme Court of Canada excluded DNA evidence that had led to the accused being convicted of sexual assault (the samples in question did not involve semen). The police in that case had not informed the accused that the samples would be used in their investigation and possibly be used as evidence. The Supreme Court decided that the accused had not waived his rights or consented to the taking of the samples by the police.

Following this case, legislation authorizing the seizure of bodily samples for DNA testing was quickly approved by Parliament. Authorization involves a judge's hearing an application and granting a warrant if probable cause is present. But how far can the police go in terms of seizing a person's bodily samples? Can the police "conscript" an individual into providing them with self-incriminating evidence?

The Supreme Court then heard an appeal involving DNA used to secure a conviction of murder (*R. v. Stillman* [1997]). In this case, a 17-year-old New Brunswick youth had been convicted of the murder of a young woman. The victim had disappeared after a party she had left in the company of Stillman. Six days later, her body was recovered. She had been sexually assaulted and bitten on her abdomen and had died from blows to the head. Arrested just hours after the discovery of the body, Stillman met his lawyers at the police station. They advised Stillman not to cooperate with the authorities if they wanted to take any bodily samples or to submit to an interrogation. After the lawyers left, the police proceeded to violate this directive. They took the bodily samples they wanted from the accused and then interrogated him for an hour. When the police took a break in their questioning, they agreed to contact Stillman's lawyers and request their presence at the interrogation. In the meantime, the accused went to the washroom, blew

Continued on next page

Investigating: The Seizing of DNA Samples: *R. v. Stillman* (1997) *(Continued)*

his nose, and threw the used tissue into the wastebasket. The police seized the tissue for DNA testing.

When the police took their evidence to a Crown prosecutor to receive approval for a charge, the prosecutor refused, telling them the evidence was still insufficient. Stillman was released, only to be rearrested a few months later. This time, the police obtained teeth impressions and an oral swab, a process that took about two hours to complete. This time the evidence was considered sufficient, and Stillman was subsequently found guilty of murder and sentenced in adult court to life imprisonment. As a 17-year-old, however, he could apply for parole after eight years. His conviction was upheld by the New Brunswick Court of Appeal.

On appeal to the Supreme Court, the defence argued that the teeth impressions and oral swabs had been obtained improperly by the police. The Supreme Court ruled that the police had reasonable and probable grounds to suspect Stillman of the crime. However, they also ruled that the seizures could not be justified by the police as necessary because they could be thrown away or hidden. The majority of the justices viewed the taking of the teeth impressions as especially offensive, although they had been taken by a dentist. In the court's final decision, the hair and dental seizures were deemed the result of "the abusive exercise of raw physical authority by the police." The court also wrote that "if there is not respect for the dignity of the individual and the integrity of the body, then it is but a very short step to justifying the exercise of any physical force of the police if it is undertaken with the aim of solving crimes." In addition, the court felt that while the seizure of the discarded tissue had violated Stillman's right not to be subject to unreasonable search and seizure, it could be admitted as evidence. Parliament responded to the Supreme Court decision by allowing for warrants to obtain bodily impressions if there are reasonable grounds for believing that an offence had been committed and that it would be in the best interests of the administration of justice to serve such a warrant (see s. 487.091 of the Criminal Code).

powers of search and seizure. This is particularly true for the use of personal electronic devices such as laptop computers and cell phones. These items are able to contain large amounts of personal and private information about individuals. Despite the fact that most Canadians use a computer and/or a personal electronic device, no special provisions for searching have been introduced into the Criminal Code as Parliament feels the existing provisions governing search warrants are acceptable. However, the Supreme Court of Canada has indicated the need to protect the integrity of personal information. In *R. v. Plant* (1993), the Supreme Court of Canada stated that s. 8 of the Charter should "protect a biographical core of personal information which individuals in a free and democratic society should wish to maintain and control from dissemination to the state."

What Are the Requirements for Search Warrants?

The "Reasonableness" Test

This test, as it applies to searches and seizures, generally refers to the question of whether the police have overstepped their authority. Most searches are judged to be unreasonable if an officer lacks sufficient information to justify the search. The appropriate standard of proof is one of "**reasonable and probable grounds**" rather than proof beyond a reasonable doubt; in other words, a search warrant can be granted only if the request for it is accompanied by facts that indicate to the court a crime has been committed or is being committed.

Particularity

Particularity refers to the search warrant itself. A search warrant must specify the place to be searched and the reasons for searching it. When the police request a search warrant, the warrant must identify the premises and the personal property to be seized, and it must be signed by a police officer. The facts and information justifying the need for a search warrant are set out in an affidavit requesting the warrant.

Warrantless Searches in Exigent Circumstances

A case involving a warrantless search is liable to be deemed illegal and thrown out of court. However, in Canada, a warrantless search can be considered reasonable under some **exigent** (i.e., immediate) **circumstances**. But what are those circumstances in Canada? When can a police officer conduct a search without a warrant? After all, the Canadian courts have ruled that the police cannot go on "fishing expeditions" for evidence. The important considerations here are the circumstances of the case and how the police conduct their activities.

Criminal Justice Focus

Search Warrants and Electronic Devices

Should a search warrant that grants police the authority to search a residence automatically include the right to search a computer or cell phone? Or should the police have to apply for a search warrant that specifically states that they will be searching for a certain electronic device? In the past few years the Supreme Court has increasingly heard cases concerning the privacy of individuals and the reasonableness of police searches of computers and other electronic devices.

R. v. Vu (2013)

In 2007, the police were informed that someone could be stealing electricity and subsequently obtained a search warrant authorizing a search of a residence. The warrant permitted the police to search the residence in order to locate evidence for the theft of electricity, the identity of the occupant of the property as well as "computer generated notes." The warrant did not specifically refer to computers or personal electronic devices that might be found in the residence. In their search the police found marijuana, two computers, and a cell phone. The police reasonably believed the computers or cell phone would contain information authorized in the warrant and subsequently searched the computers, allowing them to identify the defendant. At trial, the defendant argued that the search had violated his s. 8 Charter rights as the police did not have specific authorization to search the computers.

The trial judge agreed and excluded most of the evidence found by the search. In his decision to acquit the defendant, the judge held while the police received judicial pre-authorization for a general warrant, they needed a specific warrant to search the computers, reasoning that computers were not the same as filing cabinets or cupboards since computers have the capacity to store vast amounts of data. On appeal the B.C. Court of Appeal held that there had been no violation of the defendant's s. 8 Charter rights, and they set aside the acquittal and ordered a new trial on the grounds that the warrant had properly authorized the searches.

On appeal, the Supreme Court held that "specific, prior" judicial authorization is required prior to any search of electronic devices containing personal or other information. The Court also stated that if the police locate a computer in the course of their search and their warrant does not specifically authorize a search of the device, they can seize the device, secure the data, and then seek a warrant. The Supreme Court upheld the B.C. Court of Appeal's decision to set aside the defendant's acquittal at trial and ordered a new trial. In their decision, the Supreme Court held that while computer searches not expressly pre-authorized violate an individual's right to be free from unreasonable search and seizure, the evidence taken from the computers by the police should not have been excluded by the trial judge as the breach was "not serious" in the circumstances.

RTimages/Shutterstock

The increase in the use of electronic devices has created issues for the police when they wish to search them for evidence.

R. v. Fearon (2014)

Are the police able to conduct a warrantless search of mobile digital devices? In 2009, the defendant was arrested in an unarmed robbery of a jewellery kiosk in Toronto. When he was arrested, the police found a cell phone in his possession and quickly looked through the texts and photographs. The officer found a text that said "We did it," as well as a photograph of a hand-gun. The defendant was convicted at trial and then appealed, arguing the police violated his s. 8 Charter rights when they searched his cell phone without a warrant. The Ontario Court of Appeal upheld his conviction, and the case was then appealed to the Supreme Court of Canada. In a 4–3 decision, the Supreme Court ruled that police are able to search digital devices without a warrant incidental to arrest, subject to certain conditions, which are

- the arrest must be lawful;
- the search must be truly incidental to the arrest;
- only recently sent or drafted e-mails, texts, or photographs and the call log can be viewed, although other searches may be justified in certain circumstances; and
- the police must take detailed notes of what they examine on the device and how they examine it.

The majority of the Court felt that "prompt access" to the contents of a cell phone on arrest can help police identify accomplices and locate and preserve evidence that might be lost or destroyed.

After *R. v. Feeney* in 1997, Bill C-16 was introduced by the federal government to address that ruling; they established two more exceptions to the requirement that a police officer obtain a search warrant before entering a dwelling (an existing exception allowed the police to enter a dwelling while in "hot pursuit" of a suspect). The two new exemptions are where a police officer

- has reasonable grounds to suspect that entry into the dwelling house is necessary to prevent bodily harm or death to any person; or
- has reasonable grounds to believe that entry is necessary to prevent the imminent loss or destruction of evidence.

In addition, illegal searches are not always ruled to be unreasonable. In *R. v. Heisler* (1984), for example, the Alberta Court of Appeal ruled that searching an individual's purse when the individual entered a rock concert was not illegal even though there had been no prior reasonable grounds. And in *R. v. Harris* (1987), Justice Martin of the Ontario Court of Appeal stated that minor or technical defects in a warrant would not automatically make unconstitutional a search or seizure under s. 8 of the Charter.

Drug convictions are sometimes appealed on the issue of warrantless searches. In such cases, police officers observe possession of the drug but don't have time to obtain a search warrant prior to the use or selling of it. In *R. v. Collins* (1987), police officers in British Columbia, while conducting a heroin investigation, observed two suspects in a village pub. When one individual left to go to his car, the police approached him, searched the car, and found a quantity of heroin. Back in the pub, an officer approached the other suspect and proceeded to grab her by the throat to prevent her from swallowing any evidence. The suspect dropped a balloon containing heroin. The trial judge ruled the search unreasonable because the police had used unnecessary force. The Supreme Court of Canada, however, overturned this decision, stating that there was nothing to suggest that the collection of evidence in this manner made the trial unfair.

In determining the reasonableness of a search, the courts examine the following issues:

- Whether the information predicting the commission of a criminal offence was compelling.
- Whether the information was based on an informant's tip, and whether the source was credible.
- Whether the information was corroborated by a police investigation before the decision to conduct the search was made.

The police are permitted to take into account the accused's past record and reputation, provided that such information is relevant to the circumstances of the search.

Searches Incident to an Arrest

Another exception to the search warrant requirement involves **searches incident to an arrest**. This power is granted to the police by the common law and allows the police to search the suspect for weapons and evidence of a crime without first obtaining a search warrant. For a search incident to arrest to be lawful, the arrest itself must be lawful. This means there must be reasonable grounds for believing that a suspect committed an indictable offence; in other words, the police cannot make an arrest solely to assist their investigation.

The courts have allowed a search incident to arrest on a number of grounds, including the following:

- The need to protect the arresting officers.
- The need to prevent the arrestee from destroying evidence in his or her possession.
- The intrusiveness of the lawful arrest being so great that the incidental search is of minor consequence.
- The fact that the individual could in any event be subjected to an inventory search at the police station.

The Supreme Court of Canada unanimously agreed in *Cloutier v. Langlois* (1990) that most searches are to be based on reasonable grounds but that searches incidental to arrest need not be. In this case, the police stopped a motorist for making an illegal right-hand turn. The officers found that the motorist had several unpaid traffic fines. The driver became agitated and abusive toward the police, who then ordered him out of the vehicle and frisked him. The motorist later sued the police officers for assaulting him. The Supreme Court ruled that reasonable grounds are not necessary for a frisk search incident to an arrest, and that such searches are necessary for "the effective and safe enforcement of the law [and] ensuring the freedom and dignity of individuals." Here, the police were justified in believing that the search was necessary for their safety. In most cases, frisk searches at the time of arrest will probably be considered constitutional. In addition, searches of the immediate vicinity of a crime scene will generally be accepted if the search can be justified on the basis of "prompt and effective discovery and preservation of evidence" (*R. v. Lim* [1990]).

However, the courts have also stated that before conducting a frisk search, the police must inform the suspect of the right to counsel. But the police do not have to wait until the suspect contacts a lawyer before a search is made.

The Supreme Court has placed the following limits on the common law and the right to search an individual incident to arrest:

- The police have discretion over whether a search is necessary for the effective and safe application of the law.

Steve Baxter/E+/Getty Images

When can a police officer conduct a warrantless search of a motor vehicle?

- The search must be for a valid criminal objective (e.g., to check for weapons or to prevent an escape).
- The search cannot be used to intimidate, ridicule, or pressure the accused to gain admissions.
- The search must not be conducted in an abusive way.

Warrantless Searches in Motor Vehicles

The Supreme Court of Canada has established that a **warrantless search** of a vehicle may be reasonable if grounds exist for believing that the vehicle contains drugs or other contraband. However, the power to search a vehicle without a warrant must be found in statute or in common law (e.g., a search can be conducted incident to a valid arrest).

The legality of searching motor vehicles has been a difficult issue for the police. Can a police officer search the interior of a vehicle, a locked suitcase, or a closed briefcase? In *R. v. Mellenthin* (1992), the Supreme Court of Canada ruled that the accused's rights had been violated when, at a police check stop, the accused was questioned about the contents of a bag. The suspect handed over the bag, which was found to contain narcotics. However, the officer had not suspected that the accused was in possession of illegal drugs when he asked to search the bag. The Supreme Court has ruled that the purpose of a police check stop is to detect impaired drivers or dangerous vehicles, not to conduct unreasonable searches. In *Mellenthin*, there was no informed consent.

Other Types of Warrantless Searches

The Doctrine of Plain View

The police can search for and seize evidence without a warrant if the illegal object is in **plain view**. For example, if a police officer arrives at a home in response to an incident of domestic violence and notices marijuana on the coffee table, the officer can seize the evidence and arrest the suspect. However, if the officer suspects that more drugs are in the house, the officer will have to apply for and receive an authorized search warrant before investigating further. Also, if an officer arrests a suspect in a kitchen, the kitchen cupboards can be looked into, but only if it can be shown later that the search was more than a "fishing expedition." Justification clearly exists when there is a report of a weapon but no weapon is visible. A police officer who suspects that the weapon was placed in a cupboard just before he or she arrived may decide to check all the cupboards.

Reasonable Grounds

If a police officer stops a motor vehicle because of a defective taillight and the driver leans over, the officer may become suspicious that an illegal item is being hidden. Nothing in the act of leaning over can, by itself, make a police officer suspicious, but when the officer talks to the motorist and the motorist appears nervous and says nothing, an experienced officer can come to the reasonable conclusion that the motorist is hiding something. This may give the officer reasonable cause to search the vehicle (Salhany 1986).

The provision for "reasonable grounds" is found in s. 101(1) of the Criminal Code. It allows a police officer to search without a warrant when the officer believes they have reasonable grounds for believing that an offence is being committed or has been committed. The section also deals with prohibited weapons, restricted weapons, firearms or ammunition, and evidence of an offence that is likely to be found on a person, in a vehicle, or in any place or premises other than a dwelling place. In *R. v. Singh* (1983), the accused fit the description of a suspect wanted for interrogation about a multiple shooting. The incident had occurred just a few minutes before, when the suspect was seen in the same vicinity. When stopped by police, the suspect had a noticeable bulge in his pocket and refused to make eye contact with the police. The police then searched the suspect and found the weapon used in the crime. In this case, the Ontario Court of Appeal ruled that there had been no unreasonable search and seizure as specified by s. 8 of the Charter of Rights.

Similarly, in *R. v. Ducharme* (1990), police officers noticed a man running into a lane with a full garbage bag at 3 a.m. When they stopped the individual, they noticed that the man's hands were cut and bleeding. An officer searched the bag, without consent, and found 32 cartons of cigarettes. It was later reported that the glass door of a store had been broken and that cigarettes had been stolen from inside. The accused was convicted, but appealed the case, arguing that the police had performed an improper search. However, the British Columbia Court of Appeal ruled that since the search occurred peacefully in a public place, no invasion of the body occurred; under incriminating conditions it was "reasonable" for the officer to search the garbage bag. It was not necessary to arrest the accused before looking into the bag. In this case, the courts ruled that police officers can search if they have reasonable grounds for suspicion.

Section 489 of the Criminal Code also permits police officers to seize items not mentioned on a warrant. The key issue here is that the officer must believe on reasonable grounds that the item in question has been obtained by, or has been used in, the commission of an offence.

Consent Searches

Police officers may also make a warrantless search when an individual voluntarily **consents to the search**. Those individuals who choose to consent to a search are waiving their constitutional rights. Thus, the police may have to prove in court that the consent was voluntarily given to them.

The major legal issue in most consent searches is whether the police can prove that consent was given to them voluntarily. In *R. v. Wills* (1992), the Supreme Court of Canada provided guidelines for establishing whether voluntary consent was given:

- The giver of the consent had the authority to give the consent in question.
- The consent was voluntary in the sense that it was free from coercion and not the result of police oppression, coercion, or other external conduct that negated the freedom to choose whether the police should continue.
- The giver of the consent was aware of the right to refuse to give consent to the police to engage in search.
- The giver of the consent was aware of the potential consequences of giving the consent.

What Is the Right to Legal Counsel?

According to s. 9 of the Charter of Rights and Freedoms, everyone has the right not to be arbitrarily detained or imprisoned. But even if detention is justified, the **right to legal counsel** found in s. 10 of the Charter "emerges in the face of any detention" (Abell and Sheehy 1993:269). The Charter protects the right to counsel as well as the right to be informed of the right to counsel. Section 10(b) of the Charter states:

> 10. Everyone has the right on arrest or detention
>
> (b) to retain and instruct counsel without delay and to be informed of that right

Section 10(b) of the Charter gives an arrested individual the right to contact a lawyer without delay. This means that when an accused requests counsel, that request must be allowed. The right to legal advice and assistance is fundamental to ensure fairness in our criminal justice system. It is important for the accused to be able to access legal counsel as soon as possible after being arrested. Numerous issues have been raised over s. 10(b), including what the right to counsel encompasses, when and how the police must inform the accused of the right to counsel, what the accused must do to assert the right to counsel, and when it is reasonable to limit the right to counsel under s. 1 of the Charter (ibid.:269). The detained or accused person's right to counsel has been affirmed by the Supreme Court: for example, the police are required to inform the individual of his or her right to and availability of legal counsel; the police are required to allow the individual the opportunity to talk to a lawyer; and the police are required to stop questioning the individual until he or she has talked to a lawyer.

The accused must be given a reasonable opportunity to consult a lawyer. The accused must also have the right to talk to legal counsel privately. However, the accused cannot delay the investigation by deciding to contact counsel after several hours. The burden is on the accused to prove that it was impossible to contact a lawyer at the time the police offered him or her the opportunity to do so (*R. v. Joey Smith* [1989]).

The right to counsel in Canada is not absolute. It is available only to someone who is under arrest or being detained. In *R. v. Bazinet* (1986), the suspect voluntarily agreed to accompany the police to the police station. While answering questions about a murder, the suspect confessed to committing the crime. At this point, the police informed him of his right to counsel. On appeal, the court ruled that the police had followed proper procedure, since there was no evidence to indicate that the accused felt he had been deprived of his liberty and that he had to accompany the police.

What happens once a suspect asks to see a lawyer when they are being interrogated? Can the police continue to interrogate that person while waiting for the lawyer to appear? Recent cases decided by the Supreme Court have significantly impacted a detained or arrested individual's right to legal counsel during a police interrogation. In *R. v. Singh* (2007) (see Chapter 2), the Supreme Court held that, once the accused has consulted with legal counsel, the police may continue their interrogation although the accused has indicated they do not want to talk anymore. Although Mr. Singh repeatedly told the police officers he did not want to answer any questions, they continued to question him until he made an incriminating statement. The trial judge admitted the incriminating statement, ruling that the police had not violated Mr. Singh's s. 7 Charter right to silence.

The right to a lawyer is not a continuing right. Once the right has been complied with, that is the end of the right under s. 10(b). There is no right to have legal counsel present at any subsequent interviews between the accused and the police, as it is assumed that the lawyer will have given the appropriate information to the client in terms of what to say (or not say) to the police. In *R. v. Sinclair* (2010), the Supreme Court held that an accused individual who has already spoken to a lawyer does not have the constitutional right to further consultation during a subsequent interrogation, even if the accused asks to speak to their lawyer. However, the police cannot engage in trickery in order to obtain information that violates the accused's right to silence. If that happens, it may be held that this is a violation of s. 7 of the Charter.

The Supreme Court of Canada has established a high threshold for an accused to waive the Charter right to legal counsel. Individuals who elect to give up the right to counsel must first appreciate the consequences of doing so. If they do not—that is, if the police do not explain the consequences to them—anything they tell the police will be excluded. In *R. v. Black* (1989), the police obtained a statement from an intoxicated individual known to them as an alcoholic with a Grade 4 education. The accused was originally charged with the attempted murder of another woman. She contacted her lawyer by telephone, and a few hours later the victim died. Then the police advised her that she was being charged with first degree murder. The accused asked to speak to her lawyer again, but the lawyer could not be reached. The officers then suggested she speak to another lawyer, a suggestion she refused. Shortly after this, the police questioned the accused again and she confessed to the crime. The Supreme Court ruled that since the accused had not waived her right to a lawyer, the police had violated her right to legal counsel, and consequently her statement was excluded from the evidence. However, when the police are interrogating an individual and their jeopardy changes significantly, the police are required to readvise them of their right to legal counsel.

How long does an accused have to make a call? It depends on the seriousness of the charge. In *R. v. Joey Smith* (1989), the accused was arrested for robbery. After 9 p.m., he asked to contact a lawyer. Finding only a business telephone number, he decided to try again in the morning, despite police recommendations that he call that evening. The accused refused. When the police questioned him later, he made a statement "off the record" that was later used as evidence to convict him. On appeal, the Supreme Court of Canada ruled the statement to be admissible, because the crime was not considered a serious offence. Had it been a serious offence, he should have been granted an additional opportunity to contact legal counsel.

SUMMING UP AND LOOKING FORWARD

Section 8 of the Charter recognizes the right to be secure from unreasonable searches and seizures. What constitutes a "reasonable expectation" of privacy depends on the case. The police can search individuals, their homes, as well as their possessions in order to obtain evidence. Searches either are accompanied by a warrant, or may be warrantless in a variety of situations. They must be reasonable—that is, the appropriate standard of proof is one of "reasonable and probable grounds" rather than proof beyond a reasonable doubt. Searches are oftentimes made by the police incident to an arrest, but they can also be conducted after an individual gives their consent to the police.

Section 10(b) of the Charter protects the right to counsel as well as the right to be informed of the right to counsel. The right to legal advice and assistance is fundamental to ensure fairness in our criminal justice system. It is important for the accused to be able to access legal counsel as soon as possible after being arrested. The right to counsel in Canada is not absolute. It is available only to someone who is under arrest or being detained.

The police collect a substantial amount of evidence during their interrogations of suspects. Usually, interrogations occur in police stations, but the police have collected evidence from what is referred to as "jailhouse interrogations" in the past. These are discussed in the next section.

Review Questions:

1. Define both search and seizure.
2. What is the "reasonableness" test?
3. What is involved in a search incident to an arrest?
4. When are the police required to notify a suspect that they are entitled to legal counsel?
5. Is the right to legal counsel an absolute right in Canada? Explain.
6. Is the right to legal counsel a continuing right in Canada? Explain.

Interrogations

The police rely on **interrogations** (or questioning) of suspects to gather information about a crime. Suspects can be questioned numerous times and these are usually conducted in private. The police may videotape interrogations conducted in a police facility in order to prove that all proper rules and procedures are followed. Still, the police may decide to use other types of interrogations outside of a police facility, such as a jailhouse, to gain information allowing them to charge someone for a crime. There is much controversy over such types of interrogations as they may provide unreliable evidence leading to wrongful convictions.

According to s. 7 of the Charter, everyone has the right to life, liberty, and security of the person, and the right not to be deprived thereof except in accordance with the principles of fundamental justice. This protects the accused against the superior resources of the police; however, the police have the power to deprive an individual of their life, liberty, or security as long as they respect the fundamental principles of justice. Once arrested, many suspects choose to remain silent, and since both oral and written statements are admissible in court, police officers sometimes stop their questioning until defence counsel are present. If the accused decides to answer the questions, they may decide to stop at any time and refuse to answer more questions until a lawyer arrives. Suspects may waive this right only if they are aware of what they are doing and are able to contact a lawyer at any time if they so wish. It is recommended procedure that the police inform the suspect of the right to silence and counsel before starting their questioning.

The purpose of interrogating a suspect is to obtain information—in these cases, the investigators probably don't have enough information to arrest someone. When the police have a suspect in custody, interrogations (referred to as **custodial interrogations**) may provide incriminating evidence to the police which can lead to a determination of guilt in a court trial (Vrij 1998). Custodial interrogations may also unearth information about stolen property, accomplices, and the involvement of the suspect in other unsolved crimes. However, the primary goal of a custodial interrogation is to solicit a confession from the suspect (McConville and Baldwin 1982). The importance of a confession by the suspect cannot be underestimated, as Wigmore (1970) notes that nothing has a greater impact on a judge and/or jurors than a confession made by a suspect. This is because voluntary confessions are readily admitted into court as evidence. Canadian courts have traditionally held that an out-of-court statement by an accused person constitutes appropriate evidence as long as the statement was given voluntarily. In a pre-Charter case, *R. v. Rickett* (1975), it was determined that when an issue arises over the voluntariness of a statement, it must be proved beyond a reasonable doubt that the statement was voluntary.

Questions are sometimes raised about interrogations when a suspect confesses to a crime. If a statement is made involuntarily, they are most likely to be excluded as they may have been illegally obtained. This raises questions about why people confess; in particular, why do they confess to a crime they never committed? Concerns about false confessions have been raised in recent decades, particularly as they have been shown to lead to wrongful convictions and imprisonments.

What are some of the techniques used by the police to elicit information during an interrogation? Leo (1996) studied the interrogation techniques practised by three U.S. police departments. After watching and analyzing videotaped custodial interrogations he constructed three categories to explain the strategies used by the police. The **conditioning strategy** involves the police providing an environment in which the suspect is encouraged to think positively of the interrogator(s) and subsequently cooperate with the authorities. This lowered the suspect's anxiety level and achieved a sense of trust. The **de-emphasizing strategy** is the second technique, and in it interrogators inform suspects that their rights are unimportant and that the most important task at hand is to empathize with the victims and their families. Leo noted that when this technique is used, suspects rarely if ever think of stopping the interrogation in order to contact a lawyer for advice. In the third technique, the **persuasion strategy**, investigators inform suspects that if they don't tell their side of the story at that time, only the victim's will be heard during the trial.

According to Williams (2000), while the Charter has significantly increased the rights of the accused in our criminal justice system, this has not led to significant changes in police interrogations. This is largely because suspects do not appreciate "the nature and significance of their rights given problems with the clarity and adequacy of their communication" (ibid.:224). Another reason is that interrogations fall within the workings of the informal criminal justice system. Thus the police use a number of techniques that, while legal, are innovative in the sense that they are designed specifically to get the suspect to confess to the crime (see *Investigating: Police Interrogations, "Mr. Big," and R. v. Oickle*). These techniques are oftentimes successful, but they are not always so, as in the case of Guy Paul Morin, who was charged and wrongfully convicted of murdering a young girl at the end of an interrogation (Makin 1992:184–208).

False confessions are usually made and typically videotaped after hours and hours of intense interrogation. It's "a myth to think that getting a suspect to recap a confession on videotape after dozens of hours of intense interrogation is putting the truth before a jury, because one can't evaluate a confession without seeing the context in which it was taken" (Drizin, in Saulny 2002:5). Another expert believes that time is the "invisible force" operating during interrogations. Kassin (in Saulny 2002:5) says that what happens over time "is that the suspect gets tired, and there is an intensification of techniques. The suspect is getting

Investigating: Police Interrogations, "Mr. Big," and *R. v. Oickle*

In *R. v. Hebert* (1990), a suspect was arrested for robbery and informed the police that they chose to remain silent. The police then placed an undercover officer in the same cell, where the suspect made self-incriminating statements. The Supreme Court of Canada held that when the police use trickery to obtain self-incriminating statements they are inadmissible. According to the Court, this right occurs only when a suspect is arrested or placed in detention.

But what about individuals who are suspected of committing a crime but who haven't been arrested or detained? Are there any constraints upon police powers prior to arresting a suspect? Recent cases in Canada have brought attention upon police interrogation techniques when they are trying to obtain information prior to arresting a suspect. One such question deals with what is called the "Mr. Big" procedure. These are undercover operations in which police construct a fictitious criminal organization and then, posing as members of this organization, befriend a suspect. Slowly the undercover officers involve the suspect into their activities. Suspects are told there are benefits to joining the organization and negative consequences if they don't. These operations usually terminate with a meeting between the suspect and the leader of the organization ("Mr. Big"), who uses various incentives to have the suspect confess to the specific crime (usually a murder) under investigation. Since the statements made by suspects have until recently been admissible in court under Canadian law, the suspect is most commonly convicted of the crime and sentenced to a lengthy period of incarceration.

How many "Mr. Big" confessions have there been over the past two decades and how successful have they been? Approximately 180 police stings of this type were used by the RCMP in British Columbia between 1997 and 2004, with 80 percent of these considered to be "successful," which means it either eliminated a suspect or provided evidence to the prosecution (Hutchinson 2004:RB2). Across Canada, the RCMP has indicated that it has used this technique in at least 350 cases and there has been a 75 percent success rate and, of these, a 95 percent conviction rate (Smith et al. 2009). According to information provided by the RCMP on its website, prior to 2010, 95 percent of all Mr. Big cases resulting in a prosecution lead to a conviction (Keenan and Brockman 2010:52).

Critics argued that this approach, which can involve significant amounts of money being offered to suspects if they impress Mr. Big, is sure to lead to false confessions as it "could increase the chances that innocent persons might confess to crimes they do not commit" (Keenan and Brockman 2010:47). Nowlin (2004:383) believes that this technique possesses "dubious reliability," while Penney (2004:296) states that this type of interrogation technique could result in false confessions and argues that any evidence obtained through it should not be admitted as evidence in court.

Are the confessions obtained by the Mr. Big technique allowed as evidence into Canadian courts? If so, why? The issue of the voluntariness of confessions obtained from a suspect was originally determined in *The King v. Warickshall* (1783), when the English courts ruled that the use of certain techniques such as threats and/or promises to gain confessions were involuntary and not admissible in court. If an issue about the nature of a confession was raised in court, the Crown had to prove beyond a reasonable doubt that the statement given by the suspect to the authorities was voluntary. In Canada, the first Supreme Court case involving the admissibility of evidence obtained by an undercover officer was *Rothman v. The Queen* (1981). In this case, evidence was given by a suspect to his cellmate, who was actually an undercover officer portraying a truck driver. The defence raised the issue that the confession was obtained by "trickery." The majority of the Supreme Court disagreed on the basis of what became known as the "community shock" test. Specifically, a confession obtained by an undercover police officer would be excluded if their conduct was so shocking that it would bring the administration of justice into disrepute. It was determined that a police officer portraying a truck driver to obtain information that would lead to a conviction was not shocking to the community. What would be shocking, according to the Court, was a police officer pretending to be an officer of the court (e.g., duty counsel) and asking their client questions about their involvement in the offence in question.

Since *Rothman* was a pre-Charter case, questions were raised about its applicability to cases after the introduction of the Charter. In *R. v. Oickle* (2000), the Supreme Court ruled there had to be some restrictions on the inducements made by the police but also that courts "should be wary not to unduly limit police discretion." In this case, the accused admitted to seven counts of arson after being interrogated by the police. The trial court judge ruled the statements made by the accused were admissible but the Nova Scotia Court of Appeal acquitted the defendant on all counts since his statements were not voluntary due to the psychologically oppressive techniques used by the police.

On appeal, the Supreme Court held that an inducement does not automatically lead to the exclusion of the statement, as it recognized that the police might have to offer suspects some type of inducement in order to obtain the confession. What was not allowed was when there is a *quid pro quo* offer, such as offering the

Continued on next page

Investigating: Police Interrogations, "Mr. Big," and *R. v. Oickle* (*Continued*)

suspect some other benefit after they have confessed or when the suspect's "will is overborne." They ruled a number of police interviewing techniques were not acceptable, including offers of leniency, stating that another family member or friend would not be charged and using "shock" tricks such as pretending to be a priest or legal aid lawyer. Acceptable police interview techniques include offers of some type of counselling not conditional on a confession, minimizing the seriousness of the offence, and using a "good cop/bad cop" routine.

In *R. v. Hart* (2014), the Supreme Court further tightened the rules governing "Mr. Big" stings. The defendant was convicted of two counts of first degree murder in 2007 based entirely on confessions he made to undercover officers. On appeal to the Newfoundland Court of Appeal, two of the three confessions were ruled to be "doubtfully reliable and coerced" and in violation of his Charter rights. In its ruling in this case, the Supreme Court of Canada recognized that these types of stings can be abusive yet at the same time provide the police with "valuable evidence." The Court determined the Crown must now prove that such confessions are admissible at trial by meeting a two-stage test:

1. the Crown must determine that any such confessions are reliable and will not unfairly prejudice the accused at trial; and
2. the judge must then examine the police conduct during the investigation to ensure, for example, that confessions are not coerced or by taking advantage of any vulnerabilities (e.g., mental health problems) the defendant might have.

the message that denial is not escape, so they offer something else." When people are later asked why they falsely confessed, the main reason they give "is something like 'I just wanted to go home'" (ibid.). Kassin and Wrightsman (1985) identified three types of false confessions:

- *Voluntary false confessions*. In these situations, an individual voluntarily confesses to a crime he or she did not commit. These people may be giving a false confession to protect someone else; or establishing an alibi for another crime that is more serious; or they may be in physical fear of the person who is actually guilty.
- *Coerced-complaint false confessions*. Coerced-complaint confessions usually are the result of an intense custodial interrogation. Suspects may finally agree with police statements that falsely implicate them in a crime in order to end an extremely uncomfortable situation, or in order to receive a promised benefit for admitting (falsely) to involvement in the crime.
- *Coerced-internalized false confessions*. In this type of false confession, the suspect, who may be anxious, emotional, and/or tired of being repeatedly interrogated, may come to falsely recall an involvement in a crime and confess to it, though having had nothing to do with it.

According to Kassin (1997), false confessions of this type share two elements:

1. a vulnerable suspect, such as a person whose memory is malleable because of "youth, interpersonal trust, naivete, suggestibility, lack of intelligence, stress, fatigue, alcohol or drug use"; and
2. the presentation of false evidence (such as false conclusions of polygraph tests or what accomplices have said by the police in order to convince the suspect that they are, in fact, guilty).

What happens when a confession is introduced during a trial? In Canada, a rule of criminal evidence is that no statement made by the accused to the police is admissible in court on behalf of the prosecution unless it is first shown that it was made voluntarily. Furthermore, it must be shown that the confession was the result of the accused's conscious operating mind. When the prosecution offers to place into evidence any statement made by the accused to the police, a hearing known as a *voir dire* is held in the absence of the jury, in order to ascertain whether these conditions have been met. The trial judge who conducts the hearing must determine whether the statement was made voluntarily and that there weren't any threats or promises that made the accused confess to the police.

The Charter of Rights and Freedoms is also relevant here. Mewett and Nakatsuru (2000:171) state that "the first and prime point to bear in mind is that even if there has been a Charter violation in the obtaining of a confession, s. 24(2) does not necessarily exclude it from the trial." They add that the exclusion of evidence is not automatic, in that evidence shall be excluded only if it can be established that it violates s. 24(2) of the Charter; that is, "having regard to all the circumstances, the admission of it in proceedings would bring the administration of justice into disrepute."

Other sections of the Charter have an influence on the admissibility of evidence, including ss. 10(a) and 10(b).

In addition, s. 7, which bears on the right not to be deprived of liberty except in accordance with the principles of fundamental justice, may be relevant since the Supreme Court of Canada has ruled that there is a right to silence protected by s. 7. Under the Charter, the Supreme Court has looked carefully at how the police have obtained confessions from the accused and whether or not their actions were in accordance with the principles of fundamental justice. In *R. v. Broyles* (1991), for example, the Supreme Court held that an accused's right to silence had been infringed on by the police after they arranged a prison visit between an accused and his friend who was wearing a wiretap. In the course of the visit, incriminating statements by the accused were recorded.

Jailhouse Interrogations

Over the past two decades there have been a number of inquiries into the wrongful convictions of individuals who were convicted of murder but later exonerated when it was discovered that they had not committed these crimes. In two of these inquiries (Ontario's *Commission of Proceedings Involving Guy Paul Morin* [1998] and Manitoba's *Inquiry Regarding Thomas Sophonow* [2001]), much attention focused on the role of **jailhouse interrogations**, in particular jailhouse informants and the evidence they supplied to the police—evidence that was instrumental in gaining convictions later proved to be wrongful. A **jailhouse informant** is "an inmate, usually awaiting trial or sentencing, who claims to have heard another prisoner make an admission about his case" (Winograde 1990:755). Both inquiries criticized the use of jailhouse informants, raising questions about their reliability and the fact that they were willing, with some persuasion, to say anything in order to benefit from their cooperation. In the Sophonow case, for example, before the third trial at least 11 jailhouse informants volunteered to assist the prosecution. The Crown and the police scrutinized the volunteers and selected three of them, largely on the basis of their "credibility" and "reliability."

Why has the testimony of jailhouse informants been used in the courts when it is acknowledged that their testimony may not be truthful and may lead to false convictions? In the Anglo-American criminal justice system, various types of informants have been used for centuries. As early as the 13th century, the English common law was using the **approver system**, whereby an individual charged with a capital offence could obtain a pardon by formally accusing other persons of a serious crime. If the accusation turned out to be correct (as determined by whether or not the individual named was found guilty), the approver would be granted freedom. However, if the accusation failed, the approver would be put to death. This system created a number of problems; for example, it encouraged blackmail, and individuals who became approvers came to be seen as "manipulative, abusive and desperate" (Zimmerman 1994:155).

Despite the pitfalls of using jailhouse informants in criminal cases, it was once accepted practice across Canada. There are no statistics to indicate how often evidence obtained from jailhouse informants is used in Canada; usually the public becomes aware that informants have been used only after a formal inquiry has been called to investigate a wrongful conviction or after a released informant later reveals to the press how many times, and for which cases, they have supplied evidence to the prosecution. In the United States, it has been estimated that in 20 percent of cases in which individuals were wrongfully convicted, the prosecution used jailhouse informants (Scheck et al. 2000). The *Inquiry Regarding Thomas Sophonow* (2001:71) noted some of the dangers of using jailhouse informants:

- Jailhouse informants are polished and convincing liars.
- All confessions of an accused will be given great weight by the jurors.
- Jurors will give the same weight to "confessions" made to jailhouse informants as they will to a confession made to a police officer.
- Jailhouse informants rush to testify, particularly in high-profile cases.
- They always appear to have evidence that could only have come from someone who committed the offence.
- Their mendacity, and their ability to convince those who hear them, make them a threat to the principle of a fair trial as well as to the administration of justice.

Much of the concern here focuses on the impact on juries of statements by jailhouse informants. The leading Canadian case in this matter is *R. v. Vetrovec* (1982). In this case, the defendants had been convicted on a charge of conspiracy to traffic in heroin. The trial judge had warned the jury about the issues relating to convicting the defendants on the basis of the uncorroborated testimony of an accomplice. On appeal, the Supreme Court of Canada rejected any suggestion that jailhouse informants not be allowed to testify. Instead, the focus was to be on the credibility of the witnesses and whether their testimony could be corroborated (as opposed to the quality of the evidence). The Supreme Court cautioned against placing informants in different categories, with only some categories requiring that warnings about their testimony be given to the jury. In its decision the Supreme Court gave trial judges guidance about warning jurors concerning the evidence supplied by jailhouse informants by noting that they should warn the jury about such evidence. The Supreme Court stated that it was to be left to the discretion of the trial judge whether to give "a clear and sharp warning to attract the attention of the juror to the risks of adopting, without more information, the evidence of the witness." This "clear and sharp warning" is now commonly referred to as the **Vetrovec warning**. The warning has to contain the following four elements:

- Drawing the attention of the jury to the testimonial evidence requiring special scrutiny.
- Explaining why this evidence is subject to special scrutiny.
- Cautioning the jury that it is dangerous to convict on unconfirmed evidence of this sort, though the jury is entitled to do so if satisfied that the evidence is true.
- That the jury, in determining the veracity of the suspect evidence, should look for evidence from another source tending to show that the untrustworthy witness is telling the truth as to the guilt of the accused.

In 2000, the Supreme Court heard another case having implications for evidence supplied by jailhouse informants as well as for the "Vetrovec warning." In *R. v. Brooks* (2000), the defendant was accused of murdering his girlfriend's 19-month-old daughter. Part of the evidence used to convict Brooks was given by two jailhouse informants, who said they had heard the defendant say he killed the child to stop her crying. The trial judge, however, decided that the jury did not have to hear the "Vetrovec warning," and defence counsel did not ask that the warning be given to the jury. Brooks was found guilty of first degree murder. The Ontario Court of Appeal overturned the lower court's decision and ordered another trial, having ruled that the jury should have been warned that the jailhouse informants who supplied evidence to the prosecution had lengthy records of dishonesty and psychiatric disorders. The Supreme Court, in a 4–3 decision, restored Brooks's conviction, but also concluded that trial judges have a significant obligation to caution jurors about the unreliability of jailhouse informants' testimony.

The Morin Inquiry criticized the Crown's use of two jailhouse informants. The commissioner concluded that both informants were liars who would say anything to further their own ends. The Sophonow Inquiry noted a number of factors involving the prosecution and police. Sophonow had been tried three times and convicted twice of murdering a young woman in Winnipeg. It also noted that there had been questionable police interrogations of Sophonow and that the Crown had failed to disclose relevant evidence to the defence. The commissioner also strongly criticized the Crown for relying on evidence supplied by jailhouse informants. One of the informants had 26 fraud charges dropped in exchange for his testimony that he had heard Sophonow confess. Another jailhouse informant, who received cash, had been a prosecution witness in at least eight other cases. According to the commissioner, former Supreme Court Justice Peter Cory (*Inquiry regarding Thomas Sophonow* 2001:71), jailhouse informants are "a dangerous group" as "their testimony can all too easily destroy any hope of holding a fair trial and severely tarnish the reputation of Canadian justice."

CP PHOTO/ Pool-Winnipeg Free Press/ Wayne Glowacki

Thomas Sophonow was awarded $2.6 million after DNA evidence cleared him of the 1981 murder of a waitress. He had spent four years in prison.

As a result of the findings of these two commissions, several provinces introduced reforms to ensure that jailhouse informants are carefully scrutinized. In Alberta, for example, Crown prosecutors are required to get a second opinion from their peers before using evidence supplied by jailhouse informants, and in British Columbia, regional Crown counsels must consult with the local Crown before deciding whether a jailhouse informant will be allowed to testify. Ontario reformed their system by first requiring jailhouse informants to be vetted by a special committee consisting of senior ministry lawyers (Joyce 2000). After the Ontario guidelines were established, between 1998 and 2004, of the 56 potential jailhouse informants, 30 were approved to testify and 26 were denied. In 13 other cases during the same time period, no recommendation was issued because a defendant either pleaded guilty or the police themselves recognized independently that an informant was unreliable. By 2009, Ontario "had effectively ended the use of jailhouse informants . . . " (Makin 2009).

SUMMING UP AND LOOKING FORWARD

The police rely on interrogations (or questioning) of suspects to gather information about a crime. Suspects can be questioned numerous times and these are usually conducted in private. The police may videotape interrogations conducted in a police facility in order to prove that all proper rules and procedures are followed. Still, the police may decide to use other types of interrogations outside of a police facility, such as a jailhouse, to gain information allowing them to charge someone for a crime. Issues continue to be raised about police conduct during interrogations, such as what types of procedures are used to obtain statements from suspects during this stage of evidence gathering. For example, interrogations as they may provide unreliable evidence leading to wrongful convictions.

Questions about jailhouse interrogations have typically been raised after it is revealed that informants have been used after a formal inquiry has been called to investigate a wrongful conviction or after a released informant later reveals to the press how many times, and for which cases, they have supplied evidence to the prosecution. Due to concerns about the evidence supplied by jailhouse informants, the Supreme Court has given trial judges guidance about warning jurors concerning the evidence supplied by jailhouse informants by noting that they should warn the jury about such evidence. The Supreme Court stated that it was to be left to the discretion of the trial judge whether to give "a clear and sharp warning to attract the attention of the juror to the risks of adopting, without more information, the evidence of the witness." This "clear and sharp warning" is now commonly referred to as the Vetrovec warning.

Police use of deadly force and the use of deadly force against the police are discussed in the next section. Police misconduct, as well as different approaches to holding the police accountable for their actions, are among the topics in the next section.

Review Questions:

1. Why are interrogations so important to the police?
2. What are the different types of strategies used by the police during interrogations?
3. What are the legal issues involved when "Mr. Big" operations are used?
4. What are the different types of false confessions according to Kassin and Wrightsman?
5. What are the dangers of using jailhouse interrogations? How has the Supreme Court dealt with this issue?

Police and the Use of Deadly Force

A defining characteristic of the police is that they possess the **legitimate use of force**. In some circumstances the police use **excessive force**—that is, they use more force than necessary to get control of suspects as well as to protect themselves and others. On occasion, the use of force by police officers leads to the use of deadly force.

Deadly force is defined as force that is used with the intent to cause bodily injury or death. Police use of deadly force refers to those situations where the police use firearms in encounters with citizens. But citizens may be injured or killed as the result of other types of force used by the police. For example, choke holds, which can cause death, ought to be included in any definition of deadly force (Fyfe 1988). High-speed chases ending in death can also be seen as a type of deadly force; however, such cases are not included here because the deaths that occur are unintentional and often accidental.

Until 1995, the Criminal Code permitted the shooting of a "fleeing felon" without any consideration as to whether the suspect presented a danger to a police officer or other citizens (Roach 1999). This was challenged in the trial of a Toronto police officer who shot and wounded a Black male suspected of purse snatching. In this case (*R. v. Lines* [1993]), the prosecutor successfully argued that the shooting was inconsistent with the victim's rights to life and security as provided by the Charter of Rights and Freedoms—specifically, that it deprived both victims and potential victims of police shootings of life and security of the person in that the Criminal Code "authorized lethal force regardless of the seriousness of the offence or the threat posed by the suspect" (ibid.:232).

As a result of *Lines*, Parliament introduced a new defence (found in s. 25[4] of the Criminal Code) authorizing police officers to use deadly force in order to prevent a suspect from fleeing if the officer "believes on reasonable grounds that the force is necessary for the purpose of protecting the police officer . . . or any other person from imminent or future death or grave bodily harm."

Subsection (1) of s. 25 of the Criminal Code states that any individual, including a peace (police) officer, can use "as much force as necessary" in the "administration of the law" if they act "on reasonable grounds." Furthermore, a police officer, in order to be justified in using deadly force, must believe on "reasonable grounds" that force is necessary in order to protect himself or herself or an individual in their care from "death or grievous bodily harm."

Stansfield (1996, 2000) points out that this approach to deadly force raises a number of problems. First, the phrase "as much force as necessary" suggests that police can use as much force as they feel is necessary to resolve any particular incident. Second, it does not state exactly how much force should be used. In the first case where a police officer was convicted of manslaughter under this section of the Criminal Code, the officer received a conditional sentence (see Chapter 11) and 180 hours of community service. This sentence was reached on the basis of the defendant's previous record as a police officer and because he was given false information that the Aboriginal protestors at Ipperwash, Ontario, were in possession of weapons (*R. v. Deane* [1997]).

A number of mechanisms have been implemented to control the use of deadly force by police. While the Criminal Code clearly states that a police officer does not have to be physically attacked before using potentially deadly force, it does say that police officers have to follow a reasonable standard for the use of force. In brief, force is to be considered excessive when, after the officer has evaluated all the circumstances at the time of the incident, the force is unreasonable. However, even when police investigators and Crown prosecutors determine that excessive force was used, it is difficult to gain a conviction. Police officers who are witnesses to potential criminal offences committed by their colleagues have always been reluctant to assist Crown prosecutors. This problem has led to a revision of the Ontario Police Act, which now states that officers must cooperate with any investigation.

Deadly Force Used against Police Officers

Police officers can of course be the *recipients* of deadly force. The danger of their daily work was underscored in 2014 when three RCMP officers were shot and killed responding to a call about an armed individual in Moncton, New Brunswick, and in 2005 when four RCMP officers were also shot and killed while conducting an investigation near Mayerthorpe, Alberta. The death of a police officer on duty is a rare event in Canada; on average, two or three officers are killed each year. In comparison, approximately 70 police officers are shot and killed each year in the United States.

Between 1961 and 2009, a total of 133 police officers have been killed in the line of duty (Dunn 2010). The decade in which the highest numbers of police officers were killed was the 1980s: between 1980 and 1989, 63 officers were killed. Dunn (2010) investigated the deaths of Canadian police officers murdered in the line of duty for the years 1961–2009 and found that police officers were most likely to be murdered during a robbery investigation, which accounted for almost one-quarter (23 percent) of all killings (see Figure 7.1).

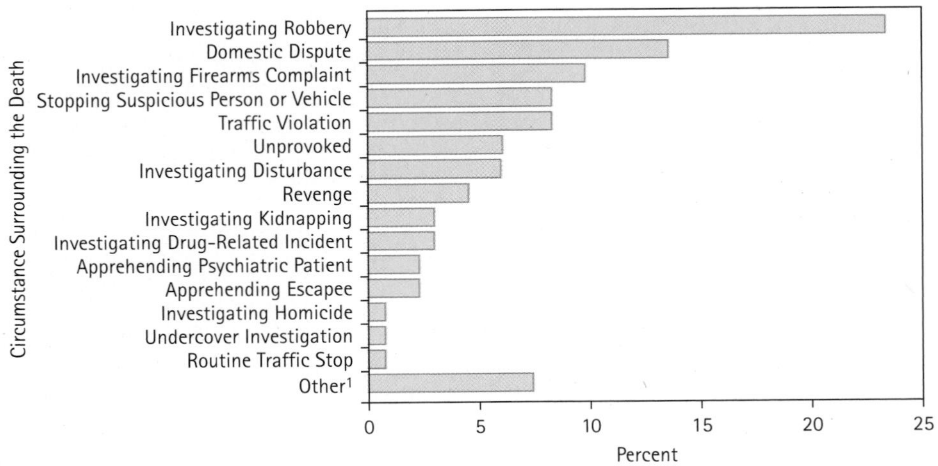

FIGURE 7.1 Homicides against Police Officers, by Type of Circumstance, Canada, 1961–2009

[1] Includes all other situations not otherwise stated. For example, riot control, suicide situations, investigations of criminal incidents not listed above.

Source: Sara Dunn, "Police Officers Murdered in the Line of Duty, 1961 to 2009." *Juristat*, Vol. 30, No. 3 (October 26, 2010), p. 7, Statistics Cana da Catalogue no. 85-002-X, http://www.statcan.gc.ca /pub/85-002-x/2010003/article/11354-eng.htm. Reproduced and distributed on an "as is" basis with the permission of Statistics Canada.

Police Misconduct

Ever since the first police forces were formed, police misconduct and the abuse of police powers has been a concern (Lundman 1980). Since the police are a key agency of social control, reports of misconduct and the abuse of power have created tension between the police and the public. The inability to control police officer discretion and misconduct has led to crises for police organizations (Mastrofksi 2004). Over time, police misbehaviour has received attention from police researchers, administrators, and policymakers. The attention from researchers has focused upon the extent and type of misconduct, how it permeates police organizations, whether or not there are certain types of police officers who are the source of most of the misconduct, and strategies for controlling officers. This issue is important as police agencies are concerned about issues that relate to police accountability, as well as the selection, hiring, and retention of police officers.

Police misconduct (also referred to as **police deviance**) is a broadly used term in the criminal justice literature (Martin 1993). It can be defined as "a generic description of police officer activities which are inconsistent with the officer's legal authority, organizational authority, and standards of ethical conduct" (Barker and Carter 1986:1–7). Police misconduct is usually subdivided into three categories: occupational deviancy, abuse of authority, and selective enforcement of the law. **Occupational deviancy** is defined as "criminal and noncriminal [behaviour] committed during the course of normal work activities or committed under the guise of the police officer's authority" (ibid.: 4). Examples of police occupational deviancy include misconduct such as sleeping on duty, insubordination, and misuse of firearms.

Police misconduct has been investigated and oftentimes publicized, so examples of it are not difficult to find. A common type of police misconduct is the use of excessive force by the police. Claims have been made throughout the 20th century that Canadian police have used excessive force. Jamieson (1973) and Brown and Brown (1978) found that various police forces across Canada have harassed and intimidated striking workers. The police have also been accused of relying on excessive physical force to obtain confessions from suspects (Hagan 1977), with some saying they "push the law to its limits, slip through the loopholes and employ technicalities" and that they cannot be trusted "to obey the rules society imposes on the way they question suspects" (Woods, in Martin 1993:161). This led Brannigan (1984:57) to conclude that "the police appear to routinely trample over the rights of accused people."

A third type of police misconduct involves the **selective enforcement of laws**—an approach to enforcement encountered in the lived experience of certain populations. These "routine incidents of misconduct reflect and reinforce race, class, and gender bias in a myriad of ways" (Martin 1993:149). The selective enforcement of the law as it applies to marginalized women became an issue in Vancouver when the disappearance of more than 50 women led to accusations that the police were indifferent to their fate. Over-policing of Aboriginal peoples and members of other minority groups have led to accusations of racial profiling by the police.

"Problem" Police Officers: Early Warning Systems

Some people believe all police officers use illegitimate force, while others argue that only a small proportion of officers (identified as **"problem" police officers**) account for the majority of such actions. What is a "problem" police officer? First identified during the 1970s, Goldstein defined them as being "well known to their supervisors, to the top administrators, to their peers, and to the residents of the areas in which they work" but that "little is done to alter their conduct" (1977:171).

Some researchers (e.g., Sherman 1974) argue that "problem" police officers are indicative of problems that exist within entire police departments. They contend that police departments can be categorized according to the level and type of misconduct found within them. Three categories have been developed:

- *Rotten apples.* This term refers to police departments that have a few problem police officers (that is, "rotten apples"), who use their position for illegal personal gain or who resort to the force that society has authorized to engage in questionable behaviour with suspects and/or members of marginalized groups. Sometimes a number of "rotten apples" work together; if they do, they are sometimes referred to as "rotten pockets."
- *Pervasive but unorganized misconduct.* Here, a majority of police personnel are engaged in questionable activities but cooperate little with one another, if at all.
- *Pervasive and organized misconduct.* Here, almost all of the members of a police department are involved in systemic and organized misconduct.

The most common view held today is that a small number of police officers account for a large amount of citizen complaints. In fact, it has become a truism among police administrators that less than 10 percent of police officers generate 90 percent of all the problems faced by police services. Lersch and Mieczkowski (1996), in their study of a large police agency in the Southeastern United States, found that 7 percent of all police officers were "chronic" offenders who generated a disproportionate number (33 percent) of complaints from the public. These "high-volume" officers were younger and less experienced and were accused of using force after a proactive encounter they had personally initiated.

Criminal Justice Insight

What Is the Impact of Body-Worn Cameras?

Edmonton Sun/Sun Media

A body-worn video camera.

Police organizations in Western countries (e.g., Canada, the United States, and the United Kingdom) are now experimenting with body-worn cameras. The deaths of Sammy Yatim in Toronto in 2013 and Michael Brown in Ferguson, Missouri in 2014 have led to suggestions that the outcomes of these cases may have been different if the police officers involved were wearing body-worn cameras. For example, in his report focusing upon reducing the lethal force incidents of the Toronto Police Service, former Supreme Court Justice Iacobucci suggested that one benefit of providing body-worn cameras to all first responders would be to "ensure greater accountability and transparency for all concerned."

Supporters of body-worn cameras argue that this technology will change police officer behaviour during their encounters with citizens. Initial experiments into the use of body-worn cameras in the United States have reported positive results. The Rialto, California police reported that after the implementation of body-worn cameras, citizen complaints against the police declined by 88 percent in a year—from 24 to 3. In addition, the use of force by officers declined by 60 percent, from 61 to 25 incidents (Farrar 2013). In the United Kingdom, one police organization reported a 14.3 percent reduction in citizen complaints during the first six months of the project compared to the previous six months. In addition, there were no complaints made against those officers wearing cameras (Goodall 2007).

Critics of this technology have raised numerous issues, such as privacy concerns, who has access to them, and the financial, resource, and storage costs to police organizations (see Table 7.1).

TABLE 7.1 Perceived Benefits and Concerns with Officer Body-Worn Cameras

Benefits	Concerns
Increased transparency and legitimacy	Citizens' privacy
Improved police officer behaviour	Officers' privacy
Improved citizen behaviour	Officers' health and safety
Expedited resolution of complaints and lawsuits	Training and policy requirements
Improved evidence for arrest and prosecution	Logistical and resource requirements, including data storage and retrieval
Opportunities for police training	

Source: Michael D. White. (2014). *Police Officer Body-Worn Cameras: Assessing the Evidence*. Washington, D.C.: Office of Community Oriented Policing Services, p. 18, http://ojpdiagnosticcenter.org/sites/default/files/spotlight/Police%20Officer%20Body-Worn%20Cameras.pdf.

The Christopher Commission's investigation of the Los Angeles Police Department (LAPD) after the beating of Rodney King identified 44 problem police officers (or less than 0.5 percent of the LAPD officers), with each averaging 7.6 complaints for excessive force or for improper tactics, compared to only 0.6 for all other officers. In 1981, the U.S. Commission on Civil Rights, in its report *Who Is Guarding the Guardians?*, recommended that all police departments create an "early warning system" to identify problem police officers "who are frequently the subject of complaints or who demonstrate identifiable patterns of inappropriate behavior" (U.S. Commission on Civil Rights 1981:81).

An **early warning system** is a data-based police management tool for identifying officers whose actions are problematic. It is designed to permit a police service to identify problem police officers before they create a situation requiring formal disciplinary action. Administrators can then warn the officers in question and provide appropriate counselling and/or training to assist them in

CANADIAN PRESS/Adrian Wyld

RCMP Commissioner Robert Paulson says antiquated rules prevent swift and decisive action against rogue police officers.

changing their behaviour. There are two types of early warning systems, which vary in terms of their objectives. The **comprehensive personnel assessment system** collects a wide range of data and has the ability to look at a large number of issues. These types of systems require sophisticated technology and administrative commitment. The **performance problem system** employs a narrower approach, and it most commonly is used to focus upon a small number of performance issues.

Early warning systems have three basic components: selection, intervention, and post-intervention monitoring. In the **selection phase**, various criteria are applied in order to identify officers who should be placed in the system. These criteria include citizen complaints, the use of firearms, the use of force, civil litigation, incidents involving resisting arrest, and high-speed pursuits and vehicular damage. The primary goal of an early warning system is to change the behaviour of police officers who have been identified as problems. **Intervention strategies** are based on a combination of deterrence and education and it is hoped that those police officers who go through this strategy will change their behaviour in response to the perceived threat of punishment. Early warning systems also include **post-intervention monitoring** in order to ensure that the officers in question improve their performance.

Police Accountability: The Role of Citizen Oversight

While police organizations may provide excellent training, practise culturally sensitive policing, and develop excellent rapport with local residents, problems such as police misconduct and the use of excessive force will no doubt surface. The question then becomes, who shall police the police? The rule of law "requires full and impartial investigations of suspected serious police wrongdoing . . ." (Editorial 2012:163). The police in a democracy are accountable to both the law and the public. This means the police have to conform to the appropriate legal standards of due process and be responsive to the citizens they serve. One important issue concerning **police accountability** is that these two aspects of accountability can conflict with each other (Walker 2001). The public wants effective crime control, but some of the approaches used by the police to accomplish this goal may conflict with legal principles. How is a balance to be struck between these two types of accountability?

In Canada, a **Royal Commission** (or an **inquiry**) can be struck to investigate a specific incident; this is rare, however, and usually happens only long after the fact. A Royal Commission was appointed to investigate the wrongful conviction of Donald Marshall, Jr., a Mi'kmaq man who served almost 12 years for a murder he did not commit. And the Aboriginal Justice Inquiry in Manitoba focused on the criminal justice response to the deaths of two Aboriginal people in that province, Helen Betty Osborne and JJ Harper. The ensuing reports were critical of how the police conducted themselves in their investigations.

Much more common approaches to ensuring police accountability are internal investigations, citizen oversight, and civil liability. With **internal investigations**, the police themselves investigate allegations of wrongdoing by police officers. Many observers are critical of this approach, arguing that it is inherently biased in favour of the police and that when an officer is found guilty of wrongdoing, the resulting penalties are too lenient. A. Alan Borovoy, then-general counsel of the Canadian Civil Liberties Union, argues that this approach is flawed as it "will scare off many potential complainants" and because "investigating officers will have a conflict of interest" (2000:A3). To illustrate his concerns, he points to the evidence collected by the Donald Marshall inquiry. That inquiry found that an RCMP officer appointed to evaluate the prosecution of Marshall soon after he started to serve his sentence found no wrongdoing by investigators in Sydney, Nova Scotia, where the crime occurred. When this issue was raised at the hearings years later, another member of the RCMP stated that "police officers are like a fraternity. You feel a certain loyalty to one another."

A second approach—and the most common one today—to ensuring police accountability with respect to conduct is to establish a separate **civilian review agency** to investigate allegations of police misbehaviour (Walker 2001:5) (see also *Investigating: The Civilian Review and Complaints Commission for the RCMP*). This opens the complaints process to individuals who are not police officers. In this way, it is hoped the police are made accountable to the public (Finn 2000).

Investigating: The Civilian Review and Complaints Commission for the RCMP

What happens when a member of the public wants to make a complaint against the RCMP in the belief that one of its officers engaged in misconduct? Some people think that complainants must file with a provincial organization where the incident took place. This is not so: complaints against RCMP officers can be lodged with any RCMP member, the Civilian Review and Complaints Commission for the RCMP (the Commission; formerly

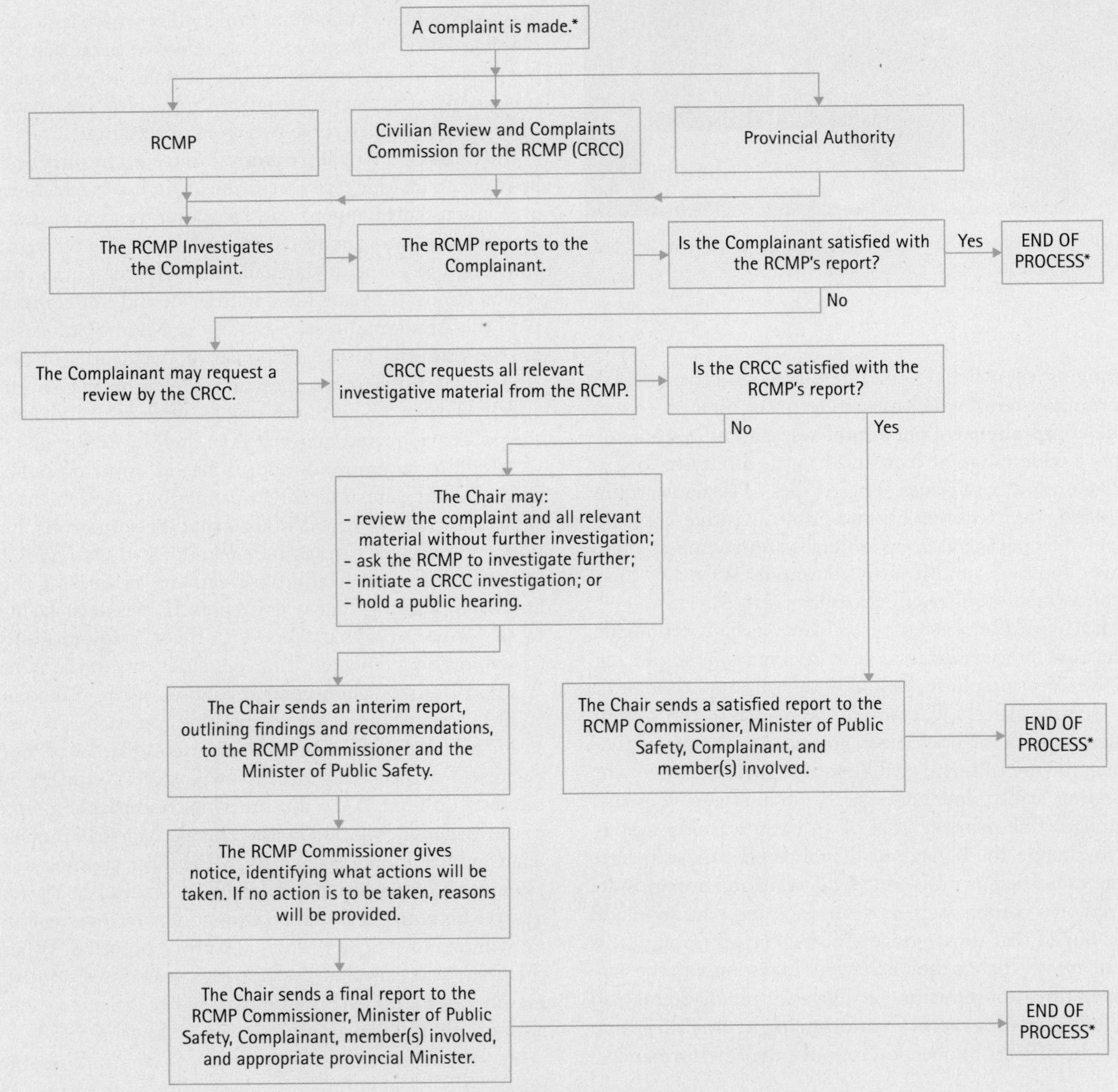

FIGURE 7.2 The Civilian Complaint and Review Process in the RCMP

Source: Civilian Review and Complaints Commission for the RCMP, http://www.crcc-ccetp.gc.ca/en/complaint-and-review-process-flowchart. Reproduced with the permission of the Civilian Review and Complaints Commission for the RCMP, 2015.

Investigating: The Civilian Review and Complaints Commission for the RCMP (*Continued*)

known as the Commission for Public Complaints Against the RCMP), or with the provincial authority responsible for receiving complaints against police in the province in which the subject of the complaint took place. Figure 7.2 shows the complaint and review process.

- The Commission is an agency of the federal government, distinct and independent from the RCMP. Its mandate is to:
  - receive complaints from the public about the conduct of RCMP members.
  - conduct reviews when complainants are not satisfied with the RCMP's handling of their complaints.
  - initiate complaints and investigations into RCMP conduct when it is in the public interest to do so;
  - review specified activities; and
  - report findings and make recommendations.

The Commission is an independent agency and does not act as an advocate either for the complainant or for RCMP members.

In 2013–14, the Commission (operating at the time as the Commission for Public Complaints Against the RCMP) processed 3,622 general enquiries and formal complaints. It issued a total of 207 review reports during the same year, and in 183 reports (88 percent) the Commission was satisfied with the RCMP's handling of the complaint. In 24 reports (12 percent), the Commission was not satisfied with the RCMP's disposition of the complaint and, in most cases, made recommendations to address deficiencies.

Various types of citizen oversight of the police have existed for more than 50 years in North America. In the 1960s, the idea of oversight was viewed as radical by almost everyone except civil liberties groups. Slowly the idea became accepted and today such bodies are found in the United Kingdom, the United States, Australia, and New Zealand (see Exhibit 7.2 for some of the reasons given by people who support and who criticize civilian oversight committees). In Canada, the first civilian oversight agencies were established in the 1980s in Toronto, in the provinces of Manitoba, British Columbia, and Quebec, and (federally) for the RCMP.

The first citizen review board in Canada was formed in Toronto in 1981. It enabled members of the public to

EXHIBIT 7.2 The Pros and Cons of Citizen Oversight

Those who favour citizen oversight committees make a number of arguments in favour of them, including these:

- Police misconduct is a serious problem, and internal police complaint systems have failed to address the real issues leading to these problems.
- Citizen oversight committees are more thorough and fair than the police's own internal reviews.
- Citizen oversight committees find in favour of more complaints.
- Such committees lead to more disciplinary actions against police officers.
- Such committees do more to deter the types of police behaviour that lead to complaints.
- Such committees are viewed as independent by citizens and therefore provide greater satisfaction among complainants.
- Such committees lead to greater professionalization within police organizations; they also improve the quality of policing.

Critics of civilian oversight point out that this approach achieves few of its stated goals and can actually make matters worse. They identify the following problems with it (among others):

- Police misconduct is not as serious a problem as it is made out to be.
- Police officers and organizations are capable of and do conduct thorough and fair investigations.
- Internal police investigations into police wrongdoing actually find in favour of complainants more often than do citizen oversight committees.
- Police departments hand out harsher disciplinary sanctions to those officers who have been found to be involved in wrongful conduct than citizen oversight committees.
- Internal police disciplinary approaches deter more police officers from engaging in misconduct.
- Internal police investigations are actually more satisfying to complainants.
- Citizen oversight committees actually do more harm than good in that they limit the crime control initiatives of police officers and undermine the authority of police executives.

Source: Walker, S. 2001. *Police Accountability: The Role of Citizen Oversight.* Belmont, CA: Wadsworth.

direct their complaints to a non-police organization. This board was created after an investigation into the Metropolitan Toronto Police Force (as it was then known) by Judge D. R. Morand of the Ontario Supreme Court recommended that a citizen review board be formed. In his investigation, Morand uncovered evidence of false arrests, cover-ups, and false charges, as well as a conspiracy among police officers to protect one another from legal action. This led to the passing of the Police Force Complaints Act, which makes it possible to investigate allegations of police brutality. This legislation established a commission for investigating complaints in which both the police and civilian authorities have input.

In 1990, a new Ontario Police Services Act received Royal Assent, making Ontario the first province in Canada to create a civilian oversight agency. It expanded the powers of the Police Complaints Commissioner to the entire province. This new legislation also created the Special Investigations Unit (SIU), a civilian oversight agency, as a response to concerns expressed during the hearings of the Task Force on Race Relations in 1988. During these hearings, some presenters had expressed concern about the manner in which the police conducted their investigations involving officers of other police services, a process that was criticized for its potential lack of objectivity and conflict of interest. The SIU is intended to be an independent agency of the provincial government and is composed of civilian investigators. Its jurisdiction is limited to the criminal investigation of police actions that result in serious injuries. Complaints involving police activities not involving serious injury or death are handled by other agencies.

The third mechanism for controlling police misconduct is **civil liability**. In this approach, individual police officers can be held liable for their misconduct and sentenced to a period of incarceration (although this rarely occurs), or the police service itself can be sued. Citizens can sue the police for negligent investigation, abuse of public office and for Charter of Rights and Freedoms damages. In 1998, for example, a rape victim successfully sued the Toronto Police Service for failing to warn her that a serial rapist was attacking women in her neighbourhood. An Ontario court awarded her $220,000 (Gatehouse and Eby 2000).

What Is the Importance of Police Legitimacy?

In Chapter 1, it was noted that the legitimacy of the various institutions of our criminal justice system is important as it is a part of the rule of law. Legitimacy is largely based on citizens' perceptions of fairness and equity, particularly on the basis of the fairness of procedures. Tyler (1990:80) found that procedural justice has a significant influence "on generalizations from experiences to attitudes toward legal authorities, law, and government."

Tyler believes four elements (**participation, neutrality, trustworthiness of authorities**, and **treatment with dignity and respect**) are key to understanding **procedural fairness**. What do each of these four elements refer to?

- *Participation* refers to the extent to which individuals believe they have control over the process, especially in terms of having the opportunity to present their side of the story to the decision makers.
- *Neutrality* occurs when decision makers do not allow the personal characteristics of individuals to influence decisions and treatment during the process.
- *Trustworthiness of authorities* refers to the degree to which decision makers can be trusted to behave fairly.
- *Treatment with dignity and respect* is based on whether or not decision makers treat individuals with dignity and respect for their rights.

While these four elements apply to all stages of the criminal justice system, they especially apply to the police as it is their actions that determine who enters into the criminal justice system. If citizens feel that the police are not fair or are disrespectful in their actions, their level of legitimacy decreases. Research into police legitimacy in the United States (e.g., Mazerolle et al. 2013) has found that people generally care more about how the police treat them than about the outcomes of their contact. This means that the quality of treatment, decision-making fairness, the ability to tell their side of the story, and the neutrality of police officers (i.e., procedural justice) lead to positive perceptions of the police by citizens, not only at the time of their interaction but also in terms of their generalized views of the police in our society.

SUMMING UP AND LOOKING FORWARD

One of the defining characteristics of the police is that they can legitimately use force in order to gain control of suspects as well as to protect themselves and citizens from injury and death.

One type of force is deadly force. The Criminal Code authorizes police officers to use deadly force in order to prevent a suspect from fleeing if the officer "believes on reasonable grounds that the force is necessary for the purpose of protecting the police officer . . . or any other person from imminent or future death or grave bodily harm." The police are also the recipients of deadly force. On average two or three officers are killed each year in Canada.

Citizens oftentimes have concerns about the conduct of the police. There are various explanations of police misconduct: one is the "rotten apple theory," which says that there are a few bad officers who are recruited but during training they can't be identified. Another suggests that police officers start their careers as good officers but then turn bad due to the socialization processes that occur during training and their experiences in the field (see also Chapter 5). Many remedies that attempt to control police misconduct are punitive. These include, for example, civilian oversight, criminal punishment, civil lawsuits, and administrative sanctions. Alternative, non-punitive measures are now being used to deal with "problem" police officers, such as early warning systems designed to detect misconduct and then improve police behaviour.

Review Questions:

1. According to the law, when can the police use deadly force?
2. Define police misconduct. What are the different types of police misconduct?
3. What is an "early warning system" and when is it used?
4. What are the different ways that can be used to deal with police misconduct?
5. What are the benefits of having a system of civilian oversight of the police?

Critical Issues in Canadian Criminal Justice

HEAT EMISSIONS (FLIR) AND THE REASONABLE EXPECTATION OF PRIVACY

The purpose of s. 8 of the Charter of Rights and Freedoms is "to protect individuals from unjustified State intrusion upon their privacy (*Hunter v. Southam Inc.* [1984]) by granting individuals "a reasonable expectation of privacy" (*R. v. Evans* [1996]). In both of these cases, the Supreme Court of Canada decided that individuals can establish that a search or seizure violated their s. 8 rights if they can show that they had a reasonable expectation of privacy in the item seized, the place searched, or both. If an individual is unable to demonstrate a reasonable expectation of privacy, and that the expectation of privacy was unjustifiably intruded upon, then the state or its representatives cannot have violated the individual's rights under s. 8.

However, emerging technologies can potentially test the limits of a person's privacy in our society. Some of these emerging technologies may be used by the police in their investigation of criminal activity. One of the problems associated with emerging technologies "has been the degree to which they create novel privacy concerns by making knowable and meaningful information and data that previously existed but weren't susceptible to being captured or conclusively comprehended through ordinary human senses" (Bailey 2008:283). One such example of this is the forward looking infrared camera (FLIR). This technology allows the police to monitor the heat emissions emerging from a residence and which may indicate that an excessive amount of electricity is being used, perhaps for a marijuana grow operation.

What is the relationship among new technologies, police powers, and the expectation of privacy by citizens? While the right to privacy in Canada is not explicitly protected by the Charter of Rights and Freedoms, it is protected indirectly through other constitutional provisions, most notably the s. 8 protection against unreasonable search and seizure. The issue for s. 8 is the determination of whether or not the "expectation of privacy should be considered reasonable in the circumstances of a challenged search and seizure by state agents" (ibid.).

This relationship was considered by the Supreme Court of Canada in *R. v Tessling* (2004). In this case, the police received a tip that Mr. Tessling was growing a large amount of marijuana in his home. Since a tip alone is not enough to establish "reasonable and probable grounds" for a search warrant, the police decided to look for other evidence that Mr. Tessling was involved in a marijuana grow operation. They decided that since grow operations use a great deal of artificial light and emanate a large amount of heat, they flew over the house and took a picture of the heat energy coming from the house using a forward looking infrared (FLIR) camera in order to determine whether or not a large amount of electricity was being used. The tip, together with the FLIR picture, was used to obtain a search warrant. When the police entered Mr. Tessling's house, they found large amounts of marijuana, drug-trafficking paraphernalia, as well as some weapons.

Continued on next page

Critical Issues in Canadian Criminal Justice (*Continued*)

The case revolved around the issue of whether or not heat produced from within a residence entitled to a high level of privacy after the heat was emitted outside. Mr. Tessling was found guilty in the lower courts for possessing 120 marijuana plants and was handed an 18-month sentence. Mr. Tessling then appealed the verdict to the Ontario Court of Appeal. During the hearing, the Crown admitted that without the FLIR images, there was insufficient evidence to support a search warrant. A key question in this case was whether or not the use of the FLIR device constituted an unreasonable search within the meaning of s. 8 of the Charter of Rights and Freedoms.

The Court of Appeal ruled in favour of Mr. Tessling, holding that individuals have a reasonable expectation of privacy in the heat energy that emits from their residence and, as such, FLIR "merits a warrant because the detected heat may come from 'perfectly innocent' private activities, such as taking a bath or using lights at unusual hours" (Tibbetts 2004:A13). Their decision was based on the view that escaping heat is a product of activity occurring within a home—and that an individual's home is viewed as his castle. Furthermore, they noted a growing consensus in society that marijuana is not a particularly harmful drug, making it more palatable to exclude the evidence (Makin 2004:A12).

The Ontario Court of Appeal decision "was based on two basic premises: (1) despite the fact that the imaging takes place outside the home, FLIR technology reveals information about activities taking place within the home and that (2) the FLIR device reveals information that could not be otherwise be observed or quantified" (Boucher and Landa 2005:70). The court held that the use of FLIR was a significant intrusion into the privacy of the home and should be unlawful in the absence of a warrant. They also noted that the intrusion was "almost Orwellian in its theoretical capacity" and disproportionate to the seriousness of producing marijuana. In addition, the breach of privacy in the heat emission "was deemed by the Court of Appeal to be so serious that it could not survive the test for exclusion under section 24(2) of the Charter" (ibid.:71).

The Supreme Court of Canada, in a 7–0 decision, upheld Mr. Tessling's conviction, rejecting the concerns noted by the Ontario Court of Appeal. The Supreme Court held that Mr. Tessling did not have a reasonable expectation of privacy as the information disclosed by the FLIR camera was meaningless. The Supreme Court justices took the view that such technology was both non-intrusive in its operations and mundane in the data it is capable of producing. It is clear, to repeat, that at present no warrant could ever be granted solely on the basis of a FLIR image. According to the decision by the Supreme Court,

> . . . external patterns of heat distribution on the external surfaces of the house is not information in which the respondent had a reasonable expectation of privacy. The heat distribution, as stated, offers no insight into his private life, and reveals nothing of "biographical core of personal information." Its disclosure scarcely affects the "dignity, integrity, and autonomy" of the person whose house is subject of the FLIR image. (*R. v. Tessling* [2004], para. 63)

The Supreme Court of Canada also chose not to focus on the theoretical capacity of the technology as the Ontario Court of Appeal did, but rather on its actual capacity. According to the Supreme Court,

> . . . the reasonableness line has to be determined by looking at the information generated by existing FLIR technology, and then evaluating its impact on a reasonable privacy interest. If, as expected, the capability of FLIR and other technologies will improve and the nature and quality of the information hereafter changes, it will be a different case, and the courts will have to deal with the privacy implications at that time in light of the facts as they then exist.

In its decision, the Supreme Court identified a set of criteria it considered to be appropriate to determining whether or not privacy interests had been violated in this particular instance:

1. What was the subject matter of the FLIR image?
2. Did the respondent have a direct interest in the subject matter of the FLIR image?
3. Did the respondent have a subjective expectation of privacy in the subject matter of the FLIR image?
4. If so, was the expectation objectively reasonable? In this respect, regard must be had to:
    a. the place where the alleged "search" occurred;
    b. whether the subject matter was in public view;
    c. whether the subject matter had been abandoned;
    d. whether the information was already in the hands of third parties; if so, was it subject to an obligation of confidentiality?
    e. whether the police technique was intrusive in relation to the privacy interest;
    f. whether the use of surveillance technology was itself objectively unreasonable;

Critical Issues in Canadian Criminal Justice (*Continued*)

g. whether the FLIR heat profile exposed any intimate details of the respondent's lifestyle, or information of a biographical nature.

The impact of this decision, according to Boucher and Landa (2005:73), is that it appears that the police are free to use FLIR technology in its current format, and probably other versions of the technology, without a warrant, provided that the investigative technique does not reveal core biographical information about a person and so long as the technology does not permit the police to "see" inside a person's home. Prior to this decision, the jurisprudence on whether the police could use certain investigative technologies without a warrant was inconsistent. Certain decisions severely restricted the use of advanced technology without a warrant . . . Others took a narrower view of how far privacy interests extend, particularly in the information captured was exposed to the public at some level, and did not reveal intimate details. The latter approach is the one adopted by the Supreme Court in *Tessling* (ibid.:68).

Questions

1. Do you agree with the Supreme Court of Canada that the use of FLIR is "non-intrusive" and therefore does not violate the reasonable expectation of privacy?
2. The decision by the Supreme Court stated that since FLIR imagery does not allow the police to see inside a person's home it does not violate a person's reasonable expectation of privacy. Do you agree with this statement?
3. Do you believe that the police should be free to use FLIR and other technology whenever they choose to, with out a warrant? What restrictions, if any, will this place on an individual's guaranteed Charter rights?
4. With technology constantly evolving at a very quick pace, what implications does this have for the future of people's expectation of privacy in Canada?

SUMMARY

A key issue for our criminal justice system is the balancing of the powers of the state with the privacy rights of the police. In most cases the police have to apply for a warrant prior to a search, but there are certain situations that this is not necessary.

KEY WORDS: reasonable expectation of personal privacy, search warrant, warrantless search

What Are the Legal Powers of the Police?

Police powers are frequently invoked by the police and used to enforce to the criminal law. In some instances the police may prefer to use their discretionary powers and use informal means to deal with an issue.

KEY WORDS: discretion, situational variables, extralegal factors, community factors, investigative detention, arrest, lay an information, summons, laying an information first, laying an information second, reasonable grounds, appearance notice

Do the Police Have Discretion? (p. 212)
What Factors Affect a Police Officer's Decision to Arrest? (p. 212)
What Is Investigative Detention? (p. 212)
How Do the Police Arrest Someone? (p. 214)

Search and Seizure

One of the most fundamental rights of Canadians is the right to protection against unreasonable search and seizure. People have the right to be left alone by the government and its agents unless there are grounds for allowing such intrusion.

KEY WORDS: search, seizure, reasonable and probable grounds, particularity, exigent circumstances, searches incident to an arrest, warrantless searches, plain view, consent searches, right to legal counsel

What Are the Requirements for Search Warrants? (p. 218)
Other Types of Warrantless Searches (p. 221)
What Is the Right to Legal Counsel? (p. 222)

Interrogations

Jailhouse Interrogations (p. 227)

Interrogations are fundamental to police work, as the police may be able to gather important evidence or a confession at this time. Much controversy exists over the interrogation techniques used by the police as they may lead to wrongful convictions.

KEY WORDS: interrogations, custodial interrogations, conditioning strategy, de-emphasizing strategy, persuasion strategy, false confessions, jailhouse interrogations, jailhouse informant, approver system, Vetrovec warning

Police and the Use of Deadly Force

Deadly Force Used Against Police Officers (p. 230)
Police Misconduct (p. 231)
"Problem" Police Officers: Early Warning Systems (p. 231)
Police Accountability: The Role of Citizen Oversight (p. 233)

A defining characteristic of the police is that they possess the legitimate use of force. In some circumstances the police use excessive force, that is, they use more force than necessary to get control of suspects as well as to protect themselves and others. On occasion, the use of force by police officers leads to the use of deadly force. Police misconduct involves officers engaging in activities that are inconsistent with their legal authority. To combat police misconduct, early warning systems have been put into place. A variety of approaches have bene developed to ensure police accountability to citizens.

KEY WORDS: legitimate use of force, excessive force, deadly force, police misconduct, police deviance, occupational deviancy, selective enforcement of laws, "problem" police officers, early warning system, comprehensive personnel assessment system, performance problem system, selection phase, intervention strategies, post-intervention monitoring, police accountability, Royal Commission (inquiry), internal investigations, civilian review agency, civil liability

What Is the Importance of Police Legitimacy?

Police legitimacy is important as it impacts the public's perception not only of the police, but also of other parts of the criminal justice system.

KEY WORDS: participation, neutrality, trustworthiness of authorities, treatment with dignity and respect, procedural fairness

Critical Thinking Questions

1. Should guilty individuals go free because the police did not follow established legal procedures when they were arrested?
2. Should evidence that is obtained illegally always be excluded from trial?
3. Should the police be able to search a cell phone without a search warrant?
4. Why do the police value interrogation?
5. Where do you think that technological advances such as body-worn cameras have the greatest impact—a reduction in the complaints against the police or the reduction of police misconduct?
6. Should there be greater legal constraints placed upon police techniques such as "Mr. Big"?
7. What do you think is the best way to ensure greater police accountability for their actions?
8. Do you think the current approaches to reviewing possible police misconduct are satisfactory? Do you think there is a better system that could be implemented?

Weblinks

Some of the most controversial aspects of the criminal justice system occur when people confess to a crime they did not commit. How does this happen? For two interviews about this topic, go to YouTube and watch the following: Saul Kassin, "False Confessions" (09:11), and Fudged Forensics & Faulty Witnesses, "The Science of Justice" (1:10:06).

Court Cases

Alderton v. R. (1985), 17 C.C.C. (3d) 204.

Beare v. R. (1988), 1 S.C.R. 525, 68 C.R. (3d) 193.

Borden v. R. (1994), 92 C.C.C. (3d) 321.

Brown v. Durham Regional Police Force (1998), 131 C.C.C. (3d), 21 C.R. (5th).

Caslake v. R. (1998), 1 S.C.R. 51.

Cloutier v. Langlois (1990), 53 C.C.C. (3d) 257.

Hunter v. Southam Inc. (1984), 14 C.C.C. (3d) 97.

King v. Warickshall (1983), Eng. Rep. 234 (K.B. 1783)

New Brunswick (Minister of Health and Community Services) v. G.(J.) (1999), 3 S.C.R. 46.

R. v. Andrews (1989), 56 D.L.R. (4th) 1.

R. v. Bazinet (1986), 25 C.C.C. (3d) 273.

R. v. Black (1989), 50 C.C.C. (3d) 1.

R. v. Brooks (2000), 1 S.C.R. 270.

R. v. Broyles (1991), 3 S.C.R. 595.

R. v. Brydges (1990), 53 C.C.C. (3d) 330.

R. v. Bryntwick (2002), O.J. No. 3618 (Ont. S.C.J.).

R. v. Charles (1987), 36 C.C.C. (3d) 286.

R. v. Collins (1987), 1 S.C.R. 265.

R. v. Deane (1997), O.J. No. 3057 (Prov. Ct.) (Q.L.).

R. v. Ducharme (1990), Unreported, British Columbia Court of Appeal.

R. v. Evans (1996), 1 S.C.R. 8.

R. v. Fearon (2014), S.C.C 77.

R. v. Feeney (1997), 2 S.C.R. 117.

R. v. Fitt (1996), 267 S.C.C.

R. v. Godoy (1997), 7 C.R. (5th) 216.

R. v. Golub (1997), 34 O.R. (3d) 743.

R. v. Harris (1987), 57 C.R. (3d) 356.

R. v. Hart (2014), 2 S.C.R. 544.

R. v. Hebert (1990), 2 S.C.R. 151.

R. v. Heisler (1984), 11 C.C.C. (3d) 97.

R. v. Joey Smith (1989), 50 C.C.C. (3d) 97.

R. v. Lim (1990), 1 C.R.R. (2d) 136 (Ont. H.C.J.) 145.

R. v. Lines (1993), O.J. No. 3248 (Gen. Div.).

R. v. Mack (1988), 44 C.C.C. (3d) 513.
R. v. Mellenthin (1992), 3 S.C.R. 615.
R. v. Moran (1987), 21 O.A.C. 257 (C.A.).
R. v. Oickle (2000), 36 C.R. (5th).
R. v. Plant (1993), 3 S.C.R. 281.
R. v. Rickett (1975), 28 C.C.C. (2d) 297.
R. v. Simmons (1988), 297 S.C.C.
R. v. Sinclair (2010) 2 S.C.R. 310.
R. v. Singh (1983), 8 C.C.C. (3d) 38.
R. v. Singh (2007), 3 S.C.R. 405.
R. v. Stillman (1997), 97 C.C.C. (3d) 97.
R. v. Storey (1990), 53 C.C.C. (3d) 316.
R. v. Tessling (2004), 3 S.C.R. 432.
R. v. Turpin (1989), 48 C.C.C. (3d) 8.
R. v. Vetrovec (1982), 1 S.C.R. 811.
R. v. Vu (2013), 3 S.C.R. 657.
R. v. Wills (1992), 70 C.C.C. (3d) 529.
R. v. Wise (1992), 253 S.C.C.
Rothman v. The Queen (1981), 59 C.C.C.
Stillman v. R. (1997), 113 C.C.C. (3d) 321.

Suggested Readings

Boucher, S. and K. Landa. 2005. *Understanding Section 8: Search, Seizure, and the Canadian Constitution*. Toronto: Irwin Law.

Horner, J.J. 2007. *Canadian Law and the Canadian Legal System*. Toronto: Pearson.

Keenan, K. and J. Brockman. 2010. *Mr. Big: Exposing Undercover Operations in Canada*. Fernwood: Halifax.

Marin, R. 1997. *Policing in Canada: Issues for the 21st Century*. Toronto: Carswell.

Mewett, A.W. and S. Nakatsuru. 2000. *An Introduction to the Criminal Process in Canada*. 4th ed. Toronto: Thomson Canada.

Tanovich, D. 2006. *The Colour of Justice: Policing Race in Canada*. Toronto: Irwin Law.

References

Abell, J. and E. Sheehy (eds.). 1993. *Criminal Law and Procedure: Cases, Context, Critique*. North York, ON: Captus Press.

Bailey, J. 2008. "Framed by Section 8: Constitutional Protection of Privacy in Canada." *Canadian Journal of Criminology and Criminal Justice*: 279–306.

Barker, T. and D. Carter. 1986. *Police Deviance*. Cincinnati, OH: Anderson.

Bilodeau, S. 2001–02. "Investigative Detention." *LawNow* 26:42–43.

Borovoy, A. Alan. 2000. "Who Will Police the Police?" *National Post*, June 6, p. A9.

Boucher, S. and K. Landa. 2005. *Understanding Section 8: Search, Seizure, and the Canadian Constitution*. Toronto: Irwin Law.

Bowal, P. and K. Bowal. 2011. "Whatever Happened to . . . Feeney?" *LawNow* 35:31–33.

Brannigan, A. 1984. *Crimes, Courts, and Corrections: An Introduction to Crime and Social Control in Canada.* Toronto: Holt, Rinehart, and Winston.

Brown, L. and C. Brown. 1978. *An Unauthorized History of the RCMP*, 2nd ed. Toronto: Lewis and Samuel.

Commission on Proceedings Involving Guy Paul Morin. 1998. Toronto: Ontario Ministry of the Attorney General.

Coughlan, S. 1998. "Developments in Criminal Procedure: The 1996–97 Term." *Supreme Court Law Review* (2d):285.

Dunn, S. 2010. *Police Officers Murdered in the Line of Duty.* Ottawa: Canadian Centre for Justice Statistics.

Editorial. 2012. "Reforming Public Complaints Against the RCMP." *The Criminal Law Quarterly*, 2&3:163–66.

Farrar, W. 2013. *Self-Awareness to Being Watched and Socially Desirable Behaviour: A Field Experiment on the Effect of Body-Worn Cameras and Police Use-of-Force.* Washington, DC: Police Foundation.

Finn, P. 2000. *Citizen Review of Police: Approach and Implementation.* Washington, DC: Government Printing Office.

Fyfe, J. 1988. "Police Use of Deadly Force: Research and Reform." *Justice Quarterly* 5:165–205.

Gatehouse, J. and C. Eby. 2000. "Rape Victim and Family Sue Toronto Police Force for $4.5 Million." *National Post*, October 12, p. A9.

Goldstein, H. 1977. *Policing a Free Society.* Cambridge, MA: Ballinger.

Goodall, M. 2007. *Guidance for the Police Use of Body-Worn Video Devices.* London: Home Office.

Hagan, J. 1977. *The Disreputable Pleasures.* Toronto: McGraw-Hill Ryerson.

Hiebert, J.L. 2002. *Charter Rights: What Is Parliament's Role?* Montreal and Kingston: McGill-Queen's University Press.

Hutchinson, B. 2004. "RCMP Turns to 'Mr. Big' to Nab Criminals." *National Post*, December 18:RB1–RB2.

Inquiry Regarding Thomas Sophonow. 2001. Winnipeg: Government of Manitoba.

Jamieson, S. 1973. *Industrial Relations*, 2nd ed. Toronto: Macmillan.

Joyce, G. 2000. "Prison Snitches in Spotlight." *Winnipeg Free Press*, June 18, B2.

Kassin, S.M. 2008. "False Confessions: Causes, Consequences, and Implications for Reform." *Current Directions in Psychological Science* 17:249–53.

Kassin, S.M. 1997. "The Psychology of Confession Evidence." *American Psychologist* 52:221–23.

Kassin, S.M. and L.S. Wrightsman. 1985. "Confession Evidence." *In The Psychology of Evidence and Trial Procedure*, edited by S.M. Kassin and L.S. Wrightsman. New York: Hemisphere.

Keenan, K. and J. Brockman. 2010. *Mr. Big: Exposing Undercover Operations in Canada.* Fernwood: Halifax.

Leo, R.A. 1996. "The Impact of Miranda Revisited." *Journal of Criminal Law and Criminology* 86 (Spring):621–92.

Leo, R.A. 1992. "From Coercion to Deception: The Changing Nature of the Police Interrogation in America." *Crime, Law and Social Change* 18:35–39.

Lersch, K. and S.T. Mieczkowski. 1996. "Who Are the Problem Prone Police? An Analysis of Citizen Complaints." *American Journal of Police* 15:23–42.

Lundman, R. 1980. *Police and Policing: An Introduction*. New York: Holt, Rinehart, and Winston.

Makin, K. 2009. "Jailhouse Informants Virtually Phased Out." *The Globe and Mail*, April 14, p. A5.

Makin, K. 2004. "Top Court Frees Police to Use Infrared Devices." *The Globe and Mail*, October 30, p. A12.

Makin, K. 1998. "Police Allowed to Enter If 911 Called, Top Court Says." *The Globe and Mail*, December 4, p. A6.

Makin, K. 1992. *Redrum the Innocent*. Toronto: Penguin.

Martin, D. 1993. "Organizing for Change: A Community Law Response to Police Misconduct." *Hastings Women's Law Journal* 4:131–74.

Mastrofski, S. 2004. "Controlling Street-Level Police Discretion." *Annals* 593:100–18.

Mazerolle, L., E. Antrobus, S. Bennett, and T. Tyler. 2013. "Shaping Citizen Perceptions of Police Legitimacy: A Randomized Field Trial of Procedural Justice." *Criminology* 51:33–63.

McConville, M. and J. Baldwin. 1982. "The Role of Interrogation in Crime Discovery and Conviction." *British Journal of Criminology* 22:165–75.

McGahan, P. 1984. *Police Images of a City*. New York: Peter Lang.

Mewett, A.W. and S. Nakatsuru. 2000. *An Introduction to the Criminal Process in Canada*, 4th ed. Scarborough, ON: Carswell.

Nicol, J.A. 2002. "'Stop in the Name of the Law': Investigative Detention." *Canadian Criminal Law Review* 7(2):223–52.

Nowlin, C. 2004. "Excluding the Post-Offence Undercover Operation from Evidence: 'Warts and All.'" *Canadian Criminal Law Review* 8:382–414.

Penney, S. 2004. "What's Wrong with Self-Incrimination? The Wayward Path of Self-Incrimination in the Post-Charter Era Part II: Self-Incrimination in Police Investigations." *Criminal Law Quarterly* 48:280–336.

Roach, K. 1999. *Due Process and Victims' Rights: The New Law and Politics of Criminal Justice*. Toronto: University of Toronto Press.

Salhany, R.E. 1986. *Arrest, Seizure, and Interrogation*, 3rd ed. Toronto: Carswell.

Saulny, S. 2002. "Why Confess to What You Didn't Do?" *New York Times*, December 8, p. 5.

Scheck, B., P. Neufeld, and J. Dwyer. 2000. *Actual Innocence: Five Days to Execution, and Other Dispatches from the Wrongfully Convicted*. New York: Doubleday.

Sherman, L.W. 1974. *Police Corruption: A Sociological Perspective*. Garden City, NY: Doubleday.

Smith, S.M., V. Stinson, and M. W. Patry. 2009. "Using the 'Mr. Big' Technique to Elicit Confessions: Successful Innovation or Dangerous Development in the Canadian Legal System?" *Psychology, Public Policy, and Law* 15:168–93.

Stansfield, R.T. 2000. "Use of Force by and against Canadian Police." Pp. 70–76 in *Criminal Justice in Canada: A Reader*, edited by J.V. Roberts. Toronto: Harcourt Brace and Company Canada.

Stansfield, R.T. 1996. *Issues in Policing: A Canadian Perspective*. Toronto: Thompson Educational Publishing.

Tibbetts, J. 2004. "Infrared Cameras No Threat to Privacy." *Winnipeg Free Press*, October 30.

Tyler, T. 1990. *Why People Obey the Law*. New Haven, CT: Yale University Press.

U.S. Commission on Civil Rights. 1981. *Who Is Guarding the Guardians?* Washington, DC: U.S. Commission on Civil Rights.

Vrij, A. 1998. "Interviewing Suspects." Pp. 124–46 in *Psychology and Law: Truthfulness, Accuracy, and Credibility*, edited by A. Memon, A. Vrij, and R. Bull. London: McGraw-Hill.

Walker, S. 2001. *Police Accountability: The Role of Citizen Oversight*. Belmont, CA: Wadsworth.

Wigmore, J.H. 1970. *Evidence* (Vol. 3). (Revised by J.H. Chadbourn). Boston: Little, Brown.

Williams, J.W. 2000. "Interrogating Justice: A Critical Analysis of the Police Interrogation and Its Role in the Criminal Justice System." *Canadian Journal of Criminology*, April:209–40.

Winograde, J. 1990. "Jailhouse Informants and the Need for Judicial Use Immunity in Habeas Corpus Proceedings." *California Law Review* 78.

Zimmerman, C. 1994. "Toward a New Vision of Informants: A History of Abuses and Suggestions for Reform." *Hastings Constitutional Law Quarterly* 22.

CHAPTER

8

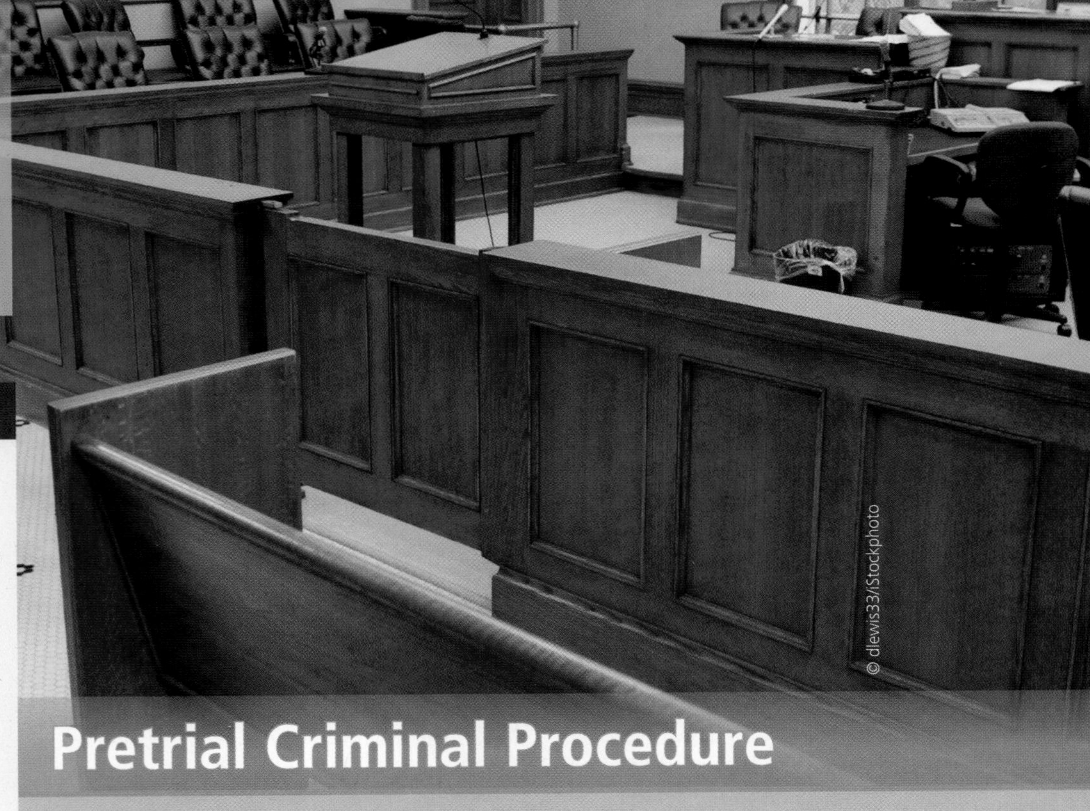

Pretrial Criminal Procedure

Learning Objectives

After completing this chapter, you should be able to:

- Differentiate among the ways in which an accused can be compelled to appear in court.
- Understand the difference between interim release and pretrial custody.
- Understand the importance of being granted bail.
- Recognize the role of legal aid and distinguish among the different types of legal aid.
- Understand the importance of the prosecutorial screening process.
- Understand the role and importance of disclosure.
- Distinguish among the different types of pleas.
- Recognize the importance of plea bargaining.
- Understand the process of selecting a jury.

When a justice receives an information, it is a "momentous occasion" as a person goes from being a suspect to being accused of a crime, as from this time on the criminal justice system will "be focused on proving the guilt of one particular person" (Coughlan 2008:150). Once this happens, the rules and principles of criminal procedure have to be followed. This involves a balance between the interests of the state and the rights of the accused. As discussed in Chapter 1, competing values between crime control and due process exist within the criminal justice process—that is, between the interest of the state to protect the security of its members and the interests of these people to liberty and privacy. The interests of victims may also be a significant factor in any case, and if so, these tend to favour the crime control approach (Roach 1999).

But what criteria are used to decide whether or not to charge a suspect? One of the most important decisions is to charge someone with a criminal offence. But how is this decision made? It typically is based on the **strength of the case**, which refers to the amount of evidence (e.g., physical evidence and eyewitnesses) available and that will be used to **prove guilt beyond a reasonable doubt**. Other influences on the decision to charge include what is referred to as the **social structure of the case**. These are (1) the seriousness of the offence, (2) the accountability of the offender, and (3) the organizational pressure to "win" cases. In any decision to charge, a number of questions about the social structure of the case have to be answered, including the characteristics of the alleged victim and the accused, whether or not the victim and accused were acquainted, and who the witnesses are for each side (Black 1989:24). This means that only "strong" or "winnable" cases may be pursued (Frohmann 1991).

It is important to realize that since each case can vary from all others, there can be significant amounts of discretion in deciding whether or not to charge an individual and what to charge them with. In other words, there may be attempts to "individualize justice" (see the section "What Happens during Prosecutorial Screening?"). There may be a decision not to prosecute the accused and instead send them to a diversion program. Regardless of the approach taken in any given case, when an accused is prosecuted, convicted, or sentenced, for justice to be achieved it has to be delivered "in accordance with rules and principles that express values of legality, legitimacy, and fairness" (Coughlan 2008:6).

Compelling Appearance, Interim Release, and Pretrial Detention

An individual who has just been arrested without a warrant may be taken to the police station, where the police record the criminal charges and obtain other information relevant to the case. This process is commonly referred to as **lodging a complaint**, and it usually includes a description of the suspect and, if necessary, circumstances relating to the offence. What actually happens to the accused next depends on the charge. If the charge is for a lesser offence, in all likelihood the accused will be released immediately by the officer in charge; after this, the police will lay an information and have a summons issued against the accused. If the accused lives more than 200 kilometres away or is not a resident of the province, that person may be required to deposit a sum of not more than $500. This is standard operating procedure in Canada, and it expedites the processing of such cases and saves the police from having to search for the accused to serve an arrest warrant or summons. The purpose of this process is to allow as many accused as possible to leave the police station as soon as possible (s. 497 of the Criminal Code).

Since often there has been no judicial intervention in these cases (e.g., the police have arrested the accused while the crime was in progress), it is important for the police to swear an information and present it to a justice of the peace as soon as possible. If an arrest warrant has been issued after a justice of the peace signs an information, it may contain an "**endorsement**" authorizing the officer in charge at the police station to release the accused on similar grounds to those for being arrested without a warrant. Justices hold discretionary powers (s. 507 of the Criminal Code) as they have to consider whether it is necessary to take a specific action or require an accused to answer the charges.

Those charged with indictable offences punishable by more than five years' imprisonment, those charged who the police believe will not appear at their trial, and those arrested with an arrest warrant that has not been endorsed by a justice of the peace that would allow the accused to be released are usually processed at the police station. This processing may involve fingerprinting and photographing the accused.

As we saw in the previous chapter, individuals detained may be released by a police officer by a summons or on an appearance notice. This is the usually the case for **s. 553 offences**. If a person is arrested without a warrant and taken into custody, they will be brought before the officer in charge or another peace officer. These individuals may decide to release the individual (s. 498 of the Criminal Code). What happens to people who are not released by the officer in charge at a police station? The Criminal Code (s. 503) requires that all such individuals be brought before a justice of the peace:

- when a justice of the peace is available within a period of 24 hours after the arrest, without unreasonable delay, and, in any event, within that 24-hour period; and
- when a justice of the peace is not available within a 24-hour period, as soon as possible.

The purpose of the above provisions is to ensure that individuals remain in custody for as short a time as possible.

If the accused is charged with a **s. 469 offence**—murder, for example—a Superior Court justice decides whether the accused will be placed in a detention facility. Here, a **reverse onus** applies—that is, it is up to the accused to show why they should be released. Among the reasons for detention are these:

- The accused is charged with an indictable offence while already on judicial interim release or is in the process of appealing another indictable offence.
- The accused commits an indictable offence but is not a resident of Canada.
- The accused allegedly has broken a previous interim release order.
- The accused has committed or conspired to commit an offence under ss. 4 and 5 of the Controlled Drugs and Substances Act (i.e., trafficking, exporting, or importing).

The prosecutor almost always has to **show cause**—that is, demonstrate that detaining the accused is justified (s. 515 of the Criminal Code). Our criminal justice system presumes that the accused is innocent and should

THE CANADIAN PRESS/Ben Lemphers

An ever-increasing number of individuals charged with a criminal offence are being held in remand centres across Canada prior to their trials.

Investigating: Case Processing

There are many paths that a criminal trial can take as it makes its way through adult criminal court in Canada. These variations in case processing depend on several factors including the seriousness of the offences being heard, and the elections made by the Crown and the accused. For most cases, the trial process in adult provincial/territorial criminal courts will include some or all of the elements listed below.

- *First Appearance:* The first appearance in court is usually a bail hearing in a provincial court, where the court must determine if the accused should be released pending trial. Most offences require the Crown to show that the accused is either a danger to the community or a risk to flee prosecution before a remand order is given. However, several offences are classified as reverse onus offences, where the accused must show cause why his detention is not justified—Criminal Code s. 515(6).
- *Crown Elections:* The Crown is eligible to elect the type of proceeding for hybrid offences, which are also known as "dual procedure" offences. The defining Criminal Code sections for hybrid offences specify that the Crown may try the case in one of two ways: (1) as a summary conviction offence—the least serious offence type, which also carries a lower maximum penalty; or (2) as the more serious indictable offence. If the Crown elects to try the case as an indictable offence, the accused faces the possibility of a prison sentence that, depending on the offence, ranges between no minimum sentence to life in prison.
- *Defence Elections:* Where permitted under the Criminal Code, the accused may elect to be tried in adult provincial/territorial criminal court or in Superior Court—with or without a jury. If the accused elects to be tried in Superior Court, a preliminary inquiry may be held. (See Preliminary Hearings below.) The defence is not eligible to elect the mode of trial for summary conviction offences, or offences identified under Criminal Code ss. 469 or 553. These Criminal Code sections identify offences that are the absolute jurisdiction of a single court level, Superior Court and provincial/territorial court, respectively.
- *Preliminary Hearings:* The purpose of the preliminary inquiry process is to determine if there is sufficient evidence in the case to proceed to trial in a higher court level, Superior Court. The provincial court judge will commit the case for trial in Superior Court if the evidence is compelling and there is a reasonable expectation of a judgment against the accused. However, if the evidence is not convincing, the judge must stop the proceedings against the accused—and the court finding will be recorded as "discharged at preliminary."
- The preliminary inquiry process is a way for the accused to review all of the Crown's evidence before proceeding to the higher court. The defence is permitted to question all of the Crown witnesses and to review any prosecution exhibits related to the charges, which helps the accused's counsel prepare for trial.
- *Fitness Hearings:* When the accused's mental health is brought into question, the court will order a psychiatric examination. In the fitness hearing that results, the accused will be found fit for trial or remanded in custody until the Lieutenant Governor of the province permits release.
- *Trial:* The trial begins with the accused entering a plea of guilty, guilty of a lesser charge, not guilty, or special plea (i.e., previous conviction, previous acquittal, or pardon—Criminal Code s. 607). In some cases, the accused may refuse to enter a plea, and the court will enter a plea of not guilty on behalf of the accused. A guilty plea will usually result in an immediate conviction, but the court may also refuse to accept a guilty plea if that plea is given with conditions, or if the court feels that the accused does not understand that the plea is an admission of guilt.

A plea of not guilty will result in a trial, where the evidence against the accused is heard and the court will make a judgment on that evidence. The final disposition, or decision, of the court will be either (1) guilty of the offence charged, (2) guilty of an included offence, (3) not guilty of the charged offence, or (4) not guilty on account of insanity. The court may sentence the accused immediately following a finding of guilt; however, the court may also delay the sentencing to a later date so that all relevant factors can be considered prior to imposing a sentence on the accused.

Source: Julian V. Roberts and Craig Grimes, "Adult Criminal Court Statistics, 1998/99." *Juristat*, Vol. 20, No. 1 (March 2000), Statistics Canada Catalogue no. 85-002, p. 6. Reproduced and distributed on an "as is" basis with the permission of Statistics Canada.

be released, and released without conditions, unless the Crown can show that it is necessary to hold that person. In Canada, there is what is referred to as a **ladder approach** to bail; that is, the prosecution must justify greater degrees of restrictions on the accused (s. 515[2] of the Criminal Code). A number of conditions may be imposed when the accused is released—for example, an obligation to report to a police officer. The prosecutor may want the accused to enter into some form of recognizance. Any accused released may be requested to deposit an amount of money with the court. A cash deposit is preferred, since the accused may disappear after paying.

Our criminal justice system prefers that a **surety** (an individual who will monitor the accused until the trial) be found who will agree to be indebted to the court for a specified amount of money if the accused does not appear on the appointed date. The surety may have to provide a cash deposit if the accused fails to appear.

Alternatively, the accused may be requested to deposit an amount of money with the court. Both a surety and a cash deposit may be required if the accused is not a resident of the province or lives more than 200 kilometres away from where he or she is being held. Of course, the accused may be detained if the justice of the peace feels it is necessary, but the reasons must be recorded.

The continued detention of the accused in custody can be justified only on one or more of the following conditions (s. 515[10] of the Criminal Code):

- Where the detention is necessary to ensure his or her attendance in court in order to be dealt with according to law.
- Where the detention is necessary for the protection or safety of the public, having regard to all the circumstances, including any substantial likelihood that the accused will, if released from custody, commit a criminal offence or interfere with the administration of justice.
- On any other just cause being shown and without limiting the generality of the foregoing, where the detention is necessary in order to maintain confidence in the administration of justice, having regard to all the circumstances, including the apparent strength of the prosecution's case, the gravity of the offence, the circumstances surrounding its commission, and the potential for a lengthy term of imprisonment.

Often the suspect will be released only after agreeing to certain conditions set by the court—for example, to reside at a particular residence or not to communicate with certain witnesses (s. 515[2] of the Criminal Code).

Most bail hearings are quick. The officer in charge of the investigation makes a recommendation to the Crown prosecutor concerning whether the accused should be released and, if so, whether any conditions should be placed on the release order. Depending on the seriousness of the charge, the background of the offender, and/or the attitude and circumstances of the accused, the bail hearing may take longer. Sometimes it develops into a formal hearing. When there is a debate at a bail hearing about releasing the accused, it typically involves issues relating to the conditions of release rather than whether or not the accused should be released.

The First Appearance

Following the laying of charges, defendants make their first appearance in court. At this time, the charges are read to the defendant. A number of other decisions may occur at this stage, including decisions about bail and the appointment of legal aid lawyers.

What Is Bail and Does It Achieve Justice?

The bail hearing can be "the most important step for an accused person in the criminal process" (Linden, in Friedland 2004:98). In the 1960s, a study of bail discovered that summonses were not widely used in Canada: in excess of 90 percent of all individuals were arrested instead of being summoned, and almost all (85 percent) of those arrested were held in custody prior to their first court appearance; 24 percent of those who had a court case were not found guilty (Friedland 1965). If someone was released on bail, it was because they were able to pay the amount of money (or property) set by the justice to guarantee that they would appear at their trial. Friedland concluded that the then-practice of releasing individuals was "ineffective, inequitable, and inconsistent . . ." (ibid.:172).

At that time, efforts were being made in the United States to rectify this same issue. The pivotal study that led to changes there was known as the Manhattan Bail Project, conducted in New York City in the early 1960s. The Vera Institute, a private, non-profit research organization dedicated to improving the criminal justice system, designed an experimental pretrial release program that studied individuals who could not afford bail to see how

CP PHOTO/Aaron Harris

Every day, police vans enter the gated entrance to Toronto's Old City Hall, taking accused persons to their bail hearings.

many would appear in court for their trials after being released back into the community following their initial court appearance. The researchers found that the appearance rate of those released on their own recognizance was consistently the same as or better than the rate of those released on monetary bail. As a result of these findings, release-on-recognizance programs were developed, and did much to change the nature of the bail process across North America.

This project also led to the introduction of different types of pretrial release. One such innovation became known as **station house release**, which involves issuing a suspect a citation to appear in court at a later date and thus bypasses the costly exercise of pretrial detention. Overall, this experiment found that most suspects released back into the community appeared in court on the duly appointed date. As a result of these studies, "the prevailing view became that release should be available, regardless of financial circumstances, unless overwhelming factors preclude it" (Anderson and Newman 1993:216).

In Canada, Parliament changed the operation of bail system in 1972 when the Bail Reform Act was passed. This Act established the system of interim release. As amended four years later, the Act is the basis for bail in Canada today. Its creation was largely the result of the Ouimet Committee, which recommended that suspects not be placed in detention unless it was thought to be the only means to ensure that the accused would appear in court.

The Bail Reform Act prefers that most offenders be released into the community pending trial. This legislation instructs police officers to issue an appearance notice to the accused rather than make an arrest unless officers feel that the public would be placed in jeopardy or the accused has committed a serious indictable offence. In addition, for most offences, the officer in charge of the lockup must release the person charged and compel that person to appear in court by a summons, by promise to appear, or on his or her own **recognizance**. In essence, the Act attempts to make the system more just by making cash bail "an exceptional condition, almost a last resort" (Friedland 2012:319). Due to increases in the remand population (see *Critical Issues in Criminal Justice* at the end of this chapter), some provinces have introduced a number of alternatives, including how the bail system is administered (see *Criminal Justice Insight*).

There have been a number of criticisms directed at how the Bail Reform Act is practised across Canada. Recent research in Ontario found that 50 percent of all accused persons are released prior to their first court appearance, but that number is lower than before (Webster et al. 2009). Hamilton and Sinclair (1991) reported that Aboriginal people accused of a crime in Manitoba were more likely to be denied bail than non-Aboriginal people and that they also spent longer periods of time in pretrial detention. The Ontario Commission on Systemic Racism in the Ontario Criminal Justice System found that the accused who were Black were more likely to be remanded to custody than non-Blacks. And for those who do receive bail, there are now more conditions attached than before (John Howard Society of Ontario 2013:5).

Some have recognized difficulties within the practice of the bail system itself. Sometimes the quality of information placed before the court in a bail hearing is insufficient in order for an in-depth consideration of risk of further violence. Even if the court orders the alleged offender to sign a peace bond, they may still violate the order and contact the victim at a later date, with tragic results. This system, according to some, "appears too cursory, too prone to error, delay and information falling through the cracks" ("Tragedies Are . . ." 2008:A12).

Criminal Justice Insight

Increases in the Remand Population: Alternatives and Responses

As an alternative to remand, some provinces/territories consider bail supervision for adults and/or youth awaiting trial. Bail supervision is a recognizance order (promise to appear) that incorporates supervision of the accused person in the community (e.g., reporting to a probation officer, respecting curfew hours).

Table 8.1 presents 2008/2009 information on the number of annual admissions and average daily counts of adults on bail supervision for those provinces and territories where information was available.

In response to the growing remand population, some provinces/territories have hired additional prosecutors, paralegals, and clerical staff in order to increase the efficiency of the court process (e.g., Government of Saskatchewan 2010; Manitoba Department of Justice 2010). As well, some courts now use videoconferencing for routine hearings in order to expedite bail hearings and to reduce the costs associated with transporting accused persons to and from courthouses (e.g., Government of Alberta 2007; Government of Ontario 2010; Provincial Court of Manitoba 2005; Government of Saskatchewan 2010). Many jurisdictions have also increased the number of custodial spaces either by constructing new facilities or by expanding existing ones (e.g., Government of Alberta 2007; Government of British Columbia 2009; Government of Saskatchewan 2010).

Note: While Newfoundland and Labrador, Quebec, Ontario, Manitoba, Saskatchewan, Alberta, British Columbia, and Yukon offer bail supervision as an alternative to remand, data are available only for Saskatchewan, British Columbia, and Yukon.

Source: L. Porter and D. Calverly, "Trends in the use of remand in Canada." *Juristat* (May 27, 2011), Statistics Canada Catalogue no. 85-002-X, p. 12, http://www.statcan.gc.ca/pub/85-002-x/2011001/article/11440-eng.pdf. Reproduced and distributed on an "as is" basis with the permission of Statistics Canada.

TABLE 8.1 Admissions and Average Daily Count of Adults on Bail Supervision, by Selected Province and Territory, 2008/2009

Province or Territory	Number of Admissions	Average Daily Count
Saskatchewan	1,773	881
British Columbia	14,880	8,740
Yukon	537	219

Source: Adult Correctional Services Survey and Adult Key Indicator Report, found in L. Porter and D. Calverly, "Trends in the use of remand in Canada." *Juristat* (May 27, 2011), Statistics Canada Catalogue no. 85-002-X, p. 12, http://www.statcan.gc.ca/pub/85-002-x/2011001/article/11440-eng.pdf. Reproduced and distributed on an "as is" basis with the permission of Statistics Canada.

What Is Legal Aid and Does It Achieve Justice?

Section 10(b) of the Charter of Rights and Freedoms states that all Canadians have the "right to retain counsel without delay" for criminal cases. This right may involve the use of **legal aid** lawyers for those who cannot afford to retain private counsel and who earn under a certain income. In the earliest days of our criminal justice system, defence lawyers played an important role in the protection of the accused by providing free (**pro bono**) legal aid as an expression of social responsibility. In recent decades, however, formal legal aid programs have been developed, with the result that legal aid systems across Canada are "viewed both as an aspect of social welfare and an important component of an effective justice system" (Johnstone and Thomas 1998:2).

Since the introduction of the Charter of Rights and Freedoms, the role of legal aid has changed. In *R. v. Manninen* (1987), the accused person had the impression that the right to legal counsel was based on his ability to afford this service. Because that view was not corrected by the police, the Supreme Court held that the accused had not been able to use his right to counsel. It followed that s. 10(b) of the Charter had been violated. Today, s. 10(b) has been judicially interpreted to mean that any person arrested must be informed by the police of the existence and availability of duty counsel and legal aid in the jurisdiction (*R. v. Brydges* [1990]). In *Brydges* (at 43), the Supreme Court held that s. 10(b) imposed two duties on the police. "First, the police must give the accused or detained person a reasonable opportunity to exercise the right to retain and instruct counsel," and second, "the police must refrain from questioning or attempting to elicit information from the detainee until the detainee has had that reasonable opportunity." This right was expanded in *R. v. Pozniak* (1994), when the Supreme Court ruled that when a toll-free number had been established by local or provincial authorities, the police had to inform the detained individual that it could be used to contact duty counsel or a legal aid lawyer.

In recent years, Charter decisions have extended the use of legal aid in our criminal justice system. In *R. v. Prosper* (1994), the Supreme Court decided on the issue of whether or not s. 10(b) of the Charter imposed a substantive constitutional obligation on governments to provide free and immediate legal counsel to individuals detained by the authorities. The Supreme Court ruled unanimously that this obligation did not exist. Its decision was based on the reasoning that the original drafters of s. 10(b) of the Charter had turned down the idea of free duty counsel as part of the protections given to detainees and that "such an obligation would almost certainly interfere with governments' allocation of limited resources by requiring them to expend public funds on the provision of a service" (*R. v. Prosper* [1994], at 267).

Some, however, consider legal aid such an important part of our criminal justice system they feel its provision should become a Charter right. The approach established in *Prosper* was modified somewhat in 1999 when the Supreme Court held that government-funded legal counsel must be provided, although only in limited circumstances in order to ensure that s. 7 and the principles of fundamental justice are met. In *New Brunswick v. G.(J.)* (1999), the Supreme Court held that a constitutional obligation exists when a province removes a child from the family home and a parent seeks to challenge the court order. While the ruling in this case in effect extended s. 7 beyond the criminal law to family law and custody hearings, the justices made it clear that this obligation on provincial authorities existed only to ensure a fair trial under s. 7 when the parents lacked the financial and mental capacity to serve as their own counsel.

Legal aid offices are typically located in central urban locations and close to law courts.

Others argue that this right should be extended in certain criminal cases, so that a judge can order legal aid for an accused who will serve time in a federal or provincial correctional facility if convicted. In addition to rights granted to the accused during their initial appearance in the Canadian criminal justice system, the rights of the defendant are recognized as well, including the right to a legal aid lawyer in certain conditions—for example, when an appeal of the case is heard or during parole revocation hearings. The right to legal aid continues to be expanded. In September 1999, the Supreme Court of Canada ruled that prisoners who face solitary confinement have a right to legal aid (Makin 1999).

Prior to a system of legal aid being introduced, defendants who could not afford their own lawyers were susceptible to local provisions for free legal representation. This system was obviously problematic, with many critics. The first province to provide a legal aid system was Ontario, in 1967. The last was Yukon, in 1979. In 1973, the federal government began providing funds to provincial legal aid programs; to receive funding, a program had to offer criminal law services when an accused was charged with an indictable offence or when the accused faced the loss of liberty or livelihood in a summary conviction offence. Governments are the major source of revenue for legal aid plans. The cost of providing criminal legal aid services was $644 million in 2008–09; in 2012–13 it had increased to $770 million (see Figure 8.1). The federal government has reduced its contribution over the years, with the result that provincial governments have had to pay more of the costs. In 2010–11, the federal government contributed $112 million to the 13 provincial/territorial legal aid plans, the same amount as the previous year, but, after factoring in inflation, this amount was less than the previous year.

Financial cutbacks to legal aid (which mostly occurred in the mid-to-late 1990s) have had a strong negative impact. Legal aid is now a "directionless program that is hampered by federal funding cuts, patchwork of services from province to province and no national standards to ensure poor people have access to justice" and that it "is

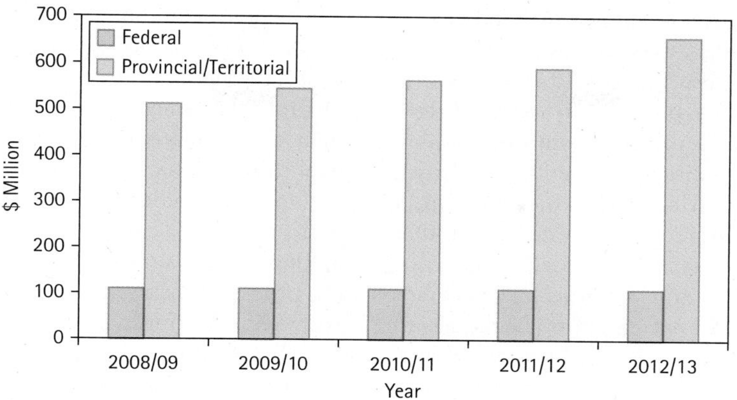

FIGURE 8.1 Federal, Provincial, and Territorial Contributions to Legal Aid, 2008/09 to 2012/13

Sources: Statistics Canada. Table 258-0006 Provincial and territorial government contributions to legal aid plans, CANSIM, http://www5.statcan.gc.ca/cansim/a26?lang=eng&id=2580006; and Statistics Canada. Table 258-0005 Federal government contributions to provinces and territories for legal aid, CANSIM, http://www5.statcan.gc.ca/cansim/a26?lang=eng&id=2580005. Reproduced and distributed on an "as is" basis with the permission of Statistics Canada.

only given to Canada's poorest of the poor—and only when they face jail terms if convicted" (Tibbetts 2002). Yet legal aid is considered such an important component of ensuring access to justice for the poor that a legal aid expert at the Canadian Bar Association commented that the federal government should establish minimum legal aid standards. And the Chief Justice of the Supreme Court of Canada, Chief Justice Beverley McLachlin, stated in 2002 that governments should treat legal aid as an essential service. This idea of legal aid as an essential service was raised again in 2011, when a public commission into legal aid (Foundation for Change) in British Columbia released its report. According to the report, the continuing failure to increase funding for legal aid "is failing needy individuals and families, the justice system, and our communities" and that it "should be fully funded as an essential public service" (Doust 2011:7). These statements reflect the belief that all Canadians have the right to a fair trial, and that even in times of government restraint, certain basic duties are unavoidable (Davison 2000:16). In 2012–13, there were over 276,000 applications for adult criminal legal aid across Canada. Approximately 47 percent of these applications were approved (see Figure 8.2).

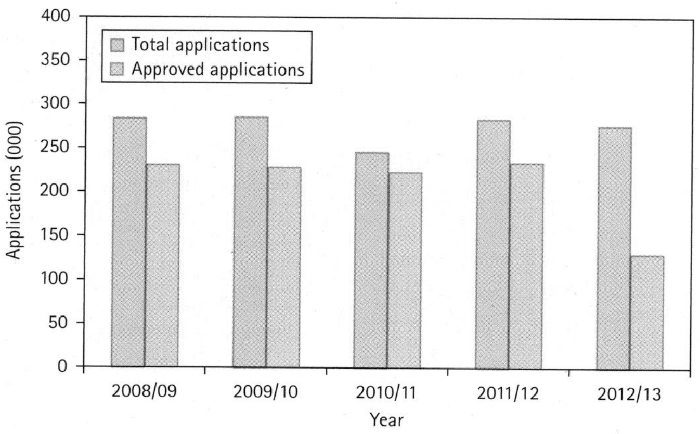

FIGURE 8.2 Criminal Legal Aid Applications and Approved Applications, 2008/09 to 2012/13

Source: Statistics Canada. Table 258-0010 Approved legal aid applications, by staff and private lawyers and type of matter, CANSIM, http://www5.statcan.gc.ca/cansim/a26?lang=eng&id=2580010; and Statistics Canada. Table 258-0009—Legal aid applications, by type of matter, CANSIM, http://www5.statcan.gc.ca/cansim/a26?lang=eng&id=2580009. Reproduced and distributed on an "as is" basis with the permission of Statistics Canada.

Historically, three models for providing legal aid for those who qualify have been used in Canada: **judicare**, the **staff system model** (also referred to as the **public defender model**), and a combination of these two approaches, referred to as the **mixed or combined model**. The judicare model has traditionally operated in British Columbia, Ontario, and Alberta. In this program, a qualified legal aid recipient received a certificate to that effect. The benefits of this system included lower costs, the availability of services, and the efficiency inherent in having one lawyer handle the case from beginning to end. Usually lawyers are paid a set fee for their services, but this amount is typically too low to cover their costs. Rural areas are better served by this system, since the population base is too small to justify the maintenance of a permanent legal aid office funded by the government; it is far less costly to allow clients to select legal counsel from those already in the area. Other benefits of this system are as follows: (1) legal aid recipients can select their own lawyer, (2) normal lawyer–client relationships can be maintained for poor defendants, and (3) clients can select lawyers whom they feel will best serve their interests (Burns and Reid 1981).

The staff system has operated in Saskatchewan, Newfoundland and Labrador, Nova Scotia, and Yukon. In this system, the lawyers are in effect employees of the provincial government. One benefit of this system is that the lawyers involved are salaried—which ensures that the client receives competent legal counsel—and take no money for their services from their clients or their clients' families. Another advantage is that the public defenders representing a legal aid case are able to contact other public defenders; this allows them to benefit from group resources and expertise. Private-practice lawyers can also be used in this model, especially when a conflict of interest arises or if a staff lawyer is unavailable for the case.

The benefits of this approach include the following (ibid.: 414–16):

- Better representation, because lawyers are specialists, with some becoming spokespersons for the poor.
- Lower costs.
- Greater efficiency, because the system is centralized.
- Better service of the interests of clients, because lawyers are salaried and therefore do not need to use legal tactics that benefit them.

The mixed system is practised on Prince Edward Island as well as in Manitoba, Quebec, New Brunswick, the Northwest Territories, and Nunavut. In these jurisdictions, the legal aid recipient has the right to choose legal counsel, either staff or private, from a panel of lawyers providing legal aid services (Johnstone and Thomas 1998).

Due to less funding, a shift has occurred in the service delivery approach to legal aid programs across Canada. This shift has been to place the onus onto individuals to find what they need within the justice system on their own. This is referred to as the **self-help model**. According to Buckley (2010:6), legal aid services have become "unbundled," which means that legal aid providers are able to help more people by giving legal information, advice, and representation at various stages of the process. Clients usually don't have ongoing representation, "but must figure out how the legal information they have received applies to them and advocate for themselves much of the time." What will happen if the funding for legal aid does not increase? According to Doust (2011:9) "without adequate legal aid, we all fail in our social obligation to ensure that every citizen . . . has available at least the basic necessities of their lives so they can adequately sustain themselves and their families."

SUMMING UP AND LOOKING FORWARD

This chapter begins by discussing the criteria used by the police when deciding whether to charge a suspect and what to charge them. This decision is largely based upon the strength of the case as well as other influences known as the social structure of the case. If an individual is not released by the police on a summons or appearance notice, they will be brought to a police station. They may be released by the officer in charge, but if not they will be held until a bail hearing.

The law governing bail presumes innocence and protects the right to a fair trial by allowing most people to be released. The Crown may decide that the accused be held in pretrial custody prior to their court case. If the accused receives bail, they may be released with conditions, or have a surety to monitor them when they are in the community. Since a bail hearing can be "the most important step for an accused person in the criminal process" a number of studies into the practice of bail have found certain flaws.

Legal aid is important part of an access to justice as it allows those who cannot afford a privately retained lawyer to access legal assistance. Section 10(b) of the Charter states all Canadians have the "right to retain counsel without delay" for criminal cases. A number of issues are relevant here, including the funding of criminal legal aid.

What are the next steps in the pretrial process? These include the plea, the preliminary hearing, and disclosure. An important question to consider is how each one promotes justice.

Review Questions:

1. Why is the strength of the case the most important issue on the list of influences on prosecutors' decision to charge?
2. Why are some people released on a summons or a promise to appear while others are taken to the police building for further actions by the police?
3. Why is bail considered to be the most important step for an accused person in the criminal process?
4. What are some of the ways that our legal aid system can be improved over the short term? Over the long term?

What Happens during Prosecutorial Screening?

Once the police arrest and lay charges against a suspect, it is not automatic that a prosecutor will proceed with the case. For various reasons, many defendants are never brought to trial. Crown prosecutors "have virtually unfettered discretion as to when to charge, what to charge, when the charge should be reduced or dropped" (Stuart and Delisle 1995:525). Thus the prosecutor has the power to decide among trying the case in court on the charges laid, or plea bargaining, or staying proceedings, or dismissing the charges outright. In addition, in hybrid offences, the prosecutor has the discretion to proceed by way of indictment or summary conviction. The prosecutor's discretionary powers exist at all levels of criminal trials. The courts have been reluctant to limit prosecutorial discretion—the Supreme Court of Canada ruled in *R. v. Beare* (1988) that prosecutorial discretion does not violate the principles of fundamental justice, stating that it is an essential component of our criminal justice system.

The right of prosecutors to choose whether or not to proceed with cases is a major source of case attrition (see Chapter 1). Prosecutors use a screening process to determine what to do with a given case. Several factors are often involved with case screening:

- The most important factor in the decision whether or not to prosecute is not the prosecutor's belief in the guilt of the accused, but whether there is sufficient evidence for a conviction. If prosecutors decide there is strong evidence in the case (e.g., overwhelming physical evidence, a confession, and a number of reliable and credible witnesses), the decision to prosecute is easier (Boland et al. 1992).
- Prosecutors have case priorities—that is, with all cases being hypothetically equal, the prosecutor will take a violent criminal to court before someone charged with vandalism.
- The record of the accused is also a significant factor. If the accused has committed a large number of prior offences, the prosecutor will usually decide to prosecute that offender before prosecuting a first-time offender. Sometimes prosecutors decide to pursue all cases that fall into a certain category, such as domestic violence, gang-related activity, or drunk driving.
- An important consideration can be the nature of the witnesses; that is, how cooperative they are (or are not). For example, some cases involving domestic violence are dropped because the witnesses will not cooperate with the prosecutor. A violent crime is more likely to be pursued in court when it involves strangers rather than family members.
- The credibility of victims (or witnesses) can influence the decision to proceed with a case. If the victim or witness is a prostitute or drug addict, and the defendant an upstanding citizen, prosecutors may be reluctant to have a trial, particularly a jury trial during which 12 citizens will be deciding who is more trustworthy.
- A prosecutor may decide to drop a case against the accused if that person will be testifying against someone else in another trial. For example, if the accused is a small-time drug dealer, the prosecutor may drop all charges for information leading to the arrest and conviction of a major supplier.

These case-processing decisions become integrated into a strategy for the prosecutor's office (see Exhibit 8.1).

EXHIBIT 8.1 Models of Prosecutorial Decisions

A number of models have been developed to guide prosecutors regarding when to proceed with the case to court and when to drop or stay charges (Jacoby 1979):

- The **transfer model**. In this model, very little screening occurs and prosecutors charge most of the accused after they receive the case from the police. The key factor here is the amount of resources available to a prosecutor's office: if it has ample resources, more cases will be heard in court.
- The **unit model**. Here, individual prosecutors are given significant amounts of discretion to do as they like with each case. There is not much organizational guidance, and little specific policy given to prosecutors.

Continued on next page

EXHIBIT 8.1 Models of Prosecutorial Decisions (*Continued*)

- The **legal sufficiency model**. Here, cases are screened according to their legal elements. If there are sufficient legal grounds, the case will probably be prosecuted.
- The **system efficiency model**. In this model, cases are disposed of in the quickest possible way. Only those cases where there is a high probability of success will be prosecuted; those which are not as clear-cut will be rejected as too time consuming (even if they may end with a conviction) because there are not enough resources.
- The **trial sufficiency model**. Here, a case proceeds to court only if a conviction is likely. Resources are secondary, given the prosecutor's feeling that the case will end in a conviction.
- The **defendant rehabilitation model**. Here, the prosecutor's decision rests on whether it is possible to rehabilitate the defendant. Under this model, alternatives (e.g., treatment programs) are sought out before the case goes to court as long as the accused agrees to participate.

What Is the Right to Disclosure?

As we saw in Chapter 2, s. 7 of the Charter imposes a duty on the prosecution to disclose all the evidence it would be using in the trial as well as any other evidence the defence might find useful. This ruling has had a tremendous impact on the activities of both prosecutors and police (see *Investigating: The Issue of Disclosure* for a further discussion of disclosure).

What Are the Different Types of Pleas?

In most cases an accused who appears in criminal court for an indictable offence enters what is known as a **general plea**—that is, a plea of guilty or not guilty. Three other pleas (referred to as **special pleas**) are available to the accused: **autrefois acquit, autrefois convict,** and **pardon**. An estimated 90 percent of accused plead guilty prior to trial or when they appear in a lower court for the first time. If the accused pleads not guilty to an indictable offence (a common plea in the more serious and complex cases), a trial date is set that is acceptable to both the

Investigating: The Issue of Disclosure: Stinchcombe, O'Connor, and McNeil

Disclosure is one of the most important features of our criminal justice system. The Law Reform Commission of Canada contends that disclosure of relevant information among all the parties involved in a court case is an important factor in the fairness and efficiency of the Canadian justice system. According to that commission, fairness in our criminal justice system depends largely "upon the quality of information available to litigating parties. . . . Our rules of criminal procedure, however, do not provide for such disclosure, although the preliminary inquiry is commonly used by defence counsel as an opportunity to discover the strength and the scope of the Crown's case" (Law Reform Commission of Canada 1974:1).

However, clear guidelines as to exactly how disclosure should operate were never developed. The lack of any principles governing disclosure was one of the most important legal issues that emerged from the investigation into the wrongful conviction of Donald Marshall in Nova Scotia. One of the problems with the original court case was the lack of disclosure among all the parties involved during both the pretrial actions and the subsequent trial (Brucker 1992). The investigation that followed Marshall's release found that both the police and the prosecution had withheld information from the defence. That withholding, together with the failure of the defence counsel to seek disclosure from the Crown, was a major contributing factor in the wrongful conviction. According to the final report on Marshall's wrongful conviction, if "the police are not candid in their dealing with Crown prosecutors, the whole policy on disclosure may go for naught. It is trite to say that a dishonest cop who wishes to subvert the system may do so, and rules are not likely to completely contain such abuse" (House of Commons Debates 1986). As a result, recommendations were made in the hope that guidelines on disclosure would emerge and that the authorities would comply with them in order to achieve the "sound administration of criminal justice." One of the problems with this case was the lack of clear directives concerning the role of disclosure during the prosecution.

Investigating: The Issue of Disclosure: Stinchcombe, O'Connor, and McNeil *(Continued)*

Donald Marshall was wrongfully convicted of murder. His case highlighted the need for disclosure in Canadian criminal trials.

The guidelines for disclosure emerged from the decision reached by the Supreme Court of Canada in *R. v. Stinchcombe* (1991). This case involved an Alberta lawyer who was convicted in the Alberta Provincial Court of misappropriating funds from a client. Stinchcombe argued the client had actually made him a business partner; thus, he had done nothing wrong. He appealed his conviction to the Alberta Court of Appeal, but the appeal was dismissed. The Supreme Court of Canada decided to hear the case, however, perhaps because it saw the opportunity to develop clear directives concerning disclosure in criminal trials.

The key issue concerned certain information given to the police after the preliminary inquiry but before the actual trial. This information involved a taped statement given to the RCMP by Stinchcombe's secretary. The tape supported the claim that Stinchcombe was innocent. The Crown prosecutor informed the defence of this taped statement but declined to indicate the exact nature of its contents. In addition, the secretary refused all offers to be interviewed by the defence. During the trial, defence counsel discovered that the secretary was not going to be called as a witness by the Crown. As a result, the defence requested that the judge make the Crown disclose the contents of the taped statement. The judge refused, since there was no obligation on the part of the Crown either to put the witness on the stand or to disclose her statements.

The Supreme Court of Canada overturned the decision made by the lower court. In a unanimous 7–0 vote favouring Stinchcombe, it ruled that Crown prosecutors must disclose to the defence any information in serious criminal matters that is capable of affecting the accused's ability to prepare a defence—and to do so early enough to allow the accused time to prepare that defence. However, this rule is not absolute and is subject to judicial interpretation. For example, the police are not required to give the name of any informant who supplies them with information relevant to a case. The Supreme Court decision is based on the fundamental right of the accused to give full answer and defence to the charges. However, the Court also ruled that "the defense has no obligation to assist the prosecution and is entitled to assume a purely adversarial role."

The rules governing disclosure fall into two categories: (1) **first-party production** and (2) **third-party production** (Brannagan 2011). First-party production is governed by the *Stinchcombe* test, while *O'Connor* governs third-party production. Third-party records aren't typically in the control of the Crown, and that's why these types of records are not included in the first-party disclosure information that the Crown is legally required to hand over to the accused. In their decision in *R. v. O'Connor*, the Supreme Court created a two-part test to determine if the accused can access third-party records that are beyond the first-party disclosure test as set out in *Stinchcombe*. In the first stage, the accused has to make an application to the trial judge for the production of the third-party records which they feel are necessary for their defence. If the accused is successful at the first stage, they then have to submit to the second stage. Here, the trial judge has to balance the competing interests at issue; that is, the right of the accused to mount a full answer and defence, with the privacy rights of the third party which would be required to produce the documentation. The Supreme Court, in *R. v. McNeil*, has stated that "with few exceptions, the accused's right to access information necessary to make full answer and defence will outweigh any competing privacy interest."

Continued on next page

Investigating: The Issue of Disclosure: Stinchcombe, O'Connor, and McNeil *(Continued)*

In January 2009, the Supreme Court unanimously ruled in *R. v. McNeil* that police have to hand over records of the discipline and misconduct of its officers as part of its disclosure obligation to the defence in criminal proceedings. In *McNeil*, the accused was charged with the possession of crack cocaine for the purpose of trafficking. The main witness at the trial was the arresting officer. While McNeil was awaiting sentencing after being convicted at trial, it was learned that the arresting officer in the case was standing trial for a number of criminal offences, and had no fewer than 71 pending Police Act offences concerning the ongoing use, sale, and transportation of narcotics. This led to questions about the officer's credibility at McNeil's trial. Until this time, an individual had to ask for police records in the third-party disclosure context. In their *McNeil* ruling, the Supreme Court joined together the Crown and the police, thereby creating a situation where the police are now categorized under the Stinchcombe disclosure rules. According to the *McNeil* ruling,

> The necessary corollary to the Crown's disclosure duty under Stinchcombe is the obligation of police (or other investigating state authority) to disclose to the Crown all material pertaining to its investigation of the accused. For the purposes of fulfilling this corollary obligation, the investigating police force, although distinct and independent from the Crown at law, is not a third party. Rather, it acts on the same footing as the Crown.

The implication of this case is that if judges are satisfied that a record has relevance to the current case, the record will be produced to the defence.

Stinchcombe created guidelines about disclosure for both the police and prosecutors. But what about guidelines for the defence counsel? This issue came before the courts in the trial of Ken Murray (*R. v. Murray* [2000]). Murray was the first lawyer hired to defend Paul Bernardo, whose crimes (along with those of his wife, Karla Homolka) had made national headlines. Following a 71-day search of his residence by the police, Bernardo instructed Murray to take from the house some videotapes he had hidden. About a month later, Murray viewed the six horrific tapes and, despite their damaging content, decided they could be used to direct some of the attention from the crimes away from his client (Homolka had already struck a plea bargain with the Crown). For the next 17 months Murray kept the videotapes in his possession, without informing the authorities about them or their contents. About a month before the trial, Bernardo suggested to his lawyer that the tapes shouldn't be used in his defence. Faced with an ethical dilemma, Murray withdrew from the case. The lawyer who took over handed them to the police through an intermediary (Blatchford 2000).

Murray was charged under s. 139(2) of the Criminal Code with attempting to willfully obstruct the course of justice in that he had failed to disclose the tapes to the police. Murray's defence rested in part on the grounds that the law society's *Professional Conduct Handbook* states only that a lawyer must not suppress "what ought to be disclosed." In June 2000, Murray was acquitted of the charges in the Ontario Superior Court, with the trial judge ruling that there was reasonable doubt concerning Murray's actions "after considering the accused's evidence in the context of the evidence as a whole" (ibid.:33). As a result of this trial, the Law Society of Upper Canada established a panel to deal with the ethical questions faced by lawyers when they uncover incriminating evidence (Abbate 2000). But some legal commentators felt that the practical lesson to be gleaned from this case "may simply be not to touch anything that smells of evidence" ("Smoking Guns" 2000:409).

Sources: Abbate 2000; Blatchford 2000; Law Reform Commission of Canada 1974; "Smoking Guns" 2000; Tochor and Kilback 1999. The quoted extract is from "Discovery in Criminal Cases," Law Reform Commission of Canada, 1974, Justice Canada.

prosecution and the defence. In most cases, the accused is released under the same terms and conditions he or she was previously given.

The presiding judge at the initial appearance is a provincially appointed judge. What happens next is determined by the type of charge—that is, whether it is an indictable, hybrid, or summary conviction. If the accused is charged with a **summary conviction offence**, the trial is held in a **summary conviction court**. The information is read to the accused, who is then asked whether he or she pleads guilty or not guilty. If the accused pleads not guilty, a date will likely be set for a trial before a provincial court judge, since it is typical in larger communities that the court docket will be full on that particular day. An accused who pleads guilty will be sentenced immediately or remanded until the judge has the opportunity to hear submissions concerning the sentence. The Criminal Code allows for remands of up to eight days, unless the accused consents to a longer adjournment. (Accused in custody generally enforce their eight-day rights.) If the charge is for an indictable offence (e.g., a gaming offence), because it is under the absolute jurisdiction of a provincially appointed judge (a s. 553 offence), trial may proceed right away (Mewett and Nakatsuru 2000) (see Exhibit 8.2).

EXHIBIT 8.2 Court Jurisdiction Over Criminal Code Offences, Sections 469 and 553

If the accused is charged with a Supreme Court exclusive offence (a s. 469 offence), the presiding provincial court judge has no jurisdiction to try the case and so sets a date for a trial to be heard by a superior court judge. These cases must be heard by a superior court judge and jury unless, in special circumstances, the Attorney General of the province allows the case to be heard by judge alone. In all other criminal cases involving indictable offences, the accused has the right to select trial by superior court judge alone or by provincial court judge alone.

In Canada, it is possible to have a trial even if the accused pleads guilty. To the trial court judge, the Crown prosecutor usually makes a brief statement of the case's facts and of other information considered relevant to the case. At this time, the accused may disagree with certain or all aspects of the prosecutor's statement. The judge then inquires into the nature of the disagreement; if the judge decides there is substance to the disagreement, he or she advises the accused to withdraw the plea of guilty and instead enter a plea of not guilty. If the accused pleads guilty to a lesser offence, the judge may decide to proceed with the more serious charge if it arose from the same factual circumstances.

In these situations, the Crown prosecutor may decide to accept the guilty plea and not proceed on the original (and more serious) charge. The presiding judge need not accept this guilty plea; if not, the trial continues with the original charge. Mewett and Nakatsuru (2000:117) point out that a Crown prosecutor's decision to accept a plea of guilty to a lesser charge depends on a number of factors, including "the seriousness of the charge, avoiding the necessity for witnesses to testify, the public interest, the likelihood of securing a conviction on the more serious charge, and so on." Thus, a plea bargain made between the defence and prosecution may not be accepted by the trial court judge.

An individual's plea of guilty must be a free and voluntary act. Once it is accepted, the accused gives up his or her constitutional rights, including the right to cross-examine witnesses and to have a trial by jury (if applicable). However, a judge may decide to review the evidence, and if it appears that the accused wishes to change his or her plea, the judge has the discretion to allow the change. Clearly, then, a judge must exercise caution when accepting the accused's plea of guilty. The judge must believe that the facts of the case warrant the plea and that the accused has made it voluntarily. The accused, if not represented by defence counsel, must be informed of the right to make a plea voluntarily, and the judge may insist on the presence of a defence lawyer before the plea is accepted by the court. In addition, the judge has the right to allow the accused to withdraw a plea of guilty if he or she was "in a disturbed state of mind at the time" of the guilty plea (*R. v. Hansen* [1977]).

Section 469 Offences

The offences listed below are the exclusive jurisdiction of superior criminal courts:

- treason
- alarming Her Majesty
- intimidating Parliament or Legislature
- inciting mutiny
- seditious mutiny
- piracy
- piratical acts
- attempting to commit any of the above offences
- murder
- conspiring to commit the above offences
- being an accessory after the fact to high treason, treason, or murder
- bribery by the holder of a judicial office

Section 553 Offences

- theft, other than theft of cattle
- obtaining money or property on false pretences
- possession of property obtained, directly or indirectly, from the commission of an indictable offence
- defrauding the public, or any person, of any item
- mischief under subsection 430(4) of the Criminal Code
- keeping a game or betting house
- betting, pool selling, bookmaking, etc.
- placing bets
- offences involving lotteries and games of chance
- cheating at play
- keeping a common bawdy-house
- driving while disqualified
- fraud in relation to fares
- counselling, attempts to commit, or being an accessory to any of the offences listed above

Source: From KENNEDY/SACCO. *Crime Counts*, 1E. © 1996 Nelson Education Ltd. Reproduced by permission. www .cengage.com/permissions.

What Is the Purpose of a Preliminary Inquiry?

A **preliminary inquiry**, or **preliminary hearing**, is held when an accused is charged with an offence that must be tried by a judge and jury, or when the accused elects to be tried by a judge and jury or by a judge alone. There is no preliminary inquiry for summary conviction offences. If an accused elects trial in a provincial court before a preliminary inquiry is held, they waive their right to a preliminary inquiry.

The purpose of this inquiry is twofold:

1. to see whether there is enough evidence collected by the Crown prosecutor (and by the defence, if it wishes to make the same determination) to proceed to a criminal trial, and
2. to protect the accused from being placed on trial unnecessarily.

During the preliminary inquiry, a provincial court judge or justice of the peace examines the evidence and hears witnesses in order to determine whether a reasonable jury (or a judge when there is no jury) would find the accused guilty. The intention of the preliminary inquiry is *not* to determine guilt. In other words, the Crown prosecutor does not have to convict the accused but only to introduce sufficient evidence to make the guilt of the accused a reasonable expectation (Mewett and Nakatsuru 2000).

The preliminary inquiry is conducted in much the same way as a regular trial. It is usually open to the public. The accused can request a prohibition of the publication of the proceedings either until charges are discharged or, if a trial is held, until the trial is over. The publication ban order is mandatory when requested by the accused at the opening of the inquiry, but discretionary when the prosecutor applies for it.

The prosecution presents its evidence as well as any witnesses. The accused has the right to cross-examine any or all witnesses and to challenge the prosecutor's evidence. It is not necessary for the prosecution to present all the evidence it has as long as it provides *sufficient* evidence to the judge that a reasonable case can be made against the accused. After the prosecutor presents the evidence, the judge informs the accused that he or she has heard the evidence and asks whether the accused wishes to reply to the charge. Rarely does a defendant decide to discuss the evidence, but, if so, whatever the accused says is written down and might be used against him or her during the actual trial. The next step allows the accused to call any witnesses he or she feels merit attention.

After all the evidence is presented to the court, the judge decides whether the prosecution has provided sufficient evidence to prosecute the accused. If the judge believes the evidence is sufficient, a trial is scheduled; if it is insufficient, the charges are dropped and the defendant is freed. The judge weighs the evidence just as if it were evidence at a criminal trial. A presiding judge who decides there is insufficient evidence to proceed will discharge the accused. This discharge does not mean the accused is acquitted; rather, it means the accused cannot be tried on that information and that the proceedings on that information are ended. If fresh evidence is brought to light about the case, the prosecution usually proceeds by way of a **direct indictment**. This allows the Crown prosecutor, after receiving the permission of the Attorney General or a Deputy Attorney General, to bypass the preliminary inquiry and indict the accused directly.

In the real world, the accused often waives the preliminary inquiry with the consent of the prosecutor, especially if he or she knows what evidence the prosecutor will be using at trial. In Canada, the accused usually has the right to waive the preliminary inquiry. A defendant is most likely to waive a preliminary inquiry for one of three reasons:

1. The accused has decided to enter a plea of guilty.
2. The accused wants to speed up the criminal justice process and have a trial date set as early as possible.
3. The accused hopes to avoid the negative publicity that might result from the inquiry.

In December 2003, a new policy (Bill C-15A) amending the operations of preliminary inquiries came into effect in Canada. Preliminary inquiries are no longer automatic in this country; instead, they must be explicitly requested by either the Crown prosecutor or the defence lawyer. Those who request an inquiry must produce a list of the issues they would like covered and the witnesses from whom they would like to hear. There is also now greater scope for having written statements introduced during the preliminary hearing; thus, witnesses are no longer always obligated to appear in person.

Recently, much debate has focused on the role of and need for preliminary inquiries in the Canadian criminal justice system. A number of provincial justice ministers and Attorneys General feel that preliminary inquiries should be eliminated altogether because of the costs and time delays they involve. They also argue that these inquiries place witnesses and victims in a vulnerable position as they must suffer through traumatic interrogations in addition to the questioning they would face during a criminal trial. Supporters of preliminary inquiries point out that they offer defence lawyers their only opportunity to examine witnesses prior to a client's trial. In addition, such inquiries are necessary because they ensure that cases will proceed to trial only if there are sufficient grounds. Bill C-15A represented a compromise between the two positions and was seen as guaranteeing that the rights of the defendant would not be compromised. It was an attempt to strike "a balance that would permit such functions as discovery and screening, without unduly prolonging the process or making it unfair." The amendments were also an attempt to make the preliminary inquiry "a more efficient, more effective and more limited procedure" (Baer 2005).

What Is Plea Bargaining?

There is no formal definition of plea bargaining in the Criminal Code. As a general definition, plea bargaining has been defined as "any agreement by the accused to plead guilty in return for the promise of some benefit" (Law Reform Commission of Canada 1975:45). According to this definition, plea bargaining involves the idea that justice can be purchased at the bargaining table. Since the Law Reform Commission wrote this definition, however, it has been acknowledged that this practice involves more than an accused bargaining with the Crown in exchange for some reduction in punishment. To better recognize the multitude of ways in which plea bargaining takes place in our criminal justice system, Perras (1979:58–59) defined it as "a proceeding whereby competent and informed counsel openly discuss the evidence in a criminal prosecution with a view to achieving a disposition which will result in the reasonable advancement of the administration of justice."

Plea bargaining exists because it serves a variety of purposes (Wheatley 1974):

- It improves the administrative efficiency of the courts.
- It lowers the cost of prosecution.
- It permits the prosecution to devote more time to more important cases.

In the real world, plea bargaining involves a large number of activities, including discussions about charges, sentences, the facts of the case, and procedural issues. Plea bargaining can occur before the trial starts, but it can also be done during the trial when the defendant and defence counsel perceive a benefit in pleading guilty. Sometimes during a judge-alone trial, the judge initiates a discussion in their chambers about the possibility of a plea bargain between the prosecutor and defence lawyer. This is referred to as **mid-trial bargaining**, and it is frowned upon by provincial Courts of Appeal as it excludes the defendant and it raises questions about the presumption of innocence (*R. v. Poulos* [2015]).

Plea bargaining agreements, then, can take several forms but are typically designed to expedite the trial. Most plea bargaining occurs between the accused, the defence lawyer, and the Crown prosecutor. A number of different types of plea bargaining identified (see Table 8.2).

As noted above, Crown prosecutors are obligated not only to serve the public interest but also to ensure that justice is done. They have a professional obligation to plea bargain with the accused, and they must do so on the basis of fairness, openness, accuracy, non-discrimination, and the public interest. Section 10(b) of the Charter of Rights and Freedoms states that plea bargaining is an essential aspect of prosecutorial discretion in criminal cases. Crown prosecutors may either initiate or respond to a plea bargain, and the plea bargain should be offered to the accused as soon as possible.

TABLE 8.2 Types of Plea Bargaining

Charge Bargaining	The reduction of the charge to a lesser or included offence The withdrawal or stay of other charges or the promise not to proceed on other possible charges
Sentence Bargaining	A promise to proceed summarily rather than by way of indictment A promise not to appeal against the sentence imposed at trial A promise to arrange sentencing before a particular judge
Procedural Bargaining	A promise by the Crown prosecutor to dispense of the case at a specified future time if, on the record and in open court, the accused is prepared to waive the right to trial within a reasonable time
Fact Bargaining	A promise by the Crown prosecutor not to volunteer certain information about the accused A promise not to mention a circumstance or the offence that might be interpreted by the judge as an aggravating factor
Label Bargaining	An attempt by the defence to ensure that the accused is not charged with an offence that carries a negative label

Even after a plea bargain has been agreed on among the accused, the defence lawyer, and the Crown prosecutor, the sentence must still be determined by the judge assigned to the case. A joint recommendation on sentencing by the prosecutor and the defence lawyer is not binding on a judge. Judges, however, are legally obligated not to reject a joint submission unless it is contrary to the public interest and the recommended sentence would bring the administration of justice into disrepute. If a judge decides that the recommended sentence is not lawful, the accused will not be able to withdraw the guilty plea. In Canada, it is rare for lawyers to discuss plea bargains privately with a judge. However, during a pretrial conference—that is, an informal meeting held in a judge's office—a full and free discussion of the issues raised can take place without prejudice to the rights of the parties in any of the proceedings occurring afterward (s. 625.1 of the Criminal Code). During these conferences, issues can be considered with the general goal of ensuring a fair and expeditious hearing. A pretrial conference can be held at the request of the Crown prosecutor, the accused, or the court. In the case of a jury trial, a pretrial conference is mandatory (s. 625.1[2] of the Criminal Code).

Prosecutors prefer to devote their time to serious crimes or to cases in which they have a good chance of securing a conviction, so they may agree in other cases to accept a guilty plea to a lesser charge; doing so saves the court's time and money and reduces the risk that the prosecution will lose the case should it proceed to trial. In addition, the prosecutor may gain information about other criminals that will help solve other crimes.

Plea bargaining has been both criticized and defended by a wide variety of individuals and sectors in the criminal justice system. Many of the criticisms are voiced by crime control advocates, who contend that it is unfair, that it is hidden from public scrutiny, and that it results in too much leniency. Other critics focus on the impact that plea bargaining has on the integrity of the criminal justice system. They point out that it undermines many of the system's core values because it avoids due process standards designed to protect the accused. It is also pointed out that innocent persons may feel compelled to plead guilty to crimes they never committed.

Advantages of plea bargaining include the fact that it increases the efficiency of our criminal justice system. Also, it reduces the costs of operating that system as well as the workloads of prosecutors so that they can pursue more serious criminal cases. It may also reduce the trauma felt by victims because it means they won't be cross-examined in a criminal trial.

The practice of plea bargaining will probably continue to be debated vigorously. The arguments of both supporters and critics will no doubt ensure that it stays within the bounds of the principles of our criminal justice system. That said, there will surely be cases where it is appropriate to review plea bargaining. The Law Reform Commission (1975:14) once referred to plea bargaining as "something for which a decent criminal justice system has no place." Yet, it later changed its view, calling plea bargaining a normal practice in the criminal justice system, and in 1989, it commented that plea bargaining is not a "shameful practice" (Law Reform Commission 1989:8).

SUMMING UP AND LOOKING FORWARD

The Crown prosecutor starts to evaluate which cases should be brought to trial. This includes a screening process that can involve a variety of decisions, illustrated by different models. Once the decision is made to proceed, the Crown has to disclose all relevant information about the case to the defence. The plea is made in front of a provincially appointed judge, but ultimately the case may be heard by a superior court judge. A preliminary inquiry may be held to determine if there is enough evidence collected by the Crown prosecutor (and by the defence, if it wishes to make the same determination) to proceed to a criminal trial, and to protect the accused from being placed on trial unnecessarily.

Not all cases are dealt with formally in a courtroom: many are concluded on the basis of a plea bargain. This involves the defendant making an agreement with the prosecution and the result is less punishment. There are many different ways in which plea bargaining takes place in our criminal justice system. Plea bargaining has been described by Perras (1979) as "a proceeding whereby competent and informed counsel openly discuss the evidence in a criminal prosecution with a view to achieving a disposition which will result in the reasonable advancement of the administration of justice."

Review Questions:

1. Do you think prosecutors have too much latitude in their decisions concerning how to proceed with individual cases?
2. Do you think the defence should also be required to disclose any and all information it has collected and that might impact the trial?
3. Do you think preliminary hearings still have an essential role to play in our criminal justice system?
4. Why do you think those who work in the criminal justice system (i.e., insiders) typically view plea bargaining differently than out insiders?

What Is the Right to a Speedy Trial and How Has It Impacted the Criminal Courts?

One of the most serious problems facing the courts today is delays in hearing criminal cases. Delays may arise for any number of reasons, such as plea bargaining, procedural and evidentiary issues, and court cancellations. These delays may contravene s. 11(b) of the Charter, which guarantees that any person charged with an offence has the right "to be tried within a reasonable time."

Section 7 of the Charter considers the right to a speedy trial to be part of fundamental justice. This right was clarified in *R. v. Askov* (1990). In this case, three men charged with weapons offences were denied bail in November 1983. The men were released on bail in May 1984, but their court trial was put over until September 1985 due to a backlog of cases. The lawyers for the accused argued that their clients' right to a fair trial had been unfairly violated by courtroom delays. The presiding judge agreed, but the Ontario Court of Appeal overturned that decision. However, the Supreme Court of Canada agreed with the trial judge. When the Supreme Court made its decision, it identified four factors for a judge to rule on when unreasonable delay had occurred:

1. The **length of the delay**. No absolute time limit was identified by the Supreme Court. However, it did rule that "it is clear that the longer the delay, the more difficult it should be for a court to excuse it." This factor is to be balanced with the other factors, including "the standard maintained by the next comparable jurisdiction in the country."
2. The **explanation for the delay**. Two key factors were identified: (a) the conduct of the Crown and (b) systematic or institutional delays. In addition, the accused cannot unduly cause a delay in the proceedings; if the accused were to make a deliberate attempt to delay the trial, the courts would not rule in his or her favour and the burden of proof would lie with the accused.
3. **Waiver**. An accused who permits a waiver is indicating that he or she understands the s. 11(b) guarantee to a speedy trial and is, in effect, agreeing to waive that guarantee.
4. **Prejudice to the accused**. The Crown may proceed with the case when, despite a long delay, no resulting damage was suffered by the accused.

The impact of *Askov* was enormous. Almost 50,000 criminal charges were permanently stayed in Ontario during the next 11 months, including a number of cases involving charges of sexual assault, assault, and fraud (*R. v. Morin* [1992]). Within two years, however, the Supreme Court of Canada had reconsidered the issue of speedy trials. In *Morin*, it ruled that a delay of between 14 and 15 months in a case involving charges of impaired driving did not violate s. 11(b) of the Charter. In this case, the Supreme Court changed its direction by ruling that the protection of society was served by allowing "serious cases to come to trial, that administrative guidelines are not limitation periods, and the importance of evidence of prejudice" (Stuart 1995:347). Since *Morin*, the number of cases stayed due to unreasonable delay has fallen dramatically. This change came about mainly because provincial governments provided more resources to the courts and investigated other strategies, such as diversion programs. Most cases in Canada are now heard within one year of the first court appearance. In fact, many cases are dealt with in a single appearance, usually within the first four months of the initial court appearance.

When Is There a Stay of Proceedings?

What happens when an individual commits a crime a number of years before charges are laid? Judges in Canada have the discretion to stay the proceedings when they believe such a situation abuses the rights of the accused. A delay in the charging and prosecution of an accused for a sexual offence cannot justify a stay of proceedings, however. Sometimes the information concerning a sexual offence will come to the attention of the police years after the reported incident occurred. The police may take months or years to decide that they have the reasonable and probable grounds to lay charges.

In *R. v. L. (W.K.)* (1991), the accused was charged in 1987 with 17 counts of sexual assault, gross indecency, and assault involving his two daughters and stepdaughter. The victims complained to the police in 1986, although the first incident had reportedly occurred in 1957 and the last in 1985. The trial judge stayed the proceedings, since to do otherwise would have violated the right of the accused to fundamental justice. Both the British Columbia Court of Appeal and the Supreme Court of Canada ruled that the trial should not have been stayed. The Supreme Court ruled that the fairness of a trial is not automatically jeopardized by a lengthy pre-charge delay. In fact, such a delay may favour the accused, since the police may find it more difficult to find witnesses and corroborating evidence, if needed.

In some cases, the complainant may make charges of illegal sexual activity on the part of the accused but not wish the case to proceed to court and give evidence.

This is what happened in *R. v. D.(E.)* (1990), and the police decided not to proceed with the charges on the condition the accused agree to have no more contact with the family. Four years later, the victims decided to press charges against the accused, and charges were laid by the police. The accused argued that his rights had been violated. The judge agreed that this case would constitute an abuse of process and ordered a stay of proceedings. The Crown appealed and won. The Court of Appeal rested its decision on the fact that the accused had given no formal statement to the police in 1984 and had talked to them on a "non-caution, no-charge basis." The appeal court stated that an abuse of process would have occurred only if the prosecution had unfairly reneged on the expectations it expressed to the accused.

The Jury

The right to a jury trial has existed in Canada for almost 300 years. The right to be tried by a jury of one's peers is one of the oldest protections of individual liberty in our criminal justice system. It is designed to protect the accused from the powers of the state, from arbitrary law enforcement, and from overzealous prosecutors and biased judges (Hans and Vidmar 1986; Levine 1992). The right to trial by jury is still considered important enough in our legal system that it was included in the Charter of Rights and Freedoms for any charge in which an accused could be imprisoned for five years or more (Davison 2005). As we have seen, this does not mean that every accused selects to be tried by a jury; the bulk of the offences that go to trial are electable offences, and the accused often selects to be tried by judge alone. This right is enshrined in the Charter of Rights and Freedoms (ss. 11[d] and 11[f]). However, in comparison to other Western countries, such as the United States, the law in Canada provides for jury trials in only the more serious criminal offences.

The specific role of a **jury** in our legal system today is similar to that of a judge trying a case alone—that is, it is "to decide the facts from the trial evidence present and to apply the law (provided by the judge) to those facts to render a verdict" (Vidmar and Schuller 2001:130). The role of the jury is twofold:

1. enhancing the fairness of any particular trial, and
2. enhancing confidence in the administration of justice as a whole (Law Reform Commission of Canada 1982).

The jury must be representative of the community, be independent and impartial, and approach the trial with an open mind. The Supreme Court, in *R. v. Sherratt* (1991), held that the right to representativeness is an essential aspect of the right to trial by jury: "The perceived importance of the jury and the *Charter* right to jury trial is meaningless without some guarantee that it will perform its duties impartially and represent, as far as possible and appropriate in the circumstances, the larger community." In its role, the jury is to make its decision about the guilt or innocence of the accused based on its evaluation of the evidence. Since jurors are members of the community where the alleged criminal offence occurred, it serves as the conscience of the community as opposed to the opinion of one person (i.e., the judge).

During the past few years, the Supreme Court has ruled on a number of issues relevant to juries. In *R. v. N.S.* (2012), a woman alleged to have been sexually assaulted wanted to testify in her niqab. The defence lawyer argued that if he couldn't see her face, he would be constrained in his ability to cross-examine her. He also pointed out that a judge's or jury's ability to assess her credibility could be limited. In their ruling, the Supreme Court held that trial judges can permit a witness to wear the niqab when her evidence isn't controversial or when her credibility is not in question. At the same, questions were raised about background checks made by police at the request of prosecutors about potential jurors and whether these actions violated the right to a fair trial as well as privacy rights of those who were investigated. In a trilogy of cases, the Supreme Court ruled it was acceptable for prosecutors to request the police to check the backgrounds of potential jurors (referred to as **jury-vetting**) as long as the information they obtain is disclosed to the defence prior to the jury being selected. This issue received national attention in 2008, when it was revealed by the Crown in Barrie, Ontario, that the police there had been using their data bases to check on potential jurors. It was later found out that 18 of the 55 Crown offices in Ontario had also conducted these types of checks, with the police using their resources to inform the Crown which potential jurors could be eliminated.

In 2013, the Supreme Court of Canada ruled on issues concerning both the representativeness and the impartiality of the jury. Individuals selected to be jurors come from the community in which the trial is being heard (see *Criminal Justice Focus*). The final selection of jurors may not be entirely representative of the community, but the original group of people from which they were selected (called a **jury array**) will have been more representative because they were randomly selected to be potential members of the jury. Trial court judges have held that the selection of a jury array that excluded inhabitants of First Nations communities was not representative (*R. v. Nahdee* [1993]); neither was an array that included too few women (*R. v. Nepoose* [1991]). And in

R. v. Kokopenace (2013): Members of First Nations Communities and the Right to a Representative Jury

Up until 2001 Indian and Northern Affairs Canada compiled lists of First Nations members on the list of potential jurors when band electoral lists were not available. Starting in 2001, it no longer compiled these lists due to privacy concerns. In Ontario, concerns were raised by First Nations peoples about the jury selection process. This led to a government investigation into this issue. The final report, *First Nations Representation on Ontario Juries* (2013), was written by former Supreme Court of Canada Justice Mr. Justice F. Iacobucci. Among his conclusions was that the jury selection system for identifying potential jurors in Ontario was unrepresentative of all First Nations peoples living on reserves. He added that while his study focused exclusively on Ontario, this issue also exists in other Canadian provinces as well as other countries (e.g., Australia and the United States).

Mr. Kokopenace was convicted of manslaughter by a non-Aboriginal jury in Kenora, Ontario, in 2008. In that year, the jury roll in Kenora consisted of 699 individuals, of whom 29 (4.1 percent) were on-reserve residents of First Nations communities. The First Nations population in the area at that time was approximately 33 percent (Perkel 2013). His jury was selected from a panel of 175 potential jurors, only eight of whom were living in a First Nations community. Prior to his sentencing, the defence applied for a mistrial, claiming Mr. Kokopenace's Charter rights to a representative jury were violated since the jury roll was improperly compiled. The trial judge refused to adjourn the sentencing in order to hear the mistrial application. After Mr. Kokopenace was found guilty of manslaughter, the defence appealed the trial judge's decision to the Ontario Court of Appeal, arguing that the lack of proper representativeness of members of First Nations communities violated his ss. 11(d), 11(f), and 15 Charter rights to the Ontario Court of Appeal.

In a 2–1 majority, the Ontario Court of Appeal ruled that the constitutional right to a representative jury (ss. 11(d) and 11(f) of the Charter) requires the Government of Ontario to take reasonable steps to ensure that Aboriginal peoples were included in the jury roll, but that they had not done so. As a result, Mr. Kokopenace's Charter rights to a representative jury were violated. His s. 15 appeal was dismissed as the justices held that the defence did not provide sufficient evidence for this claim. The Court of Appeal also noted that the right to a representative jury is qualified; that is, "it does not require a jury roll in which each group is represented in numbers equivalent to its proportion in which each group is represented in numbers equivalent to its proportion of the population of the jury as a whole." The Ontario government subsequently appealed this ruling to the Supreme Court of Canada, and in May 2015 the Supreme Court of Canada, by a 5–2 majority, held that there were reasonable attempts made to ensure the jury had adequate Aboriginal representation. As a result, Mr. Kokopenace's original conviction was restored.

Richard Lautens/GetStock.com

Former Supreme Court Justice Iacobucci investigated the issue of the representativeness of First Nations on juries.

R. v. Sherratt (1991), the Supreme Court held that the jury must consist of individuals who are impartial.

According to Davison (2005:38), the most basic value of the jury is that it is democratic. This means that the jury brings representatives of the community, with their varying life experiences, occupations, and common sense, into a setting usually (perhaps too often) occupied exclusively by lawyers and judges bound up in the legal principles and precedents and outcomes. At its heart, the jury represents society, and the prevailing views in society, about what should be penalized and what ought not.

When Is There a Right to a Jury Trial?

Before a case is heard in court, the accused may have the right to decide between a trial by judge and jury or by judge alone. In Canada, the right to a jury trial is found in s. 11(f) of the Charter of Rights and Freedoms, which states that any person charged with an offence has the right to trial by jury where the maximum punishment for the offence is imprisonment for five years or more. In *R. v. D.(S.)* (1992), this five-year rule was challenged by the accused, who had been charged with an offence carrying a maximum punishment of less than five years. The court held that no principle of fundamental justice had been violated, as no right exists that entitles the accused to a jury trial in every criminal case. Note also that most indictable offences are electable and that many accused persons decide not to be tried by judge and jury. An illustration of a criminal trial being tried by judge alone is shown in Figure 8.3.

Once an accused has been convicted and further proceedings take place on the basis of the conviction,

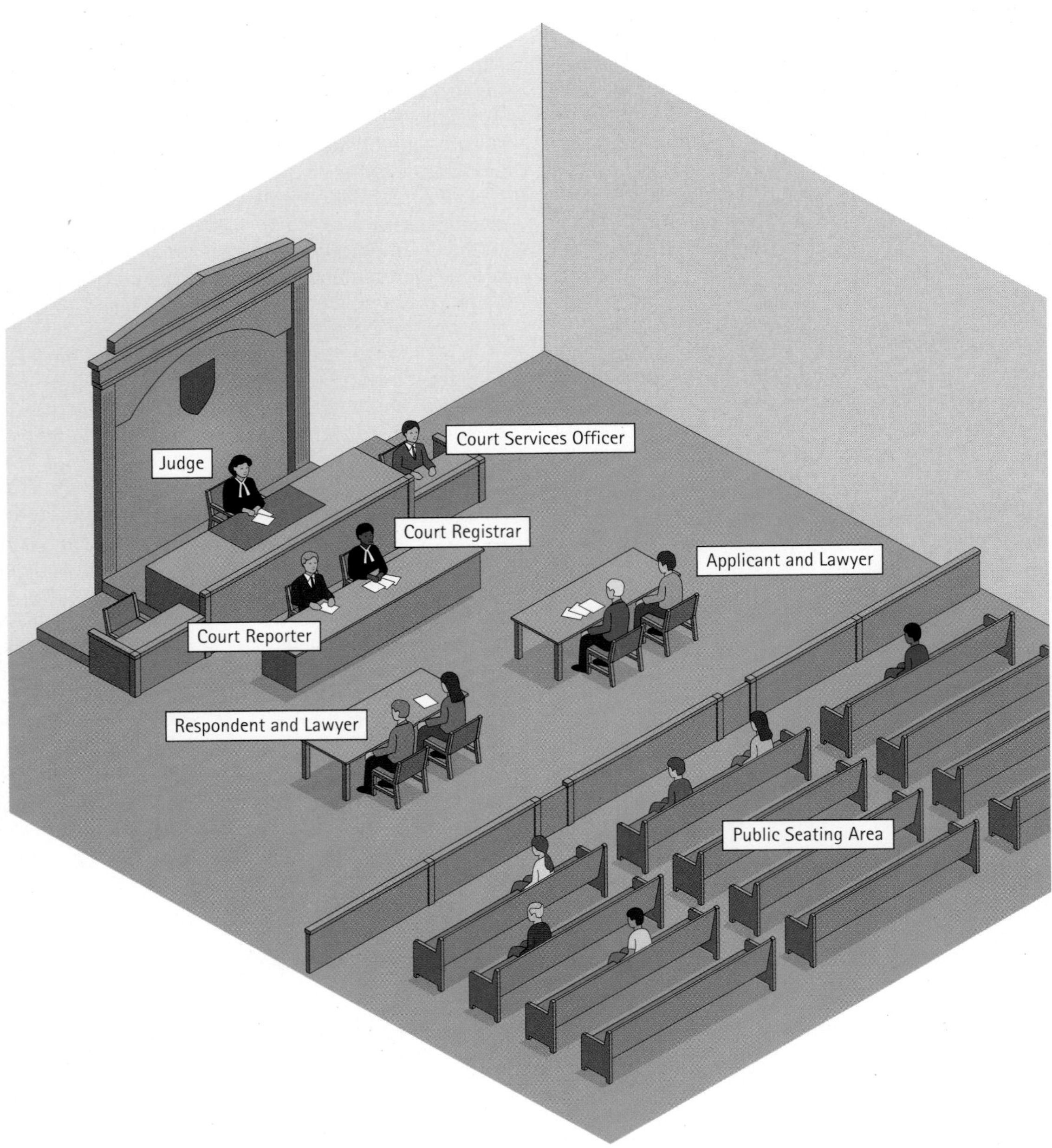

FIGURE 8.3 Layout of a Typical Courtroom Hearing Cases by Judge Alone in Canada

there can be no additional jury trial. For example, when convicted murderer Paul Bernardo was declared a dangerous offender, his defence lawyer made no attempt to have the case heard by both a judge and jury, since Bernardo had already been found guilty and, as such, was not an individual "charged with an offence" as specified in s. 11(f) of the Charter. This was based on a previous case heard by the Supreme Court of Canada, which ruled that it is wrong to allow an individual already convicted to have the right later on to request a jury trial (*R. v. Lyons* [1987]).

A jury usually does not have input into the sentence imposed on the accused after the finding of guilt. Juries do, however, assist in the determination of a sentence at two points in our legal system. One is when the accused is found guilty of second degree murder. Here, the jury will be asked to make a recommendation on the length of time the accused should have to wait (i.e., more than 10 years) before being eligible to apply for parole. The other is during a "faint hope" hearing (see Chapter 13).

How Is a Jury Selected?

If the accused decides to be tried by a judge and jury, jury selection follows. Jury selection is a four-step procedure. Three of these occur outside the court and are a provincial responsibility; the fourth takes place inside the court and is governed by the Criminal Code. The three out-of-court stages are as follows:

1. The assembly of a source list of persons who may be qualified, under provincial law, to serve as jurors (most but not all provincial jury acts specify some or all of the sources to be consulted when the list is prepared).
2. A determination of the identity of those on the source list who are qualified to serve, according to the relevant provincial jury act, and the disqualification or exemption from service of those on the list who, for various reasons, are usually also specified in the appropriate jury act.
3. The selection from the names remaining on the source list of a jury panel, whose members are, as appropriate, summoned to appear in court in accordance with the procedures set out in each provincial jury act.

A list of initial candidates is then compiled. The way this is done varies from province to province. This initial list, referred to as a jury array or **jury roll**, provides the government with the names of citizens who are potential jurors. Each province has a jury act that specifies who may be selected for the jury array. Section 626 of the Criminal Code allows each province to determine the qualifications for potential selection. This section precludes discrimination on the basis of sex.

A number of individuals from the juror array appear in court (the number varies widely from jurisdiction to jurisdiction), where an in-court selection process follows. The framework for this in-court procedure is found in s. 631 of the Criminal Code. The purpose of this process is to determine which of the prospective jurors are impartial. Canadian trial judges do not have the authority to determine the impartiality of prospective jurors (in the United States, judges do have this authority). The judge can ask the assembled panel of prospective jurors whether, if selected, they might be unable to serve on the jury (e.g., because of a health problem). The judge may excuse those who indicate they have concerns.

In Canada, the decision to select a jury is held by two layperson triers. To select the first juror, two individuals are randomly chosen and sworn to serve as triers. The triers listen to prospective jurors as they respond in turn to questions approved by the court. The triers must decide, after each response, whether the candidate is impartial. Once the candidate is deemed to be impartial, another prospective juror is called forward; the process continues until another impartial juror is found. When this happens, one of the original two triers is replaced. However, even if the triers decide that a juror is impartial, either the Crown prosecutor or the defendant may exercise a peremptory challenge, making the triers call another prospective juror. Once the twelfth juror is called, the jury is sworn.

There are two types of challenges in Canada: the **challenge for cause** (where a reason must be given for, and a determination made about, the validity of the challenge) and the **peremptory challenge** (where no questioning of prospective jurors takes place and where no cause need be stated as to why a potential juror is being eliminated). The purpose of both challenges is to eliminate jurors considered by either side to be unqualified or not impartial. In this process, the prosecution and the defence lawyer may challenge potential jurors in order to assess their appropriateness to sit on the jury. Potential jurors may be questioned under oath about such things as their personal background, occupation, residence, interest in the case, and attitudes about certain relevant issues; typically, though, the court allows only one or two specific questions—approved by the trial judge—to be put forward. Any citizen who is thought to have a bias for or against the accused—for example, a person who is a friend of the accused or who has already formed an opinion—will be eliminated. Sometimes potential jurors are not questioned at all—the Crown prosecutor and defence lawyer may simply look at the potential juror and/or the information they have about that person (which consists of name, address, and occupation) and use a peremptory challenge.

If there is a challenge for cause, a reason must be provided and the judge must determine whether the reason has merit. For either side, the usual approach is to challenge for cause first, as the number of peremptory challenges is limited. A potential juror may be challenged if, for example, he or she was convicted of an offence and incarcerated for more than 12 months, or is physically unable to serve on the jury, or cannot speak either official language of Canada, or is a non-Canadian or a landed immigrant (Criminal Code provisions, cited by Mewett and Nakatsuru 2000). If a potential juror is challenged peremptorily, no reason need be given.

Challenges for cause are rare in Canada (Vidmar 1999). Most challenges are peremptory, but the number of such challenges is limited. Section 634(1) of the Criminal Code was changed in 1992 to allow both the prosecutor and defence to exercise 20 peremptory challenges when the accused is charged with high treason or first degree murder, 12 challenges when the accused is charged with all other offences punishable by imprisonment of five years or more, or four peremptory challenges for all other offences. Different numbers of challenges open to the Crown apply in cases where there are accused being jointly tried.

Challenges for cause are used to determine whether prospective jurors are indifferent. Canadian courts have not allowed questions that are not relevant to showing partiality—the presumption is that all potential jurors will follow their oath. Historically, questions involving the possible racial bias of jurors have not been allowed in Canada. In 1993, the Ontario Court of Appeal was the first court to acknowledge the possibility of juror racial prejudice. In this case, *R. v. Parks* (1993), a Black male was accused of murdering a White male during a cocaine transaction in Toronto. Here, the Court of Appeal held that "it was essential for the accused to be able to ask potential jurors about their racial bias." The Court of Appeal "hoped that allowing one question would legitimate the trial process as fair and nondiscriminatory" (Roach 1999:228). Many judges, however, interpreted this ruling as being applicable only to the Toronto area. However, the Court of Appeal stated later on that one question could be asked throughout the province. The Court of Appeal also clarified what type of question could be asked: general questions related to the offence in question could not be asked. This question cannot be used for trials involving defendants who are gay or Vietnamese, because of "the lack of evidence of systemic discrimination against these groups."

This issue soon resurfaced. In *R. v. Williams* (1996), a trial judge in British Columbia refused to allow an Aboriginal male to ask a question to potential jurors relating to their potential biases. This ruling was appealed to the British Columbia Court of Appeal, which upheld the decision of the trial judge. This case was then appealed to the Supreme Court, which ruled in favour of the accused. And in *Mankwe v. R.* (2001), the Supreme Court held that the defence may question potential jurors about their views about Black people. This case involved a Black male who had been convicted by a jury of sexually assaulting a woman working for an escort agency in his apartment. The Supreme Court ordered a new trial, and ruled his lawyer could ask potential jurors whether they believed that Black people

- commit more crimes in Canada than other Canadians;
- have a greater propensity to commit crimes of violence;
- are more likely to commit crimes of a sexual nature than other races; and
- have a greater tendency to lie than people of other races do.

Table 8.3 summarizes the decisions from the *Parks*, *Williams*, and *Mankwe* cases.

Only the trial judge has the right to "**stand aside**" a prospective juror, and then only in limited circumstances. A judge may ask a juror to stand aside for reasons of personal hardship or any other reasonable cause (s. 633 of the Criminal Code). Exempting a prospective juror allows

TABLE 8.3 The Leading Cases Regarding the Potential Racial Bias of Jurors

Case	Year	Decision
R. v. Parks	1983	The Ontario Court of Appeal held it was essential for the accused to ask potential jurors about their possible racial biases.
R. v. Williams	1996	The Supreme Court of Canada overturned a British Columbia Court of Appeal that upheld a lower court judge not to allow an Aboriginal to ask a question to potential jurors about their possible racial biases.
Mankwe v. R.	2001	The Supreme Court of Canada held that the defence may question potential jurors about their view of Blacks.

the judge, in those situations where a full jury has not yet been sworn, to call back jurors in the hope that both sides can agree to allow them to serve as jurors. In these cases, however, the recalled jurors are subject to the same challenges as the other jurors (s. 641 of the Criminal Code).

Between 1992 and 2011, all juries in Canada consisted of 12 individuals. Until 1992, courts in Yukon and the Northwest Territories were allowed to select only six individuals. However, the Court of Appeal of the Northwest Territories held that such a jury was in violation of s. 15 of the Charter. Sometimes cases are tried by a jury of 11 because a judge has the power to discharge a juror because of illness or any other reasonable cause. A trial may continue as long as 10 jurors remain; if the number falls below 10, the jury must be discharged and the process started over, as specified by s. 634 of the Criminal Code.

In August 2011, the Fair and Efficient Criminal Trials Act (also known as the "mega-trials" legislation) came into effect. This legislation was designed to assist with large or complex cases (**mega-trials**) involving illegal activities such as terrorism, drug trafficking, and gang-related crime in order to ensure that cases arrive in court more efficiently than in the past. These trials are usually problematic to deal with since they typically involve a number of charges laid against numerous individuals, multiple witnesses, significant amounts of evidence, and lengthy delays, which may increase the likelihood of a mistrial.

The first mega-trial in Canada was heard in Ontario during the 1970s (*R. v. McNamara* (No. 1) [1981]; also referred to as the dredging conspiracy case), where 20 personal and corporate defendants were charged in a seven-count conspiracy indictment stemming from an alleged bid-rigging scheme extending over eight years. The trial lasted 197 court days over 15 months. At the conclusion of the evidence, defence counsel addressed the jury for seven days, the Crown prosecutor for 11 days, the judge's charge to the jury lasted seven days, objections to the charge continued for 11 days, and the jury deliberated for 14 days. The 20 accused individuals were charged with a total of 53 offences. The jury brought in 40 guilty pleas against 13 of the accused, found various accused not guilty of nine offences, and was unable to reach a verdict on four counts. In a 320-page judgment, the Ontario Court of Appeal unanimously affirmed the jury's verdict on all but seven counts, for which it ordered new trials. That decision was upheld by the Supreme Court of Canada four years later (*Canadian Dredge & Dock Co. v. The Queen*).

Issues related to mega-trials occurred again in 2011, when a Quebec Superior Court judge ordered that 31 of 155 accused persons be released due to the inability of the courts to handle the case efficiently (*Auclair v. R.*). He had criticized prosecutors for going forward with such a large trial without making sure that the criminal justice system could handle it efficiently. He pointed out that it was unlikely that the accused would have their court case until at least six years after their arrests. He held that the anticipated delays infringed upon the accused's s. 11(b) Charter right to be tried within a reasonable time period. In 2014, the Supreme Court upheld the Quebec judge's decision to stay the charges (*R. v. Auclair* [2014]).

The Fair and Efficient Criminal Trials Act amended the Criminal Code by allowing for

- A case management judge to assist with the preliminary stage of a trial by making decisions on preliminary issues such as imposing deadlines on the various parties, hearing guilty pleas, assisting the parties to identify issues with the evidence, and assisting those involved to identify the witnesses to be heard.
- A reduction in the number of processes required prior to the trial by holding hearings prior to dealing with multiple accused and charges where appropriate.
- The introduction of measures to better protect the identity of jurors so that they are able to better perform their duties.

At the end of October 2011, another amendment introduced by the Fair and Efficient Criminal Trials Act came into force—allowing the swearing in of 14 jurors. In mega-trials it was not uncommon for jurors to be discharged before a trial was over; if the number of jurors went below 10, there would have to be a new trial. This new amendment will prevent this from occurring. If more than 12 jurors remain after the judge's charge to the jury, there will be a random selection process to select the 12 jurors that will decide the verdict.

SUMMING UP AND LOOKING FORWARD

Some individuals may receive a stay of proceedings if the state has not been able to collect enough evidence to charge the suspect. Defendants have the right to a speedy trial to bring a case to court. It is important that our criminal justice system treats everyone fairly and does not discriminate against anyone. Most cases in Canada are tried within one year of the first court appearance. Many of these cases are dealt with in a single appearance, usually within four months of the initial court appearance.

A key aspect of the criminal justice system is that it treats all individuals fairly and does not discriminate against any one individual or individuals on the basis of, for example, race or gender. Jury trials (if used) are important parts of our system of criminal justice as they are thought to enhance the fairness of any particular trial and lead to greater confidence in the administration of justice as a whole. A recent Ontario investigation led to questions about the fairness of jury representation for residents of First Nations communities. There have been questions about the jury selection process over the past decades, resulting in the Supreme Court allowing a limited number of questions that can be asked to potential jurors about their views on issues relating to the race of the defendant. In recent years, mega-trials have led to changes in the way juror selection is conducted.

This chapter reviewed many of the criteria involved in pretrial criminal procedure; the next chapter covers aspects of criminal trials. Criminal trials are considered by many to be the high point of the formal criminal justice system. Yet, as we saw in Chapter 1 in our discussion of the crime funnel, in many cases a number of other solutions have already been achieved, such as plea bargaining to a lesser offence or no charges being laid at all.

Review Questions:

1. Do you think a stay of proceedings is always just and fair?
2. Do you think that the way governments resolved the issue of speedy trials (after the Askov and Morin cases) led to greater fairness in the criminal justice system?
3. Do you think other groups in our society should have equal representation on juries? Which ones?
4. Do you think that the revisions concerning the selection of jurors in mega-trials overcome the problems such trials faced before this legislation was passed?

Critical Issues in Canadian Criminal Justice

THE ISSUE OF CREDIT FOR PRETRIAL CUSTODY

In 2010/11, the rate of adults under correctional supervision was about the same as it was the previous year, but 7 percent lower than a decade ago. Significant changes occurred in the manner in which these adults were being supervised. In 2000–01, the percentage of adults in remand was 40 percent, while 58 percent were serving a sentence in custody. A decade later, these proportions had changed considerably, to 53 and 47 percent, respectively (see Figure 8.4). Also, on any given day in 2010/11, there were approximately 38,000 adults in custody across Canada. Of these, 36 percent were serving a sentence in a federal correctional institution

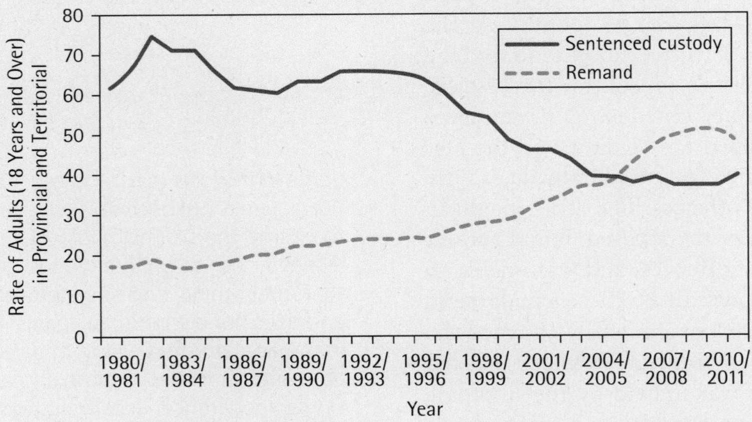

FIGURE 8.4 Average Counts of Adults in Provincial and Territorial Custody, by Type of Custody Status, 1980/81 to 2010/11

Source: Mia Dauvergne, "Adult correctional statisitcs in Canada 2010–2011." *Juristat* (October 11, 2012), Statistics Canada Catalogue no. 85-002-X 2012, p. 9, http://www.statcan.gc.ca/pub/85-002-x/2012001/article/11715-eng.pdf. Reproduced and distributed on an "as is" basis with the permission of Statistics Canada.

Critical Issues in Canadian Criminal Justice (*Continued*)

(two years or more), 34 percent were being held on remand, and 29 percent were in a provincial or territorial correctional facility (Dauvergne 2012).

One reason for the increased use of remand custody has been changes in the Criminal Code. Section 515(10) of the Criminal Code provides the reasons for which custodial remand is justified. It states that the prosecutor must "show cause" in order to justify the detention of the accused in custody. In the case of certain specified offences, for example murder, the onus is upon the accused to show cause as to why they should not be detained in custody. Traditionally, the detention of accused persons can be justified on the basis that (1) it is shown there is a risk they will not appear for their court date; and (2) they are considered to be a danger to themselves or to others. In 1997, this section of the Criminal Code was expanded to allow the use of remand when "the detention is necessary in order to maintain the confidence of justice having regard to all the circumstances." Two years later, in 1999, another amendment was added to ensure that the safety concerns of both victims and witnesses are taken into consideration in decisions involving remand. In addition, non-compliance with court orders has increased, with police-reported data indicating an increase of 40 percent in such violations over the past decade (Silver 2007).

In March 2009, the federal government introduced legislation (Bill C-25) in an attempt to limit judicial discretion in granting credit for pre-sentence custody. The most common credit for pretrial custody at the time of sentencing in Canada is two for one—six months in pretrial custody ends up being 12 months toward the sentence. The proposed legislation, entitled An Act to amend the Criminal Code (limiting credit for time spent in pre-sentencing custody), if passed, will limit judicial discretion when it comes to sentencing offenders. It is also referred to as the Truth in Sentencing Act. Truth-in-sentencing laws are used by over 40 states in the U.S. to mandate that violent offenders serve at least some of their sentence in prison (Sobel et al. 2002). While they were first enacted in 1984, most truth-in-sentencing laws came into existence after the U.S. Congress passed the federal Violent Crime Control and Law Enforcement Act (1994). The Act awards grants to states to expand prison space to punish violent offenders, if they can prove that offenders convicted of violent crimes (e.g., murder, manslaughter, sexual assault, robbery) serve at least 85 percent of their sentence. "Truth in sentencing" is a general term that has a number of goals:

- To restore truth to the sentencing process by eliminating situations in which offenders are released by a parole board after serving less than the minimum term to which they were sentenced.
- To increase the percentage of the term actually served in prison, with the purpose of reducing crime by keeping inmates imprisoned for a longer period.
- To control the use of prison space by giving correctional officials the benefit of predictable terms and policymakers advance notice of the impact that sentencing statutes will have on prison populations.

The new legislation (Bill C-25) passed on February 22, 2010, amending s. 719(3) of the Criminal Code, which had stated:

> 719.(3) In determining the sentence to be imposed on a person convicted of an offence, a court may take into account any time spent in custody by the person as a result of the offence.
>
> Under the new legislation, this section was replaced by the following:
>
> (3) In determining the sentence to be imposed on a person convicted of an offence, a court may take into account any time spent in custody by the person as a result of the offence but the court shall limit any credit for that time to a maximum of one day for each day spent in custody.
>
> (3)(1) Despite subsection (3), if the circumstances justify it, the maximum is one and one-half days for each day spent in custody unless the reason for detaining the person in custody was stated in the record under s. 515(9.1) or the person was detained in custody under s. 524(4) or (8).
>
> (3)(2) The court shall give reasons for any credit granted and shall cause those reasons to be stated in the record.
>
> (3)(3) The court shall cause to be stated in the record and on the warrant of committal the offence, the amount of time spent in custody, the term of imprisonment that would have been imposed before any credit was granted, the amount of time credited, if any, and the sentence imposed.
>
> (3)(4) Failure to comply with s. (3)(2) or (3)(4) does not affect the validity of the sentence imposed by the court.

Continued on next page

Critical Issues in Canadian Criminal Justice (*Continued*)

Bill C-25 placed a limit on the amount of credit that can be given for time served in remand to a ratio of one day for one day unless exceptional circumstances exist, although Parliament did not define what those circumstances might be. If an exceptional circumstance is determined, a judge is able to grant a ratio of 1.5 to 1, but the court is required to explain the reasons for the additional credit. These circumstances do not apply to those individuals who have violated conditions of bail or who have been denied bail due to their criminal record (Casavant 2009). A judge may decide to give less credit than one-for-one, including no credit whatsoever.

Why did the two-for-one pretrial credit sentence continue to exist as a part of the Canadian criminal justice system for so long? One reason given is that pretrial detention facilities across Canada are often overcrowded, sometimes with two or three individuals sharing the same cell. Individuals may be locked down for 18 hours or more each day, and there are very few programs or activities available. Another reason is that pretrial custody did not count toward parole eligibility. For example, if an individual was denied bail and spent six months in pretrial custody before being found guilty in court and subsequently sentenced to four years with a two-for-one credit, they will be able to apply for parole after having served 18 months. In comparison, an accused who is granted bail and receives the same four-year sentence can apply for parole after serving 16 months in custody. According to one defence lawyer, two-for-one credit "is only fair, given the jail conditions and the fact that the time does not count towards parole" (Kari 2008:A5).

In *R. v. Wust* (2000), the Supreme Court of Canada upheld the lower court decision to grant the defendant a credit of one year for their pretrial custody of 7.5 months, although in this case the credit resulted in a period of incarceration below the mandatory minimum sentence. According to the Supreme Court of Canada, mandatory minimum sentences must be interpreted and administered in a manner consistent with the criminal justice system's overall sentencing approach.

Yet, according to court decisions in Ontario, two-for-one credit is not a right. The Ontario Court of Appeal in 2006 held that the credit is not automatic, particularly when a judge determines someone remains a danger to society and has very little chance of being granted early parole. In *R. v. Francis* (2006), the Court of Appeal upheld a lower court decision not to apply the two-for-one credit because the offender posed "a serious danger to society and that he would not likely receive parole."

In 2007, the Ontario Court of Appeal once again ruled on the two-for-one credit. In *R. v. Thornton* (2007), it upheld a lower court decision not to grant credit for pretrial custody when it appeared that an offender was taking advantage of this system by intentionally accumulating time in pretrial custody so as to reduce his sentence.

The Supreme Court of Canada decided a trilogy of cases in 2014 involving appeals against the new federal legislation limiting pretrial credit. In all of these cases (*R. v. Summers* [2014]), *R. v. Clarke* [2014], and *R. v. Carvery* [2014]), the Supreme Court held that judges are to give 1.5 days of credit for every one day spent in pretrial custody.

Questions

1. Should credit for pretrial custody be eliminated entirely?
2. Are there other policies that could be introduced to reduce the number of individuals in pretrial custody?
3. Why didn't Parliament offer any consideration what the exceptional circumstances might be in Bill C-25?
4. Why do you think many judges are deciding against the provisions limiting pretrial custody introduced by the federal government?
5. Do you think the federal government should introduce a truth-in-sentencing policy for all sentences or only for certain types of offences, such as serious violent crimes?

SUMMARY

In our criminal justice system, there are rules and laws governing pretrial criminal procedure to ensure that justice is achieved.

KEY WORDS: strength of the case, prove guilt beyond a reasonable doubt, social structure of the case

Compelling Appearance, Interim Release, and Pretrial Detention

This section reviews how an accused is compelled to appear in court after he or she has been arrested. It is presumed that almost all persons charged with a criminal offence will be released unless the Crown can prove that further detention is needed.

KEY WORDS: lodging a complaint, endorsement, s. 553 offences, s. 469 offences, reverse onus, show cause, ladder approach, surety

The First Appearance

What Is Bail and Does It Achieve Justice? (p. 249)
What Is Legal Aid and Does It Achieve Justice? (p. 251)

Following the laying of charges, defendants make their first appearance in court and the charges are read to them. Other decisions may be made at this time, such as bail and the appointment of legal aid lawyers.

KEY WORDS: station house release, recognizance, legal aid, pro bono, judicare, staff system model (public defender model), mixed or combined model, self-help model

What Happens during Prosecutorial Screening?

Prosecutors screen cases to determine what approach should be taken with each case. A number of factors are involved with case screening, including the prosecutor's belief in the guilt of the accused and case priorities.

KEY WORDS: transfer model, unit model, legal sufficiency model, system efficiency model, trial sufficiency model, defendant rehabilitation model

What Is the Right to Disclosure?

The right to disclosure is found in s. 7 of the Charter. It imposes a duty on the prosecution to disclose all evidence it will be using in a trial and any other evidence the defence might find useful.

KEY WORDS: first-party production, third-party production

What Are the Different Types of Pleas?

An accused charged with an offence can plead guilty, not guilty, or one of three special pleas. When the accused pleads guilty, they are admitting they did, in fact, do the act in question (*actus reus*) and had the necessary mental state (*mens rea*). If a person pleads not guilty, the Crown has to prove they committed the offence.

KEY WORDS: general plea, special pleas, autrefois acquit, autrefois convict, pardon, summary conviction offence, summary conviction court

What Is the Purpose of a Preliminary Inquiry?

A preliminary inquiry is held when an accused is charged with an offence that has to be tried by a judge and jury, or when they elect to be tried by a judge and jury or by a judge alone.

KEY WORDS: preliminary inquiry (preliminary hearing), direct indictment

What Is Plea Bargaining?

Plea bargaining involves an accused agreeing to plead guilty in return for some sort of benefit.

KEY WORDS: mid-trial bargaining, charge bargaining, sentence bargaining, procedural bargaining, fact bargaining, label bargaining

What Is the Right to a Speedy Trial and How Has It Impacted the Courts?

When Is There a Stay of Proceedings? (p. 263)

Everyone charged with a criminal offence has the right to a speedy trial. Judges look at a number of factors when determining if this right has been violated.

KEY WORDS: length of the delay, explanation for the delay, waiver, prejudice to the accused

The Jury

When Is There a Right to a Jury Trial? (p. 266)
How Is a Jury Selected? (p. 267)

The members of the jury are the triers of fact in criminal trials. Jurors are selected after a process that involves different types of challenges.

KEY WORDS: jury, jury-vetting, jury array, jury roll, challenge for cause, peremptory challenge, stand aside, mega-trials

Critical Thinking Questions

1. Do you think that the way the bail system is set up delivers justice?
2. Do you think that our legal aid system achieves justice?
3. Do you think that both the defence and prosecution should have to disclose all information they have collected but is also important to the other actors?
4. Why do you think it took so long for the courts to formally recognize that jurors might be biased? Are there any other biases that you feel should be recognized by the courts?

Weblinks

For a discussion of various issues related to jury duty, see the following video from the Ontario government available on YouTube: "Jury Duty and You" (15:12). For a video on bail, which features the Bail Compliance Unit in Ontario, watch "16x9: Before the Courts: Inside Canada's Bail System" (16:03).

Court Cases

Auclair v. R. (2011), QCCS 2661.

Canadian Dredge & Dock Co v. The Queen (1985), 1 S.C.R. 662.

Mankwe v. R. (2001), O.J. S.C.C.

New Brunswick (Minister of Health and Community Services) v. G.(J.) (1999), 3 S.C.R. 46.

R. v. Askov (1990), 59 C.C.C. (3d) 449.
R. v. Auclair (2014), 1 S.C.R. 83.
R. v. Beare (1988), 45 C.C.C. (3d) 57 (S.C.C.).
R. v. Brydges (1990), 53 C.C.C. (3d) 330.
R. v. Carvery (2014), S.C.C. 27.
R. v. Clarke (2014), S.C.C. 28.
R. v. D.(E.) (1990), 57 C.C.C. (3d) 151.
R. v. D.(S.) (1992), 72 C.C.C. (3d) 575.
R. v. Francis (2006), Ontario Court of Appeal ONCA 41.
R. v. Hansen (1977), 37 C.C.C. (2d) 371.
R .v. Kokopenace (2015), SCC 28.
R. v. Kokopenace (2013), ONCA 389.
R. v. L (W.K.) (1991), 64 C.C.C. (3d) 321.
R. v. Lyons (1987), 37 C.C.C. (3d) 1.
R. v. Manninen (1987), 34 C.C.C. (3d) 385.
R. v. McNamara (No. 1) (1981) 56 C.C.C. (2d) 193 (Ont. C.A.).
R. v. McNeil (2009), S.C.C. 3.
R. v. Morin (1992), 278.
R. v. Murray (2000), 186 D.L.R. (4th) 125.
R. v. N.S. (2012), 3 S.C.R. 726.
R. v. Nahdee (1993), 26 C.R. (4th) 109 (Ont. Ct. Gen. Div.).
R. v. Nepoose (1991), 85 Alta. L.R. (2d) 8 (Q.B.).
R. v. O'Connor (1995), 123 C.C.C. (3d) 487 (B.C.C.A.).
R. v. Parks (1993), 15 O.R. (3d) 324, 24 C.R. (4th) 81.
R. v. Poulos (2015), O.J. No. 1282.
R. v. Pozniak (1994), 92 C.C.C. (3d) 472.
R. v. Prosper (1994), 3 S.C.R. 236.
R. v. Sherratt (1991), 1 S.C.R. 509.
R. v. Stinchcombe (1991), 3 S.C.R. 326, 68 C.C.C. (3d) 1.
R. v. Summers (2014), S.C.C. 26.
R. v. Thornton (2007), Ontario Court of Appeal ONCA 366.
R. v. Williams (1996), 106 C.C.C. (3d) 215 BCCA.
R. v. Wust (2000), 1 S.C.R. 455.

Suggested Readings

Friedland, M. 1965. *Detention Before Trial.* Toronto: University of Toronto Press.

Horner, J. 2007. *Canadian Law and the Canadian Legal System.* Toronto: Pearson.

Mewett, A. and S. Nakasuru. 2000. *An Introduction to the Criminal Process in Canada.* Toronto: Carswell.

Paciocco, D., S. Skurka, and D. Tanovich. 1997. *Jury Selection in Criminal Trials: Skills, Science, and the Law.* Toronto: Irwin Law.

Stuart, D. 2014. *Justice in Canadian Criminal Law,* 6th ed. Toronto: Carswell.

Trotter, G. 2013. *Understanding Bail in Canada.* Toronto: Irwin Law.

References

Abbate, G. 2000. "Lawyers to Get Code of Conduct on Evidence." *The Globe and Mail*, November 30, p. A8.

Anderson, P. and D. Newman. 1993. *Introduction to Criminal Justice*, 5th ed. Toronto: McGraw-Hill Ryerson.

Baer, N. 2005. "Modern Justice: Recent Criminal Code Updates Aim to Make the Justice System Sleeker, Techno-Friendly and Fair." *Justice Canada* 2.

Black, D. 1989. *Sociological Justice*. New York: Oxford University Press.

Blatchford, C. 2000. "Ken Murray's Not-So-Excellent Adventure." *Canadian Lawyer* 24(10):28–33.

Boland, B., P. Mahanna, and R. Scones. 1992. *The Prosecution of Felony Arrests, 1998*. Washington, DC: Bureau of Justice Statistics.

Brannagan, C. 2011. "Police Misconduct and Public Accountability: A Commentary on Recent Trends in the Canadian Justice System." *Windsor Review of Legal and Social Issues* 30:61–90.

Brucker, T. 1992. "Disclosure and the Role of the Police in the Criminal Justice System." *Criminal Law Quarterly* 35:57–76.

Buckley, M. 2010. *Moving Forward on Legal Aid: Research on Needs and Innovative Approaches*. Ottawa: Canadian Bar Association.

Burns, P. and R. Reid. 1981. "Delivery of Criminal Legal Aid Services in Canada: An Overview of the Continuing 'Judicature versus Public Defender' Debate." *UBC Law Review* 15:403–29.

Casavant, L. 2009. *Bill C-25: Truth in Sentencing Act*. Parliamentary Information and Research Service. Ottawa: Library of Parliament.

Coughlan, S. 2008. *Criminal Procedure*. Toronto: Irwin Law.

Dauvergne, M. 2012. *Adult Correctional Statistics in Canada, 2010/11*. Ottawa: Canadian Centre for Justice Statistics.

Davison, C. 2005. "The Values of a Jury Trial." *LawNow* 30:37–38.

Davison, C. 2000. "A Right to Fairness: Legal Aid." *LawNow* 24:14–16.

Doust, L. 2011. *Foundation for Change: Report of the Public Commission on Legal Aid in British Columbia*. Vancouver, B.C.

Friedland, M. 2012. "The Bail Reform Act Revisited." *Canadian Criminal Law Review* 16:315–22.

Friedland, M. 2004. "Criminal Justice in Canada Revisited." *The Criminal Law Quarterly* 48:419–73.

Friedland, M. 1965. *Detention Before Trial*. Toronto: University of Toronto Press.

Frohmann, L. 1991. "Discrediting Victims' Allegations of Sexual Assault: Prosecutorial Accounts of Case Rejections." *Social Problems* 38:213–26.

Hamilton, A. and C. Sinclair. 1991. *Report of the Aboriginal Justice Inquiry of Manitoba*, vol. 1. Winnipeg: Queen's Printer of Manitoba.

Hans, V. and N. Vidmar. 1986. *Judging the Jury*. New York: Plenum.

House of Commons Debates. 1986. 26 May. Hansard VI: 62.

Jacoby, J. 1979. "The Charging Policies of Prosecutors." Pp. 75–97 in *The Prosecutor*, edited by W. McDonald. Beverly Hills, CA: Sage.

John Howard Society of Ontario. 2013. *Reasonable Bail?* Toronto: John Howard Society of Ontario.

Johnstone, R. and J. Thomas. 1998. *Legal Aid in Canada: 1996–97*. Ottawa: Juristat.

Kari, S. 2008. "Pretrial Credit on Trial." *National Post*, August 5, p. A5.

Law Reform Commission of Canada. 1989. *Plea Discussions and Agreements*. Ottawa: Law Reform Commission of Canada.

Law Reform Commission of Canada. 1982. *Report on the Jury*. Ottawa: Law Reform Commission of Canada.

Law Reform Commission of Canada. 1975. *Criminal Procedure: Control of the Process*. Ottawa: Minister of Supply and Services Canada.

Law Reform Commission of Canada. 1974. *Discovery in Criminal Cases*. Ottawa: Justice Canada.

Levine, J. 1992. *Juries and Politics*. Pacific Grove CA: Brooks/Cole.

Makin, K. 1999. "Punished Prisoners Win Access to Legal Aid." *The Globe and Mail*, September 16, p. A3.

Mewett, A. and S. Nakatsuru. 2000. *An Introduction to the Criminal Process in Canada*, 4th ed. Scarborough, ON: Carswell.

Perkel, C. 2013. "Killer's Conviction Tossed over Lack of Aboriginals on Ontario Juries." *The Canadian Press*. Retrieved March 2, 2015 (http://www.citytnews/2013/06/14/).

Perras, D. 1979. "Plea Negotiations." *Criminal Law Quarterly* 22:58–73.

Roach, K. 1999. *Due Process or Victims' Rights: The New Law and Politics of Criminal Justice*. Toronto: University of Toronto Press.

Silver, W. 2007. *Crime Statistics in Canada, 2006*. Ottawa: Canadian Centre for Justice Statistics.

"Smoking Guns: Beyond the Murray Case." 2000. *Criminal Law Quarterly* 43:409–10.

Sobel, W., K. Rosich, K. Kane, D. Kirk, and G. Dubin. 2002. *The Influence in Truth-in-Sentencing Reforms on Changes in States' Sentencing Practices and Prison Populations*. Washington, DC: Urban Institute Justice Policy Center.

Stuart, D. 1995. "Prosecutorial Accountability." Pp. 330–54 in *Accountability for Criminal Justice: Selected Essays*, edited by P.C. Stenning. Toronto: University of Toronto Press.

Stuart, D. and R. Delisle. 1995. *Learning Canadian Criminal Law*. Scarborough, ON: Carswell.

Tibbetts, J. 2002. "Legal Aid System Falling Apart, Justice Department Report Says." *National Post*, February 19, p. A5.

Tochor, M. and K. Kilback. 1999. "Defence Disclosure: Is It Written in Stone?" *Criminal Law Quarterly* 43:393–408.

"Tragedies Are All Too Foreseeable." 2008. *The Globe and Mail*, April 29, p. A12.

Vidmar, N. 1999. "The Canadian Criminal Jury: Searching for a Middle Ground." *Law and Contemporary Problems* 62:141–72.

Vidmar, N. and R. Schuller. 2001. "The Jury: Selecting Twelve Impartial Peers." Pp. 126–56 in *Introduction to Psychology and the Law*, edited by R.A. Schuller and J.R.P. Ogluff. Toronto: University of Toronto Press.

Webster, C., A. Doob, and N. Myers. 2009. "The Parable of Ms. Baker: Understanding Pretrial Detention in Canada." *Current Issues in Criminal Justice* 21:79–102.

Wheatley, J. 1974. "Plea Bargaining: A Case for Its Continuance." *Massachusetts Law Quarterly* 59:31–41.

The Courts and Criminal Trial Procedure

Learning Objectives

After completing this chapter, you should be able to:

- Differentiate between the burden of the court and the burden on the accused hypotheses.
- Differentiate among the due process, crime control, and bureaucratic models of the criminal courts.
- Understand how criminal courts are organized.
- Understand the central roles of defence lawyers, Crown prosecutors, and judges.
- Understand the legal rights of the accused in a criminal trial.
- Understand the key elements of the criminal trial.
- Understand the appeal process and be able to differentiate among the different types of appeals.

The criminal courts play an important role in our criminal justice system. As discussed in the previous chapter, the Supreme Court has held that the police have a constitutional obligation to inform suspects of their right to retain legal counsel. But assuming that a case goes to trial, is it possible for someone to represent themselves? And if so, what happens when they do?

Due to the increasing costs of litigation, more and more Canadians have been representing themselves instead of hiring lawyers to look after their cases as they progress through all the stages of the criminal justice system up to and including a trial in criminal court. In March 2006, Madam Justice Marvyn Koenigsberg of the Supreme Court of British Columbia commented during a Toronto conference on access to justice that lawyers' fees "are completely beyond the reach" of most Canadians (Blackwell 2006:A6).

Sometimes defendants fire their lawyers and end up representing themselves in criminal court even though the charges against them are serious. In *R. v. Phillips* (2003), for example, the defendant, who was charged with attempted murder and other serious offences, fired several of his lawyers before the trial. He represented himself in the trial, during which he refused to cross-examine witnesses, presented no evidence in his own defence, and failed to follow the judge's instructions about possible defences. Upon his conviction, he appealed to the Alberta Court of Appeal, which dismissed his case. The appeal court judges noted that the trial court judge had considered a number of relevant factors pertaining to the defendant, including the fact that he could have afforded to pay a lawyer to represent him, his attempts to delay the trial, his ability to conduct his own defence, and the nature of the charges. The majority on the appeal court decided that "while an accused person has a constitutional right to a fair trial, there is no constitutional right to funded legal counsel in every case, nor is representation by a lawyer a prerequisite to a fair trial." These judges held that the defendant had been capable of defending himself and thus had received a fair trial.

Our adversarial system of criminal justice relies upon the effectiveness of legal counsel for both the prosecution and defence in order to discover the truth concerning the actions of the accused. In theory, every individual accused of a crime comes to court protected by the presumption of innocence and the promise of effective representation by well-prepared defence counsel. Since there has been a decline in the amount of funding for legal aid (see Chapter 8), more individuals are self-representing if they want to go to court, raising questions about access to justice. According to Doust (2011:8), when litigants involved in criminal trials have to represent themselves, "it is extremely difficult, if not impossible, to either resolve the matter without a trial or even to expedite the process." In Canada, the right to legal representation is based on the need for fairness, and this applies to representation at trial. Most cases, however, are completed before a court trial. During 1999–2000, for example, cases in the criminal courts made up just 9 percent of all cases, compared to cases where the accused was convicted with a guilty plea (53 percent) and those otherwise terminated by the court without a trial (Pereira and Grimes 2002). Even for those cases that do reach a formal court trial, the early stages of the legal process are important; research indicates that critical decisions about cases are made at all stages of the criminal justice process (Hann et al. 2002). Many important decisions are made during the earliest stages of case processing. As Currie (2003:10) has noted, while "criminal trials may be more demanding than the pre-trial stages with respect to legal technicalities, the earlier stages are, nevertheless, adversarial, formal and complex." But what factors should be taken into account when considering whether legal counsel is necessary for a fair trial? In *R. v. White* (1977), the trial judge gave the following list:

- The characteristics of the accused such as financial situation, language skills, and education.
- The complexity of legal and evidentiary matters.
- The possible outcome—for example, the possibility of imprisonment.

The extent of **self-representation** at all stages in the criminal process is significant. In their study of nine provincial courts across Canada, Hann and colleagues (2002) found that significant percentages of the criminally accused were being convicted without ever being represented by legal counsel. For example, they found that the rate of not having legal representation varied among the courts studied. At the first appearance, for example, the percentage of individuals charged with a criminal offence not represented by legal counsel varied in the different sites studied between 5 and 61. For the second appearance, that percentage was between 2 and 38, while for the third court appearance it was between 1 and 32 percent. For bail hearings, the percentage of unrepresented accused varied between 3 and 72. When the accused entered a plea, between 6 and 41 percent were unrepresented, while at the final appearance, 6 to 46 percent of all accused were unrepresented.

This has led to the development of the **burden of the court** hypothesis, which has two components. The first posits that the rising number of legally unrepresented accused is placing considerable pressure on other court actors (i.e., prosecutors and judges) who must then assist the accused. For example, our system of disclosure obligates the defence counsel to request disclosure from the prosecution. However, in those cases where the accused is "self-representing," the prosecutor is obligated to ensure that the accused is informed of the right of disclosure and to assist the accused in determining how the disclosure process will proceed. According to Hann and colleagues (2002), the perception of the various court officials interviewed was that the sheer numbers of legally unrepresented were leading to "a greater burden on and increased workloads for the court" (Currie 2003:15). For example, over a 10-day period in March 2003, court workers in Winnipeg helped 764 self-representing individuals file documents (this number of hours included both criminal and non-criminal matters). Court workers invested 67 hours of their time in person and 14 hours on the telephone to help people going to court without a lawyer. This increase in the number of people representing themselves in court is undermining the basic principle of the adversarial court process (O'Brien 2004:A5).

The second component of the "burden of the court" hypothesis is that the self-representing accused will slow down the court process because judges, in order to ensure fair process, will have to intervene in order to help the accused. The most commonly cited errors made by the self-represented at trial found by Hann et al. are noted in Table 9.1. In their study, Hann and colleagues (2002) concluded that the "burden of the courts" hypothesis is not supported. These researchers, however, also concluded that the data support a **burden on the accused** hypothesis. For example, the accused often self-represent for ill-advised reasons—perhaps they believe that they cannot wait for a lawyer to argue the case. This can lead to worse consequences when a sentence is determined.

Self-represented litigants also are attempting to appeal their cases. In 2013, it was reported that approximately 14 percent of all filings before the B.C. Court of Appeal were made by self-represented litigants (Vancouver Sun 2014).

What Are the Models of the Criminal Courts?

The most popular model of our criminal courts is adversarial, with the state in a contest against the accused, with a number of legal protections in place for defendants. This approach is most commonly found in the *due process* and *crime control models* (see Chapter 1). A third model, the *bureaucratic model* (also referred to as the *organizational model*)

TABLE 9.1 Most Frequently Cited Errors Made by Unrepresented Accused at Trial

Stage	Error or Omission
Trial	• Not demanding a trial or a dismissal on trial days when the Crown witnesses have failed to show up. • Not reading the disclosure or learning the Crown's case against them. • Going to trial where there are no real triable issues. • Deciding to testify when they should not, or thinking that they "are supposed to" testify. • Making accidental and damaging admissions, e.g., "Yes, I hit her but she hit me too." • Not calling the witnesses they need. • Not availing themselves of processes which can help them, such as a hearing on the confession. • Not asking for a directed verdict when the Crown has not proved its case. • Not understanding the available defences. • Not seeing the relevance of evidence. • Not being able to effectively scrutinize witness testimony without a lawyer. • Poor cross-examination, including that which makes them look bullying or abusive.
Sentencing	• Not knowing what arguments to make at sentencing. • Not knowing the best arguments to use (or not use) with particular judges. • Not knowing the mandatory sentences for certain offences. • Not mentioning improvements they have made in their lives since the offence, e.g., getting a job or taking treatment. • Not being aware of or asking for a certain type of sentence, e.g., conditional discharge or intermittent sentence. • Not speaking up to argue against the imposition of unworkable conditions of sentence when they are discussed or read out in court, conditions which must then be altered—or will be violated.

Source: Legal Aid Research Series-Court Site Study of Adult Unrepresented Accused in the Provincial Criminal Courts Part 1: Overview Report. Figure 5.4 Most Frequently Cited Errors Made by Unrepresented Accused at Trial, p. 27, http://www.justice.gc.ca/eng/rp-pr/csj-sjc/ccs-ajc/rr03_la2-rr03_aj2/rr03_la2.pdf. Department of Justice Canada, September 2002. Reproduced with the permission of the Department of Justice Canada, 2015.

focuses instead on the workloads of the criminal courts, the high number of guilty pleas made at the first appearance, and the importance of hearing and deciding cases in as speedily and efficiently a manner as possible (see *Criminal Justice Insight* later in this chapter).

The Due Process Model

The primary focus of our court system to ensure justice is achieved through criminal trials that are fair; that is, protecting individual citizens from the unfair advantages held by the agents of the state. Fairness is the most important consideration, much more so than convicting people. Rights guaranteed to individuals by the Charter of Rights and Freedoms, such as the right to a jury trial, the right to defence counsel, and the right to face the accuser in the courtroom, are viewed as "equalizers" that ensure the various parties in a court trial enjoy as equal a footing as possible. According to this model, the best way to attain fairness is through **adjudication**, which refers to decision making in an open court. This approach emphasizes the adversarial nature of our court system (see Chapter 1): (1) a neutral and impartial judge makes the decisions; (2) the prosecution and the defence have an equal chance to present relevant evidence; and (3) a highly structured set of procedures (e.g., constitutional safeguards) must be followed during the trial. It is through this system, due process advocates argue, that truth is discovered and upheld by the courts.

The Crime Control Model

This approach stands in contrast to the due process model by arguing that while safeguarding individual liberties is important, it is secondary to protecting society (and law-abiding citizens) from criminals. The police are not allowed to engage in abusive behaviour, but the courts do allow them to utilize devious techniques to outwit offenders. With regard to the courts, this model emphasizes punishment; it is the courts' responsibility to ensure that offenders are punished for their actions and for the harms they have inflicted. The main goal of the courts is not to ensure that the accused is given a "fair" chance, but rather to achieve justice through deterrence and harsh punishments. Constitutional rights are there to protect the law-abiding citizen, not the accused.

The Bureaucratic Model

In the **bureaucratic model**, there is a stronger focus on the day-to-day operations of the courts. While punishing criminals and protecting their constitutional rights is still a concern, the main focus is on the bureaucratic process—in particular, on the speed at which the courts can work. The length of court trials is a paramount factor here, and so is the number of appearances the accused has to make (thereby taking up valuable court resources, including time). As we saw at the beginning of this chapter, the authorities are deeply concerned about the length of court trials and about backlogs as well (a number of individuals each year are sentenced to serve their punishment in a correctional facility, but then released because they have already served a considerable amount of time waiting for the trial to start). In this model, success for judges and the court system is measured in terms of the speed at which cases are moved along rather than whether or not justice has been served. According to some observers, the adversarial nature of our courts is reflected less in the confrontation between the accused and the accuser, than in the tension between the ideals of justice and the realities of the bureaucracy (Feeley 1981).

How Are the Canadian Criminal Courts Organized?

The Canadian criminal justice system encompasses a variety of provincial and federal courts. In fact, there are in effect 14 different court systems at work in Canada: 13 provincial/territorial and 1 federal. These systems all differ from one another other in certain ways (see Figure 9.1).

An overview of the basic principles of our court system is necessary in order to understand how the courts in Canada are organized. Each court has a geographical jurisdiction: provincial and territorial courts are responsible for cases arising within their boundaries, and the Supreme Court of Canada has jurisdiction over the entire country. The provinces and territories vary in how they provide court services. Generally, however, in larger cities and towns there are permanent courts (**provincial/territorial courts** and **provincial/territorial superior courts**) while in rural areas, if there is no permanent court, services are offered by **circuit courts**.

Provincial courts are divided into courts of limited jurisdiction and courts of general jurisdiction. **Courts of limited jurisdiction** (in the bigger centres there are usually a number of these) "specialize" in certain areas, such as

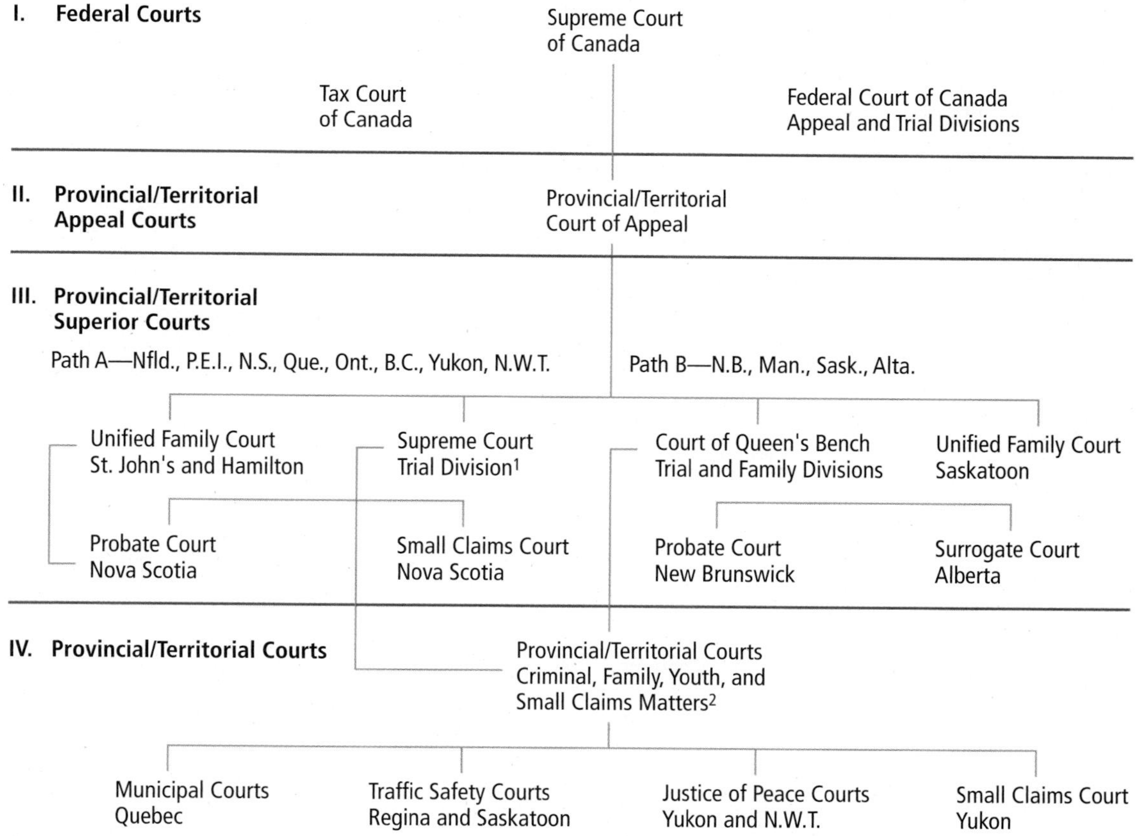

FIGURE 9.1 The Organization of the Canadian Courts

[1] Known as Superior Court of Justice in Ontario and the Superior Court in Quebec.

[2] Known as Ontario Court of Justice in Ontario and the Court of Quebec in Quebec. Small claims matters in P.E.I., New Brunswick, and Manitoba are heard in Superior Court. In Quebec, family matters are heard in Superior Court, Family Division.

Source: From KENNEDY/SACCO. *Crime Counts*, 1E. ©1996 Nelson Education Ltd. Reproduced by permission. www.cengage.com/permissions.

motor vehicle violations. The proceedings are presided over by a single judge, who makes the decisions. Most minor criminal cases are decided in these courts. Justices of the peace (or magistrates, as they are known in some provinces) are part of this level of courts. In most jurisdictions, these individuals provide law enforcement agents with search and seizure warrants, summonses, and subpoenas, as well as remand warrants (i.e., they conduct bail hearings).

Courts of general jurisdiction deal with the most serious criminal offences. Depending on the type of offence, the case may be decided by a judge and jury or by a judge sitting alone. To take the caseload pressure off these courts, some provinces have introduced what are referred to as special subject-matter courts. For example, a number of provinces now have courts that specialize in family violence and drug offences. Each province/territory also has **appeal courts**. In these, a number of judges hear and decide on cases where the convicted individual or the Crown prosecutor is appealing a decision made by the lower courts.

The Supreme Court of Canada is essentially an appeal court, in the sense that it has authority over all provincial/territorial appeal courts as well as those cases originally heard by the federal court system. The Supreme Court has final authority over all public and private law in Canada. This includes all federal, provincial, and municipal laws, as well as all common law, legislation, and constitutional interpretation (Bowal 2002). It usually hears between 70 and 90 cases a year, and more than half of these are **leave of appeal cases**; that is, they are "hand-picked by subcommittees of three Supreme Court judges because they involve legal issues of general importance" (Greene et al. 1998:100). The remaining cases are serious criminal cases that either the accused or the Crown has a right to have heard by the Supreme Court; these are known as **"as of right" appeals**. In these, there has been a dissent over the case in a provincial/territorial appeal court concerning a question of law, or a provincial/territorial appeal court has overturned a trial court acquittal (see Figure 9.2).

The Supreme Court "creates" criminal justice policy in two different ways. The first is known as **judicial review**, which refers to the Court's power to decide whether a law or policy created by a province/territory is constitutional. This is also referred to as the "lawmaker" role. Many of the cases discussed in this text have involved appeals to the Supreme Court; if they are heard there, a judgment (i.e., a judicial review) will be made of the province's right to establish the law on which the case was based. The second area is the Supreme Court's authority to interpret the law, also referred to as the **law interpreter** role. Here, the Supreme Court interprets statutory laws as they have been applied to specific situations. Many of the cases discussed or mentioned in this text involve the Supreme Court interpreting a specific piece of legislation or ruling on a specific law enforcement issue—for example, the granting of search warrants (e.g., the *Feeney* decision on search warrants). When seven Supreme Court justices were asked whether they saw one of these two areas as more important than the other, all of them indicated that both were important (Greene et al. 1998).

It is common practice to refer to the "lower" and "higher" courts in Canada. The **lower courts** are the provincial courts, which try all provincial and summary conviction offences; **superior courts** hear only indictable offences. The **higher courts** encompass the provincial appeal courts, such as the Ontario Court of Appeal.

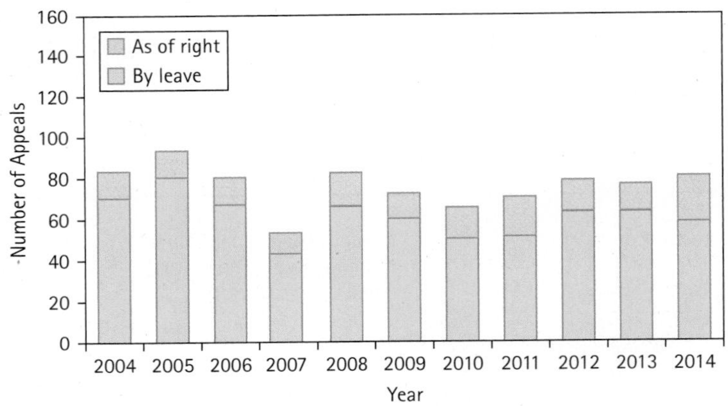

FIGURE 9.2 Appeals Heard by the Supreme Court of Canada, 2004–14: As of Right/By Leave

Source: Supreme Court of Canada: Statistics 2004 to 2014, page 7. Reproduced with the permission of the Supreme Court of Canada, 2015. http://www.scc-csc.gc.ca/case-dossier/stat/cat3-eng.aspx and http://www.scc-csc.gc.ca/case-dossier/stat/cat3-eng.aspx

jiawangkun/Shutterstock

The Supreme Court of Canada building, located in Ottawa.

Appeal courts are also known as the **courts of last resort**, meaning that they are the final authority in cases under their jurisdiction. Nonetheless, all individuals have the right to apply for leave to appeal to the Supreme Court of Canada, even if the provincial appeal court denies their application for an appeal.

The Court System

The word "court" refers to a complex part of the criminal justice system. Before a case enters the criminal court, the only elements of it that exist are suspected criminal offences, allegations of wrongdoing, police investigations, charges, and issues concerning bail. The only proof required prior to a criminal trial is **probable cause**; in order to convict a defendant in a criminal case, a higher standard of proof—**beyond a reasonable doubt**—must be met. This higher standard is meant to ensure that only those individuals who are found guilty (also referred to as **legal guilt**) are punished, not those who are thought to be guilty (also known as **factual guilt**). Higher standards of proof also contribute to higher levels of public confidence in both the fairness and the accuracy of the criminal justice system.

Anyone who has been arrested and who has entered a plea then faces a number of decisions that have a significant impact on the determination of guilt and innocence—as well as on any punishment in the event of a finding of guilty. Besides the defendant, four other key participants emerge during the court proceedings: Crown prosecutors, defence counsel, judges and juries, and victims and witnesses. Only a court or a court-appointed official can decide whether to detain an accused prior to trial, and only the courts can decide on a defendant's guilt or innocence. In addition, the court must decide on the appropriate type and length of sanction. Note that the word "court" is used here in reference to a number of different places or individuals. It can be a room where a case is being heard, or a group of judges (e.g., the Supreme Court of Canada), or a single judge.

A judge is an **officer of the government** who is in charge of a court of law. The duties of a judge include deciding which evidence can be admitted in trial, which questions are appropriate to ask, and how procedural issues are to be settled. In a jury trial, the judge also has to charge (i.e., instruct) the members of the jury about the evidence and charges before they adjourn to the jury room to decide on the guilt or innocence of the accused. If the trial is to be decided by judge alone, he or she determines the guilt or innocence of the accused.

SUMMING UP AND LOOKING FORWARD

Criminal trials are central to the finding of guilt or innocence and they attempt to reconcile the rights of the accused with the protection of society and the rights of victims. Three different models are used to analyze the functions of the criminal court system. In Canada, the courts are divided on the basis of provincial/territorial and federal jurisdictions. Each provincial/territorial court system is divided into courts of limited jurisdiction, courts of general jurisdiction, and courts of appeal. The Supreme Court of Canada hears all appeals from the provincial/territorial courts as well as the federal courts. "Lower courts" refers to the provincial courts, while the superior courts hear only indictable offences. The higher court is a term used to refer to the provincial/territorial appeal courts.

While the criminal trial is commonly viewed as the venue for discovering the truth, the criminal courts don't always follow this image. The idea of two opposite sides arguing for truth with adversarial tactics is not what necessarily happens in trials; instead, the courts can be characterized as engaging in negotiated deals, and disposing of cases in as quick and efficient a manner as possible. What actually happens in these courts on a day-to-day basis, particularly the provincial/territorial lower and superior courts, is referred to as the daily business of the courts, and this is discussed in the next section.

Review Questions:

1. What is the "burden on the accused" hypothesis?
2. What are the main differences among the three different models of the criminal courts?
3. What is the difference between courts of limited jurisdiction and courts of general jurisdiction?
4. How does the Supreme Court of Canada develop criminal justice policy?

Procedural Justice and the Courts

Most if not everyone agrees that the goal of the courts is to be fair in their resolution of conflicts and accurately administer the law. The courts have to take people and their issues seriously as this impacts upon their acceptance of the final decision and whether or not people will abide by the decisions of the court. According to Tyler (2007/08:31), "whether people feel that justice has been achieved is central to their trust and confidence in the court system." Not everyone in Canada feels the criminal courts are doing a good job. For example, in her analysis of perceptions of the criminal courts by Aboriginal and non-Aboriginal women, Brennan (2011) reported that only 39 percent of Aboriginal women and 41 percent of non-Aboriginal women included in the 2009 General Social Survey (see Chapter 4) indicated that they perceived the criminal courts to be doing a good job in terms of ensuring a fair trial for the accused.

Why are so few people satisfied with the courts in terms of their ability to ensure a fair trial? And how can these perceptions be changed? According to Tyler, one first has to recognize what the goals of the judicial system are. Tyler suggests there are three goals of the judicial system:

1. providing people with a forum in which they can obtain justice as defined by law;
2. dealing with people's issues in such a way that they will accept and abide by the court decision; and
3. retaining and enhancing the public's trust of the court and confidence in the courts, the judiciary as well as the law.

According to Tyler, gaining the public trust is essential to developing and maintaining the legitimacy of the legal system. How is this accomplished? People are more likely to agree and abide by a decision if it is made through a fair procedure. This type of approach "legitimates the decision and creates commitment to obeying it that is found to persist into the future" (Tyler 2007/08:28).

What are the court experiences that should be emphasized and practised by the courts that will enhance the public trust in them and lead to greater satisfaction and compliance with judicial decisions? According to Tyler (2007/08:30–31), the following are necessary:

1. *Voice*—people want to tell their side of the story prior to any decision being made;
2. *Neutrality*—judges should practise transparency and be open about how the rules are being applied and how their decisions are being made;
3. *Respect*—when people bring their issues to court, they want their cases to be treated with respect by the judiciary; and
4. *Trust*—people want judges to listen to and consider their issues in a fair and just manner, and not be biased in any of their rulings and decisions.

The perceptions of the criminal courts could increase if the judiciary could indicate that they are listening to people and considering their arguments, and show how they have taken these into account when making their decisions.

How Does the Court System Operate in Canada?

The criminal trial is viewed as the way in which due process protections are followed in order to ensure a fair trial. Court procedures are controlled by law, tradition, and judicial authority. These procedures govern, among other things, who may speak, when they may speak, and in what order they may speak. In addition, what can and cannot be said in court is dictated by the rules of evidence, and any questions about the admissibility of evidence are settled by the judge.

What Is the Reality of the Daily Business of the Courts?

Most cases—even those cases involving serious violent crimes—are commonly heard in the provincial (as opposed to the superior) courts. In their analysis of almost one million court cases across Canada over three years (1998–99 to 2000–2001), Webster and Doob (2007:57) found an "increasing inclination of both prosecutors and defence lawyers in hybrid offence cases (i.e., cases in which the Crown can opt to proceed summarily . . . or by way of indictment, whereby the accused can choose the court in which the case is resolved) to opt for trial in the Provincial Court."

Studies and reports about Canada's provincial courts have consistently found that in most cases the accused pleads guilty, on first appearance in court, to the charge as laid. For example, Ericson and Baranek (1982) found that 91 of 131 accused individuals (70 percent) pleaded guilty to at least one charge when they appeared in court. Only 21 pleaded not guilty; 15 were found guilty on at least one criminal charge, and 6 were acquitted. Seventeen had their charges withdrawn or dismissed. In the remaining two cases, the accused did not appear in court to face the charges. A study by the Ontario government of cases in process during 1998 found that 91.3 percent of all criminal cases were resolved without a trial. Just over 75 percent of these cases were resolved prior to the trial, while the remaining 15 percent were resolved on the actual date of the trial (Ontario Ministry of the Attorney General 1999). In British Columbia, a 2010 public commission into legal aid reported that over 80 percent of all criminal trials were resolved before trial (Doust 2011).

In the lower courts, the police may play an important role in prosecutorial discretion. Crown prosecutors often have little time to prepare for a case; for the sake of expediency they must then rely on information provided by the police. Prosecutors sometimes follow the suggestions of the police officer involved in the investigation (Ericson 1981). Desroches (1995:244) found that the police work closely with Crown prosecutors "to avoid lengthy trials that tie up courts, judges, police officers, prosecuting attorney, and witnesses." If the police succeed in obtaining a statement of guilt from the accused, they can bargain with the defence counsel from a position of strength. In most of these cases (about 60 percent), the accused are offered no concession for their guilty pleas. And those who are able to reduce the number of charges against them in return for a guilty plea are given no guarantee of a shorter sentence.

Prosecutors can of course use their own discretion to stay proceedings, withdraw charges, or dismiss the charges altogether. For example, they may decide, given the circumstances of a case, to use their discretion to expedite matters for the victims. Prosecutors have been known to use their discretion to settle cases before the trial in order to speed up the decision making in the criminal justice system and to protect child victims from the trauma of appearing and testifying in court (Campbell Research Associates 1992). Other reasons for prosecutors' deciding not to prosecute a case include insufficient evidence, witness problems, due process problems, a plea on another charge, and referral to another jurisdiction for prosecution. For example, Vinglis and colleagues (1990) found that Crown prosecutors in Ontario withdrew charges in drunk driving cases because witnesses were not available, errors were found by prosecutors in the technical requirements of the Criminal Code, the police failed to collect available evidence, the evidence did not substantiate the charge, and/or the information was improperly worded. Cases were also dismissed because the accused was charged in a number of different cases, the prosecutor decided to dismiss charges in exchange for a guilty plea, the accused agreed to attend a diversion program, or the accused was wanted for a more serious crime in another jurisdiction.

The Defence Lawyer

Defence counsel represents the legal rights of the accused in criminal proceedings and tries to ensure that the criminal justice system operates fairly. Some people believe that the defence lawyer's goal is to work out the best deal for the client with the prosecutor; in fact, an important part of the defence lawyer's role is to ensure that the client's legal rights are protected. To achieve this goal, defence lawyers typically examine all the evidence collected by the police—the evidence that will be used by the prosecutor in the case as per the Stinchcombe rule (see Chapter 8)—in order to assess the strength of the Crown's case in the proving of the defendant guilty beyond a reasonable doubt. This examination can, of course, lead a defence lawyer into conflict with the police, prosecutors, witnesses, and victims, who may feel that they are being attacked. But the role of the defence lawyer is not to criticize anyone as an individual; rather, it is to assess the validity and reliability of the evidence and testimony being used by the prosecutor. Defence lawyers, then, are "a check brake upon the vast machinery of the state—police officers, Crown prosecutors, and judges—as it seeks to deprive individual citizens of their liberty and freedom" (Davison 2006:39–40).

The defence lawyer is also responsible for preparing the case, as well as for selecting a strategy for attacking and questioning the prosecutor's case. Since most defendants are not trained in the operation of the law, they are unsure of how to proceed. A defence lawyer ideally helps their client understand what is happening in court and the consequences of the charges if the client is found guilty. The defence lawyer sometimes hires individuals to investigate certain aspects of the case or contact other experts in the field to get a second opinion.

Some of the most significant work of the defence lawyer relates to their discussion of the case with the police and the prosecutor. The defence has probably worked with the investigating officers and the prosecutors on past occasions. Usually, they discuss the strength of their client's case and assess the chances of gaining a satisfactory plea bargain.

The defence lawyer represents the accused at all stages of the criminal justice process, including bail hearings, plea negotiations, and preliminary inquiries. If the trial is to be decided by a jury, defence lawyers question prospective jurors. If the client is convicted, they will argue for the lightest possible sentence. A defence lawyer who loses a case and who is dissatisfied with the sentence or with a legal issue may file an appeal in the hope that the appeal court will either reverse the lower court's decision or reduce the sentence.

Throughout the trial process, the formal function of the defence lawyer is to "exercise his professional skill and judgment in the conduct of the case . . . [and] fearlessly uphold the interest of his client without regard to any unpleasant consequence to himself or any other person" (Martin 1970:376). If the accused admits to the defence lawyer that they committed the crime in question, the lawyer, if convinced that the admission is true, can contest the case by objecting to such legal issues as the form of the indictment and the admissibility or sufficiency of the evidence. However, that lawyer cannot suggest that another individual committed the crime, nor can they introduce any evidence believing it false or for the purpose of establishing an alibi for the accused. (See Exhibit 9.1 for a selection of the powers held by defence lawyers.)

Criminal defence lawyers are commonly asked how they can defend someone they know is guilty. According to the Canadian Bar Association's (1987) *Code of Professional Conduct*, defence lawyers are required—even when they know the client is guilty as charged—to protect that client as much as possible. Our legal system insists that accused individuals have the legal right to use every legitimate resource to defend themselves. This means that defence lawyers are required to question the evidence given by witnesses called by the prosecution and attempt to point out that the evidence taken as a whole "is insufficient to amount to proof that the accused is guilty of the offence charged"; however, "the lawyer should go no further than that" (Martin 1970:376). Some view the role of defence lawyers as necessary to protect the integrity of our legal system; if they refuse to protect the guilty, "the right of a defendant to be represented by counsel is eliminated and with it the entire traditional trial" (Swartz 1973:62).

EXHIBIT 9.1 Selected Powers of Defence Lawyers

The powers of defence counsel include the following:

- making sure that full disclosure is provided by the Crown
- making sure that all matters related to the accused's case are fully explored and properly adjudicated
- making sure that all evidence given to them by the Crown was collected in accordance with constitutional standards
- making sure that all evidence relevant to the accused's case is presented at trial
- cross-examining Crown witnesses
- when an accused is convicted, making sure that the punishment is proportionate to the seriousness of the offence
- making sure that all apparent errors made during the trial are appealed

The Crown Prosecutor

Crown prosecutors play a pivotal role in the courts, as it is they who present the state's case against the defendant. According to the CBA's *Code of Professional Conduct*, the primary duty of Crown prosecutors is not to gain a conviction but rather to enforce the law and maintain justice by presenting all the evidence relevant to the crime being tried in criminal court. Thus, for example, the prosecutor must disclose "to the accused or defence counsel . . . all relevant facts and known witnesses" that could influence "the guilt or innocence, or that would affect the punishment of the accused." As such, the role of the Crown prosecutor differs significantly from that of defence counsel. This role was articulated by a member of the Supreme Court of Canada, who stated in *Boucher v. The Queen* (1955):

> [i]t cannot be over-emphasized that the purpose of a criminal prosecution is not to obtain a conviction, it is to lay before a jury what the Crown considers to be credible evidence relevant to what is alleged to be a crime. Counsel have a duty to see that all available legal proof of the facts is presented: it should be done firmly and pressed to its legitimate strength but it must also be done fairly. The role of the prosecutor excludes any notion of winning or losing; this function is a matter of public duty. In civil life there can be none charged with greater personal responsibility. It is to be efficiently performed with an ingrained sense of the dignity, the seriousness and the justness of judicial proceedings.

Crown prosecutors are instructed that during their assessment of the evidence, "a bare prima facie case is not enough; the evidence must demonstrate that there is a reasonable prospect of conviction. This decision requires an evaluation of how strong the case is likely to be when presented at trial" (Government of Canada Department of Justice, Federal Prosecution Service Deskbook, s. 15.3.1). Assuming that the evidence test is met, an important consideration for prosecutors is to consider the public interest, such as crimes against children and the elderly, as well as organized crimes and the use of weapons.

Many prosecutors are torn between maintaining an impartial role in the courts and attempting to find the defendant guilty as charged. Grosman (1969:63) says there is pressure on prosecutors to gain as many convictions as possible. This pressure to succeed at trial stems from two factors. The first is that in order to "maintain his administrative credibility and to encourage guilty pleas the prosecutor must demonstrate that he is able [to] succeed consistently at trial." If he failed to demonstrate this ability, more cases would be taken to court, because the defence would feel that it had a good chance to gain a favourable result for its client. The second consideration is that "confidence in present administrative practices is maintained only if the acquittal rate is not substantial." So to maintain their credibility, prosecutors attempt to gain as many guilty verdicts as possible. As a result, caseload pressure forces prosecutors to decide on the outcome of a case more on the basis of expediency than on that of justice. This has led to criticisms that the justice system provides little more than **assembly-line justice** (see Chapter 1).

Some argue that this role makes prosecutors more powerful by enabling them to define the parameters of a court case. For example, the prosecutor presents the Crown's side of the case in an opening address to the judge before the jury has heard anything else. While the opening address may be criticized in court, it makes a significant first impression. Karp and Rosner (1991:74) have argued that in the David Milgaard case, the Crown prosecutor gave a "damning and convincing argument" to the jury, taking "full advantage" of the tradition that allows the Crown to speak first, and providing "a lengthy exposition of what he expected the forty-two witnesses to say when called to the stand." A large number of responsibilities are associated with the trying of cases, such as examining court documents sent by a variety of individuals—including coroners and the police—in order to determine whether further evidence is required. Crown prosecutors can be held civilly liable if their decisions are malicious or an abuse of process (see Exhibit 9.2).

EXHIBIT 9.2 Selected Powers of Crown Prosecutors

The powers of the prosecution include the following:

- detaining the accused in custody
- instructing the police to investigate alleged offences
- deciding whether or not to stay or proceed with charges
- negotiating pleas
- electing to proceed by way of summarily or by indictment
- deciding whether or not to appeal a decision

Investigating: Malicious Prosecution

As the common law developed, an important issue was raised: Can the Crown be held liable for any of its actions if they were maliciously pursued or were an abuse of process? The answer was no, because it was held that the King could do no wrong. Today, it is widely believed that our legal system is designed and operates in such a way as to prevent innocent people from being wrongfully harmed as they are investigated and/or processed by the justice system. In addition, the right to a fair trial has been repeatedly supported by the courts and legislatures. In recent decades, however, a number of mistakes, including wrongful convictions, have occurred as a result of errors made by representatives of the Crown (i.e., Crown prosecutors and the police). These errors had a serious impact on the lives of the citizens involved.

In 1989, the Supreme Court of Canada, in *Nelles v. Ontario* (1989), rejected the idea that Crown prosecutors are immune from civil liability. Susan Nelles was a nurse at the Toronto Hospital for Sick Children. After a number of infant deaths, she was charged with four murders. Her case was discharged after the preliminary inquiry with the judge citing a lack of sufficient Crown evidence. She then successfully started a civil action against the police and the Attorney General of Canada. In its decision, the Supreme Court developed a four-part test to determine whether the Crown should be held liable for malicious prosecution.

The Supreme Court ruled that the plaintiff must prove the following four elements before the courts can decide that a Crown's prosecution was malicious. This test does not make it easy for the plaintiff, since "the last thing society needs are police and prosecutors afraid to do their respective jobs" (Hughson 2004:34):

Continued on next page

Investigating: Malicious Prosecution *(Continued)*

- The proceedings must have been initiated by the defendant.
- The proceedings must have terminated in favour of the plaintiff.
- Reasonable and probable grounds must have been absent.
- There must have been malice, or a primary purpose other than that of carrying the law into effect.

When Susan Nelles's case was finally heard in the Ontario courts, a key issue revolved around prosecutorial immunity. While she settled with the police for $190,000, she continued her case against both the Ontario government and the Attorney General of Ontario. The immunity defence was heard by the Supreme Court, which decided in 1989 that Ms. Nelles could continue her case against the Attorney General for malicious prosecution but not the Crown of Ontario itself, as it had immunity under provincial legislation. In 1991, Ms. Nelles settled with the Ontario government for $60,000 (the amount of her legal fees).

The Supreme Court has had to deal with the issue of malicious prosecution in a number of cases since *Nelles*. In *Proulx v. A.G. of Que*. (2001), for example, it ordered the Quebec Crown to pay Benoit Proulx $1.1 million, "saying that it perverted the man's murder prosecution to obtain a wrongful conviction" (Makin 2001:A11). Proulx successfully sued the Quebec government for malicious prosecution after the Quebec Court of Appeal acquitted him of his jury conviction for murder and was critical of the evidence used against him at trial, "saying the case was built on flimsy evidence and conjecture, bolstered by unlawful interrogations and unfair traps" (ibid.). In addition, the Supreme Court modified the third element of the Nelles test by stating that this test is to be met on the basis of whether or not there is a reasonable likelihood of conviction based on admissible evidence.

In *Dix v. Canada (A.G.)* (2002), Dix successfully sued the Attorney General of Canada on behalf of the RCMP as well as the Crown prosecutor involved in the case. Dix had been charged for a double homicide. His charges were stayed after allegations of misconduct were made against the Crown prosecutor. The police had used evidence from "questionable" jailhouse informants; the case then fell apart when Dix's lawyer suggested that the Crown prosecutor "had misrepresented evidence at one of Mr. Dix's bail hearings in January, 1997" (Powell and Rusnell 1999:A8). The Court of Queen's Bench judge immediately halted the trial and appointed a new prosecutor. On reviewing the evidence, the new prosecutor reported that there was no reasonable likelihood of conviction. At his request, the judge dismissed the charges against Dix.

In *Miazga v. Kvello Estate* (2009), a Crown prosecutor prosecuted parents accused of sexual assault by their foster children. The claims were outrageous, and included claims of ritual killings of babies and animals. The prosecution continued against the parents, although "the allegations were unbelievably preposterous" (Bowal and Horvat 2011:59). The children later recanted all of their allegations.

The Supreme Court found no liability on the part of the prosecutor, stating that malice was not established. A plaintiff bringing a malicious prosecution lawsuit must prove a negative—an absence of reasonable and probable cause for prosecuting. A prosecutor must believe in the guilt of the accused according to their professional judgment of the strength of the case, and that belief must be reasonable in the circumstances. The Supreme Court pointed out that malice is a question of fact; that is, it requires evidence that the prosecutor was motivated by an improper purpose. In order for someone to bring a malicious prosecution lawsuit today, they will have to prove that the prosecutor deliberately intended to abuse their prosecutorial powers. Requiring proof of an improper purpose, the malice requirement protects prosecutors from incompetence, honest mistakes, and gross negligence. This means that "only the most egregious case of bad faith prosecution will be punished by civil damages. Under this new standard, it is unlikely that Nelles would have won her case against the Attorney General of Ontario" (Bowal and Horvat 2011:59).

The scope of prosecutorial work is extensive. Prosecutors' duties encompass the entire criminal justice system from investigation and arrest through bail and trial sentencing to appeals. One possible result of this involvement is overload. Gomme and Hall (1995) studied Crown prosecutors in one Canadian province between 1990 and 1992 to find out whether prosecutors are prone to work-related stress. They found that prosecutors routinely prosecuted six to ten trials each day in provincial court five days each week. The number of trials increased to between 12 and 14 during peak periods. The impact of this workload "severely constrains the time available to undertake the careful preparation required to ensure that the quality of legal work meets prosecutors' personal and professional standards" (ibid.:193). They found that prosecutors were susceptible to work overload and excessive strain, leading to questions about their professional effectiveness and whether justice is compromised.

Judges

The role of judges in our criminal justice system includes upholding the rights of the accused and arbitrating any disagreements that arise between a prosecutor and defence lawyer during a trial. In addition, judges who act as triers of fact in cases decide whether the defendant is guilty or innocent; in such cases, they also determine the type and length of sentence. It is important that judges be viewed as objective; only when they are seen as impartial will their decisions on rules of law and procedure be viewed as acceptable by all the parties involved. Some of the powers held by judges in our criminal justice system are identified in Exhibit 9.3.

Section 11(d) of the Charter states that, "Any person charged with an offence has the right . . . to be presumed innocent until proven guilty according to law in a fair and public hearing *by an independent and impartial tribunal*." The words "independent" and "impartial" are distinct from each other. Impartiality generally refers to the court deciding cases based on the merits, without bias, and not being influenced by any of the parties involved or by any outside force. Judicial independence is an *unwritten* constitutional principle. Independence generally refers to the objective, institutional relations between the court and the government. A court is considered to be independent only if the following three objectives are met:

1. security of tenure (i.e., judges cannot be dismissed except for cause);
2. financial independence (i.e., judges' salaries and benefits have to be established by law); and
3. administrative independence (i.e., judges should not be manipulated by the assignment of judges to cases or the setting of court lists).

Canada's constitution gives the federal Cabinet the power to appoint provincial superior trial court judges, provincial/territorial court of appeal judges, federal court judges, and tax court judges, and to identify judges who could be appointed to the Supreme Court of Canada. Provincial Cabinets have the power to appoint judges to the provincial court system below the level of the superior court. Appointments of provincial court judges are determined by three distinct non-partisan appointment procedures. In Ontario and Quebec, judicial nominating committees seek out the best candidates and recommend them to the Attorney General for review and appointment; in Alberta and British Columbia, provincial judicial councils screen applicants, who are then recommended to the Attorney General; and in Saskatchewan and Newfoundland and Labrador, judicial councils comment on the qualifications of candidates proposed to them by the Attorney General (Greene 1995). In the remaining provinces, patronage continues to be evident in judicial appointments; in 1985, the Canadian Bar Association reported that patronage remained an important criterion in provincial court appointments (McCormick and Greene 1990). Russell (1987) points out that though many good lawyers have been appointed to judgeships in return for their favours, some inappropriate appointments have been made as well.

CP PHOTO/Tom Hanson

In 2000, Beverley McLachlin was sworn in as the first female Chief Justice of the Supreme Court of Canada.

EXHIBIT 9.3 Selected Powers of Judges

The powers of judges include the following:

- deciding questions of fact
- deciding questions of law
- applying the law to the facts
- interpreting and applying the Charter

SUMMING UP AND LOOKING FORWARD

Most criminal cases are heard in the lower courts, and the rate of individuals pleading guilty during their first court appearance is high. Defence lawyers represent the legal rights of the accused and try to ensure that their client's legal rights are protected. Other aspects of the role of defence lawyers include making sure that there is full disclosure and cross-examining witnesses for the Crown.

Crown prosecutors represent the state's case against the accused. While one of the roles of prosecutors is to convict the accused of their offences, their primary duty is to enforce the law and maintain justice. The burden of proof in a criminal trial is upon the prosecution, as they must prove its case against the accused. This means prosecutors have to conform to the appropriate legal procedures and rules. The duties of prosecutors also include negotiating pleas and deciding to elect to proceed by way of summary or indictment. The standard of proof in a criminal trial is "beyond a reasonable doubt." Judges uphold the rights of the accused and resolve all disputes between defence lawyers and prosecutors. Other duties of judges include deciding questions of fact and interpreting and applying the Charter. In the next section, criminal trial procedures are examined—more specifically, the legal rights of the accused.

Review Questions:

1. How does the daily business of the courts differ from the view that the criminal court is the location of an adversarial form of justice?
2. For what purposes can prosecutors use their discretionary powers?
3. What are the key roles of defence lawyers?
4. What are the key roles of prosecutors?
5. What are the key roles of judges?

Criminal Trial Procedure

The criminal trial is the start of the **adjudication** stage of the criminal justice system. It is also the centrepiece of our court system. If the accused pleads guilty, a date is set for the sentencing (see Chapter 10). However, if the accused elects to be tried in court, various alternatives exist, depending on the charge. One choice the defendant can make is trial by judge and jury. Jury trials are relatively rare in Canada; Thomas (2004) found that during 2003–04, only about 2 percent of all cases were heard at the superior court level in the six reporting jurisdictions. Since these are usually high-profile cases, they attract much media attention; this is why so many Canadians believe that they are typical of what happens in the Canadian justice system.

What Legal Rights Exist in Criminal Trials?

The point of a criminal trial "is for the prosecution to prove, according to law, the guilt of the accused" (Mewett and Nakatsuru 2000:133). This means that the prosecutor must prove that the defendant committed the act in question and had the appropriate mental element at the time the criminal offence was committed. Every trial involves certain legal principles concerning the rights of the accused; these are specified in the Charter of Rights and Freedoms and in rules of evidence. These rights were introduced to ensure that the accused would be given a fair trial. Discussed below are the most fundamental rights that accused persons possess in the Canadian legal system.

The Presumption of Innocence

According to s. 11(d) of the Charter, everyone has the right "to be presumed innocent until proven guilty according to law in a fair and public hearing." The burden of proving guilt in a court of law lies with the state (i.e., the prosecutor). Even if the accused is factually guilty, the prosecutor still has to convince a judge or jury that the defendant is legally guilty.

The Right of the Accused to Confront the Accuser

The right of the accused to confront the accuser is essential to a fair trial, since it controls the type of evidence used in court. **Hearsay evidence**—that is, second-hand information—is accepted as evidence only in rare circumstances, such as, for example, when it is information divulged by a dying person. This is what happened in a famous American criminal case involving the Ford Motor Company and one of its vehicles, the Pinto (Cullen et al. 2006). In this case, it was ruled that a deathbed statement made to a nurse by a victim of a traffic accident involving a Pinto could be entered into the court record, even though it could not be corroborated. This evidence proved to be a major factor in the outcome of the case.

Furthermore, the accused (usually through the defence lawyer) has the right to **cross-examine** all witnesses and victims who testify for the prosecution. Cross-examination allows the defence to challenge (and perhaps thus discredit) any statement or testimony given by a prosecution witness or a victim.

Child sexual assault legislation allows a child to testify outside the courtroom when the accused is charged with certain sexual offences. Judges are permitted to allow a child to testify from behind a screen or via closed-circuit television from another room in the courthouse. However, the provisions in this legislation protecting children from the sight of the alleged abuser have not always been accepted outright by members of the judiciary. In *R. v. Ross* (1989), the Nova Scotia Court of Appeal upheld the constitutionality of the provision, ruling that "the right to face one's accusers is not, in this day and age, to be taken in a literal sense. . . . It is simply the right of the accused person to be present in court."

The use of videotape as the sole evidence of the victim's testimony, however, has proved to be more problematic. In *R. v. Meddoui* (1990), heard in the Court of Queen's Bench of Alberta, the trial judge accepted the videotape of the victim as evidence. However, in another case that same year (*R. v. Thompson* [1990]), the use of videotape was ruled as violating ss. 7 and 11(d) of the Charter. In the future, therefore, the use of videotape as prima facie evidence will likely be rare in Canadian courts.

The Right to a Public (Open) Trial

Do members of the public have the right to attend criminal trials in Canada? And do the members of the media have the right not only to attend criminal trials but also to publish reports on what they heard in the case? Courts are public institutions and therefore accessible to the public. But what about the ability to access and publish documents in the media related to a case? The principle of openness allows the media to access and publish such materials unless a judge considers that the application "would render the proper administration of justice unworkable" (*C.B.C. v. New Brunswick Attorney General* [1996]). In Canada, this principle of openness is not absolute as there are some federal and provincial restrictions limiting the ability of the public or media to access and publish information pertaining to a criminal case. Federal legislation, for example, gives the trial judge the discretion to order a publication ban of information that would disclose the identity of the complainant or witness in sexual offences (s. 486(3) of the Criminal Code). However, in these cases a judge has no discretion when the complainant or a witness is under the age of 18 and applies for a publication ban (in these cases, a prosecutor can also apply for a ban on publication). Section 276(3) of the Criminal Code prohibits discussions that involve the admissibility of evidence about the sexual activity of the defendant.

In other cases, however, what are the rights of the media to report on the facts and identities of the individuals involved? The judicial tradition in Canada has been to "interfere as little as possible with the fundamental right of freedom of expression. . . . Publicity is the burden that citizens of democratic countries must bear when they go to court" ("An Excessive Use . . ." 2004).

The right of individuals to attend a public trial and publish materials about it is referred to as the **open court principle**. In the pre-Charter common law rule concerning bans on publishing, the right to a fair trial was emphasized over the free-expression interests of those affected by the ban. This meant that the common law "required that those seeking a ban demonstrate that there was a real and substantial risk of interference with the right to a fair trial" (Eastwood 2004:36). While this issue is not addressed explicitly by the Charter, s. 2(b) guarantees freedom of the press and other forms of the mass media. However, freedom of the press is limited by s. 1 of the Charter, where it has been held that freedom of the press is not an absolute. A discussion of the most fundamental rights that accused persons possess in the Canadian legal system follows.

Publication Bans

While most criminal trials are open to reporting by the media, a public trial is for the benefit of the accused. Section 11(d) of the Charter states that any person charged with an offence has the right "to be presumed innocent until proven guilty according to law in a fair and public hearing." This means that justice cannot be served by secret court trials.

Publication bans are mandatory on the evidence and information produced at bail hearings. This is because bail hearings can disclose prejudicial information about defendants, such as their prior criminal record, that will likely be inadmissible at trial. Since bail hearings are held in open court, journalists are free to report the submissions of legal counsel, the reasons for the ruling by the judge, whether the bail application was granted or denied, and the conditions, if any, placed on those individuals released. Only after an accused's completed trial has finished can this information be made public and this may be years later. A number of media outlets disputed this mandatory ban in 2010, arguing that it is an unjustifiable breach of free speech and the public's right to know. The Supreme Court of Canada upheld the publication ban, with the majority holding that the fair access to bail and a fair trial outweighs the negative limits placed on the media as well as the fact that the ban is temporary (i.e., the information can be made public after the trial is completed). However, the dissenting justice stated that a "mandatory ban on the evidence heard and the reasons given in a bail application is a ban on the information when it is of most concern and interest to the public" and that such a ban is "a profound interference with the open-court principle" (*Toronto Star Newspapers Ltd. v. Canada* [2010]).

As noted earlier, the accused can ask the judge to order a ban on the publication of certain evidence emerging in a preliminary inquiry. In such a case, the name of the accused can be published, but specific evidence presented in court cannot, as "this might jeopardize the ability of the accused to receive a fair trial" (Boyd 1995:41). The rationale is that the media could give out information that biases potential jurors or judges. As a result, great care is taken to protect the accused.

These cases typically involve issues concerning the effects of pretrial publicity and whether publicity will influence the right of the accused to a fair trial. The Supreme Court ruled in *Dagenais v. CBC* (1994) that the right to a fair trial does not take precedence over the right to a free press; in this way it rejected the approach taken in the pre-Charter common law. It now requires instead "a balance to be achieved that fully respects the importance of the rights that have come into conflict" (Eastwood 2004:35). In *Dagenais*, the members of a Catholic religious order charged with physically and sexually abusing young boys in their care applied to a superior court judge for an injunction restraining the CBC from showing the miniseries *The Boys of St. Vincent* on television. The Court of Appeal agreed, but limited the extent of the injunction to Ontario and Montreal. The Supreme Court stated that the common law rule was inappropriate since it emphasized the right to a fair trial over the right to freedom of expression. When Charter rights come into conflict, Charter principles require a balance that respects both. The Supreme Court then set out a modified common law rule (referred to as a "test") that would be used in future cases to establish the fairness of a trial:

> A publication ban should only be ordered when:
>
> (a) such a ban is necessary to prevent a real and substantial risk to the fairness of a trial, because reasonably available alternative measures will not prevent the risk; *and*
>
> (b) the salutary effects of the publication ban outweigh the deleterious effects to the free expression of those affected by the ban.

The judgment in *Dagenais* "held the promise of a new era of open courts. Press freedom would no longer automatically rank behind other constitutional freedoms" (Makin 2003:A8). Yet publication bans have continued to be granted in large numbers since *Dagenais*, largely as a result of the priority given to protecting the privacy of groups in Canada. However, due to a "jurisdictional oddity," provincial appellate courts cannot hear challenges to publication bans (s. 40[1] of the Supreme Court Act). Instead, someone wanting to challenge a publication ban must obtain leave to appeal to the Supreme Court, a process that is "costly and usually doomed because the court can only hear a tiny proportion of cases" (ibid.).

In order for a publication ban to be granted by the courts, both the criteria noted in *Dagenais* must be satisfied. A question arises from this issue: Just how much does pretrial publicity influence jurors? Freedman and Burke (1996:257) studied the effects of pretrial publicity in the Paul Bernardo case to evaluate whether it would have posed a real and substantial risk to the fairness of the trial. In their study of 155 adults who served as mock jurors in this case—a case aptly described as "one of the most sensational cases in Canadian history"—they found that pretrial publicity had only a limited negative effect on the verdict. This led the researchers to conclude "there was no relation between the amount heard and ratings of guilt or verdicts either before or after the trial account."

There are other reasons why a publication ban may be sought in Canada, such as to protect the techniques used by the police in an undercover operation. In *R. v. Mentuck* (2001) a publication ban was sought by the Crown prosecutor because it was felt that the facts of the case (which involved an undercover police operation) could jeopardize the identity of police officers as well as reveal the operational methods used by the police in similar undercover operations. The trial judge granted a one-year ban concerning the identity of the undercover police officers but refused to order a publication ban regarding the operational methods. The Crown appealed the decision to the Supreme Court of Canada. The Supreme Court stated that the protection of rights in the Charter of Rights and Freedoms, such as the right to a fair trial, was "not the only legitimate objective under which a judge can consider the common law discretion to grant a publication ban" (Eastwood 2004:37). However, the Supreme Court noted that it could not directly apply the "test" it had established in *Dagenais* since the publication ban applied for in *Dagenais* was based on protecting the accused's right to a fair trial, whereas in *Mentuck* the publication ban had been applied for in order to protect the safety of undercover police officers as well as to keep from public knowledge the type of police operation used. To properly assess the issue of a publication ban in *Mentuck*, the Supreme Court replaced the "fairness of the trial" test established in the first criterion of *Dagenais* with "the proper administration of justice."

In terms of the publication ban concerning the identity of the undercover police officers, the Supreme Court accepted the one-year publication ban as decided by the trial judge. The Supreme Court decided that the ban on identifying the officers was "necessary and there is no reasonable alternative." The request for a publication ban concerning the operational methods of the police was held as unnecessary by the Supreme Court, which stated that the publication of this information "does not constitute a serious risk to the efficacy of police operations, and thus to that aspect of the proper administration of justice." The reality of the risk must be "well-grounded in evidence." Furthermore, the Supreme Court stated that "the benefits this ban promises are, at best, speculative and marginal improvements in the efficacy of undercover operations and the safety of officers in the field, but the deleterious effects are substantial. Such a ban would seriously curtail the freedom of the

CP PHOTO/Jacques Boissinot

Television cameras record the opening day of an appeal trial involving two biker club members convicted of manslaughter in 1996; Wednesday, March 15, 2000, at the courthouse in Quebec City.

press in respect to an issue that may merit widespread public debate."

Another important issue involving publicity and criminal cases is whether trials should be televised as a matter of right. The situation in Canada is different from that in the United States, where in 1981 the U.S. Supreme Court removed all constitutional obstacles to the use of television over the complaints of the accused. As a result, during the summer of 1995 many Canadians watched live TV coverage of the O.J. Simpson trial, though they could view only artists' sketches of the Paul Bernardo trial.

According to s. 486(1) of the Criminal Code, a judge has the right to exclude the public for all or part of the trial if they feel it is in the "interest of public morals, the maintenance of order, or the proper order of administration." Exclusion is most commonly ordered when a child or mentally challenged person is about to testify and the judge believes that exclusion will assist the witness.

One of the most controversial decisions a judge can make is to exclude the media. Rarely are members of the media banned from the courtroom. It is more common for a superior court judge to issue a non-publication order to protect "the integrity of the court." In addition, s. 486(3) expressly allows a trial judge to ban the publication of anything that would identify the names of the complainant or witnesses in trials involving sexual offences.

The Right to a Fair Criminal Trial

A criminal trial is a formal process that strictly follows rules of evidence, procedure, and criminal law. The formality and rigidity implied by this definition stand in sharp contrast to trials shown on many television shows and in movies, which present the courtroom as a "no-holds barred" arena in which defence lawyers and prosecutors ask leading questions, act in a prejudicial manner, and win cases through courtroom trickery. The reality is that every criminal trial follows a particular procedure that must be observed by all parties involved. As a result, trials are complicated events, and the judge has to make decisions about technical questions of procedure and about what evidence is allowed to enter the court.

The key actors are the prosecutor and defence lawyer, who present their case as persuasively as they can and in a manner that they hope is most likely to lead to an adjudication in their favour. Prosecutors use police reports, testimony from witnesses and victims, and physical evidence in an attempt to persuade the court that the defendant is guilty. The defence lawyer tries to point out weaknesses in the prosecutor's case, and at the same time presents evidence beneficial to the accused. The defence lawyer tries to ensure that his or her client's constitutional rights are protected. Since only one side can win, both the prosecutor and the defence lawyer will assess the trial in order to see whether an appeal is necessary.

The Opening Statement

Once the jury has been selected and the trial begins, the criminal charges are read to the jurors by a court employee. Both the prosecutor and the defence lawyer then have the right to make opening statements to the jury. In Canada, the prosecutor presents the first opening statement. This statement usually includes a summation of the criminal charges, the facts of the case, and the Crown's plan on how it will proceed. However, the prosecutor cannot be biased or impartial in his or her opening comments, since the prosecutor's role is to assist the jury in arriving at the truth. In other words, Crown prosecutors have a duty to be impartial, and this duty precludes any notion of winning or losing. They must guard against stating information that is likely to excite and inflame the jury against the accused. Nor may they "express a personal opinion as to the guilt of the accused or state that the Crown [is] satisfied as to the accused's guilt" (Salhany 1986:274).

The defence can choose not to make an opening statement. The defence lawyer, too, outlines the case but informs the jury of how he or she intends to show that the defendant is innocent of all charges. This plan entails describing how he or she will prove the prosecution's case to be inadequate.

Prosecutors cannot promise evidence that they will not be bringing to court. If they mention the name of a particular witness and the testimony they expect from that witness, and this individual does not appear, the judge may rule the statement was prejudicial toward the accused and subsequently set aside any verdict of guilt. In addition, the prosecutor cannot mention any evidence that he or she knows will be inadmissible and cannot mention the prior record of the accused, if one exists.

If the trial does not involve a jury, the opening statements can be brief, as the judge is probably knowledgeable about the case, the appropriate rules of law, and some of the evidence, which may already have been discussed in a preliminary inquiry.

All evidence submitted in the court in an attempt to prove the defendant innocent or guilty must meet the highest standard of proof. The standard is "**guilty beyond a reasonable doubt**," and it is viewed as the basis for reducing the risk of mistaken conviction if there are questions about certain facts presented during the trial. The standard goes hand in hand with the belief that it is better to release one hundred guilty individuals than to convict one who is innocent.

Criminal Justice Insight

Amount of Time to Complete Criminal Court Cases in Canada, 2011–12

As we have seen, the Charter guarantees that accused persons have a fundamental right to be brought to trial in a timely manner. But how long does it take to carry out a trial from the first court appearance to case completion? While there is no specific time limit for court cases to be completed, an 8- to 10-month length is felt to be acceptable. In 2011–12, cases involving two or more charges took longer to complete than single-charge cases—147 and 81 days, respectively.

In 2011–12, the median amount of time it took to complete a court case was 117 days, 2 fewer days than the previous year. However, this was more than the median time it took a decade ago, which was 101 days. Figure 9.3 illustrates the median length of cases in each province and territory for 2011–12.

Variations in the length of time depend on the type of case. Figure 9.4 reveals that the longest median length for types of cases in 2011–12 was for homicide cases (386 days), followed by other sexual assault cases (308 days).

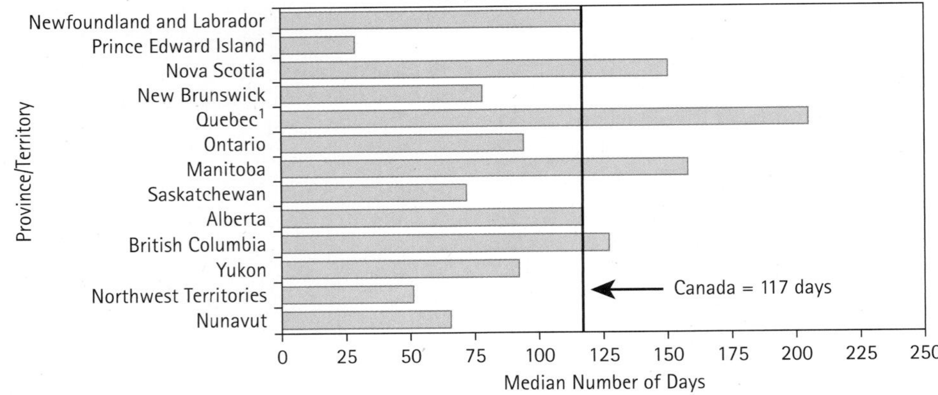

FIGURE 9.3 Median Length of Cases Completed in Adult Criminal Courts, by Province and Territory, 2011–12

[1] The median length of case completion in Quebec may be over-estimated given that data from municipal courts, which tend to handle the least serious matters, are unavailable.

Note: The median represents the mid-point of the number of days taken to complete a case, from the first to last court appearance. A case is one or more charges against an accused person or company that were processed by the courts at the same time and received a final decision. Data exclude information from superior courts in Prince Edward Island, Quebec, Ontario, Manitoba, and Saskatchewan as well as municipal courts in Quebec to the unavailability of data. There are many factors that may influence variations between jurisdictions; therefore, comparisons should be made with caution.

Source: Jillian Boyce, "Adult criminal court statistics in Canada, 2011/2012." *Juristat* (June 13, 2013), Statistics Canada Catalogue no. 85-002-X, p.17, http://www.statcan.gc.ca/pub/85-002-x/2013001/article/11804-eng.pdf. Reproduced and distributed on an "as is" basis with the permission of Statistics Canada.

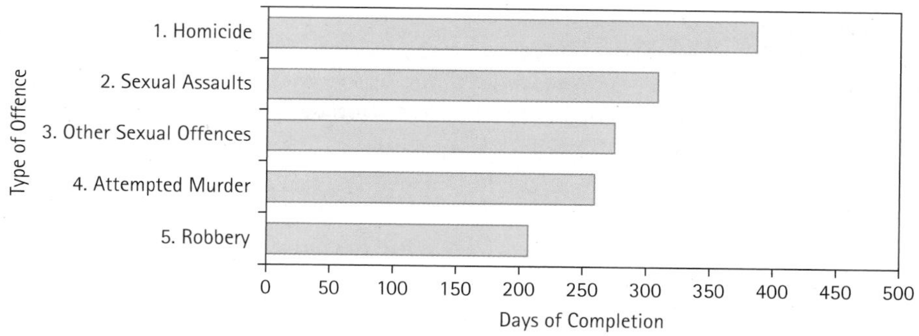

FIGURE 9.4 The Five Longest Cases to Complete in Adult Criminal Court, by Type of Offence, Canada, 2011–12

Source: Jillian Boyce, "Adult criminal court statistics in Canada, 2011/2012." *Juristat* (June 13, 2013), Statistics Canada Catalogue no. 85-002-X, p.17, http://www.statcan.gc.ca/pub/85-002-x/2013001/article/11804-eng.pdf. Reproduced and distributed on an "as is" basis with the permission of Statistics Canada.

Trial Evidence

Once the opening statements have concluded, the prosecution starts its case by presenting evidence. Usually the first evidence to be presented is testimony provided by sworn witnesses (e.g., police officers, medical examiners, and victims). This type of testimony consists of reports from the witnesses on anything that they saw, heard, or touched. Sometimes it involves the opinions of witnesses; for example, an eyewitness may give an opinion as to whether the defendant seemed confused. **Expert witnesses** are specialists in certain areas that apply to the case. For example, a medical examiner can give expert testimony on the time of death or on how injuries occurred. No more than five expert witnesses may be used by the prosecution or defence without the approval of the judge.

When the prosecution finishes its questioning, the defence has the right to cross-examine the witness. Cross-examination can focus on the oral and written statements of the witness. Testimony is only one form of evidence that may be used during a trial. Other types of evidence are as follows:

- **Real evidence.** This type of evidence consists of exhibits such as weapons, clothing, and fingerprints. Real evidence must be original. However, photographs and duplicates may be introduced as evidence.
- **Direct evidence.** This type of evidence consists of the observations of eyewitnesses.
- **Circumstantial evidence.** This type of evidence proves a subsidiary fact from which the guilt or innocence of the accused may be inferred.

All evidence presented in court is governed by the rules of evidence. The judge acts as an impartial arbitrator and rules on whether certain types of evidence are allowed into the trial. Judges may decide to exclude certain evidence. One such type of evidence that is excluded is known as hearsay evidence. This is information that a witness hears from someone else. The courts have ruled that such information represents a denial of the defendant's right to cross-examination, since witnesses do not have the ability to establish the truth of the information.

Courtesy of Valerie Van Brocklin and Alaska State Troopers.

One of the most important roles of a police officer is to give expert testimony during court trials.

The Defence Lawyer's Presentation of Evidence

The defence lawyer has the right to introduce any number of witnesses at a trial or none at all. If he or she does introduce a witness, the prosecution has the right to cross-examine that individual. One of the most critical decisions a defence lawyer makes is whether to have his or her client give testimony under oath. During a criminal trial, the defendant has the right to be free from self-incrimination (i.e., the right to remain silent), which means that the accused has the right not to testify.

The Closing Arguments

Section 651 of the Criminal Code determines whether the prosecution or defence presents their closing argument first. If the defence presents evidence or the defendant testifies, the defence must address the jury before the prosecution does. If no defence evidence is called, the prosecutor presents his or her evidence first. During their closing arguments, both prosecution and defence are allowed to offer reasonable inferences about the evidence and to show how the facts of the case prove or disprove the defendant's guilt. However, they are not allowed to comment on evidence not used during the trial.

The Charge to the Jury

After the defence lawyer and the prosecutor make their final presentations to the court, the judge instructs the jury, or **charges the jury**, as to the relevant principles of law that they have to take into account when deciding on the guilt or innocence of the defendant. The judge includes information such as the elements of the alleged offence, the evidence required to prove each charge, and the degree of proof required to obtain a guilty verdict. It is essential for the judge to clearly explain the relevant laws and evidence requirements as well as the meaning of reasonable doubt. In addition, judges must instruct the jury on the procedures they should use when making their decision. These instructions are important, since they may prove to be the grounds for an appeal.

On paper, these instructions seem simple and reasonable. In reality, they may confuse jurors and lead them to make incorrect evaluations of the evidence or to select the wrong verdict. The final instructions given to the jury apply to issues of evidence and testimony and usually include mention of the following:

1. the definition of the crime with which the defendant is charged;
2. the presumption of the defendant's innocence;
3. the burden of proof that lies with the prosecution; and
4. the fact that if, after discussion, there remains reasonable doubt among the jurors as to the guilt or innocence of the defendant, he or she must be acquitted.

The judge also instructs jurors about the possible verdicts they might consider. While the jury may reach a verdict on the guilt or innocence of the defendant on the original charge, it often has the option to decide on the degree of the offence (e.g., second degree murder or manslaughter).

The Verdict

After the judge reviews the case and the charges, the jury moves to a separate room to consider the verdict. The jury verdict in a criminal case must always be unanimous. Juries may take a few hours, a number of days, or many weeks to review all aspects of the case before reaching a decision.

If the jury remains deadlocked after a lengthy deliberation, it may return to the courtroom and inform the judge of this. The judge may ask the jurors to return to the jury room for a final attempt to arrive at a verdict; in most cases the judge specifies a time limit. If all reasonable attempts to reach a verdict fail, a **hung jury** results. In such cases, the judge dismisses the jury and declares a mistrial. It is then up to the prosecution to decide whether to retry the case—a decision that must be made within a specified time period. If a new trial is ordered, a new jury has to be appointed.

When the jury reaches a verdict of guilty, the judge sets a sentencing date. In the interim, the judge can request a pre-sentence report from a probation officer before imposing a sentence. In such cases, the defence lawyer can start the process of appeal. Defendants may be released while awaiting sentencing or may be held in custody.

The jury plays no role in sentencing except in cases of second degree murder. In such cases, it can make a recommendation to the judge that the length of time before parole be increased from 10 years to a longer period, which cannot exceed 25 years. However, this is a recommendation only, and the trial judge is not bound to accept it.

Jury nullification has occurred when a jury does not follow the court's interpretation of the law in every situation, thereby *nullifying* (i.e., suspending) the requirements of strict legal procedure. In a typical case of nullification, a jury chooses to disregard what the judge told it about specific aspects of the law or evidence because it considers the application of the law to the defendant to be unjust.

Jury nullification can occur in two ways. The first is when a verdict of guilty is reached and the judge decides the verdict is erroneous. In such a case, the judge may refuse to abide by the verdict and may instruct the jury to acquit the defendant. The second occurs when the judge requests a jury to *arrest* its verdict of guilty and acquit the accused.

Appeals

Canada's criminal justice system allows all those convicted of a crime a direct criminal appeal. Both the defendant and the prosecution have the right to appeal the decision in a case. An individual has the right to appeal a conviction, or the sentence, or being found mentally unfit to stand trial (because of a mental disorder).

If the trial involved an indictable offence and was heard by a provincial judge, by a federally appointed judge without a jury, or by a judge and jury, the appeal is taken to the provincial court of appeal. The accused may appeal the conviction if it involves a **point of law** (i.e., the trial judge made an incorrect legal ruling), a **question of fact** (i.e., the trial judge drew the wrong inference from the facts of the case), or the length of the sentence. The prosecution may appeal an acquittal on issues involving a point of law or a sentence but not on the basis of questions of fact. In addition, the terms of an appeal for the prosecution depend on whether the trial involves an indictable or a summary conviction offence. In a summary conviction case, the prosecutor can appeal against either a dismissal or the sentence. In an indictable offence case, the prosecution can appeal the sentence if the accused was acquitted, if it was found that the accused was not criminally responsible on the basis of a mental disorder, or if the accused was found unfit to stand trial (Mewett and Nakatsuru 2000).

There are limits to the length of time that may pass before an appeal is filed. However, extensions can be obtained for a variety of reasons. During an appeal it is not uncommon for the convicted individual to apply for bail or some other form of pretrial release. The appeal court can order a new trial, or it can acquit the convicted individual, if it finds that the trial judge made an error in law, that the verdict was unreasonable and not supported by the evidence, or that a miscarriage of justice took place. If it appears that the position of the prosecutor is no longer valid, the appeal court usually grants an acquittal. If it decides that there is still enough evidence for the prosecutor to argue the case, it will order a new trial. If the appeal court decides that the appeal registered by the prosecution is valid, it normally grants a new trial. However, it can convict and sentence the accused if the trial was by judge alone and enough evidence was presented to the court.

For summary conviction offences, the convicted individual usually appeals a conviction or sentence to a federally appointed judge in a superior court. Again, the accused may be released pending the outcome of the appeal. It is rare for a summary conviction offence to be heard by the Supreme Court of Canada, and then only if the case involves an important legal issue.

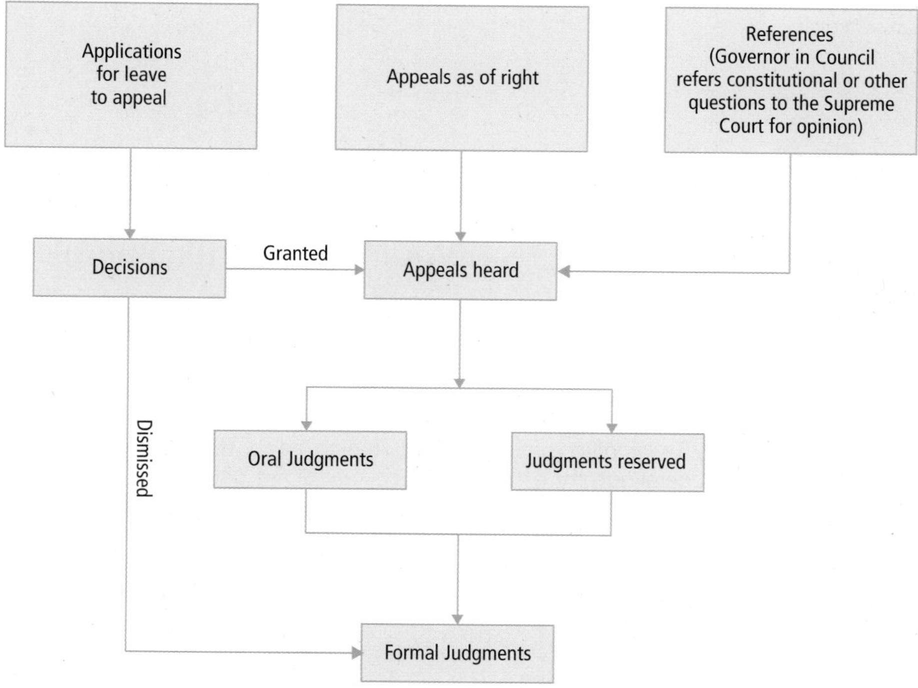

FIGURE 9.5 The Appeal Process in the Supreme Court of Canada

Source: Supreme Court of Canada: Statistics 2004 to 2014, p. 3. Reproduced with the permission of the Supreme Court of Canada, 2015. http://www.scc-csc.gc.ca/case-dossier/stat/cat3-eng.aspx and http://www.scc-csc.gc.ca/case-dossier/stat/cat3-eng.aspx

The Supreme Court decides which cases it will hear from three sources (see Figure 9.5). The first (and most common) is known as **leave to appeal**. This usually involves appeals made by another court (typically a provincial court of appeal or the Federal Court of Appeal). For the Supreme Court to hear the case, a panel of three judges of the Supreme Court must grant it permission. These cases involve a question of public importance or raise an important issue of law. The second source are those cases referred to as **"as of right" appeals**, which usually are serious criminal cases where, for example, there is "a dissent on a point of law in the court of appeal, and appeals from provincial references" (Supreme Court of Canada 2015:1). The third source is those referred to the Supreme Court by the federal government and most often raise constitutional issues. **References** by the federal government require the Supreme Court to give their opinion on a question referred to it by the Governor in Council (i.e., the Governor General acting on behalf of the federal cabinet).

SUMMING UP AND LOOKING FORWARD

The criminal trial is the start of the adjudication stage of the criminal justice system. It is also the centrepiece of our court system. If the accused pleads guilty, a date is set for the sentencing (see Chapter 10). However, if the accused elects to be tried in court, they are afforded a number of legal rights, such as the right to confront the accuser and the right to a public trial. While all criminal trials are supposed to be open to the media, publication bans are sometimes ordered to ensure the fairness of the trial.

Criminal trials follow a set of procedures that follow the requirements found in the rules of evidence, procedure, and the criminal law. These procedures include an opening statement, the presentation of evidence by both defence and prosecution, the closing arguments, and, if the case involves a jury, the charge to the jury by the judge. Cases can be appealed to the provincial and territorial appeal courts, with the Supreme Court of Canada being the appeal court of last resort.

What happens if someone is found guilty? The focus then turns to the sentencing phase of the cases, which is the subject of the next chapter.

Review Questions:

1. What are the legal rights found within the criminal trial?
2. Why are publication bans placed into effect by the courts?
3. What are the different types of trial evidence?
4. How does a judge charge a jury?
5. What are the different types of appeals heard by the Supreme Court of Canada?

Critical Issues in Canadian Criminal Justice

JUDICIAL INDEPENDENCE AND THE MANDATORY VICTIM SURCHARGE

As was noted earlier in this chapter, a central feature of our criminal justice system is the traditional independence of the judiciary. One of the key roles of judges is that they maintain, create, interpret, and apply the law. But what happens when this role is substituted by the idea of "supremacy of Parliament"? This conflict is found in the recent introduction by the federal government of the mandatory victim surcharge passed by Parliament in October 2013 (Bill C-37, the Increasing Offenders' Accountability for Victims Act).

A federal victim surcharge was passed in 1988 and proclaimed in 1989. A surcharge is a monetary penalty imposed on offenders at the time they are sentenced. The purpose of a surcharge is to provide funding for support services for victims of crime within the province (s. 737[7] of the Criminal Code). It imposes payment on offenders who were convicted of any Criminal Code offences or a Controlled Drugs and Substances offence involving controlled or restricted drugs, as well as those individuals who received an absolute or conditional discharge. Under the original legislation, offenders were required to pay a surcharge of a maximum of up to 15 percent of any fine imposed and up to $35 for other dispositions, with judges having discretion on whether or not to impose any surcharge.

The purpose of this legislation was to help cover the cost of providing services to victims as well as to make offenders more accountable for their actions. When two studies reviewed the impact of the new federal surcharge (in British Columbia and Ontario), it was discovered that judges oftentimes ignored or forgot to impose it. The reasons included lack of awareness of the surcharge on the part of judges, concerns about how the surcharge was going to be used, the hardship faced by those convicted who couldn't afford to pay the surcharge, and that when a sentence of imprisonment was imposed, the belief that imposing a fine made the sentence disproportionate to the seriousness of the offence (Roberts 1992; Axon and Hann 1994).

To address this situation, new surcharge provisions designed to address these concerns were introduced in 1999. The new legislation stated that the only exception to imposing the surcharge was when an offender could prove undue hardship for either themselves or their dependants (s. 737[5] of the Criminal Code). In addition, when the surcharge was waived, courts were now required to provide the reasons and record them in the court record (s. 737[6] of the Criminal Code).

However, the expected revenues from the new provisions regarding the collection of surcharges were never achieved. The federal ombudsman for the victims of crime asked the federal government to make the surcharges mandatory. Key to this request was a study conducted in New Brunswick in 2006, which found that provincial court judges regularly waived the surcharge without giving a reason. The report concluded that in about two-thirds of the cases studied, the surcharges were waived and that very few judges gave a written reason why they decided to waive the fine. An important finding of the report was that "the primary criterion judges used for waiving the federal victim surcharge was the perception of the offender's ability to pay" (Law and Sullivan 2006:vii).

As a result, the federal government decided to change the law governing victim surcharges (s. 737 of the Criminal Code). According to federal Justice Minister Peter MacKay, the position of the federal government is to protect both society and victims: "Our government has been categorical: The justice system is going to be centred on the protection of society and the redress of victims. Our government will transform the justice system so that it is no longer centred on the welfare of criminals" (MacKay, in Seymour 2015).

The new legislation amended s. 737 of the Criminal Code, which previously allowed judges to waive fines for impoverished people. Judges are now no longer able to waive a fine. Instead, they are now required to place a surcharge of 30 percent on top of any fine imposed by the court or, if there is no fine, $100 per summary conviction count or $200 per indictable offence. The Act ensures that "the victim surcharge is applied in all cases without exception," except when local programs exist that permit an offender to do community service. The purpose of the amendments was to increase the amount of money available for the victims of crime as well as to make offenders more accountable for their actions.

The new legislation was controversial as soon as it was passed. It was pointed out that about half of those individuals convicted in court are on welfare, and would be unable to pay the new surcharges. Some judges reportedly refused to follow the new law almost immediately once it came into effect. For example, one judge started to issue $1 fines, leading to a 30 cent surcharge. Another judge decided to allow an offender 50 years to pay a $100 fine, while at least one other judge told the individual convicted in their court that they would have no time to pay, sentenced the offender to a day for defaulting on the payment of the fine, and then made the jail sentence overlap with the time they were already serving. Provincial government spokespersons noted that at least three provinces don't allow offenders to go to a community service program to pay off their fine (a fine option program). Others pointed out that if a judge fines someone $50, for example, they would have to pay a 30 percent surcharge, or $15. But if they were to receive a sentence considered to be more lenient, such as a conditional discharge (see Chapter 10), they would have to pay at least a $100 fine.

A key turning point occurred when an Ontario court justice gave a mentally ill alcoholic offender who was arrested after stealing from an Ontario government liquor store 50 years to pay a $100 surcharge. Later, the judge found out that a 1999 Ontario government order-in-council required all surcharges to be paid within 50 days. The judge then informed defence lawyers that they would have to appeal their cases on constitutional grounds. Another Ontario judge declared the mandatory surcharge unconstitutional without being asked to do so by the defence, a case that is scheduled to be heard in the Ontario Superior Court sometime in 2015.

One issue focuses upon the removal of a judge's discretion to waive the surcharge when they realize that it would create undue hardship for an offender. For some, a judge's "ability to exercise discretion within the law, and to consider all of the circumstances in imposing sentence, is the bedrock of a fair and humane justice system" (Opinion 2013:A16). Another issue is that the new mandatory law is disproportionate to those who can't afford to pay the surcharge. As one judge pointed out, when there is a mandatory law, judges "have no opportunity to assess the very thing they are supposed to be assessing" (Westman, in Fine 2013:A4). Another issue concerns where the boundaries of judicial independence should be. As one judge notes, there are principles at stake in these issues, with "the greater principle is

Continued on next page

Critical Issues in Canadian Criminal Justice (*Continued*)

one of justice, and I take comfort that, in the scheme of things, it's more important to stand up for what is just" (Westman, in Fine 2013:A4).

Questions also have been raised regarding the money collected from the surcharge. The funds from the surcharges don't necessarily go directly into compensating crime victims in a province. Rather, the monies are sent to victims' funds to be used for various community programs to assist victims of crime. According to the Ontario Ministry of the Attorney General, the total amount of victim surcharges collected during 2013–14 ($1,235,272) was approximately 5 percent more compared to the previous year, when the surcharge wasn't mandatory. This total made up less than 3 percent of the total amount of money collected from surcharge fines collected in Ontario during 2013–14. The greatest amount of victim surcharges (over $44 million) came from provincial offences such as Highway Traffic Act violations (Kari 2014).

Questions

1. Should judges have total independence when making their decisions, or should they abide by the "supremacy of Parliament" when a conflict between the two arises?
2. When an impoverished person is found guilty of an appropriate criminal offence, should judges have the power to waive fines? Do you think judges should be able waive fines for any other groups of people?
3. Do you think all provincial/territorial jurisdictions should have legislation that allows all offenders to enter a community service program to pay off their fine? Why do you think some provinces do not have this type of legislation?
4. Should all monies collected from the victim surcharge go directly toward compensating crime victims in the province or territory?

SUMMARY

This chapter begins with a discussion of the increasing number of individuals who are representing themselves in criminal trials. This places a significant burden on the accused during the trial.

KEY WORDS: self-representation, burden of the court, burden on the accused

What Are the Models of the Criminal Courts?

The Due Process Model (p. 280)
The Crime Control Model (p. 280)
The Bureaucratic Model (p. 280)
How Are the Canadian Criminal Courts Organized? (p. 281)

Various models have been constructed that interpret the operation of the criminal courts. Our court systems are according to jurisdiction (federal and provincial/territorial), and these courts are divided into different levels.

KEY WORDS: adjudication, bureaucratic model, provincial/territorial courts, provincial/territorial superior courts, circuit courts, courts of limited jurisdiction, courts of general jurisdiction, appeal courts, leave of appeal cases, "as of right" appeals, judicial review, law interpreter, lower courts, superior courts, higher courts, courts of last resort

The Court System

Prior to a case being heard in the criminal court, the only proof required is probable cause. Since the accused is presumed innocent until proved guilty, it is up to the prosecutor to prove guilty beyond a reasonable doubt.

KEY WORDS: probable cause, beyond a reasonable doubt, legal guilt, factual guilt, officer of the government

How Does the Court System Operate in Canada?

The reality of the daily business of the criminal courts differs from the ideal process. The key actors in the courts are the defence lawyer, prosecutor, and judge. The prosecutor represents the interests of the state, while defence lawyers provide essential services to their clients. Judges are impartial participants.

KEY WORDS: assembly-line justice

Criminal Trial Procedure

The criminal trial is the start of the adjudication stage of the criminal justice system. If the accused pleads guilty, a date is set for sentencing. If they plead not guilty, a trial date is set.

KEY WORDS: adjudication, hearsay evidence, cross-examine, open court principle

The Right to a Fair Criminal Trial

This section provides an overview of the major procedures followed during a trial in the criminal courts.

KEY WORDS: guilty beyond a reasonable doubt, expert witnesses, real evidence, direct evidence, circumstantial evidence, charges the jury, hung jury, jury nullification

Appeals

When can there be an appeal? This section outlines the basis upon which there can be an appeal.

KEY WORDS: point of law, question of fact, leave to appeal, "as of right" appeals, references

Critical Thinking Questions

1. Do you think a self-representing individual should be able to cross-examine the individual they victimized in a criminal trial?
2. Should the police have more discretion over which charges are heard in court? Why or why not?
3. Why do so many accused plead guilty when a principle of our adversarial system is that the prosecution prove its case beyond a reasonable doubt?
4. Should criminal court trials in Canada be televised, as they are in the United States?
5. Describe the problems associated with pretrial publicity. What is the *right to know*, and should it overrule the right to a fair trial?

Weblinks

For an interview with Beverley McLachlin, Chief Justice of the Supreme Court, search in your Web browser for "The Agenda with Steve Paikin: Chief Justice Beverley

McLachlin" (25:06). For some contemporary issues facing the Canadian courts, search YouTube for "Clearing a Pathway to Justice—Law Society of BC" (8:33).

Court Cases

Boucher v. The Queen (1955).

C.B.C. v. New Brunswick (Attorney General) (1996), 3 S.C.R.

Dagenais v. Canadian Broadcasting Corp. (1994), C.C.C. (3d) 289.

Dix v. Canada (A.G.) (2002), A.J. 784.

Miazga v. Kvello Estate (2009), 3 S.C.R. 339.

Nelles v. Ontario (1989), 2 S.C.R. 170.

Proulx v. A.G. of Que. (2001), 3 S.C.R. 9.

R. v. Meddoui (1990), 61 C.C.C. (3d) 345.

R. v. Mentuck (2001), 3 S.C.R. 442.

R. v. Phillips (2003), ABCA 4.

R. v. Ross (1989), 49 C.C.C. (3d) 475.

R. v. Thompson (1990), 59 C.C.C. (3d) 225.

R. v. White (1977), 32 C.C.C. (2d) 478.

Toronto Star Newspapers Ltd. v. Canada (2010), 1 S.C.R. 721.

Suggested Readings

Borovoy, A. 1988. *"At the Barricades": A Memoir*. Toronto: Irwin Law.

Cullen, F.T., G. Cavender, W.J. Maakestad, and M.L. Benson. 2006. *Corporate Crime under Attack: The Fight to Criminalize Business Violence*, 2nd ed. Lexis Nexis.

Glasbeek, A. 2010. *Feminized Justice: The Toronto Women's Court (1913–34)*. Vancouver: UBC Press.

McCormick, P. 1994. *Canada's Courts*. Toronto: James Lorimer.

Salhany, R. 2013. *The Practical Guide to Evidence in Criminal Cases*, 8th ed. Toronto: Carswell.

References

"An Excessive Use of Publication Bans." 2004. *The Globe and Mail*, September 20, p. A12.

Axon, L. and R. Hann. 1994. *Helping Victims through Fine Surcharges*. Ottawa: Department of Justice.

Blackwell, R. 2006. "Judges Decry Trend of Citizens Playing Lawyer." *The Globe and Mail*, March 10, p. A6.

Bowal, P. 2002. "Ten Differences." *LawNow* 26(6):9–11.

Bowal, P. and K. Horvat. 2011. "Whatever Happened to . . . The Prosecution of Susan Nelles." *LawNow* 36(1):55–60.

Boyd, N. 1995. *Canadian Law: An Introduction*. Toronto: Harcourt Brace Canada.

Brennan, S. 2011. *Violent Victimization of Aboriginal Women in the Canadian Provinces, 2009*. Ottawa: Canadian Centre for Justice Statistics.

Campbell Research Associates. 1992. *Review and Monitoring of Child Sexual Abuse Cases in Hamilton-Wentworth, Ontario*. Ottawa: Department of Justice.

Canadian Bar Association. 1987. *Code of Professional Conduct*. Ontario: Canadian Bar Association.

Cullen, F.T., G. Cavendar, W.J. Maakestaad, and M. Benson. 2006. *Corporate Crime under Attack: The Fight to Criminalize Business Violence*, 2nd ed. LexisNexis.

Currie, A. 2003. *The Unmet Need for Criminal Legal Aid: A Summary of Research Results*. Ottawa: Department of Justice Canada.

Davison, C.B. 2006. "In Defence of Defence Counsel." *LawNow* 30:39–40.

Desroches, F.J. 1995. *Force and Fear: Robbery in Canada*. Scarborough, ON: Nelson Canada.

Doust, L.T. 2011. *Foundation for Change: Report of the Public Commission on Legal Aid in British Columbia*. Vancouver, BC: Public Commission on Legal Aid.

Eastwood, P. 2004. "Publication Bans Since *Dagenais*." *LawNow* 28:35–37.

Ericson, R. 1981. *Making Crime: A Study of Detective Work*. Toronto: University of Toronto Press.

Ericson, R. and P.M. Baranek. 1982. *The Ordering of Justice: A Study of Accused Persons as Defendants in the Criminal Process*. Toronto: University of Toronto Press.

Feeley, M. 1981. *Felony Arrests: Their Prosecution and Disposition in New York Court*. New York: Vera Institute.

Fine, S. 2013. "The New Face of Judicial Defiance." *The Globe and Mail*, December 14, 2013, p. A14.

Freedman, J.L. and T.M. Burke. 1996. "The Effect of Pretrial Publicity." *Canadian Journal of Criminology* 38:253–70.

Gomme, I.M. and M.P. Hall. 1995. "Prosecutors at Work: Role Overload and Strain." *Journal of Criminal Justice* 23:191–200.

Greene, I. 1995. "Judicial Accountability in Canada." Pp. 355–75 in *Accountability for Criminal Justice: Selected Essays*, edited by P.C. Stenning. Toronto: University of Toronto Press.

Greene, I., C. Baar, P. McCormick, G. Szablowski, and M. Thomas. 1998. *Final Appeal: Decision-Making in Canadian Courts of Appeal*. Toronto: Lorimer.

Grosman, B. 1969. *The Prosecutor: An Inquiry into the Exercise of Discretion*. Toronto: University of Toronto Press.

Hann, R.G., J. Nuffield, C. Meredith, and M. Svoboda. 2002. *Court Site Study of Adult Unrepresented Accused in the Provincial Criminal Courts: Part I—Overview Report*. Ottawa: Department of Justice Canada.

Hughson, B.F. 2004. "Malicious Prosecution." *LawNow* 28:32–34.

Kari, S. 2014. "Logic of Victim Surcharge Questioned." *Law Times News*. March 3. Retrieved March 3, 2015 (www.lawtimesnews).

Karp, C. and C. Rosner. 1991. *When Justice Fails: The David Milgaard Story*. Toronto: McClelland & Stewart.

Law, M., and S. Sullivan. 2006. *Federal Victim Surcharge in New Brunswick: An Operational Review*. Ottawa: Department of Justice.

Law Reform Commission of Canada. 1975. *Criminal Procedure: Control of the Process*. Ottawa: Minister of Supply and Services Canada.

Makin, K. 2003. "Lawyer Laments Rise in Publication Bans." *The Globe and Mail*, October 31, p. A8.

Makin, K. 2001. "Innocent Man Wins in Top Court." *The Globe and Mail*, October 19, p. A11.

Martin, J. 1970. "The Role and Responsibility of the Defence Advocate." *Criminal Law Quarterly* 12.

McCormick, P. and I. Greene. 1990. *Judges and Judging: Inside the Canadian Judicial System*. Toronto: Lorimer.

Mewett, A.W. and S. Nakatsuru. 2000. *An Introduction to the Criminal Process in Canada*, 4th ed. Scarborough, ON: Carswell.

O'Brien, D. 2004. "More Representing Selves in Court." *Winnipeg Free Press.* January 31, p. A5.

Ontario Ministry of the Attorney General. 1999. *Report of the Criminal Justice Review Committee*. Toronto: Ministry of the Attorney General.

Opinion. 2013. "A Little Judgment Would Be No Crime." *The Globe and Mail*, December 10, p. A16.

Pereira, J. and C. Grimes. 2002. *Case Processing in Criminal Courts, 1999/00*. Ottawa: Canadian Centre for Justice Statistics.

Powell, K. and C. Rusnell. 1999. "To Tell the Truth." *National Post*, January 18, p. A8.

Public Safety Canada. 2013. *Corrections and Conditional Release Statistical Review*. Ottawa: Public Safety Canada.

Roberts, T. 1992. *An Assessment of Victim Fine Surcharge in British Columbia*. Ottawa: Department of Justice.

Russell, P. 1987. *The Judiciary in Canada: The Third Branch of Government*. Toronto: McGraw-Hill Ryerson.

Salhany, R.E. 1986. *Arrest, Seizure, and Interrogation*, 3rd ed. Toronto: Carswell.

Seymour, A. 2015. "Is the Victim Surcharge the Next Supreme Court Failure for the Conservative Agenda?" *Ottawa Citizen*, January 10. Retrieved March 9, 2015 (http://ottawacitizen.com/politics/is-the-victim-surcharge-the-next-supreme-court-failure).

Supreme Court of Canada. 2015. *Statistics 2004 to 2014*. Ottawa: Supreme Court of Canada.

Swartz, M.A. 1973. Quoted in J. Caplan, *Criminal Justice*. Mineola, NY: Foundation Press.

Thomas, M. 2004. *Adult Criminal Court Statistics, 2003/04*. Ottawa: Canadian Centre for Justice Statistics.

Tyler, T. 2007/2008. "Procedural Justice and the Courts." *Court Review: The Journal of the American Judges Association*, 44:26–31.

Vancouver Sun. 2014. "Self-Represented Litigants Need Help in Court: Report." April 2. Accessed March 6, 2015 (www.canada.com/vancouversun/news/westcoastnews/story.html).

Vinglis, E., H. Blefgen, D. Colbourne, P. Culver, B. Farmer, D. Hackett, J. Treleaven, and R. Solomon. 1990. "The Adjudication of Alcohol-Related Criminal Driving Cases in Ontario: A Survey of Crown Attorneys." *Canadian Journal of Criminology* 32:639–50.

Webster, C. and A. Doob. 2007. "Superior Courts in the Twenty-first Century: A Historical Anachronism?" Pp. 57–84 in *Canada's Trial Courts: Two Tiers or One*, edited by P. Russell. Toronto: University of Toronto Press.

CHAPTER 10

Sentences and Dispositions

Learning Objectives

After completing this chapter, you should be able to:

- Differentiate among the major philosophical rationales of sentencing traditionally used by our criminal justice system.
- Differentiate between the two most recent rationales of sentencing.
- Identify the sentences available to judges.
- Distinguish between the "sentence" and the "disposition."
- Identify the reasons why alternatives to traditional forms of sentencing in Canada appeared, specifically Aboriginal sentencing and healing circles.
- Identify the causes of wrongful convictions.
- Identify why mandatory minimum sentences were introduced.
- Identify the impact of mandatory minimum sentences upon gun-related crimes.
- Explain why victim impact statements were introduced and identify their impact upon sentences.

Sentencing has been defined as "the judicial determination of a legal sanction to be imposed on a person found guilty of an offence" (Canadian Sentencing Commission 1987:153). According to Roberts and Cole (1999:4), this brief definition includes "all the traditional elements, namely that the sanction must be legal, it must be imposed by a judge, and it can follow a criminal conviction." This needs to be distinguished from the actual sentence (the disposition) imposed on the offender. A **disposition** refers to "the actual sanction imposed in sentencing" (Law Reform Commission of Canada 1974:4) or "the judicial determination of legal sanction to be imposed on a person found guilty of an offence" (Canadian Sentencing Commission 1987:153).

Of course, before someone receives a disposition, they must plead guilty or be found guilty in a court of law. One can assume that a person who admits to having committed an offence will be found guilty. The issue then becomes the type and length of the disposition. If the crime involves a serious, violent act, is it not reasonable to expect a lengthy period of imprisonment as the disposition? One would think so, yet the events of the court trial and the factors surrounding the commission of the offence may have significant weight in determining the final disposition.

The sentencing decision remains a crucial component of our criminal justice system. According to Blumstein and his colleagues (1983:1), the sentencing process

> . . . is the symbolic keystone of the criminal justice system. In it, the conflicts between goals of equal justice under the law and individualized justice with punishment tailored to the offender are played out, and society's morals and highest values—life and liberty—are interpreted and applied.

Sentencing involves handing out a punishment to the convicted offender. It has been argued that punishing criminals serves two ultimate purposes:

1. the "deserved infliction of suffering on evil doers"; and
2. the "prevention of crime" (Packer 1968:36–37).

When an individual is convicted, a punishment must be handed out. The question then becomes, "What is the appropriate sentence that indicates the disapproval of society?" Sentences can mean a fine, probation, community service, imprisonment, an intermittent sentence, or a recognizance to keep the peace. As well, a judge may combine certain of these punishments—for example, a fine and a probation order can be combined into what is known as a **split sentence**. Perhaps because of the number of sentencing options open to judges, sentences have come under heavy criticism. Critics argue that sentences are too lenient or too long. It is rare that everyone agrees on their appropriateness in any given criminal case.

Although almost everyone agrees that offenders "should be punished in some way, there is far less consensus about the purpose of punishment" (Roberts and Cole 1999:5). These purposes are embedded in the principles that guide our criminal justice system (see Chapter 3). Any sentence can reflect one of these purposes or a combination of them. If any specific purpose of sentencing can be said to exist, it is closest to specific deterrence—that is, to reduce "the crime rate by stopping the criminal activities of apprehended offenders and deterring others from committing crimes" (Anderson and Newman 1993:288). The best way to achieve this is, of course, open to opinion and debate.

What Are the Philosophical Rationales of Sentencing?

To answer the above questions, we need to consider the six basic goals of sentencing. While these goals are presented as separate and distinct from one another, sentences in Canada can reflect a combination of them (Doob 1992). Traditionally, four rationales have been given for a punishment imposed by the courts: deterrence, selective incapacitation, rehabilitation, and justice. As we have seen (Chapter 3), two newer rationales, healing and restoration, have received greater attention in recent years.

Deterrence

By punishing an offender, the state indicates its intent to control crime and deter potential offenders. **Deterrence**, the oldest of the four main sentencing goals, refers to the protection of society through the prevention of criminal acts. This is accomplished by punishing offenders in accordance with their offence. Too lenient a sentence might encourage people to engage in criminal activity because they would not fear the punishment for their offence; too severe a sentence might reduce the ability of the criminal justice system to impose punishment that is regarded as fair and impartial, and might actually encourage more criminal activity. For example, if all convicted robbers were to receive a minimum of 10 years for their crimes, they might kill their victims if those victims are the only witnesses able to identify them. For the deterrence approach to work, it must strike a balance between fear and justice among both offenders and law-abiding citizens.

When people say that sentencing has a deterrent effect, they are usually referring to two types of deterrence: specific and general. **Specific deterrence** attempts to discourage, through punishment, an individual offender from committing another crime (or recidivating) in the future. **General deterrence** refers to a sentence that is severe enough to stop people from committing crimes. To date, there is some evidence that specific deterrence works, but only in certain instances, such as in domestic violence (Sherman and Berk 1984). However, many more studies have found that specific deterrence does not stop people from committing a second crime once they serve their sentence for a first offence (Fagan 1989; Wheeler and Hissong 1988). General deterrence, by punishing an offender, is intended to have an impact on the members of society. Specific deterrence is intended to discourage individuals from engaging further in the behaviour that led to their conviction and sentencing; it is predicated on an individual's wish to avoid the pain of punishment in the future.

The objectives of general and specific deterrence may be incompatible. For example, a husband who assaults his wife may best be deterred from spousal assault by participating in emotional response therapy. This sentence may not be in the best interests of general deterrence, however, if the punishment is not perceived as adequate to deter members of society from engaging in the same behaviour. Another reason why deterrence can be difficult to achieve is that it relies on the certainty and speed of punishment. If the punishment for a crime is harsh but the risk of being apprehended is low, it is doubtful that potential offenders will be deterred.

Selective Incapacitation

Selective incapacitation is the removal or restriction of the freedom of offenders, making it almost impossible for them to commit another crime during their period of incarceration. An offender who is considered a significant risk to society may be sentenced to a long term in prison. Incarcerating those individuals (referred to as **chronic offenders**) who commit the most heinous and/or the greatest number of criminal offences is thought to reduce the crime rate. In essence, the goal of incapacitation is to prevent future crimes by imprisoning individuals on the basis of their past criminal offences. At the present time, incapacitation is achieved mainly by imprisoning offenders for very lengthy periods of time, by implementing punishments such as the "three strikes" laws in the United States.

The incapacitation and deterrence approaches both focus on punishing criminals for the express purpose of protecting society. However, selective incapacitation differs from deterrence in that it favours much longer sentences. Supporters of this approach argue it is an effective way to achieve crime prevention. Ehrlich (1975) declared boldly that a 1 percent increase in sentence length leads to a 1 percent decrease in the crime rate. Zedlewski (1987) concluded that for every $1 spent on incarcerating an offender, there is a $17 saving to society in terms of social costs. Critics of this approach believe it is flawed since it does not include **proportionality** for specific types of criminal offences. That is, how can we be sure that punishing a robber to life imprisonment will reduce the crime rate? Perhaps a much shorter punishment would ensure that that offender would not commit another robbery on release from prison. Another argument is that incapacitating criminals protects society only while the offender is in prison. Some argue that after offenders have served their prison terms, they may actually be more predisposed to committing more crime (Clear 1980).

Courtesy of Office of the Correctional Investigator, 2009–2010 Annual Report, http://www.oci-bec.gc.ca/cnt/rpt/pdf/annrpt20092010-eng.pdf, p. 30.

The exterior of a federal correctional facility.

Rehabilitation

A sentencing approach emphasizing **rehabilitation** is based on the belief that many (but not all) offenders can be treated in such a way that, once released, they will live crime-free lives in their communities. Attempts are therefore made to "correct" the behaviour and/or personality of offenders through a variety of programs. Supporters of rehabilitative sentences argue it is fairer and more productive to treat certain offenders rather than punish them without treatment. The purpose of this sentencing approach is to treat the social and psychological problems of offenders in the hope of returning them to society as law-abiding citizens. Since every offender is potentially different in the type and length of treatment they need, supporters of this approach argue that a variety of programs should be available to assist in the treatment. Rehabilitation-based sentencing is predicated on reform in the future rather than on the criminal act committed.

The success of rehabilitation programs has been strongly contested. Many argue that a **"get tough" approach** (i.e., a deterrence or incapacitation approach) to sentencing and punishment is more successful in controlling crime. But others point to recent findings that the rehabilitation approach does succeed, especially when treatment programs and offender needs are matched effectively (Andrews et al. 1990). Rehabilitative sentences, in contrast to those based on the deterrence and incapacitation approaches, do not always include imprisonment. In fact, offenders may be sentenced to serve their punishment in the community if more appropriate services are available to them.

The Justice Model

According to the **justice model**, offenders should be punished no more or less severely than their actions warrant. Specifically, the severity of the sentence should depend on the severity of the crime—that is, the essence of punishment should be to punish offenders with fairness and justice and in proportion to the gravity of their criminal offences. Offenders are to be punished because they deserve to be: "their punishment should fit the crime" (Durham 1988). This approach specifies that all punishments should be equally and fairly given to those with the same number of prior criminal convictions and who have committed the same crime. The focus is on the crime committed rather than on any attributes of the individual. **Extralegal factors** such as race, gender, and social class are not to be considered. Different individuals who commit the same offence may receive different sentences, but only because of mitigating or aggravating factors. The actual sentence imposed should be based on the crime committed. This model is not concerned with the likelihood of treatment success or a reduction in the crime rate.

The justice model differs from the deterrence and incapacitation approaches in that it (1) focuses on an offender's past behaviour as the rationale for sentencing rather than on his or her future criminality and the protection of society; and (2) believes that sentences, while determinate, should be shorter rather than longer. This means that for a specific criminal offence, justice model advocates would support a sentence of five years (with no parole); in contrast, supporters of the deterrence and incapacitation approaches would prefer a longer sentence (also with no parole). In theory, then, the justice model favours a sentencing approach with shorter periods of punishment (including community-based punishments).

Healing

Healing is multifaceted. It can mean different things to different people depending on the context in which it is used. Healing, "for many Aboriginal people, is the objective of justice, and justice derives from the restorative/transformative processes of healing. Hence, healing is a broad notion that encompasses restorative justice" (Proulx 2005:35). Proulx also points out that healing encompasses such activities as the reintegration of victims and offenders at the individual *and* community levels.

Justice is an essential component of healing, but the type of justice envisioned differs from that of the dominant society. According to Henderson and McCaslin (2005:6), justice as healing is "concerned with equitable processes or ceremonies to resolve conflicts with more than substantive rules." Healing can also involve justice as a **lived experience**. The Law Commission of Canada (1999:22–23) points out that justice viewed in this way involves "a process of negotiation and agreement between parties to a conflict. By searching for truth in this sense, parties are better able to comprehend each other's position. In turn, this encourages a better understanding of their own behavior."

Sentencing circles provide the offender, the victim, and the community with the opportunity to start the healing process. The Native Law Centre (2006) identifies various options available to sentencing circles, including these:

- Peer counselling.
- Community service work.
- Mediation.
- Aboriginal spiritual activities such as sweat lodges, as well as forgiveness/sacrifice ceremonies.
- Aboriginal cultural activities, such as powwows.
- Talking and healing circles.
- Curfew rules and regulations respecting residency.
- "Western" sentences, such as fines, incarceration, probation, house arrest, and electronic monitoring (usually for six months).

Office of the Correctional Investigator 2013-2014 Annual Report, http://www.oci-bec.gc.ca/cnt/rpt/pdf/annrpt/annrpt20132014-eng.pdf, p. 43.

The interior of an Aboriginal healing lodge located within a federal correctional facility.

Restoration

Restorative justice focuses mainly on **repairing the harm** that has been done as the result of a crime. Responses to crime "should not, primarily, punish or rehabilitate the offender but set the conditions for repairing as much harm as possible the harm caused" (Walgrave 2005:5). This is to be accomplished by examining the harm done to both the victim and the community. And while a maximum punishment should be listed for all offences, there shouldn't be a minimum punishment. Preference is given to a wide range of sentences available to a judge at the lower limits. This means that fines, community service, compensation, reconciliation, and apologies are to be preferred over imprisonment for many crimes.

According to White and Haines (2002), the restoration approach encompasses the following elements:

- *Parsimony*—that is, the criminal justice authorities must be able to justify the sentences handed out.
- *Control*—that is, over those who have power by virtue of their positions within the criminal justice system.
- *Reprobation*—specifically, the criminal justice system should place offenders in positions where they can experience community disapproval.
- *Reintegration* of offenders back into society.

In addition, sentences under this model would be shorter than those imposed under the incapacitation model.

EXHIBIT 10.1 Sentencing Options

Judges in Canada have a number of dispositions available to them when punishing a convicted offender. These include the following:

- *Imprisonment*. Canada has always imprisoned offenders, be it for the purpose of deterrence, incapacitation, rehabilitation, or justice. A sentence of imprisonment can be served in either a federal or a provincial correctional facility (see Chapter 12). In recent years, governments have been trying to limit the use of imprisonment except for the most serious offences.
- *Intermittent sentences*. These sentences allow offenders to serve their time on an intermittent basis (such as weekends) so that they can continue to engage in other activities (e.g., employment). By law, such sentences are limited to a maximum of 90 days.
- *Fines*. These can be levied by judges in combination with incarceration and probation or independently of other types of punishments. When a judge chooses to punish an offender with a fine only, it indicates that the judge considers the offender not to be a threat to the community and thus not in need of supervision.
- *Restitution and community service*. While fines are payable to a government, restitution and community service are paid to injured parties. These punishments are also referred to as "reparations." Restitution is a payment made directly to the victim; community service is an attempt to make the offender do something that will benefit the community.
- *Probation*. With this criminal sanction, offenders are allowed to spend their sentence (or part of it) in the community under supervision, provided that they follow certain conditions set by the court (see Chapter 11).
- *Restorative justice*. Some judges feel that when an offender has committed a non-serious crime, the relationship between the offender and the victim can be "healed" by having them meet and discuss the offence.
- *Absolute and conditional discharges*. An offender who receives an absolute or conditional discharge is not considered to have been convicted of an offence. A conditional discharge means that an offender is discharged with conditions and will be supervised as if on probation. An absolute discharge means that the offender does not need any supervision.
- *Community-based sanctions*. This approach emphasizes non-criminal alternatives to traditional punishments. These include referral to substance abuse or behavioural modification programs.
- *Conditional sentence*. A conditional sentence of imprisonment means that the execution of the prison sentence is suspended. A conditional sentence is more serious than probation but less serious than imprisonment.

Sentencing Patterns in Canada

What sentences do convicted people receive for their criminal actions? As identified in Exhibit 10.1, judges may have a number of options available to them in most cases when they are selecting a sentence. A recent analysis of sentencing practices used information from all jurisdictions in Canada during 2011–12. The adult criminal courts completed just under 386,500 cases involving 1,160,307 charges in 2011–12, a 5.3 percent decrease compared to the previous year. Of the cases completed in the adult criminal courts, 87 percent were for Criminal Code offences. The remaining 13 percent involved federal statutes. Of the cases involving the Criminal Code, the "crimes against person" category accounted for 22 percent, while the "crimes against property" and "Other Criminal Code" categories represented 25 and 5 percent, respectively; "administration of justice" offences accounted for 28 percent and "Criminal Code traffic" accounted for 20 percent (Boyce 2013).

During 2011–12, the most frequently occurring offences completed in court were impaired driving (11 percent), theft (10 percent), common assault (10 percent), failure to comply with a court order (9 percent), and breach of probation (8 percent). Between 2010–11 and 2011–12, every type of case involving violent crime decreased. Overall, there were approximately 3,000 fewer violent crime cases in 2011–12 than the previous year. The largest reductions were found in homicide (−11 percent) and robbery (−10 percent). In comparison, there was a reduction of just over 8,000 cases completed in the adult courts involving property crimes between 2010–11 and 2011–12, as well as reductions of almost 2,000 administration of justice offences and 2,500 "other Criminal Code" offences.

Criminal Justice Insight

GUILTY CASES IN ADULT CRIMINAL COURT, 2011–2012

During 2011–12, the accused was found guilty in 64 percent of the cases disposed of in the adult criminal courts. In 32 percent of the cases, the most serious offence was resolved by a decision to stay or withdraw charges, and 3 percent of all cases resulted in an acquittal. The remaining cases involved other decisions (e.g., the accused was found unfit to stand trial, or a finding of guilt was not recorded) (see Figure 10.1).

When a defendant was found guilty, the most common sentence handed out in 2011–12 was probation (45 percent), followed by custody (35 percent) (see Figure 10.2).

In the crime against the person category, the highest "guilty" percentage was "other sexual offences" (69 percent), followed by robbery (65 percent), and major assault (53 percent). For crimes against property, the highest "guilty" percentage was for "other property offences" (73 percent), break and enter (70 percent), and fraud (65 percent). The majority (86 percent) of all custodial sentences were for six months or less. Almost 4 percent of guilty cases resulted in a sentence to federal custody of two years or more (see Figure 10.3).

The findings of this study of the adult provincial criminal court caseload during 2011–12 also included the following:

- The violent crime category was the most likely to include a sentence of probation (75 percent).
- Cases involving violent crimes resulted in a finding of guilt 50 percent of the time, compared to property crimes (61 percent), administration of offences (72 percent), and other Criminal Code offences (60 percent).
- The median length of a probation order was 365 days.
- Cases involving an outcome of guilt for being unlawfully at large had the greatest likelihood of a custodial sentence (85 percent), followed by homicide (83 percent), attempted murder (80 percent), and robbery (80 percent).

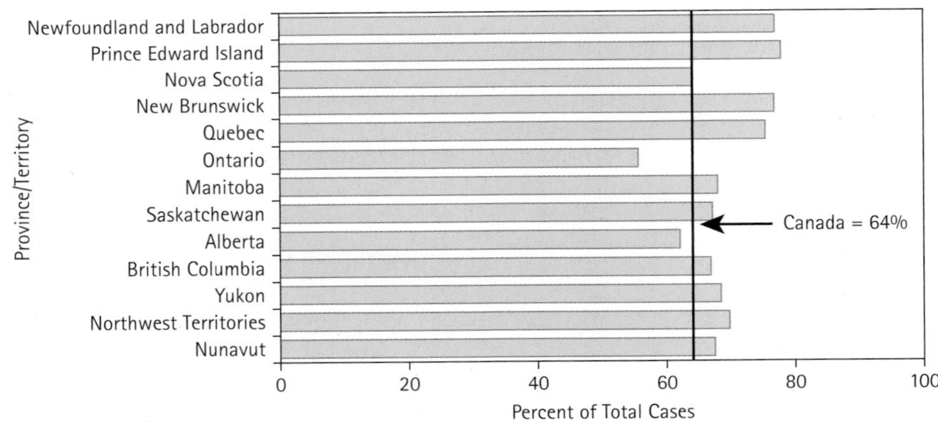

FIGURE 10.1 Guilty Cases in Adult Criminal Court, by Province and Territory, 2011–12

Source: Jillian Boyce, "Adult Criminal Court Statistics in Canada, 2011/2011." *Juristat* (June 2013), Statistics Canada Catalogue no. 85-002-x, p. 8, http://www.statcan.gc.ca/85-002-x/2013001/article/11804-eng.pdf. Reproduced and distributed on an "as is" basis with the permission of Statistics Canada.

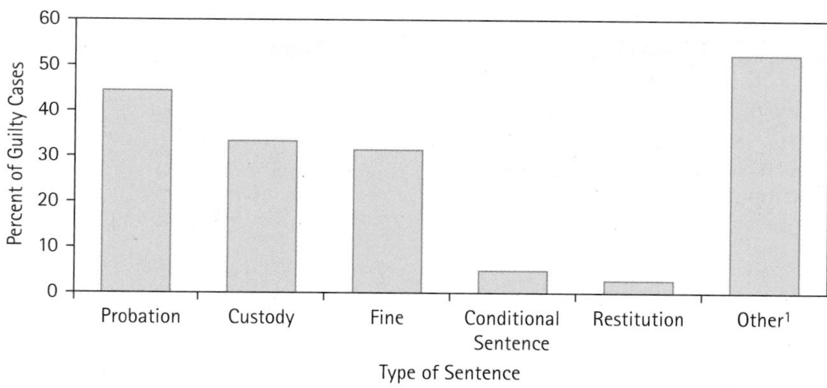

FIGURE 10.2 Guilty Cases in Adult Criminal Court, by Type of Sentence, Canada, 2011–12

[1] Includes, for example, absolute and conditional discharge, suspended sentence, community service order, and prohibition order.

Source: Jillian Boyce, "Adult Criminal Court Statistics in Canada, 2011/2011." *Juristat* (June 2013), Statistics Canada Catalogue no. 85-002-x, p. 11, http://www.statcan.gc.ca/85-002-x/2013001/article/11804-eng.pdf. Reproduced and distributed on an "as is" basis with the permission of Statistics Canada.

- Fines were most frequently imposed when the accused was found guilty of impaired driving (88 percent) and drug possession (48 percent).
- The median length for a period of custody across Canada was 30 days.
- The median amount for fines was $1,000.
- The median period of incarceration for violent crimes was 75 days; for property offences it was 45 days.
- The median prison sentence for attempted murder was 1,733 days, while for break and enter it was 161 days.

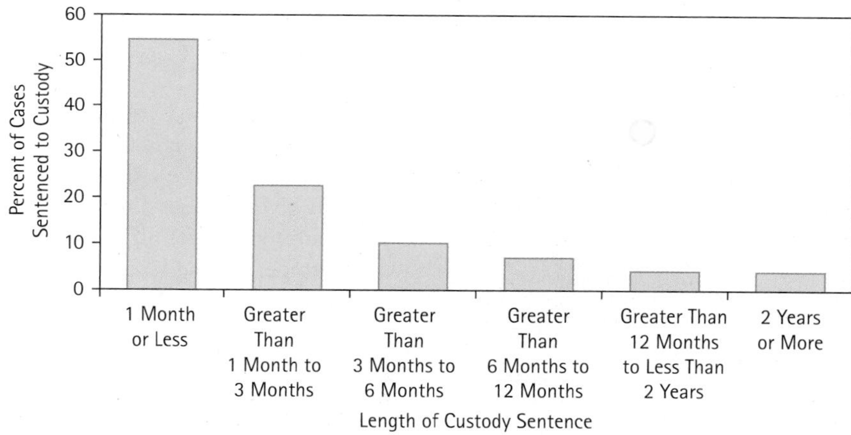

FIGURE 10.3 Guilty Cases in Adult Criminal Court, by Length of Custody, Canada, 2011–12

Source: Jillian Boyce, "Adult Criminal Court Statistics in Canada, 2011/2011." *Juristat* (June 2013), Statistics Canada Catalogue no. 85-002-x, p. 12, http://www.statcan.gc.ca/85-002-x/2013001/article/11804-eng.pdf. Reproduced and distributed on an "as is" basis with the permission of Statistics Canada.

SUMMING UP AND LOOKING FORWARD

The criminal court system in Canada consists of varying types of courts: federal, provincial, and territorial. Criminal courts have the responsibility of deciding the guilt or innocence of the accused, as well as determining an appropriate sentence if the accused pleads guilty or is found guilty by a judge and/or jury.

There are a number of philosophical rationales of sentencing. Sentences are oftentimes used in combination today in Canada. Deterrence refers to the protection of society through the prevention of criminal acts. There are two types of deterrence: specific and general. Specific deterrence attempts to discourage an offender from committing a crime, while general deterrence refers to a sentence that is severe enough to stop people from committing a crime. Selective incapacitation is the removal of certain individuals (commonly referred to as chronic offenders) from society for lengthy periods. Rehabilitation emphasizes the idea that offenders should be treated, while the justice model believes that more serious crimes should receive more severe sentences. More recent developments in the area of sentencing are healing, which uses ceremonies such as sentencing circles rather than substantive rules, and restoration, which focuses mainly upon repairing the harm that results from a crime.

In 2011–12, approximately 386,000 cases involving almost 1.2 million Criminal Code and other federal statute offences were completed in the adult criminal courts, a 6 percent decrease from the previous year. More than three-quarters of these cases were nonviolent, and about 64 percent of them resulted in an outcome of guilty. Probation was the most common sentence, followed by some form of custody. In 2011–12, the median length of custodial sentences was 30 days.

To better understand the sentencing process, it is important to consider the laws governing sentencing in Canada, particularly the principles and purposes of sentencing. These are discussed in the next section.

Review Questions:

1. What is the difference between general and specific deterrence?
2. Discuss how healing differs from the traditional approaches to sentencing.
3. What are the major elements of a restoration approach to sentencing according to White and Haines?
4. Define probation. How commonly is it used as a sentence? Why?
5. Which sentencing options include the possibility of a period of incarceration?

Sentencing Law in Canada

In 1994, then-Justice Minister Allan Rock introduced Bill C-41, which proposed to reform the sentencing system as well as intermediate punishments (see Chapter 11). At the beginning of September, 1996, **Bill C-41** (known as the Sentencing Reform Bill) was proclaimed, bringing about a significant change in the sentencing system in Canada. It also included a statement about the purpose of sentencing in Canada (see Exhibit 10.2). The bill had three objectives:

> (1) to provide a consistent framework of policy and process in sentencing matters;
>
> (2) to create a system of sentencing policy and process approved by Parliament; and
>
> (3) to increase public accessibility to the law relating to sentencing (Daubney and Parry 1999:33).

It also introduced conditional sentences as a sentencing option for judges (see Chapter 11). Bill C-41 was an attempt to achieve a **balanced approach** to criminal justice by giving judges direction when considering community alternatives for offenders in appropriate situations while also permitting longer periods of incarceration for high-risk, violent offenders.

Section 718 identifies 10 objectives of **just sanctions** (see Exhibit 10.3). Since judges can typically sentence an offender by "selecting" one of the following objectives, and since most of these sentencing objectives have existed for years, "the result is little more than a legislated statement of the status quo. To this extent, s. 718 codifies current judicial practice" (Roberts and von Hirsch 1999:53).

A statement concerning the **fundamental principle of sentencing** is found in s. 718.1, which declares that a sentence must be proportionate to the seriousness

EXHIBIT 10.2 The Purpose of Sentencing

Bill C-41 included a statement about the purpose of sentencing (s. 718). The following are excerpts:

> The fundamental purpose of sentencing is to contribute, along with crime prevention initiatives, respect for the law and the maintenance of a just, peaceful and safe society by imposing just sanctions that have one or more of the following objectives:
>
> - to denounce unlawful conduct;
> - to deter the offender and other persons from committing offences;
> - to separate offenders from society, where necessary;
> - to assist in rehabilitating offenders;
> - to provide reparations for harm done to victims or the community; and
> - to promote a sense of responsibility in offenders, and acknowledgment of the harm done to victims and to the community.

These purposes include all of the traditional purposes of sentencing such as deterrence, justice, incapacitation, and rehabilitation. Significantly, s. 718(e) highlights the federal government's interest in restorative justice as it relates to the "reparation for harm done to victims and the community and in promoting a sense of responsibility in offenders and acknowledgment of the harm done to the victims and to the community" (Daubney and Parry 1999:34). In addition, the bill's emphasis on "least restrictive measures" directs sentencing judges to use incarceration only when other sentencing alternatives (e.g., community penalties) are inappropriate. This is consistent with Parliament's decision to emphasize restorative justice.

of the offence and the degree of responsibility of the offenders. According to the Department of Justice (2005:2), it is the combination of the "**principle of proportionality** and the emphasis on the facts relating to both the offence and the offender" that sets Canada's sentencing approach apart from those of other countries. This section has introduced a number of other sentencing principles as well (see Exhibit 10.4). Overall, these principles provide a general framework for guiding sentencing judges and courts and for encouraging flexibility by judges. Over time, provincial courts of appeal and the Supreme Court of Canada "are providing more detailed guidance as to how the various principles should be applied to categories of offence and offenders" (ibid.).

One of the most controversial cases in recent Canadian sentencing history is *R. v. Gladue* (1999). This case involved s. 718.2(e) of the Criminal Code, which states "all available sanctions other than imprisonment that are reasonable in the circumstance, should be considered for all offenders, with particular attention to aboriginal offenders." Jamie Tanis Gladue, an Aboriginal woman, was charged with the second degree murder of her husband. She had reason to believe that he was having an affair, and an argument ensued, during which Ms. Gladue stabbed him in the heart

EXHIBIT 10.3 The Objectives of Just Sanctions

The 10 objectives are:

- denunciation
- individual deterrence
- general deterrence
- incapacitation
- reparation to the individual
- restitution to the community
- the promotion of a sense of responsibility in offenders
- acknowledgment of the harm done to victims
- acknowledgment of the harm done to communities
- the creation of opportunities to assist in the offender's rehabilitation

EXHIBIT 10.4 The Principles of Sentencing in Canada

Section 718.2 of the Criminal Code specifies a number of sentencing principles:

(a) a sentence should be increased or reduced to account for any relevant aggravating or mitigating circumstances relating to the offence or the offender, and, without limiting the generality of the foregoing,

(i) evidence that the offence was motivated by bias, prejudice or hate based on race, national or ethnic origin, language, colour, religion, sex, age, mental or physical disability, sexual orientation, or any other similar factor; or

(ii) evidence that the offender, in committing the offence, abused the offender's spouse or child;

(iii) evidence that the offender, in committing the offence, abused a position of trust or authority in relation to the victim shall be deemed to be aggravating circumstances; or

(iv) evidence that the offence was committed for the benefit of, at the direction of or in association with a criminal organization;

(b) a sentence should be similar to sentences imposed on similar offenders for similar offences committed in similar circumstances;

(c) where consecutive sentences are imposed, the combined sentence should not be unduly long or harsh;

(d) an offender should not be deprived of liberty, if less restrictive sanctions may be appropriate in the circumstances; and

(e) all available sanctions other than imprisonment that are reasonable in the circumstances should be considered for all offenders, with particular attention to the circumstances of Aboriginal offenders.

with a knife. Following the preliminary inquiry and the selection of the jury, she pleaded guilty to the charge of manslaughter. She was then sentenced to three years in prison with a 10-year firearms prohibition, a sentence typically handed out to those convicted of manslaughter in Canada.

The trial judge noted a number of mitigating factors in this case. These included her supportive family, the treatment for alcoholism she had been undergoing since the incident, her remorse, and her guilty plea. Aggravating factors included the fact that she had stabbed her husband twice, had intended to seriously harm him, and had committed a serious crime (Lash 2000).

When handing down the sentence, the trial judge noted that Ms. Gladue was Cree but that she lived "off reserve" and was therefore not entitled to the special consideration due to her on account of her Aboriginal status as stipulated in s. 718.2(e). The case was appealed to the British Columbia Court of Appeal on the basis of her attempts to "rehabilitate herself" since the offence, the 17 months she had waited prior to her trial to start, and the fact that the trial judge failed to consider her Aboriginal status. Again Ms. Gladue lost. She then appealed the verdict to the Supreme Court of Canada. The Supreme Court considered only one factor in her appeal—whether or not the trial judge had given appropriate attention to her Aboriginal status. It was decided that Ms. Gladue was to receive a conditional sentence (see Chapter 11) of two years less a day, to be served in the community. The Supreme Court justices, in reaching their judgment, commented on the discrimination experienced by Aboriginal people in the criminal justice system, noting also "the excessive imprisonment of Aboriginal people is only the tip of the iceberg insofar as the estrangement of the Aboriginal peoples from the Canadian justice system is concerned."

This decision was quickly followed by two similar cases, also in British Columbia. In the first, a Métis woman who had stabbed her common law husband to death was given a conditional sentence, enabling the defendant to look after her five-year-old daughter. And in July 1999, the British Columbia Supreme Court used the same section to reduce a life sentence to 20 years' imprisonment for a 37-year-old Métis man.

In March 2012, the Supreme Court, in *R. v. Ipeelee* (2012), revisited its decision in *Gladue* but as it applied to a long-term offender designation. Mr. Ipeelee was a

39-year-old Inuk man who had been drinking alcohol since he was 11 years of age. He had been in and out of custodial facilities for numerous crimes since 1985. In the case under consideration, he had been sentenced to six years for a sexual assault, and later was given a long-term supervision order, and sentenced to an extra 10 years with that designation (see Chapter 3). This meant that if he reoffended, he could be returned to custody for violating the designation's terms. When he broke the conditions of his long-term supervision order, the judge sentenced him to three years' imprisonment. On appeal to the Supreme Court, the issue in this case became "how to determine a fit sentence for a breach of a long term supervision order in the case of an Aboriginal offender in particular." After considering the principles of sentencing as determined in *Gladue*, the length of his imprisonment was reduced to one year. The reasoning by the Supreme Court was based on that there were few culturally relevant programs in Kingston, Ontario, where he was living at the time he breached his long-term supervision order. In addition, he had already served 18 months of his order with no legal-related issues, and the justices felt that a one-year sentence was sufficient for him to become involved with an alcohol treatment program.

How Do Judges Decide on a Sentence?

Many people argue that those who commit serious crimes should receive lengthy sentences. When this doesn't happen, judges are often criticized for being too lenient. Judges do not reach their sentencing decisions in an arbitrary way, however. Their options are restricted by law (these restrictions are referred to as the **structure of sentencing**). For example, it is impossible for a judge to sentence an offender to life imprisonment for a summary conviction offence, since that sentence is outside what is allowed by law. But judges do have certain parameters within which they can individualize sentences on the basis of the offender's characteristics (e.g., prior record) as well as on **mitigating circumstances** or **aggravating circumstances** surrounding the crime itself (Exhibit 10.5). They cannot, however, use unfettered discretion in every case. In some instances, such as first and second degree murder and manslaughter, fixed minimum sentences apply that the judge cannot change.

There are, however, a number of sentencing principles (see above) that judges are required to follow when deciding on an appropriate sentence. In *R. v. Priest* (1996), the Ontario Court of Appeal listed a number of principles that the trial judge in that case had broken. This case involved a 19-year-old first-time offender who had pleaded guilty to a charge of breaking and entering. The accused had cooperated fully with the authorities after he was caught and had returned to the owner all the items stolen. The Crown prosecutor requested a sentence of 30 to 60 days with probation. The trial judge, without discovering anything new about the accused (but noting the large number of break and enter charges on the court docket), sentenced the accused to one year on the basis of general deterrence. According to Edgar (1999), the Ontario Court of Appeal noted some of the principles that the judge had broken in this case:

- Prevalence of crime in an area is not to be the primary consideration in sentencing. It can only be one consideration among many.
- A custodial sentence on a first-time offender should not be imposed without either a presentence report or some other very clear information about the accused's background and circumstances.

EXHIBIT 10.5 Aggravating and Mitigating Circumstances

Aggravating Circumstances	Mitigating Circumstances
Previous convictions of the offender	First-time offender
Gang activity	Employment record
Vulnerability of the victim	Rehabilitative efforts since the offence was committed
Planning and organization	Disadvantaged background
Multiple criminal incidents	Guilty plea and remorse
Use or threatened use of a weapon	The length of time it took to prosecute or sentence the offender
Brutality	Good character

- Proportionality requires the sentence to reflect the seriousness of the offence, the culpability of the offender, and the harm occasioned by the offence.
- The role of the courts requires the imposition of appropriate sentences, not unduly harsh ones. A just society is not promoted by sentences that are far beyond those imposed for similar offences in other parts of the province.

If certain principles govern the sentencing decisions of judges in a province, what is the source of judicial discretion? Is it the personal preferences of a particular judge, the seriousness of the crime, the defendant's race, the quality of the arguments made by the defence attorney and Crown prosecutor during the trial, or perhaps the impact of the crime on the victim(s)? All of these factors may in some way contribute to the judge's decision.

Judges' sentencing decisions can be based on a number of factors, most commonly the objective factors involved in an offence (e.g., the seriousness of the offence) and the characteristics of the offender (e.g., prior criminal record). But they can also be based on other documents that focus upon the convicted offender and his or her prior record, notably the **presentence report** (Exhibit 10.6). Presentence reports are prepared for judges by probation officers in order to help judges determine an appropriate sentence. Hogarth (1971) conducted a study of judges' sentencing practices and reported that most judges were satisfied with the information about offenders they obtained from presentence reports. He also found that they were most generally used for serious offences such as assaults causing bodily harm and robbery, and that the family background of offenders was considered by judges to be an essential piece of information in 61 percent of the cases, compared to an offender's attitude toward rehabilitation, the mental condition of the offender, and the use of alcohol and other drugs—all of which were cited by the judges as essential less than 20 percent of the time. Later studies by Hagan (1975) and Boldt et al. (1983) found that judges in Canada followed the recommendations by probation officers in approximately 80 percent of the cases. In contrast, Gabor and Jayewardene (1978) reported that only 43 percent of the judges they studied followed a probation officer's recommendation for a community-based penalty.

In a study of 11 cities as well as Prince Edward Island and Nunavut, Bonta et al. (2005) sought to determine the views of judges, probation officers, Crown prosecutors, and defence counsel on presentence reports. One of their key interests was to evaluate the impact of these reports upon a judge's determination of a sentence. They reported that 60 percent of the judges would prefer to see presentence reports include sentencing recommendations. Almost all judges (94 percent) indicated that they would follow a recommendation of a community placement (especially a conditional sentence). In

EXHIBIT 10.6 Presentence Reports and the Criminal Code

Section 721 of the Criminal Code gives the legislative authority for the presentence report. Probation officers prepare a report when requested by the court "for the purpose of assisting the court in imposing a sentence or in determining whether the accused should be discharged pursuant to s. 730." The court can request a presentence report only after an offender has been found guilty or enters a plea of guilty.

A significant amount of discretion may be found in what is contained in a presentence report. However, the Criminal Code specifies that the following information will be included:

> (3)(a) . . . offender's age, maturity, character, behaviour, attitude and willingness to make amends;
>
> (3)(b) . . . history of previous dispositions under the *Youth Criminal Justice Act* and of previous findings of guilt under this Act and any other Act of Parliament;
>
> (3)(c) . . . history of any alternative measures used to deal with the offender, and the offender's response to those measures; and
>
> (3)(d) . . . any matter required by any regulation made under subsection (2), to be included in the report.

Subsection 2 refers to the type of offence that may require a report and the content of the form. While there is some mandatory content to be included in each presentence report, there is also considerable discretion in the Criminal Code to allow each province to determine what other information should be included.

addition, judges held positive attitudes toward offender rehabilitation. According to Bonta and his colleagues, information on treatment needs "were valued by all the key actors in the sentencing process and judges were particularly interested in treatment recommendations" (ibid.:23).

If you were a judge with the responsibility for deciding which offenders are to be incarcerated and which are to stay in the community, how would you decide? What criteria would you use? As noted in Exhibit 10.1, criminal sentences in Canada vary widely, from a discharge to life imprisonment. This variation originates in the Criminal Code, which sets out the maximum punishment for each offence. When you make your sentencing decision, it is of concern not only to the offender but also to the community, the police, and the victims. And of course your decision may be a mistake. What happens, for example, if you decide to sentence a convicted offender to probation and while that person is serving that sentence they commit a series of violent crimes? Would you change your sentencing approach in the future, or would you view the probation order and its consequences as an aberration?

In Canada, judges enjoy a substantial amount of discretion in terms of both the type and the severity of the sentences they can hand down. Only a few offences specify a minimum or a mandatory punishment. For most offences, the Criminal Code specifies a maximum punishment and then allows judges the discretion to select the appropriate sentence. This does not mean that judges can select any punishment they wish, for they are governed by three factors that are integral to the sentencing process in Canada. The first two determine the sentencing options available to the judge; the third frames the options from which a judge selects a sentence:

- The direction given in the statutes (generally the Criminal Code) in relation to the particular offence (see Exhibit 10.7).
- Rules and principles that offer guidance to the judge as to which dispositions should be used.
- The personal characteristics of the judge.

Still, judges in Canada are able to individualize sentences; for example, they can select a sentence from a wide range of purposes "whereby any sentence can be justified" (Doob and Webster 2006:351). Since judges have a number of sentencing options available to them, as we've seen, they must first determine what they hope to accomplish with the sentence. Sentencing always has at least one of the following objectives: deterrence, selective incapacitation, rehabilitation, or justice. These are important to sentencing because our system of justice is supposed "to accomplish some social utility beyond merely solving crimes and catching criminals" (Anderson and Newman 1993:288).

EXHIBIT 10.7 Sentencing Multiple Murderers

Between 1976, when capital punishment was abolished, and 2011, the harshest sentence a convicted offender could receive for killing two or more persons (i.e., a multiple murderer) was life in prison with no chance for parole for 25 years (see, however, the discussion of the faint hope clause in Chapter 13). In 2011, this situation changed when an amendment to the Criminal Code, the Protecting Canadians by Ending Sentencing Discounts for Multiple Murders Act, was passed. This legislation gave sentencing judges the discretion to impose consecutive parole ineligibility periods for offenders convicted of multiple murders. In their decision, judges can consider

1. the character of the offender,
2. the nature and circumstances of the offence, and
3. any jury recommendations prior to deciding to impose consecutive 25-year parole ineligibility periods.

The first case in which a multiple murder handed down one of these sentences occurred in 2013 in Edmonton, when an armoured car guard shot and killed three of his colleagues and seriously wounded another guard. Originally charged with first degree murder in the three deaths, in a plea bargain he pleaded guilty to one count of first degree murder, two counts of second degree murder, and one count of attempted murder. He was sentenced to 40 years' incarceration before he could be eligible for parole.

The longest sentence handed out under the new law occurred in 2014 in Moncton, when Justin Bourque pleaded guilty to three counts of first degree murder and two counts of attempted murder for killing three members of the RCMP and wounding two others. He received five life sentences, with no chance of parole for 75 years. Mr. Bourque will be eligible for parole when he is 99 years of age. In handing down the sentence, the trial judge stated that the sentence had to be proportionate to the seriousness of the offence and that his main concern was deterrence.

Sentencing and Healing Circles

In the past 20 years, much attention has been paid to the **overrepresentation** of Aboriginal people in the federal and provincial correctional systems. Despite the many provincial and federal inquiries into this issue, and that in 1996 the federal government introduced s. 718.2(e) in an attempt to reduce the overrepresentation of Aboriginals in custody, Aboriginal people continue to be sentenced to incarceration at a higher rate than their proportion within the general population (see Figure 10.4). Dauvergne (2012) found that 20 percent of all adults in federal sentenced custody during 2010–11 were Aboriginal, about seven to eight times higher than the proportion of Aboriginal people in the adult population (3 percent) as a whole.

According to Perreault (2014),

- Aboriginal adults accounted for 28 percent of admissions to sentenced custody in 2011–12.
- Aboriginal adults accounted for 25 percent of admissions to remand and 21 percent of admissions to probation and conditional sentences.
- The overrepresentation of Aboriginal adults is greater for Aboriginal women compared to Aboriginal men. In 2011–12, Aboriginal women accounted for 43 percent of all women admissions to provincial and territorial sentenced custody and 37 percent of all women admitted to remand, compared to 27 and 23 percent for Aboriginal males.

Based on similar evidence, Quigley (1994:271) recommended an attempt "to decrease the preponderance of Aboriginal people within the prison system." One proposal has been to reintroduce sentencing and healing circles, in which a group of Elders participate with a judge in the sentencing process in an attempt to heal the accused, the victim, and the community. Some of the benefits of sentencing circles are identified in Exhibit 10.8.

The nature of **sentencing circles** varies across Canada, but some features are common to all. Quigley (ibid.:288) notes that modern sentencing circles are a hybrid of traditional Aboriginal community justice and the Western legal system: "sentencing circles are a variation in procedure, not necessarily a change in the substance of sentencing." Judges retain the right to give final approval to a sentence imposed by a sentencing circle. In some ways, a sentencing circle operates much like the Western legal system. For example, any dispute on a factual matter is resolved by calling for evidence and through the examination and cross-examination of witnesses. The difference is that, through discussions within the sentencing circle, "respected members of the community, the victim, the police, the accused, the family of the accused, Crown and defence counsel, and the judge try to jointly arrive at a decision that is acceptable to all."

Jurisdictions vary regarding which types of offences can be heard by sentencing circles. Generally, though, these offences are minor in nature, typically involving property crimes. Serious violent crimes are usually not allowed to be heard by a sentencing circle, although there are exceptions (see the discussion of Hollow Water in Chapter 3).

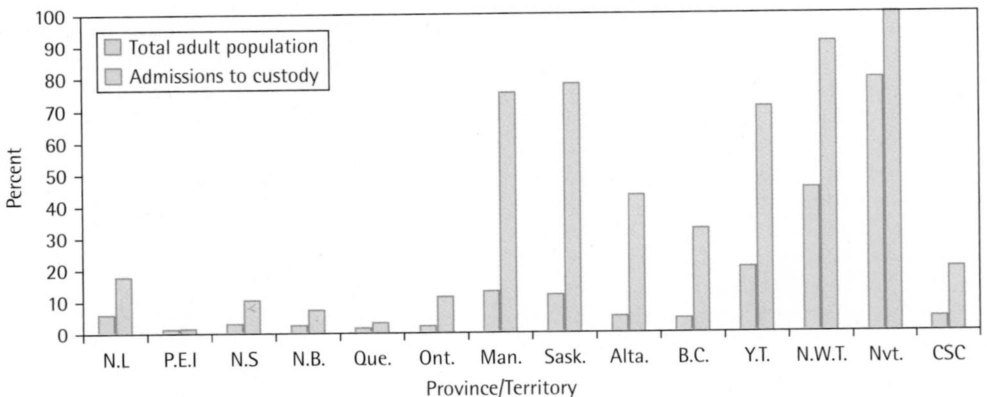

FIGURE 10.4 Admissions to Sentenced Custody by Aboriginal Identity and Proportion of Aboriginal People in Total Population, by Jurisdiction, 2011–12

Source: S. Perreault, "Admissions to adult correctional services in Canada, 2011/2012." *Juristat* (March 27, 2014), Statistics Canada Catalogue no. 85-002-x, p. 6, http://www.statcan.gc.ca/pub/85-002-x/2014001/article/11918-eng.htm. Reproduced and distributed on an "as is" basis with the permission of Statistics Canada.

EXHIBIT 10.8 The Benefits of Sentencing Circles

The benefits of sentencing circles are many. According to a Yukon court, they include the following:

1. The monopoly of professionals is reduced.
2. Lay participation is encouraged.
3. Information flow is increased.
4. There is a creative search for new options.
5. The sharing of responsibility for the decision is promoted.
6. The participation of the accused is encouraged.
7. Victims are involved in the process.
8. A more constructive environment is created.
9. There is greater understanding of the limitations of the justice system.
10. The focus of the criminal justice system is extended.
11. There is greater mobilization of community resources.
12. There is an opportunity to merge the values of Aboriginal nations with those of the larger society (*R. v. Moses* [1992]).

A number of other criteria are considered in determining whether a sentencing circle will be held. In *R. v. Joseyounen* (1995), the following criteria were set out:

- The accused must agree to be referred to the sentencing circle.
- The accused must have deep roots in the community in which the sentencing circle is held and from which the participants are to be drawn.
- There are Elders or respected non-political community leaders willing to participate.
- The victim is willing to participate and has not been coerced into participating.
- The court should determine beforehand whether the victim is suffering from battered woman syndrome. If she is, she should receive counselling and be accompanied by the support team in the circle.
- Disputed facts must be resolved in advance.
- The case must be one in which the court is willing to depart from the usual range of sentencing.

CP PHOTO/ Winnipeg Free Press/ Joe Bryksa

Sentencing circles bring offenders, victims, their families, community members, and Elders together to discuss the impact of a crime. The meeting is conducted in a circle, which is designed to reduce hierarchy and promote the sharing of ideas.

A number of circumstances exist where the sentencing circle is not appropriate, such as the following:

- A term of incarceration in excess of two years is realistic.
- There have been frequent repeat offences or the offence is indictable.
- The attitude of the offender prohibits his or her involvement.
- There are no community sentencing options available to the circle.
- The community is not prepared to be involved in the circle (Native Law Centre 2006).

Once a sentence has been agreed on, it is not automatically accepted by the Western legal system. For example, the Saskatchewan Court of Appeal overturned the sentence handed down by a sentencing circle to Ivan Morin (*R. v. Morin* [1995]). Morin, a 34-year-old Métis, was convicted in 1992 of robbing a gas station of $131 and choking a female attendant. He was sentenced to jail for 18 months instead of the six to eight years requested by the Crown. The Crown had proposed its sentence based on Morin's 34 prior criminal convictions, which ranged from drunk driving and small-time break-ins to attempted murder and kidnapping. Even so, the trial judge accepted the recommendation of the sentencing circle. The Crown appealed the case, arguing that Morin was using the sentencing circle to receive the lightest sentence possible and showed neither real remorse nor interest in rehabilitation. The Saskatchewan Court of Appeal, in its review of the case, noted that judges should accept the decisions of sentencing circles in cases where

1. the accused agrees to be referred to a sentencing circle;
2. the accused has deep roots in the community in which the circle is held;
3. the Elders are willing to support the offender; and
4. the victim voluntarily participates.

Since Morin appeared to be trying to take advantage of the lighter sentences associated with sentencing circles, the appeal court accepted the argument presented by the Crown and increased the sentence. Such appeals, however, are rare.

Healing circles have both supporters and detractors. Some offer only cautious support (Clairmont 1996; LaPrairie 1998; Roberts and LaPrairie 1996). Clairmont (1996) studied three such programs in three different communities and concluded that "in all programs the objectives relating to victims and community reconciliation have proven elusive to date." Clairmont notes that it is especially important for these programs to involve the community at large. LaPrairie (1998) reports that victims often find healing programs to be less positive experiences than do the offenders and that only about 30 percent of the families of offenders and victims considered that offenders had been dealt with appropriately. As LaPrairie notes, "these findings are not . . . to suggest a lack of merit in the projects identified above or in pursuing **local justice** in aboriginal communities . . . [but] to identify the need for greater clarity in the development and delivery of local justice services."

SUMMING UP AND LOOKING FORWARD

The law on sentencing is the result of Bill C-41 (1996). The goals of this Bill were to establish a fundamental purpose of setting a consistent framework in sentencing policy, with sentences to be approved by Parliament, as well as to increase public accessibility to the law as it related to sentencing. The fundamental purpose of sentencing is to contribute, along with crime prevention initiatives, respect for the law and the maintenance of a just, peaceful, and safe society by imposing just sanctions. A fundamental principle of sentencing is that a sentence must be proportionate to the seriousness of the offence and the degree of responsibility of an offender. It is this principle of proportionality and the emphasis on the facts concerning both the offence and the offender that sets Canada apart from other Western nations.

One section of Canada's new sentencing law became controversial: s. 718.2(e) states that all available sanctions other than imprisonment that are reasonable in the circumstance should be considered for all offenders, with particular attention to Aboriginal offenders. The Supreme Court of Canada upheld the constitutionality of this section in *R. v. Gladue* and later included long-term supervision orders in *R. v. Ipeelee*.

Judges consider a number of factors when they decide a sentence, including various aggravating and mitigating factors that appear in the crime. Judges are required to follow a number of sentencing principles when they are determining a sentence. These include the prevalence of crime in an area, proportionality, and appropriate sentences. Presentence reports provide judges with information that assists them in determining an appropriate sentence.

Alternatives to Western-based approaches to sentencing have appeared in recent decades, in particular sentencing circles. Criteria have been established to determine whether a sentencing circle will be held; for example, the accused must agree to be referred to the sentencing circle, the accused must have deep roots in the community, and the victim willingly agrees to participate. Benefits of sentencing circles include the participation of lay persons, an increase in the information flow, and the involvement of victims.

In recent years, a number of issues related to sentencing have been raised, including wrongful convictions and an increase in the number of mandatory minimum sentences. In addition, efforts have been made to increase the participation of victims in the sentencing process. These issues are discussed in the next section.

Review Questions:

1. What are "just" sanctions and how are they related to the purpose of sentencing?
2. Discuss the details of the decision made by the Supreme Court in *R. v. Gladue*.
3. Why are presentence reports important for judges?
4. What factors are integral to the sentencing process in Canada and thereby limit some of the discretion held by judges?
5. What are the criteria to determine whether or not a sentencing circle will be held?

Miscarriages of Justice: Wrongful Convictions

One of the most important principles in our criminal justice system is that a person is innocent until proven guilty. A number of cases have emerged over the past two decades that have raised the issue of miscarriages of justice in Canada, specifically **wrongful accusations** and **wrongful convictions**. While the criminal justice process is supposed to operate on the basis of the principles of due process, an increasing number of incidents are coming to the attention of the public and the authorities that lead to questions surrounding the legitimacy of the process. In 2014 over 40 wrongful convictions had been documented in Canada, starting with the Steven Truscott case in 1959. By the spring of 2015, there had been at least 23 exonerations of individuals across Canada.

In the United States, Scheck and his colleagues (2000) reported that more than 25 percent of all prime suspects were excluded prior to trial as a result of DNA testing conducted in 18,000 criminal cases. In other words, 4,000 of the prime suspects in cases were wrongly accused. Radelet et al. (1992) estimated that at least 23 individuals had been wrongfully executed in the United States. And, again in the United States, Liebman and colleagues (2000) found serious, reversible errors in almost 70 percent of the thousands of capital cases they studied over a 23-year period (1973–95). A study of the 200 individuals in the United States to be exonerated by DNA evidence found that they served an average of 12 years in prison, 176 were convicted of sexual assault, and 14 were on death row (Conway 2007:14).

There is no systematic record of the number of wrongful convictions, but in the United States, Huff et al. (1986) attempted to empirically estimate the number of wrongful convictions by surveying all the Attorneys General in the United States as well as the following in the state of Ohio: all presiding judges of the common plea courts; all county prosecutors, public defenders, and sheriffs; and the chiefs of police of seven large cities. They defined wrongful convictions as "cases in which a person (is) convicted of a felony but later . . . found innocent beyond a reasonable doubt, generally due to a confession by the actual offender, evidence that had been available but was not sufficiently used at the time of the conviction, new evidence that was not previously available, and other factors." The results were startling—based on the surveys, the researchers conservatively estimated that about 0.5 percent of all felony convictions were incorrect. That is, of every 1,000 individuals convicted of a serious crime, five are actually innocent of the charge(s). Huff (2004) points out that while a percentage of less than one may not seem high, in 2000 in the United States an average of seven million people were convicted of serious crimes, meaning that there could have been 34,250 persons wrongfully convicted in that year! As of June 2012, at least 292 wrongfully convicted individuals have been exonerated by DNA in the United States according to the American Innocence Project (www.innocenceproject.org).What causes wrongful convictions? According to research in the United States, a number of factors consistently appear in almost all cases of wrongful conviction. These include relying on jailhouse informants for evidence, perjury, misleading police lineups, forensic errors, false or coerced confessions, police and prosecutor misconduct (including the withholding of evidence), eyewitness error, community pressure for a conviction, ineffective legal counsel, and the "ratification of error" (i.e., the tendency of individuals working in the criminal justice system to "rubber-stamp" decisions made at the lower levels as cases move through the next stages of the system). In most cases, more than one factor has been found that contributed to a wrongful conviction—in some cases, most of the above-noted reasons may have been in play. While some of the reasons have been previously discussed (see the "Mr. Big" technique and jailhouse interrogations in Chapter 7), other prominent reasons are discussed below.

Eyewitness Error

Eyewitness error is viewed as the main cause of wrongful convictions. For example, Huff and colleagues (1986) reported that 79 percent of their respondents ranked witness error as the most frequent type of error resulting in a wrongful conviction. Scheck et al. (2000) point out that in 84 percent of the DNA exonerations they studied, charges ultimately proved to be incorrect were laid against the accused on the basis of mistaken eyewitness identification. A number of researchers, such as Loftus (1979), Loftus and Doyle (1991), and Penrod (2003), have studied eyewitness identification extensively and how it can be "significantly affected by psychological, societal, cultural, and systemic factors, and how police line-ups should and should not be conducted to ensure fairness to suspects" (Huff 2004:110). In the United States, 75 percent of the cases in which the first 200 individuals were exonerated by DNA were found to include eyewitness error identification (Conway 2007:A14).

A number of jurisdictions have created groups to investigate and recommend the best way to eliminate erroneous eyewitness identifications. Some of the recommendations propose to bring about procedural reforms in order to improve the accuracy and reliability of eyewitness identifications, especially the identification process as administered by law enforcement personnel. Five procedural issues have been highlighted: instructions to witnesses, witness confidence statements, documentation of identification procedures, photo arrays, and live lineups. Some of their recommendations include the following:

- Videotaping of the identification procedure;
- Eliciting a statement of the witness's confidence in the identification;
- Documenting the lineup with a colour photograph of the lineup as the witness viewed it, and documenting the logistics of the identification procedure, including date, time, location, persons present, etc.;
- Urging that lineups and photo arrays be conducted "double-blind" whenever practicable, that is administered by persons unaware of the accused's identity; and

- Advising witnesses orally or in writing about the details of the identification procedure before it begins, and that the person who committed the crime may or may not be in the photo array or lineup.

These procedures have been implemented by many if not all police agencies; for example, they have been used in Canada by the RCMP since 2003.

Forensic Errors

DNA analysis has resulted in the exoneration of many wrongfully convicted individuals (Scheck et al. 2000). But in some cases, faulty evidence submitted by forensic scientists, called **forensic errors**, has led to wrongful convictions. An analysis of the first 200 individuals in the United States exonerated by DNA discovered that in 110 of them, mistakes or other problems with forensic science were found (Conway 2007:A14). Three of these wrongful conviction cases involved experts testifying in misleading ways or misstating what was in the lab reports. It has been estimated that between 52 and 57 percent of all wrongful conviction cases in the United States are due to questionable or improper forensic science.

In Canada, the Manitoba Justice Department established a committee (the Forensic Evidence Review Committee) to review potential murder convictions on the basis that flawed hair analysis had tainted two murder convictions in that province; this has led to a further review of both cases (Smith 2004). One of these cases (*R. v. Unger*) led to the federal justice minister ordering a new trial, but the province of Manitoba decided not to prosecute the individual. This committee was established by the Manitoba government after James Driskell won his freedom after serving more than 13 years in prison. DNA evidence proved that he had been wrongfully convicted on the basis of forensic hair analysis, which until the mid-1990s had been a commonly used scientific approach in Canadian courts. After a review of 492 convictions during the previous 15 years, it was concluded that none warranted retesting hair samples using DNA samples to see whether mistakes were made (MacAfee 2005:A5). In addition, the investigation of pediatric forensic pathology in Ontario (and, notably, the practices of pathologist Dr. Charles Smith) by the Commission of Inquiry into Pediatric Forensic Pathology (the Goudge Commission) reported that he had made significant errors in at least 20 cases he handled for the Ontario Chief Coroner's Office (Makin 2008a:A4). In addition, the oversight and accountability mechanisms that existed in Ontario at that time "were not only inadequate to the task, but were inadequately employed by those responsible for using them" (Goudge Commission Press Release 2008).

CP PHOTO/ Frank Gunn

In his report, Judge Goudge accused Dr. Charles Smith of making "false and misleading statements" in criminal cases. At least 12 people were wrongfully convicted and went to jail, while another eight were wrongly accused on the basis of Dr. Smith's reports.

Police and Prosecutorial Misconduct

Based on their study of post-conviction DNA exonerations of the wrongfully convicted, Scheck and colleagues (2000) concluded that 63 percent involved **police and/or prosecutorial misconduct**. An inquiry into three wrongful conviction murder cases in Newfoundland found that these cases had been "botched largely because of a dysfunctional Crown 'culture' that was overzealous and unquestioningly accepted police theories" (Makin 2006:A7). The report's author added that "by failing to view evidence objectively and becoming over aggressive in their pursuit of legal victories . . . prosecutors played an instrumental role in the wrongful convictions" (ibid.). Other concerns in this category relate to the use of false or misleading evidence, tampering with witnesses, and failing to disclose exculpatory evidence (Huff 2004). One of the recommendations to correct these issues is for the police to record all of their interrogations. In the United States, Garrett (2010) reports that in his study of 42 individuals who confessed to a crime but were later exonerated by DNA, only 58 percent were recorded and almost all of the confessions were contaminated in some way. Recording interrogations reduces coercive questioning by the police as well as providing an accurate record of any discussions between the accused and police (see Chapter 7).

Sentencing Reforms

Various sentencing reforms, such as **mandatory minimum sentences**, sentencing guidelines, and truth-in-sentencing, have been implemented in a number of Western countries (most notably in the United States) over the past three decades. The intent of these sentencing reforms has been to curtail the discretion given to judges in order to sentence offenders, and thereby reduce the disparate treatment found within the courts. These reforms also shifted the primary focus of corrections from rehabilitation to deterrence and selective incapacitation, making the responses to crime much more severe and tangible (Morris and Tonry 1990). A considerable number of these reforms have brought mandatory minimum sentences into criminal justice policies.

Mandatory Minimum Sentences in Canada

One of the most controversial aspects of Bill C-10, the Safe Streets and Communities Act (see Chapter 1), is its provisions for mandatory minimum sentences. Two sections of Bill C-10 included mandatory minimum sentences: (1) amendments to the Criminal Code (sexual offences against children), which introduced seven new mandatory minimum sentences for certain sexual offences committed against young persons that were already within the Criminal Code, increasing the existing mandatory minimum sentences for seven offences, and proposing two new offences that have mandatory minimum sentences attached to them; and (2) amendments to the Controlled Drugs and Substances Act (CDSA), which were designed to provide for mandatory minimum sentences for certain drug crimes (when Bill C-10 came into force, there were no mandatory minimum sentences under the CDSA).

Mandatory minimum sentences in Canada have existed since the Criminal Code was codified in 1892. At that time, six offences (for such criminal acts as committing fraud upon the government and corruption in municipal affairs) had mandatory minimum sentences. Gradually, mandatory minimum sentences were introduced into the Criminal Code, typically as a response to issues involving serious criminal offences. Nineteen offences containing mandatory minimum sentences were introduced in 1995, when a number of firearms-related laws (Bill C-68) were passed which mandated a minimum prison sentence for offenders committing any of the identified 10 violent crimes with a firearm. Later, similar legislation was introduced for sexual offences involving young persons in 2005 and for gang-related gun crimes or gun use in relation to designated serious crimes and a longer minimum sentence upon a second conviction. Today, the Criminal Code contains over 70 criminal offences when a mandatory minimum sentence must be handed down by a judge following a conviction. Most of these sentences fall into four categories: murder, breaking and entering (to steal a firearm and robbery to steal a firearm, both of which came into force in May 2008), firearms offences (originally introduced in 1995), and sexual offences involving young persons. In addition, there are mandatory minimum sentences for a number of other offences, such as impaired driving when the defendant has a previous conviction for the same offence. When considering a mandatory minimum sentence, a judge may have to consider a number of factors, for example whether the offence is prosecuted as either an indictable or summary offence, or if it is the first offence committed by the offender.

When one refers to a mandatory minimum sentence, what they are actually referring to is a "mandatory period of imprisonment" as most, if not all, mandatory minimum sentences apply to individuals convicted of specific designated crimes. As a crime-reduction strategy, mandatory minimum sentences is "a method of achieving in-capacitation" (see Chapter 3) as it attempts "to guarantee that certain offenders do a certain amount of prison time by curbing the discretion of judges" (Walker 1994:87).

The idea of mandatory minimum sentences has been controversial, with individuals taking strong positions as to whether or not such sentences are, in fact, effective. Supporters of mandatory minimum sentences emphasize the need to ensure that "crime does not pay" and view lengthy prison terms as an effective way of increasing the cost of offending. They argue that these sentences

- act as a deterrent;
- prevent future crimes by incapacitating the offender by removing them from society;
- reduce sentence disparity by giving clear guidelines to judges so that all offenders across Canada will receive similar, minimum amounts of time when convicted of the same offence;

- respond to the public concern that offenders are held accountable for their criminal convictions through imprisonment.

Persons opposed to mandatory minimum sentences point out that they have significant negative effects, including entrenching some offenders in criminal careers, and that the effects of increasing criminal justice sanctions are complex and may contradict what common sense would appear to dictate. According to the critics of mandatory minimum sentences, then, they

- have little or no deterrent effect, as deterrence occurs from the fear of being caught, as opposed to the length of the sentence;
- are an inflexible penalty structure that limits judicial discretion, leading to sentences out of proportion to the blameworthiness of an individual offender or the seriousness of the offence;
- shift decisions about the appropriate punishment from judges to prosecutors, who are able to decide whether to stay or withdraw charges, or plea bargain to avoid a mandatory minimum sentence;
- may lead to individuals not guilty of any offence to plead guilty to an offence they have not committed as they want to avoid being tried for an offence that carries with it a mandatory minimum sentence;
- may increase prison populations; and
- may be inconsistent with the fundamental principles of sentencing as set out in s. 718.1 of the Criminal Code.

The Supreme Court of Canada has, on occasion, struck down mandatory sentences considered to be too severe. In *R. v. Smith* (1987), the Supreme Court struck down a mandatory seven-year period of imprisonment for importing narcotics. The justices held that drug importing offence covered many substances of varying degrees of danger, disregarded the quantity imported, and ignored the reason why the individual was importing the drug and any prior convictions. In *R. v. Nasogaluak* (2010), however, the Supreme Court ruled that a sentencing judge cannot override a clear statement of legislative intent and reduce a sentence below a statutory mandated minimum, without exceptional circumstances. If there are exceptional circumstances, the Court stated that a sentence reduction below the mandatory minimum may be appropriate under s. 24(1) of the Charter. Provincial courts have raised concerns about the appropriateness of mandatory sentences. In *R. v. Smickle* (2012), an Ontario Superior Court judge struck down the mandatory minimum sentence for possession of a loaded gun (which came into force in 2008, as part of the Tackling Violent Crime Act), finding that the minimum three-year sentence for a first-time offender violated s. 12 of the Charter which provides that "Everyone has the right not to be subjected to cruel and unusual punishment." Instead, she sentenced Mr. Smickle to a 12-month sentence, three months which were to be spent in custody. Her decision was appealed to the Ontario Court of Appeal and, in 2014, they sentenced Mr. Smickle to an additional 12 months' incarceration and permanently stayed the sentence, pointing out that it had been five years since he was initially charged, and recognized his law-abiding lifestyle since his release.

There is no exception in Canada for those judges in Canada who want to use discretion to deviate from the mandatory minimum sentences in exceptional cases. However, various judges across Canada have decided that, in certain cases, mandatory minimum sentences are **disproportionate** to the crime committed and have ruled that they violate the Charter rights of the defendants. In *R. v. Lloyd* (2014), for example, a judge in British Columbia sentenced Mr. Lloyd to 191 days of imprisonment for three counts of drug possession for the purpose of drug trafficking, a sentence which was well short of the mandatory minimum sentence of one year. According to the judge, imposing the mandatory minimum sentence would constitute cruel and unusual punishment, thereby violating s. 12 of the Charter. And in 2013 the Ontario Court of Appeal, in a series of decisions, struck down the mandatory minimum sentences for gun possession enacted by the federal Conservative government as unconstitutional, ruling that the laws could see people serving a minimum three-year sentence for a licence infraction. As such, the Court stated that there would be a "cavernous disconnect" between the severity of the offence and the mandatory sentence.

One of the basic questions about mandatory minimum sentences is whether it will reduce crime. There is little doubt that the supporters of mandatory minimum sentences view the use of imprisonment as a solution to crime. However, in the United States, which has a long history of using mandatory minimum sentence policies, research on the deterrent impact of imprisonment is equivocal at best. The general deterrent impact of imprisoning more people under mandatory minimum sentencing policies upon the crime rate is debatable. Some (e.g., Visher 1987) determined that a doubling of the prison population in the United States led to only a small (6 to 9 percent) reduction for the rates of crimes for the offences of robbery and burglary. And while Spelman (2000) estimated that doubling the prison population would reduce the most serious crimes in the United States by 20 to 40 percent, the financial costs would be high: he estimated they would be as high as $20 billion. In comparison, the impact of the specific deterrent effect on prisons is open to question, as evidence indicates that getting tougher with mandatory minimum sentences appears not to scare past or future offenders from committing crimes (Cullen and Jonson 2011). A detailed examination of research studies that evaluated the impact of these types of sentences in the United States led a researcher to state that "no individual evaluation has demonstrated crime reduction effects attributable to enactment or implementation of a mandatory minimum sentence law" (Tonry 2009:95). Tonry (2006:45) also points out that mandatory penalties will not produce just outcomes and usually are subverted by various actors in the criminal justice system (e.g., prosecutors, police, and juries) who "do not like laws that prescribe punishments they believe to be too severe, and often they find ways to avoid it."

Mandatory Minimum Sentences in Canada: The Issue of Gun-Related Crimes

A mandatory minimum sentence is a statutorily determined punishment that must be applied to all those who are convicted of a specific crime. A mandatory minimum sentence is one form of **determinate sentence**; another type is referred to as **truth in sentencing**. Truth-in-sentencing laws require offenders to serve at least a certain amount of their sentence. They usually focus on violent offenders and limit or eliminate altogether parole eligibility for these designated offenders.

Mandatory minimum sentences for gun-related crimes became an issue in the 2006 federal election, even though some of the existing offences in the legislation governing gun-related crimes already utilized mandatory minimum sentences. The new legislation proposed by the federal government in May 2006 called for stronger penalties for the use of firearms. At the core of the new legislation was "tougher" mandatory minimum sentences; the hope was that it would deter these types of offences. According to then-federal Justice Minister and Attorney General of Canada Vic Toews, by "ensuring that tougher mandatory minimum sentences are imposed for serious and repeat firearms crime, we will restore confidence in the justice system, and make our streets safer." He added that there would be "clear consequences for gun crime—prison sentences that are in keeping with the gravity of the offence" (Department of Justice 2006). He also "insisted that mandatory minimum sentences have reduced crime in the United States" (Clark 2006:A1). However, his comments about reducing crime were countered by the chair of the criminal law section of the Canadian Bar Association, who said that such laws "limit a judge's discretion to apply the fairest sentence," and added that the "best available data seem to suggest that a high sentence does not deter, and more likely it is the probability of being caught that will deter . . . you increase the probability of someone being caught by increasing resources to police agencies" (ibid.).

Canada already had introduced mandatory minimum sentences for firearms-related offences. Nineteen of these offences were established in 1995 when Bill C-86, which contained new firearms legislation, was passed (Gabor 2002). Stronger sanctions were added to these existing laws on December 1, 1998. One of the new sections (s. 109 of the Criminal Code) identifies four offence categories for which, on conviction, the judge must prohibit the possession of a wide range of weapons, including firearms and crossbows. These categories include (1) serious offences (i.e., those with a maximum term of incarceration of 10 years or more); (2) several listed weapons offences and criminal harassment (stalking); and (3) offences involving weapons while the individual was under a previous prohibition order. In addition, for a person convicted of a listed offence for the first time, the prohibition order must be for at least 10 years after release from a correctional facility (or after the trial, if that person was not sentenced to a period of incarceration). Any subsequent order involving the same person has to be for life. The second new section (s. 110 of the Criminal Code) allows judges to impose a prohibition order for the following:

1. crimes involving violence with a maximum sentence of less than 10 years; and
2. crimes involving weapons while the accused is not under a prohibition order.

Once again, the order must be for a minimum of 10 years, and the judge must give reasons for not imposing this sentence (Edgar 1999).

In May 2006, Bill C-10 was introduced to toughen sentencing for crimes involving firearms by enhancing the mandatory minimum penalty provisions of the Criminal Code. Under the proposed legislation the use of a firearm during the commission of a serious offence would be subject to escalating mandatory minimum penalty sentences. If, for example, an offence is related to gang activity, or if a restricted or prohibited firearm such as a handgun is used in the commission of an offence, the proposed legislation would establish a minimum penalty of five years on the first offence; seven years if the accused has one prior conviction for using a firearm to commit an offence; and 10 years if the accused has more than one prior conviction for using a firearm to commit an offence.

The other significant changes proposed by Bill C-10 in its original form included the following:

- Adding the new offence of "breaking and entering to steal a firearm" with a mandatory minimum penalty of one year for a first offence, three years for a second offence, and five years for a third or subsequent offence.
- Adding a new offence of "robbery to steal a firearm" with a mandatory minimum penalty of three years for a first offence, and five years for a second or subsequent offence.
- Escalating the mandatory minimum penalties for several firearm-related offences in the Criminal Code that already have an existing minimum term of imprisonment of one year, such as possessing a prohibited or restricted firearm with ammunition, possessing a firearm obtained through the commission of an offence, trafficking in a firearm, and importing or exporting a firearm without authorization. Bill C-10 proposed an increase of the mandatory minimum penalties for these offences to three years for a first offence, and five years for a second and subsequent offence.
- Escalating the mandatory minimum penalties for several firearm offences in the Criminal Code that already have a current minimum term of imprisonment for four years, such as the use of a firearm in the commission of an attempted murder, aggravated sexual assault, kidnapping, and robbery. Bill C-10 would increase the mandatory minimum penalties for these offences to five years for a first offence, seven years for a second offence, and 10 years for a third or subsequent offence.

At the end of May 2007, the proposed two new offences—breaking and entering to steal a firearm and robbery to steal a firearm—were removed from the original version of the bill and are not subject to any mandatory minimum term of imprisonment. In addition, for the remaining offences contained in Bill C-10, the mandatory minimums for a third or subsequent offence were not placed back into the bill. In addition, for those offences that currently have a mandatory minimum sentence of one year, the new mandatory minimums would be three years for the first offence, and five years for the second and subsequent offences.

As noted earlier, Bill C-10 was later combined with four other bills to form Bill C-2—the Tackling Violent Crime Act. On February 27, 2008, the Senate passed the new bill and these provisions came into force on May 1, 2008.

Victim Participation in Sentencing

In the 1980s, a significant issue was raised in Western legal systems: the right of victims to participate in the trial, typically through **victim impact statements**. Proponents of this reform argued that integrating victims into the court system and guaranteeing their right to that involvement would recognize victims' wishes for status in court proceedings (Hall 1991). Others added that recognizing victims would increase their dignity, underscore that real individuals had suffered at the hands of a criminal, and promote fairness by giving victims the right to be heard in court (Henderson 1985; Kelly 1984; Sumner 1987).

Opponents of this reform argued that establishing victims' rights would challenge the very basis of the adversarial legal system—in particular, the idea that crime is a violation against the state rather than against an individual (Ashworth 1993). Others pointed out that recognizing victims in our legal system would place too much pressure on the judge, promote vindictiveness on the part of the victims, and lead to more court delays, longer trials, substantial increases in legal costs to the state, and disparity in sentencing. Some noted that judges themselves are reluctant to consider the feelings and concerns of victims when it comes to sentencing offenders. The courtroom is their domain, and while outsiders can inform the judiciary of their experiences, there is no guarantee that the victims will have any influence on its decisions (Grabosky 1987; Miers 1992; Rubel 1986).

Since 1989, when the federal government enacted Bill C-89, victims in Canada have had the right to file a

The Constitutionality of Mandatory Minimum Sentences and Gun-Related Offences

In *R. v. Nur* (2015), the Supreme Court of Canada, in a 6–3 decision, held that Parliament does not have unlimited constitutional powers to enact mandatory minimum sentences when the harshness of the punishment outweighs the seriousness of the offence. The majority of the Supreme Court held the three- and five-year mandatory minimum sentences for illegal firearms to be cruel and unusual punishment, and thereby in contravention of s. 12 of the Charter. In this case, the Supreme Court upheld the 2013 ruling of the Ontario Court of Appeal, which heard six appeals concerning the constitutionality of mandatory minimum sentences for firearms offences. The Court of Appeal ultimately struck down the three-year mandatory minimum sentence for first-time convictions, on indictment, for possessing a loaded prohibited or restricted firearm with ammunition, or possessing an unloaded prohibited or restricted firearm with ammunition readily available, as well as the five-year mandatory minimum sentence for second and subsequent convictions. The reasoning behind the Ontario Court of Appeal decision was that the law is too broad and could, "in theory, lead to otherwise law-abiding gun owners being subjected to grossly disproportionate punishments for what are, in essence, licensing violations involving little or no moral fault, and little or no danger to the public" (Schmitz 2015:1–2).

In their decision, the majority of the Supreme Court held that firearms "are inherently dangerous and the state is entitled to use sanctions to signal its disapproval of careless practices and to discourage gun owners from making mistakes. . . But a three-year term of imprisonment for a person who has essentially committed a licensing infraction is totally out of synch with the norms of criminal sentencing set out in s. 718 of the Criminal Code and legitimate expectations in a free and democratic society." They also said that Parliament could have achieved the goal of appropriate sanctions by creating an offence focusing on those actions that endanger the lives of others, "rather than a sweeping law that includes in its ambit conduct attracting less blameworthiness for which the mandatory minimum sentence would be grossly disproportionate."

The minority argued Parliament's efforts to control weapons offences and protect the public with mandatory minimum sentences was "valid and important." They added that the majority of the Court based their opinion "on questionable assumptions or loose conjecture" and that the law allowed prosecutors to proceed by way of summary conviction, which does not allow for mandatory minimum sentences.

How does a court decide if a mandatory minimum sentence is disproportionate—that is, unconstitutional? It is based on a two-stage analysis: (1) a specific inquiry and (2) a general inquiry. These are based on two Supreme Court of Canada cases, one of which involved an appeal of a seven-day minimum sentence for knowingly driving while prohibited (*R. v. Goltz* [1991]), and an appeal by a first-time offender appealing their conviction of criminal negligence causing death, the punishment for which was a four-year mandatory minimum sentence (*R. v. Morrisey* [2000]). In both of these cases the Supreme Court did not find a violation of the Charter.

The specific inquiry requires a court to consider what an appropriate sentence would be if there were no mandatory minimum sentence. The following have to be considered:

- The gravity of the offence,
- The personal characteristics of the offender,
- The particular circumstances of the case,
- The actual effect of the punishment upon the individual,
- The penological goals and sentencing principles upon which the punishment is founded, and
- A comparison with punishments imposed for other crimes in the same jurisdiction.

The general inquiry occurs when a minimum mandatory sentence is not found to be grossly disproportionate when applied to an offender. In this stage, the focus is not upon the actual offender, but rather the question is how the sentence will be grossly disproportionate for other offenders.

victim impact statement (see Exhibit 10.9). In this document, they detail the effects of the crime on them. This statement is forwarded to the judge for consideration in sentencing. These forms are an attempt to bring victims into the criminal justice system by allowing them an opportunity to influence sentencing, either through a written statement or by speaking before a judge in the courtroom. By this means, a victim can tell the court about the impact of the crime and in some cases recommend a sentence.

The impact of such statements on sentencing is largely unknown, since judges rarely allude to them. However, some judges have made it a habit to mention them in certain cases, especially when there were aggravating circumstances in the offence that severely traumatized the victim. In this situation, some judges have handed down tougher sentences.

During the 1980s and 1990s, provincial governments across Canada passed victims' rights legislation. The first jurisdiction in Canada to introduce a Victims' Bill of Rights was Manitoba, in 1986. Since then, all other provinces and the federal government have passed victims' rights legislation. In June 1996, Ontario proclaimed Bill C-23, known as the Victims' Bill of Rights. This bill outlined the principles and standards for the treatment of victims in the criminal justice system—for example, it allowed for greater access to information for the victim, for the right to have property involved in a criminal offence returned as quickly as possible, and for the victim's right to input during sentencing. The federal government expanded its legislation on victims in September 1996, when it passed Bill C-41. Amendments were made to the Criminal Code in 1999 that specifically codified the rights of victims of crime in order to increase their participation. This bill also made it possible for victim impact statements to be admitted during sentencing, provided for restitution to the victims, and enabled victims to attend some parole hearings (Bacchus 1999).

Prior to the 1999 amendments, researchers discovered that victim impact statements were not being used by victims in many cases. In 1988, a two-year study evaluating the use of victim impact statements in Winnipeg was published. The findings "revealed little of great significance, save for the opposition demonstrated by law enforcement and judicial officials to the introduction to these statements" (Young 2001:24). Also in 1988, the federal justice department conducted a series of studies exploring their use in five Canadian cities. This report found that the use of victim impact statements varied hugely among cities, from a low of 14 percent of cases to a high of 83 percent. Around this time, Giliberti (1990) conducted a six-city study that examined various aspects of victim impact statements and their use in the courts.

Part of Giliberti's study evaluated the effect of victim impact statements on victims. To their surprise, the researchers found that these statements made no difference to victims' degree of satisfaction with the justice system. According to the victims, the most important feature of the program was that it enabled them to discuss the offence and its effects and to have this information given to the court. The program also provided them with useful feedback about the case as it progressed through the system, and allowed them to contact someone should they experience any difficulties. But it was also reported that the impact of this program was the same for participants and non-participants in terms of the level of their participation in the criminal justice system. Involvement in the program made no difference regarding satisfaction with how the case was handled or the likelihood of reporting future incidents to the police. It was found that most victims held negative attitudes toward sentencing both before and after their cases were heard.

The effect of victim impact statements on the criminal justice system varied across the six cities that Giliberti studied. For example, in Victoria, B.C., few victim impact statements were used in court when their use was controlled by prosecutorial discretion. Prosecutors indicated that they did not use them because they contained no new information, because too many were vague or contained largely irrelevant information, because they were of doubtful accuracy, and because they contributed to higher operating costs of the criminal justice system. In Toronto, prosecutors felt that victim impact statements could play a significant role in court, and as a result two-thirds of the victim impact statements in Toronto were entered into court trials as exhibits and one-third were used as Crown submissions.

For all Crown prosecutors, victim impact statements had the greatest impact in sexual assault and sexual abuse cases. Also, these statements were considered helpful in raising prosecutors' awareness of

EXHIBIT 10.9 Rights of Victims in Canada

In May 1988, Parliament passed Bill C-89, which addressed victims' rights. These rights are defined as follows:

1. A victim has the right to be treated with courtesy, compassion, dignity and respect for the privacy of the victim;
   - the right to access social, legal, medical, and mental health services that are responsive to the needs of the victims' dependants, spouse or guardian; and
   - the right to have property stolen from a victim returned to the victim as soon as possible.
2. Subject to the limits imposed by the availability of resources and to any other limits that are reasonable in the circumstances of each case, a victim has the right to be informed of:

   (i) the name of the accused,
   (ii) the specific offence with which the accused is charged,
   (iii) the scope, nature, timing and progress of prosecution of the offence,
   (iv) the role of the victim and other persons involved in the prosecution of other offence and of any opportunity to make representations on restitution and the impact of the offence on the victim,
   (v) court procedures, and
   (vi) crime prevention measures;

   - the right to be informed by law enforcement, court, health and social services personnel, at the earliest possible opportunity of the services, remedies and mechanisms to obtain remedies available to a victim; and
   - while waiting to give evidence at a proceeding in respect to an offence, the right to be kept apart, where necessary, from the accused and the accused's witnesses to ensure the safety of the victim and the victim's family and to protect them from intimidation and retaliation.

On April 15, 1999, amendments were tabled to the Criminal Code that strengthened the rights of victims of crime in the criminal justice system:

- ensure that victims are informed of their opportunity to prepare a victim impact statement at the time of sentencing;
- ensure that victims have the choice to read the victim statement aloud;
- require that victim impact statements be considered by courts and Review Boards following a verdict of not criminally responsible on account of mental disorder;
- extend to victims of sexual or violent crime up to age 18 protections that restrict personal cross-examination by self-represented accused persons;
- require police officers and judges to consider the victim's safety in all bail decisions;
- allow victims and witnesses with a mental or physical disability to have a support person present when giving testimony; and
- make it easier for victims and witnesses to participate in trials by permitting the judge to ban publication of their identity where it is necessary for the proper administration of justice.

In February 2013, the federal Conservative party announced its intention to introduce legislation that would create a Victims' Bill of Rights. They introduced Bill C-32, An Act to Enact the Canadian Victims Bill of Rights Act, and it received Royal Assent in February 2015. The new law created the following statutory rights for victims of crime:

Right to information: Victims have the right to general information about the criminal justice system and available victim services and programs, as well as specific information about the progress of the case, including information relating to the investigation, prosecution, and sentencing of the individual who harmed them.

Right to protection: Victims have the right to their security and privacy considered at all stages of the criminal justice system, to have reasonable and necessary measures to protect them from intimidation and retaliation, and to request their identity be protected from public disclosure.

Right to participation: Victims have a right to convey their views about decisions to be made by criminal justice professionals and have them considered at various stages of the criminal justice process, and to present a victim impact statement.

Right to restitution: Victims have the right to have the court consider making a restitution order for all offences for which there are easy-to-calculate financial losses.

the long-term emotional impact on victims—an impact that had not been captured in other documents available to prosecutors (Roberts 1992:67). Victim statements had some impact on judges. Thirteen judges responded to the question "Have victim impact statements actually affected sentences that you have passed?" Seven of them said yes, six answered no. However, in British Columbia, Roberts (ibid.:77) reported a "minor change" in sentences imposed by judges in cases where a victim impact statement was used, while "occasionally sentences have been dramatically higher." According to Roach (1999:291), these low rates of victim participation indicated that victim impact statements "have not emerged as a major criminal justice issue" in this country and that these low rates of participation may be the result of victims' reluctance "to expose their suffering to adversarial challenge."

Roberts and Edgar (2006) researched the perceptions and experiences of judges in three Canadian provinces concerning victim impact statements in their courtrooms. Their survey focused upon two questions relating to the use of victim impact statements in Canada: (1) do victim impact statements serve a useful purpose at sentencing? and (2) have the reforms made in the late 1990s had an impact on the participation of the victim in the sentencing process? The researchers reported that judges had responded positively to both of these questions. According to Roberts and Edgar (ibid.:27), there is little doubt that judges "found victim impact statements to represent a unique source of information that is relevant to the principles of sentencing." In addition, the researchers found that victim impact statements were used in only a minority of cases proceeding to sentencing. They were unable to conclude that these low participation rates were the result of decisions made by the victims or for reasons related to the administration of justice. It is clear, however, that judges do not need victim impact statements in minor cases in order to determine the impact of a crime upon a victim (D'Avignon 2001). A minority of the participating judges indicated they were not supportive of victims attempting to influence their sentencing decisions. Any recommendations made by victims about sentencing are to be through the Crown prosecutor's sentencing recommendations rather than the victim impact statement itself.

SUMMING UP AND LOOKING FORWARD

Numerous incidences of wrongful convictions have led to numerous miscarriages of justice being recorded in Canada. Why do these occur? A number of factors have gained prominence in the attempt to explain wrongful convictions. The most accepted reason is eyewitness error, followed by forensic errors, and then police and prosecutorial misconduct. All of these have been found by researchers studying wrongful convictions, either by themselves or in combination with other factors. While mandatory minimum sentences have existed in Canada since the Criminal Code was codified in 1892, they have become a popular approach in numerous laws passed by Parliament. Supporters of these types of approaches believe they act as a deterrent to prevent future crimes, and that offenders are held responsible for their actions. Critics argue that they have little or no deterrent effect, shift decisions about appropriate punishments from judges to prosecutors, and may increase the prison population. In recent years, however, a number of judges have decided not to follow what is stipulated by not handing out the required punishment. This has led to constitutional challenges, for example in gun-related crimes, and a number of these have been successfully upheld by the Supreme Court of Canada.

Victims' rights have also been addressed at the sentencing stage through the introduction of victim impact statements. Since 1989, victims in Canada have had the right to file a victim impact statement. The development of victim rights is a key concern for the victims' rights movement. Victims' lack of rights within the adversarial justice system has led various federal governments to introduce various pieces of legislation, but some argue that it is hard to discern any real benefits for victims. As a result, the federal Conservative government introduced Bill C-30 to increase the rights of victims in the Canadian criminal justice system. Some, however, argue that such legislation has done little to improve the actual position of victims.

But what about offenders? While some believe most offenders should be incarcerated, in reality many serve their sentence in the community. Significant numbers of offenders are also placed into the community as part of their release from incarceration. What is the purpose of using the community as part of the sentence or as part of the release process? The next chapter discusses offenders in the community.

Review Questions:

1. What is the most accepted reason as to why miscarriages of justice occur?
2. Why do supporters of mandatory minimum sentences feel that they will lead to a reduction in crime?
3. Why has the Supreme Court ruled against mandatory minimum sentences for gun-related offences?
4. Will the reforms aimed at improving the rights of victims lead to significant changes within our criminal justice system?
5. Should victims be allowed a greater degree of participation in the criminal trial process?

Critical Issues in Canadian Criminal Justice

MANDATORY MINIMUM SENTENCING LAWS: DO THEY ACHIEVE THEIR GOALS?

At the present time in Canada, there are upward of 70 mandatory minimum sentences (MMS). They can be placed into five different categories: first and second degree murder (first introduced in 1976), firearms offences (originally introduced in 1995), sexual offences involving children (first enacted in 2005), breaking and entering (originally introduced in 2008), and drug offences (introduced in 2012). In addition, a number of other offences, such as impaired driving, child prostitution, and betting, have mandatory minimum sentences if the offender has a prior conviction for the same offence.

Under mandatory minimum sentencing laws, offenders are required to spend some time (the mandatory minimum amount of time specified by law) incarcerated in a correctional facility. Under MMS, the laws remove both judges' and correctional officials' discretionary powers. Judges are unable to hand out a sentence that doesn't include the length of time to be served by the law (e.g., probation). In *R. v. Ferguson* (2008), the Supreme Court of Canada, in a 9–0 ruling, upheld Parliament's right to create MMS and to have them enforced by judges (Foot 2008:A4). In *Ferguson*, a police officer was convicted of shooting an unruly prisoner during a stationhouse altercation in 1999. Originally charged with second degree murder, the first two trials ended with hung juries, but Mr. Ferguson was eventually convicted of manslaughter. The judge granted him a "constitutional exemption" from the mandatory minimum sentence of four years, saying that the sentence was "grossly disproportionate" to his offence, imposing a two-year conditional sentence instead. The Alberta Court of Appeal later reversed that decision, and substituted the MMS of four years. On appeal, the Supreme Court unanimously held that there was no constitutional exception that gave them the power to avoid imposing a mandatory minimum sentence. They upheld the right of Parliament to create MMS, eliminating the idea that judges can deviate when a particular sentence appears to be unconstitutionally cruel and unusual. According to the Supreme Court, the law "mandates a floor below which no one cannot go. . . . To go below this floor on a case-by-case basis runs counter to the clear wording of the sections and the intent that it evinces. . . . Bad law, fixed up on case-by case basis by the courts, does not accord with the role and responsibility of Parliament to enact constitutional laws for the people of Canada." In 2007, a special five-judge panel of the Ontario Court of Appeal ruled in *R. v. Panday* (2007) that judges cannot undercut MMS by showing leniency to the accused who "lived under virtual house arrest awaiting their trials" (Makin 2007:A11). Not everyone is supportive of these decisions; as one observer stated, they may lead to unjust decisions by the courts in exceptional cases (Roach 2008:4).

According to the U.S. Sentencing Commission (1991), the principles of MMS include the following:

- *Equality*. Similar offences receive similar sentences.
- *Certainty*. Offenders and the public know that offenders will serve the minimum prison time that the law prescribes.
- *Just deserts*. Dangerous offenders and criminals who use guns deserve mandatory long prison terms.

Continued on next page

- *Deterrence*. Mandatory prison sentences deter crime by sending the strong message that those who "do the crime" really will "do the time."
- *Incapacitation*. Mandatory prison terms protect public safety by locking up dangerous offenders and criminals who use guns.

Do MMS achieve these goals? It seems logical that they would, and such laws have been extremely popular in the United States. Most of these laws were introduced in the United States starting in the 1970s, and some of the original statutes dealt with the use and selling of drugs. Perhaps the best known mandatory minimum sentencing law is New York's drug law, introduced in 1972. Under these laws, the possession of or sale of heroin or other narcotics was punished by mandatory minimum prison sentences of one to fifteen years, with maximum sentences ranging up to life imprisonment. If they were released, offenders were placed on parole for the rest of their lives, and pleas to lesser charges were not allowed. The New York City Bar Association studied the impact of this law on drug offences. Researchers compared arrests, indictments, and convictions in 1973 (a year prior to the law being passed) with 1975 (more than a year after the law had taken effect). Arrests had fallen by 20 percent, the rate of indictments had dropped from 39 percent to 27 percent, and the number of convictions had gone from 6,033 to 3,147 (Association of the Bar of the City of New York 1977). It was not until March 2009 that these laws were repealed (Peters 2009).

It is also argued that mandatory minimum sentencing laws have an incapacitation effect, specifically by removing from the streets those criminals who use guns. According to Tonry (1996), most of the mandatory minimum sentencing laws in the United States were introduced during the 1980s and early 1990s, and many of these statutes dealt with the use of firearms in serious crimes. Following is a review of selected American research into the use of mandatory minimum sentencing laws for gun-related crimes and the impact of those laws on crime.

Loftin and McDowell (1981) studied the effects of the Michigan firearms law, which required a two-year mandatory sentence for serious crimes committed with a firearm. In particular, they were interested in the impact of the new law on the certainty and severity of sentences as well as on the number of serious violent crimes in Detroit. As part of this new law, the Detroit prosecutor announced that the new policy would include a strictly enforced ban on plea bargaining in these cases. In their study of cases processed between 1976 and 1978, Loftin and McDowell found little change in either the certainty or the severity of sentences for firearms-related murders and armed robberies. However, they did find that the law significantly increased the expected sentences for firearms-related assault cases.

According to Loftin and McDowell, two factors explain their findings. First, the expected MMS for murders and robberies did not increase because offenders convicted of these crimes were already receiving longer sentences. Second, the sentences increased for assaults because the sentences handed out prior to the new law had been lighter—probation and suspended sentences were typical. These shorter sentences were explained as the result of the relationship between the offender and victim. In many cases, the offender and victim knew each other, and as a result prosecutors regularly settled these cases with a plea bargain to a lesser offence. Based on their data, Loftin and McDowell concluded that the mandatory minimum sentencing laws associated with the new gun law did not significantly change the number or type of violent offences committed in Detroit.

Three years later, Loftin and McDowell (1984) published their study of the Florida felony firearm law, which mandated a three-year prison sentence for anyone possessing a firearm or attempting to commit any of 11 specified serious crimes. After analyzing the data for three Florida cities (Miami, Tampa, and Jacksonville), they concluded that the new law did not have a measurable deterrent effect on violent crime. These same two researchers studied the effect of a mandatory minimum sentencing law in Philadelphia and Pittsburgh, Pennsylvania, and reported that the new sentencing laws had reduced the number of homicides but that their effect on assaults and robberies was inconclusive.

Further analyses of the nationwide effects of mandatory minimum sentencing law in the United States have not reported any effects on crime prevention. Kleck (1991), in his study of 170 cities in 1980, found that the new laws were not related to the rates of homicide, assault, or robbery. And Marvell and Moody (1995) studied the effects of mandatory minimum sentencing laws on crime and prisons and reported little evidence to support the contention that such laws have any effects on either crime rates or firearm use. On the basis of these and other studies, the best that can be said about the impact of mandatory minimum sentencing laws on gun-related crimes is that the findings are mixed, with some effects being found for certain offences but minimal effects for most crimes.

Evaluations of mandatory minimum sentencing laws have reported that their potential impacts are not as significant as supporters think they will be. This has been attributed to the fact that these laws, once passed, are generally altered by implementation practices, reinterpretation, changes in the legal statutes, court rulings, and the passage of subsequent legislation. Of these, most evaluations have pointed to adaptations to implementation practices by significant criminal justice actors as being the most common mechanism that alters the goals of mandatory minimum sentencing laws. Research has found that, despite the claim that all offenders are treated equally on the basis of the crime committed and/or their prior record, this is not always the case. Berg (2005) reported that prosecutors used their charge reduction discretion to circumvent "three strikes" MMS for some defendants. He discovered three-strike MMS were circumvented for some groups of individuals. In particular, these sentencing laws were less likely to be used for males, Hispanics, and, to a lesser extent, African Americans. Farrell (2003) found that African Americans, males, and those convicted after choosing to have a court trial were more likely to receive mandatory minimums for offences involving firearms. And Ulmer et al. (2007), in their analysis of the use of mandatory minimums for individuals sentenced for drug crimes or for three-strike offences, found that prosecutors used their discretion in their use of the mandatory minimums. Specifically, they found prosecutors' decisions to be influenced by such things as prior record, the type of conviction (i.e., negotiated guilty pleas significantly assisted defendants in avoiding mandatory minimums), gender, and race (Hispanics were more likely to receive mandatory minimums).

Tonry argues that when MMSs are introduced, prosecutors and, to a lesser degree, judges find ways to circumvent them, either by dismissing cases at earlier stages or plea bargaining to other charges that do not carry mandatory minimums. What results is a small net increase in incarceration after the MMP statutes are brought into force. Without an increase in incarceration, it is not surprising that researchers most typically do not find a deterrent effect. Hofer (2000) studied the use of mandatory firearm penalties in the U.S. federal sentencing system and found that the use of the penalty varied by jurisdiction. He was investigating the charging practices of s. 924c of the United States Sentencing Commission, a law that mandates a five-year term for offenders who use firearms during the commission of a crime within the federal system. He found that the mandatory firearm penalty was not applied uniformly; in fact, the penalty was not applied in 41 percent of the bank robbery and drug trafficking cases in which it was warranted. However, when the penalty was applied, offenders were sentenced according to the law.

This process of adaptation is commonly referred to as "**the law of criminal justice hydraulics**." Walker (2007:62) refers to this as "an increase in the severity of the penalty will result in less frequent application of that penalty." An important corollary of this law is that "the less often a severe penalty is applied, the more arbitrary will be the occasions when it is applied." Walker uses the death penalty as an example, pointing out that since it is a severe penalty, it exerts "an enormous amount of pressure" on courtroom actors to avoid its application (e.g., plea bargaining, reducing a charge, and appealing every possible issue).

Others have referred to another aspect of this process that they refer to as the "**hydraulic displacement of discretion**" or "**system hydraulics**" (Heumann and Loftin 1979; Miethe 1987). This refers to the fact that any change made within the criminal justice system will have an effect on the other components of the system. That is, the introduction of a sentencing reform such as a mandatory minimum sentencing law potentially affects the operation not only of the courts but of the police and the correctional systems as well. Feeley (1983) points out that reforms in one area of the criminal justice system are likely to alter the operations in other areas of the system, leading to results other than those that were originally intended.

Three interrelated system-level effects have been found to be associated with the introduction of MMS. These include a shift in the balance of courtroom power, increased prosecutorial authority, and changes in how plea bargains are made. It has been found that when mandatory sentencing laws are introduced, prosecutors find themselves with greater authority than all other system participants. In particular, prosecutors are now in a position to determine which cases will be prosecuted while judges lose much of their authority over sentencing. Some of the implications of this shift to greater prosecutorial authority include "decisions are no longer as public as was previous when judges were in authority; their decisions are rarely subject to review and do not occur in open court." The introduction of mandatory sentencing laws has also been found to give prosecutors enhanced plea bargaining powers, providing them "with a valuable tool with which to ensure that severe sanctions are imposed in appropriate cases" (Merritt et al. 2006:12).

According to Feeley (1983), some of the important issues to consider when implementing mandatory minimum sentencing laws include the following:

- The importance of understanding and accepting the limitations of mandatory minimum sentencing law reforms—what can and cannot be accomplished.
- The need to understand the limitations of mandatory minimum sentencing laws that are inadequate in dealing with complex situations to which they must be applied.
- The dangers of creating laws for symbolic appeal rather than for actual effect.
- The importance of understanding criminal justice system dynamics and the interrelationships between the various actors before implementing reforms.

Continued on next page

Critical Issues in Canadian Criminal Justice (*Continued*)

Questions

1. What plausible effects may result from removing sentencing discretion from prosecutors in cases involving mandatory minimum punishments? What effects do you predict will happen?
2. Why do you think mandatory minimum sentences don't have the deterrent effect that they were created to provide? Do you believe prosecutors should have more power to determine the outcome of cases than judges?
3. How dramatically do you think the Canadian number of individuals sentenced to the federal prison system will increase as a result of the new mandatory minimum sentences?
4. If the mandatory sentences introduced by the Conservatives don't have a dramatic increase on the prison population, how could one explain this?

SUMMARY

Sentencing has been defined as "the judicial determination of a legal sanction to be imposed on a person found guilty of an offence" (Canadian Sentencing Commission 1987:153). A disposition refers to "the actual sanction imposed in sentencing" (Law Reform Commission of Canada 1974:4) or "the judicial determination of legal sanction to be imposed on a person found guilty of an offence" (Canadian Sentencing Commission 1987:153).

KEY WORDS: sentencing, disposition, split sentence

What Are the Philosophical Rationales of Sentencing?

Sentencing is typically considered to be the highest-profile component of our entire criminal justice system. This is because it involves the disposition, and it determines how long and where the convicted offenders must serve their punishment. Sentencing follows certain patterns across Canada, although there can be variations among provinces.

KEY WORDS: deterrence, specific deterrence, general deterrence, selective incapacitation, chronic offenders, proportionality, rehabilitation, "get tough" approach, justice model, extralegal factors, healing, lived experience, sentencing circles, restorative justice, repairing the harm

Sentencing Law in Canada

Sentencing law establishes the framework for the sentences handed out in Canada. These laws establish both the principle and purpose of sentences.

KEY WORDS: Bill C-41, balanced approach, just sanctions, fundamental principle of sentencing, principle of proportionality

How Do Judges Decide on a Sentence?

Judges do not have unfettered discretion to decide on what type of sentence is appropriate in a case. There are mitigating and aggravating circumstances that have to be considered, as well as the restrictions found in the relevant laws.

KEY WORDS: structure of sentencing, mitigating circumstances, aggravating circumstances, presentence report

Sentencing and Healing Circles

As a result of the overrepresentation of Aboriginals in custody, some jurisdictions have instituted sentencing and healing circles in an attempt to reduce the incarceration rate of Aboriginal peoples. The decisions reached by a sentencing circle in criminal cases are typically reviewed by the Western legal system to determine if it is appropriate.

KEY WORDS: overrepresentation, sentencing circles, healing circles, local justice

Miscarriages of Justice: Wrongful Convictions

Eyewitness Error (p. 321)
Forensic Errors (p. 322)
Police and Prosecutorial Misconduct (p. 322)

Despite the procedural safeguards found in our criminal justice system errors are made by the courts, particularly when someone is convicted of a crime they didn't commit. This is referred to as a "miscarriage of justice."

KEY WORDS: wrongful accusations, wrongful convictions, eyewitness error, forensic errors, police and/or prosecutorial misconduct

Sentencing Reforms

Mandatory Minimum Sentences in Canada (p. 323)
Mandatory Minimum Sentences in Canada: The Issue of Gun-related Crimes (p. 325)

In recent years, the federal Conservative government has passed legislation that has introduced new types of sentences (e.g., "truth in sentencing") or increased the number of mandatory minimum sentences.

KEY WORDS: mandatory minimum sentences, disproportionate, determinate sentence, truth in sentencing

Victim Participation in Sentencing

While it is a key purpose of our criminal justice system to punish those individuals who have broken the law, it is necessary to treat all parties involved in a criminal act fairly. It is important that our system of justice gain the confidence of the victims of crime.

KEY WORDS: victim impact statements

Critical Thinking Questions

1. Why is sentencing considered by many to be the most critical phase in our system of justice?
2. What are some of the arguments for and against using factors other than the crime itself in deciding an appropriate sentence for a convicted offender?
3. Compare the four traditional types of philosophical rationales for sentencing with the two most recent approaches. What are the main differences between these two categories?
4. Should all criminal court judges be elected?
5. Should public opinion affect sentencing decisions made by judges?
6. Should victims play a larger role in the sentencing of offenders? How could victims be given a greater role?

7. Should Aboriginal sentencing circles be used for offenders charged with a violent crime?
8. What aspects of the criminal justice system should be changed in order to decrease wrongful convictions?

Weblinks

To see the Supreme Court hearing of *R. v. Nur*, watch the following program on YouTube: "(Guns) Mandatory Minimums: Her Majesty the Queen, et al. v. Hussein Jama Nur, et al." (2:12:35).

Court Cases

R. v. Ferguson (2008), 1 S.C.R. 96.

R. v. Gladue (1999), 1 S.C.R. 688.

R. v. Goltz (1991), 3 S.C.R. 485.

R. v. Ipeelee (2012), S.C.C. 13.

R. v. Joseyounen (1995), 6 W.W.R. 438.

R. v. Lloyd (2014), BCPC 11.

R. v. Morin (1995), 9 W.W.R. 696.

R. v. Morrisey (2000), S.C.R. 90.

R. v. Moses (1992), 11 C.R. (4th) 357.

R. v. Nasogaluak (2010), 1 S.C.R. 206.

R. v. Nur (2015), S.C.J. No. 15.

R. v. Panday (2007), Ont. C.A. 597.

R. v. Priest (1996), 110 C.C.C. (3d) 289 (Ont. C.A.).

R. v. Smickle (2012), ONSC 602.

R. v. Smith (1987), 1 S.C.R. 1045.

R. v. Unger (1993), M.J. No.363 (Man. C.A.).

Suggested Readings

Makin, K. 1998. *Redrum the Innocent*, rev. ed. Toronto: Penguin.

Roberts, J. and D.P. Cole (eds.). 1999. *Making Sense of Sentencing*. Toronto: University of Toronto Press.

Sanghia, B., K. Roach, and R. Moles. 2010. *Forensic Investigations and Miscarriages of Justice: The Rhetoric Meets the Reality*. Toronto: Irwin Law.

Sher, J. 2001. *"Until You Are Dead": Steven Truscott's Long Ride into History*. Toronto: Knopf Canada.

Tonry, M. 1996. *Sentencing Matters*. New York: Oxford University Press.

References

Anderson, P.R. and D.J. Newman. 1993. *Introduction to Criminal Justice*, 5th ed. Toronto: McGraw-Hill Ryerson.

Andrews, D.A., I. Zinger, R. Hoge, J. Bonta, P. Gendreau, and F. Cullen. 1990. "Does Correctional Treatment Work? A Clinically Relevant and Psychologically Informed Meta-Analysis." *Criminology* 28:393–404.

Ashworth, A. 1993. "Victim Impact Statements and Sentencing." *Criminal Law Review:* 498–509.

Association of the Bar of the City of New York. 1977. *The Nation's Toughest Drug Law: Evaluating the New York Experience*. Washington, DC: Drug Abuse Council.

Bacchus, S. 1999. "The Role of Victims in the Sentencing Process." Pp. 217–29 in *Making Sense of Sentencing*, edited by J.V. Roberts and D.P. Cole. Toronto: University of Toronto Press.

Berg, D. 2005. "Making the Crime Fit the Penalty: The Role of Prosecutorial Discretion Under Mandatory Minimum Sentencing." *Journal of Law and Economics* 48:591–625.

Blumstein, A., J. Cohen, S.E. Martin, and M.H. Tonry (eds.). 1983. *Research on Sentencing: The Search for Reform*, Vol. 1. Washington, DC: National Academy Press.

Boldt, E.D., L. Hursch, S.D. Jonson, and K.W. Taylor. 1983. "Presentence Reports and the Incarceration of Natives." *Canadian Journal of Criminology* 25:269–76.

Bonta, J., G. Bourgon, R. Jesseman, and A.K. Yessine. 2005. *Presentence Reports in Canada 2005–03*. Ottawa: Public Safety and Emergency Preparedness Canada.

Boyce, J. 2013. *Adult Criminal Court Statistics in Canada, 2011/2012*. Ottawa: Canadian Centre for Justice Statistics.

Canadian Sentencing Commission. 1987. *Sentencing Reform: A Canadian Approach*. Ottawa: Minister of Supply and Services.

Clairmont, D. 1996. "Alternative Justice Issues for Aboriginal Justice." *Journal of Legal Pluralism and Unofficial Law* 36:125–58.

Clark, C. 2006. "Crackdown Takes Aim at Guns, Sentencing." *The Globe and Mail*, June 6, pp. A1, A5.

Clear, T. 1980. *Harm in Punishment*. Boston, MA: Northeastern University Press.

Conway, C. 2007. "The DNA 200." *The New York Times*, May 20, p. A14.

Cullen, F.T. and C.L. Jonson. 2011. *Correctional Theory: Context and Consequences*. Thousand Oaks, CA: Sage.

D'Avignon, J. 2001. *Victim Impact Statements: A Judicial Perspective*. Winnipeg: University of Manitoba.

Daubney, D. and G. Parry. 1999. "An Overview of Bill C-41 (The Sentencing Reform Act)." Pp. 31–47 in *Making Sense of Sentencing*, edited by J.V. Roberts and D.P. Cole. Toronto: University of Toronto Press.

Dauvergne, M. 2012. *Adult Correctional Statistics in Canada, 2010/2011*. Ottawa: Canadian Centre for Justice Statistics.

Department of Justice. 2006. *Minister of Justice Proposes Tougher Mandatory Minimum Prison Sentences for Gun Crime*. Ottawa: Department of Justice Canada. Retrieved May 17, 2006 (www.justice.gc.ca).

Department of Justice. 2005. *Fair and Effective Sentencing—A Canadian Approach to Sentencing Policy*. Ottawa: Department of Justice Canada. Retrieved February 15, 2006 (www.justice.gc.ca).

Doob, A.N. 1992. "Community Sanctions and Imprisonment: Hoping for a Miracle But Not Bothering Even to Pray for It." *Canadian Journal of Criminology* 32:415–28.

Doob, A.N. and C.M. Webster. 2006. "Countering Punitiveness: Understanding Stability in Canada's Imprisonment Rate." *Law & Society Review* 40:325–65.

Durham, A. 1988. "The Justice Model in Historical Contexts: Early Law, the Emergence of Science, and the Rise of Incarceration." *Journal of Criminal Justice* 16:331–46.

Edgar, A. 1999. "Sentencing Options in Canada." Pp. 122–36 in *Making Sense of Sentencing*, edited by J.V. Roberts and D.P. Cole. Toronto: University of Toronto Press.

Ehrlich, I. 1975. "The Deterrent Effect of Capital Punishment: A Question of Life and Death." *American Economic Review* 65:397–417.

Fagan, J. 1989. "Cessation of Family Violence: Deterrence and Dissuasion." Pp. 100–51 in *Crime and Justice: A Review of Research*, vol. 11, edited by L. Ohlin and M. Tonry. Chicago: University of Chicago Press.

Farrell, J. 2003. "Mandatory Minimum Firearm Penalties: A Source of Sentencing Disparity." *Justice Research and Policy* 5:95–115.

Feeley, M. 1983. *Court Reform on Trial: Why Simple Solutions Fail*. New York: Basic Books, Inc.

Foot, R. 2008. "Court Backs Minimum Sentences." *National Post*, March 1, p. A4.

Gabor, T. 2002. *Mandatory Minimum Penalties: Their Effects on Crime, Sentencing Disparities, and Justice System Expenditures*. Ottawa: Department of Justice Canada.

Gabor, T. and C. H. S. Jayewardene. 1978. "The Pre-sentence Report as a Persuasive Communication." *Canadian Journal of Criminology* 20:18–27.

Garrett, B.L. 2010. "The Substance of False Confessions." *Stanford Law Review* 62:1051–1119.

Giliberti, C. 1990. "Study Probes Effectiveness of Victim Impact Statements." *Justice Research Notes* 1:1–8.

Goudge Commission. 2008. *Commissioners Statement on Release of the Report. Oct. 1, 2008*. www.attorneygenderal.jus.gov.on.caéinquirieségoudgeéindex.html.

Grabosky, P.N. 1987. "Victims." Pp. 143–57 in *The Criminal Injustice System*, vol. 2, edited by G. Zdenkowski, C. Ronalds, and M. Richardson. Sydney, Australia: Pluto Press.

Hagan, J. 1975. "The Social and Legal Construction of Criminal Justice: A Study of the Presentencing Process." *Social Problems* 22:620–37.

Hall, D.J. 1991. "Victim Voices in Criminal Court: The Need for Restraint." *American Criminal Law Review* 28:233–66.

Henderson, J.S.Y. and W.D. McCaslin. 2005. "Exploring Justice as Healing." Pp. 3–9 in *Justice as Healing: Indigenous Ways*, edited by W.D. McCaslin. St. Paul, MN: Living Justice Press.

Henderson, L.N. 1985. "The Wrongs of Victims' Rights." *Stanford Law Review* 37:937–1021.

Heumann, M. and C. Loftin. 1979. "Mandatory Sentencing and the Abolition of Plea Bargaining." *Law and Society Review* 13:393–430.

Hofer, P. 2000. "Federal Sentencing for Violent and Drug Trafficking Crimes Involving Firearms: Recent Changes and Prospects for Improvement." *American Criminal Law Review* 37:41–73.

Hogarth, J. 1971. *Sentencing as a Human Process*. Toronto: University of Toronto Press.

Huff, C.R. 2004. "Wrongful Convictions: The American Experience." *Canadian Journal of Criminology and Criminal Justice* 46:107–20.

Huff, C.R., A. Rattner, and E. Sagarin. 1986. "Guilty until Proven Innocent: Wrongful Conviction and Public Policy." *Crime and Delinquency* 34:518–44.

Kelly, D.P. 1984. "Victims' Perceptions of Criminal Justice." *Pepperdine Law Review* 11:15–22.

Kleck, G. 1991. *Point Blank: Guns and Violence in America*. New York: Adline de Gruyter.

LaPrairie, C. 1998. "The 'New' Justice: Some Implications for Aboriginal Communities." *Canadian Journal of Criminology* 40:61–79.

Lash, J. 2000. "Case Comment: *R. v. Gladue*." *Canadian Woman Studies* 20:85–91.

Law Commission of Canada. 1999. *From Restorative Justice to Transformative Justice*. Ottawa: Law Commission of Canada.

Law Reform Commission of Canada. 1974. *Studies on Sentencing: Working Paper 3*. Ottawa: Information Canada.

Liebman, J.S., J. Fagan, V. West, and J. Lloyd. 2000. "Capital Attrition: Error Rates in Capital Cases, 1973–1995." *Texas Law Review* 78:1839–65.

Loftin, C. and D. McDowell. 1984. "The Deterrent Effects of the Florida Felony Fire-arms Law." *Journal of Criminal Law and Criminology* 75:250–59.

Loftin, C. and D. McDowell. 1981. "'One with a Gun Gets You Two': Mandatory Sentencing and Firearms Violence in Detroit." *American Academy of Political and Social Sciences* 455:150–67.

Loftus, E.F. 1979. *Eyewitness Testimony*. Cambridge, MA: Harvard University Press.

Loftus, E.F. and J. Doyle. 1991. *Eyewitness Testimony: Civil and Criminal*, 3rd ed. New York: Klouwer.

MacAfee, M. 2005. "Manitoba Review of Hair Evidence Turns up Little." *The Globe and Mail*, September 21, p. A5.

Makin, K. 2008. "Deeply Flawed Coroner's Office Condemned." *The Globe and Mail*, October 2, p. A4.

Makin, K. 2007. "'Bail Is Not Jail,' Ontario Appeal Court Rules." *The Globe and Mail*, September 12, p. A11.

Makin, K. 2006. "Prosecutors Must Share Blame for Botched Cases, Report Says." *The Globe and Mail*, June 22, p. A7.

Marvell, T. and C. Moody. 1995. "The Impact Study of the Enhanced Prison Terms for Felonies Committed with Guns." *Criminology* 33:247–81.

Merritt, N., T. Fain, and S. Turner. 2006. "Oregon's Get Tough Sentencing Reform: A Lesson in the Justice System." *Criminology & Public Policy* 5:5–36.

Miers, D. 1992. "The Responsibilities and the Rights of Victims of Crime." *Modern Law Review* 55:482–505.

Miethe, T. 1987. "Charging and Plea Bargaining Practices under Determinate Sentencing: An Investigation of the Hydraulic Displacement of Discretion." *Criminology* 25:155–76.

Morris, N. and M. Tonry. 1990. *The Future of Imprisonment*. New York: Oxford University Press.

Native Law Centre. 2006. "Sentencing Circles: A General Overview and Guidelines." Saskatoon: University of Saskatchewan. Retrieved January 15, 2006 (www.usask.ca/nativelaw/publications).

Packer, H.L. 1968. *The Limits of the Criminal Sanction*. Palo Alto, CA: Stanford University Press.

Penrod, S. 2003. "Eyewitness Identification Evidence: How Well Are Witnesses, Police Performing? *Criminal Justice* 18:36–47.

Perreault, S. 2014. *Admissions to Adult Correctional Services in Canada, 2011/2012*. Ottawa: Canadian Centre for Justice Statistics.

Peters, J.W. 2009. "Legislation to Overhaul Rockefeller Drug Laws Moves Ahead Swiftly." *The New York Times*, March 1, p. 19.

Proulx, C. 2005. *Reclaiming Aboriginal Justice, Identity and Community*. Saskatoon, SK: Purich.

Quigley, T. 1994. "Some Issues in the Sentencing of Aboriginal Offenders." Pp. 269–98 in *Continuing Poundmaker and Riel's Request*, edited by R. Gosse, J.Y. Henderson, and R. Carter. Saskatoon: Purich.

Radelet, M.L., H.A. Bedau, and C. Putnam. 1992. *In Spite of Innocence*. Boston, MA: Northeastern University Press.

Roach, K. 2008. "The Future of Mandatory Minimum Sentences after the Death of Constitutional Exceptions." *The Criminal Law Quarterly* 54:1–4.

Roach, K. 1999. *Due Process and Victims' Rights: The New Law and Politics of Criminal Justice*. Toronto: University of Toronto Press.

Roberts, J.V. and D.P. Cole. 1999. "Introduction to Sentencing and Parole." Pp. 3–30 in *Making Sense of Sentencing*, edited by J.V. Roberts and D.P. Cole. Toronto: University of Toronto Press.

Roberts, J.V. and A. Edgar. 2006. *Victim Impact Statements at Sentencing: Judicial Experiences and Perceptions: A Survey of Three Jurisdictions*. Ottawa: Department of Justice.

Roberts, J.V. and C. LaPrairie. 1996. "Circle Sentencing: Some Unanswered Questions." *Criminal Law Quarterly* 39:319–55.

Roberts, J.V. and A. von Hirsch. 1999. "Legislating the Purpose and Principles of Sentencing." Pp. 48–62 in *Making Sense of Sentencing*, edited by J.V. Roberts and D.P. Cole. Toronto: University of Toronto Press.

Roberts, T. 1992. *Assessment of the Victim Impact Statement Program in British Columbia*. Ottawa: Department of Justice, Research and Sentencing Directorate.

Rubel, H.C. 1986. "Victim Participation in Sentencing Proceedings." *Criminal Law Quarterly* 28:226–50.

Scheck, B.C., P.J. Neufeld, and J. Dwyer. 2000. *Actual Innocence*. New York: Double-day.

Schmitz, C. 2015. "Bar Reviews Call for Safety Valve after Mandatory Minimum Ruling." *The Lawyers Weekly* 34(May 1):1–2.

Sherman, L.W. and R. Berk. 1984. "The Specific Deterrent Effects of Arrest for Domestic Assault." *American Sociological Review* 49:261–72.

Smith, G. 2004. "Faulty Hair Analysis of Hair Samples Sparks Calls for Case Reviews." *The Globe and Mail*, September 16, p. A7.

Spelman, W. 2000. "What Recent Studies Do (and Don't) Tell Us About Imprisonment and Crime." Pp. 419–94 in *Crime and Justice: A Review of Research*, Vol. 27, edited by M. Tonry. Chicago: University of Chicago Press.

Sumner, C.J. 1987. "Victim Participation in the Criminal Justice System." *Australia and New Zealand Journal of Criminology* 20:195–217.

Tonry, M. 2009. "The Mostly Unintended Effects of Mandatory Penalties: Two Centuries of Consistent Findings." Pp. 65–114 in *Crime and Justice: A Review of Research*, Vol. 38, edited by M. Tonry. Chicago: University of Chicago Press.

Tonry, M. 2006. "Criminology, Mandatory Minimums, and Public Policy." *Criminology & Public Policy* 5:45–56.

Tonry, M. 1996. *Sentencing Matters*. New York: Oxford University Press.

Ulmer, J.T., M. Kurlchek, and J. Kramer. 2007. "Prosecutorial Discretion and the Imposition of Mandatory Minimums." *Journal of Research in Crime and Delinquency* 4:427–58.

U.S. Sentencing Commission. 1991. *Mandatory Minimum Penalties in the Federal Criminal Justice System*. Washington, DC: U.S. Sentencing Commission.

Visher, C. 1987. "Incapacitation and Crime: Does a 'Lock 'em Up' Strategy Reduce Crime?" *Justice Quarterly* 4:513–43.

Walgrave, L. 2005. "Towards Restoration as the Mainstream in Youth Justice." Pp. 3–25 in *New Directions in Restorative Justice: Issues, Practice, Evaluation*, edited by E. Elliott and R. Gordon. Cullompton, Devon: Willan.

Walker, S. 2007. *Sense and Nonsense about Crime and Drugs: A Policy Guide*, 6th ed. Belmont, CA: Wadsworth.

Walker, S. 1994. *Sense and Nonsense about Crime and Drugs: A Policy Guide*, 3rd ed. Belmont, CA: Wadsworth.

Wheeler, G. and R. Hissong. 1988. "Effects of Sanctions on Drunk Drivers: Beyond Incarceration." *Crime and Delinquency* 34:29–42.

White, R. and F. Haines. 2002. *Crime and Criminology: An Introduction*. New York: Oxford University Press.

Young, A.N. 2001. *The Role of the Victim in the Criminal Process: A Literature Review—1989 to 1999*. Ottawa: Department of Justice Canada.

Zedlewski, E.W. 1987. *Making Confinement Decisions*. Washington, DC: Government Printing Office.

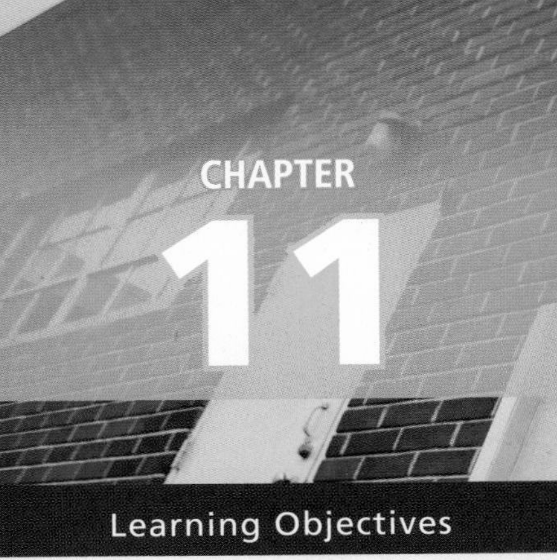

CHAPTER 11

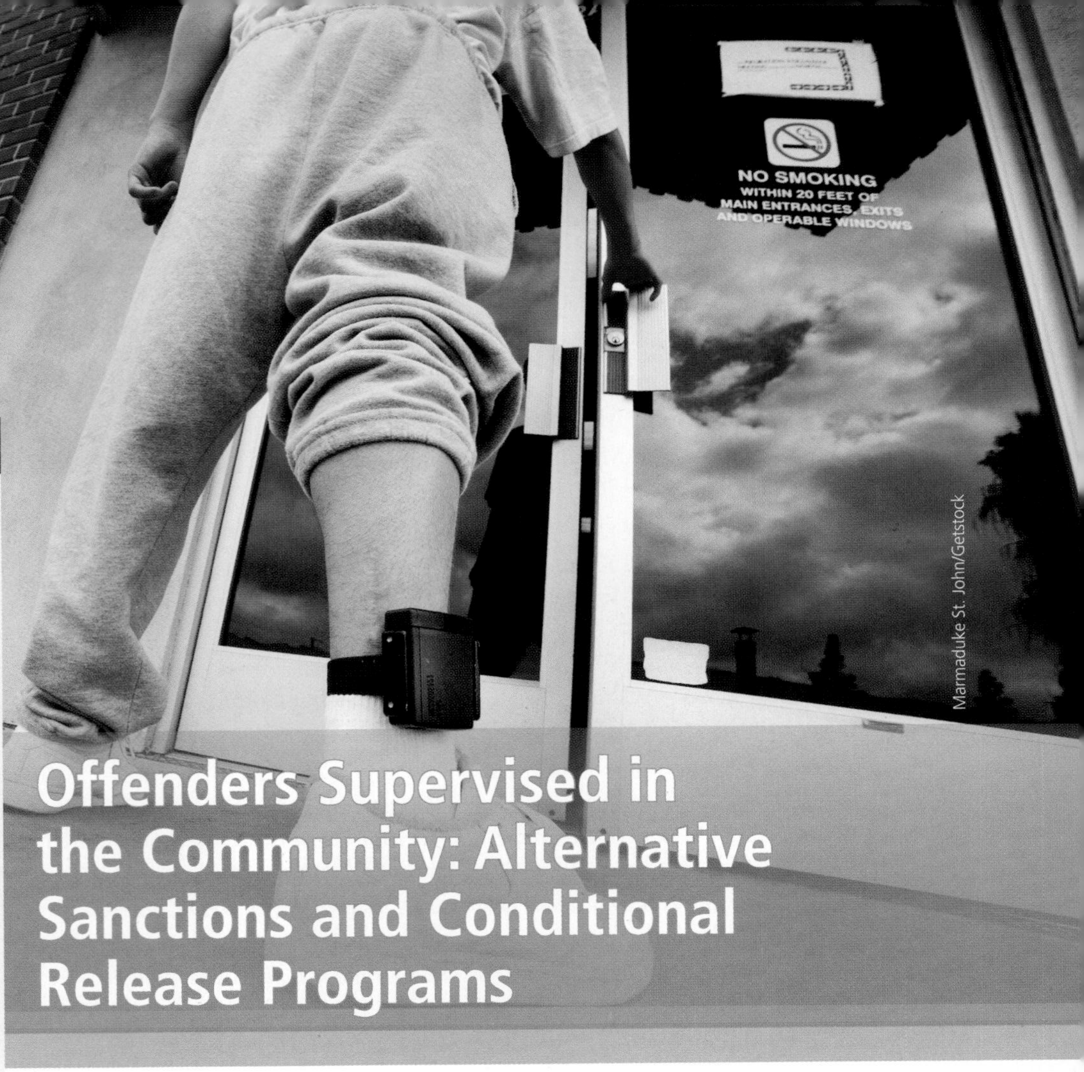

Marmaduke St. John/Getstock

Offenders Supervised in the Community: Alternative Sanctions and Conditional Release Programs

Learning Objectives

After completing this chapter, you should be able to:

- Understand the role of alternative sanctions in Canada.
- Understand the extent to which probation is used as an alternative sanction.
- Differentiate between probation and the conditional sentence of imprisonment.
- Understand the changes to conditional sentences since it was introduced.
- Understand the impact of intermediate sanctions.
- Differentiate between alternative sanctions and conditional release programs.
- Understand the different types of conditional release programs.
- Understand the recidivism rates for the different types of conditional release programs.
- Understand why problem-solving courts were created and their main features.
- Understand how problem-solving courts are a type of alternative sanction.

Once an accused is sentenced, they proceed to the final stage of the criminal justice system—the correctional system. People can be placed into a correctional facility (incarceration) or into the community (probation and parole) or a combination of both. While incarceration receives the most attention, most people aren't incarcerated as the majority of those convicted serve their sentence in the community. The administration of adult correctional services in Canada is a shared responsibility between the federal and provincial/territorial governments. Generally, the **federal correctional system** has jurisdiction over those offenders serving a sentence of custody of two years or more as well as those offenders on conditional release (e.g., full parole or day parole) in the community. **Provincial and territorial correctional systems** are under the authority of provincial/territorial governments, who are responsible for offenders serving custodial sentences of two years less a day, in remand awaiting trial or sentencing, as well as those serving a community sentence, for example, probation.

In 2010–11, there were on average approximately 163,000 adults serving their sentence in the correctional system. The majority of adult offenders (77 percent) were serving their sentence in the community, while the other 23 percent were incarcerated. Since 2000–01, the rate of adult offenders in the community has declined by approximately 10 percent, while the rate of adults incarcerated has increased by 5 percent (see Exhibit 11.1).

How do we know how many people are serving a sentence in the community and in a correctional facility? There are two ways offenders are counted in Canada. The first is by counting an admission each time an individual enters custody or a community supervisions program. This means that an individual may be counted more than once in a year. For example, someone who moves from remand to sentenced custody to community supervision is counted three times. The second way offenders are counted is by looking at where

EXHIBIT 11.1 Status of Adults on Initial Entry into Correctional Services

As mentioned earlier, information on adults in the correctional system is generally analyzed using average counts or admissions data. However, another way to examine the involvement of adults in the correctional system is by looking at the legal status of individuals at the point of initial entry into the system. This method is similar to counting admissions, yet each person is counted only once regardless of a change in legal status.

In 2010–11, data on the initial entry of adults into correctional services were available for six provinces (Table 11.1). Consistent with previous years, these data showed that in four of the six reporting provinces (New Brunswick, Ontario, Saskatchewan, and Alberta) remand was the most common point of initial entry. In the other two provinces (Newfoundland and Labrador and Nova Scotia), the commencement of a probation sentence was the most common point at which adults entered the correctional system.

TABLE 11.1 Status of Adults into Correction Services, by Type of Supervision and Province, 2010–11

Type of Correctional Services	Newfound-land and Labrador	Nova Scotia	New Brunswick	Ontario	Saskatchewan	Alberta
Custody	37.0	48.2	63.1	65.9	54.4	81.5
Remand	15.4	27.9	29.9	53.7	38.7	60.3
Sentenced custody	15.8	12.7	24.2	5.3	13.7	21.2
Intermittent sentences	5.0	3.69	2.3	3.3	0.8	0.0
Other temporary detention	0.8	3.8	6.6	3.6	1.2	0.0
Community supervision	63.0	51.8	36.9	34.1	45.6	18.5
Probation	42.7	42.3	26.6	30.5	26.6	16.2
Conditional sentences	20.3	9.4	10.3	3.7	9.5	2.3
Bail supervision	n/a	n/a	n/a	n/a	9.5	n/a
Total correctional services	**100.00**	**100.00**	**100.0**	**100.0**	**100.0**	**100.0**

Note: Figures may not add up due to rounding.

Source: Mia Duavergne, "Adult correctional statistics in Canada, 2010/2011." *Juristat* (October 2012), Statistics Canada Catalogue no. 85-002-x, p. 16, http://www.statcan.gc.ca/pub/85-002-x/2012001/article/11715-eng.pdf.

someone enters the correctional system, regardless of a change in their status (see Figure 11.1).

This chapter examines the various types of ways that offenders are placed into the community while serving their sentences. The main alternatives to imprisonment used in conjunction with the correctional system in Canada are probation, conditional sentences, parole, and three types of intermediate punishment—intensive supervision probation, home confinement and electronic monitoring, and day fines. These are sometimes referred to as **community corrections**, the main purpose of which is to administer and monitor diversion programs, pretrial supervision, and community-based sanctions. Community correctional services are also responsible for a number of additional justice activities that best fit within the community corrections context; these include drafting presentence reports and operating fine option programs (Calverley and Beattie 2005). Many of these programs are available across Canada, but in some jurisdictions a number of these programs are either not available or of limited availability.

Both probation and conditional sentences are forms of community-based sanctions. Probation has existed in Canada for more than a century; conditional sentences were not implemented until 1996 as part of the package of reforms proclaimed when Bill C-41 was passed (see Chapter 10). Intermediate punishments have been used in the United States for a number of decades and, depending on the jurisdiction in Canada, are beginning to be used more commonly.

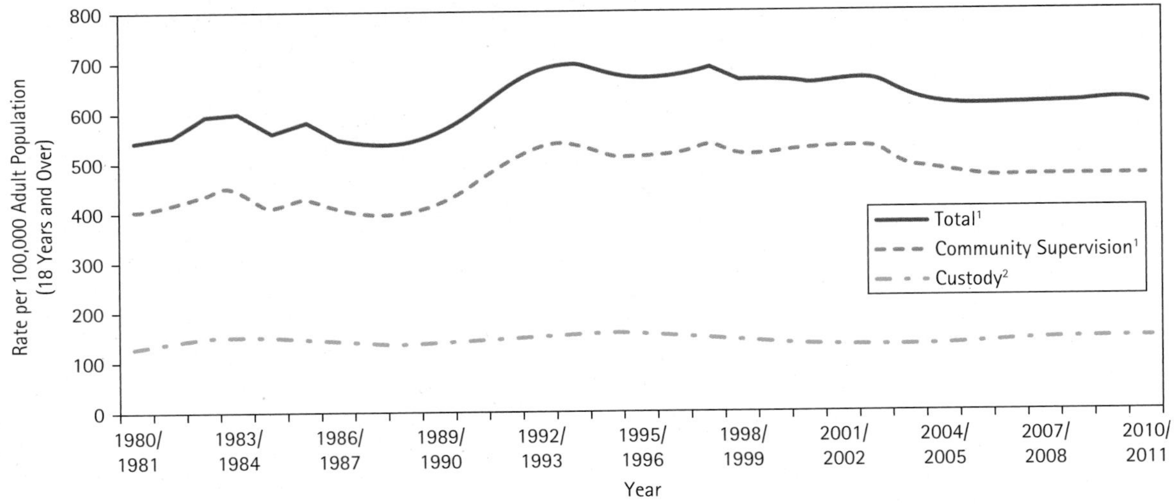

FIGURE 11.1 Average Counts of Adults under Community Supervision and in Custody, Canada, 1980–81 to 2010–11

1. Includes adult offenders under provincial and federal community supervision. Due to the unavailability of data for certain years, the following jurisdictions have been removed in order to make comparisons over time: Newfoundland and Labrador, Prince Edward Island, Nova Scotia, New Brunswick, the Northwest Territories, and Nunavut.
2. Includes adult offenders in provincial and federal custody. Due to the unavailability of data for certain years, the following jurisdictions have been removed in order to make comparisons over time: Prince Edward Island and Nunavut.

Note: Counts are based on the average number of adults under community supervision and in custody on any given day. Rates are calculated per 100,000 adult population (18 years and over) using revised July 1st population estimates from Statistics Canada, Demography Division. Rates may not match those previously published in other reports.

Source: Mia Duavergne, "Adult correctional statistics in Canada, 2010/2011." *Juristat* (October 2012), Statistics Canada Catalogue no. 85-002-x, p. 5, http://www.statcan.gc.ca/pub/85-002-x/2012001/article/11715-eng.pdf. Reproduced and distributed on an "as is" basis with the permission of Statistics Canada.

Community Release under Attack

In the early 1970s, all forms of community sanctions, especially parole, came under attack by an outraged public that felt any program with the goal to place offenders into the community as part of their sentence was soft on criminals. These criticisms were followed by a series of policy changes developed by criminal justice practitioners, who argued that all community sanctions were too discretionary and were failing to protect the due process rights of offenders. Critics also asserted that the rehabilitation ideal and its related treatment programs, which had been designed to reintegrate offenders into the community, were misplaced. For many reasons, parole was abolished in a number of American states, beginning with Maine in 1975. By 1984, the number of states without parole had increased to 11, although the following year Colorado reinstated parole after having abolished its parole board in 1979. In 1987, the Canadian Sentencing Commission recommended the elimination of parole in this country, but its proposals were never implemented.

"Nothing Works"

In 1974, Robert Martinson published an article that was to have a tremendous impact on how community sanctions would operate over the following decades. Titled "What Works? Questions and Answers about Prison Reform," this article questioned the very existence of rehabilitation. This essay was drawn from a larger work (Lipton et al. 1975) that assessed 231 studies of treatment programs operating between 1945 and 1967. At the end of his article, Martinson (1974:25) commented that with "few and isolated exceptions the rehabilitative efforts that have been reported so far have had no appreciable effect on recidivism."

In his last section—"Does Nothing Work?"—he pointed out that the studies he had just reviewed were no doubt flawed in many ways, and that these flaws might explain why he had not been able to find any significant treatment successes. Even so, he concluded (ibid.:49) that it might be impossible for rehabilitation-based programs to overcome or reduce "the powerful tendencies of offenders to continue in criminal behavior."

Most people who read Martinson's article failed to heed his acknowledgment that rehabilitation might work sometimes. Instead, as Walker notes (1984:168), the phrase "**nothing works**" became an instant cliché for critics—one that exerted enormous influence on both popular and professional thinking. Five years later, Martinson (1979:244, 252) clarified his position: "Contrary to my previous position, some treatment programs do have an appreciable effect on recidivism. . . . Some programs are indeed beneficial. New evidence from our current study leads me to reject my original conclusion. . . . I have hesitated up to now, but the evidence in our surveys is simply too overwhelming to ignore."

Although his original article is one of the most frequently cited in criminology, his second remains virtually ignored (Cullen and Gendreau 1989). By the time his second article appeared, the critique of rehabilitation was too powerful and entrenched. Martinson himself, after reviewing the few research projects on parole, concluded that when parolees and non-parolees were compared, parole had at best only a delaying effect on recidivism (Waller 1974). This doubt cast on the benefits of parole led to questions concerning the grounding of parole in rehabilitation (Canadian Sentencing Commission 1987).

Probation

Probation is based on the idea that some offenders are not dangerous criminals who threaten society and, as a result, may serve all or part of their sentence in the community. A judge gives probation at the sentencing, after suspending the offender's sentence; however, a judge cannot suspend a sentence for an offence that has a specified minimum punishment. A probation order can be imposed either as a single sentence or as a **split sentence**. With the latter, an offender is required to complete another punishment (e.g., pay a fine or serve a period of time not exceeding two years) before going on probation. In Canada, probation is a required accompaniment to a suspended sentence or conditional discharge.

For adult offenders, the maximum length of a probation order is three years. The proportion of offenders receiving probation as part of their sentence has continually increased over the past decade or so. In 2011–12, 45 percent of all guilty cases received probation either on its own or in combination with other sanctions, compared to 43 percent in 2006–07 and 37 percent in 1996–97. The median length of probation orders has remained consistent since 1994–95, at about 365 days (one year).

Probation typically involves an offender being released into the community under the supervision of a provincial probation service. It is, in essence, a contract between an offender and the state in which the former promises to abide by the conditions mandated by the court. If the offender breaks the conditions of probation, a federal statute, or the Criminal Code, a breach of probation has occurred and he or she is guilty of an offence (s. 733[1] of the Criminal Code). **Mandatory conditions** of probation include remaining within a particular jurisdiction, reporting to a probation officer as required, keeping the peace, keeping authorities informed about changes of residence, refraining from contact with criminal associates, and notifying the court or probation officer of any change in employment or occupation (s. 732.1[2] of the Criminal Code). The court may impose other conditions deemed reasonable "for protecting society and for facilitating the offender's successful reintegration into the community" (s. 732.1[3][h]). **Optional conditions** may include drug counselling, avoiding contact with children (e.g., if a child molester is placed on probation), or performing a specified community service order. It is noteworthy that reporting to a probation officer is also an optional condition of probation (s. 732.1[3][a] of the Criminal Code). In the event of a new offence, the court may revoke the probation order and, in the case of a suspended sentence, impose any sentence that could have been handed out if the sentence had not been suspended. Alternatively, the court may make changes to the optional conditions as deemed by the court (s. 733.2[5][d][e]).

Judges have considerable discretion when determining whether to give probation. Section 731 of the Criminal Code states:

> Where an accused is convicted of an offence, the court may, having regard to the age and character of the accused, the nature of the offence and the circumstances surrounding the commission
>
> (a) . . . suspend the passing of sentence and direct that the accused be released on the conditions prescribed in a probation order.

Probation has been the most common community-based punishment, and it is constantly being revised. For example, when Bill C-41 (see Chapter 10) was proclaimed, it included probation as a punishment for firearm offences. Section 100 of the Criminal Code provides for prohibition orders against the possession of firearms, ammunition, or explosive devices. These orders are imposed on offenders who have been convicted or discharged in connection with offences involving violence, threats of violence, or firearms. Courts are now required (s. 731.1) to consider Section 100 of the Criminal Code before imposing a probation order (Daubney and Parry 1999).

Bill C-41 also made allowances for the **long-term supervision** (sometimes referred to as **super-probation**) of certain offenders in the community (see Chapter 3). Section 753.1 of the Criminal Code focuses on individuals the courts find to be **dangerous offenders**. A judge who decides there is a possibility that an offender will be a high-risk threat to the safety of a community, or that the offender might reoffend once released, can order the offender to be placed on probation while in the community for a period of up to 10 years. The supervision may be attached to parole, and would begin after parole has been successfully completed.

The Use of Probation as a Sanction

Probation is the most common form of community sanction in Canada. Of the 246,985 total guilty cases in 2011–12, 110,885 (45 percent) were handed down sentences involving probation, a slight decrease (from 46 percent) from the previous year. The number of admissions to probation steadily increased between 1999–2000 and 2008–09. Figure 11.2 shows the increase in the number of individuals on probation between 1980–81 and 2010–11.

In 2011–12, probation was most likely to be part of a sentence in the category of crimes against the person (75 percent), compared to 60 percent of offenders in the category of crimes against property and 54 percent in the category of other Criminal Code. The most common offence in the category of crimes against the person where probation was used was criminal harassment (stalking), at 90 percent; common assault and uttering threats had probation orders attached to the sentence (80 percent and 79 percent, respectively). The most common offences in the category of crimes against property in which a probation order was used were mischief (71 percent) and break and enter (54 percent). In the category of other Criminal Code, the most common use of probation was for prostitution (52 percent) (see Table 11.2).

Who Is Eligible for Probation?

Many people believe that probation is granted to first-time offenders who commit minor property offences. However, probation is commonly given to individuals convicted of violent offences. There are two reasons why most violent criminals are given a sentence of probation: (1) the violent crimes that most commonly receive probation are less serious and therefore warrant a lenient response, and (2) the offender's prior criminal record suggests this is appropriate. Regarding (1), according to Roberts (1999), the majority of all violent crimes are considered relatively minor. Regarding (2), the accused's prior criminal record has a strong impact on sentencing patterns. Roberts (ibid.:95) points out that "property offenders are more likely to have prior convictions than violent offenders [and] are more likely to have been sentenced to probation in the past. This may discourage judges from imposing probation on this second (or third) occasion."

Studies of probation orders indicate that some offenders are sentenced to lengthy probation terms. In 2011–12, for example, six offences had a median length of probation sentence of 545 days or longer (see Table 11.2). The offences that led to long probation orders tended to be serious, and probation was usually imposed in combination with incarceration. Offenders found guilty of five violent crimes (homicide, attempted murder, robbery, sexual assault, and other sexual offences) who receive probation as part of their sentence get the greatest amount of probation (two years), while for other offences (i.e., criminal harassment and "other violent offences") offenders

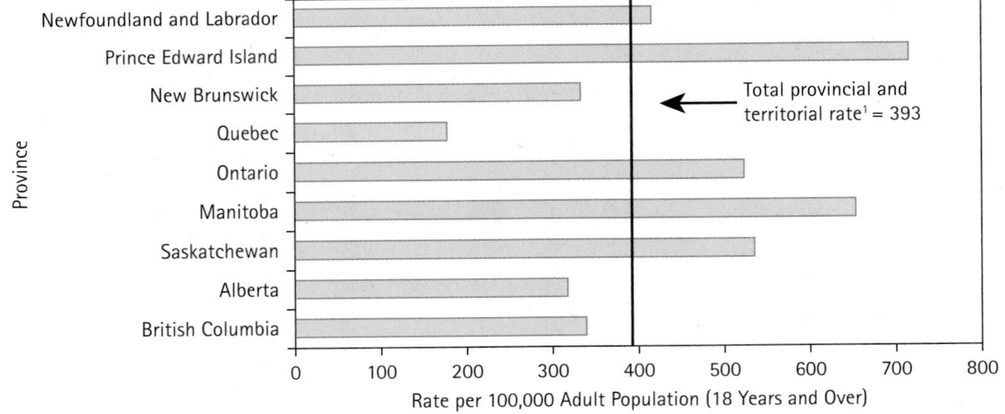

FIGURE 11.2 Average Counts of Adults on Probation and Conditional Sentences by Type of Supervision, 1980–81 to 2010–11

1. Excludes Nova Scotia due to the unavailability of 2010/2011 data on adult offenders under community supervision.

Note: Counts are based on the average number of adults on probation on any given day. Rates are calculated per 100,000 adult population (18 years and over) using revised July 1st population estimates from Statistics Canada, Demography Division. Rates may not match those previously published in other reports.

Source: Mia Duavergne, "Adult correctional statistics in Canada, 2010/2011." *Juristat* (October 2012), Statistics Canada Catalogue no. 85-002-x, p. 14, http://www.statcan.gc.ca/pub/85-002-x/2012001/article/11715-eng.pdf. Reproduced and distributed on an "as is" basis with the permission of Statistics Canada.

TABLE 11.2 Guilty Cases Completed in Adult Criminal Court, by Type of Offence and Select Sentence, Canada, 2011–12

		Custody			Probation			Fine		
Type of Offence[1]	Total Guilty Cases	Number	%	Median Length (days)[2]	Number	%	Median Length (days)[3]	Number	%	Median Amount ($)[4]
Violent offences	**46,255**	**15,677**	**34**	**75**	**34,796**	**75**	**365**	**3,083**	**7**	**400**
Homicide	132	109	83	1,825	14	11	730	6	5	1,100
Attempted murder	40	32	80	1,733	8	20	730	0	0	. . .
Robbery	2,391	1,917	80	440	1,233	52	730	16	1	375
Sexual assault	1,610	873	54	360	1,059	66	730	39	2	500
Other sexual offences[5]	1,551	1,008	65	150	1,147	74	730	58	4	500
Major assault[6]	10,986	5,076	46	90	7,677	70	365	662	6	500
Common assault	17,791	2,626	15	30	14,276	80	365	1,411	8	400
Uttering threats	8,948	2,987	33	30	7,058	79	365	767	9	300
Criminal harassment	1,609	483	30	45	1,446	90	545	65	4	400
Other violent offences	1,197	566	47	154	878	73	540	59	5	300
Property offences	**54,561**	**21,605**	**40**	**45**	**32,572**	**60**	**365**	**7,226**	**13**	**250**
Theft[7]	24,918	9,896	40	30	13,492	54	365	4,275	17	250
Break and enter	7,477	4,412	59	161	4,946	66	540	213	3	500
Fraud	8,101	2,804	35	60	5,294	65	365	806	10	300
Mischief	7,857	1,555	20	17	5,545	71	365	1,095	14	300
Possess stolen property	5,047	2,258	45	45	2,583	51	365	780	15	400
Other property offences	1,161	680	59	82	712	61	540	57	5	250
Administration of justice offences	**60,723**	**29,904**	**49**	**15**	**20,449**	**34**	**365**	**13,420**	**22**	**250**
Fail to appear	2,243	889	40	8	587	26	365	731	33	200
Breach of probation	25,353	14,092	56	20	9,394	37	365	4,713	19	250
Unlawfully at large	2,144	1,833	85	20	450	21	365	118	6	300
Fail to comply with order	24,887	11,109	45	10	7,496	30	365	6,175	25	200
Other admin. of justice offences	6,096	1,981	32	18	2,522	41	365	1,683	28	300
Other Criminal Code offences	**9,866**	**3,886**	**39**	**90**	**5,307**	**54**	**365**	**1,854**	**19**	**250**
Weapon offences	5,901	2,292	39	69	3,076	52	365	1,132	19	250
Prostitution	313	79	25	3	175	56	365	81	26	250

(Continued)

TABLE 11.2 Guilty Cases Completed in Adult Criminal Court, by Type of Offence and Select Sentence, Canada, 2011–12 *(Continued)*

		Custody			Probation			Fine		
Type of Offence[1]	Total Guilty Cases	Number	%	Median Length (days)[2]	Number	%	Median Length (days)[3]	Number	%	Median Amount ($)[4]
Disturbing the peace	868	160	18	10	391	45	365	278	32	250
Residual Criminal Code offences	2,784	1,355	49	124	1,665	60	540	363	13	300
Total Criminal Code (excl. traffic)	**171,405**	**71,072**	**41**	**30**	**93,124**	**54**	**365**	**25,583**	**15**	**250**
Criminal Code traffic offences	**43,420**	**7,313**	**17**	**34**	**6,801**	**16**	**365**	**33,670**	**78**	**1,100**
Impaired driving	34,780	3,235	9	30	3,752	11	365	30,633	88	1,200
Other Criminal Code traffic offences	8,640	4,078	47	45	3,049	35	365	3,037	35	900
Total Criminal Code offences	**214,825**	**78,385**	**36**	**30**	**99,925**	**47**	**365**	**59,253**	**28**	**1,000**
Other federal statute offences	**32,159**	**8,276**	**26**	**90**	**10,960**	**34**	**365**	**12,951**	**40**	**300**
Drug possession	7,582	828	11	9	2,588	34	365	3,726	49	300
Other drug offences[8]	6,478	2,600	40	180	1,942	30	365	492	8	1,000
Youth Criminal Justice Act	979	313	32	9	347	35	365	282	29	230
Residual federal statute offences	17,120	4,535	26	90	6,083	36	365	8,451	49	250
Total	**246,984**	**86,661**	**35**	**30**	**110,885**	**45**	**365**	**72,204**	**29**	**800**

Notes:

... not applicable

[1] Cases that involve more than one charge are represented by the most serious offence.

[2] Custodial sentence lengths exclude time spent in custody prior to sentencing and/or the amount of credit awarded for time spent in presentence custody. Also excludes cases in which the length of the custody sentence was unknown or indeterminate.

[3] Excludes cases in which the length of the probation sentence was unknown or greater than three years.

[4] Excludes cases in which the amount of the fine was unknown.

[5] Includes, for example, sexual interference, invitation to sexual touching, child pornography, luring a child via a computer, and sexual exploitation.

[6] Includes, for example, assault with a weapon (level 2) and aggravated assault (level 3).

[7] Includes, for example, theft over $5,000, theft $5,000 or under, as well as motor vehicle theft.

[8] Includes drug trafficking, production, importing, and exporting.

Note: Cases may involve more than one type of sentence and/or other sentences not shown, therefore, percentages do not total 100. A case is one or more charges against an accused person or company that were processed by the courts at the same time and received a final decision. The median represents the midpoint, where exactly half the custody sentences are above and half are below. Data exclude information from superior courts in Prince Edward Island, Quebec, Ontario, Manitoba, and Saskatchewan as well as municipal courts in Quebec due to the unavailability of data.

Source: Jillian Boyce, "Adult Criminal Court Statistics in Canada, 2011/2012." *Juristat*, June 2013, p. 2727. Statistics Canada catalogue no. 85-002-X. Reproduced and distributed on an "as is" basis with the permission of Statistics Canada.

are given a median probation term of two years. Two other violent offences—criminal harassment and "other violent offences"—have a median probation length of 18 months (Dauvergne 2012). In 2010–11, there was one property offence where the median length of the probation order exceeded one year—break and enter, which had a median length of 540 days.

The Conditional Sentence of Imprisonment

One of the most controversial sections of Bill C-41 was the creation of the **conditional sentence**. Sometimes these are referred to as **house arrest**, as these types of sentences typically require an offender to remain in their home except for limited, court-restricted reasons such as employment, shopping once a week, and so on. This sentence was created in order to inject restorative considerations into the sentencing process (Roach 2000b). The conditional sentence is a sentence of imprisonment of less than two years that the offender serves in the community under both optional and mandatory conditions. Section 742.2 states that a conditional sentence may be imposed under the following conditions:

(a) the Criminal Code does not set a minimum term of imprisonment;

(b) the court imposes a sentence of less than two years; and

(c) the court is satisfied that allowing the offender to serve the sentence in the community would not endanger the safety of the community and would be consistent with the fundamental purpose and principles of sentencing as set out in ss. 718 to 718.2 of the Criminal Code. The court may, for the purposes of supervising the offender's behaviour in the community, order that the offender serve the sentence in the community, subject to an offender's complying with the conditions of a conditional sentence order under s. 742.3.

A conditional sentence is meant to be an alternative to imprisonment. The hope is that such sentences will reduce the number of incarcerated individuals. When a court imposes a conditional sentence, it "has essentially substituted the community for jail as the place where the sentence is to be served, as long as conditions set out in its order are respected" (Daubney and Parry 1999:42). Roach (2000a:26) points out that conditional sentences "were defined as sentences of imprisonment that should be served under strict conditions in the community." Mandatory conditions include law-abiding behaviour, appearing before the court when ordered, remaining within a specific set of boundaries unless the court grants permission to leave, and informing the court or supervisor of any change in address or occupation. Optional conditions include those which are possible in most probation orders, such as attending a treatment program and providing support and care for dependants. The most common options used to date include curfews, mandatory medical or psychiatric treatment, and orders preventing offenders from contacting other persons. The least used option is home confinement and electronic monitoring (Roberts et al. 2000).

In terms of punishment, sentencing judges have situated conditional sentences between incarceration and probation. In *R. v. Proulx* (2000), the Supreme Court clarified the differences between conditional sentences and probation. While the terms of a conditional sentence may appear to be similar to those available under probation, there are differences in purposes as well as in enforcement procedures. Conditional sentences should be more punitive than probation with regard to restrictions on liberty, such as house arrest. Besides restrictions on movement, tougher conditions than those imposed under probation may be used. Rehabilitation is the primary objective of probation; conditional sentences are intended to fulfill the principles of **denunciation** and **rehabilitation** (Lonmo 2001). According to the Supreme Court (in *Proulx*), offenders serving a conditional sentence of imprisonment are subject to conditions that should allow them to engage in rehabilitation, but like incarceration, conditions are also to be punitive and "restrictive of the offender's liberty . . . such as house arrest or strict curfews. . . ." A conditional sentence does not have to be the same length as a period of incarceration—for example, a six-month period of incarceration can mean a one-year conditional sentence. In addition, the Supreme Court also ruled that when an offender breaches a conditional sentence without a reasonable excuse, they will presumably serve the rest of the sentence incarcerated.

In 2006, as part of its Speech from the Throne, the Liberal-controlled federal government introduced legislation that would end the use of conditional sentences for serious offences. Under the proposed reforms, a conditional sentence would no longer be an option for anyone convicted of an offence prosecuted by indictment and that carries a maximum prison sentence of 10 years or more. Those who committed serious crimes, such as designated violent and sexual offences, major drug offences, crimes against children, and impaired driving causing death or bodily harm, would be ineligible for a conditional sentence. In addition, select weapons offences, such as an assault with a weapon causing bodily harm, would be ineligible when prosecuted by indictment. When they were elected, the new Conservative-led federal government reintroduced legislation and on December 1, 2007, it came into force. It amended s. 742.1 of the Criminal Code in order that indictable offences punishable by 10 years or more that qualify as either serious personal injury offences (e.g., sexual assault, aggravated sexual assault, or sexual assault with a weapon), terrorism offences, or criminal organization offences be ineligible from receiving conditional sentences. Since they were first introduced, the rate of people serving a conditional sentence has increased moderately. However, in recent years, due to the changes by the various federal governments, their use has decreased slightly. In 2010–11, the rate of offenders on a conditional sentence was approximately 4 percent lower than the previous year (Dauvergne 2012). Exhibit 11.2 discusses conditional sentences and the Safe Streets and Communities Act.

What Is the Impact of Conditional Sentences?

Have conditional sentences reduced the number of offenders sentenced to a period of imprisonment? Community sanctions may lead to the use of formal responses to minor criminal acts, expanding the scope of the criminal justice system. According to Worrall (1997:25), community penalties "create a new clientele of criminals who are controlled by other mechanisms. The boundaries between freedom and confinement become blurred. The 'net' of social control is thus thrown even wider into the community, its thinner mesh designed to trap even smaller 'fish.'" The issue here, as it is for all alternative sanctions, is that conditional sentences may lead to "**net widening**." Net widening occurs when offenders are diverted into a new program (such as conditional sentencing) even though they are not really the individuals for whom the program was originally intended. As a result, those individuals placed in the new program are given harsher sanctions than they would have received had the program never been launched in the first place. In other words, the argument is that people who receive conditional sentences would normally have received probation—and since a large number of people are now receiving conditional sentences, more people need to be placed on probation. The end result is that more people are placed under the supervision of the authorities.

Supporters of conditional sentences believed that incarceration rates would decrease after they were introduced. Critics argued that the opposite would happen—that judges would hand down the "more severe" conditional sentence to those offenders who in the past would have received probation. Reed and Roberts (1999) conducted an analysis of conditional sentences, which on the surface suggested that they were helping bring down incarceration rates; however, they were reluctant to attribute this decrease to conditional sentences. In fact, they felt that this decline in custodial admissions "cannot be attributable to the introduction of conditional sentence, since . . . admissions to custody had

EXHIBIT 11.2 Bill C-10, the Safe Streets and Communities Act, and Conditional Sentences

In September 2011, the Minister of Justice introduced Bill C-10 (the Safe Streets and Communities Act; see Chapter 1). The legislation (which passed in March 2012) was designed to further restrict and eliminate the use of conditional sentences. For example, all offences of violence prosecuted by way of indictment have now been removed, as have a number of drug offences and theft over $5,000. The complete list of offences included in Bill C-10 included the following:

- Offences for which the law prescribes a maximum sentence of 14 years or life.
- Offences prosecuted by indictment and for which the law prescribes a maximum sentence of imprisonment of 10 years that
  - results in bodily harm;
  - involves the import/export, trafficking, and production of drugs; or
  - involves the use of weapons.
- Offences specified below when prosecuted by indictment:
  - Prison breach
  - Criminal harassment
  - Sexual assault
  - Kidnapping, forcible confinement
  - Trafficking in persons—material benefit
  - Abduction of a person under 14
  - Theft over $5,000
  - Motor vehicle theft
  - Breaking and entering a place other than a dwelling house
  - Being unlawfully in a dwelling-house
  - Arson for fraudulent purpose

If no other punishment was considered to be suitable, an individual may be placed into a correctional facility. It was estimated by then-Parliamentary Budget Officer Kevin Page that these changes would cost the provinces (based on 2008–09 data) around $137 million. This figure includes the cost of a trial for offenders who decide to have a court trial whereas previously they would have pleaded guilty and been placed on a conditional sentence. Based on the fact that the daily cost of incarceration is $160, compared to community supervision at $10, Page estimated that about 3,800 more offenders across Canada will be incarcerated. The cost to taxpayers to place these offenders into a custodial facility will increase to $41,000 from $2,600.

been declining for several years before conditional sentences were introduced." In other words, fewer offences were being committed, and as a result fewer charges were being laid; therefore, fewer offenders were being admitted to correctional facilities. They went on to point out that the best way to assess the impact of conditional sentences would be to compare sentences of admission to both federal and provincial correctional facilities, since the percentage of these admissions "should have declined by the number of conditional sentences imposed" (ibid.:9).

Reed and Roberts's analysis indicates that the total number of sentences of imprisonment handed down has changed little since conditional sentences were introduced in late 1996. They found that in the year prior to the establishment of conditional sentences, 35 percent of sentences imposed in eight jurisdictions across Canada involved a term of imprisonment; in 1997–98, with more than 22,000 conditional sentences imposed, the proportion of terms of imprisonment remained at 35 percent. Roach (2000a:26), after looking at the first two years of the use of conditional sentences, commented that the data "strongly suggests conditional sentences have resulted in net widening." However, Belanger (2001), after examining data on the types of sentences (e.g., custody, probation, a conditional sentence) that offenders were receiving, reported that the number of sentences involving a term of custody had dropped from 60 percent to 49 percent, while probation orders had increased from 40 percent to 42 percent. This led Belanger (ibid.:13) to conclude that "these data would imply that net widening is not occurring at the national level." Roberts and Gabor (2004:102) found that there had been net widening in five of the nine provinces studied and that the national effect of this was "a very small degree of net widening (1 percent)." They also found that while there was "a significant negative correlation between changes in the rate of custody and the volume of conditional sentences," a considerable proportion of the drop in custody rates could be explained "by variables other than the introduction of conditional sentencing." In other words, judges were using other alternatives to imprisonment besides conditional sentences (ibid.:100).

Intermediate Sanctions

The various types of community supervision traditionally used rehabilitation as an approach to dealing with offenders. Probation officers have been regarded as caseworkers or counsellors whose primary task is to help offenders adjust to society. Surveillance and control are minimal compared to what offenders encounter elsewhere in the criminal justice system. Over the past two decades, **intermediate sanctions** have been introduced in an attempt to introduce more control over offenders who have been released into the community.

Intermediate sanctions include programs usually administered by probation departments, such as intensive supervision probation, home confinement, fines, electronic monitoring, and restitution orders. These sanctions are also referred to as **judicially administered sanctions**, because most often it is judges who sentence offenders to these programs. Intermediate sanctions are an outgrowth of justice model–based policies; it is this model that first stirred interest in alternative sanctions (see Chapter 3). A major concern relating to these programs is that a large number of offenders serving these types of sentences might recidivate and subsequently be placed in a correctional setting. If intermediate sanctions are to succeed, care must be taken to maintain high-quality programs and to screen the offenders who participate in them.

Intermediate sanctions were originally based on a deterrence perspective and first introduced in the belief that they would reduce prison overcrowding and substantially reduce the costs of placing offenders in the correctional system. Early advocates also believed that such programs would protect the community by exerting more control over offenders than traditional probation services. It was also hoped that these new forms of punishment would discourage potential offenders from committing crimes and help rehabilitate offenders through mandatory treatment orders reinforced by mandatory substance-abuse tests and the firm revocation of violators (Byrne et al. 1992).

The idea of intermediate punishments is popular for several reasons. First, there is the strong belief that the costs associated with these programs are somehow lower. The direct costs of administering and supervising an intermediate punishment program are generally thought to be much less than those of running a prison. Indirect cost savings result when offenders on intermediate sanctions are required to find employment, thus generating income, paying taxes, and participating in community service projects and other such activities—activities that would not be possible if they were imprisoned (Rackmill 1994).

Second, some jurisdictions require participants to help pay for the costs of the program. Byrne et al. (1989) point out that intensive supervision probationers usually have to pay a probation supervision fee of $10 to $50 per month, as well as any court-ordered fines and restitution payments. Intermediate punishments also save money by diverting large numbers of offenders away from prison. Collectively, this should save millions of dollars each year, provided that a substantial number of intermediate punishment programs are in place.

Third, intermediate punishments can result in sentences that are seen as fair, equitable, and proportional (Morris and Tonry 1990). Sending violent criminals to prison makes sense, but shouldn't those convicted of fraudulent offences be given a lighter punishment, albeit one that maintains some degree of control? Such a system, Tonry and Will (1990) argue, establishes fairness and equity in sentences not involving incarceration, as it can increase the punishment for those who are reconvicted of an offence but for whom a prison sentence is inappropriate. Intermediate punishments also provide stronger control than normal community supervision. In theory, they also lead to greater deterrence, because the greater amount of surveillance makes it likely that anyone violating the terms of the program will be caught and punished. Furthermore, offenders under intermediate punishment should also commit fewer offences, because the conditions of the program limit their opportunities to engage in such activities. According to Petersilia and Turner (1993), closer surveillance will likely uncover more technical rule violations. Exhibit 11.3 outlines some of the criticisms of the use of intermediate punishments.

What Is Intensive Supervision Probation?

Intensive supervision probation (ISP) is the most common form of intermediate punishment today (Petersilia 2004). It can be used across jurisdictions or for a specific program. For example, when Manitoba instituted its high-risk probationer program, it contained an intensive supervision component. The popularity of ISPs stems from the notion that they can reduce prison populations, eliminate the need to build costly new prisons, and prevent the negative impact of imprisonment on offenders. They are also seen as promoting public safety by ensuring that all offenders are subject to intensive surveillance; in this way, they reduce the opportunities for involvement in criminal activities (Petersilia 1987). See Exhibit 11.4 for a comparison of ISP and regular probation.

ISP programs are not designed for leniency but rather for punishment. As one policymaker stated in reference to these programs, "We are in the business of increasing the heat on probationers . . . to satisfy the public's demand for just punishment. . . . Criminals must be punished for their misdeeds" (Erwin 1986:24).

Offenders do not have an easy time in ISP programs; usually, ISP involves several contacts with a probation officer every week, residence only in approved locations, random drug and alcohol tests, and one year's minimum involvement. In fact, because of the intrusive nature of these programs, many offenders choose not to participate when given the chance, even if the alternative is prison. Petersilia and Turner (1993) report that in Oregon, 25 percent of the offenders they studied who were eligible for an ISP program preferred prison instead.

Evaluation of ISP Programs

Early evaluations of two ISP programs in the United States led to the rapid spread of ISPs across that country and, to a lesser degree, Canada. Expectations were high. As Petersilia (1993) points out, the rapid expansion of ISP programs was based on a number of hopeful assumptions. The first assumption was that many offenders present only a medium risk and should neither be placed on routine probation nor sent to prison. Instead, they should be

EXHIBIT 11.3 Intermediate Punishments and the Penal Harm Movement

Critics argue that the benefits of intermediate punishments have not been achieved. Instead, they argue that these programs have brought about a new era of punitive punishments that simply incarcerate more offenders than before (Morris and Tonry 1990). Clear (1994) believes that these new punishments reflect the "penal harm movement"—a series of seven interrelated components based on the assumption that crime rates can be reduced if more offenders are punished and placed under the control of criminal justice agencies. His argument is related to net widening in the sense that it contends that more, not fewer, offenders will be placed in these programs.

The components of the "penal harm movement," when combined, create what Clear refers to as the punishment paradigm. The components in this paradigm are as follows:

1. The "root causes" of crime, such as social inequality, racism, and poverty, cannot be changed or have no relevance to the causes of crime.
2. Any programs developed and implemented to combat the root causes of crime are misplaced and will not reduce the crime rate.
3. Criminals will only be deterred if the criminal justice system ensures that they receive enough pain for their wrongs.
4. Prisons are an effective means of reducing crime because they keep criminals off the street.
5. Society will be much safer with large numbers of criminals in prison.
6. Offenders in the community should be controlled, not incarcerated, through a variety of programs known as intermediate punishments, such as house confinement, electronic monitoring, and intensive supervision probation
7. If crime rates do not decrease, more punishment, community control, and prisons will be needed.

EXHIBIT 11.4 Selected Differences between Intensive Supervision Probation and Regular Probation

How is ISP different from regular probation? The most commonly cited advantage to ISP is that probation officers in these programs have fewer clients—usually between 15 and 40. According to Thompson (1985), ISP programs are also unique in the following ways:

1. Supervision is extensive. Probation officers have multiple weekly face-to-face contacts with offenders, as well as collateral contacts with employers and family members.
2. Supervision is focused. Monitoring activities focus on specific behavioural regulations governing curfews, drug use, travel, employment, and community service.
3. Supervision is ubiquitous. Offenders are frequently subjected to random drug tests and unannounced curfew checks.
4. Supervision is graduated. Offenders commonly proceed through ISP programs in a series of progressive phases—each of which represents a gradual tempering of the proscriptions and requirements of ISP—until they are committed to regular supervision as the final leg of their statutory time on probation.
5. Supervision is strictly enforced. Penalties for new arrest and non-compliance with program conditions are generally swift and severe.
6. Supervision is coordinated. ISP offenders are usually monitored by specially selected and trained officers who are part of a larger specialized, autonomous unit.

placed in the community, but under more stringent conditions than those enforced by regular probation programs. The second assumption was that ISPs are cost-effective because they mean that fewer people are sentenced to prison. The third assumption is that ISPs provide stronger crime control than regular probation but less control than prison. Once judges understand that ISP offers stricter control than regular probation, they will show more willingness to apply this form of community sentencing.

Three key findings appeared over and over in evaluations of ISPs. First, most ISP participants were not prison-bound offenders. In fact, many of the offenders who ended up in ISPs should have been placed in regular probation programs. From the perspective of those who created ISPs, this problem was caused not by the original guidelines but rather by judges who ignored those guidelines. Judges were placing lower-risk offenders on ISPs, and as a result, ISPs were "widening the net," since the number of people assigned to regular probation programs and prison remained the same.

Second, the re-arrest rates for ISP participants increased after they were placed under tighter supervision. Instead of reducing criminal activity, ISP programs were actually *increasing* it, leading to higher incarceration rates and system costs. Petersilia and Turner (1993) found little difference in re-arrest rates after one year (38 percent for ISP participants and 36 percent for regular probationers). The study also indicated that a much higher percentage of ISP participants were being arrested for technical violations (70 percent versus 40 percent of regular probationers). As a result, 27 percent of ISP participants had been sent to a correctional facility after one year, compared to 19 percent of regular probationers.

Third, recidivism rates were lower in ISP programs that included a rehabilitative component. Byrne and Kelly (1989:37), for example, found that "58 percent of the offenders who demonstrated improvement in the area of substance abuse successfully completed the one-year at risk, as compared with only 38 percent of those who did not improve." These researchers concluded that crime control could be achieved, but only through the use of rehabilitation measures.

Jolin and Stipak (1992) reported that drug treatment programs led to a significant reduction in offenders' drug use (from 95 percent at the time they started the program to 32 percent at the completion of the program). Latessa (1995) found that high-risk clients fared no worse, and sometimes better, than random samples of regular probationers when they participated in ISPs with a treatment component. Finally, offenders sentenced to treatment-based ISPs were found to have lower recidivism rates than a matched group of regular probationers (21 percent versus 29 percent)—a finding attributed to the fact that ISP participants received "significantly more treatment services" (Gendreau et al. 1994:34). Gendreau and Little (1993), after systematically reviewing 175 evaluations of intermediate sanction programs, concluded that "in essence, the supervision of high-risk probationers and parolees must be structured, [be] intensive, maintain firm accountability for program participation, and connect the offender with prosocial networks and activities."

Home Confinement and Electronic Monitoring

Home confinement (HC) and **electronic monitoring** (EM) are designed to restrict offenders to their place of residence. In this way, the offender can maintain family ties and continue to work and to use community programs and resources. The introduction of EM technology is considered to be "the most significant development in intermediate sanctions in the last 30 years" (Mair 2006:57). The use of EM in some Western nations is now so common that it appears to have "become normalized as a criminal justice tool" (ibid.).

But how can correctional officials be sure that offenders are following their probation orders and remaining at home during the designated times? This issue has been solved by electronic monitoring, which tells officials at a central location whether the offender is ignoring the home confinement agreement by violating a curfew order. The hope is that by increasing the certainty of detection, EM will deter those sentenced to HC from reoffending.

Just as with ISP, HC and EM started slowly but became popular within a few years. In 1986, only 95 offenders were on EM programs in the United States. Within a year, however, this number had increased to 2,300 and by 1993 it was reported that there were 10,000 individuals who had been using EM (Camp and Camp 1993). The use of EM in many American states has continued to grow. At the end of June 2009, for example, the state of Florida alone had slightly fewer than 2,400 offenders on EM (Bales et al. 2010). In 2012, about 200,000 offenders in the United States were wearing some type of electronic monitor. In 2011, it was estimated that there were 70,000 offenders using EM in the United Kingdom. The interest in EM is based largely on the assumption that it saves money while ensuring effective surveillance. The savings extend beyond keeping individuals out of a custodial facility, as EM has the potential to create significant savings in opportunity costs because offenders placed behind bars will lose their jobs and no longer be able provide for their families or provide tax revenue for their communities (see Figure 11.3).

Canada has been slow to introduce house arrest and EM, even though the Supreme Court of Canada ruled in *R. v. Proulx* (2000) that conditional sentences should include house arrest as the "norm, not the exception." In the same ruling, the Court "virtually mandated the use of electronic monitoring as part of many conditional sentences" (Makin 2000:A8). The federal and provincial governments have been criticized for not using EM more frequently. In 1999, the Ontario Court of Appeal commented that EM could be used more often—a comment apparently not embraced by provincial authorities (Makin 1999). Seven provinces, including Saskatchewan, Alberta, and British Columbia, have used EM for a small number of participants, while Ontario has had over 200 participants in its program.

At the federal level, the Correctional Service of Canada (CSC) tested electronic monitoring anklets on volunteer parolees from 2008 to 2011. Bill C-10, the Safe Streets and Communities Act (2012), included legislation

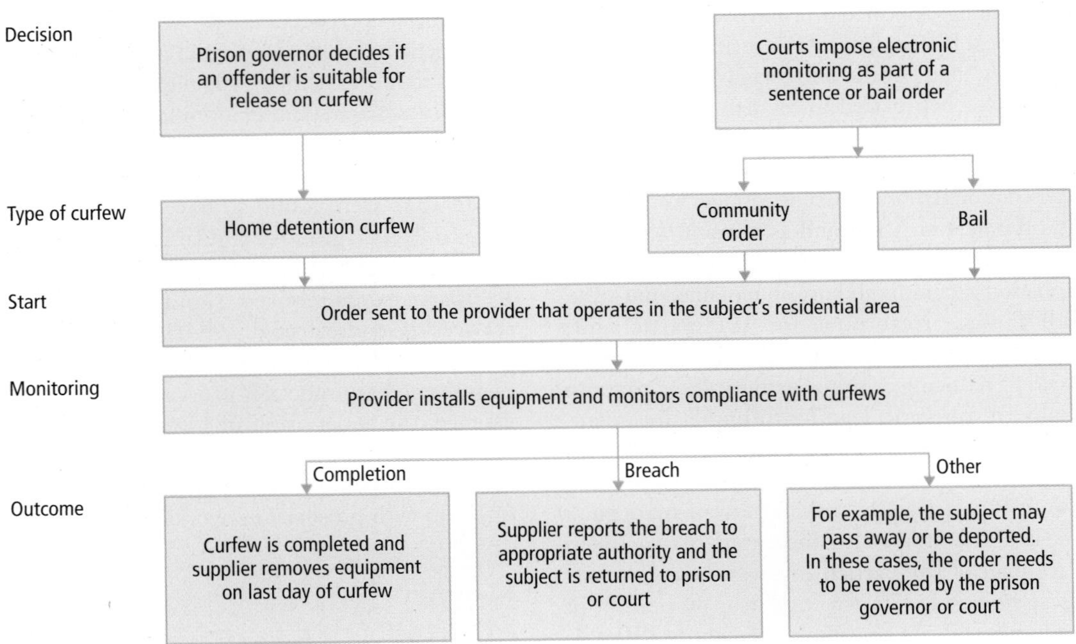

FIGURE 11.3 Overview of the Electronic Monitoring Process in the United Kingdom

Source: The Ministry of Justice's electronic monitoring contracts report, National Audit Office (November 19, 2013), p. 8, http://www.nao.org.uk/wp-content/uploads/2013/11/10294-001-MoJ-Electronic-Monitoring_final.pdf.

allowing CSC to use electronic monitoring devices with designated high-risk offenders with geographic restrictions on temporary absences, work release, parole, statutory release, and long-term supervision. In early 2015, the CSC announced plans to implement an electronic monitoring project using anklets to track up to 300 high-risk offenders (Harris 2015).

How Effective Are Home Confinement and Electronic Monitoring Programs?

According to Clear and Hardyman (1990), early supporters of intermediate punishment programs such as ISP made exaggerated claims that these programs would revolutionize corrections—that they would result in better crime control, reduced prison populations, fiscal savings, and greater public safety. Of course, more modest claims—for example, that there are little if any cost savings, and only a minimal increase in public safety—would have led to diminished support for these programs and made them more difficult to implement.

ISP, HC, and EM programs have been viewed as **panaceas** for the control of crime. As a consequence, little attention was initially paid to what these programs hoped to accomplish, and thus researchers found it difficult to say whether these programs had achieved their goals. As Tonry (1990:180) has commented, ISP programs have succeeded not in terms of achieving their stated goals, but rather in serving "latent bureaucratic, organizational, political, professional, and psychological goals of probation departments and officers."

In an evaluation of the EM programs in three provinces (British Columbia, Saskatchewan, and Newfoundland), Bonta et al. (1999) compared 262 participants in EM programs with a group of offenders who were either incarcerated or on probation. The recidivism rates were 26.7 percent for the EM participants, 33.3 percent for the probationers, and 37.9 percent for those incarcerated. The lower recidivism rates of the EM participants were attributed to the fact that they were lower-risk offenders and were less likely to recidivate anyway. When the researchers introduced into their analyses the risk levels of all the offenders they studied, the differences in the recidivism rates could not be attributed to the type of sanction. The researchers concluded that EM programs do not reduce the recidivism of offenders more effectively than custody or probation. This study also raised questions about net widening—specifically, whether EM programs were targeting low-risk offenders who would otherwise have received a community sanction. The researchers' findings led them to question whether EM programs are more cost-effective, whether they really contribute to greater public safety, and whether attempts to reduce criminal behaviour might not be served better by treatment programs. Bonta et al. (2000:73) posit that the impact of EM varies with the intended outcomes. If such a program is designed solely to achieve program completion, then the surveillance and control nature of EM "may ensure that offenders complete a period of supervision without incident." In fact, they found that completion rates were high in the various provincial programs regardless of the amount of time offenders spent in them (from an average of 37.3 days in British Columbia to 71.6 days in Newfoundland and 139.3 days in Saskatchewan). However, if the desired outcome of an EM program is to reduce recidivism, "EM has questionable merit" (ibid.).

CP PHOTO/ John Woods

In an attempt to reduce the number of car thefts in Winnipeg, in 2008 the provincial government introduced electronic anklets for young thieves identified as high-risk repeat offenders. This program, along with a number of other programs, led to the reduction of car thefts in excess of 60 percent in the following year compared to the previous year.

Fines

In 2011–12, a fine was imposed in 29 percent of all guilty cases, a figure that has remained relatively constant during the past decade, but lower than the 44 percent in 1996–97. Over these same years, there has been a trend toward slightly higher fines: in 1994–95, the median for all fines was $410; by 2000–01, it was $500; by 2006–07, it was $758, and in 2011–12 it was $800. In Canada, **fines** can be imposed alone or in conjunction with other sanctions, with this exception: if the offence carries a minimum or a maximum penalty of more than five years, the offender cannot receive a fine alone (see Table 11.3).

During 2011–12, the cases involving a fine as the most frequently imposed sentences were impaired driving (88 percent), drug possession (49 percent), other Criminal Code offences—traffic (35 percent), and failure to appear (33 percent). Not surprisingly, fines are rarely used as the most severe sanction in the category of crimes against

TABLE 11.3 Fines Used as Punishment in the Different Categories of Crime, 2011–12

Type of Offence[1]	Total Guilty Cases	Fine		
		Number	%	Median Amount ($)[4]
Violent offences	46,255	3,083	7	400
Homicide	132	6	5	1,100
Attempted murder	40	0	0	n/a
Robbery	2,391	16	1	375
Sexual assault	1,610	39	2	500
Other sexual offences[5]	1,551	58	4	500
Major assault[6]	10,986	662	6	500
Common assault	17,791	1,411	8	400
Uttering threats	8,948	767	9	300
Criminal harassment	1,609	65	4	400
Other violent offences	1,197	59	5	300
Property offences	54,561	7,226	13	250
Theft[7]	24,918	4,275	17	250
Break and enter	7,477	213	3	500
Fraud	8,101	806	10	300
Mischief	7,857	1,095	14	300
Possess stolen property	5,047	780	15	400
Other property offences	1,161	57	5	250
Administration of justice offences	60,723	13,420	22	250
Fail to appear	2,243	731	33	200
Breach of probation	25,353	4,713	19	250
Unlawfully at large	2,144	118	6	300
Fail to comply with order	24,887	6,175	25	200
Other admin. of justice offences	6,096	1,683	28	300
Other Criminal Code offences	9,866	1,854	19	250
Weapon offences	5,901	1,132	19	250
Prostitution	313	81	26	250
Disturbing the peace	868	278	32	250
Residual Criminal Code offences	2,784	363	13	300
Total Criminal Code (excl. traffic)	171,405	25,583	15	250
Criminal Code traffic offences	43,420	33,670	78	1,100
Impaired driving	34,780	30,633	88	1,200
Other Criminal Code traffic offences	8,640	3,037	35	900
Total Criminal Code offences	214,825	59,253	28	1,000
Other federal statute offences	32,159	12,951	40	300
Drug possession	7,582	3,726	49	300
Other drug offences[8]	6,478	492	8	1,000
Youth Criminal Justice Act	979	282	29	230
Residual federal statute offences	17,120	8,451	49	250
Total	**246,984**	**72,204**	**29**	**800**

[1] Cases that involve more than one charge are represented by the most serious offence.
Notes 2 and 3 are not applicable to fines and as a result are not included.
[4] Excludes cases in which the amount of the fine was unknown.
[5] Includes, for example, sexual interference, invitation to sexual touching, child pornography, luring a child via a computer, and sexual exploitation.
[6] Includes, for example, assault with a weapon (level 2) and aggravated assault (level 3).
[7] Includes, for example, theft over $5,000, theft $5,000 or under, as well as motor vehicle theft.
[8] Includes drug trafficking, production, importing, and exporting.

Note: Cases may involve more than one type of sentence and/or other sentences not shown, therefore, percentages do not total 100. A case is one or more charges against an accused person or company that were processed by the courts at the same time and received a final decision. The median represents the midpoint, where exactly half the custody sentences are above and half are below. Data exclude information from superior courts in Prince Edward Island, Quebec, Ontario, Manitoba, and Saskatchewan as well as municipal courts in Quebec due to the unavailability of data.

Source: Jillian Boyce, "Adult Criminal Court Statistics in Canada, 2011/2012." *Juristat* (June 2013), Statistics Canada Catalogue no 85-002-x, pp. 27–28, http://www.statcan.gc.ca/pub/85-002-x/2013001/article/11804-eng.pdf. Reproduced and distributed on an "as is" basis with the permission of Statistics Canada.

the person. The offences in this category for which fines were used most often were uttering threats and common assault (at 9 and 8 percent, respectively, followed by major assault (at 6 percent) (Boyce 2013).

Questions about the fairness of fines have surfaced over recent decades in Canada. In most jurisdictions, judges receive little guidance on how and against whom to impose fines, but it is agreed that once the facts of a case are considered, judges use fines as a sanction in an appropriate manner. In the 1970s, some provincial governments attempted to develop **fine option programs** as alternatives for people who could not pay the fines imposed on them by the courts. (Community service was a common option.) According to a report on fines by the Law Reform Commission (1975), fines can discriminate against poor offenders. It noted that 57.4 percent of Aboriginal admissions to provincial institutions in Saskatchewan in 1970–71 were for non-payment of fines, compared to 24.7 percent of non-Aboriginal admissions. The inability to pay fines is a significant reason why Aboriginal offenders are overrepresented in provincial and territorial correctional facilities; since Aboriginal people can experience high rates of unemployment in their communities, fines are not reasonable options for them (Frideres and Robertson 1994:110). As the *Report of the Alberta Task Force on the Criminal Justice System and Its Impact on the Indian and Métis People of Alberta* (Alberta 1991) stated, the use of custody for fine defaulters does not fulfill the principle of proportionality and the purposes of sentencing, which includes the protection of the community as well as deterrence.

One approach to avoiding the incarceration of fine defaulters was to have defence counsel introduce information about the accused's ability to pay a fine into the court record, subject to cross-examination by the Crown prosecutor. It was also possible for a judge to request that this information be included in a presentence report. Bill C-41 simplified the process of including this information when it introduced the provision that the court "may fine an offender under this section only if the court is satisfied that the offender is able to pay the fine." If the offender cannot pay, other alternative sanctions are to be considered, including probation, a conditional sentence, an absolute or conditional discharge, or incarceration.

Another alternative is **day fines**. The concept of day fines was introduced in Finland in 1921 and is based on the idea that a fine can satisfy the idea of proportionality by assessing an offender's net income as well as the seriousness of the crime. Day fines (in contrast to the current fixed-fine system) are weighted by a daily-income value taken from a chart similar to an income tax table; the offender's number of dependants is also considered. Evaluations of day fine programs in the United States have found that they are generally successful, in that they increase the amount of money collected from fines while at the same time reducing the number of arrest warrants for failure to pay. Even when the fine cannot be paid in full, most offenders pay at least some of the amount owed to the state (Hillsman 1990).

Intermediate Sanctions: How Well Do They Work?

In 1985, Sawyer called intermediate sanctions the future of corrections. But have they lived up to this? More than 20 years later, we are in a position to examine whether they have achieved their goals, particularly in the areas of reducing prison populations, saving money, and deterring crime. The results of several American evaluations are reviewed below.

Do Intermediate Sanctions Reduce Prison Crowding?

This question is perhaps the most critical of all. Advocates of ISPs have long argued that they decrease the number of offenders incarcerated. However, as Morris and Tonry (1990:223–34) point out, these advocates base their contention on the belief that most individuals convicted of a serious crime are sent to prison—an assumption that Morris and Tonry indicate is incorrect in that "most felonies never were or are not now punished by imprisonment." In reality, most offenders placed in ISPs would otherwise have been placed in regular probation programs or given suspended sentences instead of being sent to prison. Tonry (1990:178) also argues that some ISPs may "fill more prison beds than they empty" because so few offenders from prison are actually placed in these programs. ISPs are generally filled by low-risk offenders who normally would have been placed on regular probation.

Petersilia (1987:156–57), in her review of five EM programs, found that most offenders sentenced to them were not from prison, but rather were on regular probation. With few exceptions, "participants in the program had only been convicted of misdemeanors."

Are Intermediate Sanctions a Cost-Saving Alternative?

One of the most common arguments in favour of ISPs is that they cost less than incarceration programs. Most of these arguments are based on average per-offender costs, which many have pointed out is a misleading approach to evaluating the financial savings of ISPs. One reason for this is the length of time that offenders are sentenced to prison or to an ISP. Morris and Tonry (1990) point out that it is misleading to directly compare costs, because if the average offender serves 12 months in an ISP at a cost of $3,000 per month but would otherwise have served three months in prison at a total cost of $14,000 the ISP costs more, not less.

Comparing per-offender costs is misleading for another reason: it assumes that all offenders are diverted into ISPs from prison. In fact, many ISP participants (a figure that varies from 50 percent to 80 percent, depending on the jurisdiction and the type of program) have been diverted from regular probation programs. According to Tonry (1990:182), ISPs' "costs per day are six times higher than the cost of ordinary probation." Moreover, the greater the number of individuals placed in an ISP directly from the courts, the less the savings because fewer people are being taken out of prison.

Furthermore, most cost comparisons look only at the costs of building a new prison but ignore the costs of operating an ISP, which is labour-intensive. If 25 offenders in an ISP require the hiring and training of four to eight new employees, this "increases direct outlays in the form of salaries and expanded overhead expenses, but also produces longer-term financial commitments in the form of employment benefits and pensions" (U.S. General Accounting Office 1990:27).

When all costs, both direct and marginal, are factored in, any savings may be limited. For example, Petersilia and Turner (1993:309) studied 14 programs and reported that in "no site did intermediate sanction programs result in cost-savings during the one year follow-up period." This was due mainly to the large number of technical violations, revocations, and incarcerations and the cost of court appearances, resulting in costs up to twice as high as those for routine probation and parole supervision.

Another argument in favour of intermediate punishments is that many of them charge a fee to the offenders participating in them. Renzema and Skelton (1990:14) point out that in the programs they reviewed, about two-thirds of the participants paid fees. The average cost was $200 a month, with probationers paying "an average of $155 a month while inmates pay an average of $228 a month. A few programs charge clients as much as $15 a day for monitoring."

Tonry (1990) has pointed out a significant error made by those who evaluate the cost savings of ISPs: they fail to include the cost of recidivists. Since offenders in these programs may be caught for technical violations or new crimes and be sent to prison, the additional time incarcerated must also be factored into any comparison of costs. With recidivism rates at about 40 to 50 percent, taking incarceration time into account in the cost-benefit analysis would substantially increase the costs of these programs.

Can Intermediate Sanctions Control Crime?

The third point raised by advocates of ISPs relates to their effectiveness in controlling crime. It is argued that more intensive supervision cannot help but reduce crime. Basing their arguments on the recidivism rates reported in early evaluation studies, they emphasize that ISPs have the potential both to "control offenders in the community and to facilitate their growth to crime-free lives" (Morris and Tonry 1990).

However, some studies have found that many offenders released from ISPs committed serious crimes. Even low-risk offenders in ISPs have been found to reoffend at a high rate on release. For example, almost 27 percent of offenders in three provinces recidivated, although they had lower risk levels than either the inmates or the probationers to whom they were being compared. According to Bonta et al. (2000), the lower recidivism rates of those in EM programs can explain their lower risk. Many studies (Petersilia and Turner 1993; Wallerstedt 1984) have found that individuals released from ISPs often have high recidivism rates and that many of their offences are serious. In addition, many researchers have reported that these programs fail to result in any reduction in crime rates. Pearson (1986:443–44), for example, concluded that "we can be confident that intermediate sanction programs at least did not increase recidivism rates."

In one of the most comprehensive analyses of its kind, Petersilia and Turner (1993) reported that in the 14 ISPs they studied, no participants were re-arrested less often, had a longer time before being re-arrested, or were arrested for less serious offences than those individuals on regular probation. When the researchers included technical violations in their recidivism measure, "the record for intermediate sanction programs looks somewhat grimmer" (Petersilia and Turner 1993:310–11). About 65 percent of the offenders in these programs recorded a technical violation, compared to 38 percent of those offenders on regular probation. The researchers also found no support for the argument that offenders arrested for technical violations reduced the incidence of any future criminal acts.

Do Intermediate Sanctions Work?

The concerns raised about alternative sanctions do not mean that they should be abandoned as another failed experiment. Perhaps there was too great an expectation that these programs would somehow "save" the current correctional crisis by reducing prison populations and recidivism, besides making communities safer. As Finckenhauer (1982) has noted, the history of corrections is filled with great expectations but, at the same time, littered with one failed panacea after another. New programs are attractive because they always promise to do so much, at a minimal cost. When programs are poorly conceived and implemented and, as a result, fail to reach their goals, it is not surprising that they are labelled as another program that "didn't work."

Yet a number of important lessons can be learned by examining the rise and growth of alternative correctional programs, particularly the rapid growth in intermediate sanctions. One lesson is that the number of offenders entering the correctional system is beyond the control of criminal justice officials. Political demands for tougher penalties and a "war on crime" can have a significant impact on the operations of all facets of our criminal justice system. The police are under more pressure to arrest and charge more alleged criminals; the courts are under more pressure to deal with these alleged offenders more speedily. But when offenders enter the correctional system, often with long sentences, correctional officials have a hard time knowing where to put them.

Underlying ISPs is the justice model. The results to date have revealed not only that specific programs do not reach their objectives, but also that the justice model preference of alternative sanctions is open to question. However, evidence is emerging that some intermediate punishment programs, when merged with rehabilitation-based principles, achieve more favourable results (Gendreau et al. 1994). Researchers who have evaluated programs and who have seen the high rates of recidivism in these programs have recommended the inclusion of rehabilitation. For example, in their study of the Florida Community Control Program, Smith and Akers (1993:228) noted that "a more persuasive model might move back in the direction of community reintegration and propose that occupation skill enhancement, education, substance abuse treatment, behavior modification and other practices be added to the principle of closely supervising home confinement." And in their analysis of the 14 sites experimenting with intermediate supervision probation, Petersilia and Turner (1993:321) reported that in the three California locations included in their study, offenders who "received counselling, held jobs, paid restitution, and did community service were arrested 10–20 percent less often than were other offenders."

These comments are consistent with a growing literature on the importance of introducing effective rehabilitative components into ISPs. Any such program would have to identify which offenders are to receive treatment. This means that the principles of risk, need, and responsivity must be introduced (see Chapter 12) (Andrews et al. 1990). Fulton et al. (1997:68), in their analysis of ISPs, commented that when they are combined with effective rehabilitation-based approaches they may be more effective if more policymakers call for "abandoning ISPs that seek only to control and punish offenders in favour of programs that give equal primacy to changing offenders." As Petersilia and Turner (1993:320) point out, placing drug-dependent offenders into an ISP that "forbids drug use, provides frequent drug testing, and provides no assured access to drug treatment virtually guarantees high violation rates." The potential for intermediate sanctions with a strong rehabilitative component exists, but only if such programs "provide the opportunity to channel offenders into treatments that address criminogenic needs—sources of criminality that are not targeted and affected by surveillance and punishment" (Cullen et al. 1995).

SUMMING UP AND LOOKING FORWARD

While many individuals who break the law will be punished for their actions by being sent to a correctional facility, a number of options exist for individuals who are found guilty of certain criminal offences. In Canada, as in most Western societies, there is a distinction between serious criminal acts that require the offender to serve time in a correctional facility and less serious criminal acts that potentially allow the offender to remain in the community.

There are different types of mechanisms by which those individuals who are convicted of a crime can remain in the community. For example, an offender may be fined, placed on probation, or be sent to a provincial/territorial or federal correctional facility. Those individuals who receive a community sentence mostly serve their sentences in the community, as alternatives to custody. While these types of sentences vary, all of them involve some type of direct supervision of offenders. They are used for a variety of purposes, including punishment, the protection of society, and rehabilitation. Overall, these approaches are seen as being more effective punishments than custody. Probation is the first type of community service discussed in this chapter, as it is the most common type of community sentence in Canada. Each province/territory has its own probation service, as most offenders who are sentenced receive a term of probation at their sentencing. About 20 years ago the federal government introduced another type of alternative type of custody (conditional sentence). Questions have been raised about the possibility of alternatives to custody having a net-widening impact and having latent factors that must be understood. Various types of intermediate punishments have been introduced (mostly in the United States) since the 1980s. These were introduced by the claims that they better deter crime, provide greater protection for the public, are less expensive, and are more effective in reducing recidivism. The federal government is responsible for conditional release programs such as full parole and statutory release. The programs release offenders into the community from federal correctional facilities prior to the end of their sentence.

A large number of issues have been raised about community sentences and conditional release programs. Some are pessimistic about the effectiveness of these types of sentences and conditional release programs to effectively reduce criminal behaviour, while others don't think they are harsh enough. Others question the decisions of probation and parole officers to release offenders into the community. According to some critics, community sentences widen the net by bringing offenders into the criminal justice system who would better be dealt with normally on an informal basis.

Review Questions:

1. What is the rationale for having alternative sanctions?
2. What are the advantages and disadvantages of alternative sanctions?
3. Is net widening an inevitable result of alternative sanctions?
4. What are the limits that have been placed on conditional sentences since their introduction?
5. What are the purposes of the various kinds of intermediate punishments?
6. Are intermediate punishments successful in terms of reaching their goals?

Conditional Release Programs

Conditional release programs include **full parole, day parole, statutory release**, and **temporary absences**. The number of individuals on conditional release programs has generally remained stable since 2008–09 (see Figure 11.4). Full parole allows offenders to serve a portion of their sentence in the community until that sentence has expired. Most inmates in the federal correctional system can apply to the **Parole Board of Canada** (PBC) for full parole after serving one-third of their time or seven years, whichever is shorter. Offenders who face steeper eligibility requirements include those serving life sentences or sentences of preventive detention. Offenders serving a sentence of two years less a day in a provincial institution are eligible to apply for parole after serving one-third of their time. Ontario and Quebec are the only provinces to operate their own parole boards. The PBC has authority over all provincial inmates in all other provinces. An offender released on full parole is placed under the supervision of a parole or probation officer and is required to follow general and specific conditions similar to those granted probationers. As with all types of conditional release, offenders can be reincarcerated if they fail to meet the conditions of their parole or if they break the law. Figure 11.5 overviews when offenders can become eligible for the different types of conditional release throughout their sentence.

Day parole differs from full parole in that it is granted only for short periods of time, to a maximum of four months. However, it is renewable for a period of up to one year. Most offenders in federal and provincial correctional facilities become eligible for day parole six months before they are eligible for full parole. The PBC has the authority to grant day parole to offenders in both federal and provincial correctional institutions (see *Investigating: Accelerated Parole Review*). **Provincial parole boards** do not have the power to grant day parole.

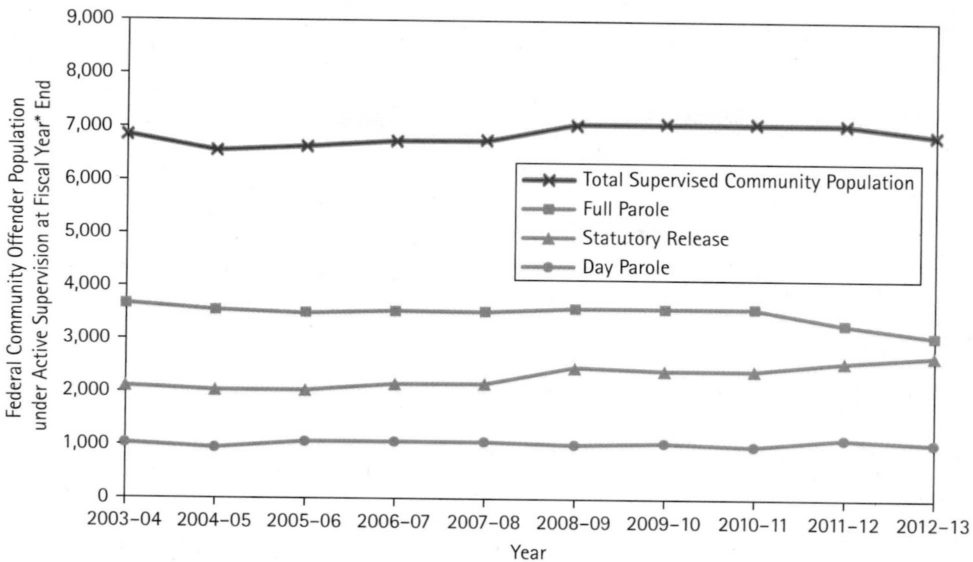

FIGURE 11.4 The Supervised Federal Offender Population in the Community Has Remained Stable since 2008–09

*A fiscal year runs from April 1 to March 31 of the following year.

Source: Corrections and Conditional Release Statistics Overview Annual Report 2013, Fig C20, p. 71, Public Safety Canada. Reproduced with the permission of the Minister of Public Safety and Emergency Preparedness Canada, 2015. https://www.publicsafety.gc.ca/cnt/rsrcs/pblctns/crrctns-cndtnl-rls-2013/crrctns-cndtnl-rls-2013-eng.pdf.

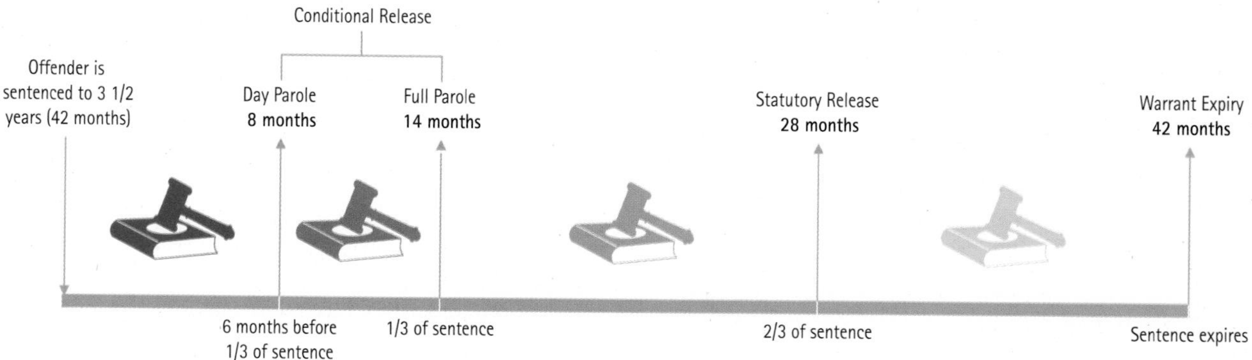

FIGURE 11.5 Offenders Can Be Eligible for Different Types of Release throughout the Length of Their Sentence

Day Parole: Day parole is a conditional release that is granted or denied by the Parole Board. Offenders serve the remainder of their sentence under CSC supervision in community facilities.

Full Parole: Full parole is a conditional release that is granted or denied by the Parole Board. Offenders serve the remainder of their sentence in a location of their choice in the community, and must report to parole officers or the police.

Statutory Release: Statutory release is a legislated release that allows offenders other than those with a life sentence, to serve the final third of their sentence in the community in a location of their choice, unless they are required to reside within a community facility under CSC supervision.

Warrant Expiry: Warrant expiry is a required release at the end of an offender's sentence. It is a full release for offenders who were considered too dangerous to return to the community under statutory release.

Source: *Report of the Auditor General of Canada (2014)*, Office of the Auditor General of the Canada, p.13. http://oag-bvg.gc.ca/internet/English/parl_oag_201405_04_e_39335.html Reproduced with the permission of the Minister of Public Works and Government Services, 2015.

Investigating: Accelerated Parole Review

Accelerated parole review (APR) was included into conditional release programs with the passing of the Corrections and Conditional Release Act (CCRA) (1992). APR was created to permit non-violent federal offenders with a low risk of reoffending to be released as early as possible to serve the rest of their sentence under supervision in the community. This enabled the CSC and PBC to focus more of their resources upon offenders sentenced for a violent or serious drug-related offence and considered to be a high risk to reoffend.

The idea behind APR was to allow accelerated processing of parole applications by offenders serving their first sentence of incarceration who were not convicted of an offence involving violence or a serious drug-related offence for which a court had stipulated a specific parole eligibility date. APR guaranteed that an offender's case would be reviewed in advance by the PBC in order that offenders be granted parole as soon as possible. Offenders entitled to APR benefited from a presumption in favour of parole; that is, the PBC could not refuse parole unless it is of the opinion that there were reasonable grounds to believe they would commit a violent offence prior to the expiration of their sentence. In order to benefit from APR, offenders had to meet a number of conditions:

- they must be serving their first sentence in a penitentiary;
- they must not have been convicted of murder or of being an accomplice to murder;
- they must not have been sentenced to imprisonment for life;
- they must not have committed an offence related to terrorism or organized crime;
- they must not have been sentenced for an offence set out in Schedule I of the CCRA;
- they must not have been convicted of an offence set out in Schedule II to the CCRA in respect of which the court has ordered that the offender not be eligible for parole before serving at least half of their sentence; and they must not have been the subject of a decision revoking day parole.

Between 1992 and 1997, APR applied only to full parole; that is, after an offender served one-third or seven years of his or her sentence (whichever was the shortest). The CCRA was amended in 1997 to allow offenders on day parole to apply for APR. This meant offenders entitled to APR were eligible for day parole after serving one-sixth of their sentence or six months (whichever is the longest).

Since its inception there have been numerous criticisms directed at APR. For example, some critics were concerned about selecting offenders serving their first sentence in a federal custodial facility, pointing out that most of these individuals already had served time, but in a provincial/territorial custodial institution. Other critics argued that allowing offenders to gain APR distorted the sentence handed out by the sentencing judge, especially in the case of offenders receiving lengthy sentences. In response to the publicity of various Ponzi schemes and the conviction of some of those individuals who had been operating them (see Chapter 4), people became concerned that these offenders could soon be released on APR. As a result, Parliament agreed to look at APR.

In September 2009 a private member's bill was introduced into Parliament proposing to end APR for granting day parole. If the bill had passed, it meant that offenders would have to wait to apply for APR at full parole review (as existed between 1992 and 1997). In addition, the federal government asked the CSC to review APR. In October 2007, the CSC submitted its report, A Roadmap to Strengthening Public Safety: Report of the Correctional Service of Canada Review Panel (2007), which recommended ending APR on the basis that offenders granted APR generally had a higher recidivism rate compared to other types of parole. In its review, the CSC noted that in 2007–08, 6 of the 831 offenders granted APR had their parole revoked for committing a violent offence, while another 72 had their APR revoked for committing a non-violent offence. In comparison, under the regular parole process, 6 of the 527 offenders released had their parole revoked as a result of committing a violent offence, and another 22 had their parole revoked for committing a non-violent offence. The CSC Review Panel also stated that APR should be abolished since they deemed it necessary to emphasize that parole is not a right, but rather it has to be earned. The federal government then introduced Bill C-53, which failed to receive Royal Assent before the proroguing of Parliament. In June 2010, the Conservatives introduced this legislation as Bill C-59, An Act to amend the Corrections and Conditional Release (accelerated parole review), and to make consequential amendments to other Acts in order to abolish APR. It passed Parliament and received Royal Assent at the end of March 2011. The impact was felt almost immediately, as Howard Sapers, the Correctional Investigator, noted that the increase in the number of federal female offenders in custody was largely due to the government abolishing APR.

Temporary absences (TAs) are granted for four main reasons—medical, compassionate, administrative, and family and community contact. Such absences can last from a few hours up to 15 days. A **medical TA** is granted when an offender requires treatment not available in a correctional facility. An example of a **compassionate TA** is when a family member falls seriously ill or dies. Family and community contact TAs are granted to allow offenders to participate in community activities that contribute in their adjustment in the community. An **administrative TA** is given when an offender needs to make contact with community agencies prior to his or her release (Grant and Belcourt 1992). TAs may be escorted or unescorted. An offender on an **escorted temporary absence** must be accompanied by a representative of the correctional facility. An escorted TA may be granted at any time after sentencing. TAs are the responsibility of the superintendent of the institution, under the authority of the CSC.

Federal offenders not granted parole may, under statutory release, be released into the community before the sentence's expiration. Provincial inmates can gain early release for earned remission (good behaviour) and not be supervised in the community; federal offenders released under statutory release are supervised in the community as if they were on parole. However, all inmates leaving a correctional institution on statutory release must, before their release, have their cases reviewed by the PBC. The Corrections and Conditional Release Act (CCRA) allows the board to detain an offender on statutory supervision beyond and up to the normal release date. Furthermore, the board has the power to specify that an offender released on statutory supervision will live in a community residential facility if it feels that the offender will be a threat to the community or will commit a crime before the termination of his or her sentence.

The PBC does not grant parole to every applicant; in fact, in most years, fewer than 50 percent of applications succeed. Just over 46 percent of federal and provincial applicants for full parole succeeded in 2012–13. Of the 3,234 male inmates who applied for full parole in 2012–13, only 912 (28 percent) succeeded. And of the 230 women serving a federal sentence who applied for full parole, 90 (39 percent) succeeded. Offenders who were successful in obtaining their first full parole served almost 46 percent of their sentence. Women who were granted their first full parole served slightly less of their sentence than their male counterparts (45 percent compared to 47 percent, respectively).

In comparison, the success rates for those applying for day parole were much higher. Only 70 of the 356 women (19.7 percent) who applied for day parole were denied, while the success rate for males was 66.5 percent (2,817 of the 4,233 males who applied were successful). Overall, offenders granted their first day parole served about one-third of their sentence. Males granted their first day parole served almost the same amount of time as females (38.8 percent compared to 38.3 percent, respectively) (Public Safety Canada 2013).

It is possible that an inmate will never be released on a conditional release program; in such cases, the inmate is detained until the warrant expiry date. Detainees fall into one of three categories. The first category includes those convicted of offences found in Schedule I of the CCRA. This category is especially likely to contain offenders who are thought likely to commit another offence causing death or serious injury if released into the community through a conditional release program. The second category, too, contains those convicted of offences found in **Schedule I**—specifically, sexual offences involving children. The third category contains those convicted of **Schedule II offences**. This category is most likely to contain those believed likely to commit a serious drug offence while on a conditional release program. According to the PBC's own statistics, the number of inmates detained increased from 184 in 1991–92 to a high of 484 in 1995–96; in 2012–13, the number was 232, which was the highest number since 2003–04, when the number of individuals detained was 279 (Public Safety Canada 2013).

How Effective Are Conditional Release Programs?

There is much disagreement in Canada today regarding the effectiveness of conditional release programs. Much of this debate has focused on the administration of parole. Roberts (1988), in his study of attitudes toward the Parole Board of Canada, found that two-thirds of Canadians considered the board too lenient. Another study, this one conducted by the Canadian Criminal Justice Association (1987), found that most Canadians felt the board was releasing too many offenders. Adams (1990:11) found that most Canadians held negative views about parole. Most of the people he interviewed said that offenders "get off too soon, that parole is virtually automatic after one third of the sentence and that the nature of the offender's crime and concurrent risk to society are not given proper consideration." Adams (ibid.) also reported that while parole is actually part of the offender's sentence, it is "not viewed generally by the public as part of the 'punishment' for a crime."

Since offenders commit different types of crimes and have different criminal backgrounds, is it fair to treat all offenders on conditional release programs the same way? Also, offenders have their conditional release orders revoked for different reasons—for example, for a technical violation such as missing a curfew, or for a conviction for an indictable offence while under the supervision of the parole board. The PBC measures the effectiveness of conditional release on the basis of three factors:

(1) the rate of success;
(2) the number of charges for serious offences committed by offenders while on release in the community, by release type, in eight offence categories that emphasize violent crimes (murder, attempted murder, sexual assault, major assault, hostage taking, unlawful confinement, robbery, and so-called sensational incidents such as arson); and
(3) post-warrant-expiry recidivism.

What Are Recidivism Rates?

A key factor in assessing the success of an offender on a conditional release program is the **recidivism rate**. In general, recidivism means the readmission, because of a violation, of an offender to an institution. This rate is usually expressed in terms of the number of readmissions within a particular period of time.

The two most common categories applied when measuring recidivism are technical violations and convictions for new offences. A **technical violation** has occurred when an offender breaks a condition of the release program. This type of violation does not count as a new criminal offence. Nouwens et al. (1993) illustrate the concept of technical violations by discussing a "fraud offender who was told to abstain from alcohol and drugs while on release [and who] decides to celebrate his new-found freedom by getting drunk at a party. The police are called . . . and find out the offender is on parole." Other examples of technical violations include failing to stay within a specified geographical location and failing to maintain a job.

Recidivism rates are considered the most important figures for assessing the success or failure of a conditional release program. In 2012–13, the success rate for all offenders on full parole was 85 percent. Parole was revoked for breach of conditions in 134 cases (11 percent), for non-violent offences in 39 cases (6.1 percent), and for violent offences in three cases (0.3 percent) (see Figure 11.6). The rates of successful completion for day parole were higher than those for full parole. The success rate for all offenders was 89.3 percent. Nine percent of day paroles were revoked for a breach of conditions. In addition, 1.5 percent of individuals were revoked for a non-violent offence, and another 0.1 percent for a violent offence (see Figure 11.7).

Of the three conditional release programs, offenders on statutory release had the highest recidivism rates (see Figure 11.8). The success rate for all offenders on

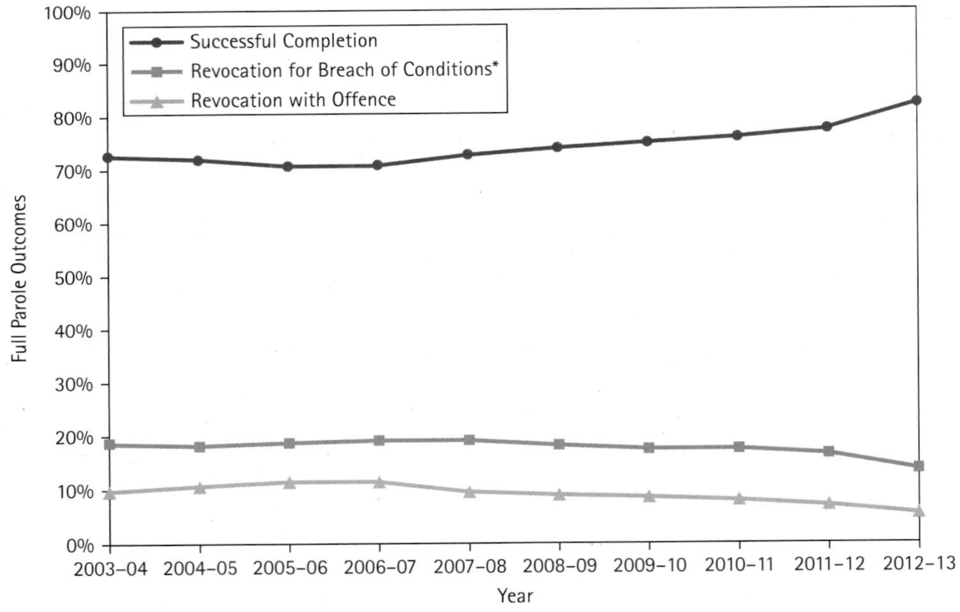

FIGURE 11.6 The Majority of Full Paroles Are Successfully Completed

*Revocation for Breach of Conditions includes revocation with outstanding charges.

Source: Corrections and Conditional Release Statistics Overview Annual Report 2013, Figure D8, p. 91 https://www.publicsafety.gc.ca/cnt/rsrcs/pblctns/crrctns-cndtnl-rls-2013/crrctns-cndtnl-rls-2013-eng.pdf Reproduced with the permission of the Ministry of Public Safety and Emergency Preparedness Canada 2015.

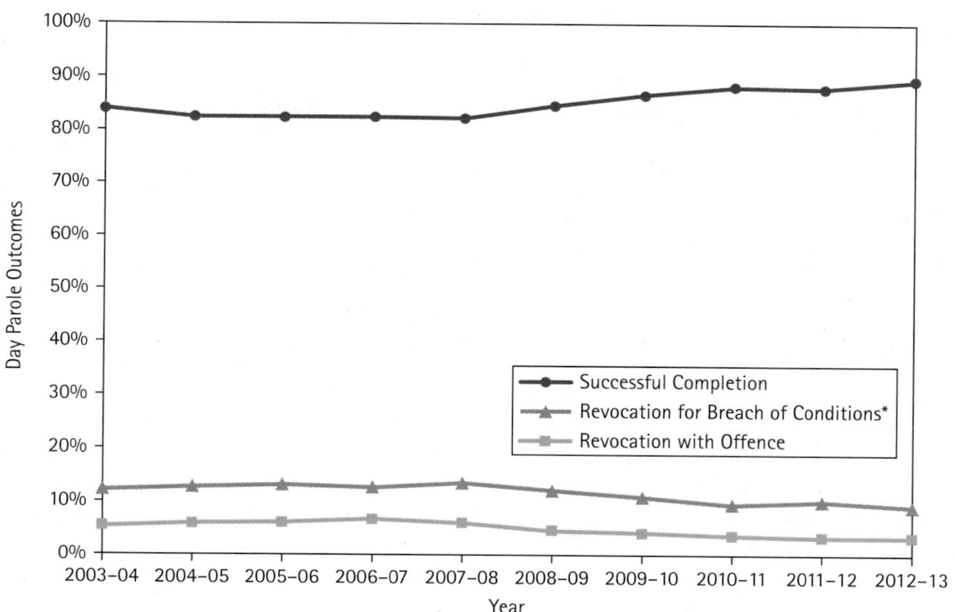

FIGURE 11.7 The Majority of Day Parolees Are Successfully Completed

*Revocation for Breach of Conditions includes revocation with outstanding charges.

Source: Corrections and Conditional Release Statistics Overview Annual Report 2013, Figure D7, p. 89 https://www.publicsafety.gc.ca/cnt/rsrcs/pblctns/crrctns-cndtnl-rls-2013/crrctns-cndtnl-rls-2013-eng.pdf. Reproduced with the permission of the Ministry of Public Safety and Emergency Preparedness Canada 2015.

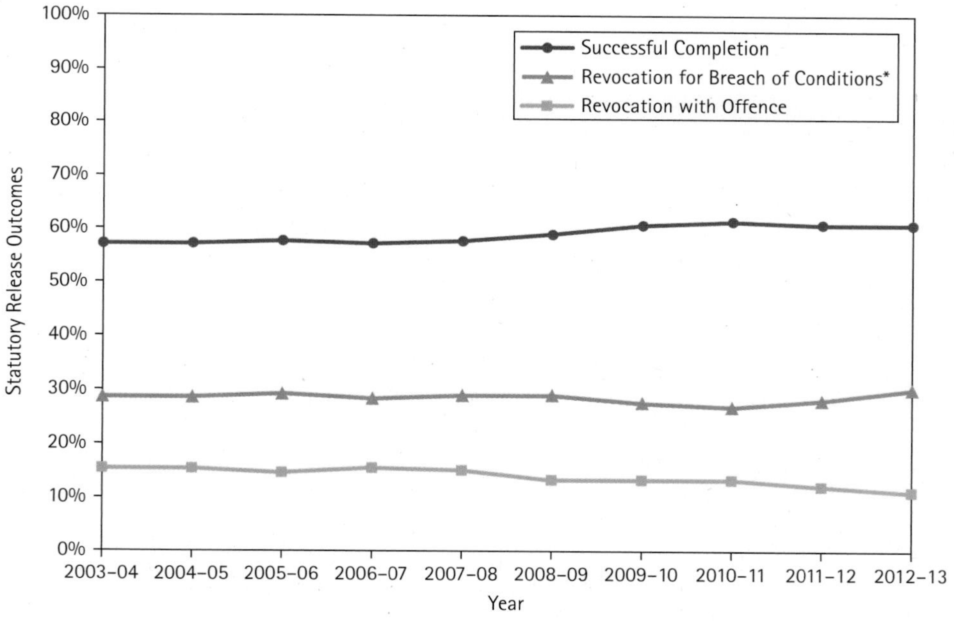

FIGURE 11.8 Statutory Releases Have the Lowest Rates of Successful Completion

*Revocation for Breach of Conditions includes revocation with outstanding charges.

Source: Corrections and Conditional Release Statistics Overview Annual Report 2013, Figure D9, p. 93 https://www.publicsafety.gc.ca/cnt/rsrcs/pblctns/crrctns-cndtnl-rls-2013/crrctns-cndtnl-rls-2013-eng.pdf Reproduced with the permission of the Minister of Public Safety and Emergency Preparedness Canada, 2015.

statutory release was 60.6 percent. In 2012–13, 30.7 percent of statutory releases were revoked for a breach of conditions; 7.1 percent were revoked for a non-violent offence and another 1.5 percent were revoked for a violent offence (Public Safety Canada 2013).

Recidivism rates can also be measured in terms of the different lengths of time that offenders are on a conditional release program. Nouwens and colleagues (1993) compared the **short-term** and **long-term recidivism** rates of 1,000 federal offenders. Short-term recidivism was measured by looking at those offenders released over a three-year period (April 1, 1990 to March 31, 1993). The percentage of supervised offenders readmitted to a correctional facility for technical violations was 2.8 percent; for those readmitted for a new offence, it was 2 percent. Long-term recidivists were defined as those offenders released during a 10-year period (April 1, 1975 to March 31, 1985). Over this 10-year period, 15,418 offenders were released on full parole. Of these, 72 percent (11,704) completed their sentence without being returned to custody for any reason. After these individuals had completed their parole, about 10 percent committed a new offence, for which they were returned to the federal correctional system. Over the same period, 27,124 offenders were released on mandatory supervision. Fifty-seven percent completed their sentence successfully; 24 percent had their release revoked for technical violations; and 19 percent were readmitted for a new offence. Thirty-four percent of those offenders who successfully completed their statutory release supervision were readmitted to a federal institution after their sentence was finished.

A profile of readmissions to federal correctional institutions over a six-year period conducted by the CSC found a substantial difference between recidivism rates for those on full parole and those on statutory release. Of the 8,751 offenders released on full parole, 30 percent were readmitted, compared to 58 percent of the 17,769 offenders placed in statutory release. The majority of offenders returned to a federal institution for violating the terms of their conditional release did so within 12 months of release. Also, 81 percent of all offenders who failed on full parole or statutory release were readmitted within 24 months. After 24 months, however, the incidence of inmates being returned to a federal institution dramatically declined. According to the CSC (1990:12), "after the two-year follow-up point, the number of offenders returning to federal institutions dropped to 2 percent and gradually tapered off each subsequent year. At the six-year follow-up point, fewer than 1 percent of offenders were readmitted." This study revealed that for offenders on statutory release, the critical point for readmission to a federal institution arrives within six months of release, whereas for offenders on full parole, the second six-month period is the most critical.

Criminal Justice Insight

Parole and the Life Means Life Act

In March 2015, the federal Conservative government introduced legislation that would introduce life without parole for some murderers. The proposed legislation (the Life Means Life Act) would amend both the Criminal Code and the CCRA to ensure that people who commit designated offences would receive a mandatory life sentence without the chance of parole. The designated offences are

(1) first degree murder that is planned and deliberate and that involves sexual assault, kidnapping or forcible confinement, terrorism, the killing of police officers or corrections officers, or conduct of a "particularly brutal nature," and
(2) high treason.

The proposed bill will give the courts the discretion to impose a life sentence without the chance of parole for

(1) any other first degree murder where a sentence of life without parole is not mandatory, and
(2) second degree murder where the murderer has previously been convicted of either a murder or an intentional killing under the Crimes against Humanity and War Crimes Act.

The legislation will also allow an individual serving a life without parole sentence to apply to the Minister of Public Safety for exceptional release after serving no less than 35 years.

Critics of the legislation pointed out that homicide rates are at their lowest in decades (see Chapter 4). In addition, others point out that the number of violent crimes committed by someone being supervised on a conditional release program has decreased dramatically since 2008–09 (see Figure 11.9).

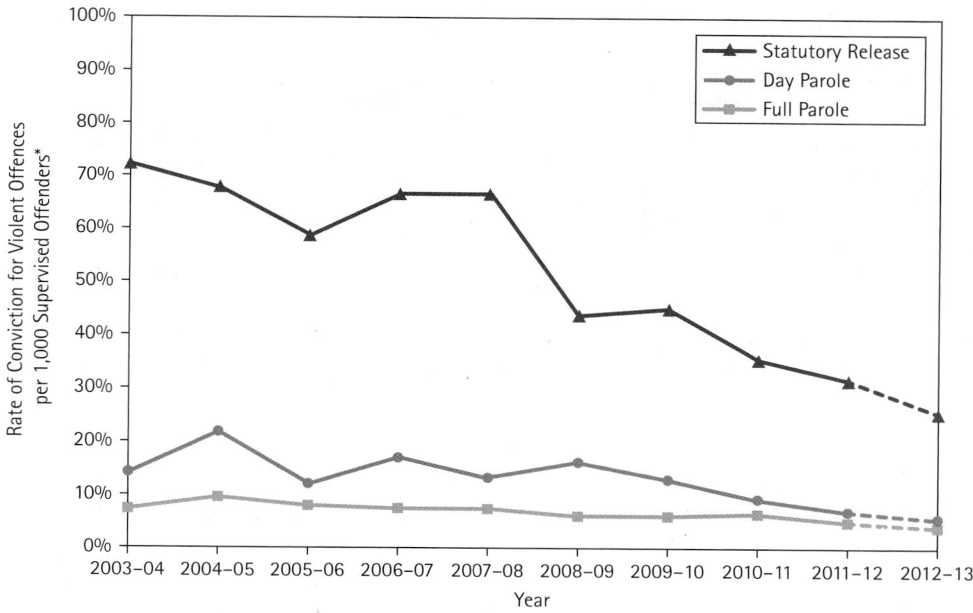

FIGURE 11.9 Over the Past Decade, the Rate of Violent Conviction for Offenders While under Supervision Has Declined

*Supervised offenders include offenders who are on parole, statutory release, those temporarily detained in federal institutions, and those who are unlawfully at large.

Source: Corrections and Conditional Release Statistics Overview Annual Report 2013, Figure D10, p. 95. www.publicsafety.gc.ca/cnt/rsrcs/pb/ctns/cttctns-cndntl-rls-2013/crrctns-cndntl-rls-2013-eng.pdf Reproduced with the permission of the Minister of Public Safety and Emergency Preparedness, 2015.

Are those who commit a violent crime such as murder bad risks for parole and at risk of reoffending once released? Edwin (1992) investigated the recidivism rates of 2,900 homicide offenders released between 1975 and 1990 to determine their success rate on full parole. Of these offenders, 658 had been convicted of first or second degree murder. The vast majority (77.5 percent) successfully completed their conditional release program, while 13.3 percent were incarcerated for a technical violation of their full parole and 9.2 percent for the commission of an indictable offence. Of the 69 indictable offences committed by the released offenders, 21 (30.4 percent) were narcotics offences, 12 (17.5 percent) were property offences, 6 (8.7 percent) involved robbery, and 17 (24.6 percent) were for "other" Criminal Code offences (ibid.:7).

Edwin also studied the full parole and supervision success rates of 2,242 offenders convicted of manslaughter between January 1, 1975, and March 31, 1990. Almost all of these offenders (93 percent) were released on a conditional release program. Forty-seven percent were released on full parole and 53 percent on statutory release supervision. Twenty-two percent of those released on full parole were reincarcerated: 14.6 percent for a technical violation, 6.5 percent for an indictable offence, and 0.5 percent for a summary conviction offence. Of those released on statutory release, 41 percent had their full parole revoked. Thirty-one percent were revoked for a technical violation of the conditions of their parole order, 10 percent for an indictable offence, and 1 percent for a summary offence.

Stys (2010) reviewed the success of federal offenders convicted of criminal organization offences (ss. 467.11 to 467.13 of the Criminal Code). In total, she identified 451 offenders convicted of a criminal organization offence between 1997 and 2009. Along with their current criminal organization offence, they were also convicted of drug offences (59.6 percent) and attempted murder (8.2 percent). Overall, 396 of the 451 offenders (87.6 percent) were identified as gang members during intake. Of this number, 418 were non-Aboriginal males, 19 were Aboriginal males, and 14 were women, and their average sentence length was 5.2 years. They were assessed, on average, as being medium risk with high needs, and with high reintegration potential. Of the 451 offenders, 332 had been released into the community. Most (76.4 percent) were released on day parole or statutory release (44.9 percent). Of those released, 42 (12.7 percent) were readmitted to a federal custodial facility. Most had their release revoked for a breach of condition (76.2 percent), while six (14.3 percent) were convicted of a new offence.

There is much public concern about the release of **special needs offenders**—such as those diagnosed with mental disorders—on conditional release programs. Porporino and Madoc (1993) compared the recidivism rates of 36 male federal offenders identified as having a mental disorder with those of a matched group of 36 federal offenders without mental disorders. During the four-year study, almost as many offenders *with* mental disorders were released (67 percent) as those without (75 percent). However, offenders with mental disorders were more likely to be released on statutory release (83 percent), while offenders without mental disorders (44 percent) were released more often on parole. In addition, Porporino and Madoc (ibid.:17) reported "a tendency for mentally disordered offenders to serve more time before release and a greater proportion of their sentence."

The same study looked at recidivism at two points during the release period: six months after release and 24 months after release. No significant differences were found in the recidivism rates between the two groups during the first six months of conditional release, although more offenders without mental disorders were returned to custody for a new offence or a new violent offence. After 24 months, however, those with mental disorders were more likely to have their conditional release suspended owing to concern about the probability of further violent offences (Madoc and Brown 1994:11). In contrast, offenders without mental disorders were more likely to have their conditional release revoked for the commission of a new offence.

Post-warrant-expiry recidivism rates are of interest to the PBC, which uses these figures as indicators of long-term effectiveness. However, offences committed after warrant expiry are beyond the control of the PBC. According to Larocque (1998:22), information concerning the recidivism rates of federal offenders after "warrant expiry on SR [statutory release] indicates that offenders reaching warrant expiry on statutory release are 3 to 4 times more likely to be readmitted to a federal institution than offenders who complete their sentence on full parole." In addition, recidivism rates are higher for all groups of offenders who have been in the community for longer periods, regardless of the type of conditional release program they were in.

SUMMING UP AND LOOKING FORWARD

Conditional release programs differ from community sentences in a number of ways. While probation is a substitute for custody, parole follows confinement in a correctional facility. Another difference is that community sentences are a sentencing option that sets the conditions for release, while parole is an option for release made by a parole board that sets the terms of the release. Community sentences are under provincial/territorial control, while almost all parole decisions are made by a national agency, the Parole Board of Canada. There are three main types of conditional release programs: full parole, day parole, and statutory release. Most offenders successfully complete full and day parole, while the lowest rate of success is experienced by those on statutory release. Recidivism can be measured in a number of ways; the most common approach is to count the individuals whose parole is revoked for any reason and who are subsequently returned to a correctional facility. In recent years, specialized courts have been introduced in an attempt to lower recidivism rates of offenders. These new types of court are the subject of the next section.

Review Questions:

1. What is the difference between day parole and full parole?
2. What happens when someone is not admitted to a conditional release program and has served his or her entire sentence?
3. What are the different types of recidivism measures? Which measure is most commonly used?
4. Why do you think that people on full parole have the lowest recidivism rate?
5. Why do you think statutory release is the least successful of all conditional release programs?

What Are Problem-Solving Courts?

Probation, conditional sentences, and all types of conditional release programs are sometimes referred to as "traditional" alternatives or forms of community corrections as they involve people who have been directed to them after having been found guilty in court. In the past 25 to 30 years, however, new alternatives to these approaches (e.g., drug courts and mental health courts) have emerged within the criminal justice systems of many Western nations (see the *Investigating* and *Criminal Justice Focus* features

Investigating: Mental Health Courts

Deinstitutionalization refers to the idea that incarceration has criminogenic effects upon individuals. As a result, there needs to be a reduction in the prison population through the establishment of community-based alternatives. Since the 1960s, there has been a deinstitutionalization of mental health cases in Canada from psychiatric and general hospitals. Some believe that one of the results of the deinstitutionalization of the mental health cases has been an increase in the number of individuals with mental illness coming to the attention of the law, being arrested and remanded and then sent to a provincial or federal correctional facility (Bernstein and Seltzer 2003). Schneider (2000) points out that during the 1990s in Canada, the number of mentally disordered individuals accused in the Canadian criminal justice system grew at a rate of over 10 percent a year. Mental disorders have also been found to be more prevalent among incarcerated offenders in Canada (Johnson 2003). In 2010–11, the Correctional Service of Canada reported that 9,200 offenders received mental health care services in federal custodial facilities; 45 percent of all men offenders and 69 percent of all women offenders received some mental health care intervention (Correctional Service of Canada 2011).

Mental health courts are a recent innovation, first emerging in the United States during the mid-1990s and designed as alternatives to incarceration. In the United States, mental health courts involve accused individuals who are eligible and agree either to participate in the court and have the criminal charges against them reduced, stayed, or dropped, or return to the regular trial court. The involvement of the accused is entirely voluntary and they may decide to leave the program at any time. In Canada, however, the approach differs. The main emphasis is upon the fitness of the accused to stand trial. The participation of the accused in this part of the mental health court is not voluntary. Once fit, however, the accused may decide to "remain within the mental health court for a bail hearing, participate in diversion, or resolve the matter with a guilty plea" (Schneider et al. 2007:6).

Mental health courts in Canada are a type of problem-solving court at the provincial level, based on the idea that law can become therapeutic by incorporating the insights of the behavioural sciences (Vandergoot 2006). Therapeutic justice provides a basis for law that attempts to combine the behavioural sciences with legal processes and procedures. According to Wexler (1994:279–80), the focus of this approach is that, "within important limits set by principles of justice, the law ought to be designed to serve more effectively as a therapeutic agent . . . [and it] enables us to ask a series of questions regarding legal arrangements and therapeutic outcomes that would likely have gone unaddressed under other approaches." In the mental health courts, therapeutic justice sees the law as "a force for providing beneficial, rehabilitative outcomes for mentally disordered accused persons" (Reiksts 2008:32).

The therapeutic justice approach impacts both the individual and the courts. At the individual level, judges are able to introduce principles from behavioural sciences by requiring offenders to participate in the process of problem solving to encourage their following of court-mandated activities. At the court level, special programs and services are introduced, representing both treatment and justice concerns.

The mental health court approach appears to be beneficial to both offenders and society. Generally, it has been found that there are high levels of satisfaction and feelings held by participants with the procedures and treatments received; reduced recidivism (Poythress et al. 2002); fewer days spent in jail by those involved with the mental health court system (McNiel and Binder 2007); and better outcomes such as reduced homelessness, frequency and levels of substance abuse, and improvements in psychosocial functioning (Cosden et al. 2005).

Despite these achievements, in some locations it has run into difficulties. For example, sometimes there is a lack of community support for programs and institutions treating mentally ill offenders. In addition, most programs accept only the non-violent mentally ill; those who are prone to violent behaviour still serve their sentences in correctional facilities without receiving the same quality of services as those who enter into a mental health court. It is also a problem to evaluate the success of mental health courts; in comparison, drug court outcomes can be determined by whether or not the participants are able to remain drug-free. For those involved in drug courts, however, the issue can be more difficult since they suffer from complex mental issues, and the multidisciplinary teams have to be sure that the participants have gained control over their illness, which can be a more difficult issue to establish.

for discussion on one type of problem-solving court, the mental health court, and the *Critical Issues* section at the end of this chapter for an in-depth discussion of the community justice type of problem-solving approach in Canada). All of these depart from the business-as-usual approach found in the traditional criminal justice system. These courts use alternative sanctions to better respond to offending as well as a willingness to spend more time on each case. Problem-solving courts vary in their approaches, as they attempt to become a significant actor in solving complex problems in a defined geographical area (such as a neighbourhood, part of a city, or a region). While many deal only with criminal cases, focusing largely on **quality-of-life offences** such as shoplifting, prostitution, and graffiti, others include more serious criminal offences, such as minor assaults and small amounts of drug possession, and some address noncriminal matters, such as housing issues and various types of code violations.

However they are organized, problem-solving courts are designed to expand the role of courts from an exclusive focus on administering the law to one which offers **community-based alternatives** to incarceration. It is hoped that by offering alternatives to incarceration, participants will reduce their involvement in, for example, crime or drug use. Key aspects of these courts that lead to their success include more judicial hearings, **individualized justice**, more treatment, greater **offender accountability**, and increased support by participants of **procedural justice**. In general, all problem-solving courts rely on a number of common principles and practices (Wolf 2007):

- *Enhanced information*—Staff are better trained in one or a variety of areas (e.g., complex issues such as addictions and mental illness) and have better information (about the defendants, victim(s), and the community context of the crime) in order that the judges, prosecutors, and other justice officials have better information.
- *Community engagement*—Citizens are engaged to assist the justice system to identify, prioritize, and solve local problems.
- *Collaboration*—Various justice officials (e.g., judges, prosecutors, defence lawyers, probation officers, and so on) are brought together with various stakeholders outside of the courthouse (e.g., social service providers, community residents, victims groups, and so on) in order to create partnerships and improve interagency cooperation, trust, and new responses to various issues.
- *Individualized justice*—Risk and needs assessments are used to connect offenders to individually tailored community-based services (e.g., job training, drug treatment).
- *Accountability*—The accountability of individuals is improved through the use of community restitution requirements and regular compliance monitoring.
- *Outcomes*—The effectiveness of programs is conducted on an ongoing basis to assess the effectiveness of the policies and programs.

Shared Operating Procedures of Mental Health Courts

Mental health courts focus their attention upon mental health treatment to assist people with emotional problems reduce their chances of reoffending. By focusing upon the need for treatment, along with providing supervision and support from the community, mental health courts provide a place for those dealing with mental health issues to avoid being incarcerated, where they will have little or no access to the treatment they need.

While mental health courts vary in their approach, most share a number of basic operating procedures:

- The theoretical basis of the court attempts to address the underlying causes of crime that traditional courts have often been unable to achieve.
- The focus is upon the mentally ill person as an individual. The first question the mental

Shared Operating Procedures of Mental Health Courts (*Continued*)

health court asks is how can the law benefit the accused in dealing with his or her mental health issues and at the same time protect the public.

- Most demand active participation by the defendant.
- The participant must be diagnosed with a mental illness, and a direct link must be established between the illness and the crime committed.
- Intervention must occur quickly; individuals must be screened and referred to the program either immediately after arrest or within three weeks.
- Once in the program, participants are closely monitored by case managers. Mental health courts use judicially monitored programs with a multidisciplinary team approach to encourage voluntary treatment over punishment.
- The multidisciplinary approach is implemented at the court level by creating a mental health court team. These teams usually consist of specially trained judges, lawyers, psychologists, psychiatrists, specially trained nurses, community caregivers, and case managers or probation officers.
- Most provide voluntary outpatient or inpatient mental health treatment, in the least restrictive manner appropriate as determined by the court, that carries with it the possibility of dismissal of charges or reduced sentencing on successful completion of treatment.
- Centralized case management involves the consolidation of cases that include the mentally ill or mentally disabled defendants (including those who violate their probation orders) and the coordination of mental health treatment plans and social services, including life skills training, placement, health care, and relapse prevention for each participant who requires such services.
- Supervision of treatment plan compliance continues for a term not to exceed the maximum allowable sentence or probation for the charged or relevant offence, and, to the extent possible, psychiatric care continues at the completion of the supervised period.
- The goal is to satisfy the traditional criminal law function of protecting the public by dealing in individual cases with the real—rather than the apparent—causes that lead to violations of the law.

SUMMING UP AND LOOKING FORWARD

Problem-solving courts are a recent innovation and attempt to reduce reoffending by keeping offenders in the community and providing them with multi-agency supports. In essence, the role of the courts is expanded from administrating the law to one in which there is a focus on remedying reoffending. These courts emphasize such issues as participant accountability, the integration of social service agencies, and a coordinated management of the court process, among others.

While this chapter has discussed those individuals who are placed on conditional release programs, we need to know more about the way in which correctional institutions operate. The next chapter looks at how prisons developed in Western societies, a variety of structural features of prisons, and the conditions facing inmates, particularly those serving longer sentences.

Review Questions:

1. Why were problem-solving courts created?
2. What are the main differences between problem-solving courts and the regular criminal justice system?
3. What are the key aspects of problem-solving courts?

Critical Issues in Canadian Criminal Justice

COMMUNITY JUSTICE

Community justice approaches are focused upon improving the conditions in neighbourhoods and increasing the public's trust in justice, accountable to the communities in which they are located, and concerned with involving local residents to identify those problems they wish to see addressed. Community justice focuses on the belief that crime not only involves an offender, an incident, or a case that needs to be processed through the criminal justice system, but also is a social problem that affects the life within the community. It appears to share a similar focus to that offered by restorative justice (see Chapter 3), but outside of a focus on community empowerment, it is quite different.

Clear and Karp (1999) believe that an effective approach to limiting crime and achieving justice is to have a more community-oriented criminal justice system. Community justice involves decentralizing authority, building community support, and allowing local citizens to work together in order to create programs that fit their local areas. Each of these initiatives includes programs involving victims, the broader community, and offenders in a process that is called "community justice." The community justice approach has been defined as "an ethic that transforms the aims of the justice system into enhancing community life or sustaining community" (Clear and Karp 2000). At the same time, it is a philosophy of justice, a strategy of justice, as well as a series of justice programs.

As a *philosophy of justice*, community justice is based on a view that differs from the traditional goals of criminal justice—the apprehension, conviction, and punishment of offenders. In contrast, community justice recognizes the importance of viewing crime and its resultant problems as central to the quality of community life. As a result, community justice not only attempts to respond to criminal activity but also includes as a goal the improvement of community life, particularly for those communities affected by high crime rates. Sampson and colleagues (1997) have referred to the quality of life that communities need to reduce crime as **collective efficacy**. They found that neighbourhoods vary in their ability to "activate informal social control." Informal social control involves residents acting proactively when they see questionable behaviour. The likelihood that residents will do such things, however, is contingent upon whether or not there is mutual trust among them. In neighbourhoods where such cohesiveness exists, residents can depend on one another to enforce rules of civility and good behaviour. Such places have "collective efficacy, defined as social cohesion among neighbours combined with their willingness to intervene on behalf of the common good" (ibid.:918).

As a **strategy of justice**, two recent innovations in the area of justice are included: community policing and environmental crime prevention. Community policing uses strategies to identify alternative ways to successfully determine the root causes of crime as opposed to relying on arrests as a way to respond to crimes. The police are encouraged to form partnerships with community members as well as decentralizing decision making to the police officers in an attempt to develop area-specific strategies for reducing crime. Environmental crime prevention involves an approach to crime prevention that starts with an analysis of why crime tends to concentrate in certain locations at certain times (Sherman et al. 1995).

Three major areas of community justice have emerged: community policing (see Chapter 6), community prosecution (also referred to as "community-oriented lawyering"), and community courts.

Community-Oriented Lawyering

The goals of community-oriented lawyering include the prevention and reduction of disorder and crime, restoration of victims and communities to more effective and healthier functioning, and empowerment of local citizens. And though prosecution is still an activity employed by prosecutors, for community-oriented lawyers it is only one tactic that can be used to solve problems in neighbourhoods and communities. Prosecutors take a leadership role in building connections and initiatives that bring together citizens, businesses, government agencies, and other criminal justice agencies in the community for the purposes of reducing crime and increasing safety (Coles and Kelling 1998). This means they are developing **accountability** at the neighbourhood level by implementing tactics that include the following:

1. Refining their core capabilities in order to enhance the prosecution of violent and repeat offenders.
2. Helping set standards for the selective prosecution of offenders and offences in the context of neighbourhood priorities.
3. Relying on civil law and the use of civil initiatives as well as criminal law and criminal sanctions.
4. Using diversion and alternatives to prosecution, sentencing, and incarceration such as mediation, treatment, community service, and restitution to victims.

To achieve the goals of community-oriented lawyering, a new approach was needed. Most significant here is that the traditional approach has been to ask, "What happened?" while the new approach attempts

Critical Issues in Canadian Criminal Justice (*Continued*)

"to reshape what will happen" (Connor 2000:28). Community-oriented lawyers approach their jobs by focusing on the problems of particular people and places rather than just crimes and legal cases.

In addition, the definition of success has changed. No longer is winning the case the only desired outcome, as increasing neighbourhood safety, preventing crime, and improving the quality of life have all become important considerations. In order to achieve these goals, community-oriented lawyers listen to the victims themselves as well as to service providers, local residents, and criminal justice agents who work in the community, such as police officers who work in community storefronts. Other changes include the sharing of information and the making of decisions based on the feelings and concerns of other members of the community. Another significant change is that court case processing is a tool, not an end in itself. Instead, other types of activity are used, such as employing non-adversarial solutions and negotiating outcomes between the parties involved.

How can the effectiveness of community-oriented lawyers be measured? Like success in community policing, success in community-oriented lawyering includes traditional outcome measures—in this case, the conviction of criminals in a court of law. But it also includes several other measures, such as the degree to which certain neighbourhood problems are solved and the effectiveness of civil sanctions and negotiated agreements used in lieu of prosecution. Other possible measures include evaluating the perceptions of safety by the residents in a designated area, increasing the involvement of citizens in crime prevention and crime reduction, improving case management procedures used by the police, and improving the ability of individual citizens and neighbourhood groups to solve problems.

Community Courts

Community courts are decentralized courts that respond directly to community concerns rather than wait for serious crimes to be committed. According to Rottman (1996), community-based justice programs share certain elements. First, they all practise some type of restorative-based justice. Second, community courts treat those involved as real individuals rather than as abstract legal persons. Third, community resources are used in the adjudication of disputes.

Rottman (1996) states that three different models exist for today's community-focused courts. The first is Navajo Peacemaking, an approach that uses Navajo traditions and principles in the judicial process. The integration of Navajo customs is most evident in the Peacemaker division of the Navajo Nation judicial branch, which emphasizes non-adversarial processes in dispute resolution. The formal aspects of this process include a peacekeeper, who is a person recognized for ability and wisdom; the parties in disagreement; their extended families; and Navajo religious ceremonies. Peacemaking gains its authority from the community.

All Peacemaker sessions take a similar approach and address problems that range from marital discord to land dispute. Peacemaking is a ceremony. First, basic rules are established and prayers are made. Then, all those in attendance become involved in the questions and answers, the peacemaker develops a problem-solving statement, agreements are made, and finally, prayers are offered once again. It is important to emphasize that there are no winners or losers, but only agreed-upon decisions. Generally these sessions last two or three hours, but some have gone on for much longer (Rottman 1996; Zion 1998).

The second approach identified by Rottman involves the return of certain types of criminal cases back into communities through the use of local or "branch" courts. The Midtown Community Court (MCC), located in Manhattan, New York City, is perhaps the most famous example of this approach. In the MCC, only minor offences are heard. But this is not just another court trial using the same actors and the same rules in a criminal courtroom that just happens to be located in a community. Instead, the community plays a significant role and is viewed as having a major role to play in the process and decision. In the MCC, community groups provide opportunities and the supervision of sentences that are served in the community. In addition, they provide other resources and services, such as treatment, support, and education. Eventually a community advisory board was created and a mediation board developed in order for disputes within the community to be resolved outside the traditional legal process.

The third type of community court identified by Rottman is the community justice centre. The community justice centre "significantly expands traditional notions about the role of courts and tests the extent to which they are capable of serving as catalysts for change" (Rottman 1996:50). The centre consists of local agencies that supervise community service sentences, local residents' groups that become involved in the legal process, and administrators who coordinate and make recommendations for programs and services to those who need them. The Red Hook Community Justice Center in Brooklyn, New York, generally hears misdemeanour criminal cases but also hears felony cases such as domestic violence and juvenile delinquency. In addition, civil cases such as landlord-tenant disputes and small claims are heard.

Continued on next page

Critical Issues in Canadian Criminal Justice (*Continued*)

Questions

1. Can community courts assume a problem-solving role within a community, bringing people together and helping to create solutions to the problems that face communities?
2. How can the sentencing strategy of a court address the effect that chronic offending has on a community?
3. Can local individuals play a role in the administration of justice?
4. How can courts best link offenders to the services they need in order to keep people from reoffending?

Summary

Alternative sanctions to custody have developed rapidly to meet the needs of both the social control system and offenders. These types of sanctions include probation, parole, and problem-solving courts. They fill a need for the state to have a significant amount of control over offenders, but at the same time, they enable offenders to live and participate in the community. This allows governments to save money, open up spaces in prison for more violent offenders, and give the appearance that sentences are fairer.

KEY WORDS: federal correctional system, provincial and territorial correctional systems, community corrections

Community Release under Attack

"Nothing Works" (p. 344)

In the 1970s there was an "attack" directed toward all types of community release, particularly parole. As a result, some jurisdictions in the United States eliminated cancelled parole. Over time, these types of programs have re-emerged, but with a rehabilitative focus.

KEY WORDS: nothing works

Probation

The Use of Probation as a Sanction (p. 346)
Who Is Eligible for Probation? (p. 346)

The most common form of alternative sanction is probation. It can be used either by itself or in conjunction with a custodial sentence. Usually there are both mandatory and optional conditions attached to a sentence of probation.

KEY WORDS: probation, split sentence, mandatory conditions, optional conditions, long-term supervision, super-probation, dangerous offenders

The Conditional Sentence of Imprisonment

What Is the Impact of Conditional Sentences? (p. 350)

Conditional sentences were introduced in 1996. They originally applied to numerous offences but in recent years the federal government has started to restrict the number and type of offences they can be used for.

KEY WORDS: conditional sentence, house arrest, denunciation, rehabilitation, net widening

Intermediate Sanctions

In recent decades, new forms of alternative sanctions have been created. One is intensive supervision probation, which is characterized by close contact between probation officers and their clients. Home confinement is increasing in popularity and is usually accompanied by electronic monitoring devices. Day fines are another alternative; these are usually directed toward offenders who are unable to pay a fixed fine because of financial constraints (i.e., poverty).

KEY WORDS: intermediate sanctions, judicially administered sanctions, intensive supervision probation, home confinement, electronic monitoring, panaceas, fines, fine option programs, day fines

What Is Intensive Supervision Probation? (p. 352)
Evaluation of ISP Programs (p. 352)
Home Confinement and Electronic Monitoring (p. 353)
How Effective Are Home Confinement and Electronic Monitoring Programs? (p. 355)
Fines (p. 355)
Intermediate Sanctions: How Well Do They Work? (p. 357)

Conditional Release Programs

Conditional release programs are available to individuals incarcerated in provincial/territorial and federal correctional facilities. The various types of conditional release programs have differing rates of recidivism.

KEY WORDS: full parole, day parole, statutory release, temporary absences, Parole Board of Canada, provincial parole boards, accelerated parole review (APR), medical TA, compassionate TA, administrative TA, escorted temporary absence, Schedule I offences, Schedule II offences, recidivism rate, technical violation, short-term recidivism, long-term recidivism, special needs offenders

How Effective Are Conditional Release Programs? (p. 363)
What Are Recidivism Rates? (p. 364)

What Are Problem-Solving Courts?

Problem-solving courts use alternative sanctions to better respond to offending as well as a willingness to spend more time on each case. While there are various types of problem-solving courts, for example mental health courts and community courts, they all share certain core principles.

KEY WORDS: quality-of-life offences, community-based alternatives, individualized justice, offender accountability, procedural justice, deinstitutionalization, collective efficacy, strategy of justice, accountability

Critical Thinking Questions

1. How closely related are the introduction of alternative sanctions and the growth of the prison population?
2. Has the potential of alternative sanctions been realized?
3. What are the strengths and weaknesses of having offenders serve their sentences in the community?
4. Why do you think Canada hasn't introduced intermediate punishments to the same degree as the United States?
5. Do you think that making parole more difficult to attain is problematic?
6. Do you think that the use of problem-solving courts should be expanded in Canada?

Weblinks

The first community court in Canada was opened in Vancouver. Watch the following videos about this court (available at www.justiceeducation.ca/resources/dcc-videos): "Introduction to the Downtown Community Court" (8:08), and "The Community Court's Story," Part I (4:11), Part II (8:08), and Part III (5:04). There are many videos on YouTube that feature mental health courts and other problem-solving courts. Watch the following video available on YouTube that features the Boston Mental Health Court, "For Mentally Ill Defendants: A Different Kind of Court" (8:06).

Court Case

R. v. Proulx (2000), 1 S.C.R. 61.

Suggested Readings

Berman, G. and J. Feinblalt. 2005. *Good Courts: The Case for Problem-Solving Justice.* NY: New Press.

Miller, J. and D. Johnson. 2009. *Problem Solving Courts: A Measure of Justice.* Lanham, MD: Rowman and Littlefield.

Morris, N. and M. Tonry. 1990. *Beyond Prison and Probation: Intermediate Punishments in a Rational Sentencing System.* New York: Oxford University Press.

Pavelka, S., A. Seymour, and B. Stuart (eds.). 2013. *Legacy of Community Justice.* Vernon, BC: J. Charlton.

Tonry, M. and K. Hamilton (eds.). 1995. *Intermediate Sanctions in Overcrowded Times.* Boston, MA: Northeastern University Press.

References

Adams, M. 1990. "Canadian Attitudes toward Crime and Justice." *Forum on Corrections Research* 2:10–13.

Alberta. 1991. *Report of the Task Force on the Criminal Justice System and Its Impact on the Indian and Métis People of Alberta*, Vol. 1. Edmonton.

Andrews, D.A., J. Bonta, and R.D. Hoge. 1990. "Classification for Effective Rehabilitation: Rediscovering Psychology." *Criminal Justice and Behavior* 17:19–52.

Bales, W.D., K. Mann, T. Blomberg, G.H. Gaes, K. Barrick, K. Dhungana, and B. McManus. 2010. *A Quantitative and Qualitative Assessment of Electronic Monitoring*. Washington, DC: National Institute of Justice.

Belanger, B. 2001. *Sentencing in Adult Criminal Courts 1999/00.* Ottawa: Canadian Centre for Justice Statistics.

Bernstein, R. and T. Seltzer. 2003. "Criminalizaton of People with Mental Illness: The Role of Mental Health Courts in System Reform." *The University of the District of Columbia Law Review* 7:143–62.

Bonta, J., J. Rooney, and S. Wallace-Capretta. 1999. *Electronic Monitoring in Canada.* Ottawa: Public Works and Government Services Canada.

Bonta, J., S. Wallace-Capretta, and J. Rooney. 2000. "Can Electronic Monitoring Make a Difference? An Evaluation of Three Canadian Programs." *Crime and Delinquency* 46:61–75.

Boyce, J. 2013. *Adult Criminal Court Statistics in Canada, 2011/2012*. Ottawa: Canadian Centre for Justice Statistics.

Byrne, J.M. and L. Kelly. 1989. *Restructuring Probation as an Intermediate Punishment: An Evaluation of the Implementation and Impact of the Massachusetts Intensive Probation Supervision Program: Final Report*. Washington, DC: National Institute of Justice.

Byrne, J.M., A.J. Lurigio, and C. Baird. 1989. "The Effectiveness of the New Intensive Supervision Programs." *Research in Corrections* 2(2):1–48.

Byrne, J.M., A. Lurigio, and J. Petersilia. 1992. "Introduction: The Emergence of Intermediate Sanctions." Pp. ix-xv in *Smart Sentencing*, edited by Byrne, Lurigio, and Petersilia. Newbury Park, CA: Sage.

Calverley, D. and K. Beattie. 2005. *Community Corrections in Canada 2004*. Ottawa: Ministry of Industry.

Camp, G. and C.G. Camp. 1993. *The Corrections Yearbook: Probation and Parole*. South Salem, NY: Criminal Justice Institute.

Canadian Criminal Justice Association. 1987. *Attitudes toward Parole*. Ottawa: Canadian Criminal Justice Association.

Canadian Sentencing Commission. 1987. *Sentencing Reform: A Canadian Approach*. Ottawa: Minister of Supply and Services.

Clear, T. 1994. *Harm in American Penology: Offenders, Victims, and Their Communities*. Albany, NY: SUNY Press.

Clear, T. and P. Hardyman. 1990. "The New Intensive Supervision Movement." *Crime and Delinquency* 36:42–60.

Clear, T.R. and D.R. Karp. 2000. "Toward the Ideal of Community Justice." *NIJ Journal*. Washington, DC: U.S. Department of Justice, National Institute of Justice.

Clear, T.R. and D.R. Karp. 1999. *The Community Justice Ideal: Preventing Crime and Achieving Justice*. Boulder, CO: Westview.

Coles, C. and G. Kelling. 1998. "Prosecution in the Community: A Study of Emergent Strategies." Paper presented at J.F. Kennedy Law School, Harvard University, Program in Criminal Justice, September.

Connor, R. 2000. "Problem-Solving Lawyers." *National Institute of Justice Journal*, January: 26–33.

Correctional Service of Canada. 2011. *Health Services Sector 2010–2011. Performance Measurement Report*. Ottawa: Correctional Service of Canada.

Correctional Service of Canada. 1990. "A Profile of Federal Community Corrections." *Forum on Corrections Research* 2:8–13.

Cosden, M., J. Ellens, J. Schnell, and Y. Yasmani-Diouf. 2005. "Efficacy of a Mental Health Treatment Court with Assertive Community Treatment." *Behavioral Sciences and the Law* 23:199–214.

Cullen, F.T. and P. Gendreau. 1989. "The Effectiveness of Correctional Rehabilitation: Reconsidering the 'Nothing Works' Debate." Pp. 23–44 in *American Prisons: Issues in Research and Policy*, edited by L. Goodstein and D. MacKenzie. New York: Plenum.

Cullen, F.T., J.P. Wright, and B.K. Applegate. 1995. "Control in the Community: The Limits of Reform?" In *The Search for Effective Correctional Interventions*, edited by A.J. Hartland. Newbury Park, CA: Sage.

Daubney, D. and G. Parry. 1999. "An Overview of Bill C-41 (The Sentencing Reform Act)." Pp. 31–47 in *Making Sense of Sentencing*, edited by J.V. Roberts and D.P. Cole. Toronto: University of Toronto Press.

Dauvergne, M. 2012. *Adult Criminal Court Statistics in Canada, 2010/2011*. Ottawa: Canadian Centre for Justice Statistics.

Edwin, G. 1992. "Recidivism among Homicide Offenders." *Forum on Corrections Research* 4:7–9.

Erwin, B.S. 1986. "Turning Up the Heat on Probationers in Georgia." *Federal Probation* 50:17–24.

Finckenhauer, J.Q. 1982. *Scared Straight! and the Panacea Phenomenon*. Englewood Cliffs, NJ: Prentice-Hall.

Frideres, J.S. and B. Robertson. 1994. "Aboriginals and the Criminal Justice System: Australia and Canada." *International Journal of Contemporary Sociology* 31:101–27.

Fulton, B., E.J. Latessa, A. Stichman, and L. Travis. 1997. "The State of ISP: Research and Policy Implications." *Federal Probation* 61:65–75.

Gendreau, P., F.T. Cullen, and J. Bonta. 1994. "Intensive Rehabilitation Supervision: The Next Generation in Community Corrections?" *Federal Probation* 58:72–78.

Gendreau, P. and T. Little. 1993. "A Meta-analysis of the Effectiveness of Sanctions on Offender Recidivism." Unpublished manuscript, University of New Brunswick, Saint John.

Grant, B.A. and R.L. Belcourt. 1992. *An Analysis of Temporary Absences and the People Who Receive Them*. Ottawa: Correctional Service of Canada.

Harris, K. 2015. "Corrections Canada Pushing Ahead with Electronic Monitoring of Offenders." March 5. CBC News. Retrieved April 1, 2015 (www.cnc.ca/news/politics/corrections-canada-pushing-ahead-with-electronic-monitoring).

Hillsman, S.T. 1990. "Fines and Day Fines." Pp. 49–98 in *Crime and Justice: A Review of Research*, vol. 12, edited by M. Tonry and N. Norris. Chicago: University of Chicago Press.

Johnson, S. 2003. *Custodial Remand in Canada, 1986/87 to 2000/01*. Ottawa: Canadian Centre for Justice Statistics.

Jolin, A. and B. Stipak. 1992. "Drug Treatment and Electronically Monitored Home Confinement: An Evaluation of the Community-Based Sentencing Option." *Crime and Delinquency* 38:158–70.

Larocque, B. 1998. "Federal Trends and Outcomes in Conditional Release." *Forum on Corrections Research* 10, 2 (May):18–22.

Latessa, E. 1995. "An Evaluation of the Lucas County Adult Probation Departments ISP and High Risk Groups." In *The Search for Effective Correctional Interventions*, edited by A.T. Hartland. Newbury Park, CA: Sage.

Law Reform Commission of Canada. 1975. *Criminal Procedure: Control of the Process*. Ottawa: Minister of Supply and Services Canada.

Lipton, D., R. Martinson, and J. Wilks. 1975. *The Effectiveness of Correctional Treatment*. New York: Praeger.

Lonmo, C. 2001. *Adult Correctional Services in Canada 1999/00*. Ottawa: Canadian Centre for Justice Statistics.

Madoc, L.L. and S.L. Brown. 1994. "Sex Offenders and Their Survival Time on Conditional Release." *Forum on Corrections Research* 6:14–17.

Mair, G. 2006. "Editorial Introduction." *Criminology & Public Policy* 5:57–60.

Makin, K. 2000. "Judge Blasts Ontario's Monitoring of Convicts." *The Globe and Mail*, January 28, p. A8.

Makin, K. 1999. "Fear Limits Use of Electronic Monitoring." *The Globe and Mail*, October 11, p. A3.

Martinson, R. 1979. "Symposium on Sentencing: Part II." *Hofstra Law Review* 7:243–58.

Martinson, R. 1974. "What Works? Questions and Answers about Prison Reform." *Public Interest* 35:22–54.

McNiel, D.E. and R.L. Binder. 2007. "Effectiveness of a Mental Health Court in Reducing Criminal Recidivism and Violence." *The American Journal of Psychiatry* 164:1395–1403.

Morris, N. and M. Tonry. 1990. Between *Prison and Probation: Intermediate Punishments in a Rational Sentencing System*. New York: Oxford University Press.

Nouwens, T., L. Madoc, and R. Boe. 1993. "So You Want to Know the Recidivism Rate." *Forum on Corrections Research* 5:22–26.

Pearson, F. 1986. *Research on New Jersey's Intensive Supervision Program: Final Report*. Washington, DC: National Institute of Justice.

Petersilia, J. 2004. "Community Corrections." In *Crime: Public Policies for Crime Control*, edited by J.Q. Wilson and J. Petersilia. Oakland, CA: Institute for Contemporary Studies.

Petersilia, J. 1993. "Measuring the Performance of Community Corrections." Performance Measures for the Criminal Justice System. Washington, DC: U.S. Department of Justice.

Petersilia, J. 1987. *Expanding Options for Criminal Sentencing*. Santa Monica, CA: Rand.

Petersilia, J. and S. Turner. 1993. "Intensive Probation and Parole." Pp. 281–336 in *Crime and Justice: A Review of Research*, vol. 17, edited by M. Tonry. Chicago: University of Chicago Press.

Porporino, F.J. and L.L. Madoc. 1993. "Conditional Release and Offenders with Mental Disorders." *Forum on Corrections Research* 5:17–19.

Poythress, N.G., J. Petrila, A. McGaha, and R.A. Boothroyd. 2002. "Perceived Coercion and Procedural Justice in the Broward Mental Health County." *International Journal of Law and Psychiatry* 25:517–33.

Public Safety Canada. 2013. *Corrections and Conditional Release Statistical Overview: 2013 Annual Report*. Ottawa: Public Safety Canada.

Rackmill, S.J. 1994. "An Analysis of Home Confinement as a Sanction." *Federal Probation* 58:45–52.

Reed, M. and J.V. Roberts. 1999. *Adult Correctional Services in Canada, 1997–98*. Ottawa: Juristat.

Reiksts, M. 2008. "Mental Health Courts in Canada." *LawNow* 33:31–34.

Renzema, M. and D. Skelton. 1990. "Trends in the Use of Electronic Monitoring: 1989." *Journal of Offender Monitoring* 3:14–19.

Roach, K. 2000a. "Conditional Sentences, Restorative Justice, Net-Widening and Aboriginal Offenders." Pp. 25–38 in *The Changing Face of Conditional Sentencing: Symposium Proceedings*. Ottawa: Department of Justice.

Roach, K. 2000b. "Changing Punishment at the Turn of the Century: Restorative Justice on the Rise." *Canadian Journal of Criminology* 42:249–80.

Roberts, J.V. 1999. "Conditional Sentencing: Issues and Problems." Pp. 77–97 in *Making Sense of Sentencing*, edited by J.V. Roberts and D.P. Cole. Toronto: University of Toronto Press.

Roberts, J.V. 1988. "Early Release from Prison: What Do the Canadian Public Really Think?" *Canadian Journal of Criminology* 30:231–49.

Roberts, J.V. and T. Gabor. 2004. "Living in the Shadows of Prison: Lessons from the Canadian Experience in Decarceration." *British Journal of Criminology* 44:92–112.

Roberts, J.V., A.N. Doob, and V. Marinos. 2000. *Judicial Attitudes to Conditional Terms of Imprisonment: Results of a National Survey*. Ottawa: Department of Justice.

Rottman, D.B. 1996. "Community Courts: Prospects and Limits." *National Institute of Justice Journal*, August: 46–51.

Sampson, R.J., S.W. Raudenbush, and F. Earles. 1997. "Neighborhoods and Violent Crime: A Multilevel Study of Collective Efficacy." *Science* 277:1–7.

Sawyer, K. 1985. "Tougher Probation May Help Georgia Clear Crowded Prisons." *Washington Post*, August 16, p. A1.

Schneider, R.S. 2000. *A Statistical Survey of Provincial and Territorial Review Boards*. Ottawa: Department of Justice.

Schneider, R.S., H. Bloom, and M. Heerma. 2007. *Mental Health Courts: Decriminalizing the Mentally Ill.* Toronto: Irwin Law.

Sherman, L., P.R. Gartin, and M.E. Buerger. 1995. "Hot Spots of Predatory Crime: Routine Activities and the Criminology of Place." *Criminology* 27:27–55.

Smith, L.G. and R.L. Akers. 1993. "A Comparison of Recidivism of Florida's Community Control and Prison: A Five-Year Survival Analysis." *Journal of Research in Crime and Delinquency* 30:267–92.

Stys, Y. 2010. *Conditional Release of Federal Offenders Convicted of Criminal Organization Offences*. Ottawa: Correctional Service of Canada. Research Report No. R-227.

Thompson, D. 1985. *Intensive Probation Supervision in Illinois*. Chicago: Center for Research in Law and Justice.

Tonry, M. 1990. "Stated and Latent Functions of ISP." *Crime and Delinquency* 36:174–91.

Tonry, M. and R. Will. 1990. *Intermediate Sanctions*. Washington, DC: National Institute of Justice.

U.S. General Accounting Office. 1990. *Intermediate Sanctions: Their Impacts on Prison Over-crowding, Costs*. Washington, DC.

Vandergoot, M.E. 2006. *Justice for Young Offenders*. Saskatoon, SK: Purich.

Walker, S. 1984. *Sense and Nonsense about Crime*. Belmont, CA: Wadsworth.

Waller, I. 1974. *Men Released from Prison*. Toronto: University of Toronto Press.

Wallerstedt, J. 1984. *Returning to Prison*. Washington, DC: National Institute of Justice.

Wexler, D.B. 1994. "Therapeutic Jurisprudence and the Criminal Justice Courts." *William and Mary Law Review* 35:278–99.

Wolf, R.V. 2007. *Principles of Problem-Solving Justice*. Washington, D.C. Bureau of Justice Assistance.

Worrall, A. 1997. *Punishment in the Community: The Future of Criminal Justice*. London: Harlow, Addison, Wesley, Longman.

Zion, J.W. 1998. "The Dynamics of Navajo Peacemaking." *Journal of Contemporary Criminal Justice* 14:58–74.

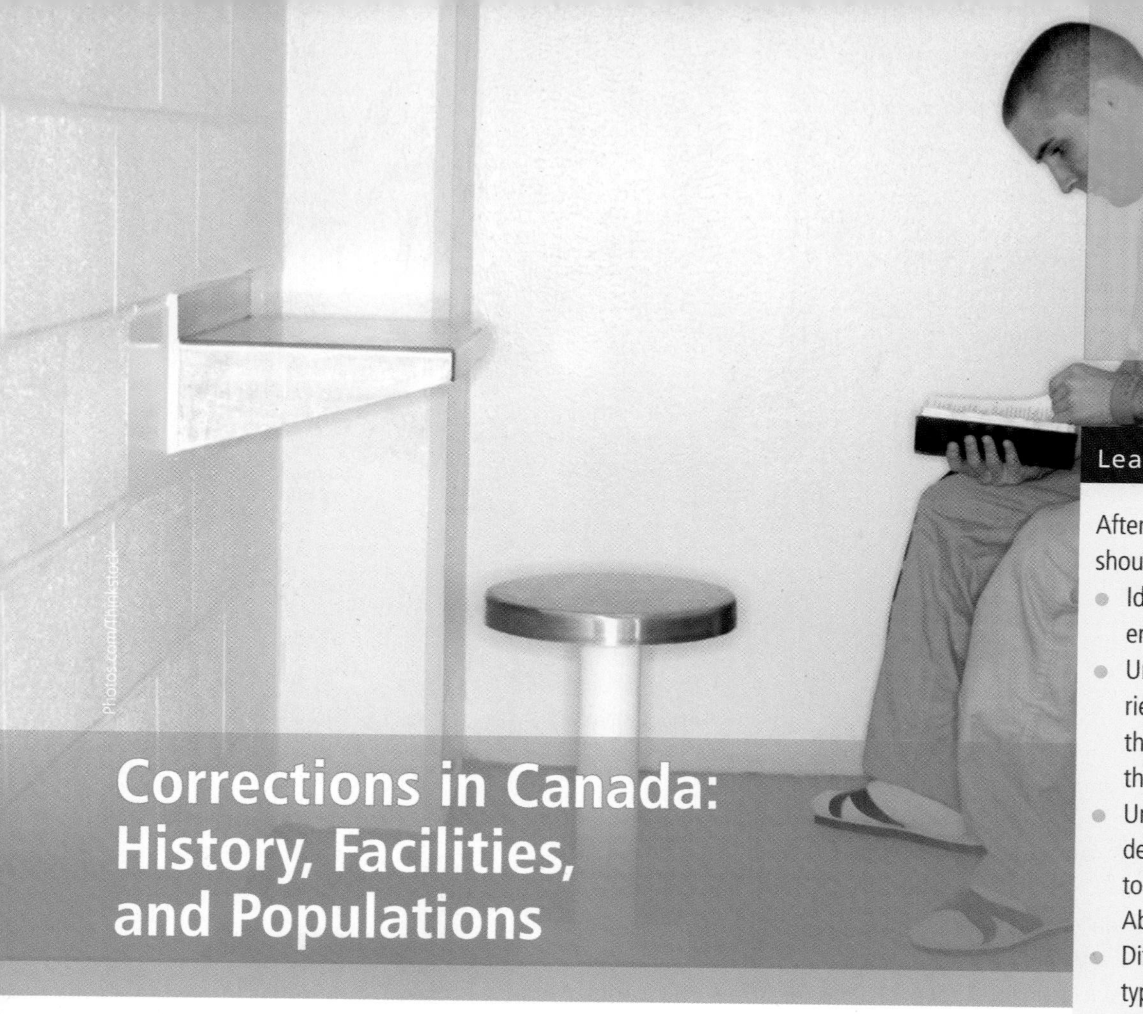

CHAPTER

12

Corrections in Canada: History, Facilities, and Populations

Learning Objectives

After completing this chapter, you should be able to:

- Identify how modern prisons emerged and developed.
- Understand the Canadian experience with corrections during the 19th and the first half of the 20th century.
- Understand the reasons for the development of approaches to corrections for women and Aboriginal people.
- Differentiate among the various types of prison architecture.
- Understand how correctional facilities use different supervision approaches to try to change offenders' behaviour.
- Understand why the rule of law exists within correctional facilities.

Offenders who have been convicted of a criminal offence may be sentenced to a period of confinement in a federal or provincial/territorial correctional institution (see Figure 12.1). Canada's correctional system was established in the early 1800s in Ontario with the opening of Kingston Penitentiary. The correctional system has grown since then in response to the growing number of individuals sentenced to a term of **incarceration**. Currently there are 250 correctional facilities across Canada; 73 of these are under federal jurisdiction and the remaining 177 are under provincial/territorial jurisdiction. Sixteen of the federal institutions are community correctional centres, with a capacity of 474 spaces (see Chapter 13). The other 57 federal institutions contain 15,151 spaces. Of these 57 federal facilities, 16 are minimum security, 19 are medium security, 7 are maximum security, and 15 are multilevel facilities.

Six of the 57 federal institutions are women's correctional facilities; five are regional women's institutions and another is an Aboriginal healing lodge for women. All of the women's institutions (except the Aboriginal healing lodge) are classified as multilevel security. There are also five regional mental health units across Canada. The remaining federal facilities are for male inmates. The federal facilities are aging—the average age of a federal custodial institution was 49 years in 2013, and five of them were built between 1835 and 1900.

In 2012–13, a total of 39,679 individuals were incarcerated in Canada. Of those in custody, 36 percent were serving a federal sentence, 28 percent were serving a provincial sentence, and 35 percent were being held in remand. Less than 1 percent of adults in custody were being detained for another reason, such as parole suspension (Perreault 2014). The rate of adult offenders in custody in Canada's correctional system on any given day was 142 offenders per 100,000 adults. The highest incarceration rates were found in the Northwest Territories (726), Nunavut (553), Yukon (355), and Manitoba (248). The lowest rates were found in the federal correctional system (52), Nova Scotia (63),

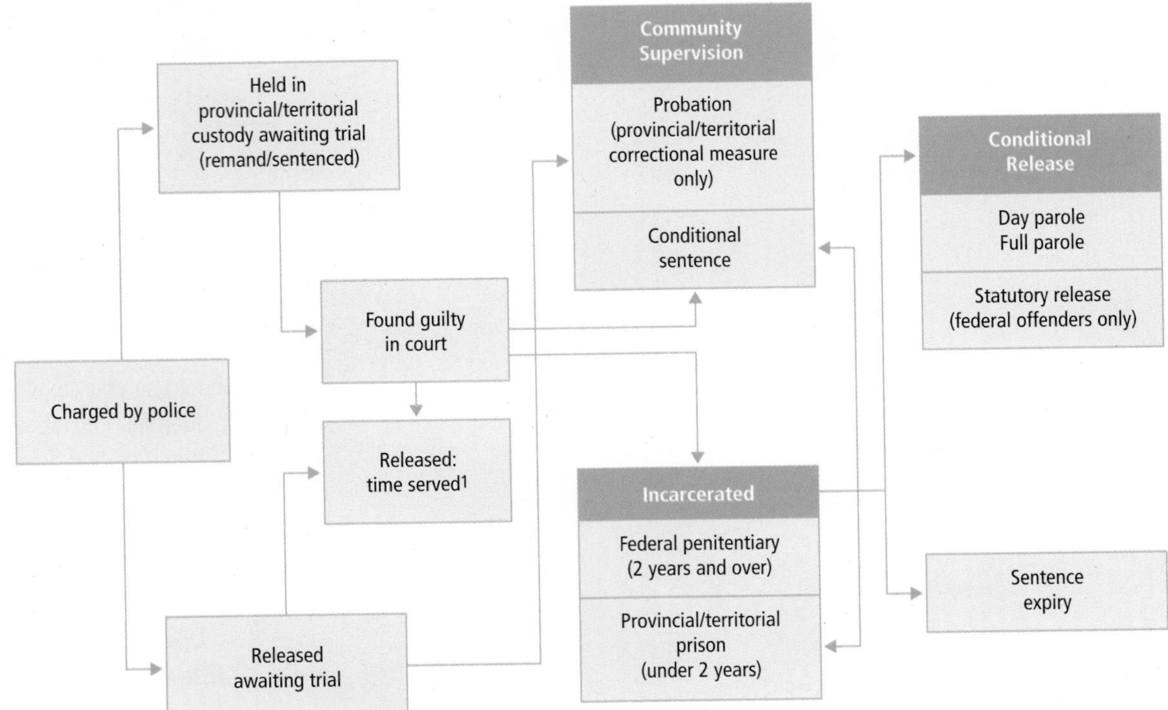

FIGURE 12.1 An Overview of Events in the Adult Correctional System (Statistics Canada)

1. An individual whose sentence approximates time already held in custody (i.e., while awaiting trial) is generally released by virtue of having already served his sentence.

Source: Micheline Reed and Julian Roberts, "ADULT CORRECTIONAL SERVICES IN CANADA, 1997–98." *Juristat* (April 1999), p. 3, Statistics Canada Catalogue no. 85-002-X, http://www.statcan.gc.ca/pub/85-002-x/85-002-x1999004-eng.pdf. Reproduced and distributed on an "as is" basis with the permission of Statistics Canada.

National Archives of Canada/PA-30472

An aerial photograph taken in 1919 of the federal Kingston Penitentiary for Men in Kingston, Ontario. The federal government announced in 2012 that it would be closing this facility.

British Columbia (66), Newfoundland and Labrador (66), and New Brunswick (70) (see Figure 12.2).

Some other statistics about imprisonment in federal correctional facilities in Canada during 2012–13 include the following (see also Figure 12.3):

- Sixty-eight percent of federal offenders were serving a sentence for a violent offence.
- The proportion of offenders admitted to a federal correctional facility with sentences between three and six years increased from 35 percent in 2003–04 to 40 percent in 2012–13.
- The proportion of offenders admitted to a federal correctional facility with sentences over six years was about 14 percent in 2012–13, a figure that hadn't changed noticeably since 2003–04.
- Forty-seven percent of all offenders entering a federal correctional facility during 2012–13 were between the ages of 30 and 49; 40 percent were between the ages of 18 and 29.
- Twenty-one percent of the federal correctional inmate population were double bunked.
- 4,850 men offenders were admitted into a federal correctional facility, an increase of 22 percent since 2003–04.
- 275 women offenders were admitted into a federal correctional facility, an increase of 16 percent since 2003–04.
- 1,080 Aboriginal offenders were admitted into a federal correctional facility, an increase of 47 percent since 2003–04 (Correctional Service of Canada 2014; Perreault 2014).

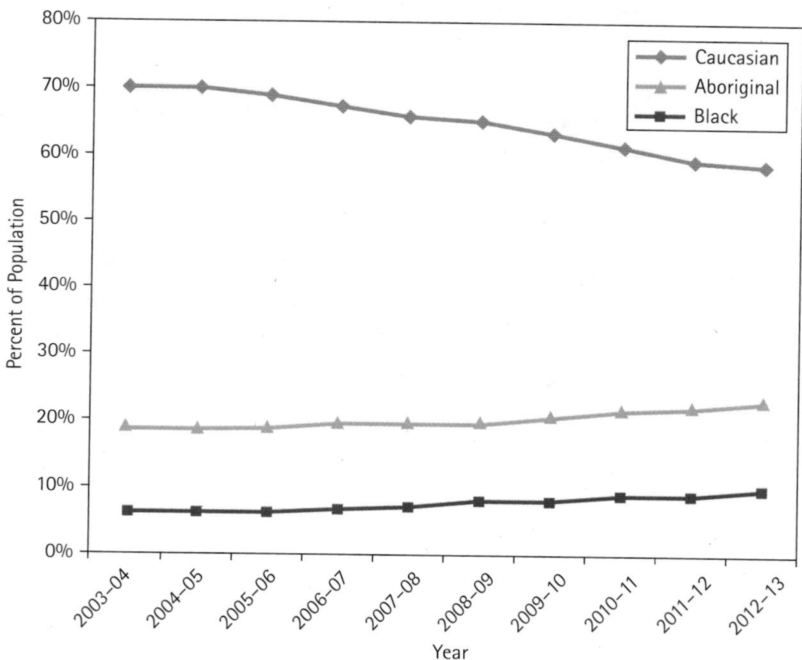

FIGURE 12.2 Ten-Year Offender Population Trends (Incarcerated and Community)

Source: Office of the Correctional Investigator, *Annual Report of the Office of the Correctional Investigator 2012–2013*, p. 6, http://www.oci-bec.gc.ca/cnt/rpt/pdf/annrpt/annrpt20122013-eng.pdf. Reproduced with permission of the Office of the Correctional Officer.

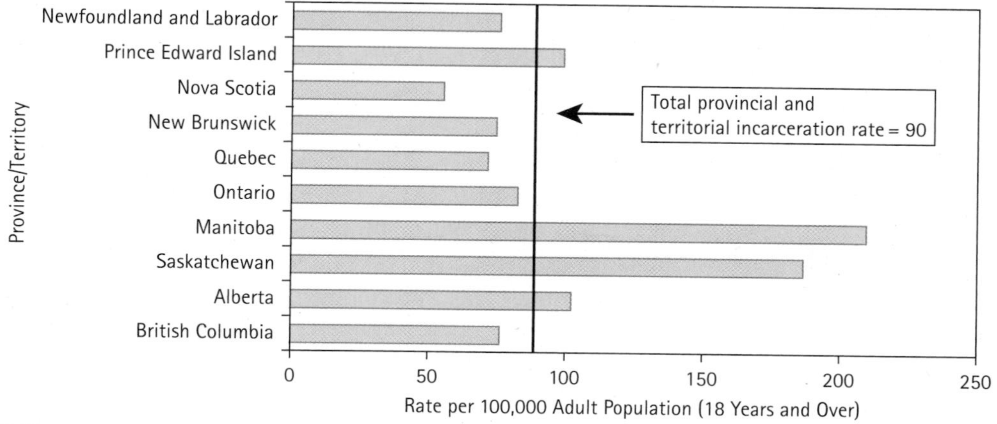

FIGURE 12.3 Average Counts of Adults in Custody (Incarceration Rates), by Province, 2010–11

Source: Mia Duavergne, "Adult correctional statistics in Canada, 2010/2011." *Juristat* (October 2012), Statistics Canada Catalogue no 85-002-X, p. 8, http://www.statcan.gc.ca/pub/85-002-x/2012001/article/11715-eng.pdf. Reproduced and distributed on an "as is" basis with the permission of Statistics Canada.

How Did the Modern Prison Develop?

The 18th century was a decisive moment in the history of social control in Europe, as imprisonment became the main way of dealing with undesirable conduct and the preferred approach to dealing with those individuals who broke the law. Until this time, people were mainly imprisoned for the following two reasons:

1. holding in custody people awaiting trial or, if they were convicted, awaiting their sentence, and
2. forcing fine defaulters and debtors to pay back what they owed (Carrabine 2006).

There is no agreed-upon history of why prisons emerged and became the dominant mode of social control.

Some believe that it was due to the work of reformers (referred to as the *Whig view*) who wanted to create a more humanitarian form of punishment. Others (referred to as *Revisionist views*) argue it was due to the advent of industrial capitalism (Rusche and Kirchheimer 1939), a response to a crisis in class relations brought about by the Industrial Revolution (Ignatieff 1978), or an attempt to create a more disciplined society (Foucault 1995). Others point out that the rise of prisons is much more complex than the above approaches offer (e.g., Garland 1990), and that there has been a failure to consider the punishment of women and Aboriginals and other minority groups, "which problematizes thinking on the role and development of incarceration" (Carrabine 2006:214).

European Antecedents to the Modern Prison

The first institutions resembling prisons emerged in Europe during the 17th and 18th centuries. Three major changes during this century dramatically influenced how most Western societies would run their correctional facilities in the coming centuries. The first was a philosophical shift away from the punishment of the body (such as flogging and torture) toward the punishment of the mind (Cohen 1985). Many people felt that punishments should focus on depriving people of their liberty instead of physically punishing them. According to Foucault (1995:11), "the punishment-body-relation [was no longer] the same as it was in the torture during public executions. The body now serves as an instrument or intermediary: if one intervenes upon to imprison it, or to make it work, it is in order to deprive the individual of a liberty that is regarded as both a right and as property."

This new approach had its clearest beginnings with the work of the Philadelphia Society for Alleviating the Miseries of Public Prisons, a society operated by the Pennsylvania Quakers. In 1794, Pennsylvania became the first state to permanently abolish the death penalty for all criminal offences except first degree murder. The Quakers were also instrumental in restructuring the first jail in America (originally built in 1776 in Philadelphia) in order to introduce a humanitarian approach to housing inmates and changing their behaviour (Taft 1956).

The second major change involved the passing of laws that made it illegal to imprison anyone who had not been convicted of a crime. This led to the **segregation** of criminals from the rest of society. Gradually, the courts began to hand out sentences involving terms of imprisonment as opposed to physical punishments. According to historians, these changes emerged slowly in different European countries at different times. Spierenburg (1995) notes that the first criminal prison in Europe was opened in Amsterdam in 1654; he adds, however, that in other parts of the country, people were still being imprisoned for non-criminal offences—a practice that continued for another 100 years or so.

The third and biggest change was the beginning of the **Age of Enlightenment**. The Enlightenment had a strong impact on the criminal justice systems of Western nations, by influencing the form and content of corrections over the next two centuries. In terms of changes in imprisonment, two figures had the greatest impact: Cesare Beccaria and Jeremy Bentham (see Chapter 3).

Beccaria (1738–1794) was a member of a progressive intellectual group that in the late 1750s began publicly criticizing Italy's criminal justice system. Basing much of their social critique on the work of like-minded thinkers in England and France, they ultimately wrote a book titled *On Crimes and Punishments*. (Beccaria was credited as sole author. The others feared that the authorities would respond harshly to their critique. Beccaria, who belonged to an aristocratic family, would probably be safe.) In this short book, Beccaria outlined a utilitarian approach to punishment. He argued that some punishments could never be justified since they were more "evil" than any potential good they could ever do. Among the punishments that Beccaria categorized as "evil" were torture and the use of **ex post facto laws** (i.e., laws passed after someone had committed a crime; the offender was then punished for actions that had not been illegal at the time). One of his strongest arguments was that punishments should be swift, since that would achieve the greatest amount of deterrence. Also, he argued that punishments should not be overly severe.

Bentham (1748–1832) was a famous British philosopher and jurist. He was a utilitarian—that is, he supported the principle that the goal of public policies (such as imprisonment) should be the greatest good for the greatest number of people. He also believed that people are motivated by pleasure and want to avoid pain and that a proper amount of punishment can deter crime (this is referred to as the "**hedonistic calculus**"). Accordingly, people by nature choose pleasure and avoid pain. Thus:

- Each individual calculates the degree of pleasure or pain from a given course of action.
- Lawmakers can determine the degree of punishment necessary to deter criminal behaviour.
- Such punishment can be effectively and rationally developed into a system of criminal sentencing.

Bentham drew up the plans for the first prison. Known as the **panopticon** (or "all-seeing"), it was designed to put utilitarianism into practice by reforming offenders. A significant feature of the panopticon was its design: the plans called for a circular structure with a glass roof and a window in each cell. This would make it easy for the staff, who were located in a circular room in the centre of the building, to observe (or "surveil") each cell and its occupant. Solid walls separated each cell from the others, ensuring that the offenders, who were housed one to a cell, could not talk to one another. No panopticon was ever built, apparently because Bentham insisted that they be built near large urban centres in order to achieve the maximum amount of deterrence. Local residents, however, opposed the building of these structures and succeeded in defeating Bentham's dream of building progressive places for incarcerating offenders.

A Brief History of Federal Correctional Facilities in Canada

It is only in recent decades that Canada, like all other Western nations, has increased its use of confinement as the main approach to punishing offenders. Between 1832, when the first federal prison was built in Kingston, and 1950, a total of eight federal prisons were constructed. During the 1950s, three federal institutions were built, followed by eight in the 1960s, five in the 1970s, and six during the 1980s. As prisons became more popular, two competing views about how they should be developed emerged in the early 19th century. One was called the *separate system* and the other the *silent system*; both of these described differing systems of prison discipline and were used in Canadian, American, and English prisons.

The first prisons in North America were built in the United States. Two different types were originally constructed. The **Pennsylvania system** (the **separate system**) reflected a strong Quaker influence: inmates were isolated not only from the outside, but also from one another. They had one hour a day to exercise by themselves in an outside yard; they were expected to spend the rest of their time in their small cells, reading the Bible provided to them, reflecting on their illegal actions, and "repenting" their crimes (Jackson 1983). This approach was designed to make those incarcerated reflect upon their behaviour and ultimately reform their ways. This approach was criticized as it was pointed out that its practice led to long-term negative psychological effects in inmates.

Another style of prison was built in Auburn, New York. Referred to as the **Auburn system** (the **silent system**), this institution held inmates in what is sometimes known as the **congregate system**. This system was based on the belief that the most efficient way for inmates to reform their actions was through hard work. During the day, inmates worked together both inside and outside the walls, although they were not supposed to talk to one another. Prisoners ate together, but also in complete silence. When the inmates were not working or eating, they were locked in their cells. This approach demanded silence on the part of all inmates as it was felt that any communication would ultimately end up with prisoners teaching others how to commit more and different types of crimes.

Different prison architectural styles characterized these different systems. The Pennsylvania prison was built on one floor; the Auburn system had a number of floors of cells built in tiers, as they were called (Rothman 1971). The Auburn system, originally built between 1819 and 1823, quickly became the most copied style of prison and ultimately was considered to be the "international prototype of a maximum-security prison" (Anderson and Newman 1993:349). The Auburn system was to become the basis for Canadian prisons. The first prisons in Canada were built by provincial authorities. The first of these was completed in 1835 in Kingston; this was followed by the New Brunswick Penitentiary (1841) and the Nova Scotia Penitentiary (1844). In 1868, the federal government took over all three of these institutions and proceeded to build four new ones over the next 12 years. While the Canadian authorities followed the Auburn model, the Pennsylvania system continued to survive in one particular form: solitary confinement. Most correctional institutions today contain within them areas set aside for more severe forms of punishment for inmates who have violated prison rules and regulations or who are considered to be troublemakers.

For the rest of the 19th century, the federal government operated its prisons in a very harsh manner. Conditions were harsh, discipline was extreme, and solitary confinement was regularly used (up to 18 months at a time). These approaches, it was argued, clearly demonstrated their "superiority [in terms of] the treatment of incorrigibles and criminal crooks" (Jackson 1983:38–39).

At the beginning of the 20th century, significant changes were introduced to the federal correctional system. Parole was introduced, correctional officials began to receive training, and inmate classification systems were developed. Also, inmates began to be housed on the basis of their needs and crimes, which led to the minimum-, medium-, and maximum-security designations. The treatment of inmates was now based on the **policy of normalization**, which specified that inmate programs were to be in a controlled environment (i.e., not an oppressive one) in order to better reflect conditions in society. Education programs and vocational training were also introduced at this time. In reality, the living conditions of inmates remained harsh; handcuffs and the ball and chain continued to be used until the early 1930s (Eckstedt and Griffiths 1988).

In 1935, the federal government decided to change its approach toward the treatment of inmates. Clear (1994:80) notes that this change came about for three reasons:

1. The correcting of offenders was now considered a "science," and as a result highly educated individuals were beginning to take more dominant positions in the correctional administration hierarchy;
2. Trained specialists were beginning to enter the institutions as case management workers and psychologists, with the goal of "correcting" offenders; and
3. The belief that offenders could be corrected was leading to an infusion of money into the correctional system.

Gradually an approach was adopted (referred to as the **medical model of corrections**) that favoured the provision of a variety of programs and therapies for "curing" inmates of their problem behaviour. It advocated medical solutions for problem behaviour, with treatments to be prescribed by "experts" in human nature, such as psychiatrists and psychologists. The impact of this new approach was immense: in 1920, there were approximately 1,200 federal inmates; by 1937, this figure had increased to 4,000. Over the same years, the number of federal correctional facilities increased, from 8 in 1937 to 19 in 1961.

Despite this change to a more rehabilitative ideal, inmates still experienced a harsh environment. Between 1932 and 1937, 16 riots broke out in federal correctional facilities. In 1937, the first of many Royal Commissions began investigating conditions in federal facilities. This commission, known as the **Archambault Commission**, produced a report that was harshly critical of the existing system. Instead of finding a system that was humane and based on the rehabilitative ideal, the commissioners found many problems. They made 88 recommendations, the general goal of which was to make federal correctional institutions more humane and progressive. But before any of these recommendations could be implemented, the Second World War began, leaving concerns about prison conditions as a low priority.

The end of the war led to a renewed interest in the federal correctional system. Of particular note was the creation, in 1953, of a committee of inquiry to study the operations and activities of the federal correctional system. The resulting report, the **Fauteux Report**, popularized the term **corrections** in Canada—a word the committee defined as "the total process by which society attempts to correct the anti-social attitudes or behaviour of the individual" (Carrington 1991:374). This report's recommendations included the provision of aftercare programs and the construction of facilities with different security classifications. It also recommended a liberalizing of the parole process, automatic review of parole, increased use of presentence reports, and the creation of a National Parole Board (now the Parole Board of Canada). However, support for rehabilitation was waning at this time, and by the early 1960s treatment programs had been reduced in favour of incarceration.

In 1963, the medical model began to decline in importance, to be replaced by the **reintegration model**. This approach favoured community-based correctional facilities, in particular the elimination of the coercive aspects of "treatment" and greater use of community resources for correcting offenders. This approach reflects the justice model of corrections (see Chapter 3), which maintains that inmates must be protected from any potential harmful actions of correctional officials through the introduction of legal rights for inmates and the increased use of community sanctions. In the mid-1970s, the Law Reform Commission of Canada committed itself to the reintegrative ideology, calling for a reduction in the use of imprisonment as a sanction. According to the Law Reform Commission of Canada (1975:25), "restricting our use of imprisonment will allow more people for other types of penalties . . . positive penalties like restitution and community service orders should be increasingly substituted for the negative and uncreative warehousing of prison."

This approach was dominant until the 1990s, when the federal government merged the reintegration model with the psychological-based **risk prediction ideology** (see Chapter 13). The dominant approach today emphasizes the increased use of community resources; the assessment of offenders' risks and needs on entering the correctional facility; and the creation of individual programs addressing those risks and needs. This approach has since become recognized in other countries as the most effective way to treat inmates.

A Brief History of Federal Correctional Facilities for Women

The earliest prison for women in Canada was located within Kingston Penitentiary. The original design called for separate units for male and female inmates; however, the first two women sentenced there were placed in the infirmary. By 1859, 68 women were serving their sentences in this facility, creating a serious problem for administrators. As Faith (1993) points out, female inmates were viewed as an "inconvenience" by prison administrators. Women continued to be moved to various locations within the penitentiary over the years; basically, they were "confined wherever and in whatever manner best served the administration of the larger male population" (Cooper 1993:5).

Construction of a separate institution for female inmates was not begun until 1914. This facility, known as the **Prison for Women (P4W)**, was actually built within the walls of the male prison in Kingston. Construction of a completely separate facility for women was begun in 1925. When it was completed in 1934, this new facility was designated as a maximum-security facility. No outside windows were built into the walls, all letters were censored, and there were no opportunities for education or vocational training of the type available to male inmates. Reports of sexual abuse and harsh living conditions led many reformers to demand that conditions be improved.

Beginning in 1968, numerous reports, investigations, and commissions investigated the P4W, and the final reports all made the same recommendation—that the facility be closed. They recommended that all inmates be located in their home provinces or in regional correctional facilities, which should be built and operated by the federal government. Many of these reports made basically the same point in support of their demands—that is, that female offenders are different from male offenders and thus should have different programs available to them. Programs were to be woman-centred—that is, all policies should be restructured to reflect the realities experienced by women as distinct from men. This was reflected in the report *Creating Choices: Report of the Task Force on Federally Sentenced Women* (1990), which advocated the empowerment of female inmates. It was recommended that women inmates be offered meaningful choices, respect and dignity, supportive environments, and shared responsibilities (Correctional Service of Canada 1990:126–35). This report also recommended that the federal government open regional facilities for women (including a healing lodge for Aboriginal women), increase programming for women, and make those programs more relevant so that when women were released they would be able to reintegrate quickly into society. Figure 12.4 shows women inmate population trends.

Two inquiries into the conditions of federally sentenced women in the P4W made a number of recommendations about how conditions for female inmates could be improved. The first was in 1989, when the federal government appointed the Task Force on Federally Sentenced Women to study the needs of female offenders, as well as their experiences, especially with regard to physical and sexual abuse. One of the goals of the inquiry was to evaluate whether the correctional model used for the male prison population was appropriate for women. The task force's final report, the previously mentioned *Creating Choices* (Correctional Service of Canada 1990), recommended that the P4W be replaced by five new correctional facilities for women, all of which would feature community-based programs.

Perhaps the most significant event in the history of federal correctional institutions for both women and men in Canada occurred in 1994, when "a series of events occurred in the Prison for Women in Kingston . . . would go on to define the new 'face' of corrections in Canada" (Erdahl 2001:43). On the evening of April 22, an Emergency Response Team made up of male correctional officers from the neighbouring federal facility in Kingston became involved in a "brief but violent physical confrontation with eight female inmates." The officers had been ordered to take the women out of their cells in the segregation unit and strip search them. The following day, these women were sent to a psychiatric centre before being returned to the P4W. A second inquiry was held in 1995 to investigate the 1994 incident. The final report of this investigation, *Commission of Inquiry into Certain Events at the Prison for Women in Kingston* (also known as the **Arbour Commission**), was released in 1996. In its report, the Commission reported that it found a "disturbing lack of commitment to the ideals of justice on the

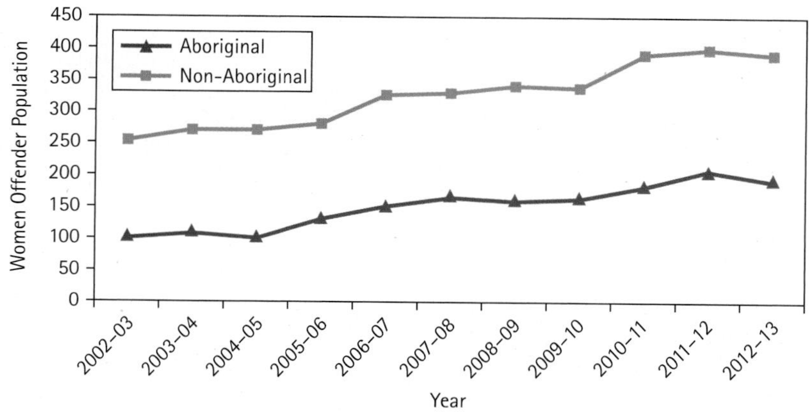

FIGURE 12.4 Ten-Year Federally Sentenced Women Inmate Population Trends

Source: Office of the Correctional Investigator, *Annual Report of the Office of the Correctional Investigator 2012–2013*, p. 36, http://www.oci-bec.gc.ca/cnt/rpt/annrpt20122013-eng.aspx. Reproduced with permission of the Office of the Correctional Officer.

part of the Correctional Service and that there should be greater judicial supervision in terms of [how] the Correctional Service manages segregation and the grievance process" (1996:196–197). The Commission of Inquiry report "serves as a scathing reminder of the injustices that are possible and of the importance for all those employed in the criminal justice system to follow the rule of law when carrying out their duties" (Barker 2009:21). The Commission made a series of recommendations, the general thrust of which was for fundamental and systematic changes for federally sentenced women. Its findings included these:

1. The CSC was not responding to outside criticism and was not prepared to give an honest and fair account of its actions. Instead, it was choosing to deny any errors in judgment and resist any criticism. Also, it was failing to properly investigate allegations of misconduct.
2. The CSC was part of a prison culture that did not value individual rights.
3. The CSC was failing to promote a "culture of rights" (Jackson 2002).

After the Commission released its report, the Correctional Service of Canada revised its mission statement to include the "rule of law." The amended mission statement read "the Correctional Service of Canada (CSC), as part of the criminal justice system and respecting the rule of law, contributes to public safety by actively encouraging and assisting offenders to become law-abiding citizens, while exercising reasonable, safe, secure and humane control."

Between 1995 and 1997, the federal government opened new women's facilities across Canada (Correctional Service of Canada 1997). These regional facilities were located in Truro, Nova Scotia; Joliette, Quebec; Kitchener and Kingston, Ontario; Maple Creek, Saskatchewan; Edmonton, Alberta; and Burnaby, British Columbia. The Burnaby facility was managed under an **Exchange of Service Agreement** between the CSC and British Columbia Provincial Corrections. In September 2002, the federal government announced that those women serving federal sentences in Burnaby would be moving to a new federal women's facility in Abbotsford. This facility opened in the fall of 2004. All of the new regional facilities included cottage-style accommodations, with each woman inmate having her own room. Communal kitchens, laundry areas, bathrooms, living rooms, and dining rooms were included in the plans for the cottages. The idea was to make the new facilities appear as close as possible to the norm of community living (Hayman 2006). When the new women's correctional facilities first opened, all women, regardless of their security level, were housed together. However, a series of violent incidents at the Edmonton facility in its first few months of operations in 1996—including two serious assaults on correctional staff, self-injury by a number of women inmates, a homicide, and seven escapes—led to all of the women classified as medium- and maximum-security risks being transferred to Alberta provincial facilities (where they would remain until late August 1996) under exchange of service agreements. Soon after, the CSC decided that for safety reasons, no women classified as maximum security would be placed in the new regional facilities.

Yet another investigation of female inmates' needs was conducted at the time of the incidents in Edmonton. The resulting report, the **Rivera Report**, concluded that some women offenders required both a secure environment and long-term intervention/treatment for needs that pre-existed their incarceration and that could be exacerbated by certain aspects of their incarceration (Watson 2004:4). One of the conclusions of this report was that the CSC should create a safe environment for at least three distinct subgroups of federally sentenced women.

It was realized that new resources would have to be built for maximum-security federally sentenced women in the new regional facilities. It was decided to place the maximum-security female offenders in small units in two federal male institutions (Springhill Institution and the Saskatchewan Penitentiary), both of which housed female inmates until 2003. A third facility, the Regional Reception Centre in Quebec, housed women inmates until 2004.

In May 1998, the **Structured Living Environment (SLE)** approach was implemented at each institution. This approach allowed higher security levels so that federally sentenced women would be able to remain in the regional facilities together with other offenders. Around-the-clock

The Edmonton Institution for Women was opened in 1995 and can accommodate up to 123 inmates. It is a multilevel facility; medium- and minimum-security inmates are accommodated in living units within a Structured Living Environment. Maximum-security inmates are accommodated in the Secured Unit.

Source: © Edmonton Institute for Women, *Correctional Service Canada's Infectious Diseases Newsletter,* Vol. 6, No. 1, http://www.csc-scc.gc.ca/text/pblct/hsbulletin/2008/no1/vol6_no1_index-eng.shtml, Correctional Service Canada, 2008. Reproduction with permission of the Minister of Public Works and Government Services, Canada. 2015.

The exterior of two living units at a women's federal correctional facility.

Source: Office of the Correctional Investigator, *Annual Report of the Office of the Correctional Investigator 2012–2013*, p. 35, http://www.oci-bec.gc.ca/cnt/rpt/annrpt20122013-eng.aspx. Reproduced with permission of the Office of the Correctional Officer.

assistance and supervision were to be provided by staff with specialized training. However, concerns were raised about having maximum-security women living so close to lower-security offenders. As a result, in 1999, **Secure Units** were introduced in order to provide high-level intervention and supervision by specialized staff for women classified as maximum security; with the exception of the women's facility at Maple Creek, Saskatchewan, all facilities currently have, or will eventually contain, Secure Units.

Unlike the federal male facilities, there is little ability or choice to transfer or move female offenders to other federal custodial facilities that are less crowded or that have a lower security ranking. This has the potential to lead to overcrowding. The Office of the Correctional Investigator (Office of the Correctional Investigator Canada 2011) reported that three of the women's facilities had requested approval so that they could "double bunk" offenders in their Secure Units. In addition, at one of the institutions the Structured Living Environment unit had been used to segregate women offenders, while other facilities were housing women in an interview room within a Secure Unit and another was planning to convert the recreational space into a dormitory.

A Brief History of Federal Correctional Facilities for Aboriginal People

Aboriginal peoples made up about 4 percent of Canada's population in 2006, yet they accounted for 20 percent of the federal custodial sentences in 2010. On any given day in 2010, approximately 2,600 Aboriginal offenders were incarcerated in federal custodial facilities. In 1991, the Royal Commission on Aboriginal Peoples was established to investigate many issues confronting Aboriginal people in the broader Canadian society, including justice issues. In response to the Commission's five-volume final report, the federal government launched the "Gathering Strength" initiative, which amounted to a plan to recast the relationship between the government and Canada's Aboriginal people. The plan was built on the principles of mutual respect, mutual recognition, mutual responsibility, and sharing.

In compliance with the Royal Commission's recommendations and the federal government's initiative, the CSC reviewed its mandate to provide services to Aboriginal offenders as reflected in ss. 79 to 84 of the Corrections and Conditional Release Act (CCRA). These clauses are intended to allow Aboriginal inmates to benefit from the positive spiritual and holistic aspects of their culture. They also invite Aboriginal communities and Elders to play an active role as service providers and advisers on policy formulation and implementation. Sections 79–84 of the CCRA focus specifically upon the Correctional Service of Canada (CSC) obligations in the area of Aboriginal corrections:

- section 80 provides that the CSC shall provide Aboriginal-specific programs;
- section 81 provides that the CSC may enter into an agreement with an Aboriginal community in order to provide services to Aboriginal offenders;
- section 82 states that the CSC shall establish a National Aboriginal Advisory Committee which shall provide advice to the CSC about the provision of correctional services to Aboriginal offenders; and
- section 84 states that where an inmate who is applying for parole has expressed an interest in being released to an Aboriginal community, the CSC shall give the Aboriginal community notice of the parole application as an opportunity to propose a plan for the inmate's release.

As a result of the obligations found in the CCRA, the CSC began to implement more programs for Aboriginal offenders. These include Aboriginal programs such as Circles of Change, In Search of Your Warrior, and Aboriginal Offender Substance Abuse Programming, and Pathways units which are located in living areas found in medium-security custodial facilities designed to address the cultural and spiritual needs of Aboriginal offenders (Table 12.1). They also began to build and operate a number of **healing lodges** across Canada (Table 12.2).

Healing lodges offer services and programs reflecting Aboriginal culture that incorporates Aboriginal peoples' traditions and beliefs. While serving their federal sentence, the needs of Aboriginal offenders are facilitated by culturally relevant programs. The needs of Aboriginal offenders are addressed through Aboriginal teachings and ceremonies—with an emphasis on spiritual values—in order to assist Aboriginal offenders in their successful reintegration. The philosophy governing this approach is one that follows a **holistic philosophy**, allowing staff and offenders to engage in

TABLE 12.1 Aboriginal-Operated s. 81 Facilities

Facility	Opening Date	Region	Bed Capacity
Prince Albert Grand Council (PAGC) Spiritual Healing Lodge	1995	Prairie – Saskatchewan	5
Stan Daniels Healing Centre	1999	Prairie – Alberta	30
O-Chi-Chak-Ko-Sipi Healing Lodge	1999	Prairie – Manitoba	18
Waseskun Healing Centre	2001	Quebec	15
Total			**68**

Source: Office of the Correctional Investigator, *Spirit Matters: Aboriginal People and the Corrections and Conditional Release Act*, p. 22, http://www.oci-bec.gc.ca/cnt/rpt/pdf/oth-aut/oth-aut20121022-eng.pdf. Reproduced with permission of the Office of the Correctional Officer.

TABLE 12.2 CSC-Operated Healing Lodges

Facility	Opening Date	Region	Capacity
Okimaw Ohci Healing Lodge	1995	Prairie – Saskatchewan	44
Pe Sakastew Centre	1997	Prairie – Alberta	60
Kwìkwèxwelhp Healing Village	2001	Pacific – British Columbia	50
Willow Cree Healing Lodge	2003	Prairie – Saskatchewan	40
Total			**194**

Source: Office of the Correctional Investigator, *Spirit Matters: Aboriginal People and the Corrections and Conditional Release Act*, p. 22, http://www.oci-bec.gc.ca/cnt/rpt/pdf/oth-aut/oth-aut20121022-eng.pdf. Reproduced with permission of the Office of the Correctional Officer.

activities that emphasize spiritual elements as well as preparing individuals for reintegrating with the community when they are released (e.g., Graveline 1998; Hart 2002). Almost all of these healing lodges are located away from urban centres.

The first healing lodge operated by the federal government was opened in 1995; this was the 30-bed Okimaw Ohci Healing Lodge in Maple Creek, Saskatchewan, for use by Aboriginal female offenders. Since that time, four more healing lodges have been opened by CSC for Aboriginal men. These are located near Hobbema, Alberta (the Pe Sakastew Centre); Chehalis, British Columbia (the Elbow Lake Healing Village); Duck Lake, Saskatchewan (the Willow Cree Healing Lodge); and Yellowknife (the Some Ke' Healing Lodge). In addition, in 1999, the federal government opened the first healing lodge within the walls of a federal correctional facility, in Stony Mountain Institution, a medium-security facility north of Winnipeg. In this healing lodge, inmates do not live in the lodge, but do attend the facility for Aboriginal programming, spiritual teachings, and ceremonies.

The CSC also has **s. 81 agreements** with Aboriginal communities to operate healing lodges. Sections 81(1) and (3) of the act state:

> 81 (1) The Minister, or person authorized by the Minister, may enter in to an agreement with an Aboriginal community for the provision of correctional services to Aboriginal offenders and for payment by the Minister, or by a person authorized by the Minister, in respect to the provision of these services . . .

An Aboriginal meeting room at a medium-security federal correctional facility.

Source: Office of the Correctional Investigator, *Annual Report of the Office of the Correctional Investigator 2012–2013*, p. 17, http://www.oci-bec.gc.ca/cnt/rpt/annrpt/annrpt20122013-eng.aspx. Reproduced with permission of the Office of the Correctional Officer.

Okimaw Ohci Spiritual Lodge.

Source: © Okimaw Ohci Healing Lodge, http://www.csc.scc.gc.ca/aboriginal/002003-2000-eng.shtml, Correctional Service of Canada, 2013. Reproduced with the permission of the Minister of Public Works and Government Services Canada 2015.

> (3) In accordance with any agreement entered into under subsection (1), the Commission may transfer an Aboriginal offender to the care and custody of an Aboriginal community, with the consent of the Aboriginal offender and of the Aboriginal community.

As part of this initiative, starting in the mid-1990s the federal government entered into agreements with Aboriginal communities and organizations relating to correctional services, including custody, for Aboriginal offenders. Since this time, at least four s. 81 healing lodges for Aboriginal offenders have been established. Healing lodges are designed to offer services and programs reflecting Aboriginal cultural traditions. Since that time, four healing lodges have been opened for Aboriginal men. These are located near Prince Albert, Saskatchewan (the Grand Council Spiritual Healing Lodge); Edmonton (the Stan Daniels Healing Centre); Crane River, Manitoba (the O-Chi-Chak-Ko-Sipi Healing Lodge); and Montreal (the Waseskun Healing Centre). To date, there is no s. 84 healing lodge for Aboriginal women.

There are a number of differences between the lodges operated by the federal government and those run by Aboriginal agencies/communities. The federal lodges focus on traditional Aboriginal cultural traditions and holistic methods and are classified as minimum-security facilities (although Okimaw Ohci also accepts medium-security offenders). Some staff of both facilities were CSC correctional officers before the lodge became a healing lodge. An offender who wants to transfer to one of these healing lodges follows the same process as for a transfer to any other correctional facility within the CSC. Between 1995, when the first healing lodge opened in Canada, and October 2001, 530 offenders resided in a healing lodge. Since 1998, over 100 individuals have been transferred to a healing lodge each year.

Healing lodges managed by Aboriginal communities are privately operated and follow guidelines as outlined in their contracts with the CSC. They do not necessarily follow the structured approach found within CSC-operated facilities. Transferring to a s. 81 healing lodge involves a slightly different process. Only those who are classified as minimum security can apply for a transfer. Once a healing lodge receives an application for a transfer to its facility, a meeting is held between the applicant and members of the healing lodge. Factors such as the applicant's involvement in traditional culture, motivation to change, commitment to the healing plan, and behaviour in the current correctional facility may influence the outcome of the application. Some healing lodges have other stipulations—for example, Waseskun has an agreement with the local community not to accept an applicant who has been convicted of a sexual offence (Trevethan et al. 2002).

Federal healing lodges have spaces for 30 to 40 individuals; the healing lodges under s. 81 offer spaces for anywhere between 10 and 75. Also, Crutcher and Trevethan (2002) report several differences between Aboriginal offenders in healing lodges and those in a minimum-security CSC facility: overall, the "residents of healing lodges appear to have a slightly more extensive criminal history than Aboriginal offenders in a minimum security" (ibid.:52). A larger proportion of healing lodge residents had been previously segregated for disciplinary infractions (25 percent versus 17 percent) and for attempted/successful escapes (34 percent versus 21 percent). Also, they were rated as at higher risk for reoffending (53 percent versus 45 percent) and as having a lower reintegration potential (45 percent versus 33 percent).

In many instances the healing lodges are operating below their capacity, although there are waiting lists to

SUMMING UP AND LOOKING FORWARD

Correctional facilities as we know them today are social institutions that confine and separate convicted criminals from the rest of society. They were first introduced in Europe during the 17th and 18th centuries. The rise and acceptance of prisons represented a move from the punishment of the body to the punishment of the mind. Key figures involved in the introduction of correctional facilities included Cesare Beccaria and Jeremy Bentham. Competing views about the structure of prisons emerged, with the Auburn approach ultimately becoming the most popular, and this approach became the type favoured in Canada. Over time, changes were made to the way inmates were treated in prisons. Rehabilitation became dominant, and various types of rehabilitation have been practised since the 1950s, for example the medical model and the risk prediction approach.

Women's correctional facilities in Canada were first placed in separate spaces and then buildings within prisons for men. The first separate women's correctional facility opened in 1934 was located near the men's federal correctional facility in Kingston, Ontario. The first correctional facility for Aboriginals was opened in 1995 in Maple Creek, Saskatchewan. Since that time, new healing lodges operated by the federal government as well as by Aboriginal communities have opened.

While the formal structure and organization of correctional facilities has been discussed, how are inmates classified and what is the profile of the people who are sent to correctional facilities? The next section outlines how inmates are classified according to security risk and how facilities differ based upon risk levels, how prison architecture and their related supervision models have changed over time, as well as the profiles of a variety of groups who are incarcerated.

Review Questions:

1. Why were prisons "invented" in Europe during the 17th and 18th centuries?
2. What are the differences between the Pennsylvania and Auburn systems of incarceration?
3. How has rehabilitation changed over time in the correctional system in Canada?
4. Discuss how the federal correctional facilities for women emerged and have developed.
5. How did the federal correctional facilities for Aboriginal peoples emerge and how have they developed?

enter these facilities. This has raised questions about the direction given to CSC's policies regarding s. 81 healing lodges. Almost 20 years after the CCRA allowed for the creation of healing lodges, an audit by CSC concluded that there wasn't a policy framework in place to support the creation of s. 81 healing lodges as well as no direction provided by the CSC in either their policies or procedures (Correctional Service of Canada 2008).

What Is the Role of Correctional Facilities in Canada?

Correctional facilities are built to make society a safer place to live. Since correctional facilities have emerged, attempts have been made to describe how they operate:

- *The custodial model.* The **custodial model** is based on the idea that prisoners are incarcerated for the purposes of incapacitation and deterrence. All decisions are made in the context of maintaining maximum security and discipline. There is tight control over inmates in all phases of prison life. This model was the first to emerge, and the early prisons built in Canada reflected this style of thinking and operation.
- *The rehabilitation model.* The emphasis of the **rehabilitation model** is on individualized treatment. Concerns about security and control are secondary to the well-being of inmates. Treatment programs are available for (and often forced on) inmates in order to help them change their criminal and antisocial behaviours. This model came into popularity in the 1950s, but that popularity began to fade in the 1970s with the emergence of critiques of rehabilitation brought about by the work of Robert Martinson and his colleagues (see Chapter 11).
- *The reintegration model.* In the **reintegration model**, correctional facilities attempt to prepare inmates for reintegration with the broader society. Facilities that take this approach help inmates work on their specific needs and risks so that they will not engage in criminal behaviour once they are living in the community again. During incarceration and their time on conditional release, responsibility and accountability are stressed. This model is the most influential one in Canada today.

Security Levels

The major objective of correctional institutions is confinement; it follows that the key factor in determining an inmate's classification level is security. On a general level, security has three components:

1. the likelihood that an inmate will escape or attempt to escape;
2. the likelihood that an inmate will place a correctional officer or another inmate in danger; and
3. the likelihood that an inmate will attempt to violate institutional rules (Anderson and Newman 1993).

Until 1981–82, the CSC employed a classification system for offenders based on the likelihood that the offender would try to escape from an institution and the potential harm to the community if he or she succeeded. Accordingly, the CSC defined three security levels as follows:

1. **Maximum security**. The inmate is likely to escape and would cause serious harm in the community.
2. **Medium security**. The inmate is likely to escape but would not cause serious harm in the community.
3. **Minimum security**. The inmate is not likely to escape, and if they did, would not cause harm in the community (Eckstedt and Griffiths 1988:191).

The CSC's parole officers assign every inmate a security classification on entry into the institution. In most cases, this is followed by an interview with a placement officer, who assesses the inmate to determine their security needs. However, this initial assessment does not necessarily determine to which type of security-level facility the inmate will be sent. An inmate classified as maximum security may be sent to a medium-security institution, depending on his or her prior record as well as the types of programs offered by the institution. Maximum-security facilities are usually surrounded by high fences or walls (depending on when they were built), which are typically around 6 metres in height and surrounded by guard towers at strategic points. Intrusion detection systems ensure that the perimeter is not "compromised." Parts of the facility are separated by gates, fences, and walls, and inmates are usually required to have special permission forms when they are moving between sections of the institution outside normal times of movement. A number of inmates live in solitary confinement, either owing to behavioural issues or out of concern that they will be attacked by other inmates, usually because of the crimes they are in prison for (e.g., sex offenders are in particular danger in prison). Maximum-security facilities usually have a number of educational and treatment programs, including adult basic education, high-school equivalency courses, and various skills development programs, such as carpentry.

Medium-security institutions are typically enclosed by chain link fences topped with barbed and razor wire. Relative to maximum-security facilities, medium-security institutions allow more freedom of movement for inmates. Many of these facilities have modern surroundings and training centres; a variety of educational and treatment facilities are also available. Minimum-security prisons usually have no fences or walls around them. In fact, any inmate can walk out of the facility, since the surrounding security is much more relaxed. There are no armed guards, no towers, and no barbed wire; nor is there any electronic surveillance equipment to ensure that prisoners stay in the institution. Staff and inmates often mingle and are indistinguishable from one another, since prison clothes are not issued. Inmates are housed in better living arrangements, in private or semiprivate rooms. In addition, inmates may be on work release programs that allow them to hold jobs during the day.

There is another type of security found within the CSC, but it focuses upon the interactions between people as opposed to the risk level of an offender. This is known as **dynamic security**, which refers to a policy objective that optimizes a safe environment for all employees, offenders, and the public through meaningful interactions. Those who have worked in this area (e.g., Liebling and Arnold 2004) point out that an approach that emphasizes respectful social relationships between prison staff and inmates leads to improved relationships and just treatment of inmates, which leads to improved conditions. It is the responsibility of all staff within federal facilities who interact directly with offenders to improve their knowledge of the offenders' activities and behaviours. This is to be accomplished by staff increasing their awareness of those factors that contribute to, or may compromise, the safety and security of the staff, offenders, and members of the public (Correctional Service of Canada 2007). Dynamic security is considered an essential component of the health and safety of all inmates and CSC personnel. According to the Correctional Investigator (Office of the Correctional Investigator Canada 2010:33) "mutual respect, along with positive and constructive interactions between staff and offenders, are the hallmarks of a healthy and safe institution."

In 2013, the CSC reported that 15.1 percent of all male and female inmates serving a custodial sentence in the federal system were in a maximum-security institution. Most offenders (62 percent) are classified as medium risk (see Figure 12.5). The remaining offenders were in either minimum-security or multilevel institutions (Public Safety Canada 2013). A multilevel facility combines features of two or more of the security levels described earlier in this section. Some facilities use the same buildings to accommodate inmates classified at different security levels; others operate separate structures for each level. The majority of female inmates in the federal system are housed in multilevel security institutions, as are a significant number of all male inmates and 35 percent of female inmates serving a custodial sentence in the provincial/territorial correctional systems.

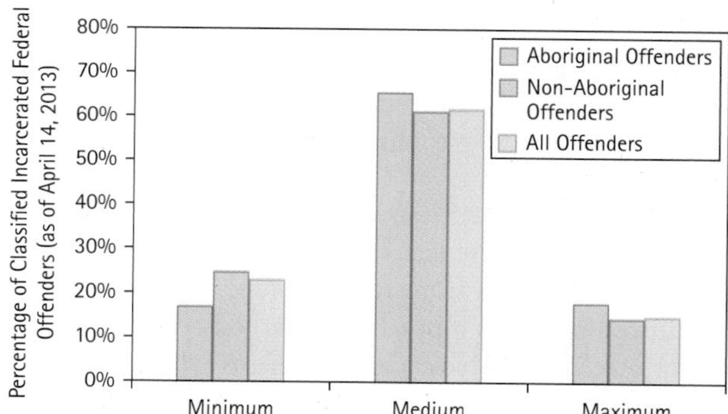

FIGURE 12.5 The Majority of Incarcerated Federal Offenders are Classified as Medium Security Risks

Source: Corrections and Conditional Release Statistics Overview Annual Report 2013, Figure C12, p. 55, https://www.publicsafety.gc.ca/cnt/rsrcs/pblctns/crrctns-cndtnl-rls-2013/crrctns-cndtnl-rls-2013-eng.pdf. Reproduced with the permission of the Minister of Public Safety and Emergency Preparedness, 2015.

Since 1981–82, the CSC has operated on the basis of seven security levels. Level 1 facilities are community correctional centres; level 2 institutions are minimum-security facilities such as forestry and work camps. Levels 3 to 5 are medium security; level 6 is maximum security. Level 7 is the highest level of security and is reserved for violent offenders. Level 7 units are often referred to as special handling units, or "super-max."

Federal female offenders are classified according to a different scale: the **Security Reclassification Management System**, which was approved for the new women's federal facilities in April 1995 and implemented in September 2005. The guidelines developed by this system govern the daily management of each facility as well as the inmates' participation in programs and activities and freedom of movement inside each facility. This system focuses on the majority of the female population in federal institutions, rather than on the few who persistently commit crimes in a violent and aggressive manner. It comprises six management levels, of which five are related to security classification and one is used exclusively for admission status (Finn et al. 1999). All female offenders are reassessed at least once a year; those who are classified as maximum security are reassessed every six months.

Prison Architecture and Correctional Facilities

Correctional facilities must confront many serious issues, including drug use, suicide, violence between inmates, and attacks on correctional officers. Some prison officials began looking at these issues and developing new ways to approach the housing, guarding, and treatment of convicted offenders. They felt that how correctional facilities were operated was just as important as why they were built. As a consequence, some correctional facilities in Canada have been moving away from traditional designs and turning themselves into **new-generation facilities**.

In traditional facilities, known as **first-generation facilities**, often there is a separate building or cluster of buildings separated from the "outside" by high walls of reinforced concrete topped with barbed wire and guard towers. Cell blocks have a linear design—that is, they are located along a long hallway. To supervise inmates when they are in their cells, correctional officers walk up and down these halls; as a result, their ability to see beyond the specific cell they are looking at is extremely limited. This style of supervision is referred to as **intermittent supervision**. There is minimal contact between correctional officers and inmates, unless the officers are responding to an incident requiring their assistance. Many inmates misbehave or engage in illicit activities since they are not under the surveillance of correctional authorities.

Second-generation facilities began to emerge in the 1960s. In these designs, correctional officers keep the inmates under constant supervision from secure control booths that overlook all of the hallways and other areas (e.g., weight rooms) where inmates gather in groups. This type of surveillance is generally referred to as **indirect supervision**. Cells are clustered around common living areas, where the inmates can watch television or meet. The cells have metal doors with unbreakable windows and usually have enough room for one or two inmates. Rooms have a bed, a desk, a sink, and perhaps a toilet. They can be made of concrete or reinforced metal bolted to the wall or floor. Overall, there is little interaction between correctional officers and inmates. Early facilities of this type continued to use reinforced concrete walls topped with barbed wire; many later facilities used fences topped with razor wire.

Because of increasing prison violence starting in the late 1960s and continuing through the 1970s, other efforts were made to change the architecture of prisons. These attempts were based on the idea that inmates' physical surroundings were having an impact on their behaviour. In addition, important changes were made in the management philosophies of correctional facilities, so as to allow for more personal contact between correctional staff and inmates. Prison officials altered the traditional designs of correctional facilities to arrive at what are now known as "new-generation" facilities (sometimes these are referred to as **third-generation facilities** or **direct supervision**). These new facilities are very different from their predecessors. The physical structure is based on a **podular design**—that is, each "pod" contains 12 to 24 one-person cells extending from a common area. These cells are usually situated in a triangle, enabling correctional officers to be in the centre of the triangle and have visual access to all, or nearly all, the living units and common areas. Daily activities, such as eating and recreational activities, take place in this common area. Other types of facilities, such as treatment and interview rooms, are located within the pod; all of this allows correctional officers greater access to and contact with inmates. Another change in these facilities is the provision of comfortable furniture and rugs, as well as a "communal" room that allows inmates to get together to watch television, listen to a radio, or make a telephone call.

The podular design also differs from the traditional model in that it allows each unit to be directly supervised (see Exhibit 12.1). Throughout the day there are physical contacts among correctional officers (who are stationed within the pod), prison authorities, and inmates. During the day, inmates must stay in common areas and

EXHIBIT 12.1 Supervision Models

According to prison officials, there are six objectives of the direct supervision model:

1. Staff, rather than inmates, control the facility and inmates' behaviour.
2. Inmates are directly and constantly supervised, and correctional officers direct and control the behaviour of all inmates.
3. Rewards and punishments are structured to ensure compliant behaviour.
4. Open communication is maintained between the correctional staff and inmates.
5. Inmates are advised of the expectations and rules of the facility.
6. Inmates are treated in a manner consistent with proper standards of conduct and are treated in a fair and equitable way regardless of their personal traits or crimes they committed.

Seven behavioural dimensions are necessary for the effective supervision and control of inmates in the pods. Many of these dimensions were developed from the general principles found in effective personnel supervision:

1. Resolving inmate problems and conflicts.
2. Building positive rapport and personal credibility with inmates.
3. Maintaining effective administrative and staff relations.
4. Managing the living unit to ensure a safe and humane living environment.
5. Responding to inmate requests.
6. Handling inmate discipline.
7. Supervising in a clear, well-organized, and attention-getting manner.

Sources: Nelson and O'Toole 1983; Gettinger 1984; Zupan 1991.

can be in their cells only with permission. This model allows correctional officials to identify problem behaviours quickly; it also allows them to observe the daily activities of all inmates. Prison officials have reported that the new-generation facilities have led to a dramatic reduction in the number of violent incidents as well as escapes (Zupan 1991). Studies have verified the positive effects that new-generation facilities have had on inmate behaviour, including lower rates of destructive behaviour, fewer escapes, and reductions in the number of suicides and violent incidents (Senese 1997). Applegate and colleagues (1999) concluded that new-generation designs were not increasing recidivism and might lead to reduced post-offence offending.

Women Inmates

In 2012–13, women accounted for 5.4 percent of all admissions into the federal correctional system. The number of women sentenced to custody varies among the provinces and territories. The percentage of women sentenced in the provinces was greatest in Saskatchewan and Alberta (both at 14 percent), while for the territories it was in Yukon (12 percent). Female offenders usually account for larger proportions of probation and conditional sentences than of custody admissions. During 2008–09, for example, they accounted for 18 percent of all admissions to probation, ranging from a low of 15 percent in Quebec and Prince Edward Island to a high of 23 percent in Saskatchewan. Nineteen percent of all admissions to conditional sentences were female, ranging from 15 percent in Quebec to 31 percent in Yukon. Women accounted for almost 13 percent of all remands during 2008–09, with the lowest percentage recorded in Nunavut while the highest was found in Manitoba.

Overall, the number of women sentenced to federal custody has remained at approximately 5 to 6 percent since 1998–99. In 2012–13, the CSC reported that 270 women were sentenced to federal custody (Public Safety Canada 2013). While the number of federally sentenced women (FSW) makes up a small proportion of the total federal offender population (4.9 percent in 2014), women are "among the fastest growing sub-populations in federal corrections today" (Office of the Correctional Investigator Canada 2014a). Over the past 10 years, the number of women offenders (both incarcerated and in the community) increased by 30 percent. This growth has been largest in the incarcerated population: since 2004–05, the number of women in federal custody has increased by almost 67 percent. In early 2014, an investigation into federally incarcerated women reported the following:

- Seventy percent of women inmates are single;
- More than 60 percent are between the ages of 20 and 29;
- Seventy-five percent are mothers to children under the age of 18;
- At the time of their arrest, 67 percent of women offenders were single caregivers;
- Almost one-half are classified as medium security;
- Just over one-half (52.4 percent) are serving a sentence of between two and four years
- Most are classified as high need and high risk;

- They demonstrate higher levels of motivation and reintegration potential compared to male inmates (Office of the Correctional Investigator Canada 2014a:26).

Exhibit 12.2 provides additional information about federally sentenced women.

Women inmates are convicted and placed in a correctional facility for different offences than men, and for fewer offences. Data from four provinces (Newfoundland and Labrador, Nova Scotia, New Brunswick, and Saskatchewan) in 2002–03 indicate that 23 percent of all women released from an adult provincial correctional institution returned to that same jurisdiction's correctional service system within two years (compared to 32 percent for men). In the federal system in 2006, 85 percent of women serving a term had either no, or only one, previous term of federal incarceration, compared to 70 percent of men inmates (Kong and AuCoin 2008).

Women and men may differ in terms of the offences for which they have been convicted. Women sentenced to a federal correctional facility are less likely than men inmates to be incarcerated for a violent crime. Nineteen percent of women were incarcerated for a violent crime, compared to 38 percent of men. The most common violent crime for which women were convicted during 2003–04 was "common assault," while the most common conviction in the category of crimes against property was "theft." Men were also most commonly convicted of these same two offences during 2003–04.

Aboriginal Inmates

A major correctional issue is the well-documented fact that Aboriginal people are overrepresented in Canada's correctional facilities. In 2010–11, 27 percent of all adults in the provincial and territorial correctional systems and 20 percent of the federal correctional system were Aboriginal. Two years later, in 2013, Aboriginal people were 23 percent of all federal inmates. This overrepresentation of Aboriginal adults in the Canadian correctional system has continually increased over the past number of years. Between 2000–01 and early 2013, the

EXHIBIT 12.2 Profile of Federally Sentenced Women, 2010

General

- As of August 2010, there were 512 federally sentenced women incarcerated in CSC facilities.
- 567 women offenders were under some form of community release supervision.
- In the last 10 years, the number of Aboriginal women in custody has increased by 86.4 percent compared to 25.7 percent over the same period for Aboriginal men.
- 34 percent of the incarcerated women offender population is Aboriginal.
- More than 65 percent of new female admissions are serving a sentence of less than three years.

Personal Histories

- 77 percent of women offenders have children. Just over half indicated having experiences with Children's Aid.
- In 2010, 86 percent of women offenders reported histories of physical abuse, and 68 percent reported a history of sexual abuse at some point in their lives, representing an increase of 19 percent and 15 percent, respectively, since 1991.
- Approximately 45 percent of women offenders reported having less than a high school education at intake.
- 64 percent supported themselves financially.

Mental Health and Addictions

- In 2009, 29 percent of women offenders were identified at admission as presenting mental health problems, and this proportion has more than doubled over the past decade.
- 31 percent of women were identified at intake as having a past mental health diagnosis, representing a 63 percent increase over the past decade.
- 48 percent of women were identified at intake as having a current need for prescribed medication.
- Since 2003, at intake, approximately 77 percent of women report abusing both alcohol and drugs.
- Just under half of women self-report having engaged in self-harming behaviour.

Source: Office of the Correctional Investigator, *Annual Report of the Office of the Correctional Investigator 2010–2011*, p. 50, http://www.oci-bec.gc.ca/cnt/rpt/pdf/annrpt/annrpt20102011-eng.pdf. Reproduced with permission of the Office of the Correctional Officer.

overall representation rate for Aboriginals in the federal inmate population increased from 17 percent to 23 percent. And from 2005–06 to 2013, there was a 43.5 percent increase in the federal Aboriginal inmate population, compared to a 9.6 percent increase in non-Aboriginal inmates (Perreault 2014). The rate of overrepresentation was higher for Aboriginal women than Aboriginal men in the federal correctional system; 33.6 percent of all FSW women in 2013 were Aboriginal.

The overrepresentation of Aboriginal people in both provincial/territorial and federal correctional facilities is consistent across all provinces and territories (see Figure 12.6). Provinces with the largest numbers of Aboriginal people in the adult population reported a larger representation of Aboriginal offenders in their sentenced admissions. The largest overrepresentation of Aboriginal offenders in sentenced custody compared to their representation in the adult population occurred in all of the western provinces (British Columbia, Alberta, Saskatchewan, and Manitoba).

According to the Office of the Correctional Investigator Canada (2012b), the gap between Aboriginal and non-Aboriginal offenders continues to widen on every indicator of correctional performance:

- Aboriginal offenders serve disproportionately more of their sentence behind bars before first release;
- Aboriginal offenders are underrepresented in community supervision programs and overrepresented in maximum-security institutions;
- Aboriginal offenders are more likely to return to prison on revocation of parole; Aboriginal offenders are disproportionately involved in institutional security incidents, use of force interventions, segregation placements, and self-injurious behaviour; and
- Most Aboriginal inmates are released on statutory release or warrant expiry, not parole.

Similar to their representation in the general population, Aboriginal adults in correctional services were younger than non-Aboriginal adults and were more likely to have served prior youth and/or adult sentences; to be incarcerated more often for a violent offence; to have a high risk rating; to have higher need ratings; to be more inclined to have gang affiliations; and to have more health problems, including fetal alcohol spectrum disorder (FASD) and mental health issues and addiction (Mann 2010). More specifically, Aboriginal adults were, on average, three years younger than their non-Aboriginal counterparts in the three provinces (30.8 years versus 33.7 years of age). In addition, the majority (42.3 percent) of Aboriginal adult offenders were between 20 and 29, compared to 35.2 percent for non-Aboriginal offenders in this same age bracket. In addition, about three-quarters of all Aboriginal adults involved in correctional services had not completed high school compared to one-third of non-Aboriginal adults. Aboriginal people were also to be less likely to have been employed at the time of their admission to correctional services compared to non-Aboriginal people (35 percent versus 44 percent) (Brzozowski et al. 2006).

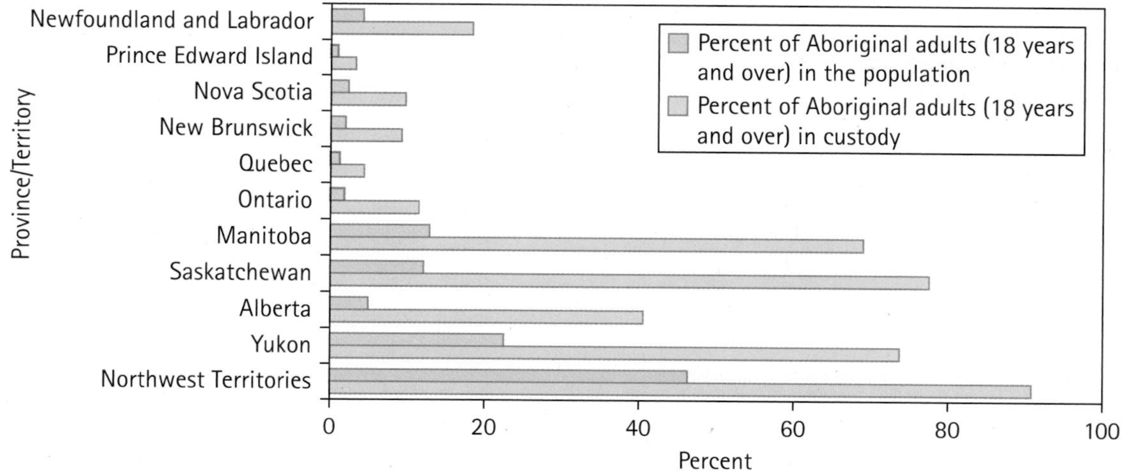

FIGURE 12.6 Aboriginal Adult Admissions to Custody, by Province and Territory, 2010–11

Source: Mia Duavergne, "Adult correctional statistics in Canada, 2010/2011." *Juristat* (October 2012), Statistics Canada Catalogue 85-002-X, p. 12, http://www.statcan.gc.ca/pub/85-002-x/2012001/article/11715-eng.pdf. Reproduced and distributed on an "as is" basis with the permission of Statistics Canada.

Black Inmates in Federal Correctional Facilities

The visible minority population (both incarcerated and those in the community) increased 40 percent between 2007–08 and 2012–13. Members of visible minority groups made up 18 percent of the total federal offender population. In 2011–12, Whites made up the largest number of inmates (62.3 percent), followed by Aboriginals (19.3 percent), Blacks (8.6 percent), Asians (5.4 percent), Hispanics (0.9 percent), and members of all other visible groups (3.4 percent). In the same five-year time span, all of the net growth in the federal incarcerated population (both incarcerated and in the community) was accounted for by increases by visible minority groups—Aboriginals (+793), Blacks (+585), Asians (+337), and all other visible minority groups (+290). In comparison, the total number of White offenders decreased (−466).

In 2011–12, there were 55 Black women incarcerated in a federal correctional facility (9 percent of the federally incarcerated women). Between 2002 and 2010 the numbers of Black women incarcerated stayed about the same, but since then their numbers have increased dramatically, up 54 percent in 2010 and another 28 percent during the next two years. Most Black women were foreign nationals, and incarcerated for Schedule II (drug) offences.

The following profile of Black inmates is based on information collected by the Office of the Correctional Investigator Canada (2013):

- From 2003–04 to 2012–13, the number of federally incarcerated Blacks increased by 80 percent (from 778 to 1,403).
- Four percent of Black inmates are women.
- The majority of Black inmates are incarcerated in federal correctional facilities located in Ontario (60 percent) and Quebec (17 percent).
- Approximately one-half of Black inmates are under the age of 30, and 8 percent are over the age of 50.
- Fifty-one percent were incarcerated for Schedule I (violent) offences and 18 percent for Schedule II (drug) offences.
- Black inmates are no more likely to be sentenced for a violent crime than any other group.
- The majority of black offenders (81 percent) are not affiliated with a gang.
- Black offenders have higher completion rates for all conditional release programs.
- Black inmates are more likely than other inmates to be placed in maximum-security facilities as well as solitary confinement.
- Black inmates are more likely to have use of force against them from correctional officers.

The following information about Black inmates is based on interviews of 73 Black inmates (30 women and 43 men) by the Office of the Correctional Investigator Canada (2013):

Nearly all Black inmates reported being discriminated against by correctional officials. The most common type of discrimination was covert discrimination, which increases their marginalization, exclusion, and isolation.

Black inmates are commonly stereotyped—as, for example, trouble-makers and gang members—which impacts official decision making with regard to security classification, program enrollment, work assignments, and recommendations for conditional release programs.

Most Black women had been convicted of drug trafficking, and reported that they were forced into trafficking drugs due to threats of violence against their families or to escape poverty.

SUMMING UP AND LOOKING FORWARD

Various models have been developed in an attempt to describe the different ways correctional facilities operate in society: the custodial model, the rehabilitation model, and the reintegration model. Correctional facilities are characterized by different security levels, which are based on the risk levels of offenders. Another type of security, dynamic security, refers to a policy objective that emphasizes a safe environment for employees, offenders, and the public through meaningful interactions. Various types of prison architecture have existed since the first prisons were built in the 18th century. First-generation correctional facilities are characterized by a cluster of buildings (or a single building) separated from the outside world by walls and/or fences. Second-generation facilities keep inmates under constant supervision from secure booths located within the correctional facility. New-generation correctional facilities use a podular style of architecture that, by design, eliminates many of the traditional features of prisons, such as allowing correctional staff greater interaction and control of inmates.

Once in prison, there is a process by which inmates internalize and legitimize a prison subculture. A prison subculture is a unique set of norms that influence inmates' behaviour. These norms are informal and unwritten, but violating them can lead to a violent confrontation. Federally sentenced women were originally placed into separate buildings within male correctional facilities. The first separate federal correctional facility for women in Canada was opened in 1934. Separate regional facilities for women were opened during the 1990s; one of these facilities was built for Aboriginal women. Aboriginal inmates are overrepresented in the federal correctional facilities. The gap between Aboriginal and non-Aboriginal inmates continues to widen on every indicator of correctional performance; for example, they are incarcerated for longer periods of time and are underrepresented in community supervision programs. During the last 20 years the federal correctional system has introduced Aboriginal programming and facilities operated by Aboriginal communities.

While the formal structure and organization of correctional facilities has been discussed, what are the conditions of confinement like? And how do people experience the prison environment? The next section overviews what happens during the prison experience, from the prison subculture to various types of conditions found when people are confined.

Review Questions:

1. What are the differences among the following types of models of prisons: the custodial model, the rehabilitation model, and the reintegration model?
2. What are the different types of security levels and how are they associated with correctional facilities?
3. What is the direct supervision model? How does it differ from other supervision models?
4. How are the separate women's facilities structured? What is the profile of federally sentenced women in terms of their personal histories?
5. What are the different types of federal correctional facilities available for Aboriginal offenders? How do they differ from non-Aboriginal facilities?

The Prison Environment

Correctional facilities are coercive institutions, and inmates have little or no control over their lives. The need to adapt to an environment that is oftentimes violent may lead people to "all kinds of reactions: anger, frustration, bewilderment, agitation, feelings of hopelessness and despair" (Cooke et al. 1990:55–56). As well, any rehabilitation efforts are conducted within an institution dominated by security concerns.

Prison Life

As prisoners are separated from the outside world, they experience a life under the constant scrutiny of prison guards and other staff, and are required to follow strict daily regimes or endure strict disciplinary sanctions. Prisons are commonly referred to as **total institutions**. According to Goffman (1961), total institutions have four distinct elements:

1. The inmate lives under the watchful eye of a centralized institutional authority.
2. The inmate shares his or her space with other inmates, who are all treated alike and who are forced to enact the same routines.
3. All of an inmate's time is tightly scheduled by a body of rules and administrative orders imposed by those in charge.
4. The entire system of enforced activities, and time and space control, is organized around the institutional goals of correction and/or treatment.

Goffman was interested in the ways that structural properties of institutions affect and alter the identities of the residents. According to Goffman, prisons are total institutions that force inmates to live regimented and dehumanizing lives. This overwhelming control forces inmates to "fight back" against this authority, leading them to commit more criminal acts. This **process of dehumanization** starts while the new inmates are being admitted, and it gives them a "clear notion of their plight." They quickly find that the requirements of the institution far outweigh any concerns about individual needs. This transition from the outside world to prison life is referred to as **civil death** by Goffman. At this time, the new inmate enters into a total institution that involves significant psychological and social changes that undermine the sense of self (see Exhibit 12.3).

EXHIBIT 12.3 The Consequences of High Rates of Incarceration

For some people, especially those who support the crime control theory of criminal justice (see Chapter 1), high rates of incarceration contribute in a significant way to a decrease in crime rates. At the core of this belief is the fact that most crimes are committed by a relatively small number of repeat offenders. A number of studies have attempted to corroborate this view, with varying results. Estimates of the number of crimes committed each year by repeat offenders range from 3 to 187 (Zimring and Hawkins 1997). If one accepts the highest estimate, every year a repeat offender spends incarcerated prevents a significant amount of criminal acts. And by locking these individuals up, it is argued that communities will become safer places to live. DiIulio (1994) has claimed that incarcerating such offenders is, in essence, a form of social justice that will save the lives of people who live in the same communities as the criminals.

Many people, including some correctional officials, note the negative consequences upon society by sending more individuals to custody as well as for longer periods of incarceration. For one, incarceration can lead to severe social consequences for both communities and the families that live in those communities. Rose and Clear (1998) argue that while offenders are viewed by many as community liabilities (e.g., victimizers) they can also be community assets (e.g., income producers, family supporters). According to Rose and Clear, while it is usually realized that incarceration can reduce community liabilities, it can also reduce community assets (which is often not realized). A key point in their argument is that the impact of incarcerating criminal offenders upon individuals will differ on the basis of the affluence and social organization of an area. In stable working class and middle class communities, the incarceration of a small number of resident criminals is probably a social benefit. In underclass communities, the overuse of incarceration will lead to a reduction of resources and the weakening of core social institutions. As a result, incarceration has differential impacts depending upon its magnitude and the type of community.

> We argue that state controls, . . . typically . . . directed at individual behavior, have important secondary effects of family and neighborhood structures . . . Thus, at the ecological level, the side effects of policies intended to fight crime by controlling individual criminals may exacerbate problems that lead to crime in the first place. (Rose and Clear 1998:441)

Others look at the impact of incarceration upon family stability. When a parent is imprisoned, their children will often suffer financial hardships, and a general deterioration of the family structure. Lacking income, families frequently move, leading to more instability. Researchers (e.g., Kjellstrand and Eddy 2011; Rowe and Farrington 1997) have found that children born to parents who have criminal backgrounds or have been incarcerated are at a greater risk of becoming involved in criminal activity themselves compared to children born to parents without such backgrounds.

The federal government of Canada's recent crime control policies, specifically the introduction of more mandatory minimum sentences, changes to parole laws, and the end of two-for-one pretrial credit, has led to a rise in the federal prison population. Between 2005 and 2013, the federal inmate population increased by 17.5 percent while in 2013–2014, the daily federal custody count averaged 15,200 incarcerated individuals. This increase is approximately equal to the creation of two or three custodial facilities. This has led to a double bunking, placing a strain on both the prison infrastructure as well as the inmates. At the present time, the federal system "is struggling to accommodate the new demands placed on it" ("The Jails . . . " 2011:A12). While the Conservatives originally estimated that 2,500 to 2,700 new spaces were needed for the increased numbers of offenders, they later revised this estimate

EXHIBIT 12.3 The Consequences of High Rates of Incarceration *(Continued)*

upward to 4,200 extra spaces. The then-federal Public Safety Minister, Vic Toews, said that the government was more than prepared for the increase in inmates expected after the *Safe Streets and Communities Act* was passed by Parliament. He also believes that the increase in spaces will alleviate the problems of violence in and in-custody deaths.

Howard Sapers, the Correctional Investigator, commented that this increase will create a situation where "inmates, staff, and, ultimately public safety is compromised by prison crowding" (Office of the Correctional Investigator 2012a:3). In his 2013–2014 report, Mr. Sapers noted that national rate of double-bunking was just under 20 percent, with some regions experiencing a 30 percent rate. This represents a 93 percent increase over five years. "Even accounting for the new 2,700 cells that will open at 37 institutions in the next year or so, the CSC still expects significant double bunking to continue in the foreseeable future" (Office of the Correctional Investigator (2014:2).

Mr. Sapers, in his 2010–11 Annual Report of the Office of the Correctional Investigator, Mr. Sapers noted his concerns about some of the Conservatives' policies and their impact upon the federal correctional system, including overcrowding:

> I am particularly concerned that the underlying principles that have guided correctional practice and operations since the enactment of the *Corrections and Conditional Release Act* in 1992 do not seem to hold the same currency as they once did—the notion of the "least restrictive" measure, the recognition that prisoners actually have retained rights, the idea that correctional authority has a duty to act fairly or that supervised and gradual community release is far safer than release at warrant expiry.
>
> To be clear, my Office is not against holding offenders to account for their criminal behavior nor with providing incentives to those who are motivated to change or who have gained insight into those aspects of their personality or lifestyle that brought them into conflict with the law in the first place. But we need to get change and reform right, as the health and welfare of our federal inmates is an important public policy issue. Today's public policy decisions will impact the lives of individuals, our communities and the public purse for decades to come . . . It is also important to understand that the serious, if unintended, effects of prison crowding reach far beyond the provision of a comfortable living environment for inmates. Aside from the immediate issue of physical capacity, prison crowding has negative impacts on the system's ability to provide safe and secure custody. It is well understood that prison crowding can lead to increased levels of tension, frustration and institutional violence, which can jeopardize the safety of staff, inmates and visitors. According to CSC data, the number of major institutional incidents increased during the reporting year – including preventable deaths in custody, violent assaults, serious bodily injury and use of force. As correctional populations increase, timely access to offender programs, treatment and meaningful employment opportunities measurably diminish, resulting in delays for the safe reintegration into the community and further exacerbating both population management and cost pressures.
>
> Given high rates of mental illness, drug addiction, violence and criminal aging membership, it is difficult to see how double-bunking can be viewed as a correctionally appropriate or sustainable solution to crowding pressures in either the short or medium terms.
>
> (Office of the Correctional Investigator, *Annual Report of the Office of the Correctional Investigator Canada 2009–2010*, pp. 5, 6, 35 http://www.oci-bec.gc.ca/cnt/rpt/pdf/annrpt/annrpt20092010-eng.pdf.)

Mr. Sapers has also noted that the effects of the new Conservative crime control policies are felt almost immediately on inmates. For example, three months after Parliament eliminated accelerated parole reviews (see Chapter 11) used to speed the release of first-time, nonviolent offenders, there already were increases in overcrowding found in federal institutions. He found that the impact of the new law is having a negative effect on inmates, in particular female offenders. More women now have to stay in prison longer to wait for a parole hearing, although there aren't enough cells. The elimination of accelerated parole has led to greater stress within the system, as the Parole Board of Canada will now face about 1,000 additional hearings a year for the lowest-risk offenders. In addition, there has been a significant increase in violence in prison. In the federal correctional system during 2013–2014 there were

- 1,293 inmate assaults and fights (a 17 percent increase in the last five years);

Continued on next page

EXHIBIT 12.3 The Consequences of High Rates of Incarceration *(Continued)*

- 1,683 use of force incidents (a 6.7 percent increase in the last five years);
- 182 inmates who incurred serious bodily harm (a 19 percent in the last five years) (Office of the Correctional Investigator 2014a:18).

He attributed these increases to crowding, lack of access to programs, and increases in the number of inmates with significant mental health issues, all of which combine to make custodial institutions into places of volatile environments.

Mr. Toews indicated that the federal government remained committed to rehabilitation programs and health resources to keep up with the increasing inmate population. But he added that while he considers concerns about the welfare of inmates to be "fine," his main concern is on the victims of crime, particularly the victims of violent crimes ("Watchdog Says . . . " 2011).

In contrast, Mr. Sapers (Office of the Correctional Investigator 2014a: 3) notes that

A sentence of imprisonment needs to be seen as an investment, an opportunity for a convicted person to make positive change in his or her life by addressing individual needs and risks that contribute to crime. Nearly all but a few offenders will eventually be returned to society. Beyond safe and humane custody, the Service's mandate rightly emphasizes preparing offenders for their gradual and structured reintegration."

Inmate Society

For decades, experts on prisons and prison life have stated that inmates form their own world—one with a unique set of norms and rules referred to as **inmate subculture** (Irwin 1980). The basis of inmate subculture, they argue, is a unique **social code** of unwritten rules and guidelines that tell inmates how to behave, think, and interact with prison staff and other inmates. Clemmer (1958) introduced the idea of inmate social codes when he wrote about life in a maximum-security prison. He identified a unique language used by prisoners, known as **argot** (Caron 1982), consisting of such words as "jointman" (a prisoner who behaves like a guard) and "yard" ($100). Clemmer also identified what he termed the "prisonization process"—the manner in which an individual assimilates into the inmate subculture by adhering to norms of behaviour, sexual conduct, and language. According to Clemmer, inmates who become the most "prisonized" are the most difficult to reintegrate into mainstream society.

When studying **prisonization**, criminologists have looked at two areas: how inmates adapt their behaviour to life behind bars, and how life in a correctional facility changes as a result of inmate behaviour. Sykes (1958) identified the **pains of imprisonment**; that is, five deprivations inflicted on inmates that constitute the defining elements of imprisonment. The five pains of imprisonment identified by Sykes were as follows:

- loss of liberty
- deprivation of goods and services
- loss of heterosexual relationships
- deprivation of autonomy
- deprivation of security

Inmate society compensates for the losses of things generally taken for granted in the outside society by creating an inmate subculture that offers differing degrees of comfort to those who successfully adjust to it. Sykes (ibid.) and Sykes and Messinger (1960) used Clemmer's work to identify the most important aspects of inmate subculture. They discovered what they called a **prison code**—that is, a system of social norms and values established by inmates to regulate their own behaviour while they were serving their time. According to Sykes (1958), these norms and values include the following:

1. Don't interfere with inmates' interests—for example, never betray another inmate to authorities.
2. Don't lose your head, and refrain from emotional displays (e.g., arguing) with other inmates.
3. Don't exploit other inmates.
4. Be tough and don't lose your dignity.
5. Don't be a sucker, don't make a fool of yourself or support guards or prison administrators over the interests of the inmates.

Sykes and Messinger (1960) identified the major theme of the inmate social code as prison or group solidarity. The greater the number of inmates who follow the inmate code, the greater the stability of the prison population and the less prison violence.

An alternative to the above model (referred to as the **deprivation model**) for understanding how inmate society develops is the **importation model** (Irwin and Cressey 1962). This model posits that inmate society is shaped by external rather than internal factors—that is, by the attributes that inmates bring with them when they enter the prison. An inmate who was engaged in criminal offences on the outside and was friends with similarly minded people will bring those norms and values into prison and keep them while incarcerated, resisting any changes to make him or her more law abiding. Conversely, an individual who abided by societal norms on the outside will be open to following those norms while incarcerated, and will be more amenable to taking programs and services while in prison.

This inmate social code has changed over the years. In the earliest studies of inmates, researchers concluded that an unwritten set of rules guided inmate conduct. An inmate's position in a prison was determined by whether they followed the prison code: those who failed to do so were ignored and rejected by the prisoners who did follow the code. Some inmates were ignored; most were relatively safe from the violent actions of others unless they "ratted out a con." Starting about two decades ago, however, correctional facilities began to change as the prison code lost some of its power to maintain social relationships among inmates. This was attributed to the rising numbers of younger offenders and drug offenders, who were originally viewed by those embedded in the traditional prison code as only "looking out for themselves" and as unwilling to follow the code and pay homage to other inmates. As a result, violence began to increase among inmates. Ricciardelli (2014:135), in her interviews with former federal inmates, reports that in Ontario correctional facilities the inmate code is not the result of deprivation or importation, but instead is focused upon "survival and negotiating risk." As such, a violation of the code could result in a violent incident. "The code was a form of informal social control that shapes behaviours in the context of rewards (i.e., safety) and punishments (i.e., victimization and risk)."

According to Dobash and colleagues (1986), women inmates experience prison and the pains of imprisonment differently from male inmates. This is referred to as the **gender-specifc pains of imprisonment**, which take into account the unique deprivations associated with women's incarceration and their responses to it. As Ishwaran and Neugebauer (2001:135) point out, female inmates "cope with the loss of emotional relationships by developing and maintaining significant relationships of 'pseudo families' with other prisoners."

Associated Press/Ed Wozniak

A large number of federal inmates have children under the age of 18. Families left behind suffer not only financial hardships but psychological and emotional problems as well.

Hannah-Moffat (2001:233) states that "one manifestation of the pains of imprisonment experienced by female inmates is self-injurious behaviour." **Self-injurious behaviour** (or **self-harm**, as it is also called) is a serious problem among women in the Canadian correctional system (see Criminal Justice Insight below). Shaw (1991) reported that 59 percent of all federal female inmates at the time of her federally sponsored study of incarcerated women had engaged in some self-injurious behaviour. Presse and Hart (1996) studied 26 patients in the Intensive Healing Program at the Prairie Regional Psychiatric Centre and found that 19 of them had injured themselves. And the 1990 *Survey of Federally Sentenced Aboriginal Women in the Community* (Sugar and Fox 1990) reported that Aboriginal women continued to slash themselves after being released in order to relieve their tension and anger. It is estimated that one-quarter of the federal women offender population has a history of engaging in some type of self-harming behaviour (Office of the Correctional Investigator Canada 2010). Fillmore and Dell (2001:105) point out that to effectively deal with self-injurious behaviour, it is important to interconnect "the health concerns of self-harm [with] the broader issues of poverty, child care support, housing, education, job training, employment, discrimination, and racism."

Another difference experienced by female inmates relates to the disruption of their family life. At the time of their offence, at least half of incarcerated female offenders are living with at least one of their children. As a result, many must make special child-care arrangements

Investigating: Use of Force Reviews Conducted by the Office of the Correctional Investigator Canada

Violence can also involve all of the inmates in a correctional facility. Culhane (1985) documented nine examples of prison violence in Canada between 1975 and 1985. She described the degradation of inmates by prison officials and the resulting prisoner violence. One such incident occurred at Archambault Prison, north of Montreal, in 1972. Although 50 inmates were identified as having actively participated in the riot, between 75 and 150 were sent to solitary confinement. These inmates were accused of "participating passively" and therefore "had to pay the social price." Complaints about this treatment reached the attention of federal politicians; a federal inquiry failed to materialize because the guards who had allegedly been involved denied that they had participated, and there was a lack of corroborating evidence (Culhane 1985; Ruby 1985).

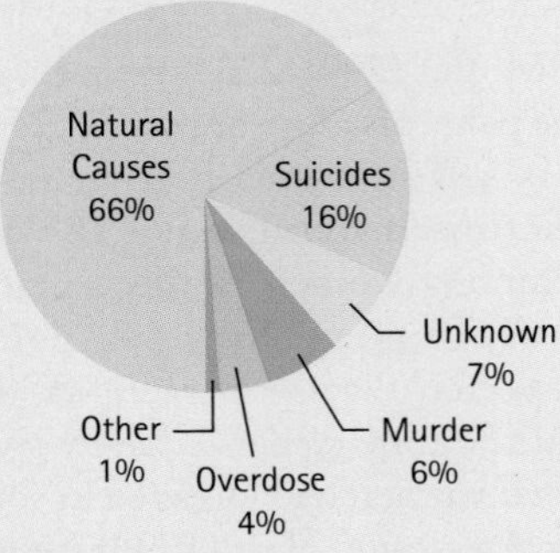

FIGURE 12.7 Reasons for Deaths in Federal Custody, Canada, 2003–13

Source: Office of the Correctional Investigator, *Office of the Correctional Investigator 2013–2014* Annual Report, p. 28, http://www.oci-bec.gc.ca/cnt/rpt/pdf/annrpt/annrpt20132014-eng.pdf. Reproduced with permission of the Office of the Correctional Officer.

Prison Deaths

In the 10-year period between 2003 and 2013, 536 inmates died in federal custody. Sixty-six percent of these deaths were classified as natural (e.g., cancer, cardiovascular disease), 16.4 percent were the result of suicides, 5.6 percent were homicides, 3.7 percent were a result of an overdose, and reasons for the remaining 7.1 percent were unknown (Figure 12.7).

In 2007, Howard Sapers, the federal correctional investigator, released a report in which he studied the 82 deaths (all homicides, suicides, and accidental deaths) that occurred in federal correctional facilities between 2001 and 2005. It was discovered that more than 60 percent of these deaths were suicides, the majority of which were by hanging. Most homicides were the result of stabbings, while drug overdoses accounted for 80 percent of all accidental deaths. In his report, Mr. Sapers accused the federal correctional system of poor recordkeeping and communication involving troubled inmates, as well as having poor policies in place to respond to emergencies and failing to routinely check on inmates to ensure that they were safe. According to Mr. Sapers, the CSC "has failed to incorporate lessons learned and implement corrective action over time and across regions, with the same errors and observations being made incident after incident" (Tibbetts 2007:A6). In his report, he did add that it may "possess a bias" since the study did not look at those cases in which the lives of inmates were saved by the actions of prison staff.

with family or friends. Some lose custody of their children to the authorities. Many provincial governments have some type of limited policy regarding mother-and-child contact, but this was not so for federally sentenced women until recently. Shaw (1991), in her survey of federally sentenced women, reported that separation from children and concerns about child custody were a major source of anxiety for incarcerated women. The federal government's Task Force on Federally Sentenced Women reported that about 70 percent were mothers, many of whom were sole supporters of their children. In addition, most women had a limited education and few marketable skills, and were either on social assistance or working at low-paying jobs when arrested (LeBlanc 1994). When the regional centres for federally sentenced women were opened the **Mother–Child Program** was established, which allows children to live with their mothers in the facility (Watson 1995). The federal Conservative party ordered stricter eligibility requirements by ministerial directive in 2008, when a woman awaiting trial for murder gave birth to a daughter. The changes meant that the age of eligibility for children was reduced to 6 from 12 years, exclusions were based on the seriousness of the crime, and participation required the approval of provincial/territorial officials. Since 2008, only 14 children were able to participate in the program (eight of them on a full-time basis). Later, a British Columbia judge held that women offenders had a right to be with their children and provincial authorities were given six months to reinstate the program (*Inglis v. British Columbia [Minister of Public Safety]* 2014). In May 2014, Corrections Service Canada announced it was adding 114 beds and 15 new rooms to women's correctional facilities to improve the mother–child program (Shingle 2014).

Prison Violence

Conflict leading to violence is an ever-present reality of prison life. Violence can involve different sets of actors: inmate versus inmate, staff versus inmate, inmate versus staff. According to official data, major assaults by inmates on other inmates declined yearly between 1983–84 and 1988–89, but started to increase in 1989–90—a trend that has continued. The CSC produces the equivalent of official police reports (i.e., the Uniform Crime Reports); however, the actual occurrence of incidents that happen within the walls is not known, so the true picture of prison violence is not available. Between 1995–96 and 1997–98, for example, 144 major assaults among inmates were recorded. In addition, there were 10 major assaults by inmates on correctional staff, 9 murders by inmates, 8 hostage takings, and 13 major fights among inmates (Correctional Service of Canada 1998). As a result of the increased violence, use of force incidents have increased in federal correctional facilities (see the *Investigating* feature).

Suicide in Prison

Suicide is the leading cause of unnatural death in Canadian prisons, accounting for approximately 20 percent of all deaths in custody in any given year. During the 10-year period between 1998 and 2008, 107 deaths (or 20 percent of all deaths in federal custodial facilities) were suicides. In 2013, the suicide rate for federal inmates was 70 per 100,000 inmates, compared to 10.2 suicides per 100,000 Canadians (Office of the Correctional Investigator Canada 2014a).

Concern over suicide rates during the early 1990s led the CSC to develop a suicide prevention program. In order to gain as much information as possible about male and female inmates who had committed suicide, Green and colleagues (1992) studied 133 suicides that occurred between 1977 and 1988. They found that most suicides were male (129, or 97 percent) and that 115 (or 80 percent) were White. The study also found that suicide was distributed across all age groups. In terms of marital status, half of those who committed suicide were single, 38 percent were married or living common-law, and 12 percent were divorced. Sixty percent had no children, 14 percent had one child, and the rest had two or more children.

The researchers reported that hanging was the most common suicide method (80 percent) among inmates. Almost all of the suicides occurred inside the inmate's own cell. In terms of offence and sentence characteristics, 51 individuals who committed suicide had committed a non-sexual offence of violence as their most recent offence, 34 had a robbery or weapons offence, 25 had a property offence, and only one individual was a first-time offender. Green and colleagues discovered that a high number of suicides occurred early on in a sentence—25 percent within 90 days of sentencing and 50 percent within a year of sentencing. In an attempt to rectify this situation, the CSC developed a comprehensive approach that encompassed assessment, prevention, intervention, treatment, support, evaluation, research, and training of staff. Specific actions included these:

1. Providing a safe, secure, and humane environment for those suffering from mental illness and for those coping with the stresses of life in a correctional environment.
2. Increasing the awareness and understanding of both management and staff concerning suicide and self-injury.
3. Developing staff skills to prevent suicide and self-harm, so that suicide risk can be identified, pre-indicators can be monitored, and crisis intervention and support services can be provided.
4. Developing and implementing support services for survivors as well as affected staff and inmates.

Between 2001 and 2010 the number of suicides in CSC correctional facilities averaged about 9 per year, compared to 14 suicides between the years 1991 and 2000. Between 2003 and 2013, the suicide rate for federal inmates was 70 per 100,000 inmates compared to 10.2 suicides per 100,000 Canadians.

Much of what was reported in the early 1990s about suicide still holds true. Most inmates who committed suicide while in federal custody between 2011 and 2014 were unmarried, White males between the ages of 31 and 40 and died by hanging. One-third were serving a sentence for a violent offence that had resulted in the death of the victim. Offenders who were serving a life sentence and those serving less than a five-year sentence were most likely to commit suicide. Information from 98 suicides in CSC correctional facilities between 2000–01 and 2009–10 found the following risk factors:

- most (58 percent) had a history of psychological problems;
- most (60 percent) had made previous suicide attempt(s);
- over one-third have a history of self-injurious behaviour; and
- most (85 percent) had been identified as having difficulties in the past with substance abuse (Office of the Correctional Investigator Canada 2014b:8).

The Office of the Correctional Investigator Canada conducted an analysis of more than 140 deaths in custody, serious assaults, and self-harming incidents during 2011–12. They found a number of problems, mistakes, and structural weaknesses, including:

- responses to medical emergencies which are either in appropriate or inadequate;
- critical information-sharing failures between clinical and front-line staff;
- recurring patterns in deficiencies in monitoring suicide pre-indicators; and
- management of mentally ill offenders too often driven by security responses rather than appropriate health and treatment (Office of the Correctional Investigator Canada 2012a).

THE CANADIAN PRES/Darren Calabrese

A view into one of the segregation cells at Kingston Penitentiary.

Gangs in Prison

Prison gangs are one of the most significant developments in Canadian prisons in recent years. Their presence is attributed to increased gang activity in general across Canada as well as to criminal justice interventions such as anti-gang legislation. Boe et al. (2003) studied the prevalence of gangs in Canadian federal correctional facilities and found that the proportion of federal inmates affiliated with a criminal organization had increased from 821 in March 1997 to 1,696 in November 2002. In 2012, there were 54 different gangs identified within the CSC. In 2012, there were 2,040 offenders (about 12 percent of all federal inmates) identified as either members or associates of criminal organizations, and this figure had grown from 1,421 in 2007. Of these offenders, 66 percent were in custody, while the other 34 percent were under various types of community supervision. Some of these offenders were associated (5) or affiliated (48) with Aboriginal gangs, with most (86 percent) serving their sentence in Alberta, Saskatchewan, or Manitoba. The number of individuals affiliated with street gangs in 2012 had increased by 269 percent over the previous 10 years—119 percent between 2000 and 2007, from 213 to 467 members. Street gangs are now the most common form of gang identified within the federal correctional system (43 percent), followed by Aboriginal gangs (24 percent), motorcycle gangs (16 percent), traditional organized crime groups (7 percent), Asian gangs (3 percent), and other types of gangs (6 percent) (Harris 2012).

Gangs in Canadian correctional facilities tend to vary according to region. Aboriginal gangs are typically concentrated in the Prairie region. Motorcycle gang members are overwhelmingly found in the Quebec region, as are members of traditional organized crime groups. Street gang members are predominantly located in the Prairie and Quebec regions, as are members of Asian gangs. White Supremacist gangs are most commonly found in the Pacific and Prairie regions.

Gang members are being blamed more and more for an increasing number of offences against both staff and other inmates. Gabor (2007) reported that about 40 percent of all prison homicides were gang related. Leger (2003) reports that the presence of gang members poses various challenges for prison officials—challenges relating to power and control issues, the availability of

Criminal Justice Insight

Self-Injury in Federal Correctional Facilities

Between 2008–09 and 2012–13, the number of self-injury incidents in the federal correctional system more than tripled (see Figure 12.8). According to the Office of the Correctional Investigator Canada (2013:17), self-injurious offenders are "often managed in maximum security segregation units or observation cells, where conditions of confinement, lack of external stimuli and limited association can result in further deterioration in mental health functioning, leading to an escalation of the frequency and seriousness of the self-injury."

In 2012–13, there were 901 reported self-injury incidents; of these, a relatively small number of the federally sentenced women offenders (37 of the 264 total, or 14 percent) accounted for 36 percent of all the incidents (see Figure 12.9). Aboriginal women accounted for almost 45 percent of all self-injury incidents.

Of the 264 federal offenders who self-injured in 2012–13, 17 engaged in chronic self-injurious behaviour. These 17 individuals accounted for 40 percent of all recorded incidents.

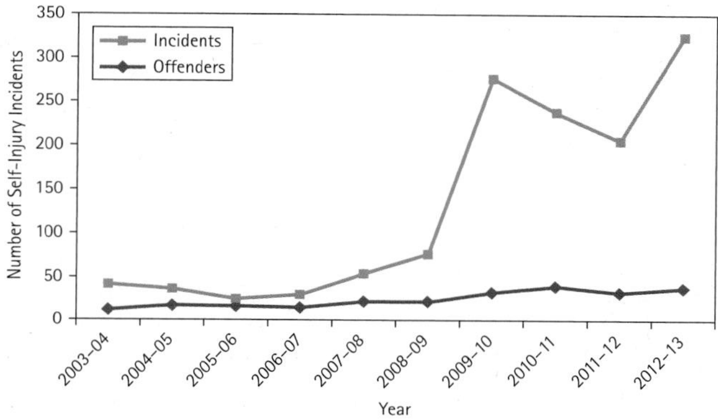

FIGURE 12.8 Number of Incidents of Self-Injury Involving Federally Sentenced Women Inmates

Source: Office of the Correctional Investigator, *Risky Business: An Investigation of the Treatment and Management of Chronic Self-Injury Among Federally Sentenced Women* (September 30, 2013), p. 3, http://www.oci-bec.gc.ca/cnt/rpt/pdf/oth-aut/oth-aut20130930-eng.pdf. Reproduced with permission of the Office of the Correctional Officer.

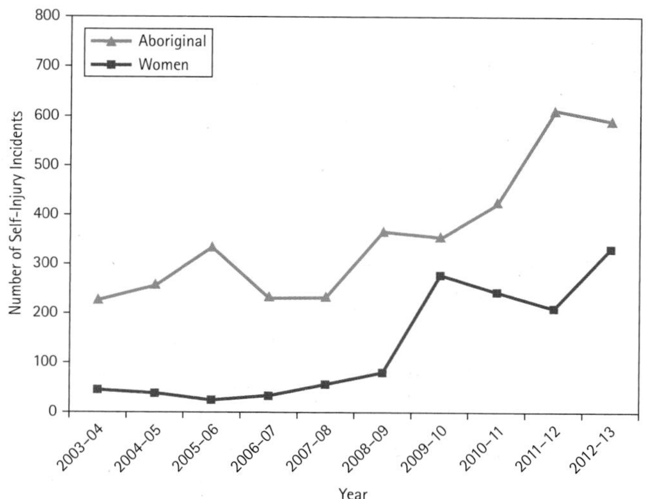

FIGURE 12.9 Self-Injurious Incidents Involving Women and Aboriginal Offenders

Source: Office of the Correctional Investigator, *Annual Report of the Office of the Correctional Investigator 2012–2013*, p. 17, http://www.oci-bec.gc.ca/cnt/rpt/annrpt/annrpt20122013-eng.aspx. Reproduced with permission of the Office of the Correctional Officer.

drugs, gang recruitment, and the intimidation and corruption of staff. These individuals are more likely to be directly involved in assaults on other inmates and staff members than are non-gang members. As a result, some gang members have been placed into Canada's Special Handling Unit (SHU), located at Ste-Anne-des-Plaines in Quebec. Howard Sapers, in an investigation into the deaths of inmates between 2001 and 2005, attributed a number of killings and suicides to gang-related activities. He noted that the federal correctional system "lacks anti-gang strategies and trained security intelligence analysts" (Tibbetts 2007:A6).

Two explanations for the emergence of gangs as powerful forces within Canadian correctional facilities are deprivation and importation. As pointed out in this chapter, the argument underlying the deprivation model is that inmates develop a social system as a way to adapt to the pains of imprisonment. Since inmates are deprived of, for example, their liberty, they develop a culture that allows them to access what imprisonment has taken from them. The importation approach emphasizes that inmates' pre-prison attitudes and values guide their behaviours as well as their responses to the internal conditions of a correctional facility. Groups often bring their illicit activities with them when they enter prison.

Does the Rule of Law Exist in Prison? Prisoners' Rights, Due Process, and Discipline

According to the Office of the Correctional Investigator Canada, there are sound reasons why the **rule of law** follows an offender into prison and why "legality does not end at the prison gate." According to the Supreme Court, individuals who are incarcerated remain citizens and still bearers of the Charter of Rights and Freedoms. And according to the CCRA, "offenders retain the rights of all members of society except those that are, as a consequence of the sentence, lawfully and necessarily removed or restricted."

According to the Office of the Correctional Investigator Canada (2013:3):

> Imprisonment does not mean total deprivation or absolute forfeiture of rights. By law, prisoners maintain the right to be treated with dignity and respect, they have the right to safety and security of the person, to be treated humanely, to not be discriminated against on the basis of ethnicity or religion and to be free from degrading, cruel, and/or inhumane treatment or punishment.
>
> Legal compliance, however important, is not the sole test of CSC's conduct. CSC staff makes thousands of discretionary decisions each year. Good decision making is about more than legal compliance. Complying with the law is the floor, not the ceiling, for setting the standard in regard to administrative fairness. Good and best practices are more than just doing the minimum.

In his book *Justice Behind the Walls: Human Rights in Canadian Prisons*, UBC law professor Michael Jackson studied two issues relating to the law and Canada's prisons. The first issue was how far recent legislation had gone toward balancing the security of society with the "residual rights of prisoners." The second issue looked at how well the Correctional Service of Canada "does at respecting the rule of law while administering the system." Jackson concluded that while the legislation doesn't "do badly at achieving the balance between security and residual rights," the Correctional Service of Canada had demonstrated its inability "to respect the rule of law, to adhere to the spirit and letter of its own rules . . ." (Ruby 2003:11).

Over the past few decades, prisons have been reformed most often through the intervention of the courts. Before the 1970s, Penitentiary Service Regulations required prison officials to provide inmates with certain basics, such as adequate food and clothing, essential dental and medical services, and sufficient time to exercise (MacKay 1986). These rights represented only the core of the Standard Minimum Rules for the Treatment of Prisoners (1957) adopted by the United Nations, which covered such issues as religion, transfers, and disciplinary procedures. Starting in 1980, inmates began to receive limited rights and access to justice within federal correctional facilities. Yet it remained difficult for them to question prison rules and regulations or the decisions of prison officials. Perhaps the most important reason why inmates lacked legal rights was that provincial and federal courts hesitated to intervene in the administration of prisons unless there were obvious, excessive, and indiscriminate abuses of power by prison officials. This policy, referred to as the **"hands-off" doctrine**, had three planks:

1. Correctional administration was a technical matter best left to experts rather than to courts, which were ill equipped to make appropriate evaluations.
2. Society as a whole was apathetic to what went on in prisons, and most individuals

preferred not to associate with or know about offenders.

3. Prisoners' complaints involved privileges rather than rights.

The effect of this doctrine was "to immunize the prison from public scrutiny through the judicial process and to place prison officials in a position of virtual invulnerability and absolute power over the persons committed to their institutions" (Jackson 1983:82).

As Naylor (2013) points out, individuals who were incarcerated lost all rights and legal recognition as legal persons—that is, they were **socially dead**. But as a result of prison disturbances during the 1970s and complaints made by inmates about their treatment during and after these incidents, government officials began inquiring into the conditions faced by those serving sentences in federal correctional facilities. The federal government established a committee to investigate prison conditions in the mid-1970s; its final report (tabled in 1977) emphatically pointed out that the prison system was not rehabilitating offenders and that "imprisonment . . . itself epitomizes injustice" (House of Commons Subcommittee on the Penitentiary System in Canada 1977:85). To alleviate this situation, the committee recommended that the rule of law (see Chapter 1) and justice be introduced into the prison system.

At the end of the 1960s, prisoners and prison-rights advocates were already challenging the hands-off doctrine in the courts over the specific issue of **due process rights** within correctional facilities. In the first such case, *R. v. Institutional Head of Beaver Creek Correctional Camp, ex parte McCaud* (1969), an inmate challenged the prison's authority to make disciplinary decisions without providing inmates with due process protections, such as the right to a fair hearing and the right to legal counsel. Also challenged were the arbitrary powers found within s. 229 of the Penitentiary Regulations, which outlined a number of activities for which inmates could be disciplined. The Ontario Court of Appeal ruled that while natural justice also applied to inmates, there were situations in which prison officials had the right to place an inmate in segregation without proper due process safeguards and the possibility of a review of the administrative decision in question. However, while the court ruled that administrative decisions are reviewable when they involve questions about the civil rights of inmates, this specific case involved a decision purely administrative in nature and therefore wasn't reviewable by the courts.

The first case to significantly challenge the administrative power of prison officials was *McCann v. The Queen* (1975). Jack McCann had been placed in solitary confinement in the British Columbia Penitentiary for 754 days under the authority of s. 2.30(1)(a) of the Penitentiary Service Regulations, which states: "Where the institutional head is satisfied that for the good maintenance of good order and discipline in the institution . . . it is necessary that the inmate should be kept from associating with other inmates." McCann argued that his period in solitary confinement infringed on his right to freedom from cruel and unusual treatment or punishment under s. 2(b) of the Canadian Bill of Rights (Jackson 1983). The court held that prison administrators had the right to place inmates in solitary confinement with no prior hearing, unless their civil rights were in jeopardy. But it ruled that the use of solitary confinement in this case did, in fact, constitute "cruel and unusual punishment" (ibid.:101–33).

However, the Supreme Court of Canada, in *Martineau v. Matsqui Disciplinary Board* (1980), formally recognized that "the rule of law must run within penitentiary walls." It also stated that although prison officials make administrative decisions, they are still subject to the duty to act fairly. In this case, two inmates at the Matsqui Institution in British Columbia had been found guilty of being in a cell where they shouldn't have been. They argued that "they were not provided with a summary of evidence against them; that the evidence of each was taken in the absence of the other; that the conviction was for an offence unknown to law; and that Martineau was never given an opportunity to give evidence with respect to the charge" (ibid.:126–27). As a result of this ruling, all those who make administrative decisions concerning the rights or liberties of inmates now have a duty to act fairly (Pelletier 1990).

The Duty to Act Fairly

What does it mean to "act fairly," especially for inmates in a correctional facility? The **duty to act fairly** involves two basic rights: (1) the right to be heard, and (2) the right to have an impartial hearing. As Pelletier (1990:26) notes, the right to be heard means that all citizens have the right "to be informed of the allegations made against them and to respond to those allegations." The right to an impartial hearing means that "a decision must not be rendered against a person for discriminatory or arbitrary reasons."

In Canada, two areas of legal concern are related to the duty to act fairly: (1) **administrative segregation** (or **solitary confinement**), and (2) discipline of inmates. What powers do prison officials have to place inmates in administrative segregation? Obviously, some situations, such as prison riots, may require immediate segregation. But what about other situations? In *McCann v. The Queen*

(1975), which was the first case to argue the fairness of the decision to segregate, Mr. Justice Heald ruled that the decision to place an inmate in solitary confinement was "purely administrative" and therefore not subject to legal review.

This interpretation was reinforced by the decision in *Kosobook and Aelick v. The Queen and The Solicitor-General of Canada* (1976). In this case, the complainants had been told that they were being placed in solitary confinement after an administrative inquiry into the stabbing of an inmate, but no charges had been laid against them. They argued that their segregation was a denial of natural justice and their right to an unbiased tribunal, the result of a decision made in an arbitrary manner, and an infringement of the Canadian Bill of Rights. They claimed that they had not been provided with due process protections and that as a result they had been held in arbitrary detention. The judge ruled that the prison authorities did not have any judicial or quasi-judicial functions, but rather performed the role of an administrative body. Thus they could not violate the Canadian Bill of Rights.

However, in *Martineau v. Matsqui Disciplinary Board* (1980), the Supreme Court of Canada ruled that correctional officials have a duty to act fairly when making disciplinary decisions. According to Cole and Manson (1990:63), this case "opened the modern era of prison law in Canada and exposed internal parole and prison processes to judicial scrutiny." In essence, the Supreme Court concluded that the rule of law must be upheld within correctional facilities. As a result of *Martineau*, the CSC changed its policies to fit more closely with the fairness doctrine. For example, in terms of administrative segregation, inmates now had the right to be heard within the correctional context, and prison authorities were obliged to (1) inform an inmate, in writing, of the reasons for the placement in segregation within 24 hours following this placement; (2) notify an inmate in advance of each review of the placement in segregation, in order to permit the inmate to present his or her case at a hearing in prison; and (3) advise the inmate, in writing, of decisions concerning his or her status.

The impact of the Charter of Rights and Freedoms has not been as great in the area of prisoners' rights as many had first expected. Some thought that it would bring about great changes, but the Supreme Court has often held in its decisions that the state can justify, within reasonable limits, intrusions into fundamental rights and freedoms afforded to Canadians (e.g., the right to freedom from search and seizure). In other words, "the concept of liberty is not an all or nothing proposition" (Jackson 2002:60). However, the Charter has had an impact in terms of procedural protections for inmates.

One way the federal government responded was to create the Office of the Correctional Investigator (OCI) (1973) after a Royal Commission examined the events surrounding recent prison riots at Kingston and Millhaven. This report recommended major changes "in the accountability and oversight of the federal correctional system," which has led the OCI to be seen by many as "an important part of safeguarding the rights of offenders" and of ensuring that inmates are treated fairly (Sapers 2006:31). The OCI has the power to investigate a broad range of offender issues and problems. While it can only recommend solutions to the problems that inmates bring to its attention, it can often get information that the inmate is requesting and that has not yet been provided by the correctional administration. Exhibit 12.4 lists several case examples that illustrate the legal rights of inmates; Exhibit 12.5 outlines mental health indicators and correctional performance.

EXHIBIT 12.4 The Legal Rights of Inmates: Selected Charter Cases

CASE	ISSUE
Sauvé v. Canada (Chief Electoral Officer) 2002	Voting rights
May v. Ferndale Institution 2005	Habeas corpus
Bacon v. Surrey Pretrial Services Centre 2010	Administrative segregation for pretrial detention
Inglis v. British Columbia (Minister of Public Safety) 2013	Cancellation of Mother–Child Program
Canada (Attorney General) v. Whaling 2014	Retroactive changes to early day parole
Mission Institution v. Khela 2014	Prison transfers

EXHIBIT 12.5 Mental Health Indicators and Correctional Performance

In May 2012, Correction Service Canada released a research report *(Federally Sentenced Offenders with Mental Disorders: Correctional Outcomes and Correctional Responses)* that summarizes the profile experiences and outcomes of federally sentenced offenders with mental health disorders:

- More likely to be considered higher risk and higher need
- More likely to be serving a sentence for a violent offence (robbery, assault, sexual assault) but less likely to be serving a sentence for homicide
- Tend to be more socially isolated for example, less likely to be married or living common-law)
- More likely to be penitentiary placed in maximum security
- Less likely to be granted parole and more likely to be released on statutory release
- More likely to serve a greater proportion of their sentence behind bars
- More likely to be revoked for technical violations of parole conditions
- More likely to incur minor and major institutional charges leading to higher rates of voluntary and involuntary segregation (Office of the Correctional Investigator Canada 2013:15).

SUMMING UP AND LOOKING FORWARD

What happens when someone is incarcerated? The conditions of confinement in correctional facilities have been found to exert long-term consequences on the behaviour of those who are exposed to it. It also leads to the creation of an inmate subculture. Early investigations described a process of prisonization and a prison code. Various models were developed in an attempt to explain what occurred within the walls when individuals are incarcerated. The deprivation model focuses upon how the inmate society develops, while the importation model looks at how elements of this society are imported from the outside world. In recent years researchers have found that the inmate culture has changed. In addition, attention is now placed on how women experience prison differently from men.

Violence can be a common occurrence. While deaths classified as "natural" are the most common type of death in a correctional facility, the next most common type of death is by suicide (the most common type of "unnatural" death). Prison gangs can be an everyday fact of prison life, with different types of gangs dominating the correctional facilities across Canada.

While the rule of law exists in correctional facilities, historically many issues related to the legal rights of inmates were ignored. The hands-off policy meant that inmates were subject to the discretionary powers of correctional staff. However, a number of court cases established that inmates have due process rights and that the rule of law must exist within correctional facilities.

Almost all inmates are ultimately released back into society. This is known as reintegration, and the federal authorities attempt to prepare inmates returning to society to have low risk of reoffending. How does this happen? Who are some of the inmates those can't be reintegrated? These as well as other issues related to the reintegration process are discussed in the next chapter.

Review Questions:

1. What is a total institution and how does it affect the nature of prison life?
2. What are the deprivations of prison life that constitute the pains of imprisonment?
3. What are some of the unique aspects of women and Aboriginal peoples being in prison in terms of their deprivations and adjustment?
4. What types of factors contribute to the dangerousness of correctional facilities?
5. How did the courts establish the rule of law in correctional facilities?

Critical Issues in Canadian Criminal Justice

THE ISSUE OF SOLITARY CONFINEMENT (ADMINISTRATIVE SEGREGATION)

According to Howard Sapers, the Correctional Investigator of Canada, one in four inmates placed into the federal correctional system in 2013 spent some time in solitary confinement (referred to as "administrative segregation" by the Correctional Service of Canada). He believes the CSC is "increasingly turning to solitary confinement to manage institutions that are crowded and lack sufficient resources to deal with high-needs inmates . . ." (Howlett 2014:A11). Mr. Sapers (Office of the Correctional Investigator Canada 2014a:26) has also noted that "there remains considerable work to be done in terms of improving the operations and accountability of the federal correctional system to safely house, treat and manage the most profoundly mentally disordered offenders. This work should not be delayed."

The use of solitary confinement with mentally disordered inmates by the Correctional Service of Canada has led to tragic results. One case involved Ashley Smith, 19, who died at the Grand Valley Institution in Kitchener, Ontario, on October 19, 2007. Smith first became involved with the criminal justice system in New Brunswick when, at the age of 14, she was sentenced to one year of probation in March 2002 for harassing phone calls and shoving strangers on the street. A year later, she was ordered to a youth centre for breach of probation. She then underwent a psychiatric assessment that mentioned she had a possible learning disorder, ADHD, and a borderline personality disorder. In October 2003, Ms. Smith, while at home on probation, threw apples at a postal worker and was subsequently returned to the youth centre.

On October 24, 2006, she received a one-year sentence for charges while she was at the youth centre. When she turned 18, Ms. Smith was then transferred to the federal women's correctional centre in Nova Scotia. In less than a year, she was transferred nine times between six different federal correctional facilities. During the time she was in federal custody, Ms. Smith never received a comprehensive psychological assessment. In September 2007, while in segregation at the Grand Valley Institution in Kitchener, Ms. Smith started to choke herself several times a day. Guards who intervened "were kicked, grabbed, or spat upon" (Ha 2009b:A6). Between August 20 and her death two months later, guards confiscated 50 ligatures from Ms. Smith. Kim Pate, Executive Director of the Elizabeth Fry Society, visited Ms. Smith at the Grand Valley Institution and filed a grievance on her behalf. Ms. Smith indicated to Ms. Pate that she wanted to be taken out of segregation and taken to a hospital. However, the letter Ms. Pate sent to correctional officials went unread until several weeks after Ms. Smith's death.

On October 15, Ms. Smith was referred to a nearby regional mental health care facility but no beds were available. Four days later, she died in her cell after tying a garrote around her neck. She had spent over a total of 2,000 days in segregation. After Ms. Smith's death, Kim Pate stated that Ms. Smith's case "is exceptional but not unique, reflecting the inability of the correctional system in dealing with mentally troubled inmates" (ibid.). A coroner's inquiry was called to investigate and, in 2013, the jury at the inquest called her death a homicide. It also recommended that there be a complete overhaul of the existing policy on solitary confinement, making 104 recommendations. The recommendations included abolishing indefinite terms of solitary confinement, replacing them with 15-day limits, implementing an annual limit of 60 days of solitary confinement, and conducting reviews of segregated inmates after 10 days instead of the existing policy of 30 days.

During an investigation of Ms. Smith's death by federal corrections investigator Howard Sapers, it was discovered that managers at the federal correctional institute had repeatedly attempted "to curb the instances where they had to report the use of force" when dealing with Ms. Smith (Ha 2009a:A5). In his report, Mr. Sapers stated that the system had failed to solve an array of problems that had previously been highlighted. He was troubled that Ms. Smith had been moved 17 times within the correctional system, had spent the final year of her life in segregation, and had not received the mental health care she required. In his report, Mr. Sapers found that the Correctional Service of Canada "violated the law by keeping Ashley in solitary confinement without review, and continually transferring her without a proper psychiatric assessment" (Ha 2009b:A6). Although the use of solitary confinement is, "by law, subject to automatic review by regional correctional authorities after six weeks, Ms. Smith never received a single such review in nearly a year of solitary" and while federal policy "forbids the transfer of suicidal inmates . . . Ms. Smith was transferred 17 times" ("Ashley Smith's . . ." 2009:A14). Mr. Sapers made 16 recommendations for improvements in a number of areas, including compliance with the law and policy in correctional operations, governance in women's corrections, and inmate complaint and grievance procedures (Meaney 2008).

In another case, Edward Snowshoe was convicted of an armed robbery in Fort McPherson, N.W.T., in 2007 and sentenced to five-and-one-half years in the federal correctional system. He was first incarcerated in the federal correctional facility in Drumheller, Alberta, and then transferred a few months later to Stony Mountain

Critical Issues in Canadian Criminal Justice (*Continued*)

Institution north of Winnipeg—a medium-security institution where there is an Aboriginal program. Mr. Snowshoe successfully completed the In Search of Your Warrior Program, a violence-prevention program for Aboriginal inmates. He also participated in a number of prison-sanctioned sweat lodges. As a result of his progress, he was transferred to an Aboriginal healing lodge 225 kilometres northwest of Winnipeg. Four weeks later he escaped; he was found and subsequently transferred back to Stony Mountain (White 2014b). He attempted suicide at Stony Mountain three times and displayed depressive behaviour (White 2014a). After his third suicide attempt, he was placed in the mental health wing and later transferred back into the general population in late January 2010. On March 1, he threatened correctional officers with a "facsimile weapon" (a juice box turned inside-out). The next day he was transferred to solitary confinement for 134 days and, in July 2010, was transferred to Edmonton Institution, a maximum-security facility. Twenty-eight days later, Mr. Snowshoe was found slumped and unresponsive in his cell (White 2015).

Questions

1. Why was solitary confinement originally introduced into correctional facilities?
2. What changes should be made to the policy of solitary confinement?
3. Should solitary confinement be restricted to a few days at the maximum?
4. Should solitary confinement be eliminated?

SUMMARY

Incarcerated offenders serve their sentence in either a federal or provincial/territorial correctional facility. Currently there are 250 correctional facilities across Canada; 73 of these are under federal control. Various types of correctional facilities exist, with differing types of risk levels.

KEY WORDS: incarceration

How Did the Modern Prison Develop?

The modern prison was invented in Europe. This idea of incarcerating convicted offenders slowly became the norm, and it became the basis of imprisonment in common law countries. Various types of correctional facilities exist in Canada: in recent decades, a number of regional women's facilities and Aboriginal healing lodges have been established.

KEY WORDS: segregation, Age of Enlightenment, ex post facto laws, hedonistic calculus, panopticon, Pennsylvania system (separate system), Auburn system (silent system), congregate system, policy of normalization, medical model of corrections, Archambault Commission, Fauteux Report, corrections, reintegration model, risk prediction ideology, Prison for Women (P4W), Arbour Commission, Exchange of Service Agreement, Rivera Report, Structured Living Environment (SLE), Secure Units, healing lodges, holistic philosophy, s. 81 Agreements

European Antecedents to the Modern Prison (p. 384)
A Brief History of Federal Correctional Facilities in Canada (p. 385)
A Brief History of Federal Correctional Facilities for Women (p. 386)
A Brief History of Federal Correctional Facilities for Aboriginal People (p. 389)

What Is the Role of Correctional Facilities in Canada?

Security Levels (p. 392)
Prison Architecture and Correctional Facilities (p. 394)
Women Inmates (p. 395)
Aboriginal Inmates (p. 396)

This section reviews the structural aspects of correctional facilities, including the different types of security levels, different types of architecture, and supervision models. In addition, a profile of women and Aboriginal inmates is provided.

KEY WORDS: custodial model, rehabilitation model, reintegration model, maximum security, medium security, minimum security, dynamic security, Security Reclassification Management System, new-generation facilities, first-generation facilities, intermittent supervision, second-generation facilities, indirect supervision, third-generation facilities, direct supervision, podular design

The Prison Environment

Prison Life (p. 399)
Inmate Society (p. 402)
Prison Violence (p. 404)
Suicide in Prison (p. 405)
Gangs in Prison (p. 406)

This section looks at what it is like to experience the conditions of confinement in correctional facilities. When people are incarcerated, they enter into the inmate subculture, with its own values and norms.

KEY WORDS: total institutions, process of dehumanization, civil death, inmate subculture, social code, argot, prisonization, pains of imprisonment, prison code, deprivation model, importation model, gender-specific pains of imprisonment, self-injurious behaviour (self-harm), Mother–Child Program, prison gangs

Does the Rule of Law Exist in Prison? Prisoners' Rights, Due Process, and Discipline

The Duty to Act Fairly (p. 409)

The rule of law exists in all correctional facilities in Canada. In this section, there is a discussion of various legal rights afforded to inmates such as due process, discipline, and the duty to act fairly.

KEY WORDS: rule of law, "hands-off" doctrine, socially dead, due process rights, duty to act fairly, administrative segregation (solitary confinement)

Critical Thinking Questions

1. Do you think that building more federal correctional facilities in Canada is a good idea?
2. Discuss "prisonization." What are the negative aspects of this process? Can we change it?
3. What can be done to reduce the pains of imprisonment?
4. Why are the pains of imprisonment felt acutely by women?
5. Do you think that the current efforts by Correctional Service Canada to facilitate the needs of Aboriginal inmates are adequate?
6. Should Correctional Service Canada improve the services it provides to the members of racial and ethnic minority groups?
7. How is it possible to ensure that correctional facilities provide procedural justice and fairness for inmates?
8. Do you think the rule of law will ever completely exist in the correctional system?

Weblinks

For an interesting view of the inside of a variety of prisons, the people who are incarcerated there, and the people who work there, watch the CBC production *Inside Canada's Prisons* (2:09:04), available on YouTube.

Court Cases

Bacon v. Surrey Pretrial Services Centre (2010), B.C.J. 1080.

Canada (Attorney General) v. Whaling (2014), S.C.J. No. 20.

Inglis v. British Columbia (Minister of Public Safety) (2014), B.C.J. No. 2708.

Kosobook and Aelick v. The Queen and The Solicitor-General of Canada (1976), 1 F.C. 540.

Martineau v. Matsqui Disciplinary Board (1980), 1 S.C.R. 602.

May v. Ferndale Institution (2005), B.C.J. No. 84.

McCann v. The Queen (1975), 29 C.C.C. (2d) 377.

Mission Institution v. Khela (2014), S.C.J. No.24.

R. v. Institutional Head of Beaver Creek Correctional Camp, ex parte McCaud (1969), 2 D.L.R. (3d) 545.

Sauvé v. Canada (Chief Electoral Officer) (2002), S.C.J. No. 66.

Suggested Readings

Faith, K. 1993. *Unruly Women: The Politics of Confinement and Resistance*. Vancouver: Press Gang Publishers.

Garrison, G. 2015. *Human on the Inside: Unlocking the Truth about Prisons*. Regina, SK: University of Regina Press.

Jackson, M. 1983. *Prisoners of Isolation: Solitary Confinement in Canada*. Toronto: University of Toronto Press.

Liebling, A. and H. Arnold. 2004. *Prisons and Their Moral Performance: A Study of Values, Quality and Prison Life*. Oxford, UK: Oxford University Press.

Ricciardelli, R. 2014. *Surviving Incarceration: Inside Canadian Prisons*. Waterloo, ON: Wilfrid Laurier Press.

Waldrum, J.B. 1997. *The Way of the Pipe: Aboriginal Spirituality and Symbolic Healing in Canadian Prisons*. Peterborough: Broadview Press.

References

Anderson, P.R. and D.J. Newman. 1993. *Introduction to Criminal Justice*, 5th ed. Toronto: McGraw-Hill Ryerson.

Applegate, B., R. Surette, and B.J. McCarthy. 1999. "Detention and Desistance from Crime: Evaluating the Influence of a New Generation Jail on Recidivism." *Journal of Criminal Justice* 27:539–48.

"Ashley Smith's Inhumane Death." 2009. *The Globe and Mail*, March 10, p. A14.

Barker, J. 2009. "The Canadian Criminal Justice System and Women Offenders." Pp. 3–30 in *Women and the Criminal Justice System: A Canadian Perspective*, edited by J. Barker. Toronto: Emond Montgomery.

Boe, R., M. Naketh, B. Vuong, R. Sinclair, and C. Cousineau. 2003. "The Changing Profiles of the Federal Inmate Population: 1997 to 2002." Research Report R-132, Ottawa, Ontario Correctional Service in Canada.

Brzozowski, J., A. Taylor-Butts, and S. Johnson. 2006. *Victimization and Offending among the Aboriginal Population in Canada*. Ottawa: Canadian Centre for Justice Statistics.

Caron, R. 1982. *Go-Boy!* Toronto: Hamlyn.

Carrabine, E. 2006. "Incarceration." Pp. 211–14 in *The Sage Dictionary of Criminology*, 2nd ed., edited by E. McLaughlin and J. Muncie. London: Sage.

Carrington, D. Owen. 1991. *Crime and Punishment in Canada: A History*. Toronto: McClelland & Stewart.

Clear, T. 1994. *Harm in American Penology: Offenders, Victims and Their Communities*. Albany, NY: SUNY Press.

Clemmer, D. 1958. *The Prison Community*. New York: Holt, Rinehart, and Winston.

Cohen, S. 1985. *Visions of Social Control*. Cambridge: Polity Press.

Cole, D.P. and A. Manson. 1990. *Release from Imprisonment: The Law of Sentencing, Parole and Judicial Review*. Toronto: Carswell.

Cooke, D., P. Baldwin, and J. Harrison. 1990. *Psychology in Prisons*. London: Routledge.

Cooper, S. 1993. "The Evolution of Federal Women's Prisons." In *Women in Conflict with the Law: Women and the Criminal Justice System*, edited by E. Adelberg and C. Currie. Vancouver: Press Gang.

Correctional Service of Canada. 2014. *Federal Offender Population—2013 Warrant of Committal Admissions—All Offenders*. Ottawa: Correctional Service of Canada.

Correctional Service of Canada. 2008. *Audit of Management of Section 81 Agreements*. Ottawa: Correctional Service of Canada.

Correctional Service of Canada. 2007. *Commissioner's Directive: Dynamic Security*. Retrieved May 16, 2012 (www.csc-scc.gc.ca/text/plcy).

Correctional Service of Canada. 2004. *Commissioner's Directive: Special Handling Unit*. Ottawa: Correctional Service of Canada. Retrieved April 16, 2006 (www.csc-scc.gc.ca).

Correctional Service of Canada. 1998. *Performance Report for the Period Ending March 31, 1998*. Ottawa: Correctional Service of Canada.

Correctional Service of Canada. 1997. *Corrections in Canada*. Ottawa: Correctional Services Canada.

Correctional Service of Canada. 1990. *Creating Choices: Report of the Task Force on Federally Sentenced Women*. Ottawa: Correctional Service of Canada.

Crutcher, N. and S. Trevethan. 2002. "An Examination of Healing Lodges for Federal Offenders in Canada." *Forum on Corrections Research* 14:52–54.

Culhane, C. 1985. *Still Barred from Prison: Social Injustice in Canada*. Montreal: Black Rose.

Dauvergne, M. 2012. *Adult Correctional Statistics in Canada, 2010/2011*. Ottawa: Canadian Centre for Justice Statistics.

DiIulio, J.J. 1994. "The Question of Black Crime." *Public Interest* 117:3–32.

Dobash R.P., R.E. Dobash, and S. Gutterridge. 1986. *The Imprisonment of Women*. New York: Basil Blackwell.

Eckstedt, J.W. and C.T. Griffiths. 1988. *Corrections in Canada: Policy and Practice*, 2nd ed. Toronto: Butterworths.

Erdahl, E. 2001. "History of Corrections in Canada." Pp. 27–48 in *Corrections in Canada: Social Reactions to Crime*, edited by J.A. Winterdyk. Toronto: Prentice-Hall.

Faith, K. 1993. *Unruly Women: The Politics of Confinement and Resistance*. Vancouver: Press Gang.

Fillmore, C. and C. Dell. 2001. *Prairie Women, Violence and Self-Harm*. Winnipeg: Elizabeth Fry Society of Manitoba.

Finn, A., S. Trevethan, G. Carriere, and M. Kowalski. 1999. *Female Inmates, Aboriginal Inmates, and Inmates Serving Life Sentences: A One-Day Snapshot*. Ottawa: Juristat.

Foucault. M. 1995. *Discipline and Punish: The Birth of the Prison*, trans. Alan Sheridan. New York: Vintage.

Gabor, T. 2007. *Deaths in Custody: Final Report*. Ottawa: The Correctional Investigator Canada.

Garland, D. 1990. *Punishment and Modern Society: A Study in Social Theory*. Oxford: Clarendon Press.

Goffman, E. 1961. *Asylums*. New York: Doubleday.

Graveline, F.J. 1998. *Circle Works: Transforming Eurocentric Consciousness*. Halifax: Fernwood.

Green, C., G. Andre, K. Kendall, T. Looman, and N. Potovi. 1992. "A Study of 133 Suicides among Canadian Federal Prisoners." *Forum on Corrections Research* 4:20–22.

Ha, T.T. 2009a. "Officials Tailored Reports Involving Use of Force on Inmate, Transcripts Show." *The Globe and Mail*, March 11, p. A5.

Ha, T.T. 2009b. "Instructed to Curtail Crushing Red Tape, Guards Watched Girl Die in Her Cell." *The Globe and Mail*, March 3, pp. A1, A6.

Hannah-Moffat, K. 2001. "Limiting the State's Right to Punish." Pp. 151–69 in *Corrections in Canada: Social Reactions to Crime*, edited by J.A. Winterdyk. Toronto: Prentice-Hall.

Harris, K. 2012. "Rise in Prison Gangs Fuelling Violence, Drug Trade." *CBC News*, October 24. Retrieved April 7, 2015 (http://cbc.ca/news/politics/rise-in-prison-gangs-fuelling-violence-drug-trade).

Hart, M.A. 2002. *Seeking Mino-Pimatisiwan: An Aboriginal Approach to Healing*. Halifax: Fernwood.

Hayman, S. 2006. *Imprisoning Our Sisters: The New Federal Women's Prisons in Canada*. Montreal & Kingston: McGill-Queen's University Press.

House of Commons Subcommittee on the Penitentiary System in Canada. 1977. *Report to Parliament*. Ottawa: Minister of Supply and Services.

Howlett, K. 2014. "Prison Watchdog Criticizes Rate of Segregation." *The Globe and Mail*, December 8, pp. A1, A13.

Ignatieff, M. 1978. *A Just Measure of Pain: The Penitentiary in the Industrial Revolution 1750–1850*. New York: Columbia University Press.

Irwin, J. 1980. *Prisons in Turmoil*. Boston: Little Brown.

Irwin, J. and D. Cressey. 1962. "Thieves, Convicts, and the Inmate Culture." *Social Problems* 10:142–55.

Ishwaran, S. and R. Neugebauer. 2001. "Prison Life and Daily Experiences." Pp. 129–50 in *Corrections in Canada: Social Reactions to Crime*, edited by J.A. Winterdyk. Toronto: Prentice-Hall.

Jackson, M. 2002. *Justice Behind Walls: Human Rights in Canadian Prisons*. Vancouver: Douglas and McIntyre.

Jackson, M. 1983. *Prisoners of Isolation: Solitary Confinement in Canada*. Toronto: University of Toronto.

Kjellstrand, J.M. and J.M. Eddy. 2011. "Parental Incarceration during Childhood, Family Context, and Youth Problem Behavior across Adolescence." *Journal of Offender Rehabilitation* 50:18–36.

Kong, R. and K. Aucoin. 2008. *Female Offenders in Canada*. Ottawa: Canadian Centre for Justice Statistics.

Law Reform Commission of Canada. 1975. *Our Criminal Law*. Ottawa: Information Canada.

LeBlanc, T. 1994. "Redesigning Corrections for Federally Sentenced Women in Canada." *Forum on Corrections Research* 6:11–12.

Leger, S. 2003. *Criminal Organizations: Identification and Management of Gangs and Criminal Organizations in CSC*. Ottawa: Correctional Service of Canada.

Liebling, A. and H. Arnold. 2004. *Prisons and Their Moral Performance: A Study of Values, Quality and Prison Life*. Oxford, UK: Oxford University Press.

MacKay, A.W. 1986. "Inmates' Rights: Lost in the Maze of Prison Bureaucracy?" *The Correctional Review* 1:8–14.

Mann, M. 2010. *Good Intentions, Disappointing Results: A Progress Report on Federal Aboriginal Corrections*. Ottawa: Office of the Correctional Investigator.

Meaney, K. 2008. "Report Cites Federal Prison Danger." *National Post*, June 25, p. A8.

Naylor, B. 2013. "Protecting the Human Rights of Prisoners in Australia." Pp. 395–416 in *Contemporary Perspectives on Human Rights Law in Australia*, edited by P. Gerber and M. Castan. Pybank, NSW: Thomson Reuters.

Office of the Correctional Investigator Canada. 2014b. *A Three Year Review of Federal Inmate Suicides (2011–2014)*. Ottawa.

Office of the Correctional Investigator Canada. 2014a. *Annual Report of the Office of the Correctional Investigator 2013–2014*. Ottawa.

Office of the Correctional Investigator Canada. 2013. *Annual Report of the Office of the Correctional Investigator 2012–2013*. Ottawa.

Office of the Correctional Investigator Canada. 2012b. *Spirit Matters; Aboriginal People and the Corrections and Conditional Release Act*. Ottawa.

Office of the Correctional Investigator Canada. 2012a. *Annual Report of the Office of the Correctional Investigator 2011–2012*. Ottawa.

Office of the Correctional Investigator Canada. 2011. *Annual Report of the Office of the Correctional Investigator 2010–2011*. Ottawa.

Office of the Correctional Investigator Canada. 2010. *Annual Report of the Office of the Correctional Investigator 2009–2010*. Ottawa.

Pelletier, B. 1990. "The Duty to Act Fairly in Penitentiaries." *Forum on Corrections Research* 2:25–28.

Perreault, S. 2014. *Correctional Services Key Indicators, 2012/2013*. Ottawa: Canadian Centre for Justice Statistics.

Presse, L.D. and R.D. Hart. 1996. "Variables Associated with Parasuicidal Behaviour of Female Offenders during a Cognitive Behavioural Treatment Program." *Canadian Psychologist* 40.

Public Safety Canada. 2013. *Corrections and Conditional Release Statistical Overview.* Retrieved March 1, 2015 (www.publicsafety.gc.ca).

Public Safety Canada. 2010. *Corrections and Conditional Release Statistical Overview.* Retrieved April 24, 2012 (www.publicsafety.gc.ca).

Ricciardelli, R. 2014. *Surviving Incarceration: Inside Canadian Prisons.* Waterloo, ON: Wilfrid Laurier Press.

Rose, D.R. and T.R. Clear. 1998. "Incarceration, Social Capital, and Crime: Implications for Social Disorganization Theory." *Criminology* 36:441–79.

Rothman, D.J. 1971. *The Discovery of the Asylum.* Boston: Little, Brown. Anderson.

Rowe, D.C. and D.P. Farrington. 1997. "The Familial Transmission of Criminal Convictions." *Criminology* 35:177–201.

Ruby, C.C. 2003. "Do Canadian Prisoners Have Rights?" *Literary Review of Canada*, November, pp. 10–11.

Ruby, C.C. 1985. "Violence In and Out of Prison." *The Globe and Mail*, June 29, p. E6.

Rusche, G. and O. Kirchheimer. 1939. *Punishment and Social Structure.* New York: Columbia University Press.

Sapers, H. 2006. "The Correctional Investigator." *LawNow* 30:3031.

Senese, J.D. 1997. "Evaluating Jail Reform: A Comparative Analysis of the Podular/Direct and Linear Jail Inmate Infractions." *Journal of Criminal Justice* 25:61–73.

Shaw, M. 1991. *Survey of Federally Sentenced Women: Report of the Task Force on Federally Sentenced Women on the Prison Survey.* Ottawa: Corrections Branch, Ministry of the Solicitor General of Canada.

Shingle, B. 2014. "Canada Expanding Rarely Used Program That Lets Mothers Live with Children in Minimum Security Prisons." *The National Post*, May 20, p. A6.

Spierenburg, P. 1995. "The Body and the State: Early Modern Europe." In *The Oxford History of the Prison*, edited by N. Morris and D.J. Rothman. New York: Oxford University Press.

Sugar, F. and L. Fox. 1990. *Survey of Federally Sentenced Aboriginal Women in the Community.* Ottawa: Native Women's Association of Canada.

Sykes, G. 1958. *The Society of Captives.* Princeton, NJ: Princeton University Press.

Sykes, G. and S. Messinger. 1960. "The Inmate Social Code." Pp. 6–9 in *Theoretical Studies in the Social Organization of the Prison*, edited by R. Cloward et al. New York: Social Science Research Council.

Taft, D.R. 1956. *Criminology*, 3rd ed. New York: Macmillan.

"The Jails Should Not Become Cages." 2011. *The Globe and Mail*, August 11, p. A12.

Tibbetts, J. 2007. "Prison Staff Blamed for Inmates' Deaths." *National Post*, June 28, p. A6.

Trevethan, S., N. Crutcher, and C. Rastin. 2002. *An Examination of Healing Lodges for Federal Offenders in Canada.* Ottawa: Research Branch Correctional Service of Canada.

"Watchdog Says Prison Violence Is on the Rise; Toews Says It Has Decreased." 2011. *The Globe and Mail*, August 9, p. A9.

Watson, L. 2004. "Managing Maximum Security Women in Federal Corrections 1989–2004." *Forum on Corrections Research* 16:3–7.

Watson, L. 1995. "In the Best Interest of the Child: The Mother-Child Program." *Forum on Corrections Research* 7:25–27.

White, P. 2015. "We Can Only Do So Much as an Institution." *The Globe and Mail*, March 6, pp. A1, A13.

White, P. 2014b. "Solitary: A Death Sentence." *The Globe and Mail*, December 6, pp. F1, F4–F7.

White, P. 2014a. "Judge's Report: 162 Days in Segregation: Then Edward Snowshoe Killed Himself." *The Globe and Mail*, July 11, pp. A1, A13.

Zimring, F. and G. Hawkins. 1997. *Crime Is Not the Problem: Lethal Violence in America*. New York: Oxford University Press.

Zupan, L.L. 1991. *Jails: Reform and the New Generation Philosophy*. Cincinnati, OH: Anderson.

© Photos 12 / Alamy

CHAPTER

13

Community Reintegration

Learning Objectives

After completing this chapter, you should be able to:

- Understand the reintegration approach.
- Understand the risk assessment process.
- Identify the criteria used by the Parole Board of Canada in its decisions to release inmates into the community.
- Understand the role of reentry courts.
- Differentiate among gender, race, age, marital status, and employment in terms of desistance.
- Understand the issues facing older inmates in correctional facilities.
- Understand the purpose and operation of the "faint hope" clause.

Although some people would like to see criminals put away in prison forever, the reality is that over 90 percent of offenders are released back into society. Some offenders are placed on probation as soon as they are sentenced or shortly thereafter, while others—considered good risks not to reoffend—are ultimately released on some type of conditional release program such as parole.

This chapter begins with a discussion on what is known as **reintegration**. It then outlines the reintegration model and how it is practised in today's federal correctional system. A discussion then follows of some of the issues relating to reintegration, such as the importance of risk prediction. The roles played by the Parole Board of Canada (PBC) and the Corrections and Conditional Release Act (1992) in this area are also reviewed. Finally, the different types of conditional release programs and the recidivism rates of those who participate in them are reviewed.

In recent years, the increasing number of inmates incarcerated in federal correctional facilities has led the federal correctional system to "become increasingly compromised in meeting its rehabilitation and reintegration mandate. There is arguably not enough educational, vocational, and meaningful work opportunities being offered . . . and declining parole grant rates are linked to the capacity of the Correctional Service to address unmet needs linked to offending" (Office of the Correctional Investigator 2014a:3). The issue of providing appropriate programming and opportunities in order to assist the reintegration of offenders has been the subject of much discussion over the past decades, especially for women and Aboriginal offenders. In the spring of 2003, for example, the Auditor General of Canada tabled a report in the House of Commons that focused upon the reintegration of women offenders. This report reviewed all aspects of the Correctional Service of Canada's (CSC) reintegration programs for women offenders. While the report noted the efforts and advances made by the CSC since 1990 in the area of facilities and programming for women, such as the construction of the Aboriginal healing lodge as well as the new federal facilities and the development of gender-based rehabilitation programs, it also advanced a variety of recommendations on issues that would lead to greater successes of women offenders reintegrating into the community.

Among the recommendations made by the Auditor General was that the CSC implement its gender-specific substance abuse program, prompting the CSC to introduce the Women Offender Substance Abuse Program in all federal facilities. This led to the CSC adjusting some of its programs so that participation was based on an open entry approach. In addition, some other programs were adjusted in order that small group or one-on-one programs became possible. In addition, some programs were changed in order that participants could enter them at an earlier date. The Auditor General also noted that in order for women offenders to better prepare for future employment opportunities, the CSC should create and introduce a Women's Employment Strategy. In addition, the Auditor General recommended that the CSC look at and evaluate those factors contributing to the large number of women whose conditional release is revoked although they have not committed a new offence (Squires 2006).

David Cooper/getstock.com

An offender released into the community. Reintegration helps offenders by connecting them with resources that allow them to support themselves in society.

The issue of reintegration for Aboriginal offenders has also been explored. More Aboriginals in federal custodial facilities are first released into the community on statutory release or at their warrant expiry date than are non-Aboriginal offenders. Between 2003 and 2008, an average of 55 percent of Aboriginal offenders had their first release at statutory release compared to 45 percent for non-Aboriginal offenders. In addition, an average of 6 percent of Aboriginal offenders were first released at their warrant expiry date, compared to 3 percent for non-Aboriginals. The proportion of Aboriginal offenders on community supervision (30 percent) is less than for non-Aboriginals (40 percent). In addition, compared to non-Aboriginal offenders, Aboriginal offenders have been found to be

- overrepresented in segregation populations,
- classified as higher risk and higher need, and
- more likely to reoffend and have their conditional release revoked more often.

According to Mann (2010), one reason that Aboriginal offenders may be detained longer and serve less time in the community is related to the appropriateness of using the same risk assessment measures for all inmates. However, the reintegration instrument used by CSC has not undergone any validation in the Aboriginal context and, as a result, questions have been raised about its relevance for Aboriginal offenders. Yet, the CSC has the mandate to develop appropriate programs for Aboriginals in federal custody to give them culturally relevant programming in order to increase the likelihood of successfully reintegrating into the community. Mann (2010:31) states that the "ongoing gaps in outcomes between Aboriginal and non-Aboriginal offenders raise serious questions pertaining to whether the good intention underlying CSC strategies and policies in Aboriginal corrections are translating to results." Some of the shortcomings noted by Mann in her report include

- limited use of legislative provisions designed to enhance Aboriginal reintegration,
- inconsistent access to Aboriginal programming, and
- lack of an Aboriginal classification instrument.

The Reintegration Approach

Reintegration has a strong theoretical basis in rehabilitation (see Chapter 3). An offender is usually considered to be "rehabilitated" once he or she is no longer viewed as a threat to the community at large and therefore able to live within the community. Since it was observed that offenders exposed to the prison subculture within custodial facilities oftentimes had a difficult time after being released, a frequent justification of conditional release programs is that they prepare offenders for reintegrating back into mainstream society.

Reintegration is essentially a process through which corrections officials (e.g., parole officers) provide offenders with incentives to follow the rules of society. In doing so, the correctional system must balance the rights of the offender with the rights of law-abiding members of a community.

In Canada, most inmates are released into the community prior to the end of their sentence. This is referred to as "reintegration," and it involves placing offenders in the **least restrictive setting** possible. Conditional releases and temporary absences are also available. The former, however, can be revoked when it is considered necessary for public safety (Motiuk and Serin 1998). Reintegration is based on two assumptions:

(1) that only the most serious offenders should be sentenced to a period of incarceration in the federal system, and
(2) that the use of alternative sanctions should be maximized. According to Latessa and Allen (1997:28), reintegration is "a broad correctional ideology stressing the acquisition of legitimate skills and opportunities by criminal offenders, and the creation of supervised opportunities for testing, using, and refining those skills, particularly in community settings."

The reintegration approach takes the position that the **key predictors of recidivism** are known and that each individual offender must be assessed in terms of these predictors so that programs can be developed that will enhance their reintegration to society. These key predictors of recidivism are as follows:

(1) "antisocial/procriminal attitudes, values, beliefs and cognitive-emotional states (that is, personal cognitive supports for crime)";
(2) "procriminal associates and isolation from anticriminal others (that is, interpersonal supports for crime)"; and
(3) antisocial personality orientations such as low self-control, impulsiveness, risk-taking, and egocentrism (Andrews 1995:37).

Recidivism is also predicted by a history of antisocial conduct going back to childhood; by poor childhood training by parents, such as inadequate support and supervision; and by "low levels of personal educational, vocational or financial achievement," including an "unstable employment record" (ibid.). Some of these predictors are static, but most are dynamic—that is, most of them can be changed. These dynamic factors are called **criminogenic needs**. To determine what the likelihood is that an offender will recidivate, the individual's risks and needs are assessed on entry into a federal correctional facility. On the basis of this assessment, correctional personnel select the proper response.

Lucie McClung, the first woman to be appointed commissioner of the Correctional Service of Canada, favoured reintegrating inmates into the community.

This approach has been practised by the CSC for a number of decades. The key piece of legislation guiding that organization, the Corrections and Conditional Release Act (CCRA), has as one of its main goals the reintegration of offenders into the community (see Exhibit 13.1). The main tool for achieving this goal is the **Offender Intake Assessment (OIA)**, during which an extensive amount of information is collected, including the offender's prior criminal record, his or her potential for violence, and the nature of the most recent offence. During the OIA, a criminal risk assessment is developed and the offender's case needs are identified. These serve as the basis for the Correctional Plan Overview, which evaluates the total case record of the offender (typically, it is updated every six months). All of this becomes the basis of the Custody Rating Scale (CRS), which is used to determine the security classification of the offender (see Figure 13.1).

The Offender Risk Assessment is based on the risks and needs of each offender. (The risk of an offender is also evaluated by the Parole Board of Canada when an inmate applies for early release on a conditional release program.) Risk assessments are intended to identify those individuals most likely to reoffend and the types of needs that correctional officials must address when developing a personalized plan to assist the incarcerated offender.

EXHIBIT 13.1 Federal Policy on Offender Reintegration

One of the purposes of the Corrections and Conditional Release Act is to help rehabilitate offenders and reintegrate them by providing programs in penitentiaries and in the community. Offender reintegration is defined as all activities and programs conducted to prepare an offender to return safely to the community and live as a law-abiding citizen. To understand offender reintegration, one must understand the variables considered in decisions about releasing offenders to the community. For each offender, the Correctional Service of Canada (CSC) does the following:

- Collects all available relevant information about the offender, including items such as the judge's reasons for sentencing and any victim impact statements.
- Assesses the offender's risk level (the likelihood that he or she will reoffend) and criminogenic needs (life functions that lead to criminal behaviour).
- Reduces the offender's risk level by increasing his or her knowledge and skills and by changing the attitudes and behaviours that lead to criminal behaviour.
- Develops and implements programs and individual interventions that effect change in areas that contribute to criminal behaviour.
- In cooperation with the offender, develops a plan to increase the likelihood that the offender will function in the community as a law-abiding citizen.
- Motivates and helps the offender follow the correctional plan and benefit from correctional programs and interventions.
- Monitors and assesses the offender's progress in learning and changing.
- Makes recommendations to the National Parole Board as to the offender's readiness for release and the conditions, if any, under which he or she could be released.
- After release, helps the offender respect the conditions of the release and resolve day-to-day living problems.
- Makes required programs and interventions available in the community.
- Monitors the offender's behaviour to ensure that he or she is respecting the release conditions and not indulging in criminal behaviour.
- If required, suspends the offender's release, carries out specific interventions, and reinstates or recommends revocation of the release as appropriate.

Source: Federal Strategic Principles of Reintegration, Thurber, A., 1998. "Understanding Offender Reintegration." Forum on Corrections Research 10:14–18. See http://www.publicsafety.gc.ca/lbrr/archives/forum%2010-1-1998%20e-eng.pdf, page 14. Reproduced with the permission of the Minister of Public Safety and Emergency Preparedness Canada, 2015.

The CSC implemented the Offender Risk Assessment and Management Strategy in 1986 and uses it to assess all inmates, except for some who may receive a very early release date (Taylor 1998).

The Theory of Risk Assessment

Underlying the OIA is the **theory of risk assessment**. This theory focuses on the social psychology of criminal behaviour. It posits that individual and social/situational factors combine to create in offenders values, cognitions, and personality contexts that facilitate criminal behaviour. To a large extent, these ways of thinking, behaving, and reacting are learned and reinforced and ultimately lead to individual differences in criminal actions.

There are three key factors in a risk assessment: **risk**, **need**, and **responsivity**. The first principle, risk, states that the level of supervision and treatment should be commensurate with the offender's level of risk. This means that the most intensive correctional treatment and intervention programs should be reserved for those offenders identified as higher risk (Andrews et al. 1990). However, as Andrews (1989:14) points out, "the belief persists that treatment services, if effective at all, only work for lower risk cases." Thus, high success rates for low-risk offenders on a conditional release program may be incorrectly interpreted to mean that those offenders benefited from treatment. This may not be so because, being low risk, they might have had high success rates even without treatment. According to Andrews (ibid.:19), "such errors involve confusing the predictive accuracy of pretreatment risk assessments with the issue of who profits from it." If high-risk offenders are improperly assessed as low risk, they will no doubt have high recidivism rates. In his research on probation supervision programs in Ottawa, Kiessling (1989) found that higher-risk cases in a regular supervision program had a recidivism rate of 58 percent, compared to 31 percent of high-risk cases placed in a high-risk supervision program. So it is essential to make a correct determination of risk in order to match the offender with the type of program from which he or she will benefit. Lipsey (1995), in his meta-analysis of 400 studies of the effectiveness of treatment programs with youth offenders, found greater reductions in reoffending when higher-risk offenders were treated than when lower-risk offenders were treated.

One essential component of risk assessment is the determination of which risks are considered static factors and

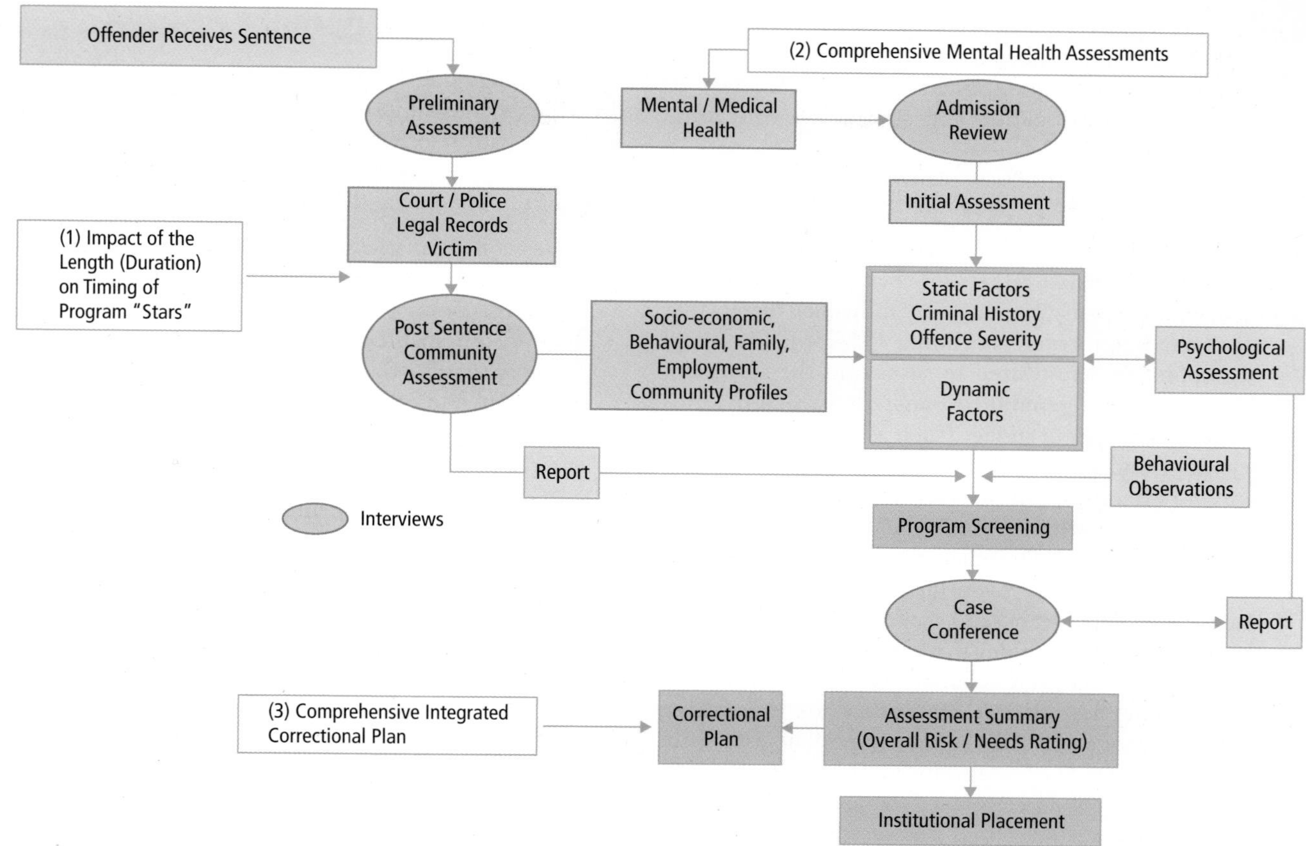

FIGURE 13.1 The Offender Risk Intake Assessment Process

Source: © Offender Intake Assessment Process, Audit of Offender Intake Assessment, http://www.csc.scc.gc.ca/publications/pa/adt-offndr-378-1-247-eng.shtml, Correctional Service Canada, 2009, p. 8. Reproduced with the permission of the Minister of Public Works and Government Services Canada, 2015.

which are considered to be dynamic. **Static factors** include the prior record of the offender as well as his or her prior record (if any) when placed in a conditional release program. **Dynamic factors** (sometimes these are referred to as "need" factors) involve those characteristics of the offender that can be changed through correctional programming. These include level of education, the level and type of cognitive thinking skills, occupational skills, and interpersonal skills. Dynamic factors differ from static factors in that they can be changed. Some needs may be viewed as criminogenic—that is, if they are not dealt with, there is a significant chance that the offender will reoffend on release.

The second principle, need, asserts that "if correctional treatment services are to reduce criminal recidivism, the criminogenic needs of offenders must be targeted" (Andrews 1989:15). Research has found that offenders with criminogenic needs are much more likely to fail when they are placed in a conditional release program and that assessments of offender risk and needs are good predictors of outcome on parole (Motiuk and Brown 1993). The combined assessment of risk associated with criminal history and need levels of offenders has been found to increase the predictive power of risk assessments (Taylor 2001). Motiuk and Brown (1993) found that higher-risk/higher-need offenders were four times more likely to fail while they were in conditional release programs than were lower-risk/lower-need offenders.

Research in this area points to the importance of distinguishing between criminogenic and non-criminogenic needs. For example, Dowden (1998) found after 9e-entry9 the need principle that non-criminogenic needs were not related to, or were negatively associated with, reductions in recidivism. Criminogenic needs, however, were positively correlated with reduced recidivism. Overall, 75 percent of the individual criminogenic need targets led to significant decreases in recidivism.

Specific needs vary among individuals. That said, Andrews (1989:15) found that the following needs can be dealt with in a rehabilitative program:

- Change antisocial attitudes.
- Change antisocial feelings.

- Reduce antisocial peer associations.
- Promote formal affection/communication.
- Promote formal monitoring and supervision.
- Promote identification and association with anti-criminal role models.
- Increase self-control, self-management, and problem-solving skills.

Responsivity, the third principle, has to do with selecting appropriate targets for change as well as styles of service. Responsivity factors are individual targets that affect the treatment goals (Bonta 1995:36). Two types of responsivity are related to success in the treatment of offenders: (1) **general responsivity**, which involves the styles or types of service (such as behavioural, social learning, and cognitive-behavioural strategies) that work for offenders; and (2) **specific responsivity**, which matches service with personality and motivation as well as ability with demographics such as age, gender, and ethnicity. In essence, this principle addresses effective correctional supervision and counselling. The assumption underlying the responsivity principle is that not all offenders are the same. Characteristics such as verbal skills, communication style, inadequate problem-solving skills, and poor social skills become important not only in classifying offenders but also in the ways that offenders themselves respond to efforts to change their behaviour, thoughts, and attitudes (ibid.). Research in this area has found that many risk factors overlap with the types of responses needed to teach offenders prosocial attitudes. An important part of this principle is that offenders need to be matched to parole officers' characteristics. Research indicates that parole officers who scored higher on interpersonal sensitivity and awareness of social rules received higher scores from their clients and were also more likely to display prosocial behaviours and to disapprove of antisocial behaviours (Andrews 1980; Andrews and Kiessling 1980).

According to Taylor (2001:15), studies related to these three principles for correctional treatment "demonstrate that assessing a variety of static and dynamic risk factors using actuarial methods, providing more intensive levels of treatment to higher-risk offenders, and targeting criminogenic needs in a manner consistent with the characteristics of the offender results in considerably reduced rates of recidivism."

Note that there is another principle, the principle of professional discretion, which states that correctional staff should use the information about offenders attained through the proper application of the risk, need, and responsivity principles in an informed manner. Professional judgment can be used to override objective-based results in exceptional cases, and this can improve the accuracy of assessments (Taylor 2001).

The Case Management Process

Case management is defined as "a systematic process by which identified needs and strengths of offenders are matched with selected services and resources in corrections" (Enos and Southern 1996:1). The essential objectives of this system are the following:

- Assess offender accountability, motivation, responsivity, engagement, reintegration potential, and level of intervention;
- Identify criminal risk and risk management strategies using actuarial tools, assessment, and professional judgment; and
- Include the offender's continuum of correctional intervention and sentence planning.

This system establishes interventions that will

(1) take into account the importance of the protection of society, staff members, and offenders;
(2) include observations of the offender's engagement and progress against his/her Correctional Plan;
(3) address dynamic factors contributing to the offender's criminal behaviour;
(4) consider factors that do not contribute to criminal behaviour but that require structure and guidance to enhance the potential for reintegration; and
(5) ensure that the result of assessments are continuously monitored in the institution and community.

The Integrated Correctional Program Model

The CSC is obligated to provide a variety of programs "directed to address criminal behaviour, reduce reoffending, and contribute to successful reintegration" (Office of the Correctional Investigator 2014b). Research indicates inmates involved in correction and interventions related to their risks and needs are less likely to reoffend (Correctional Service of Canada 2011). To better address offenders' needs, the CSC has introduced the **Integrated Correctional Program Model** (see Exhibit 13.2), which prioritizes placing inmates into programs as early as possible during their incarceration and targets multiple risk factors within single programs. Some of the key programs offered include the following:

(1) Employment and employability
(2) Family violence
(3) Offender education
(4) Substance abuse
(5) Violence prevention

EXHIBIT 13.2 The Integrated Correctional Program Model

According to the CSC, multiple risk factors contribute to an offender's criminal activity. In order to facilitate offender reintegration, the CSC attempts to address these risk factors through the Integrated Correctional Program Model (ICPM). There are three categories of programs in the ICPM, all of which are offered at moderate and high intensity levels:

(1) Multi-target programs
(2) Aboriginal multi-target programs
(3) Sex offender programs

The ICPM is based on CSC's most effective offender programs. These programs have been proven to significantly reduce reoffending. This program model focuses upon those multiple risk factors that most offenders have. In these programs, offenders learn to understand the risk factors that are linked to their criminal behaviour. The goal is to have the participants use what they have learned in demanding situations.

The ICPM has four components that complement the main program:

(1) *The introductory phase*: this consists of 10 to 11 group sessions. Each is 2 to 2.5 hours long. The goal is to provide general direction to offenders and to focus upon areas where they have trouble. Such areas could include their risks, lifestyles, and relationships, or their ability to manage emotions and thoughts.
(2) *The motivational component*: the goal is to encourage offenders who are not motivated to participate or stay in correctional programs. It also aims to help those who are having trouble understanding program concepts.
(3) *The community program*: this consists of 20 to 26 group sessions. These are each 2 to 2.5 hours long. It is offered to offenders who have not fully completed their required correctional programs while incarcerated. They learn to understand their personal risk factors as well as developing basic skills to help reduce risky or harmful behaviours before they participate in the maintenance component.
(4) *The maintenance component*: this consists of cycles of 12 group sessions, each 2 hours in length. The sessions are offered in both the institution and the community. The goal is to teach offenders how to apply the skills they have learned in the main program to real-life situations. It is hoped that this will reduce the risk of reoffending (Correctional Service of Canada 2011).

Contemporary Community Supervision in Canada

The law specifies that offenders must receive penalties for their crimes, but it also allows for the mitigation of sentences. Some offenders serve their time in a provincial or federal institution, of course, but the majority remain in the community—at home and at work—under the supervision of probation or parole officers.

Conditional release programs were originally implemented as a result of dissatisfaction with the role of prisons. Prisons are viewed as being too expensive to operate, as having harmful effects and disrupting family relationships, and as having success rates about the same as probation and conditional release programs. As previously mentioned, correctional institutions are expensive to run. Food, medical and dental services, vocational and literacy training, 24-hour security, and escorted leaves are expensive. Community sanctions are much less expensive, as indicated in Figure 13.2. Guards are not needed, and capital costs are lower since no expensive security devices are required. The offenders are usually working as well as paying taxes and supporting their family (and in some cases restitution to victims).

Community-based facilities are thought to mitigate the harmful effects of incarceration on individuals. Life in a correctional facility does not resemble life in society. The violence, controlled environment, and lack of employment programs in prisons have led many to conclude that prisons do more harm than good. Community facilities allow offenders to maintain connections to society—to work, to be in supportive relationships, and to benefit from community resources. Finally, those who live in or have contact with community facilities usually have lower recidivism rates, since they are considered lower risks. Keeping every offender in a correctional facility until the end of their sentence could be counterproductive, as it would disrupt their lives and their families and make it more difficult for them to reintegrate into society.

Community Correctional Centres

Community correctional centres (CCCs) are community-based residential facilities operated by the CSC that are available only to federally sentenced offenders who have been conditionally released into the community (see Exhibit 13.3). The participants

FIGURE 13.2 The Cost of Keeping an Inmate Incarcerated

Source: Corrections and Conditional Release Statistical Overview, 2013, Table B3, p. 26. http://www.publicsafety.gc.ca/cnt/rsrcs/pblctns/crrctns-cndtnl-rls-2013/crrctns-cndtnl-rls-2013-eng.pdf. Reproduced with the permission of the Minister of Public Safety and Emergency Preparedness Canada, 2015.

Categories	Annual Average Costs per Offender (current $)				
	2007–08	2008–09	2009–10	2010–11	2011–12
Incarcerated Offenders					
Maximum Security (males only)	135,870	147,135	150,808	147,418	151,484
Medium Security (males only)	87,498	93,782	98,219	99,519	104,889
Minimum Security (males only)	89,377	93,492	95,038	95,034	91,959
Women's Facilities	182,506	203,061	211,093	214,614	211,618
Exchange of Services Agreements	77,762	87,866	89,800	90,712	97,545
Incarcerated Average	101,664	109,699	113,974	114,364	117,788
Offenders in the Community	24,825	29,476	29,537	31,148	35,101
Total Incarcerated and Community	81,932	91,498	93,916	96,412	100,622

EXHIBIT 13.3 Profile of Community Correctional Centres

- The CSC operates 16 Community Correctional Centres (CCCs) across Canada (Atlantic: 4; Quebec: 6; Ontario: 3;* Prairie: 2; Pacific: 1) with a total bed capacity of 474 (Atlantic: 84; Quebec: 184; Ontario: 105; Prairie: 70; and Pacific: 31).
- In 2012–13, there were approximately 7,750 federally sentenced offenders supervised in the community, 439 (6%) of whom resided in a CCC.
- Over the past 10 years, CCCs have generally been operating below capacity except for those in Ontario which have been over-capacity for the past 4 years.
- Some CCCs accommodate offenders with special needs. For example, Martineau CCC in Quebec accommodates offenders with mental health needs and Chilliwack CCC in the Pacific region has 3 beds for older offenders including those with a chronic illness and/or palliative care needs. Of the 474 beds in CCCs across Canada, 76 are accessible (16%).

Costs

- In 2012–13, the 16 CCCs operated on an annual budget of $30M, which represents 12.1% of the total community corrections budget ($247M in 2012–13) and 1.1% of the overall CSC budget ($2.7B in 2011–12**). The total allocation for CCCs has remained constant over the past 3 years.***
- In 2012–13, the annual average cost to accommodate an offender in a CCC was $72,333 compared to $31,534 to supervise an offender in the community (includes parole supervision and community-based residential facility beds). In 2011–12, the annual average cost of keeping an inmate incarcerated was $117,788 per year.****

The exterior of a community correctional centre.

Source: Office of the Correctional Investigator, *Annual Report of the Office of the Correctional Investigator 2013–2014*, p. 10, http://www.oci-bec.gc.ca/cnt/rpt/pdf/annrpt/annrpt2013 2014-eng.pdf Reproduced with permission of the Office of the Correctional Investigator.

*Hamilton CCC in Ontario closed December 31, 2014, and there are currently no plans to replace it.

**Public Safety Canada, *"Corrections and Conditional Release Statistical Overview,"* 2013.

***Revised financial information was provided by CSC (August 15, 2014) after the printing of the OCI's 2013–14 Annual Report. As such, some of the financial numbers in this report do not correspond to those in the Annual Report. For example, the Annual Report states that CCCs operate on an annual budget of $17M; however, this amount only included the community supervision component, whereas the $30M reported here includes those costs as well as accommodation, heating, food, and maintenance costs. The financial data presented in this report should be considered as the most recent data available.

**** Public Safety Canada, *"Corrections and Conditional Release Statistical Overview,"* 2013.

have been released on unescorted temporary absences, day and full parole, work releases, statutory release, and long-term supervision orders. (The CCRA allows the Parole Board of Canada to add a condition of residency in a CCC to those inmates who are being released on statutory release, and who are considered to be a high risk for committing a serious violent offence.) In early 2014, the Office of the Correctional Investigator (2014b) reported that 55 percent of all residents of CCCs were on statutory release, 26 percent were on a long-term supervision order, 17 percent were on day parole, with the remaining 2 percent on full parole. Community correctional centres are categorized as minimum-security institutions in policy, but they are not required to conform to all of the institutional standards associated with such facilities. They provide a structured and secure living environment that comprises 24-hour supervision, monitoring by onsite parole officers, curfews, and sign-in and sign-out procedures.

A slight majority of offenders placed in CCCs are assessed as having high needs and low reintegration potential when they first arrive; these needs decrease significantly during their stay, and as such their reintegration increases.

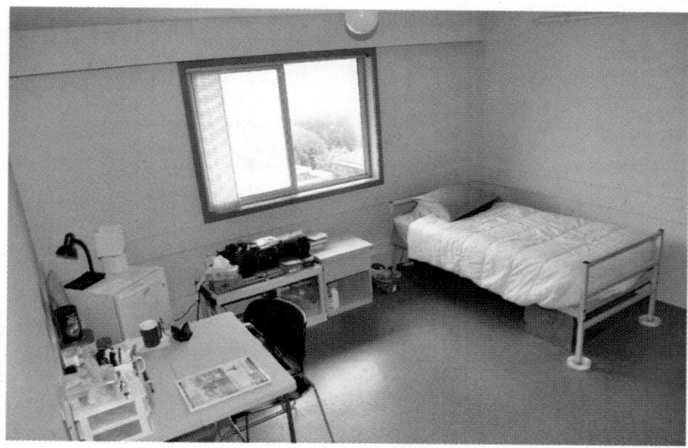

A bedroom in a community correctional centre for an individual with health care needs.

Office of the Correctional Investigator, *Annual Report of the Office of the Correctional Investigator 2013-2014*, p. 14, http://www.oci-bec.gc.ca/cnt/rpt/pdf/annrpt/annrpt20132014-eng.pdf. Reproduced with permission of the Office of the Correctional Investigator.

SUMMING UP AND LOOKING FORWARD

Within the past few decades, Canadian correctional officials have realized that failing to address the reentry of incarcerated offenders can lead to higher recidivism rates and pose a threat to public safety. Reintegration policies generally emphasize the need to start a reentry program while offenders are incarcerated and to focus on those issues and challenges offenders will face when they are released back into the community. In addition, there is an emphasis on the provision of treatment services that will assist individuals in their reintegration into society.

The reintegration approach is associated with rehabilitation. Reintegration is based on the idea that by placing offenders into the least restrictive setting possible they will perform better when they reenter society. Prior to being released back into society, offenders are assessed on the basis of certain predictors of possible recidivism. The Offender Intake Assessment (OIA) attempts to discover the key predictors of recidivism for offenders and then create a plan to address them. The OIA is based on the theory of risk assessment which attempts to look at the risks and needs of offenders and what type of responses should be used to better facilitate their reintegration. Part of the reintegration approach is to assist individuals to better interact with the broader society. Community correctional centres are community-based facilities operated by the CSC that are available to federally sentenced offenders and provide a structured and secure environment for residents.

Review Questions:

1. What is the role of reintegration in the area of corrections?
2. What are the key components of the case management process?
3. What are the major elements that complement the main Integrated Correctional Program Model?
4. What is the federal policy on offender reintegration?
5. What is the role and purpose of community correctional centres?

The Parole Board of Canada

The Parole Board of Canada plays a significant role in the conditional release (see Chapter 11) and reintegration of inmates into the community. While it once held significant discretionary powers under the Parole Act, it gradually changed its approach as a result of concerns about the lack of due process guarantees and procedural safeguards for inmates during parole hearings. For example, the Task Force on the Release of Inmates (1973) criticized the criteria for parole release for being vague and unclear, with the effect that "neither inmates nor members of the Board are able to articulate with any certainty what positive and negative factors enter the parole decision" (Task Force on the Release of Inmates 1973:32). The task force recommended that offenders be allowed to appear before the parole board members, giving them "the opportunity to hear from the decision-makers themselves the reasons for their decision" (ibid.:34). The reasons for any decision were now to be written down and a copy given to the applicant. Also, a parole hearing would now be granted when an inmate requested it. In addition, the Parole Board of Canada (then the National Parole Board) (1981) published a list of factors that its members could consider during a hearing. These included the following:

- Any criminal record, the kinds of offences and their pattern, and the length of crime-free periods between convictions.
- The nature of the current offence and its seriousness.
- The understanding the inmate appeared to have gained of the situation that brought him or her to prison, and what that individual had done about it.
- The effort the inmate had made while in prison to take training and to take advantage of educational and employment upgrading activities.
- The institutional behaviour and offences of the inmate.
- Previous parole violations, if any, of the inmate.
- The plans the inmate had for employment or training and how definite those plans were.

An important component of the legislation governing the federal correctional system (the Corrections and Conditional Release Act, which replaced the Parole Act) is what is referred to as "schedule offences." These are offences under the Criminal Code prosecuted by way of indictment. Offences found in Schedule I are violent crimes, such as murder, attempted murder, and sexual offences, as well as offences of criminal negligence in which the result was severe harm or death. Severe harm may be physical or psychological. Schedule II offences are offences under the Controlled Drugs and Substances Act and the Food and Drugs Act and are prosecuted by way of indictment. Offences included in Schedule II include all drug offences and conspiracy to commit a drug offence (charges for simple possession are excluded). The importance of these schedules lies in their influence on how offenders are classified, the types of programming they are offered, their need for a psychiatric or psychological assessment, and their qualification for a conditional release program (Leonard 1999).

Today, before offenders leave a federal correctional facility on a conditional release program, they agree to a correctional plan developed by the Parole Board of Canada with the assistance of correctional officials (such as institutional parole officers). The correctional plan outlines an individualized risk management strategy for each offender and specifies the interventions and monitoring techniques that will be required to address the risks associated with the offender's reoffending. It typically involves the placing of certain restrictions on their movement and activities. It also specifies certain constructive activities, such as working and attending counselling.

The assumption behind this approach is that people become involved in crime because of problems in their lives, such as substance abuse, lack of skill in anger management, lack of employment opportunities owing to a lack of job training and skills, and so on. The correctional plan is based on information selected from risk assessment evaluations conducted by the CSC as well as the case management group to which the offender belongs while in custody (Correctional Service of Canada 1997).

The release of an offender into the community entails the addressing of three related issues: supervision, programming, and community involvement. Supervision is the direct monitoring of and communication with offenders once they are back in the community. This is usually conducted by parole officers or trained volunteers, depending on the offender involved. Not all offenders are adequately supervised, however, according to the 1999 report by the Federal Auditor General's office. That office conducted a random sample of 150 offenders under community supervision in five major urban centres and reported that 10 to 20 percent "were not contacted with the required frequency" (Bellavance and Alberts 1999:A6). According to the CSC, supervision alone does not help offenders change. Therefore, it is combined with "programming," which requires the supervised offender to participate in programs designed to meet his or her needs. These programs are located in the community, with the idea that they will help the offender reintegrate (Correctional Service of Canada 1997).

Risk of Recidivism

In 1987–88, the Parole Board of Canada (then the National Parole Board [NPB]) came under increasing public criticism for its release decisions, especially after a series of homicides during 1987–88 committed by individuals on conditional release. At the time, some of the public felt that most offenders released into the community were potential high-risk offenders. Almost 25 years later, similar concerns led to the introduction of the Safe Streets and Communities Act (Bill C-10), which amended the conditional release provisions in the Corrections and Conditional Release Act (see Exhibit 13.4).

However, studies of inmates placed in community release programs found that rates of recidivism were related to the type of conditional release program in which offenders were placed. A profile of readmissions to federal correctional institutions over a six-year period conducted by the CSC found a substantial difference between recidivism rates for those on full parole and those on statutory release (then known as mandatory supervision). Of the 8,751 offenders released on full parole, 30 percent were readmitted, compared to 58 percent of the 17,769 offenders placed in mandatory supervision.

The majority of offenders returned to a federal institution for violating the terms of their conditional release did so within 12 months of release. Also, 81 percent of all offenders who failed on full parole or mandatory supervision were readmitted within 24 months. After 24 months, however, the incidence of inmates being returned to a federal institution dramatically declined. According to the Correctional Service of Canada (1990:12), "after the two-year follow-up point, the number of offenders returning to federal institutions dropped to 2 percent and gradually tapered off each subsequent year. At the six-year follow-up point, fewer than 1 percent of offenders were readmitted." This study revealed that for offenders on statutory release

EXHIBIT 13.4 The Safe Streets and Communities Act (Bill C-10): Changes to the Parole Board of Canada

Among the changes introduced by the Safe Streets and Communities Act were amendments to the conditional release provisions of the Corrections and Conditional Release Act.

Changes to Conditional Releases

The new Act:

- Emphasizes as a principle that Parole Board decisions should be consistent with the protection of society and be "limited to only what is necessary and proportionate to the purpose of conditional release," replacing the term "least restrictive determination consistent with the protection of society."
- States that the Parole Board of Canada considers "the nature and gravity of the offence" and "the degree of responsibility of the offender" in conditional release decisions.
- Permits the Parole Board of Canada to go forward with a decision even if offenders withdraw their application for parole within 14 calendar days.
- Increases the waiting period for reapplication for day or full parole after a negative decision from six months to one year.
- Permits offenders with a life sentence or with an **indeterminate sentence**, who previously were ineligible, to apply for parole by exception if they are terminally ill.
- Enables the imposition of residency during statutory release on offenders who present an undue risk to commit organized crime offences.
- Introduces automatic suspension of parole or statutory release when an offender receives an additional sentence.

In addition to the changes to conditional release, there were changes to detention criteria as well as for victims of crime and pardons.

Changes to Detention Criteria

The new Act expands the categories of offences subject to detention until the end of the sentence. This would include, for example, those convicted of

- child pornography,
- luring a child,
- aggravated assault of a peace officer,
- breaking and entering to steal a firearm, or
- a terrorist offence under the Criminal Code.

Changes to Victims of Crime

The Safe Streets and Communities Act amends the Corrections and Conditional Release Act to permit the Correctional Service of Canada and the Parole Board of Canada to release additional categories of information to registered victims and enshrine in law the right of victims to present a statement at the hearings.

Changes to Pardons

The Safe Streets and Communities Act replaces the term "pardon" with "record suspension." It makes individuals convicted of a sexual offence against a minor and individuals convicted of more than three indictable offences ineligible for a record suspension. There is now a waiting period for a record suspension to five years for all summary convictions and to 10 years for all indictable offences.

Source: Parole Board of Canada 2012.

the critical point for readmission to a federal institution arrives within six months of release, whereas for offenders on full parole, the second six-month period is the most critical.

Because of concerns about recidivism rates, the CSC instructed the NPB to shift its focus to risk factors as the primary consideration when considering the release of offenders. This change was introduced in November 1986, when the NPB identified its main goal as the protection of society. To achieve this goal, the board made risk assessment of future crimes by offenders after release its major focus (National Parole Board 1987). And in 1988, the NPB released its policy on pre-release detention, which was intended to identify the criteria for parole board decisions.

These policies were based on three key assumptions:

(1) that risk to society is the fundamental consideration in any conditional release decision;
(2) that the restrictions on the freedom of the offender in the community must be limited to those that are necessary and reasonable for the protection of society and the safe reintegration of the offender; and
(3) that supervised release increases the likelihood of reintegration and contributes to the long-term protection of society (Bottomley 1990; Larocque 1998; National Parole Board 1988).

In 1992, the Corrections and Conditional Release Act (CCRA) replaced the Parole Act. The new Act identified fundamental principles that were to guide the correctional system in the changing social and legal contexts of Canadian society. The CSC is now guided by a statement of principles that declares, first, that the purpose of the federal correctional system is to maintain "a just, peaceful and safe society" (Haskell 1994:45). Section 3 of the CCRA states that this purpose is to be achieved through the following means:

(1) By carrying out sentences imposed by the courts through the safe and humane custody and supervision of offenders.
(2) By assisting the rehabilitation of offenders and their reintegration into the community as law-abiding citizens through the provision of programs in penitentiaries and in the community.

Those who drafted the new Act hoped to enhance for all concerned—offenders, correctional staff, and the public—an understanding of and appreciation for the principles and purposes behind correctional decision making. To this end, it provided improved guidance for the NPB. The hope was that the board would become "more consistent and straightforward in its functioning" (ibid.:46).

To achieve its goals, the CCRA authorizes the disclosure of all relevant information to offenders (subject to certain limited exceptions) when a decision adversely affects their conditional release application. The CCRA also allows for the disclosure of some information to victims, in the hope that this will "lead to greater awareness of the legitimate reasons behind decisions that may appear arbitrary, inappropriate or even unfair" (ibid.). Furthermore, the Act requires the release of all information to the NPB about the offender's background that could affect the board's conditional release decision. This information includes the nature of the offences as well as police and prosecution files and sentencing information.

Risk Assessment

The CCRA requires the PBC to distinguish among offenders on the basis of risk factors. All board members are required to "specifically assess whether an offender will commit an offence, in particular a violent offence, while on conditional release" (Sutton 1994:21). To enhance their decision-making ability, board members are now required to take training in risk assessment as well as in the tools and research currently available.

PBC decisions, then, are made on the basis of risk assessment, risk prediction, and risk reduction. They are based on a general knowledge of the social-psychological perspective on criminal conduct, including the assumption that criminal behaviour is usually learned behaviour. When making decisions about conditional release, parole board members make assessments in five areas of an offender's situation (ibid.:22):

- behavioural history
- the immediate situation

Jw/getstock.com

A halfway house. These facilities provide a place to live as well as a range of personal and social services for offenders in the process of being reintegrated back into society.

- mental and emotional outlook favourable to criminal activity
- pro-criminal social supports
- other personal factors, including level of development, self-regulation, problem-solving skills, impulsivity, and callousness

The Task Force on Reintegration of Offenders, formed by the CSC in 1997, noted in its report that the service has been mandated to use the least restrictive measures consistent with protecting the public. As such, it recommended implementing a risk-related differentiation process that would place offenders in one of three categories on the basis of a risk/needs rating. This categorization would be carried out during the OIA process. The three levels are

(1) release-oriented intervention for low-risk offenders,
(2) institutional and community intervention for moderate-risk offenders, and
(3) high-intensity intervention for offenders in the high-risk category (Correctional Service of Canada 1997).

To assess the significance of these principles for recidivism rates, Brown and O'Brien (1993) described a study that involved a panel of psychologists and psychiatrists and their assessments of 69 randomly selected federal offenders in the forensic unit of a Canadian hospital. The most common offences were murder (41 percent of offences), a sexual offence (20 percent), and assault or manslaughter (19 percent). The panel used 15 recidivism risk factors—three demographic factors and 12 clinical factors—to complete their assessments. On the basis of risk scores, 26 offenders were identified as "good risks" for release into the community, and all succeeded in completing their terms on parole. Clearly, then, recidivism risks were a factor in the release of these high-risk offenders on parole. However, the success of these offenders on parole was in large part the result of treatment services delivered in the context of risk principles in a community setting.

Criminal Justice Focus

Pardons (Record Suspensions)

When Graham James was convicted in 2012 of sexually assaulting two hockey players he had coached (see Chapter 3), it was discovered that he had received pardons for his previous offences. This resulted in a public outcry, and the federal government decided to make changes to the pardons system and included these in the legislative changes brought about by Bill C-10. The PBC remained the government agency with complete control over granting, refusing, or revoking a record suspension (Pardon Services Canada 2010). A number of new provisions regarding pardons were introduced when Bill C-10 was passed:

- The term "record suspensions" replaced the name "pardons."
- The period of ineligibility to apply for a record suspension for a summary conviction offence was increased from three to five years.
- The period of ineligibility to apply for a record suspension for an indictable offence was increased from 5 to 10 years.
- Individuals convicted of a child sex offence are permanently barred from receiving a record suspension.
- Individuals with three or more convictions for indictable offences are permanently ineligible to receive a record suspension.
- The cost of applying for a record suspension was increased to $631 from $150.

From mid-March 2012 to December 2012, 3,693 record suspensions were granted, compared to the more than 24,000 pardons granted during 2009–10. And as of December 2012, in excess of 22,000 applications were still awaiting review under the old system (Bronskill and Cheadie 2013). The Canadian Bar Association (2011:6) has criticized the new approach, saying it makes "rehabilitation and reintegration into society more difficult, rather than improve public safety." Others have pointed out that the new approach stigmatizes individuals and makes it more difficult for them to obtain jobs.

Reentry into Society and Desistance from Crime

What can be done to reduce the possibility that individuals released from custody will commit a crime when they return to society? Efforts to answer this question have led correctional authorities to develop programs that help inmates make the transition from prison to the community. In the recent past, those programs came under the general heading of "rehabilitation," but today many correctional authorities refer to them as part of the strategy known as **prisoner reentry**. The concept of reentry refers to as encompassing "all activities and programming conducted to prepare ex-convicts to return safely to the community and to live as law-abiding citizens" (Petersilia 2003:39). One of the biggest obstacles to successful reentry is that life behind bars is very different from life on the outside. The prison, for example, insulates inmates from making decisions that are necessary to live a normal existence beyond the prison. As a result, much of the work that goes into prison reentry is based upon the types of programs available to inmates to prepare them to successfully reintegrate into society upon release. This involves understanding the risk of recidivism of offenders, as well as providing those resources within the walls to inmates so that they can successfully reintegrate (see *Investigating: Reentry Courts and Recidivism*).

Investigating: Reentry Courts and Recidivism

The beginnings of reentry courts occurred decades prior to their being established, when the U.S. incarceration rate began to increase. This rise in the prison population was not the result of a single policy, but rather a combination of various policies introduced with a focus upon getting "tough on crime." The introduction of mandatory minimum sentences and truth-in-sentencing legislation increased not only the actual number of individuals being sent to prison, but also the length of prison sentences as a whole. Most of the rise in the U.S. prison population largely occurred to the increased proportion of incarcerations per arrest (Blumstein and Beck 1999), which led to more people being sentenced to prison for the same crimes that previously were dealt with by community sanctions (Travis 2005).

Much of the attention of the new policies was placed upon drug offenders, with the introduction of longer prison sentences for drug law violations and drug-related offences (Glaze 2002). The increased use of mandatory minimum sentences, lowered weights for drug possession charges, and greater law enforcement efforts to apprehend drug offenders combined to significantly increase the number of drug offenders entering prison (Belenko 2006). From 1980 to 1996 the per capita rate of prison admissions increased by more than 930 percent (Travis 2005).

To a certain extent this increase in the incarceration rate for drug crimes started in New York State. As a result of the Rockefeller Drug Law that was introduced in 1973 (see Chapter 10), the number of drug offenders incarcerated increased. The percentage of drug offenders in New York State custodial facilities went from 11 percent in 1973 to a peak of 35 percent in 1994 (New York State Department of Correctional Services 2008). These laws had a significant impact upon certain communities, particularly in Black and Hispanic neighbourhoods. Although representing 33 percent of the New York State population, Blacks and Hispanics made up 94 percent of all individuals incarcerated under the Rockefeller Drug Laws (Drucker 2002).

Not only did these new policies have an impact upon the number of offenders entering prison, but they also increased the number of people leaving on parole. West (2008) estimated that over 725,000 inmates were being released annually, the majority (almost 80 percent) being released on parole. In 2000, the number of drug offenders accounted for 33 percent of all prison releases (Hughes et al. 2001).

The purpose of parole has been to reintegrate offenders back into the community as well as to protect the community from recidivism through parole supervision. Yet, large numbers (up to 80 percent) of those released in New York were being rearrested and sent back to prison. Much of this is the result of measures, in particular intermediate punishments, that were introduced into post-release programs designed to protect the community (see Chapter 11). These programs effectively increased the parole failure rate—in 1984, the number of individuals who successfully completed parole in New York State was 70 percent, while in 2002 it was 45 percent. The vast majority of the failures were attributed to technical violations, with 10 to 15 percent the result of new criminal offences (Glaze 2002).

Beginning in the late 1990s, as a result of the high recidivism rates, the U.S. Department of Justice started a number of reentry initiatives. Based on the drug court model, the Reentry Court Initiative was designed to provide graduated sanctions and case management in combination with needed social services that would likely produce long-lasting changes (Travis et al. 2001). The Initiative started nine pilot programs, and although they were encouraged to develop their programs to match the

Investigating: Reentry Courts and Recidivism *(Continued)*

needs of the parolees with the local community, six core elements common to all the pilot programs emerged:

- *Assessment and Planning*: Eligibility criteria and psychosocial assessment and service need identification, and multiple reentry planning partners (e.g., judge, parole offices, case managers, correctional administrators).
- *Active Oversight*: Formal court appearances and judicial involvement.
- *Management of Support Services*: Court-monitored social services.
- *Accountability to the Community:* Feedback and input provided by an advisory board, efforts made to pay fees in lieu of revocation, and involvement of victims' organizations.
- *Graduated and Parsimonious Sanctions*: The use of predetermined sanctions for violations in lieu of revocations and sanctions administered universally.
- *Incentives for Success*: Rewarding completion of program milestones (e.g., early release, graduation ceremonies to recognize achievements).

When the U.S. Department of Justice started the pilot programs it was imagined that this approach would produce successful outcomes such as those being reported by drug court evaluations at the time. In the first evaluations of the Reentry Courts (which studied participants of Reentry Courts with individuals on traditional parole programs over a three-year period), it was found that the programs had positive impacts with regard to preventing new criminal behaviour (rearrests and reconvictions). Reentry court offenders were rearrested and reconvicted less frequently. In addition, reentry participants were out for a longer period of time before they were rearrested.

However, the overall technical violations occurred more frequently for Reentry Court participants than the comparison group of traditional parolees. It was found that the traditional parolee groups were on parole for a longer period of time before they were recorded with a technical violation. This is interpreted as a "supervision effect"; that is, as a result of the smaller staff-to-parolee ratio, the Reentry Court more closely supervises its parolees, which provides for a greater opportunity to "catch" parolees violating the conditions of their parole. In addition, Reentry Court parole officials have close relationships with local service providers thereby increasing the chance that a missed appointment or a failed drug test will be reported. This additional supervision and quicker transfer of information creates a supervision effect as paroles on the reentry program are more closely monitored than those on the traditional parolee program.

In terms of recognizing issues related to recidivism, Andrews (1989) reviewed the literature on this issue and concluded that the findings from past research were consistent in outlining characteristics that indicate an increased risk of crime. These characteristics include the following: having associates who have criminal tendencies or who are antisocial in nature; pro-criminal attitudes, values, and beliefs; generalized difficulties or trouble in relationships with others; and being male. The more risk factors present, the greater the likelihood of reoffending. According to Andrews (ibid.:13), research has established "beyond question, that systematic risk assessment allows the identification of lower and higher risk groups . . . offenders in higher risk groups will be responsible for a majority of the recidivistic offences."

Of course, predictions are not always accurate. Some individuals identified as high risk may never reoffend, while some identified as low risk will. In an attempt to improve the risk classification of offenders, risk assessment criteria have been developed on the basis of behavioural and objective criteria. Behavioural criteria include cognitive-behavioural and social learning factors (Andrews et al. 1990). Objective criteria, which are the ones most commonly used when comparing offenders on conditional release programs, include such measures as race, drug abuse history, and employment status.

Programs in correctional systems across Canada (both federal and provincial/territorial) are delivered on the basis of **cognitive-behavioural therapy**. The goal of these programs is to focus upon the thinking patterns and thought processes of offenders and then have offenders participate in relevant programs such as self-control and emotional response management. Programs generally involve **structured learning environments** designed "to affect such cognitive processes as interpreting social cues, monitoring one's own thought processes, identifying and compensating for distortions in thinking, reasoning about right and wrong behaviour, generating alternative solutions, and making decisions about appropriate behavior" (Landenberger and Lipsey 2005:452).

Studies by Antonowicz and Ross (1994) and Robinson (1995) have concluded that low-risk offenders have a similar, if not better, response to treatment than high-risk offenders. Andrews (1996) has identified four significant risk factors: antisocial cognitions, antisocial associates, antisocial personality complex, and a history of antisocial behaviour.

Most research on success in conditional release programs compares recidivists with non-recidivists on a number of standard objective criteria, including gender, race, age, marital status, and employment.

Desistance from Criminal Activity

As individuals transition from incarceration to the community it is hoped that what they have learned in their programming will lead to them to desist from criminal activity. **Desistance** is "a behavioural concept, intended to describe a widespread pattern of criminal activity and inactivity identified in the longitudinal study of criminal careers" (Maruna 2006:121) Empirical research has found a number of social processes to be related with desistance. Meaningful social bonds such as stable employment and strong personal relationships can function for adults as **turning points** that lead them to engage in socially conforming behaviour through the development of **social capital** (Laub and Sampson 2003). Cognitive or motivational factors felt to lead to prosocial behaviours include self-efficacy and the acceptance of prosocial labels. As people create, develop, and invest in prosocial contacts they desist from criminal activity as they have "something to lose" by offending.

Gender

As of April 2013, there were 579 women offenders incarcerated under federal supervision in Canada. The most commonly cited offences committed by incarcerated women are drug-related offences, homicide, robbery, and assaults. Women admitted to federal custody have been found to have different treatment needs than men. In a study that evaluated federally sentenced women in terms of risk levels assessed at intake, just over half the women were identified as being low risk to reoffend, 35 percent as moderate risk, and 14 percent as high risk. On release, 62 percent of the women were identified as low risk to reoffend, 29 percent as moderate risk, and 9 percent as high risk (Taylor and Flight 2004).

Overall, women offenders often come from family backgrounds where dysfunction and trauma exist, including domestic and family violence and physical and/or sexual abuse. As the Office of the Correctional Investigator (2014a) points out, almost 80 percent of federally sentenced women have some type of substance or alcohol-related abuse. They also have histories of nonpermanent employment and low educational levels of achievement. Women are also more likely than men to have a significant mental health diagnosis at the time they are admitted into custody. In 2010–11, 29 percent of women offenders, compared to 13.5 percent of male offenders, were identified during the intake process at a federal correctional facility as having mental health problems. Just over 30 percent of women offenders compared to 14.5 percent of male offenders had previously been hospitalized for psychiatric reasons (Office of the Correctional Investigator 2012). Jones (2004) studied 483 substance-abusing women who were released on a conditional release program between January 1, 1995 and December 31, 2000. The rate of revocation was 48 percent, "considerably higher than that reported in earlier research studies." However, the researchers pointed out that the sample of their study consisted of "only substance abusing women, who are at greater risk for recidivism compared to women who do not have substance abusing problems."

A number of studies have compared male and female offenders on conditional release. These have found some differences in recidivism rates. In general, women seem to have lower recidivism rates than men. Bonta et al. (1992) 32e-entry 2,985 male and 81 female recidivists released from federal custody during 1983–84 and found that 36 percent of the women committed a new offence within three years of their release compared to 49 percent of the men. Regarding temporary absences, Grant and Belcourt (1992) reported that women (0.01 percent) were less likely to fail on this program than men (1.0 percent). However, Lefebvre (1994), in her analysis of 929 men and 44 women on day parole during 1990–91, found that the overall failure rate for women was 30 percent, compared to 27 percent for male offenders.

Reasons for parole revocation varied between women and men: 5 percent of women had committed a new offence, compared to 10 percent of men. This result supports the conclusion reached by Belcourt et al. (1993), who reported in their analysis of 968 women released from federal custody over a 10-year period that 50 percent had been readmitted for a technical violation, while 21 percent had had their release revoked for a new offence. Blanchette and Dowden (1998) state that federally sentenced women released on either full or day parole have higher success rates on day and full parole than those released on statutory release or on the expiration of their warrant.

Proper programming has a significant influence on reducing recidivism rates among federally sentenced women. Dowden and Blanchette (1998) studied 251 federally sentenced women: 143 of them were substance abusers and 108 were non-abusers. All of them had been released on either day or full parole. The researchers found that the substance abusers were at greater risk of being returned to a correctional facility. However, participation in drug treatment programs while in custody was "associated with reduced returns to custody for substance abusers; the rate approximated that of female non-abusers" (ibid.:29).

However, Correctional Service Canada's reintegration plan for federally sentenced women "is hindered by the fact that, unlike those they have for men, there are no stand-alone minimum security institutions in which to place women offenders as they prepare to make their way back to society. This is fundamentally an issue of equality" (Office of the Correctional Investigator 2010:50). The Correctional Investigator (2010, 2014a) also notes that women offenders have higher levels of motivation and a higher reintegration potential than men. The Correctional Investigator recognizes that the needs of women offenders include education, employment, as well as substance abuse counselling. As such, he questions why so much vocational training at the women's regional facilities involves "domestic" work.

Race

Most research has found that Aboriginal offenders in conditional release programs have recidivism rates higher than those of non-Aboriginal offenders. The Office of the Correctional Investigator (2012:35) noted the following about Aboriginal offenders:

- They are much more likely than others to have their parole revoked, less likely to be granted day or full parole, most often released on statutory release or held until warrant expiry date.
- They are referred to proportionately more programs than their non-Aboriginal counterparts of equivalent risk and need.
- They return to CSC custody at a higher rate of post-warrant expiry.

These outcomes have existed for Aboriginal offenders over two decades. For example, Bonta et al. (1992), in a three-year study, reported that Aboriginal offenders placed on statutory release (then mandatory supervision) had a much higher recidivism rate (75 percent) than those released on full parole (33 percent). Belcourt et al. (1993) studied the success of Aboriginal female offenders in all types of conditional release programs. They reported that Aboriginal women were overrepresented in the group returned to a correctional facility after release. Forty-four percent of Aboriginal women offenders were readmitted, compared to around 19 percent of non-Native female offenders. Dowden and Serin (2000) studied the needs of 113 Aboriginal female offenders placed in conditional release as of May 1, 1999. They found that compared to non-Aboriginal offenders, Aboriginal women were more likely to be assessed as high risk (31.9 percent versus 14.6 percent); non-Aboriginal women were more likely to be placed in the lower-risk category (72.1 percent versus 49 percent) or in the medium-risk category (13.3 percent versus 18.6 percent). Also, offenders who were released with significant needs that had yet to be addressed were more likely to recidivate. The authors concluded that when these offenders' needs are not addressed in the community, they are more likely to fail in the community.

The reasons for these differences between Aboriginal and non-Aboriginal offenders have been of concern to the CSC, various federal committees studying conditional release programs, and independent researchers. The Daubney Committee (1988:214), for example, noted that "Native inmates are often not as familiar with release preparation and the conditional release system as other inmates." Zimmerman (1992:401) reported that Aboriginal offenders "often waive the right for early release." She attributed this in part "to subtle encouragement by case management officers" (ibid.:409). It seems, then, that Aboriginal offenders are the least likely of all groups in the federal correctional system to be released on parole. This is in part due to certain parole criteria being "inherently weighted against aboriginal offenders" (ibid.:408). Johnson (1997) found that Aboriginal offenders have lower rates of application to conditional release programs in part because they mistrust the correctional system. Welsch (2000) found that less than half (48 percent, or 65 of 136 individuals) of Aboriginal offenders who could make their first application for full parole actually did so, compared to 73 percent of non-Aboriginal offenders. In addition, about 59 percent of Aboriginal offenders waived a full parole hearing on their current sentence, compared to 33 percent of non-Aboriginal offenders. In addition, of those offenders who did apply for parole, Aboriginal offenders were more likely to be classified as high risk relative to non-Aboriginal offenders (61.1 percent versus 49.9 percent), while non-Aboriginal applicants were more likely to be classified as low risk (26.4 percent versus 16 percent) or medium risk (29.4 percent versus 20.9 percent) (see Figure 13.3).

Aboriginal offenders who are granted parole are more likely to find themselves returned to prison before the expiration of the conditional release program—a fact thought to be the result of the inappropriate conditional release requirements placed on them, more stringent enforcement of release conditions, and inadequate support on their release.

Ellerby (1994:23) points out that these higher recidivism rates have made the reintegration of Aboriginal inmates into the community on conditional release programs both "difficult" and "challenging." Culturally

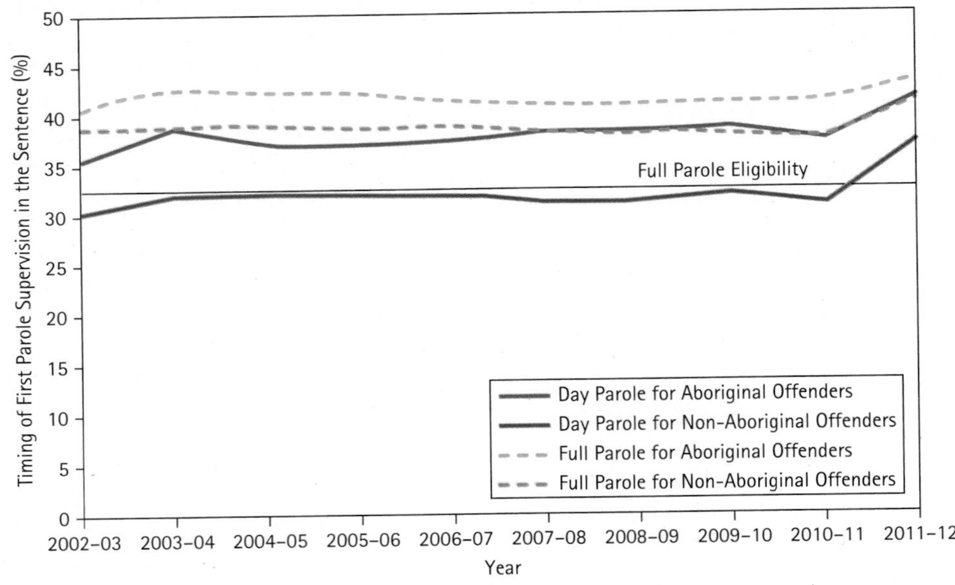

FIGURE 13.3 Aboriginal Offenders Serve a Higher Proportion of Their Sentences before Being Released on Parole

Source: 2012 Annual Report—Corrections and Conditional Release Statistical Overview, Figure D5, page 85, http://www.publicsafety.gc.ca/cnt/rsrcs/pblctns/2012-ccrs/2012-ccrs-eng.pdf. Reproduced with the permission of the Minister of Public Safety and Emergency Preparedness, 2015.

specific practices have been incorporated into the treatment process in the hope that they will "help aboriginal offenders address their offending and develop the insight and skills necessary to avoid or manage the factors that place them at risk of re-offending" (ibid.:24). Starting in 1987, the Forensic Behavioural Management Clinic in Winnipeg began to include traditional healing practices in its treatment of both Aboriginal and non-Aboriginal participants. These programs involve Elders and present an opportunity for offenders to take part in pipe ceremonies and sweat lodge ceremonies. This program has made treatment more meaningful for the program participants.

Despite the fact that Correctional Service Canada has implemented healing lodges, the Office of the Correctional Investigator (2010) identifies problems with their progress in implementing programs for Aboriginals. They found that CSC has yet to provide sufficient access to culturally sensitive programs, as well as implementing more Aboriginal core programs. They also noted the lack of initiative on the part of CSC to implement the principles identified in *R. v Gladue* (1999) and *R. v. Ipeelee* (2012) (see Chapter 10) into the case management process. Furthermore, given that Aboriginals have a high rate of being classified as "high needs"; that statutory release now represents the most common form of release for federally sentenced Aboriginals; and that there is no Aboriginal-specific classification instrument in place, there is much to do to prepare Aboriginals for reintegration.

In their 2014 report, the Office of the Correctional Investigator (2014a) noted some improvements by CSC in terms of reintegration policies for Aboriginal offenders, such as:

- Increases in escorted and unescorted temporary absences for Aboriginal offenders so they can participate in cultural activities and maintain community contacts.
- High program enrolment and completion rates in Aboriginal-specific programs and interventions.
- The creation of more Aboriginal-specific positions such as Aboriginal Community Development, Programs and Community Liaison Officers.

However, they also noted that while progress was being made, "there are still too many Aboriginal offenders whose initial custody rating scale is overridden to higher security, too many day and full parole waivers, suspensions and revocations, and statutory releases" (Office of the Correctional Investigator 2014a:44).

Black offenders are less likely to be readmitted to a federal correctional facility after being released on all types of a conditional release program; they are "generally less likely to be readmitted on a new federal sentence" (Office of the Correctional Investigator 2013:13). While most Black inmates indicated that CSC programs provided them "with important tools and strategies, they did not feel that they adequately reflect their cultural reality" (Office of the Correctional Investigator 2013:14). Black inmates have identified a number of shortcomings, including

(1) inconsistent support for cultural events at the institutional level, and
(2) a lack of community support.

Black women inmates, many of whom are foreign nationals, point out that restricted contact with both their homes and families present challenges to their reintegration as many face deportation once they have completed their sentence. Other concerns raised by Black women inmates include the following:

(1) lack of appropriate skills training (rather than laundering, folding, ironing, and sewing of clothes); and
(2) although many were incarcerated for drug trafficking, they didn't have a drug addiction or substance abuse problem. Yet, they were required to complete courses in both these areas, despite an absence of an identified need (Office of the Correctional Investigator 2013:13).

Age, Marital Status, and Employment

Sherman and colleagues (1992) have reported that recidivism may be higher among those who are unemployed and unmarried. Citing research from domestic violence studies, they argue that neither race nor a record of prior offences has an impact on reducing recidivism. They have found, rather, that "arrested persons who lacked a stake in conformity were significantly more likely to have a repeat offence than their counterparts who were not arrested" (ibid.:682). This finding suggests that those with a higher stake in conformity are more likely to complete a conditional release program.

Regarding marital status, Lefebvre (1994) found that offenders who were married or involved in common-law relationships at the time of their offence had a lower failure rate (22 percent) than those who were divorced or separated (28 percent) or single (29 percent). Studies by researchers such as Bonta et al. (1992) have consistently found that recidivism rates for single, divorced, or separated offenders are higher than for those who are married.

Lefebvre (1994) studied the impact of employment status and education on recidivism. She found that the overall failure rate for day parolees declined as the offender's level of education increased, from 29 percent for those with a Grade 8 education or less to 19 percent for those with a post-secondary education. She also found that those who were employed at the time of the offence were twice as likely to succeed on conditional release programs compared to those who were unemployed (33.9 percent versus 16.8 percent).

Other research, particularly in the United States, has found that "all but the most exceptional criminals, even violent ones, mature out of lawbreaking before middle age . . . as they age, they are no longer a risk" (Goldstein 2015:4). Involvement into the length of criminal activity by individuals (referred to as **criminal careers**) has found that, for the eight most serious crimes tracked by the F.B.I., the typical duration that adults commit these crimes (as measured by arrests) is 5 to 10 years.

Lefebvre (1994) found that the overall failure rate of her sample of day parolees was inversely related to age. For the youngest group (18 to 25 years), it was 41 percent, followed by 25 percent for those aged 26 to 40 and 14 percent for those over 40. The rate of failure owing to the commission of a new offence was 15 percent for the youngest group, 9 percent for the middle group, and 5 percent for the oldest group. Similar findings were made by Bonta and colleagues (1992), who found that recidivists were, on average, three years younger (26) than non-recidivists at the time of sentencing. In their study of female offenders, Belcourt et al. (1993) found a similar trend. Twenty-nine percent of those aged between 18 and 25 were readmitted, compared to 22 percent of those 26 to 30, 20 percent of those 31 to 45, 16 percent of those 46 to 60, and 11 percent of those over 60.

SUMMING UP AND LOOKING FORWARD

The Parole Board of Canada maintains a key role in releasing offenders into the community prior to the end of their sentence. A major concern for the authorities is the possibility or risk that offenders will reoffend (i.e., recidivate) in the future. It is thought that recidivism can be explained by a range of factors that include both the background of offenders and the inability of treatment programs in correctional facilities to successfully reform offenders. Treatment programs, especially those based on cognitive-behavioural therapy, have been developed in an attempt to stop offenders from reoffending. cognitive-behavioural therapy is an approach that attempts to alter the thought processes which may lead to criminal behaviour. It is hoped that by delivering treatment to offenders by way of cognitive-behavioural therapy that offenders' criminogenic risks will be reduced and eliminated. A wide range of interventions may be pursued at the same time to address offending behaviour. It is hoped that offenders will "rethink" their involvement in criminal activity and ultimately desist from offending.

Review Questions:

1. What are the factors considered by the Parole Board of Canada when deciding to grant early release to an offender?
2. What are Schedule I and Schedule II offences?
3. What is cognitive-behavioural therapy?
4. What is desistance?
5. Explain how age is a risk factor for reoffending?

Corrections: The Older Inmate

In 2012–13, 37 percent of all offenders admitted to a federal correctional facility were between the ages of 20 and 29 while 27 percent were between 30 and 39. The median age of the offender population has been increasing, from 30 in 1994–95 to 33 in 2012–13.

When the term **older offenders** is used, it refers to offenders aged 50 or over. In 1996, older offenders serving a federal sentence in Canada ranged in age from 50 to 90. The largest group of older offenders is between 50 and 59, where 456 offenders were serving a federal sentence in 2012–13 (435 men and 21 women), an increase from the 368 offenders (353 men and 15 women) who were serving a sentence in a federal correctional facility in 2007–08.

The number of older inmates will continue to grow in the future, since 5,335 (or about 23 percent) of the total offender population is serving a life or indeterminate sentence. Most of these individuals will be over the age of 50 before they are eligible to apply for parole (see Figures 13.4 and 13.5).

Three types of older offenders have been identified. The first group includes those who were incarcerated while young and who have remained in prison since. The second category includes chronic offenders who have been incarcerated many times before their latest term of imprisonment. Most of them are serving time for property crimes. The third category includes those

Canadian correctional facilities are increasingly home to greater numbers of inmates with special needs and elderly inmates.

Photos.com/Thinkstock

25%
20%
15%
10%
5%
0%
Percentage of Warrant of Committal Admissions
2003-04
2012-13
Under 18 18-19 20-24 25-29 30-34 35-39 40-44 45-49 50-59 60-69 70 +
Age of Offender at Admission

FIGURE 13.4 Offender Age at Admission to Federal Jurisdiction Is Increasing

Source: *Corrections and Conditional Release Statistical Overview*, 2013, Fig C6, p. 43, https://www.publicsafety.gc.ca/cnt/rsrcs/pblctns/crrctns-cndtnl-rls-2013/crrctns-cndtnl-rls-2013-eng.pdf. Reproduced with the permission of the Minister of Public Safety and Emergency Preparedness Canada, 2015.

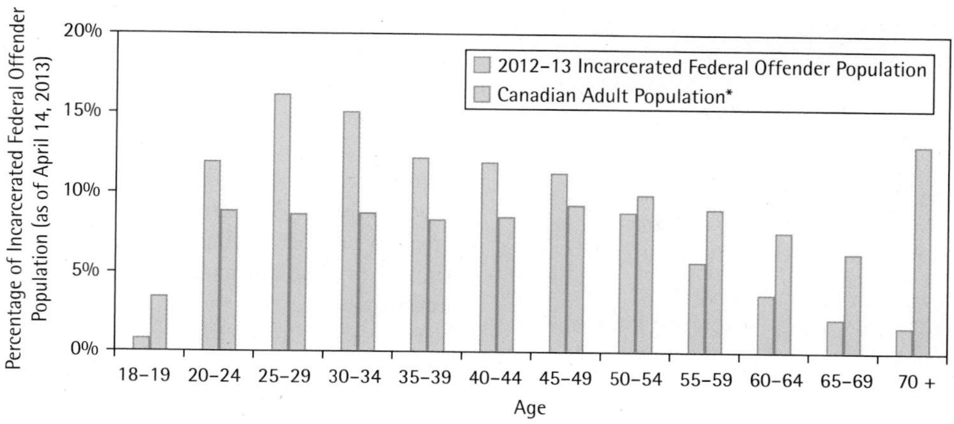

FIGURE 13.5 21% of the Federal Incarcerated Population Is Aged 50 or Over

*2013 Postcensal Estimates, Demography Division, Statistics Canada and include only those age 18 and older.

Source: Corrections and Conditional Release Statistical Overview, 2013, Fig C8, p. 47, http://www.publicsafety.gc.ca/cnt/rsrcs/pblctns/crrctns-cndtnl-rls-2013/crrctns-cndtnl-rls-2013-eng.pdf. Reproduced with the permission of the Minister of Public Safety and Emergency Preparedness Canada, 2015.

offenders who are serving their first term of imprisonment late in life. They were law-abiding for most of their life and became involved in crime only later (Aday 1994). Most of the older inmates in Canada's prisons fall into this category. Overall, older offenders are a low risk to reoffend and pose limited problems associated with control for correctional authorities. They are generally easy to manage since they are less likely to violate institutional rules. Older offenders, however, pose special problems for the correctional system, since they have a reduced ability to cope in prison and to have their needs met there. As a consequence of growing old in prison while serving a long sentence, older offenders have special needs and problems that set them apart from the rest of the adult offender population (Cowles 1990; Krebs 2009; Walsh 1989). Among other things, these needs relate to accommodation, programming, adjustment to imprisonment, the prison environment, peer relationships while in prison, family relationships, and parole issues (Uzoaba 1998). A study of older inmates in California found that 80 percent had a chronic health condition, 38 percent had hypertension, 28 percent had a heart disease, and 16 percent had cataracts (Zimbardo 1994).

Despite the high costs of incarceration, some (e.g., Goetting 1983; Walsh 1992) argue that it is inconsistent to argue that older inmates ought to be excused from serving time in a federal institution simply because costs are high. They contend that the needs of older inmates will not create a heavy financial burden on the correctional system. But they also point out that it must be recognized that older inmates require programs that meet their needs.

Specialized care is a general concern in prisons. To date, prisons have operated with young offenders in mind. Issues facing elderly offenders include "physical ambulation and accessibility, independent care and living, palliative care, and employment assistance" (Office of the Correctional Investigator 2012:21). (See also Exhibit 13.5.) Some observers (e.g., Vito and Wilson 1985; Wilson and Vito 1988) speculate that prisons will soon become geriatric centres and that staff will have to be specially trained to look after these inmates. Morton (1993:44) recommends that these staff be trained to identify physical disabilities in older inmates, to develop policies on managing the special needs of older inmates, to be sensitive to the physical and emotional difficulties experienced by older inmates, and to begin developing solutions that apply to specific institutions. In Canada's federal correctional facilities there is oftentimes very little appropriate activity provided to elderly inmates. And in many cases elderly inmates "rarely access existing counselling, educational, or vocational prison programs. Many aging offenders simply elect to spend long periods of time locked in their cells during working or programming hours" (Office of the Correctional Investigator 2012:22).

Adjustment to prison life by older prisoners is a contentious issue. Some argue that older inmates experience more psychological and emotional problems—a concern that Vito and Wilson (1985) believe is not being

EXHIBIT 13.5 Institutional and Personal Safety Issues for Elderly Offenders

According to the Office of the Correctional Investigator (2012), prison victimization research has consistently found that elderly inmates can be exploited, harassed, and assaulted by younger inmates. Research findings have found that older inmates

- are victimized by younger inmates,
- feel vulnerable to attack by younger inmates,
- prefer to live with inmates in their own age bracket, and
- may live in age-segregated protective-custody units

Source: Office of the Correctional Investigator, *Annual Report of the Office of the Correctional Investigator 2010-2011*, p. 22, http://www.oci-bec.gc.ca/cnt/rpt/pdf/annrpt/annrpt20102011-eng.pdf. Reproduced with permission of Office of the Correctional Investigator.

addressed by correctional systems. Others (e.g., Teller and Howell 1981) argue that older offenders are better adjusted, less impulsive, and less hostile than those who are younger. Sabath and Cowles (1988) found that older offenders who maintain family contacts are better adjusted than those who don't, and there is general agreement that first-time older offenders are better adjusted in prison than those who have served at least one previous term of incarceration (Aday and Webster 1979; Teller and Howell 1981).

Other issues facing older inmates arise when they leave a correctional facility. They are by then used to prison life and have established social networks. How will they survive in the outside world? Many of their friends have died or forgotten about them, so questions involving care and a place to stay become paramount. As Hassine (1996:97) points out, the elderly inmate represents "a growing underclass of dependents in a world of change."

A special category of older offenders is "lifers"—that is, inmates who have spent many years in prison. In 2013, 5,314 offenders were serving life or indeterminate sentences. They represented 23 percent of CSC's total offender population; 3,436 (64 percent) were in a custodial facility, and 1,899 (36 percent) were on conditional release. Lifers are aging—the average lifer was 49 years old in 2009, compared to 44 in 1998. The number of lifers aged 61 years or older increased by 149 percent between 1998 and 2009. During this time period, 97 percent of lifers were men and 3 percent were women. The number of women lifers has increased: between 1998 and 2009, there was a 37 percent increase of women lifers. If this trend continues, it is estimated that there will be 210 women lifers by 2019. Seventeen percent of the lifer population in 2009 were Aboriginals (Correctional Service of Canada 2010). As these individuals will in all probability spend a number of their older years in a federal institution, they pose particular issues for federal correctional authorities.

The "Faint Hope" Clause

All offenders in Canada serving life sentences have, until recently, had the ability to apply for parole and serve their sentences in the community prior to the end of their sentence. In July 1976, capital punishment was abolished in Canada with the passage of Bill C-84. This bill established mandatory life sentences, with parole eligibility specified for those convicted of first and second degree murder (25 years and 10 to 25 years, respectively). Bill C-84 also stipulated that offenders convicted of first and second degree murder would be eligible for a judicial review after serving 15 years of their sentence, and, if successful in their application, would be able to participate in a conditional release program. Section 745.6 of the Criminal Code was a component of Bill C-84 and was added to the Criminal Code when it passed.

This section, now commonly referred to as the **faint hope clause**, allowed offenders who had served at least 15 years of their sentence to apply for a reduction in the amount of time they had left to serve before the parole eligibility date specified in their sentence. As Roberts and Cole (1999:284) point out, s. 745.6 was included in the Criminal Code "out of recognition of the fact that inmates who have served well over a decade in prison may have changed"; they added that "once applications began to be heard by juries, the section becomes possibly the most controversial provision in the Criminal Code."

The faint hope clause states that any offender still serving a sentence after 15 years has the right to apply for a judicial review of parole eligibility. Application is made to the chief justice in the province/territory in which the conviction occurred. The chief justice determines whether the offender is eligible to apply, and, if so, informs the provincial justice minister of the decision. A two-stage process then begins: (1) a **preliminary hearing** followed by (2) the **actual hearing**.

The preliminary hearing considers such issues as the evidence to be allowed, as well as matters such as transportation and living facilities. The actual hearing is adversarial in nature, and the applicant is present. A jury determines whether the application has merit and decides on one of three options: (1) no change or reduction in the period before parole eligibility, (2) a reduction in the number of years of imprisonment prior to eligibility for parole, or (3) termination of ineligibility for parole, allowing the applicant immediate eligibility. If the jury selects the third option, it does not mean the offender is released right away, but rather that he or she can apply to the Parole Board of Canada for release prior to the original eligibility date (Brown 1992).

Under the original legislation, juries were not able to consider such issues as "the character of the applicant, his conduct while serving his sentence, the nature of the offence for which he was convicted and such other matters as the judge deems relevant in the circumstances." It was possible that if the jury rejected the application, the Supreme Court of Canada might hear an appeal, although s. 745 made no provision for this. If the Supreme Court were to decide in the applicant's favour, a second hearing would be ordered. In addition, juries did not have to be unanimous in their decision; only two-thirds of the jurors had to agree to allow an applicant to proceed to a Parole Board of Canada.

In December 1996, Parliament revised s. 745(6) by passing Bill C-45. The impetus for this was an application for early release from serial killer Clifford Olson. Olson gained national and international notoriety in the early 1980s when he received $100,000 from provincial authorities in return for revealing where he had buried 11 of his murder victims in British Columbia's Lower Mainland. Public outrage over his application was so great that it became an issue during the 1997 federal election.

As a result, s. 745(6) of the Criminal Code was revised (and the revision was promptly labelled the **Olson Amendment**). No longer can **multiple murderers** apply for early release. Note, however, that very few cases involving multiple victims are ever processed, and those that are unlikely ever to be approved by a jury. Superior court judges now have to review all applications and be convinced that they have a reasonable prospect of success (Roberts and Cole 1999). Another change requires the jury to reach a unanimous decision. And when a jury unanimously decides that the number of years to be served is to be reduced, it must decide by a two-thirds majority that a certain number of years must be served before the inmate can apply to the PBC for a possible reduction in the time to be served. If a jury decides that no reduction in time is to be granted, it may set another date of application. If it doesn't set a date, the inmate has to wait for another two years before applying again. These changes are retroactive, to include all individuals who committed their crimes before Bill C-45 was passed. In addition, Bill C-41 (proclaimed in 1995) made it possible for the families of victims to submit victim impact statements as evidence. (Such information was admissible before that year, but only at the discretion of the judge.)

In June 2009, the federal government introduced legislation that proposed to take away the ability of individuals convicted of first and second degree murder to apply for parole after serving 15 years of their life sentence. The proposed legislation stipulated that if someone is convicted of first or second degree murder on the day or after the new law is passed, they would no longer be able to apply for an early release. Those individuals currently serving a life sentence or awaiting sentencing would only have three months to apply for early release after serving 15 years of their sentence. If they missed the deadline, they would have to wait another five years (as opposed to the existing current two-year wait) before they could apply again. In addition, a judge would have to rule that there was a "substantial likelihood" that the jury would agree to move up their parole eligibility date (Galloway 2009). In November 2009, the bill passed the House of Commons and was referred to the Senate. The Bill died on the Order Paper at the end of December 2009, when Parliament was prorogued.

The Bill was reintroduced to the Senate (Bill S-6) in the spring of 2010 after the Conservatives were re-elected. In June 2010, a Department of Justice internal research study obtained by the Canadian Press under the Access to Information Act analyzed the faint hope clause and found that it was working as it was designed. According to the authors of the report, the faint hope clause is not "a free pass for individuals convicted of murder. . . . Those granted reduced time under faint hope do better in the community than other offenders. Lower recidivism rates . . . suggest that decisions to release early are based on fairly accurate assessments of an offender's risk to reoffend." The bill received Royal Assent in March 2011, and came into force in December 2011. The faint hope clause is no longer available for any offences committed after December 2011.

Criminal Justice Insight

How Many Judicial Review Hearings Result in Earlier Parole Eligibility?

Between the first judicial review and April 2013, there have been a total of 198 court decisions involving a judicial review; of these, 155 (78.3 percent) succeeded in the sense that a jury reduced the time to be served before possible parole (see Figure 13.6). Of these 155 successful applications, 151 (97 percent) have reached their revised eligibility date. Most of the applications have occurred in Quebec (84 applications, or 44 percent) and Ontario (40, or 20 percent). In Quebec, 77 of the applications have been successful while 21 in Ontario have been approved (Public Safety Canada 2013).

Of these offenders, 138 have been released on parole, and 91 of the successful applicants are currently being supervised in the community. Of the others, 20 are incarcerated, 21 are deceased, 2 are being temporarily detained, and 4 have been deported. Many of the applicants for judicial review had been convicted of a murder: a higher percentage of second degree (87 percent) than first degree (77 percent) murder cases has led to a reduction of the time period required to be served before parole eligibility. Most of the applications have occurred in Quebec (84 applications, or 44 percent) and Ontario (40 applications, or 20 percent). In Quebec, 77 of the applications have been successful while 21 in Ontario have been approved (Public Safety Canada 2013).

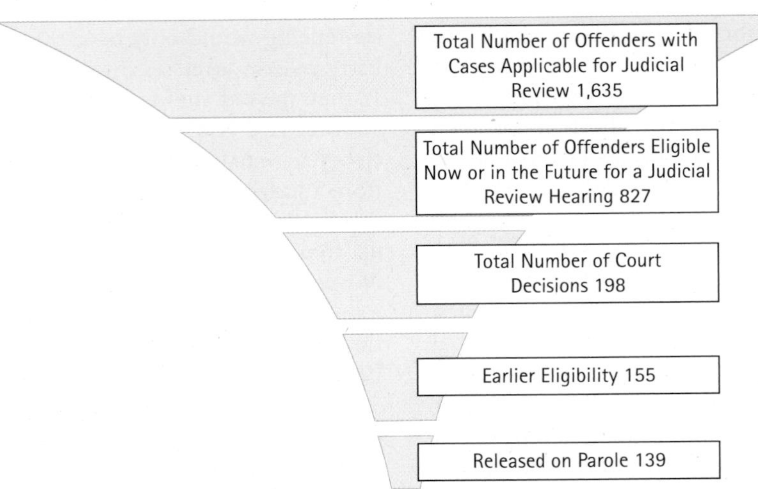

FIGURE 13.6 78% of Judicial Hearings Result in Earlier Parole Eligibility

Source: Corrections and Conditional Release Statistical Overview, 2013, Fig E2, p. 101, https://www.publicsafety.gc.ca/cnt/rsrcs/pblctns/crrctns-cndtnl-rls-2013/crrctns-cndtnl-rls-2013eng.pdf.

SUMMING UP AND LOOKING FORWARD

Numerous issues face correctional officials, including the increase in older inmates. Overall, older offenders are a low risk to reoffend and pose limited problems associated with control for correctional authorities. They are generally easy to manage since they are less likely to violate institutional rules. Older offenders, however, pose special problems for the correctional system, since they have a reduced ability to cope in prison and to have their needs met there. As a consequence of growing old in prison while serving a long sentence, older offenders have special needs and problems that set them apart from the rest of the adult offender population. For example, older inmates may not participate in programming as they may feel threatened by younger inmates or feel that the programs are not relevant to their needs.

All offenders in Canada serving life sentences have, until recently, had the ability to apply for parole and serve their sentences in the community prior to the end of their sentence. In July 1976, capital punishment was abolished in Canada with the passage of Bill C-84. This bill established mandatory life sentences, with parole eligibility specified for those convicted of first and second degree murder (25 years and 10 to 25 years, respectively). Bill C-84 also stipulated that offenders convicted of first and second degree murder would be eligible for a judicial review after serving 15 years of their sentence, and, if successful in their application, would be able to participate in a conditional release program (the "faint hope" clause). Section 745.6 of the Criminal Code was a component of Bill C-84 and was added to the Criminal Code when it passed. The faint hope clause is no longer available for any offences committed after December 2011.

Review Questions:

1. What are the different types of older offenders?
2. What are the issues facing those older offenders who are incarcerated?
3. How are older offenders victimized in correctional facilities?
4. How was the faint hope clause introduced?
5. How many applications were successful that led to a reduction of time served under the faint hope clause?

Critical Issues in Canadian Criminal Justice

CORRECTIONAL TREATMENT: "WHAT WORKS" AND GENDER-RESPONSIVE APPROACHES

In the years since Robert Martinson's article "Nothing Works" was published, there has been considerable debate over the issue of whether or not rehabilitation is effective. Various researchers (e.g., Wilson and Davis 2006) believe that some treatment programs using the most recent approach to treatment, cognitive-behavioural therapy, have failed to show that treatment has a positive impact on individuals who are released back into the community. Others argue that the continuing belief that "nothing works" is not always true. As early as 1979, Gendreau and Ross were arguing that many correctional treatment programs were, in fact, successful. According to Ross and Gendreau (1980:viii), these successful programs were "convincing evidence that some treatment programs, when they are applied with integrity by competent practitioners in appropriate target populations, can be effective in preventing crime or reducing recidivism." More recently, Lipsey and Cullen (2007) reviewed studies of correctional rehabilitation programs and discovered consistent positive effects in terms of programs reducing recidivism. They also reported that there was considerable variation in the effects of correctional treatment programs depending on the type of treatment, the implementation, and the type of offenders to which the program was applied.

Evaluations of treatment programs within correctional facilities as well as the community have found the following elements to be the most successful in terms of reducing recidivism:

- Cognitive-behavioural therapy
- Interpersonal skills training
- Individual counselling
- Behaviour modification techniques
- Integration of community programs with those found within correctional facilities to assist reentry into society (Wilson et al. 2005).

In recent years, questions have been raised as to whether this approach is applicable to all individuals. Since the research on these programs has been conducted almost exclusively upon White males, there have been questions raised about its applicability to women as well as racial and cultural groups. While the cognitive-behavioural approach does not totally ignore the issue of gender, it is considered to be of secondary importance. According to Andrews and Bonta (2006), gender is a specific responsivity factor; that is, gender should be considered in terms of how a treatment program is delivered. However, this approach rejects the idea of gender-specific assessment and treatment interventions. Andrews and Bonta (ibid.:467) state that they have "not found any evidence that the antisocial evidence of demographically defined groups is insensitive to personality, attitudes, associates, or behavioural history. Nor have we

Continued on next page

Critical Issues in Canadian Criminal Justice (*Continued*)

found that the impact of RNR (risk-needs-responsivity) adherence and breadth on future offending varies with age, race, or gender."

A number of researchers have examined the considerable differences that exist between the cognitive-behavioural and gender-responsive approaches. Some (e.g., Krisberg 2005) have discovered that most of the research conducted from the cognitive-behavioural perspective has not included females. Others (e.g., Belknap 2001) point out that a gender-responsive approach has an entirely different theoretical base; that is, instead of the psychological approach favoured by the cognitive-behavioural approach, the gender-responsive approach uses a macro-level explanation that attributes the criminal activity of women to social issues such as class and race, both of which are marginalizing forces, creating an environment in which they are able to potentially engage in destructive behaviours.

Another difference between the approaches centres upon the issue of "risk." According to the cognitive-behavioural approach, the level of risk refers to the likelihood of an individual's recidivism. This is based upon the research evidence pointing out that high-risk offenders need intensive levels of services to reduce recidivism and that medium-risk offenders need moderate levels of services (Andrews et al. 1990). Supporters of the gender-responsive approach believe that although women may have significant "needs," they are not high "risk."

Criminogenic needs are also thought to differ. The cognitive-behavioural approach makes a distinction between "general" and "criminogenic" needs. General needs refer to those areas that are not considered as strong correlates of criminal behaviour on the basis of research reports. In comparison, criminogenic needs are dynamic factors that have proven to be correlates of criminal behaviour. As such, it is necessary to target the identified criminogenic needs in order to reduce the possibility of recidivism. Supporters of the gender-responsive approach point out that the source of crime is to be found within societal factors, not within individuals. They also point out that looking at only a select number of criminogenic needs fails to lead to an understanding of the problems that are the source of women's criminal behaviour as well as the social realities in which women live (Bloom 2003).

Differences are also found in terms of program delivery. According to the cognitive-behavioural approach, it is important to recognize that cognitive restructuring is needed in order that beliefs, values, and attitudes become prosocial. In addition, cognitive skills training is required, particularly those that focus upon improving critical thinking and problem-solving skills. Those who support a gender-responsive approach believe it is more important to look at the ways in which the programs are delivered. They favour programs that are trauma-informed (i.e., aware of the history of past abuse in order to create better and more effective programs) and that are relational (i.e., the development of positive interpersonal relationships).

While the cognitive-behavioural and gender-responsive approaches may appear to be incompatible, Law (2007) notes that some recent research efforts have identified substantial overlap between them. On the basis of this research, she recommends an approach that recognizes that variability may be greater in small groups such as women offenders. Furthermore, it is necessary to look for and study gender-informed constructs as well as situational variables. Finally, it is important to have "full consultation with the women being served in the correctional system" (ibid.:35).

Questions

1. Do you think that women have different risks than men? If so, what are they?
2. Why do you think there has been so much inattention to women offenders in the criminal justice system?
3. Do you think correctional systems put women and minority groups at a disadvantage when they base their correctional programs entirely on White males?
4. Do you think that the "What Works" approach could be improved for women? Or do you think a women-focused approach is more appropriate and relevant?

SUMMARY

This chapter opens with an overview of the importance of reintegration and the challenges of developing comprehensive programs for inmates. Issues about the reintegration of both women and Aboriginal offenders are introduced.

KEYWORD: reintegration

The Reintegration Approach

Reintegration is a key component of releasing offenders into the community prior to the end of their sentence. The theory of risk assessment is discussed, as are related Correctional Service Canada policies.

KEY WORDS: least restrictive setting, key predictors of recidivism, criminogenic needs, Offender Intake Assessment (OIA), theory of risk assessment, risk, need, responsivity, static factors, dynamic factors, general responsivity, specific responsivity, case management, Integrated Correctional Program Model, community correctional centres

The Theory of Risk Assessment (p. 424)
The Case Management Process (p. 426)
The Integrated Correctional Program Model (p. 426)
Contemporary Community Supervision in Canada (p. 427)
Community Correctional Centres (p. 427)

The Parole Board of Canada

The Parole Board of Canada evaluates offenders requesting to be reintegrated into the community according to various criteria. The PBC assesses each offender's risk of recidivism during the decision-making process.

KEY WORDS: indeterminate sentence

Risk of Recidivism (p. 430)
Risk Assessment (p. 432)

Reentry into Society and Desistance from Crime

Reentry into the community starts while an inmate is incarcerated in order that they will be ready to face the challenges they will probably experience once they are released. A goal of correctional programming is that the inmates who are released from correctional facilities desist from criminal activity.

KEY WORDS: prisoner reentry, cognitive-behavioural therapy, structured learning environments, desistance, turning points, social capital, criminal careers

Desistance from Criminal Activity (p. 436)
Gender (p. 436)
Race (p. 437)
Age, Marital Status, and Employment (p. 439)

Corrections: The Older Inmate

The number of older inmates continues to increase in federal correctional facilities, and they pose a number of unique challenges for correctional officials.

KEY WORDS: older offenders

The "Faint Hope" Clause

The "faint hope" clause was introduced in 1976 when capital punishment was abolished. This clause is not available to offenders who committed their crime after 2011.

KEY WORDS: faint hope clause, preliminary hearing, actual hearing, Olson Amendment, multiple murderers

Critical Thinking Questions

1. Why is it so difficult to reintegrate offenders back into communities?
2. Are cognitive-behavioural therapies the programs to reduce recidivism?
3. What could be done to better enhance the prison conditions for older inmates?
4. Should the "faint hope" clause be reinstated?

5. What are the reasons why offenders who have been released commit other crimes?
6. What are the benefits of reentry courts?
7. Should reentry courts be introduced across Canada?

Weblinks

For a brief discussion of how California operates its reentry courts, watch the following video available on YouTube: "Parolee Reentry Courts" (2:50). For a discussion of the "What Works" approach, watch the following video available on YouTube: "Paul Gendreau: Everything You Wanted to Know about Prisons" (1:19:08). For a discussion of the issues relating to Aboriginal corrections, watch the following on YouTube: "Aboriginal Corrections Report Finds 'Systemic Discrimination'" (15:19).

Court Cases

R. v. Gladue (1999), 1 S.C.R. 688.

R. v. Ipeelee (2012), S.C.C. 13.

Suggested Readings

Andrews, D. and J. Bonta. 2010. *The Psychology of Criminal Conduct*, 5 th ed. Cincinnati, OH: Lexis Nexis.

Blanchette, K. and S.L. Brown. 2006. *The Assessment and Treatment of Women Offenders: An Integrated Perspective*. Chichester, U.K.: Wiley.

Culhane, C. 1985. *Still Barred from Prison*. Montreal: Black Rose.

Morash, M. 2010. *Women on Probation and Parole*. Boston, MA: Northeastern University Press.

Proulx, J. and S. Perrault (eds.). 2000. *No Place for Violence: Canadian Aboriginal Alternatives*. Halifax: Fernwood.

References

Aday, R.H. 1994. "Aging in Prison: A Case Study of New Elderly Offenders." *International Journal of Offender Therapy and Comparative Criminology* 38:79–91.

Aday, R.H. and E.L. Webster. 1979. "Aging in Prison: The Development of a Preliminary Model." *Offender Rehabilitation* 3:271–82

Andrews, D.A. 1996. "Criminal Recidivism Is Predictable and Can Be Influenced: An Update." *Forum on Corrections Research* 8:42–45.

Andrews, D.A. 1995. "The Psychology of Criminal Conduct and Effective Treatment." Pp. 35–62 in *What Works: Reducing Offending*, edited by J.M. McGuire. West Sussex: John Wiley.

Andrews, D.A. 1989. "Recidivism Is Predictable and Can Be Influenced: Using Risk Assessments to Reduce Recidivism." *Forum on Corrections Research* 1:11–17.

Andrews, D.A. 1980. "Some Experimental Investigations of the Principles of Differential Association through Deliberate Manipulations of the Structure of Service Systems." *American Sociological Review* 45:448–62.

Andrews, D.A. and J. Bonta. 2006. *The Psychology of Criminal Conduct*, 4th ed. Cincinnati, OH: Anderson.

Andrews, D.A., J. Bonta, and R.D. Hoge. 1990. "Classification for Effective Rehabilitation: Rediscovering Psychology." *Criminal Justice and Behavior* 17:19–52.

Andrews, D.A. and J.J. Kiessling. 1980. "Program Structure and Effective Correctional Practices: A Summary of the CaVic Research." In *Effective Correctional Treatment*, edited by R.R. Ross and P. Gendreau. Toronto: Effective Correctional Treatment.

Andrews, D.A., I. Zinger, R.D. Hoge, J. Bonta, P. Gendreau, and F.T. Cullen. 1990. "Does Correctional Treatment Work? A Clinically Relevant and Psychologically Informed Meta-Analysis." *Justice Quarterly* 8:369–404.

Antonowicz, D. and R.R. Ross. 1994. "Essential Components of Successful Rehabilitation Programs for Offenders." *International Journal of Offender Therapy and Comparative Criminology* 38:97–104.

Belcourt, R., T. Nouwens, and L. Lefebvre. 1993. "Examining the Unexamined: Recidivism among Female Offenders." *Forum on Corrections Research* 5:10–14.

Belenko, S. 2006. "Assessing Inmates for Substance-Abuse-Related Service Needs." *Crime and Delinquency* 52:94–113.

Belknap, J. 2001. *The Invisible Woman: Gender, Crime, and Justice*. Belmont, CA: Wadsworth.

Blanchette, K. and C. Dowden. 1998. "A Profile of Federally Sentenced Women in the Community: Addressing Needs for Successful Reintegration." *Forum on Corrections Research*, 10:40–43.

Bloom, B.E. 2003. *Gendered Justice: Addressing Female Offenders*. Durham, NC: Carolina Academic Press.

Blumstein, A. and A. Beck. 1999. "Population Growth in U.S. Prisons, 1980–1996." Pp. 17–61 in *Crime and Justice: A Review of Annual Research*, vol. 26, edited by M. Tonry and J. Petersilia. Chicago: University of Chicago Press.

Bonta, J. 1995. "The Responsivity Principle and Offender Rehabilitation." *Forum on Corrections Research* 7:34–37.

Bonta, J., S. Lipinski, and M. Martin. 1992. "The Characteristics of Aboriginal Recidivists." *Canadian Journal of Criminology* 34: 517–22.

Bottomley, A.K. 1990. "Parole in Transition: A Comparative Study of Origins, Developments, and Prospects for the 1990s." *Crime and Justice: A Review of Research*, vol. 12. Chicago: University of Chicago Press.

Bronskill, J. and B. Cheadie. 2013. "New Rules Make for Massive Drop in Pardons." *The Globe and Mail*, January 11 p. A4.

Brown, G. 1992. "Judicial Review: How Does It Work and How Does It Affect Federal Corrections?" *Forum on Corrections Research* 4:14–16.

Brown, R.J. and K.P. O'Brien. 1993. "How Do Experts Make Parole Recommendations and Are They Accurate?" *Forum on Corrections Research* 5:3–4.

Canadian Bar Association. 2011. *Submission on Bill C-10: Safe Streets and Communities Act*. Ottawa: Canadian Bar Association.

Correctional Service of Canada. 2011. *Integrated Correctional Program Model.* Ottawa: Correctional Service of Canada. http://www.csc-scc.gc.ca/correctional-process/002001–2011-eng.shtml. Accessed December 14, 2014.

Correctional Service of Canada. 2010. *Shaping Future Services to Lifers: Public Safety, Human Relations, and Innovation and Savoir-Faire. Lifeline 2008–2010 National Report*. Ottawa: Public Safety Canada.

Correctional Service of Canada. 2008. *Corrections and Conditional Release Statistical Overview*. Public Safety Canada. Retrieved April 24, 2009 (www.publicsafety.gc.ca).

Correctional Service of Canada. 2007. *A Roadmap to Strengthening Public Safety—Report of the Correctional Service of Canada Review Panel*. Ottawa: Correctional Service of Canada.

Correctional Service of Canada. 1997. *Basic Facts about Corrections in Canada*. Ottawa: Solicitor General of Canada.

Correctional Service of Canada. 1990. "A Profile of Federal Community Corrections." *Forum on Corrections Research* 2:8–13.

Cowles, E.L. 1990. "Programming for Long-Term Inmates." Executive Summary. *Long-Term Confinement and the Aging Inmate Population: A Record and Proceeding*. Washington, DC: Federal Bureau of Prisons.

Daubney Committee. 1988. *Taking Responsibility: Report of the Standing Committee on Justice and Solicitor-General on Its Review of Sentencing, Conditional Release and Related Aspects of Corrections*. D. Daubney, chair. Ottawa: Queen's Printer.

Dowden, C. 1998. "A Meta-Analytic Examination for Risk, Need and Responsivity Principles and Their Importance within the Rehabilitation Debate." Unpublished MA thesis. Ottawa: Department of Psychology, Carleton University.

Dowden, C. and K. Blanchette. 1998. "Success Rates for Female Offenders on Discretionary versus Statutory Release: Substance Abusers and Non-Abusers." *Forum on Corrections Research* 10:27–29.

Dowden, C. and R. Serin. 2000. "Assessing the Needs of Aboriginal Women Offenders on Conditional Release." *Forum on Corrections Research* 12:57–60.

Drucker, E. 2002. "Population Impact of Mass Incarceration under New York's Rockefeller Drug Laws: An Analysis of Years of Life Lost." *Journal of Urban Heath: Bulletin of the New York Academy of Medicine* 79:1–10.

Ellerby, L. 1994. "Community-Based Treatment of Aboriginal Offenders: Facing Realities and Exploring Realities." *Forum on Corrections Research* 6:23–25.

Enos, R. and S. Southern. 1996. *Correctional Case Management*. Cincinnati, OH: Anderson.

Galloway, G. 2009. "Tories Look to Deny Murderers 'Faint Hope' for Early Parole." *The Globe and Mail*, June 6, p. A7.

Glaze, L. 2002. *Probation and Parole in the United States*. Washington, DC: National Institute of Justice.

Goetting, A. 1983. "The Elderly in Prison: Issues and Perspectives." *Journal of Research in Crime and Delinquency* 20:291–309.

Goldstein, D. 2015. "Too Old to Commit Crime?" *The New York Times*, March 22, p. 4.

Grant, B.A. and R.L. Belcourt. 1992. *An Analysis of Temporary Absences and the People Who Receive Them*. Ottawa: Correctional Service of Canada.

Haskell, C. 1994. "The Impact of the Corrections and Conditional Release Act on Community Corrections." *Forum on Corrections Research* 6:45–46.

Hassine, V. 1996. *Life without Parole*. Los Angeles: Roxbury.

Hughes, T., D. Wilson, and A. Beck. 2001. *Trends in State Parole, 1990–2000*. Washington, DC: Bureau of Justice Statistics.

Johnson, J.C. 1997. *Aboriginal Offender Survey: Case Files and Interview Sample*. Research Report R-61. Ottawa: Correctional Service of Canada.

Jones, D. 2004. "The Revocation of Conditionally Released Women: A Research Summary." *Forum on Corrections Research* 16:31–33.

Kiessling, J. 1989. Cited in D.A. Andrews, "Recidivism Is Predictable and Can Be Influenced: Using Risk Assessments to Reduce Recidivism." *Forum on Corrections Research* 1:11–17.

Krebs, J.J. 2009. "A Commentary on Age Segregation for Older Prisoners: Philosophical and Pragmatic Considerations for Correctional Systems." *Criminal Justice Review* 34:119–139.

Krisberg, B. 2005. *Juvenile Justice: Redeeming our Children.* Thousand Oaks, CA: Sage.

Landenberger, N. and M. Lipsey. 2005. "The Positive Effects of Cognitive-Behavioral Programs for Offenders: A Meta-Analysis of Factors Associated with Effective Treatment." *Journal of Experimental Criminology* 1:451–76.

Larocque, B. 1998. "Federal Trends and Outcomes in Conditional Release." *Forum on Corrections Research* 10, 2 (May):18–22.

Latessa, E.J. and H.E. Allen. 1997. *Corrections in the Community.* Cincinnati, OH: Anderson.

Laub, J. and R. Sampson. 2003. *Shared Beginnings, Divergent Lives: Delinquent Boys at Age 70.* Cambridge, MA: Harvard University Press.

Law, M.A. 2007. "Federally Sentenced Women in the Community: Dynamic Risk Factors." *Forum on Conditional Research* 18:18–20.

Lefebvre, L. 1994. "The Demographic Characteristics of Offenders on Day Parole." *Forum on Corrections Research* 6:11–13.

Leonard, S.G. 1999. "Conditional Release from Imprisonment." Pp. 259–76 in *Making Sense of Sentencing*, edited by J.V. Roberts and D.P. Cole. Toronto: University of Toronto Press.

Lipsey, M.W. 1995. "What Do We Learn from Research Studies on the Effectiveness of Treatment with Juvenile Delinquents?" Pp. 63–78 in *What Works: Reducing Reoffending*, edited by J. McQuire. New York: John Wiley.

Lipsey, M.W. and F.T. Cullen. 2007. "The Effectiveness of Correctional Rehabilitation: A Review of Systematic Reviews." *Annual Review of Law and Social Science* 3:297–320.

Mann, M. 2010. *Good Intentions, Disappointing Results: A Progress Report on Federal Aboriginal Corrections.* Ottawa: Office of the Correctional Investigator.

Maruna, S. 2006. "Desistance." Pp. 120–23 in *The Sage Dictionary of Criminology*, 2nd ed., edited by E. McLaughlin and J. Muncie. London: Sage.

Morton, J.B. 1993. "In South Carolina: Training Staff to Work with Elderly and Disabled Inmates." *Corrections Today:* 42–47.

Motiuk, L.L. and S.L. Brown. 1993. *The Validity of Offender Needs Identification and Analysis in Community Corrections.* Research Report R-34. Ottawa: Correctional Service of Canada.

Motiuk, L.L. and R. Serin. 1998. "Situating Risk Assessment in the Reintegration Potential Framework." *Forum on Corrections Research* 10:19–22.

National Parole Board. 1988. *National Parole Board Pre-Release Decision Policies.* Ottawa: Ministry of Supply and Services.

National Parole Board. 1987. *Briefing Book for Members of the Standing Committee on Justice and Solicitor General.* Ottawa: National Parole Board.

National Parole Board. 1981. *A Guide to Conditional Release for Penitentiary Inmates.* Ottawa: National Parole Board.

New York State Department of Correctional Services. 2008. *Statistical Review: Year 2007 Court Commitments:* 14.

Office of the Correctional Investigator. 2014b. *Overcoming Barriers to Reintegration: An Investigation of Federal Community Correctional Centres*. Ottawa.

Office of the Correctional Investigator. 2014a. *Annual Report of the Office of the Correctional Investigator 2012–2013*. Ottawa.

Office of the Correctional Investigator. 2013. *Annual Report of the Office of the Correctional Investigator 2012–2013*. Ottawa.

Office of the Correctional Investigator. 2012. *Annual Report of the Office of the Correctional Investigator 2011–2012*. Ottawa.

Office of the Correctional Investigator. 2011. *Annual Report of the Office of the Correctional Investigator 2010–2011*. Ottawa.

Office of the Correctional Investigator. 2010. *Annual Report of the Office of the Correctional Investigator 2009–2010*. Ottawa.

Pardon Services Canada. 2010. "Bill C-10: The Government's Tough Stance against Criminal Record Holders." *LawNow*, http://www.lawnow.org/wp-content/uploads/2013/09/LN381.pdf. Accessed April 10, 2014.

Parole Board of Canada. 2012. *The Safe Streets and Communities Act (Bill C-10): Changes to the Parole Board of Canada*. Retrieved May 15, 2012 (www.pbc-clcc.gc.ca).

Petersilia, J. 2003. *When Prisoners Come Home: Parole and Prisoner Reentry*. New York: Oxford University Press.

Public Safety Canada. 2013. *Corrections and Conditional Release Act: Statistical Overview*. Ottawa: Public Safety Canada.

Roberts, J.V. and D.P. Cole. 1999. "Sentencing and Early Release Arrangements for Offenders Convicted of Murder." Pp. 277–94 in *Making Sense of Sentencing*, edited by J.V. Roberts and D.P. Cole. Toronto: University of Toronto Press.

Robinson, D. 1995. "Federal Offender Family Violence: Estimates from a National File Review Study." *Forum on Corrections Research* 7:15–18.

Ross, R. and P. Gendreau. 1980. *Effective Correctional Treatment*. Toronto: Butterworth.

Sabath, J. and E.L. Cowles. 1988. "Factors Affecting the Adjustment of Elderly Offenders in Prison." In *Older Offenders: Perspectives in Criminology and Criminal Justice*, edited by B. McCarthy and R. Langworthy. New York: Praeger.

Sherman, L.W., D.A. Smith, J.D. Schmidt, and D.P. Rogan. 1992. "Crime, Punishment, and Stake in Conformity: Legal and Informal Control of Domestic Violence." *American Sociological Review* 57:680–90.

Squires, K. 2006. "The Reintegration of Federally Sentenced Women: A Commentary." *Forum on Corrections Research* 18:7–8.

Sutton, J. 1994. "Learning to Better Predict the Future: National Parole Board Risk-Assessment Training." *Forum on Corrections Research* 6:20–22.

Task Force on the Release of Inmates. 1973. *Report*. Ottawa: Information Canada.

Taylor, G. 2001. "The Importance of Developing Correctional Plans for Offenders." *Forum on Corrections Research* 13:14–17.

Taylor, G. 1998. "Preparing Reports for Parole Decisions: Making the Best Use of Our Information—and Time." *Forum on Corrections Research* 10:30–34.

Taylor, K. and J. Flight. 2004. "A Profile of Federally-Sentenced Women on Conditional Release." *Forum on Corrections Research* 16:24–27.

Teller, F.E. and R.J. Howell. 1981. "The Older Prisoner: Criminal and Psychological Characteristics." *Criminology* 18:549–55.

Thurber, A. 1998. "Understanding Offender Reintegration." *Forum on Corrections Research* 10:14–18.

Travis, J. 2005. *But They All Come Back: Facing the Challenges of Prisoner Reentry*. Washington, DC: The Urban Institute.

Travis, J., A. Solomon, and M. Waul. 2001. *From Prison to Home: The Dimensions and Consequences of Prison Reentry*. Washington, DC: The Urban Institute.

Uzoaba, J.H.E. 1998. *Managing Older Offenders: Where Do We Stand?* Ottawa: Correctional Service of Canada, Research Division.

Vito, G. and D. Wilson. 1985. "Forgotten People: Elderly Inmates." *Federal Probation* 49:18–24.

Walsh, C.E. 1992. "Ageing Inmate Offenders: Another Perspective. In *Correctional Theory and Practice*, edited by C.A. Hartjen and E.E. Rhine. Chicago: Nelson-Hall.

Walsh, C.E. 1989. "The Older and Long-Term Inmate Growing Old in the New Jersey Prison System." *Journal of Offender Counselling Services and Rehabilitation* 13:215–48.

Welsch, A. 2000. "Aboriginal Offenders and Full Parole." *Forum on Corrections Research* 12:61–64.

West, H. 2008. *Prisoners in 2007*. Washington, DC: Bureau of Justice Statistics.

Wilson, D. and G. Vito. 1988. "Long-Term Inmates: Special Need and Management Considerations." *Federal Probation* 52:21–26.

Wilson, J. and R. Davis. 2006. "Good Intentions Meet Hard Realities: An Evaluation of the Project Greenlight Reentry Program." *Criminology and Public Policy* 5:303–38.

Wilson, R., A. Bouffard, and D.L. Mackenzie. 2005. "Quantitative Review of Structured, Group-oriented, Cognitive-Behavioral Programs for Offenders." *Criminal Justice and Behavior* 32:1872–204.

Zimbardo, P.G. 1994. *Transforming California's Prisons into Expensive Old Age Homes for Felons*. San Francisco: Center on Juvenile and Criminal Justice.

Zimmerman, S. 1992. "'The Revolving Door of Despair': Aboriginal Involvement in the Criminal Justice System." *University of British Columbia Law Review:* 367–426.

GLOSSARY

Aboriginal justice. A focus on justice that emphasizes a healing approach involving victims, offenders, and the community. Local communities should be able to determine what happens to offenders who commit crimes within their boundaries. *p. 94*

Absolute discharge. A sentence of the court in which no further action is taken. *p. 309*

Absolute jurisdiction indictable offence. Offences for which the accused has to be tried by a provincial court judge unless the judge determines that the case must be tried another way. These offences are found in s. 553 of the Criminal Code. *p. 63*

Accelerated parole review (APR). A policy was included into conditional release programs with the passing of the Corrections and Conditional Act (1992). APR was created to permit non-violent federal offenders with a low risk of reoffending to be released as early as possible to serve the rest of their sentence under supervision in the community. This policy ended in 2011. *p. 362*

Access to justice. This involves the idea of legal equality, acknowledging that each person is equal under the law and entitled to be treated without discrimination. *p. 8*

Actus reus. The illegal act. It involves either the commission of an act, such as an assault, or the failure to act, such as failing to take proper safety measures. *p. 44*

Adjudication. The determination of guilt or innocence of the accused by a judge. *p. 280*

Administrative regulations. The laws created by administrative agencies (in the form of rules, regulations, orders, and decisions) in order that they can carry out their responsibilities and duties. *p. 54*

Adversarial system. The procedure used to determine truth in a criminal court system. According to this system, the burden is on the state to prove the charges against the accused beyond a reasonable doubt. It is open to the defence to challenge this evidence. *p. 7*

Aggravating circumstances. Any circumstances accompanying the commission of a crime that may justify a harsher sentence. *p. 315*

Aggregate UCR Survey. Records the number of incidents reported to the police and includes the number of reported offences, the number of actual offences, the number of offences cleared by charge, the number of adults charged, the number of youths charged, and the gender of those charged. Does not include victim characteristics. *p. 122*

Appeal court. A review of lower court decisions or proceedings by a higher court. *p. 282*

Appearance notice. Issued to the accused requiring him or her to appear in court on a specific date and time. The accused is issued an appearance notice instead of being arrested. *p. 19*

Arraignment. The process whereby the accused hears the formal charges being laid and pleads either guilty or innocent. *p. 20*

Arrest. The taking into custody of a person thought to have committed a crime. The legal requirement for an arrest is "reasonable and probable grounds." *p. 18*

Assembly-line justice. The idea that the criminal justice process is similar to a production line, in that it handles most cases in as routine a manner as possible. *p. 287*

Assisted suicide. The intentional act of providing a person with the medical knowledge to commit suicide. *p. 5*

Auburn system. The prison system developed in New York in the 19th century that favoured a tier-based prison facility and congregate working conditions for inmates. *p. 385*

Bail. *See* judicial interim release hearing. *p. 20*

Beyond a reasonable doubt. The standard used to determine the guilt or innocence of an accused. *p. 283*

Broken window model. Refers to the idea that community disorder leads to criminal behaviour. *p. 192*

Case law. The judicial application and interpretation of laws as they apply in any particular case. *p. 53*

Challenge for cause. When legal counsel states the reason why a prospective juror should not be included on the jury. *p. 267*

Charge a jury. When the judge informs a jury of the relevant evidence of a case and the types of decisions the jury can reach about the accused. *p. 296*

Charge bargaining. A prosecutor's decision to reduce the number of charges against the accused in return for a plea of guilty and/or for information. *p. 261*

Citizen oversight. The process by which citizens review complaints brought against individual police officers or police services. The citizens often do not have the power to discipline misconduct, but can recommend that action can be taken by police administrators. *p. 233*

Clearance rate. Represents the proportion of all crimes that are successfully cleared by the laying of a charge or through extrajudicial measures. *p. 122*

Common law. Early English law, developed by judges, based on local customs and feudal rules and practices. Common law formed the basis of the standardized criminal law system in England. *p. 52*

Community policing. A police strategy that emphasizes the reduction of fear, community involvement, decentralization of the police force, neighbourhood police stations, and order maintenance as an alternative approach to fighting crime. *p. 169*

Comprehensive personnel assessment system. System that collects a wide range of data and has the ability to look at a large number of issues. *p. 233*

Concurrence. Forms the legal relationship between the guilty mind and the illegal act. *p. 44*

Conditional discharge. A sentence of the court that results in no further action taken for the current offence but which allows the court to sentence in some other way if another offence is committed within the time specified. *p. 22*

Conditional sentences. A sentence where the court substitutes the community for jail as the place where the sentence is to be served under strict conditions. *p. 309*

Contextual discrimination. Discrimination that arises from organizational policies within criminal justice agencies such as the police and the courts. *p. 26*

Corpus delecti. The body of circumstances that must exist for a criminal act to have occurred. *p. 42*

Courtroom work group. The informal social organization of the courtroom, comprising the prosecutor, defence attorney, judge, and other court workers. The informal relationships among the members of this group have far-reaching implications for the treatment of the accused in our criminal justice system. *p. 25*

Crime control model. An objective of criminal justice emphasizing the reduction of crime. *p. 55*

Crime Severity Index (CSI). Measures the seriousness of crime. *p. 117*

Criminal investigation. The search for people and items in order to recreate the circumstance(s) of a criminal act in the hope of identifying suspects as well as finding evidence that will assist a court in determining guilt. *p. 184*

Criminal justice funnel. The process through which individuals working within the criminal justice system decide whether or not to proceed with a case to the next step in the justice system. The overall effect is a reduction in the number of persons being prosecuted. As a result, the number of persons convicted and sentenced is much smaller than the number of persons arrested. *p. 23*

Custodial interrogation. The questioning of a suspect after that person has been taken into custody. Before any interrogation begins, the individual must be read his or her rights. *p. 224*

Cybercrime. A crime that occurs online, in the virtual community of the Internet, as opposed to the physical world. *p. 143*

Day parole. Parole granted only for short periods of time, to a maximum of four months. It is renewable for a period of up to one year. Most offenders in federal and provincial correctional facilities become eligible for day parole six months before they are eligible for full parole. *p. 22*

Deadly force. Force applied by a police officer that is likely or intended to cause death. *p. 229*

Denunciation. An objective of sentencing and punishment used in conditional sentences where the aim is to reinforce community values by indicating that certain behaviour is regarded as reprehensible and will not be tolerated. *p. 349*

Deprivation model. The theory that states that inmate aggression is the result of the frustration inmates experience at being deprived of freedom, consumer goods, and the like that are common outside prison. *p. 403*

Detention. This involves the police holding an individual for questioning, even when they do not have grounds for an arrest. The legality of detaining an individual depends on the importance of the matter being investigated and on the amount of intrusion that is necessary. *p. 19*

Determinate sentence. A period of incarceration fixed by legislature that cannot be reduced by a judge or correctional officials. *p. 86*

Deterrence. The prevention of crime before it occurs by threatening individuals with criminal sanctions. *p. 306*

Deterrence, general. A crime control policy that aims to stop potential law violators from engaging in illegal behaviour. It favours certain policies—such as long prison sentences—that underscore the fact that the pain associated with crime outweighs the gain. *p. 82*

Deterrence model. One of the four main models of criminal justice. It envisions a criminal justice system with no discretion, more police, and longer prison terms. It is related to the crime control model and the classical school of criminology. *p. 82*

Deterrence, specific. A crime control policy that advocates punishment severe enough to convince convicted offenders never again to engage in criminal behaviour. *p. 82*

Directed patrol. A police patrol strategy. Police officers are told to spend much of their patrol time in certain areas, to use certain tactics, and to watch for certain types of offences. *p. 189*

Discretion. The use of individual decision making and choice to influence the operations of the criminal justice system. All the major institutions of the criminal justice system—police, courts, corrections—make decisions that influence the outcome of cases. *p. 26*

Discrimination. The unfavourable treatment of a person and/or members of a group based on negative judgments relating to their perceived or real membership in a group. *p. 26*

Disintegrative shaming. Punishments that stigmatize and exclude individuals. *p. 99*

Disparity. The lack of uniformity in sentencing, which leads to concern about discrimination against particular groups in society. Disparity involves arbitrary differences between sentences against offenders convicted of the same crime. *p. 26*

Diversion. A policy to divert offenders who qualify away from a correctional facility and toward community-based and intermediate sanctions. *p. 343*

DNA Database. Deoxyribonucleic acid, a component of all living matter present in blood, hair, bones, nails, and bodily fluids which is used for identification purposes in criminal investigations and during a trial. *pp. 84, 173*

Drug treatment courts. Courts whose jurisdiction is limited to drug offences. Offenders selected receive treatment as an alternative to incarceration. *p. 368*

Due process model. The legally required procedure ensuring that a criminal investigation and the trial is conducted in a fair manner and protects the rights of the defendant. *p. 12*

Dynamic security. A policy objective of the Correctional Service of Canada that emphasizes a safe environment for all employees, offenders, and the public through meaningful interactions. *p. 393*

Election indictable offence. An offence for which the accused (or the accused's lawyer) may decide on which type of criminal court to be tried in. *p. 20*

Electronic monitoring (EM). A system designed to ensure whether an offender completes the terms of a court order. EM is the regulatory aspect of home confinement. *p. 353*

Employment equity. The federal policy that emphasizes that members of minority groups should be represented in the workforce. *p. 163*

Euthanasia. The act or practice of causing or hastening the death of a person who suffers from an incurable or terminal disease or condition, especially a painful one, for reasons of mercy. *p. 5*

Excuse defence. A defendant admits to committing a criminal act but contends that they cannot be held criminally liable for it as they did not possess criminal intent. *p. 48*

Fact bargaining. A type of plea bargaining in which the prosecutor decides not to introduce certain facts about the offence or offender into the court record. *p. 261*

Factual guilt. An individual charged with a criminal offence but not yet found guilty in a court of criminal law. *p. 37*

"Faint hope" clause. States that any offender still serving a sentence after 15 years has the right to apply for a judicial review of parole eligibility; no longer available for offences committed after December 2011. *p. 442*

Fear reduction. A measure for evaluating police performance. *p. 195*

Fine. One of the most common sentences in Canada. Failure to pay a fine is one of the most common reasons for the incarceration of offenders. *p. 22*

First degree murder. Planned and deliberate murder—though it does not have to be planned or deliberate when the victim is a police officer, a prison guard, an individual working in a prison, or a similar individual acting in the course of duty. *p. 130*

Fit to stand trial. Able to understand the trial proceedings and to instruct defence counsel throughout the trial. *p. 20*

Foot patrol. A type of police patrol linked to community policing. It takes police officers out of cars and places them on a beat, which allows them to strengthen ties with community residents. *p. 189*

Full parole. The early release of an inmate from prison subject to conditions established by a parole board. Full parole can be granted to inmates after they serve one-third of their sentence, unless the sentence specifies otherwise. *p. 22*

General Social Survey (GSS). A survey which asks people about their experiences as a victim. *p. 124*

Habeas corpus. A judicial order requesting that a state representative (e.g., a police officer) detaining another give reasons for the capture and detention. It is a legal device used to request a judicial review of the reasons for an individual's detention and the conditions of detention. *p. 57*

"Hands-off" doctrine. The unwritten policy favouring non-interference by the courts in the administration of correctional facilities. *p. 408*

Home confinement. A type of intermediate punishment that allows offenders to live in the community while serving their sentence. *p. 353*

"Hot spots." Concentrated areas of high criminal activity that draw the interest of the police. *p. 192*

Human smuggling. A form of illegal migration involving the organized transport of a person across a border, usually in exchange for money and oftentimes using dangerous conditions and methods. *p. 159*

Human trafficking. This involves any person who recruits, transports, receives, holds, conceals, or harbours a person, or exercises control, direction, or influence over the movements of a person, for the purpose of exploiting them or facilitating their exploitation. Trafficked persons typically are not able to, or perceive that they cannot, leave their situation. *p. 158*

Hung jury. A jury whose members are so irreconcilably divided in their opinion that they cannot reach a verdict. *p. 296*

Hybrid offence. An offence that may proceed either as an indictable or summary conviction offence. The decision on how to proceed is usually made by the Crown prosecutor. *p. 63*

Incarceration. Occurs when an offender receives a sentence that stipulates that he or she spend time in a provincial or federal correctional institution. *p. 22*

Incident-driven policing. The primary role of the police is to respond to a citizen's calls for assistance. *p. 182*

Indeterminate sentence. This type of sentence occurs when a judge determines the minimum and maximum terms of imprisonment. When the minimum term is reached, the inmate becomes eligible to be paroled. *p. 91*

Indictable offence. An offence for which the accused must, or has the right to, choose between a trial by judge and a trial by jury, with the exception of a few minor offences. *p. 63*

Individual discrimination. Discrimination that occurs when an individual employed within the criminal justice system acts in a way that discriminates against the members of certain groups. *p. 27*

Infanticide. One of the four types of murder. It was introduced in 1948, and only a woman can be charged. The Criminal Code defines an infant as a child under one year of age. *p. 130*

Information, to lay an. One lays an information when one presents to a judge a sworn written allegation alleging the individual named in the document has committed an offence. Informations are also used to obtain search warrants. *p. 19*

Institutionalized discrimination. Form of discrimination in which disparities appear in the outcomes of decisions. *p. 26*

Intensive supervision probation. A punishment-oriented form of probation in which offenders are placed under stricter and more frequent surveillance and control than conventional probation by probation officers with small caseloads. *p. 352*

Intermediate sanctions. Sanctions that are more restrictive than probation and less restrictive than imprisonment. *p. 351*

Judicare. A type of legal aid practised in Canada that combines elements of the public defender and judicare models. *p. 254*

Judicial interim release hearing (bail). The condition(s) of pretrial release, typically set by a justice of the peace, in order that an accused may live in the community prior to his or her trial. Also referred to as "bail." *p. 19*

Jury. A group of individuals whose function is to determine the guilt or innocence of the accused. A jury comprises of 12 citizens with the exception of a mega-trial, in which 14 jurors are selected (but only 12 actually determine the innocence or guilt of the defendant(s)). *p. 264*

Justice model. A model of criminal justice that emphasizes legal rights, justice, and fairness. A main feature of this model is that any punishment should be proportional to the seriousness of the crime. *p. 14*

Justification defence. This involves a defendant admitting that while they committed the criminal act in question, the act was justified in the circumstances. *p. 50*

Legal aid. A government-supported system that allows individuals who are earning below a certain amount to receive free legal services. *p. 8*

Legal guilt. An individual whose guilt has been determined by a criminal court. *p. 37*

Lower court. A general term used to describe those courts that have jurisdiction over summary conviction offences. Most pleas are made in these courts. *p. 16*

Management of demand. A police organizational strategy that categorizes requests for service and analyzes them as to their priority, resulting in differential police responses. *p. 185*

Mandatory minimum sentences. These sentences apply to individuals convicted of specific designated crimes. They attempt to guarantee that offenders convicted of certain crimes serve a certain amount of time in prison by curbing the discretion of judges. *p. 323*

Manslaughter. Unintentional homicide requiring either criminal negligence or an unlawful act. *p. 130*

Maximum-security prison. A correctional facility designed and organized to control higher-risk inmates, as well as prevent escape, with high levels of supervision and cement walls and electronic, barbed wire fences. *p. 392*

Medium-security prison. A correctional institution that houses lower-risk inmates and uses less restrictive measures to control inmates. *p. 392*

Mega-trials. Large and/or complex criminal cases (usually involving numerous charges) where various procedures are used to ensure that cases arrive in court in as timely and efficiently a manner as possible (*see also* jury). *p. 269*

Mens rea. A prerequisite of criminal conduct is the "guilty mind." *Mens rea* is based on the belief that people can control their behaviour and choose between right and wrong. It commonly is used to refer to the intent to commit a crime. *p. 42*

Minimum-security prison. A correctional facility designed to allow inmates, most of whom are low risk, a certain amount of freedom of movement and contact with the outside world. *p. 392*

Mitigating circumstances. Any circumstances accompanying the commission of a crime that may justify a lighter sentence. *p. 315*

New-generation facility. A type of correctional facility distinguished architecturally from its predecessors by a design that encourages interaction between inmates and correctional officers. *p. 394*

Normal crimes. The social characteristics of individuals charged with a criminal offence, the settings in which the alleged offence occurred, and the types of victims involved. *p. 25*

Parole. The conditional release of an inmate from an unfinished sentence of incarceration into the community. The decision to parole an individual is made by a parole board, which determines the conditions of the release. *p. 360*

Pennsylvania system. A prison system developed in the 19th century that emphasized solitary confinement for all inmates so they could reflect on individual penitence. *p. 385*

Peremptory challenge. A challenge to exclude potential jurors from serving on the jury without giving any supporting reason. *p. 267*

Performance problem system. System that employs a narrower approach than a comprehensive system; most commonly is used to focus upon a small number of performance issues. *p. 233*

Physical incivilities. Occurrences such as vacant lots and abandoned buildings that cause residents and workers in a neighbourhood to be fearful of crime. *p. 192*

Plea bargaining. A defendant pleading guilty to certain lesser charges when more serious charges are dropped or when an indication of a likely sentence is given (*see also* charge bargaining, fact bargaining, and sentence bargaining). *p. 261*

Podular design. The architectural style of the new-generation jail. "Pods" usually contain between 12 and 24 one-person cells, as well as a communal room that allows for social interaction. *p. 394*

Predictive policing. A policing strategy or tactic that develops and uses information and advanced analysis to inform forward-thinking crime prevention. *p. 200*

Preliminary inquiry. An inquiry made by a provincial court judge in a case involving an indictable offence in order to determine whether there is enough evidence to order the accused to stand trial. *p. 20*

Presentence report. An investigation, usually conducted by a probation officer, before the sentencing of a convicted offender. The report typically contains information about the offender's personal background, education, previous employment, and family as well as interviews with family members, neighbours, and employer. *p. 316*

Presumptive primary offences. Those offences for which the court shall make an order for a DNA sample unless the accused can convince the court that the impact of the order upon their privacy and security of the person is "grossly disproportionate" to the public interest in the protection of society and the proper administration of justice. *p. 88*

Primary compulsory offences. Those offences to which the court is compelled to make an order to obtain a DNA sample, such as murder, manslaughter, sexual assault, and aggravated sexual assault. *p. 88*

Prisoner reentry. A corrections strategy designed to prepare inmates for a successful return to the community and to reduce their criminal activity after release. *p. 434*

Prisonization. The socialization process through which a new inmate learns the accepted norms and values of the prison population. *p. 402*

Proactive policing. The police initiating an investigation without relying on citizen complaints. *p. 86*

Probation. A sentence that allows a convicted offender to serve his or her sentence in the community, subject to certain conditions for a designated time period. *p. 22*

Problem-oriented policing. A style of policing that emphasizes focusing on a specific crime problem. It features a proactive rather than a reactive approach to fighting crime. *p. 193*

Problem-solving courts. Those courts having jurisdiction over one specific area of criminal activity, such as domestic violence or illegal drugs. *p. 368*

Procedural criminal law. The rules that define the operations of criminal proceedings. It specifies the methods that are to be followed in obtaining warrants, conducting trials, sentencing convicted offenders, and reviewing cases in the appeal courts. Its main purpose is to describe how substantive offences are to be enforced. *p. 37*

Procedural justice. This relates to the fairness of the procedures used to arrive at a verdict of the case. *p. 7*

Public defender. A type of legal aid. Legal aid lawyers are employed by a provincial government to help with the legal defence of an accused. *p. 254*

Reactive policing. The police responding to citizens' reports of crime. *p. 182*

Recidivism rate. The repetition of criminal behaviour. It is measured by criminal acts committed by individuals under correctional supervision or technical violations of individuals on probation or parole. *p. 364*

Recidivist. A repeat offender. *p. 364*

Rehabilitation. A correctional philosophy that emphasizes the treatment of conditional offenders and their reintegration into the community. *p. 14*

Rehabilitation model. One of the four criminal justice models. It differs from the other models in its support of discretion in the system and the treatment of the offender. *p. 90*

Reintegration. The goal of corrections that focuses on preparing the offender for a return to the community. *p. 386*

Reintegrative shaming. This approach attempts to reintegrate offenders back into the community of law-abiding citizens through forgiveness and/or ceremonies that decertify the individual as deviant. *p. 99*

Release on recognizance. A judge's order that releases an accused from jail with the understanding that they will return to a later court date on their own will. *p. 250*

Restorative justice. This approach posits that an individual's conscience and significant others can be incorporated into deterrence and serve as potential sources of punishment. *p. 99*

Revised UCR system. Reports that record incident-based criminal events. Each crime incident is analyzed for a number of individual characteristics (e.g., the relationship between offender and victim) (*see also* Uniform Crime Reporting (UCR) system). *p. 122*

Rule of law. Ensures that laws are created, administered, and enforced on the basis of acceptable procedures that promote fairness and equality. *p. 8*

Search and seizure. The legal term, as found in the Charter of Rights and Freedoms, that generally refers to the searching for and confiscating of evidence by law-enforcement agents. *p. 216*

Search warrant. An authorization, granted to police officers by a judge, that authorizes officers to search a specific place. *p. 210*

Second degree murder. Any murder that is not first degree is second degree. The maximum punishment for second degree murder is life imprisonment. *p. 130*

Selective incapacitation. The incarceration for long periods of time of a select group of "chronic" offenders who commit numerous violent offences. *p. 86*

Selective incapacitation model. One of the four criminal justice models. It emphasizes long prison sentences for the small number of individuals who chronically commit violent crimes. It rejects any type of favourable discretionary actions for those offenders. *p. 86*

Self-help model. A type of legal aid in which clients don't have ongoing legal representation, but instead must rely on the information provided to them in order to determine how it applies to their specific case. In most case, they become advocates for themselves. *p. 254*

Self-report survey. A type of questionnaire asking people about the number of offences they have committed. *p. 128*

Sentence bargaining. A form of plea bargaining that involves the reduction of a sentence in return for a plea of guilty or information. *p. 261*

Sentencing. The judicial determination of a legal sanction to be imposed upon a person found guilty of an offence. *p. 22*

Sexual assault. Classified as a violent crime. Legislation introduced in 1983 created three levels of sexual assault, which emphasize that these offences involve physical violence directed against an individual. *p. 37*

Social control. Refers to the various types of organized reaction to behaviour viewed as problematic. *p. 3*

Social incivilities. Occurrences such as loitering and public drinking that cause residents and workers in a neighbourhood to be fearful of crime. *p. 192*

Social service. A view held by some police officers that their prime function is to assist the public in as many ways as possible. A purely legalistic approach is rejected except in extreme cases. *p. 155*

Staff system. A type of legal aid in which lawyers involved in a legal aid case are in effect employees of the provincial government. *p. 254*

Stare decisis. A common law doctrine under which judges are to follow those precedents established by prior decisions. *p. 52*

Statute. Laws created by legislatures in a response to changing social conditions and public opinion. *p. 53*

Statutory release. A program designed to release most incarcerated offenders who have not been able to obtain full parole and who have served two-thirds of their sentence. *p. 22*

Structured Living Environment (SLE). A Correctional Service of Canada policy which allows higher security levels so that federally sentenced women of varying risk levels are able to remain in the regional facilities together with other offenders. *p. 388*

Substantive criminal law. These describe our rights and duties as members of Canadian society. The substantive part of the criminal law prohibits various forms of conduct from which society and its members have a right to be protected. *p. 37*

Substantive justice. The accuracy or correctness of the outcome of a case. It is concerned with the truthfulness of the allegation, the accuracy of the verdict, and the appropriateness of the sentence. *p. 7*

Summary conviction offences. Minor offences tried on the basis of the information without other pretrial formalities. *p. 63*

Summons. An order by the court requiring the appearance of the accused or a witness before it on a specific date. *p. 19*

Superior court. The court where most indictable offences are tried, either by judge or by judge and jury. *p. 16*

Supreme Court exclusive indictable offence. Involves those individuals who are charged with first or second degree murder. The case is tried by a federally appointed judge and jury. *p. 63*

Suspended sentence. A prison term that is delayed by a judge's order while the convicted offender is involved in community treatment. If this treatment is successful, the individual is allowed to remain in the community. *p. 22*

Systemic discrimination. Discrimination (e.g., race and/or gender) existing in all aspects of the operations of our criminal justice system. *p. 26*

Temporary absence (TA). Permits the release of offenders from federal institutions so that they can access programs and various services within the community. *p. 363*

Temporary absence, escorted. An offender's permitted temporary absence, for a brief period, from a correctional facility, on the basis of having an escort. *p. 363*

Temporary absence, unescorted. An offender's permitted temporary absence, for a relatively long period of time, from a correctional facility, in order to integrate that individual into the outside community. *p. 363*

Total institutions. Institutions that eliminate all daily and normal inmate contact with the outside world. *p. 399*

Truth-in-sentencing. Sentences designed to ensure that convicted offenders serve a certain period of their sentence (e.g., 80 percent) in a custodial facility prior to receiving parole. *p. 325*

Uniform Crime Reporting (UCR) system. National crime statistics maintained by the RCMP in Ottawa. Offences are grouped into three categories: crimes against the person, crimes against property, and "other" crimes (*see also* Revised UCR system). *p. 121*

Victim impact statement. The option given to the victim of a crime to complete a form and detail what has happened to that victim as a result of the crime. If the victim decides to fill out the form, it is placed in the case file and may have an impact on the case, particularly at the sentencing stage. *p. 327*

Victim surveys. A method of gathering crime data that directly surveys participants to determine their experiences as victims of crime. *p. 127*

Victimless crime. Crimes for which there are no complainants or victims. It refers to consensual social exchanges punished by criminal law (e.g., drug use and selling sex). *p. 44*

Warrant. An authorization that grants an individual, usually a police officer, to do what is specified in the warrant (e.g., to arrest someone). *p. 19*

Warrantless arrest. An arrest made without first applying for a warrant for the action. This is permitted under certain circumstances such as when a police officer witnesses a crime. *p. 215*

Warrantless search. Those conditions which allow an individual, usually a police officer, to search a place without a warrant (e.g., doctrine of plain view). *p. 211*

Watchman. A style of policing that emphasizes a reactive style of policing rather than a proactive or preventive style. *p. 151*

Wedding cake model. A wedding cake–shaped model that explains why different cases receive different treatment in the criminal justice system. The cases at the top of the cake receive the most attention and have the greatest effect on public perception of criminal justice, while those cases at the bottom are disposed of quickly and typically ignored by the media. *p. 23*

Zero tolerance policing. The focus of the police is order maintenance on the streets, and it narrows police attention to suppressing those individuals who are viewed as the main sources of disorder in public places. *p. 197*

INDEX

Page numbers followed by *e*, *f*, and *t* refer to exhibits, figures, and tables respectively.

Q

R

S

T